AV. UNIVERSIDAD 1330
CABLE "OLYMPIC"
TEL. 34-80-80
MEXICO 20, D. F.

COMITE ORGANIZADOR DE LOS JUEGOS DE LA XIX OLIMPIADA

K.S. GÓRNIK ZABRZE — MANCHESTER CITY F.C.

EUROPEAN CUP WINNERS' CUP 1970

MANCHESTER CITY 2 — GÓRNIK ZABRZE 0

PIERWSZY DZIEŃ OBIEGU FDC — PPF „RUCH"

Some of the stamps on these pages are reproduced by courtesy of Stanley Gibbons Ltd.

W9-BUR-816

Cover pictures supplie
Rex Features, Synd   atrick Eagar,
Wilmik, Ed Lace   ursport, John Stoddard

encyclopedia of SPORTS

Golden Hands Books

Marshall Cavendish
London and New York

Gerry Cranham

Published by Marshall Cavendish Publications Limited
58 Old Compton Street
London W1V 5PA
©Marshall Cavendish Limited 1969/1970/1971/1975
Part of this material was first published by Marshall
Cavendish Limited in the partwork *The Game*
This volume first published 1975
Printed in Gt. Britain by Carlisle Web Offset Limited
ISBN 0 85685 113 2

This edition is not to be sold in the USA, Canada
and the Philippines

Introduction

A lone skier hurtling breakneck down an icy mountain slope . . . the hushed atmosphere of a snooker hall as a player makes a critical stroke . . . the roar of a cup final crowd as a soccer star drives the ball goalwards—just three aspects of the world of sport, a world which has been brought vividly to life in the pages of this book.

Encyclopedia of Sports is an exciting compendium of dozens of the world's leading sports. Written by experts and lavishly illustrated with over 1,000 action photographs—most of them in full colour—it describes the history, development and rules of each sport, and presents those outstanding competitors whose skills have delighted the fans through the ages.

As might be expected, *Encyclopedia of Sports* includes detailed coverage of soccer, athletics, boxing, cricket and rugby football. But this is a truly international book about a truly international subject, and its scope is world-wide—from the fine cut and thrust of fencing, to the jet-age thrills of power boat racing; from the rough and tumble of Australian rules football, to the hair-breadth skills of archery.

Detailed, knowledgable, and always interesting, *Encyclopedia of Sports* puts you right there in the grandstand. To read it is to evoke the high octane atmosphere of a Grand Prix, the thrills of downhill skiing, the gruelling grind of the marathon. For sports fans all over the world it's a must.

Martin Tyler.

Left, **An explosive shot of Margaret Court at Wimbledon in 1969. In the late 1960s she, with Billie Jean King, dominated the Women's Singles Championships at Wimbledon.** *Overleaf,* **Gerd Muller (right), the man who won the 1974 World Cup for West Germany, at home in the penalty area for his club, Bayern Munich.**

Contents

Barnaby's

Picturepoint

Right, **Dragon class yachts, a type notoriously difficult
to handle in rough conditions, racing under full spinnakers
in the Solent during Cowes Week.**

Rules of the Game

American football is played by teams of 11 men on a field 100 yards long by 53 yards 1 foot (160 feet) wide. Lines are marked across the field at 5-yard intervals. Beyond each goal-line is an area 10 yards deep called the end-zone. The ball is of the rugby type, but is slimmer and more pointed (about 12 in long by 7 in diameter at centre), allowing it to be gripped firmly in one hand; it weighs 14-15 oz. In college football the H-shaped goal-posts stand on the *end line* and are 23 ft 4 in wide, with the crossbar 10 ft high. In professional football the posts are 18 ft 6 in apart, directly over the *goal-line*. They are built to extend from a single post standing 6 ft behind the goal-line.

The players acquire their Martian appearance from the large amount of protective equipment they wear. This includes plastic helmets (usually with face guards), protective pads for shoulders, hips, ribs, and the kidney area, and soft pads to cover the knees.

The scoring methods remain similar to those of rugby—taking the ball over the goal-line, worth 6 points (called a *touchdown*, although the ball does not have to be touched down), and kicking it over the crossbar and between the uprights for a *field goal*, worth 3 points. Running the ball over the goal-line is not the only method of scoring a touchdown. Because forward passing is legal, the ball can be thrown forward to a receiver who has already run beyond the goal-line. If he catches the ball within the end-zone, it is a touchdown. After each touchdown, a *conversion* kick (worth 1 point) is allowed; it is always taken from directly in front of the posts. In college football, an alternative conversion play, worth 2 points, allows the ball to be run or passed into the end-zone. Field goals are invariably attempted from place kicks. The rules allow drop-kicking (on the half-volley), but it has virtually died out of the game.

Each game has 60 minutes of playing time, divided into four quarters of 15 minutes. The teams change ends after each quarter, and there is a 15-minute interval between the second and third quarters. As the rules call for the clock to be stopped on a number of occasions when the ball is not in play—e.g. after a score, or when the ball is carried over the sideline—and as each team can call a limited number of *time-outs* in each half (three in professional football, four in college), a football game usually lasts about 2½ hours from kick-off until the final gun.

In the professional game there is free substitution—any player can be taken out or put back into the game as frequently as required. Teams are allowed to use up to 40 players in a game, so that totally different squads are fielded for offensive and defensive play. Free substitution has also led to the rise of the specialist, particularly the field goal kicker, who enters the game only to take the kick, and leaves it immediately he has done so. College rules on substitution are only slightly less permissive. The game is controlled by field officials in vertically striped black and white shirts. There are four or five officials in college football and six in pro football.

A team that infringes the rules is penalized by having the ball moved closer to its goal line. Minor fouls—offside, deliberate delay of the game—cost 5 yards; for major offences such as rough play the offending team loses 15 yards. When an official spots a foul, he signals by dropping a small flag; play is not stopped at this point, but continues until the end of the down. Then, if Team A has committed the offence, the captain of Team B can decide whether he wishes to accept the yardage or not. If it is less than the yardage his team gained on the play, he will decline it. A code of more than 25 hand-signals is used by the officials to indicate which offence has been committed.

The rules of American football permit players on the offensive team to *block* opponents—i.e. prevent them from getting to the ball-carrier. The blocker may use his body and forearms, but never his hands. Defensive players are allowed to push blockers away. Only the ball-carrier can be tackled, rugby style.

American Football

A huddle in the middle of the field . . . a stream of complicated instructions . . . the centre snaps the ball back to his quarterback and 22 padded, helmeted giants burst into electrifying action. This is football, American style.

With its crunching tackles, its thrilling 60-yard forward passes, and its highly sophisticated tactics, football has ousted baseball as America's number one sport. Professional football alone draws more than 11 million spectators a season, an average of nearly 45,000 a game. Television relays the big games to millions of viewers every weekend in a season that lasts from mid-October to the end of December. Cameras shoot the play from all angles, and instant playbacks analyse every move in detail.

Colleges vie with each other for high-school stars, and professional teams offer the top college players contracts worth hundreds of thousands of dollars. College games are loud, boisterous, colourful affairs, surrounded by a ritual that is as much a part of the game as the pointed oval-shaped ball—the huge marching bands, prancing cheerleaders exhorting the supporters, mascots, half-time shows, and noise, noise, noise.

American football has little to do with the feet. It is a handling game, a direct but much modified descendant of rugby. It started as a college sport around the end of the 19th century, and early games were crude soccer-like affairs. It was not until Canada's McGill University took a rugby team to Harvard University in 1874 that handling of the ball gained acceptance.

From the start, rules were treated as anything but sacrosanct. They were continually modified, for the sake of clarity or to discourage unwanted types of play. Among these changes, which progressively divorced the game from rugby, were the decision to use 11-man teams, the abolition of the scrum and of fly-kicking, and the introduction of blocking.

One of the most fundamental changes was the brainchild of Yale University's coach Walter Camp, the 'father of American football'. It was designed to counter a trend familiar to modern soccer: defensive play and the 0-0 tie. Teams were hanging on to the ball, making no attempt to score. Camp solved this problem in 1882 by introducing the concept of possession. This is essentially an application of the innings of cricket and baseball, where first one team and then the other gets a chance to

1 American football is a game of fast and furious action. The offensive side has four plays called *downs,* to advance the ball 10 yards. Each play averages about 15 seconds. The ball-carrier's team-mates protect him from opponents by blocking.
2 As part of the half-time entertainment, college cheering groups form the 'stars and stripes' by holding cards in a prearranged order.
3 The Army-Navy game, a match between the US military and naval academies, West Point and Annapolis, takes place annually at the end of the college football season.

score. Camp's rule stated that the team in possession of the ball was allowed three plays (or *downs*) in which to advance the ball 5 yards. If it was successful, it retained possession and started another series of three downs; if it failed, it had to turn the ball over to its opponents. This rule, now altered to read 10 yards in four downs, has remained the heart of American football.

Another important change came in 1906. Play had become so rough, with increasing numbers of injuries and even deaths, that President Theodore Roosevelt demanded the game be cleaned up. The response of the Rules Committee was to legalize the forward

pass. This opened up the game and put an end to the concentrated power plays that were the cause of most of the injuries.

Rule changes, of major and minor importance, have been made almost every year since. American football has prospered mightily under this incessant doctoring. The 1960s saw a vast increase in its popularity, especially the professional version. And while football's attendance figures spiralled dizzily upwards, baseball's slumped, leading many to acclaim football as the number one sport in the United States.

Professional football. The first professional league in American football was formed in 1920 in the

mining areas of Ohio and Pennsylvania. Called the United States Professional Football Association, its president and star player was Jim Thorpe, the American Indian who had won the pentathlon and the decathlon in the 1912 Olympics. (He was later forced to return his medals when it was found that he had once played semi-pro baseball.) The league, which changed its name to the National Football League (NFL) in 1921, did not prosper during its first years. The turning point came in 1925 with the signing of Red Grange, already a nationally known star with the University of Illinois. The crowds began to grow, and pro football was on its way. Until

How the Game is Played

The object in American football is to advance the ball over the opposing goal-line. This is done in a discontinuous series of plays, or *downs*. After each play, the ball is placed on the ground at a spot marking the limit of forward progress on the previous play. An imaginary line drawn through this spot parallel to the goal lines marks the *scrimmage line*, from which the next play starts. All plays, except kick-offs, begin from a scrimmage in which two lines of players about 1 yard apart face each other in crouching positions. The offensive team *must* have at least 7 players on the line, as follows:

| left | left | left | centre | right | right | right |
| end | tackle | guard | | guard | tackle | end |

These are the *linemen*. The other four players behind them are the *backs*, including the *quarterback*. The centre five players on the offensive line are positioned about a foot apart, but the ends are often split wider. The formation of the backs depends on the team's style of play. Most modern formations are modifications of the basic 'T', in which the quarterback stands immediately behind the centre, with the other backs in a line about 4 yards behind him.

The defensive team can adopt whatever formation it likes; it will usually have from four to six men on the line, two or three a short distance behind (the *linebackers*), plus three or four deeper men to guard against long passes.

The team on offence can advance the ball by running or passing. (Kicking is usually employed only on fourth-down situations where possession of the ball has to be given up if the requisite 10 yards is not gained.) It receives the ball from the opening kick-off, and the player catching it attempts to run it back to the opposing goal line. If he makes it all the way, he scores a touchdown. Far more often he will be stopped while still in his own half, and his team then has four downs in which to gain 10 yards.

All teams have a large number of pre-set plays, within which every player has an assigned role. Before each play, the offensive team gathers into a circle—the *huddle*—to decide which play to use. Usually it is the quarterback who calls the plays. The team then goes to the scrimmage line, with the centre crouched over the ball. At a shouted signal from the quarterback, the centre *snaps* the ball back through his legs directly into the quarterback's hands. As soon as the ball is snapped, the two opposing lines make contact, as the defensive team tries to get to the ball-carrier, and the offensive linemen try to keep them away by blocking.

On a *running play*, the quarterback hands the ball to one of his backs, who will try either to run around one end of the line, or to run into the line and through a gap which, hopefully, his linemen have opened by blocking defenders out of the way. On a *passing play*, the quarterback drops back while his linemen form a defensive semi-circle around him, trying to prevent him from being tackled before he gets off the pass.

The ability to deceive the defensive team as to the type of play coming up is an important part of offensive tactics. Which play is actually called— a running play into the line, an end run, a long or short pass—depends on many factors, such as known weaknesses in the opposing defence, distance from the opposing goal line, or the amount of time remaining in the game. An offensive play may gain yardage, or it may be stopped at the line of scrimmage for no gain, or—particularly if the defensive team gets to the quarterback before he passes—it may lose yardage. (In this respect the game is similar to the rugby codes, where a combination of running the ball forwards, but passing it backwards, means that individual plays can gain ground or lose it.)

If a first-down play gains, say, 3 yards, then 7 yards must be gained in the three remaining downs. If the offensive team does gain 10 yards in four (or fewer) downs, they retain possession and start a new series of four downs. A team that has not gained 10 yards after three downs will usually use the fourth-down play in one of two ways. If they are within about 35 yards of the opponents' goal-line, they may attempt to kick a field goal. If they are farther away than this, they will punt the ball downfield so that their opponents, who will take over possession on the next play, will have to start their drive from as far back as possible.

The defensive team can acquire early possession of the ball by intercepting a pass, or by recovering a *fumble* (see *Glossary*). With the opposing players running hard and concentrating on a particular task, a player making an interception will often be able to run through the offensive side and score a touchdown.

1927, the professionals used the college rules, but since that time the two have always differed slightly.

By 1946, interest in pro football had grown to the point where a second league was started, the All America Conference (AAC). After four seasons, the AAC and the NFL merged, the combined league having teams in 10 cities. By the beginning of the 1960s, the NFL was spectacularly successful; franchises that had cost $500 back in the 1920s were worth millions of dollars.

Another new league, the American Football League, was formed in 1960. Although it suffered from poor play and even worse attendances, the AFL was kept alive by money from television until it was strong enough to start outbidding the NFL for college stars.

The NFL had avoided bidding wars for college players among its own clubs by adopting the draft system. Under this system a list of eligible college players is drawn up each year, and the clubs take it in turn to choose the players they want. The method also serves to maintain balance in the league, as the order of choice is the reverse of the league positions, the weakest club getting first pick. Once a club has picked a player, they are the only club allowed to negotiate with

The New York Jets in their warm-up clothes before the start of a game. The Jets won the 1969 Super Bowl game—the pro football championship.

Transworld/Jerry Cranham

Blocking A player on the offensive team using body or forearm to prevent a defender reaching the ball-carrier.

Broken field running Seen on punt and kick-off returns where the ball-carrier often has to dodge his way past defenders without the help of blocking from his team-mates.

Clipping Bringing down an opponent, who is not carrying the ball, by throwing the body across the back of his legs. It is illegal, and brings a 15-yard penalty.

Down Action is broken up into individual plays called *downs*. A down starts with the *snap* of the ball through the centre's legs, and continues until the ball next becomes dead—e.g. because the ball-carrier has been tackled, or because a touchdown has been scored. The average down lasts only about 15 seconds.

First and ten The beginning of a series of downs: first down and 10 yards to gain. A gain of 4 yards on a first down will bring up a 'second-and-six' situation.

Flanker back A back positioned wide to act as a pass receiver.

Forward pass One forward pass is allowed during each play. It is usually thrown by the quarterback, using a regular one-handed throwing motion. In a well-thrown pass the ball travels pointed end forward, spinning in flight. Accurate passes of up to 60 yards can be thrown. The pass must be caught before it hits the ground. The down is lost on an *incomplete forward pass*, i.e. when it is not held.

Fumble When the ball-carrier drops the ball or has it fairly knocked out of his hands.

Gridiron Another name for the football field, the transverse markings give it a gridiron appearance.

Necktie tackle A high tackle, around the neck. Its opposite is the *shoestring* tackle.

Offside A player who advances beyond the line of scrimmage before the ball is snapped is offside. The penalty is 5 yards.

Platooning The practice of using two different teams for offensive and defensive play.

Playbook Each player has a book containing detailed instruction of his roles within the team's rehearsed plays.

Red Dog or **Blitz** A play by the defensive team in which one or more linebackers rush through their opponents' line to get at the quarterback.

Snap The action of the centre in passing the ball back to the quarterback which starts a play from scrimmage.

Spotter A coach placed high up in the stadium where he has a bird's eye view of the game, and can sometimes see developments not apparent from ground level. He is in telephone contact with the head coach on the bench.

Straight-arm Equivalent to a rugby hand-off; can be used only by the ball-carrier.

him during the year.

The rivalry of the AFL upset this scheme, and in 1965 the New York Jets of the AFL brought matters to a head by giving Alabama University star Joe Namath a contract worth over $400,000. The prospect of a cut-throat war between the two leagues quickly led to a merger agreement, in which the AFL and the NFL agreed to conduct a joint draft of college players.

The combined league has 26 teams in 25 cities. They are divided into two sections that correspond roughly with the old NFL-AFL alignments.

In the early days of pro football it was the Chicago Bears, under coach George Halas, and the Washington Redskins, behind the passing feats of quarterback Sammy Baugh, that were the top teams. Another star quarterback, Johnny Unitas, led the Baltimore Colts to the national championship in 1958

1 High-school players are quick to recover from a fumble under pressure.
2 Cheer leaders are a major part of college football.
Pro football: **3** A Green Bay Packer runs into the San Francisco Forty-Niners' defensive barrier. **4** More successful this time, the Green Bay Packers quarterback has plenty of time to pass.
5 The ball has just been snapped from a scrimmage. The distinctive pattern of the end zone distinguishes it from the gridiron.

PROFESSIONAL CHAMPIONS

National League			
1933	Chicago Bears	1952	Detroit Lions
1934	New York Giants	1953	Detroit Lions
1935	Detroit Lions	1954	Cleveland Browns
1936	Green Bay Packers	1955	Cleveland Browns
1937	Washington Redskins	1956	New York Giants
1938	New York Giants	1957	Detroit Lions
1939	Green Bay Packers	1958	Baltimore Colts
1940	Chicago Bears	1959	Baltimore Colts
1941	Chicago Bears	1960	Philadelphia Eagles
1942	Washington Redskins	1961	Green Bay Packers
1943	Chicago Bears	1962	Green Bay Packers
1944	Green Bay Packers	1963	Chicago Bears
1945	Cleveland Rams	1964	Cleveland Browns
1946	Chicago Bears	1965	Green Bay Packers
1947	Chicago Cardinals	1966	*Green Bay Packers
1948	Philadelphia Eagles	1967	*Green Bay Packers
1949	Philadelphia Eagles	1968	Baltimore Colts
1950	Cleveland Browns	1969	Minnesota Vikings
1951	Los Angeles Rams	1970	Dallas Cowboys
		1971	*Dallas Cowboys

1972	Washington Redskins		
1973	Minnesota Vikings		
Amercian League			
1960	Houston Oilers		
1961	Houston Oilers		
1962	Dallas Texans		
1963	San Diego Chargers		
1964	Buffalo Bills		
1965	Buffalo Bills		
1966	Kansas City Chiefs		
1967	Oakland Raiders		
1968	*New York Jets		
1969	*Kansas City Chiefs		
1970	*Baltimore Colts		
1971	Miami Dolphins		
1972	*Miami Dolphins		
1973	*Miami Dolphins		
		*Winners of AFL-NFL play-off.	

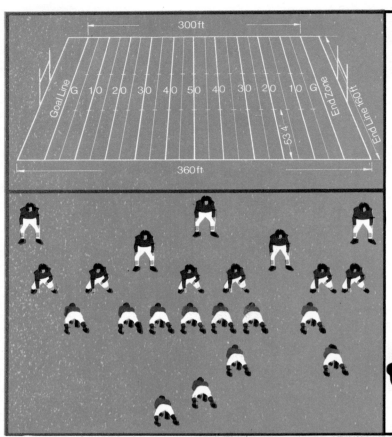

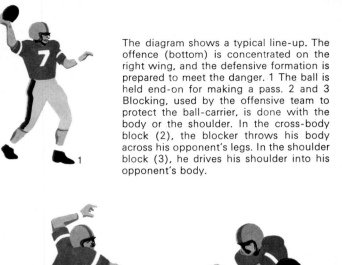

The diagram shows a typical line-up. The offence (bottom) is concentrated on the right wing, and the defensive formation is prepared to meet the danger. 1 The ball is held end-on for making a pass. 2 and 3 Blocking, used by the offensive team to protect the ball-carrier, is done with the body or the shoulder. In the cross-body block (2), the blocker throws his body across his opponent's legs. In the shoulder block (3), he drives his shoulder into his opponent's body.

Roy Castle

and 1959.

The 1960s belonged to Green Bay, a small meat-packing town in Wisconsin, whose Packers were coached by Vince Lombardi to the NFL championship five times in the 1960s. The town has a population of only 63,000, yet the stadium is regularly filled to its 50,000-plus capacity on matchdays. In 1967, when the champions of the NFL and AFL met for the first time in a game dubbed the Super Bowl, Green Bay won easily, and repeated their victory in 1968. But in 1969, the AFL's New York Jets, led by Joe Namath, upset the Baltimore Colts of the NFL, proving that the AFL was no longer an inferior league.

Professional football's 260-game season now draws an average of nearly 45,000 spectators a game. Big crowds, watching big men— few players are under 14st (196 lb) in the sport. The minimum salary for a professional is $12,000, but most players earn more, with an average of around $20,000. Cleveland full-back Jimmy Brown was paid $75,000 a year before he retired to become a Hollywood star in 1965, and today's superstars earn $100,000. Head coaches average about $40,000, but the top men such as Vince Lombardi are in the $100,000 bracket.

College football. American football is firmly established as the top college sport in the United States. Each season, from September to November, nearly 3,000 games are played, involving teams from more than 600 colleges. Total attendance is around the 27 million mark each

Looking like men from outer space, American footballers wear masses of protective equipment. Sixteen-stone giants clashing at top speed need all the padding they can get: chest and shoulder pads, rib and kidney pads, and below-the-belt protection. Pockets are built into the trousers for knee and thigh pads. The helmet, of plastic or metal, usually has a face guard. Boots are light. Even the smallest players take on a massive appearance when fully rigged out for a game.

Paul Berman.

year, a very high figure.

Oddly enough, there is no nation-wide competition to decide the national champion. Most colleges play in leagues, called *conferences*, of 8 or 10 teams, grouped together on the basis of geography and approximately equal strength. The argument over which is the nation's strongest team is resolved—on paper—by two polls, one of sportswriters, one of coaches. The two usually agree, but when they do not, co-champions are named.

Teams from different conferences do meet in the post-season bowl games—'bowl' is just another way of saying stadium, most of which are bowl-shaped. These games, held in southern and western states where the winter weather is mild, started in 1902 with California's Rose Bowl. Five of the most important bowl games are played on New Year's Day.

There are several polls—of coaches and sportswriters—that each year select the best player in each position. Thus is built up a dream-team which, although it never takes the field, gives its members the prestige of being an 'All-America Selection'.

The immense success of college football has brought its own problems. Many feel that it is merely a big business operation (with receipts of about $100 million a year) functioning as a farm system for professional football.

Right. The muscular, padded giants of American football spring into thrilling action in a big league game.

Angling

The appeal of angling is the same the world over—a final chance for man, in an increasingly urbanized society, to hunt and outwit a wild creature. There are almost as many kinds of anglers as there are species to fish for, but fundamentally they fall into three main groups. They are coarse anglers (in North America they are called *pan* anglers); game anglers, who catch fish of the salmon and trout families; and sea anglers, who include big-game fishermen.

The *coarse angler*'s quarry is anything that swims in fresh water with the exception of salmon, trout, or char. He tends to congregate where the rivers are slow, deep, and often rather muddy. There are probably at least two million coarse anglers in Britain alone, and possibly even more in France. Germany, Belgium, the Netherlands, Italy, and most central European countries have a high proportion of coarse anglers. British anglers fish mainly for pike, perch, roach, rudd, barbel, bream, dace, chub, carp, tench and eel. In addition to these, there are other species on the mainland of Europe that are unknown to British anglers, such as asp and ide.

Just as there are several species of coarse fish, so there are several kinds of coarse anglers. In Europe the main kinds are 'pleasure fishermen', who fish alone for pure recreation; 'specimen-hunters', usually dedicated hunters of the giants among certain species; and 'match fishermen' who catch large quantities of small fish in competition with each other. Match fishermen draw for *pegs* (set positions) along the bank of a river, and in big matches there may be a thousand anglers fishing from 10 miles of river bank. The winner sometimes takes home more than £1,000 in prize money. A number of European countries take part in international championships.

There are two main schools of fly-fishing for trout—*dry-fly* and *wet-fly*. A dry-fly is tied to float on the surface and it usually closely resembles an insect to which trout are 'rising' for food. A dry-fly angler deliberately fishes for a rising fish, and his art is seen at its best on clear, less turbulent rivers, such as chalk streams, where fly life is abundant.

The *wet-fly* angler excels on broken mountain rivers where he 'fishes the water' by casting his *wet* or sinking flies downstream and letting the current carry them across the 'lies' where he knows from experience that fish are waiting for food. His fly patterns resemble aquatic insects and small fish rather than actual flies. Both forms of fly-fishing can be used in still water, and reservoirs stocked with trout are fished with modified wet-fly techniques.

Sea fishing is normally confined

1 A big-game fisherman fighting an 800-lb tuna arms himself with appropriately tough equipment.

2 No need to lie! The winners stand by their catch of sailfish on the beach at Malindi in Kenya.

3 The blue waters of the Caribbean are a paradise of fighters for the big-game fisherman.

to the shallower warmer areas of the continental shelf, whether this be off Florida, Cornwall, or Queensland. Until recent times, sea angling was the slowest of all branches of the sport to make use of modern developments in tackle and technique. Now progress is so fast that, in Britain for example, more than half the sea fishing records have been broken in the 1950s and 1960s. Sea anglers all over the world are following the example of their freshwater colleagues by abandoning heavy tackle and replacing it with the lightest possible equipment for the job and in this way are increas-

ing their enjoyment of the sport.

International sea fishing festivals that now take place throughout the summer months from the Red Sea to the Kattegat have greatly helped and encouraged the spread of knowledge and technique in this branch of the sport.

In the seas around the British Isles sea anglers fish for tope, cod, black bream, ling, turbot, dogfish, skate, ray, bass, mackerel, pollack, conger eel, and some sharks, including blue, mako, thresher, and porbeagle.

But real big-game fishing is usually confined to tropical waters, where the fish are bigger and

generally great fighters. (They can, however, be found in more temperate areas. For instance, an 851-lb blue-fin tuna has been caught in the North Sea.) In earlier days Zane Gray, Ernest Hemingway, and others portrayed big-game fishing as a sport only for the very rich. In the jealously preserved waters off the Bahamas, for example, this is still largely true. But cheaper flying and package holidays are gradually bringing the sport within the reach of the ordinary angler on holiday. The quarry include blue, black, and striped marlin, sailfish, swordfish, tuna, and various large sharks.

There are also a number of smaller but lively performers such as tarpon and barracuda. The finest fishing grounds are found off Hawaii, the East and South African coasts, New Zealand, Australia, the Caribbean, and the Gulf of California. But big-game species are by no means confined to those areas, and good fishing for smaller but hard-fighting species is increasingly being developed in the Canaries, and off Madeira, Malta, Gibraltar, and Portugal.

Most coarse fishing rods are made of fibreglass or split-cane, and vary in length from the match angler's 14-footer down to a 6-foot pike spinning rod. Lines are nearly always of nylon mono-fil, the breaking strain varying from 1½ lb to 14 lb. The most popular reels are the free-running centre-pin drum type and, for long-casting, the fixed-spool reel. Most fishing is done either by float that is allowed to drift downstream, or by leger weight that keeps the bait close to the bottom.

In America, coarse fishing is known as *panfishing*. Panfish include bluegills, crappie, white and yellow perch, the sunfishes, and white, yellow, and warmouth bass. Some anglers refer to bullhead catfish and pickerel as panfish; others consider them as game fish.

Game fishing for members of the salmon family (salmon, trout, char, and grayling) is a world-wide sport, although most game fish naturally belong to the Northern Hemisphere. Sportsmen have introduced various kinds of trout into many countries, including Africa, India, Ceylon, Australia, New Zealand, and South America, where they thrive in lakes and fast, cold mountain rivers. Salmon, like sea trout, are migratory fish that spend their adult life in the sea. They live in fresh water only when they are very young and when they return to the river to spawn. This migratory urge makes them harder to establish in new waters.

Americans apply the term 'game fish' to salmon, char, trout, and other sporting species, including muskellunge (largest of all pike),

Picturepoint.

Barnaby's.

Picturepoint.

Picturepoint.

4 The slow-flowing River Ouse in Sussex is rich in many species of coarse fish, as an angler is ready to prove. Few British coarse fishermen eat their catch, in marked contrast to anglers on the Continent.
5 The fly-fisherman on the Murrumbidgee River in the Snowy Mountains of New South Wales weaves a complex pattern over the water with his all-important cast.
6 A 'wet fly' angler plays a trout on the River Ure in Yorkshire. Such fast flowing rocky streams are ideal for this method of fishing.
7 A box of lugworms—with ragworms perhaps the most popular sea-fishing bait. Lugworms are found in the sand.
8 A spot of sea fishing makes a holiday—or so it seems to the experts on Brighton pier, and the patient sightseers.

Barnaby's.

northern pike (the European species), walleye (American zander), most catfishes, and large- and small-mouth black bass.

West coast Americans and east coast Russians fish for Pacific salmon, a group of six species that die after returning to spawn. But the single species of Atlantic salmon often survives the breeding season and returns to its home three or four times from the sea.

The salmon angler fishes for both kinds of salmon when they are making their run up-river from the sea, using as a lure spinning bait or a large gaudy 'fly' that resembles no fly ever found in nature. Nobody knows why salmon accept this bait because, once they have entered fresh water, they live on fat accumulated at sea and have no further use for external food. Some of the finest Atlantic salmon fishing is found in Iceland, the east coast of Canada, Ireland, Scotland, Norway, and as far

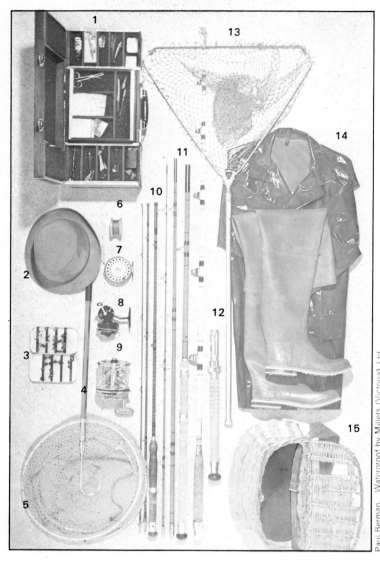

The modern angler's equipment has come a long way from the traditional bent pin on a bit of string. Shown in the picture above are: 1 tackle box (holding various hooks, spinners, and floats); 2 waterproof hat; 3 fly tin; 4 gaff; 5 keepnet; 6 sea fishing line; 7 fly reel; 8 fixed spool reel; 9 multiplier (sea reel); 10 trout fly rod; 11 match rod; 12 deep sea rod; 13 landing net; 14 waterproof jacket and studded waders; 15 creel.

Paul Berman. Waterproof by Millets (Victoria) Ltd

feathered lures or flies.

Trout fly patterns are listed in thousands, many of them *dry flies* fashioned to float on the surface film of the water. As they are virtually weightless, non-anglers may wonder how these flies can be cast with such precision to trout lying as much as 20 yards from the angler. The answer lies in the heavy line cast by all fly-fishers— a veritable hawser compared with the nylon lines of course anglers and ultra-light spinning enthusiasts. The spinner's casting weight is concentrated at the end of his line, usually in the lure itself, but the fly-fisher has no such advantage, and his casting weight must be built into the line. This heavy line may be designed to float or sink, but its weight makes the rod bend and catapult the line and fly ahead of the angler. Tied to the end of that bulky line is a length of fine nylon, usually 6-9 ft. long, at the end of which is the artificial fly.

But dry flies are not the only varieties. *Wet flies*, resembling tiny fish and other underwater creatures, are designed to penetrate the surface and sink quickly before being retrieved as the angler strips short lengths of line back through the rod rings, giving a semblance of life to his lure and prompting the trout to attack. *Streamer flies*, often tied with animal hair rather than feathers, are designed to imitate small fish and are normally retrieved at speed. *Nymphs* are patterns representing the larvae of aquatic flies rising from the bed of a lake or river to hatch at the surface.

When trout feed at the surface, ringing the water as they sip flies and other insects, the experienced angler will invariably 'fish the rise', moving carefully into position and casting only to those fish. It needs no great knowledge of entomology to offer an artificial fly that matches flies active at that time or at least common at that stage of the season. When no trout are moving, the angler may choose to 'fish the water', paying particular attention to spots favoured by trout or perhaps systematically covering every square yard of water available.

The heaviest trout tackle is that used on large reservoirs and main rivers. Anglers use rods of 9 ft. to 9 ft. 6 in. and lines known as *shooting heads*—short lengths of very heavy fly line (10 yards is normal) attached to a fine nylon line that will shoot easily through the rod rings and so ensure maximum casting distance.

It has been said that fly-fishing for trout gives a sense of enjoyment found only in this one branch of angling. Even when no fish are caught, there is satisfaction in knowing that throughout the day one has at least cast accurately and well. And then there is the pleasure which is always a part of fishing—spending long, relaxed hours in pleasant surroundings.

south as Spain.

Close seasons for salmon fishing are observed throughout the world, but opening and closing dates vary considerably from one river to another. In the British Isles, for example, an angler free to travel can enjoy his sport from New Year's Day to the end of November. But just how he fishes will depend on the state of the water and the rules governing that part of the river. And it is best if he finds out what is in store for him before he sets out.

Trout anglers are almost invariably fly-fishermen by preference. Fly-fishing began to evolve in the early Middle Ages. Until the introduction of specially dressed silk and, more recently, synthetic fibre lines, the fly was presented by allowing a light line to waft out on the breeze—a practice called *dapping*. Aided by pliant split-cane or fibreglass rods, the modern fly-fisherman casts a heavy line in such a way that the fly, which is attached to a fine nylon *cast* or line at the end of the heavy line, has to follow. The art of fly-fishing involves not only putting the fly down in the right spot, but doing it naturally and gently.

There are few areas not stocked with trout—brown trout of European origin or rainbow trout from America. In New Zealand, for example, browns were introduced from Britain in the 19th century, and rainbows followed later from California. North Island, with its thermal areas at Taupo and the Rotorua lakes and rivers, has some of the finest rainbow trout in the world, while in South Island —especially the beautiful Southern Lakes district—the brown trout is king. The so-called Brook and Lake trout, the Dolly Varden, and others of the *char* family are not trout but a separate though closely related species. All respond to

Archery

The cutting pressure of bowstring on nose and chin; the agony of blistered fingers; the *whang* of the string as the aluminium arrow cleaves the air at more than 100 mph—this is archery today. It either leaves you cold—or hooks like a drug.

Ten thousand archers from Britain, along with men and women from 40 other nations, compete regularly in one of the world's fastest-growing individual sports. World championships in target and field archery are held biennially, and target archery was reinstated for the 1972 Munich Olympic Games. Nine out of ten British archers practise their sport all the year round. In North America there are a million club and tournament archers, and millions more go bow-hunting. These are the facts. What is the attraction?

Archery's skills are easy to learn initially, but improvement becomes progressively more difficult. Hence, at one end of the competitive scale, tournament archers are known for an utter dedication. At the other end, newcomers to a club are quickly assessed, it is said—perhaps truly —by which gets priority at weekends: the mid-day meal or a day's uninterrupted shooting! The average club is a most useful foundation for the sport, welcoming beginners and giving instruction. Initial equipment, if bought new, costs little more than £10 and has a high second-hand value as an archer's skill outgrows his first equipment.

In the United States, where winters can be hard, indoor archery 'lanes'—the archery equivalent of bowling alleys—are increasing in number by a third every year. All equipment can be hired at a cost of about £1 an hour, which includes use of the lane. For this, the archer shoots in ideal conditions and then presses a button for the target to come 20 or 30 yards to him so that the arrows can be removed and the score recorded.

The annual indoor tournament in the USA is the largest archery tournament anywhere and in 1969 attracted to Cobo Hall, Detroit, almost 2,000 competing archers, each of whom would have paid around £150 to buy his equipment. Each tries to put 60 successive arrows into a 3¼-inch centre spot from a range of 20 yards—and some succeed. Altogether, about 15,000 competitive tournaments, indoor and outdoor, take place across the United States in the course of a year.

Target and *field* archery are the most competitive forms.

Target archery

In target archery any form of bow may be used, except for that rifle-like but wholly mechanical and accurate projector of bolts known as a cross-bow. A few special meetings are held each year for those who continue to enjoy shooting the traditional yew longbow—straight-limbed, about 6 ft long, and with horn *nocks* (grooves) holding the string loops.

The modern archery bow combines beauty of design and craftmanship with great efficiency in performance. It owes its tremendous resilience to a fibreglass skin, front and back, separated by tapered laminations of rock maple. The *riser*, or handle, is sculptured from attractive tropical hardwoods and gleams with synthetic lacquers. The stranded bowstring of polyester yarn travels a mere 18 inches from the fully drawn position to accelerate the arrow to a speed of well over 100 mph. The arrows themselves are of tubular aluminium alloy drawn to precision tolerances. They are carefully chosen for length, weight, and stiffness to suit the characteristics of both bow and shooter. A tournament set, straight overall to within a fraction of a thousandth of an inch, has a weight variation of less than a grain—that is, one four-hundredth of an ounce.

The target archer's bow is fitted with a sighting device, finely adjustable, not only for range but also laterally to compensate for side winds. The distance between the point of an arrow and the sighting pin is constant for any setting while the archer is at full draw. But there is no back-sight to a bow, and the accuracy with which successive arrows hit the target depends on consistency in positioning the end of the arrow that has been drawn back with the string. Most archers achieve *lateral* consistency by drawing the string to the centre of their nose and chin, and *vertical* consistency by having the index finger of their draw-hand just touching under the corner of the chin. The string is generally held by three fingers— one above and two below the arrow.

But there is infinite scope for poor shooting. The destination of each arrow depends on the set of the shoulders and wrists, on the tenseness of the hand holding the bow and, above all, on the fluidity with which the fingers of the drawing hand release the string. Here lies the fascination of the sport—its personal and perpetual challenge.

Archery requires no great physical strength—indeed it is a sport practised by all ages, and often by

Derek J. White

1 Seventy-year-old George Brown, British target archery champion in 1956 and 1960, at full draw. **2** A field archer withdraws his arrows from the animal-shaped target. The animal targets have a clearly defined centre spot surrounded by scoring lines.

J. Kember Smith

all the members of a family.

The draw-weight of women's bows is generally between 24 and 28 lb; for men the range is wider —between 35 and 45 lb. But women shoot a maximum range of 80 yards, while the men go back to 100 yards. The target at this distance is 4 ft in diameter with a centre (called the *gold*) just over 9 inches across, surrounded by four equal rings—red, blue, black, and white, in that order, working outwards. A gold is worth 9 points, the red 7, and so on down to 1 for the white.

Each target accommodates two to six archers, in two or three successive groups. The archers in a group each shoot three arrows and retire for the next group to do the same. When all have shot six arrows, the archers walk to the target to take the scores and collect their arrows before shooting again. There are a variety of different 'rounds', each comprising between 6 and 12 dozen arrows shot from different distances. The longest or longer distances are always tackled first, maintaining the ancient military tradition of shooting at an advancing enemy force. A round of 12 dozen arrows takes a full day to shoot.

Six sighting arrows are shot, but not scored, at the start of each round or day of shooting. The sport is governed by simple but effective safety rules, and some equally simple points of etiquette to ensure its fullest enjoyment. There is a traditional cry of '*Fast*!' to stop shooting in the case of some unexpected danger.

International or FITA (*Fédération Internationale de Tir à l'Arc*) rounds differ slightly from club rounds because two sizes of target face are used, and each colour is divided into an inner and outer scoring zone. This gives scoring values from 10 for an inner gold to 1 for an outer white.

Men shoot three dozen arrows at each distance: 90, 70, 50, and 30 metres. Women and juniors (under 18) shoot the same number of arrows but from 70, 60, 50, and 30 metres. At the two shorter distances a smaller target face, 80 cm across, is used, and the arrows are scored and collected after every three have been shot.

For indoor shooting, where the range is less, still smaller faces are used, and styles vary between countries. But there are neither international rules nor standard practices with indoor archery.

Field archery

Field archery has two main styles of shooting, with separate competitive classes in each. One is freestyle, and the equipment may be the same as that used by the target archer, including the use of a sight on the bow. The other style is called *instinctive* or *barebow* and, as might be expected, any attachment or mark that could be used as an aid to sighting,

or in indicating the draw length, is forbidden. An instinctive archer angles the bow so that the arrow hits the target without any deliberate or conscious aiming at all.

Field archery targets are of two types and in four sizes, between 15 and 60 cm in diameter according to the range. Shooting distances vary between 6 and 60 metres, and are not always announced beforehand. In the *field round* the outer half of the target is a black ring, and the inner part is white with a black centre spot one-sixth of the overall diameter. The outer ring scores 3 points, the inner (including the spot) 5 points. In the *hunters' round* the target is similar, but black overall, except for a white centre spot and fine ring dividing the 5- and 3-point scoring zones. Animal figures, with a clearly visible centre spot and scoring lines of similar dimensions, may also be used in both field and hunters' rounds.

A field round consists of 28 targets, or twice round a 14-target course. Four arrows are shot at each target from 10 different distances, plus one arrow at four differently spaced targets from each of four different distances. This makes a total of 56 arrows for the 14-target unit or 112 arrows for the standard round.

The hunters' round consists of the same total number of arrows, but with one arrow from each of four distance posts at every target. Two are placed between 5 and 15 metres, four between 10 and 30 metres, five between 20 and 40

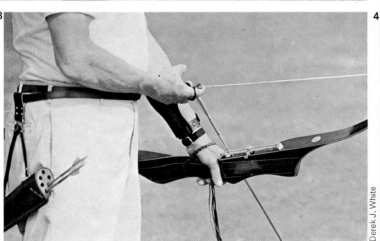

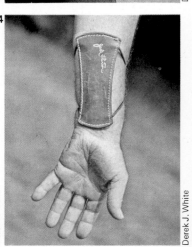

1 Close-up of the archer's target: no golds this time. The gold is the 9-inch centre worth 9 points to the marksman. The target itself is made of straw ropes.
2 Quivers vary widely in size and shape. This side-quiver is hung at the belt and is generally made of leather or similar stout material.
3 Nocking is the act of fitting the arrow onto the bowstring. The archer holds the bow obliquely across the front of his body with the bowstring resting on the inside of his forearm.
4 The arm bracer protects the arm from the bowstring.

metres, and three between 30 and 50 metres.

There are also, as in target archery, many other rounds and methods of scoring, but the field and hunters' rounds are those on which the first World Field Archery Championships were decided in August 1969.

In addition to the two main kinds of archery already described, there are many minor forms. Among them are *clout* and *flight shooting*, *popinjay*, *archery golf*, and *roving*. These forms of archery vary slightly from country to country; the rules and terms used to describe them and their equipment also vary.

Great names in archery
Two of archery's outstanding personalities were Miss B. M. Legh and Horace Ford, both of Britain. Miss Legh held the ladies' national championship 22 times between 1881 and 1922. Horace Ford was men's national champion for 12 successive years, and in 1857 scored 1251 points for the double York round shot two ways—a record that will never be broken because in 1949 two-way (i.e., back and forth) shooting was discontinued at the championships.

The archer with most world championships to her credit is Miss Kurkowska of Poland, who won in 1933, 1934, 1936, 1939,

In the Surrey archery championship at Stoke d'Abernon, ladies and gentlemen face their targets in separate competitions.

and 1947. It is remarkable that since the double FITA round was introduced, no world champion has achieved that pinnacle more than once.

History of archery
The bow and arrow were almost certainly invented many times in different parts of the world at least 10,000 years ago, but their use for target archery as a sport can be dated from the decline of the bow as a military weapon in the middle of the 1500s. Originally the bow had been a tool for man's survival. In the 1300s it became the decisive weapon during the long-drawn-out wars between England and France.

The prowess of King Henry VIII, in the early 1500s, extended to the use of the bow, and archery was popular then as a pastime among the leisured classes. King George IV is supposed to have invented the present method of scoring. When Prince of Wales he started the Toxophilite Society with some members of Finsbury Archers, an organization that had shot on Finsbury Fields (now part of central London) since the Honorable Artillery Company discarded the bow 150 years earlier.

The Royal Toxophilite Society, as it is now known, is among some 600 archery societies and clubs in Britain today. The governing body for archery in England and Wales is the Grand National Archery Society (GNAS) formed in 1951 by the fusion of several regional societies.

Twenty years earlier than

GNAS, in 1931, FITA was born. This is the international federation for shooting with the bow. The members of FITA are national amateur archery associations, one from each country. The GNAS represents Britain. The National Archery Association of the United States represents American archers, and members of other English-speaking countries are represented by the South African National Archery Association, the Archery Association of Australia, the New Zealand, Rhodesian, and Canadian archery associations, and the Irish National Archery Federation.

FITA introduced world archery championships in 1931 as a single FITA round shot over two days. The championships were held annually, except for the war years, until 1950. Now the target archery championships are held every two years, as a double FITA round shot over four days. In the alternate years, European target and field championships may be held. In 1969 the XXVth World Archery Championships were held for the first time outside Europe—at Valley Forge national park, in Pennsylvania.

Before the 1969 championships were held, American archers had provided six out of the seven world champion men and six of the seven world champion women since the double FITA round was introduced in 1957. Moreover, American women, as a team of three, have won the women's team award all but once, since it was introduced in 1957. To

underline their dominance of the sport, the United States have had both a women's and a men's team in the first three places for seven consecutive championships. At the 1972 Olympics the Americans, through J. Williams and D. Wilbur, took the gold medals.

Apart from world championships, each member country of FITA has the opportunity of holding up to 10 tournaments a year at which world records may be established, both for the FITA rounds and for the separate distances in each round.

Since 1966, FITA have also arranged competitive postal shoots for individuals and teams, and separate ones for boys and girls under 18. In 1968 an outstanding score of 1,208 was made in the junior FITA match by an Australian boy, Graeme Gwin.

Shortly before World War II, yew longbows and wooden arrows were being used. Since then composite bows, with their new materials and adhesives, and perfectly matched metal arrows, have become universal. As equipment design has improved, so has the ceiling for shooting skills, with the result that scores are now double what they were 30 years ago. The question now constantly posed is just how much higher can they go? With records still being broken every year there is no sign that any limit is in sight. Yet behind this modern sport, with its plastics-age equipment, lingers the traditional archery motto, seemingly far removed from its martial origins—*Union, Trueheart and Courtesie.*

Picturepoint

Athletics

Everybody runs, jumps and throws at some time in his life—often for sheer joy, occasionally for survival. The 'stuff' of athletics is natural human activity—an inheritance, perhaps, from the days when man's life depended on his speed, agility, strength and skill.

Athletics, the premier Olympic sport, has long enjoyed a special status with the public, and today television coverage has spread the interest to all parts of the world. The thrilling transmissions from the Mexico Olympics in 1968, which kept millions of European viewers out of their beds until the small hours of the morning, won hosts of new admirers for the sport. A British survey showed athletics to be the third most popular televised sport, after soccer and professional boxing. Ironically, in spite of the sport's popularity, attendances at meetings in most countries have progressively diminished in recent years.

Athletics is also popular with participants. To reach the highest level demands extraordinary dedication, for the standards of performance are frighteningly high. Yet athletics still has much to offer the less dedicated or physically gifted competitor. Each participant can find a grade of competition to match his or her talents and, apart from the challenge of personal rivalry, there is the unique satisfaction of an athlete's gauging his own progress with a stopwatch or tape measure.

Athletics is richly varied. The sprinter, marathon runner, pole vaulter, and hammer thrower may seem to have little in common—but they are all athletes. There is no such thing as a 'typical' athlete, for they come in all shapes, sizes, and ages—from emaciated long distance runners weighing little more than 100 lb to the muscular giants of the throwing circles; from sub-teenagers to Joe Deakin, Olympic gold medallist in 1908 and still an active runner at the age of 90.

There is no short cut to the top.

An aspiring distance running champion needs to pound out more than 100 miles each week in training. A thrower, besides paying meticulous attention to detail, has to lift prodigious weights to develop his strength. But training alone is no guarantee of success, because physical preparation cannot make a champion unless he has also the will to win. For a runner this can mean the ability to transcend the 'pain barrier' and continue at maximum effort when the going is toughest. For a field event performer, who competes 'in a vacuum', it is the knack of channelling all his skill and concentration into a brief but complicated series of movements to a greater degree of purpose than ever before.

Competitions

With the notable exception of the United States, where the system is primarily inter-collegiate, the athletics club forms the backbone of the sport. An individual, depending on his calibre, can normally make steady progress. Most countries (again excepting the U.S.) stage regional or area championships, with the successful competitors qualifying for the national championships. The results of these championships help the selectors to choose the country's international team.

Most international competitions are made up of dual or sometimes three-sided matches, and many European nations engage in up to half a dozen of these encounters each season. The United States, Canada, Australia, New Zealand, and the South American and African nations are worse off in this respect because of the long distances involved in travelling. But the U.S. almost invariably fields the strongest and most glamorous teams, and their popularity with European fans is so high that they annually arrange a number of tours in Europe.

The 'summit match', conducted on a home and away basis, is the U.S. v U.S.S.R. clash, started in

The staggered start, such as this one in a 400-metre race, compensates for the greater distance of the outside lanes.

Colour Sport

USA 110 metres hurdles star,
Willie Davenport, powers his
way to a gold medal in the
1968 Olympics at Mexico.

Moscow in 1958. The series was interrupted in 1966 when the Soviet team withdrew from a Los Angeles match for political reasons, but was resumed in 1969.

Another attractive international team competition is the European Cup. It was started in 1965, with Russia winning both men's and women's trophies that year and again in 1967.

The most important international competition of all is, of course, the Olympic Games, which actually incorporates the International Amateur Athletic Federation's world championships. These are staged every four years, as are the British Commonwealth Games, Asian Games, and Pan-American Games. The other major regional championships which, like the Olympics, are conducted on an individual and not a national team-scoring basis, are the European Championships, which are held every four years, and the All-African Games, which were first held in 1965 and were not contested again until 1973.

Events

The programme for the 1972 Olympic Games in Munich showed the wide range of events classified as athletics. There are 24 events for men: 100, 200, 400, 800, 1,500, 5,000, and 10,000 metres, marathon, 3,000 metres steeplechase, 110 metres and 400 metres hurdles, 4 by 100 metres and 4 by 400 metres relays, high jump, pole vault, long jump, triple jump, shot put, discus throw, hammer throw, javelin throw, decathlon, and the 20 kilometres and 50 kilometres road walks. Women have 14 events from which to choose: 100, 200, 400, 800, and 1,500 metres, 100 metres hurdles, 4 by 100 metres and 4 by 400 metres relays, high jump, long jump, shot put, discus throw, javelin throw, and pentathlon. Those are the standard international events, but there are many other distances outside the Olympics that are recognized for world records, such as the 100 yards and the mile, as well as cross-country running events.

Each event radiates its own appeal and contributes to the unique attraction of the sport as a whole. The 100 metres sprint is perhaps the purest of all athletic endeavours: a straightforward test of speed in which top class male competitors gobble up the distance in 45 strides and take barely 10 seconds for the journey. Men such as Olympic champions Bob Hayes and Jim Hines have reached speeds of about 27 mph at around the 60 metres mark— the stage at which maximum speed is attained.

The 200 and 400 metres races are also classified as sprints, but here the athlete must ration his effort. The classic example of an otherwise great runner paying the price for faulty pace judgement was Jamaica's Herb McKenley

1 David Hemery, gold medal winner at the Mexico Olympics, demonstrates his immaculate hurdling style. 2 Leading British steeplechaser John Jackson convincingly clears the water jump. The object is to land as far over the water as possible so as not to get soaked to the skin. 3 Valerie Peat hands over the baton to Lillian Board during a women's sprint relay. At that moment both runners should be moving at the same speed. 4 A classic 5,000 metres duel between Vladimir Kuts (3) and Chris Chataway (1) which the Englishman won in world record time

5 The 10,000 metres allows spectators nearly half an hour to get involved in the race. There was emotion aplenty when, in 1969, Britain's Dick Taylor loped round the track to beat Ron Clarke, Australia's world record-holder, in the fourth fastest 10,000 metres ever run. 6 The 1,500 metres, or the 'metric mile', has had a fascination all its own since the days of Paavo Nurmi. It nearly always resolves itself into a battle of tactics, and here the three Britons (Stewart, Douglas, and Boulter) crowd out their French rivals on the bend. 7 In the race walking events walkers must have continuous contact with the ground. The strain shows clearly as Paul Nihill breaks the tape. 8 The moment of truth—the 400 metres runners hit the home stretch. 9 The 200 metres is usually a desperate sprint, but not for world record-holder Tommie Smith!

In the 1948 Olympic 400 metres final he set such a fierce pace for the first 200 metres that he weakened disastrously in the closing stages and was overtaken by his much less fancied team-mate, Arthur Wint. Four years later, in the next Olympic 400 metres final, McKenley went to the other extreme: he held back early to such a degree that, although finishing faster than any-one else in the race, he just failed to catch yet another Jamaican colleague, George Rhoden.

The most popular races with the crowds are what are loosely called the middle distance events: 800 to 10,000 metres, plus the 3,000 metres steeplechase. These races, lasting between $1\frac{3}{4}$ minutes and half an hour, give the spectator a chance to become really involved in what is occurring on the track, and the tactical battles waged there can be wholly engrossing. Some athletes, known as front runners, are happiest when dictating a fast pace which they hope will dishearten and ultimately destroy the opposition. John Landy, Vladimir Kuts, and Ron Clarke are among those who achieved great success with these tactics. But if the front runner is not able to shake off his pursuer, then the advantage in the closing stages switches to the man who is following, should he be blessed with a good 'kick' or finishing sprint. Roger Bannister and Chris Chataway, notably in their respective duels with Landy and Kuts in 1954, proved that.

The greatest middle distance runners of all have been those equally adept at setting a mur-derous pace or, when circum-stances favour it, just tagging along behind, ready to out-sprint the field. Emil Zatopek, Herb Elliott, Peter Snell, and Jim Ryun had this enviable talent.

Few would deny that the marathon, run over a distance of 26 miles 385 yards, is the most gruelling of all athletic activities, but in a different way there is an equally exacting test of all-round ability known as the decathlon. During two successive days the athlete is called upon to sprint 100 metres, long jump, put the shot, high jump, run 400 metres, negotiate the 110 metres hurdles, throw the discus, pole vault, toss the javelin and, as a masochistic finale to the proceedings, drag his, by now, very weary body around 1,500 metres. The corre-sponding event for women, the pentathlon, is less demanding, though formidable by normal standards. It comprises the 100 metres hurdles, shot put, high jump, long jump, and 200 metres.

The four jumps (two for women) and four throws (three for women) are collectively known as the field events. The high jump and pole vault, where a visible physical barrier (the bar) has to be conquered, are increasingly being appreciated by spectators.

23

At one time field events tended to be regarded as the poor relations of the track events. But the thrills of the Mexico Olympics, when thousands in the stadium and millions before their TV screens were gripped by the sight of men catapulting themselves well over 17 feet in the pole vault, by Dick Fosbury 'flopping' his way to victory in the high jump, and not least by Bob Beamon's almost unbelievable 29-ft long jump, proved once and for all that field events are at least the equal of track events in drama, excitement, and beauty.

An Athletics Meeting

The starter in his red coat . . . the suspense of a neck-and-neck race . . . the agonized wait of a lonely jumper facing his last attempt— these are images conjured up by almost any athletics meeting, but what is usually overlooked or taken for granted is the organization that makes it all possible.

An athletics club, staging a full programme of men's and women's events in a local 'open' meeting (a meeting where athletes enter as individuals on payment of an entry fee, and where there are prizes to be won), has to start preparing at least six months in advance. The club sends the proposed date to the national governing body under whose rules the meeting must be conducted, and books the local stadium for that day. Money can be one of the main problems. The income from admission charges, sale of programmes, and entry fees is unlikely to cover the cost of stadium hire, printing, advertising, and prizes.

Many officials are needed to run the meeting. There are the track referee, track judges and umpires, the field events referee, the starter, field judges, timekeepers, lap scorers, a clerk of the course, and a sprinkling of stewards. In addition there must be an announcer, with assistants to feed him information, and a recorder to keep the official results.

Tracks and Installations

For many years athletes ran on grass, dirt, or cinder tracks that reacted unfavourably to bad weather. But in the late 1960s these outmoded surfaces were increasingly replaced with all-weather, resilient, plastic-surfaced tracks. These tracks, although initially much more expensive, save money in the long run. They provide a fast and firm surface, have permanent markings, need virtually no upkeep, do not wear out, and remain in perfect condition. They are immensely popular with athletes and have resulted in a dramatic improvement in performance. Such tracks are now used for the Olympic, Pan-American and Commonwealth Games and the European Championships.

The standard length of a running track is either 400 metres or 440 yards. It should not be less

Below A rare bird in British athletics, Arthur Rowe held the European shot-put record in 1961, and his British record still stood in 1969. He gained most of his strength at his work—he was a blacksmith. *Insert above* Since the development of the American aerodynamic javelin in 1953, 50 ft has been added to the world record. Speed and strength combine to propel the object up to 300 ft. *Insert below* Erstwhile British record holder Mike Ellis prepares to throw the 16-lb hammer. The cage protects onlookers from any stray throws.

© George König

Colour Sport

24

1 The tug-of-war is no longer an Olympic event but it is popular at British meetings. **2** Both discus and javelin date back to Greek times. Here Britain's Bill Tancred lets loose with a mighty heave. **3** Fred Alsop, fourth in the 1964 Olympic Games, performs in the triple jump. In Mexico City the world mark was beaten no less than five times. **4** American Ralph Boston won three Olympic long-jump medals, and broke the 25-year-old world record.

than 24 ft in width, and each lane must be at least 4 ft wide. Most tracks have six or seven lanes, but eight lanes are now obligatory for the major events such as the Olympics and European Championships.

The eight field events are held inside or adjacent to the track. The installations are a high jump take-off and landing area, pole vault runway and landing area, long and triple jump runways and sandpits, shot, discus, and hammer circles, and javelin run-up. A water jump for the steeplechase is located either just inside or just outside the main track.

Equipment

What equipment does an athlete need? The rules of England's Amateur Athletic Association stipulate only that 'in all events competitors must wear at least a vest and shorts which are clean and so designed and worn as not to be objectionable. The clothing must be made of a material which is non-transparent even if wet.' Other items vital to the athlete are a track suit and appropriate footwear. Many types of shoe are manufactured—with flat, corrugated, studded, or spiked soles, depending on the event for which they are required.

The only technical equipment essential for a track runner is starting blocks—and this applies only to sprinters and hurdlers. The blocks provide a firm support for the athlete's vigorous leg drive at the start of a race, and experi-

ments have indicated that the advantage of blocks (as compared with holes in the track) is about 1 ft, a significant margin in a sprint race.

Other personal items of athletic impedimenta are poles, shots, discuses, hammers, and javelins. Poles, invariably made of glass fibre where top athletes are concerned, are particularly expensive. They can easily cost £40 each, and it is not unknown for a high-flying vaulter to break half a dozen in a season.

Training and Coaching

What does it take to become, say, one of the world's great marathon runners? Courage, determination, persistence . . . and unending training. During an average week marathon runner Bill Adcocks put in 128 miles of road running in all weathers. In addition, he worked normal office hours in order to earn his living. Miler Jim Ryun made it all look so easy with a long, unfaltering stride, but behind every minute spent racing there were many hours of tortuous training well away from the public gaze. His preparations included running up to 20 miles cross-country in a day, weight training, and intensive but skilfully planned track sessions.

The bulk of Ryun's track workouts consisted of what is known as interval (or fast-slow) training. This is the staple diet of most leading middle distance runners, and involves running a certain distance over and over again at a predetermined speed with a set recovery phase between each timed run. A high quality example would be ten runs of 400 metres or 440 yards in 60 seconds, with a 200-metres or 220-yards walk or jog between each. The great Emil Zatopek, the hardest-training athlete of his era, carried this method to extremes. At one time he was running a hundred stretches of 400 metres, in two sets of 50, in a day!

Another method of training, not unlike Ryun's mixture but usually carried out away from track and stopwatch, and preferably over varied terrain, is *fartlek*, a Swedish term that literally means 'speed-play'. One of its attractions is that there is no standard formula. The athlete can mix short sprints, sustained fast striding, and long steady runs with jogging and walking in endless combinations, as the mood takes him. A third basic system of training for middle distance runners, as evolved by the New Zealander Arthur Lydiard, calls for much lengthy road running (up to 20 miles or so at a time) and hill climbing during a four-month programme, before undertaking track work.

Weight training, an optional extra for the middle and long distance runner, is necessary for most sprinters, hurdlers, and jumpers, for whom explosiveness as well as sound technique is vital. The thrower benefits most from the intensive strength training provided by various weight lifting movements.

An athlete's standard of performance depends largely on his training, particularly during the winter, but another important factor is coaching. Athletes have won Olympic titles and broken world records without any coaching at all, but most of them benefit from the guidance of a coach or training adviser. Athletes in 'technical' events such as sprinting, hurdling, jumping, and throwing are particularly dependent on a coach to correct their faults. But equally important is the coach's psychological role. Coaching, in the words of Arthur Lydiard, 'is an art, bringing the athlete right on the relevant day'.

Some coaches have produced a string of great athletes. Two of the most celebrated of champion-

1 Laying the Tartan track at Crystal Palace. A tarmac base is capped by a layer of rubberized 'cinders'. 2 The pole vault, a gymnastic event for athletes, is one of the many events demanding skill as well as pure strength.

Notice the built-up landing pit, the mobile fork-lift truck for replacing the bar, and the long run-up track. 3 V. Stepanov (USSR) high-jumps 7 ft 1½ in, but using the thick-soled shoe banned by the IAAF in 1958.

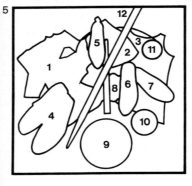

4 Today's athletes are clothed in and use an expensive array of equipment:
1 Track suit
2 Shorts
3 Vest
4 Training shoes
5 Ridge-soled road shoes
6 Spiked track shoes
7 Studded cross-country shoes
8 Starting blocks
9 Discus (4 lb 6½oz)
10 Shot (16 lb)
11 Hammer (16 lb)
12 Javelin (800 grammes)

builders in a variety of events were Dean Cromwell and 'Dink' Templeton, both of whom died in 1962. Another successful all-rounder has been Austrian-born Franz Stampfl. Once a British resident but now settled in Australia, Stampfl coached such diverse characters as Olympic 800-metres champion Ralph Doubell, first four-minute miler Roger Bannister, 1958 European 1,500-metres champion Brian Hewson, ex-world 5,000-metres record-holder Chris Chataway, multi-record-breaker Ron Clarke, 1956 Olympic steeplechase gold medallist Chris Brasher, and former world high jump record-holder Thelma Hopkins.

Many coaches specialize in one event or a group of events. Bud Winter (USA) is unrivalled in the production of great sprinters. His pupils have included Hal Davis, Ray Norton, Tommie Smith, Ronnie Ray Smith, Lee Evans, and John Carlos. In the world of middle distance running the names of Arthur Lydiard (who coached Peter Snell and Murray Halberg), Australian Percy Cerutty (Herb Elliott and John Landy), and Hungarian-born U.S. citizen Mihaly Igloi (Sandor Iharos, Laszlo Tabori, Istvan Rozsavolgyi, and Jim Beatty) are in a class of their own.

Organization
The supreme governing body in athletics is the International Amateur Athletic Federation, founded in 1912.

Each member country's athletics is controlled by a national governing body. In Britain the situation is complicated. The Amateur Athletic Association (with more than 1,000 affiliated clubs) runs men's athletics in England and Wales, while the Women's AAA, Scottish AAA, Scottish WAAA, Northern Irish AAA and Northern Irish WAAA govern their own territories. There are also some semi-autonomous bodies such as the English Cross-Country Union and the Race Walking Association. The body representing Britain and Northern Ireland on the IAAF (only one organization per nation is allowed) is the British Amateur Athletic Board.

Next to the AAA, founded in 1880, the oldest national governing bodies are the New Zealand AAA (1887), the Amateur Athletic Union of USA (1888), Ligue Royale Belge d'Athletisme (1889), and the AAU of Canada (1889).

Junior, Youth, and School Athletics
Age categories in junior athletics are bewildering, and there has been little attempt at standardization. The AAA stipulates that juniors are aged 17 and 18, youths 15 and 16, and boys 13 and 14. But the only records ratified are AAA under-19 records, which can be made in England and Wales by any United Kingdom athlete of appropriate age. Under Women's AAA rules, an inter-

1 In the now-famous Kenyan colours, Kipchoge Keino, 1968 Olympic 1,500 metres champion, strides round the Cardiff track. Keino is one of the many outstanding athletes to come from the hitherto 'dark' continent. **2** The Golden Girl of Australian athletics in the late 1950s, Betty Cuthbert, practises a start before a sprint race. She collected four 'golds' in three Olympic Games. **3** Professional running has been out of vogue for 50 years now, but this annual professional sprint, the Powderhall, still takes place in Edinburgh. Many of the competitors come from the English rugby league clubs. **4** Sheila Carey maintains form right through the tape in this relay held on London's all-weather track at Crystal Palace. Runners may 'tie-up' in close finishes, especially in the longer sprint events.

mediate is an athlete between 15 and 17 and a junior, one between 11 and 15. No official records are kept.

The IAAF does not recognize any form of junior records and there are no official age limits, but it is widely accepted internationally that a junior is one who has not reached his or her 20th birthday during the year of competition. European Junior Games were staged in 1966 and 1968, and European Junior Championships in 1970 and 1974.

Many teenage athletes have reached world standards. On an Olympic level, the youngest champions have been Maureen Caird (Australia), winner of the 1968 80-metres hurdles title, Mihaela Penes (Romania), women's javelin winner in 1964, and Bob Mathias (U.S.), decathlon gold medallist in 1948; all were 17. The youngest world record holder is Doreen Lumley (New Zealand), who was 17½ when she equalled the 100 yards record of 11.0 sec, in 1939.

Professional Athletics

For the first threequarters of this century, professional athletics was unimportant internationally, though the period after the 1972 Olympics saw the birth of a new professional group, International Track Association, which took into its ranks some of the leading athletes of the time, notably Kip Keino, Lee Evans, and Jim Ryun. Although well organized, it did not prove conclusively that it had genuine spectator appeal.

There was a time, throughout the 1800s and the early years of the 1900s, when the leading 'pros' were better than their unpaid brethren. Their meetings attracted vast crowds, and large sums of money were wagered on men such as Britain's Walter George, whose mile time of 4 min 12.75 sec in 1886 survived all onslaughts, by amateur and professional alike, until 1935.

The classic events in the professional athletics calendar are the Powderhall New Year Sprint in Edinburgh, a 120-yards handicap race carrying a first prize of £500, and the Stawell Gift 130-yards handicap in Australia, for a first prize of $1700 (Australian).

History

Nobody knows precisely when men first began to run, jump, and throw competitively, but the Olympic Games of Ancient Greece were in existence in 776 B.C. and may have begun some 600 years earlier. The first measured performance recorded for posterity was a long jump of 23 ft 1½ in, by a Spartan athlete names Chionis, in the Olympic Games of 656 B.C. Those games, the most celebrated of a cycle that included the Pythian, Nemean, and Isthmian Games, continued at four-yearly intervals (called *Olympiads*) until they were abolished in A.D. 393 by the Roman emperor Theodosius.

Running, jumping, and hammer throwing joined shin kicking, climbing the greasy pole, and grinning competitions as among the most popular features of the many fairs and festivals of medieval England. Two important developments of the 1600s were the revival of the ancient Olympic ideal, through the Cotswold Games, and the growing attraction of *pedestrianism*, or professional foot-racing.

Amateur athletics as known today began to evolve in the 1800s. The Royal Military College at Sandhurst founded an annual sports day in 1812, and five years later the world's first athletic club, the Necton Guild, came into being in Norfolk. Rugby School's Crick Run, a fearsome cross-country race described in *Tom Brown's Schooldays*, was instituted in 1837, and soon afterwards several other public schools introduced athletics into their sporting curricula. The universities followed suit, and in 1850 Exeter College Athletic Club—the oldest still in existence—was formed in Oxford.

27

1 The first verifiable
athletics meeting in history
was probably the Olympic
Games of Ancient Greece held
in 776 B.C. This frieze from
Greek pottery shows three
athletes preparing for the
contest with massage and
liniments. **2** Greek sculptor
Myron's bronze statue of the
Discobolus or Discus-Thrower
provides a remarkable study
in changing techniques. The
athlete turns his head and
body as he swings but does
not make a complete turn as
in the modern style.

A key event in athletics history
came in 1863, when England's
first open amateur meeting was
organized by the West London
Rowing Club. Two years later
the oldest of all surviving open
clubs, Mincing Lane Athletic
Club (renamed London Athletic
Club in 1866), was founded. In
the meantime the sport had
spread to Canada and the United
States, and English students were
responsible for staging the first
meeting on the European continent, in Dresden in 1874.

The world's first national
championships were, not surprisingly, the English—promoted
by the Amateur Athletic Club in
1866. But these were restricted to
'gentlemen amateurs' drawn from
the universities, the services, and
the professional classes. It was not
until 1880, when the Amateur
Athletic Association replaced the
AAC, that the championships
were thrown open to all amateurs.
Four years earlier the first
recorded instance of an international match—an unofficial
Ireland *v* England encounter—
was staged.

About the turn of the century
the British and Irish, pre-eminent
during the early years of development, were gradually overhauled
by the Americans, with their
intensive system of inter-collegiate
competition. World records were
not ratified officially by the International Amateur Athletic
Federation until 1913, but unofficial lists of best performances
at the start of 1900 show a
massive dominance by the United
States. Indeed, the only record

holder from a non-English-
speaking nation was a Swedish
javelin thrower.

The results of the first modern
Olympic Games, in Athens in
1896, tell the same story. Apart
from Australia's Edwin Flack in
the 800 and 1,500 metres, the only
non-American to win a title was
the Greek marathon runner
Spiridon Louis. Mainly on senti-
mental grounds, Louis has secured
a permanent niche in the athletes'
hall of fame, but who were the
truly great stars of the 1800s?
One who stands out is the American Lon Myers, who between 1880
and 1888 held the world's best
times for 100, 440, and 880 yards,
and reduced the quarter-mile
record from 50.4 to 48.8 sec.
Another was England's Walter

3 The shot put calls for
strength, co-ordination, and
tremendous speed of move-
ment. Russia's muscular Galina
Zybina prepares to put with
the shot tucked in her neck,
so that her body takes most
of the weight. **4** In 1969 the
1,500 metres for women was
recognized as a new
international event in
athletics. A star of the
event, flying Dutch girl Mia
Gommers is seen here
powering round the track.
5 Britain's Sheila Sherwood,
long jump silver medallist
at Mexico in 1968.
Opposite Determination is
etched on every face in a
1,500 metres heat in Athens.

George. As an amateur he won
national titles at every distance
from 880 yards to 10 miles and
set several world records, but his
finest achievements came as a
professional—notably his mile
time of 4 min 12.75 sec in 1886.
No Briton bettered that mark
until Sydney Wooderson arrived
on the scene in 1935!

As athletics has spread to every
corner of the globe, so the number
of nations producing all-time
greats has grown steadily, with the
U.S. still in the forefront. What
about the supreme athlete of them
all? No panel of experts would
agree on a single name, but any
short list must include the American Negro Jesse Owens, winner of
four gold medals in the 1936
Olympics, whose long jump record
of 26 ft 8¼ in lasted 25 years;
Paavo Nurmi, the Phantom Finn,
nine times an Olympic Games
gold medallist from 1920 to 1928,
and creator of a score of world
records between 1,500 and 20,000
metres; Czech army officer Emil
Zatopek, who defied the laws of
probability by winning the 5,000
metres, 10,000 metres, and marathon at the 1952 Olympics, in
addition to many other outstanding achievements; and perennial
Al Oerter of the United States,
whose discus victory in the 1968
Games was his fourth successive
Olympic triumph—an unprecedented feat.

Women's Athletics
The story of women's athletics
has not always been happy.
Women were forbidden, on pain
of death, from even watching the
ancient Olympic Games. Instead,
they held their own four-yearly
Heraea Games, named after the
god Zeus's wife, Hera. In 1922
England's Amateur Athletic Association declined responsibility for
women's athletics, at that time
considered unladylike by many
men. For that reason the Women's
AAA came into being. In the same
year the Fédération Sportive
Feminine Internationale (formed
in October 1921) learned that
their request for women's events
to be added to the 1924 Olympic
programme had been refused.
They defiantly went ahead and
staged their own Women's
Olympic Games in Paris—to the
fury of the International Olympic
Committee. As usual, the ladies
eventually got their way, and
women's athletics entered the
Olympic arena at the 1928 Games
in Amsterdam.

Women's athletics in the
modern era had been born in the
U.S. about the turn of the century,
but it was not until 1917 that the
first national governing body—
the French—was set up. International competition began at
Monte Carlo in 1921, when five
countries were represented, the
star of the meeting being Britain's
Mary Lines. The novelty of young
ladies appearing in a state of comparative (but exceedingly modest)
undress drew no fewer than 25,000

spectators to an international meeting at Stamford Bridge, London, in 1924. Many came to scoff, and left admiring those pioneers in their knee-length 'shorts' and flapping shirts.

Physiologically speaking, women are not as well equipped for athletics as men, and certain events such as the pole vault, hammer, steeplechase, and triple jump are considered unsuitable and officially banned. On average, women have relatively longer bodies and shorter legs than men, their hips and thighs are heavier, and their centre of gravity is lower. More fatty tissue and less muscle results in a lower strength-to-weight ratio, while the ratio of heart weight to body weight is less than a man's, as is also a woman's oxygen-carrying capacity.

But by virtue of hard training and expert coaching, these disadvantages have been reduced to the point where top girl athletes can produce performances in some events that are the envy of many male competitors. Some examples are 11.0 sec for the 100 metres by the American flier Wyomia Tyus; 22.5 sec for the 200 metres by Poland's Irenal Szewinska; and 26.2 sec for the 200 metres hurdles by Chi Cheng of Taiwan. In the high jump, Romania's long-legged Iolanda Balas has cleared 6 ft 3¼ in; in the long jump, Viorica Viscopoleanu of Romania has leaped 22 ft 4½ in. Women will never be able to run, hurdle, jump, and throw as well as men, but the gap will continue to narrow as the female side of the sport develops.

Suspicions that a few of the most prominent competitors were not in fact female at all have been the one factor hindering total public acceptance of women's athletics. But since the introduction of 'sex-tests' (by chromosome count) before major international events such as the Olympic Games, this last lingering doubt has been removed. Only one athlete is known to have failed the test, though a number of others whose status might have been in doubt chose prudently to retire rather than submit to inspection.

Progression of World Records
Each new generation of athletes

1 Athletics in the 1800s had a rather casual air about them, compared with today's high-powered training sessions. Hurdling technique in this Oxford and Cambridge meeting of 1883 is decidedly quaint. **2** Lord Burghley, later Marquess of Exeter, was a hurdling genius. Among his scores of trophies were a gold medal in the 1928 Olympics 400 metres hurdles, and three golds in the 1930 Empire Games. He threw his leg slightly across the hurdle because of an old injury. **3** World record-holder Jim Ryun kicks away from Kipchoge Keino to win another sub-four-minute mile.

confounds its predecessors with the records it achieves, yet there is no sign of any let-up.

The highly successful U.S. coach, Brutus Hamilton, when presenting his 'Table of the Ultimates of Human Effort in Track and Field' in 1934, considered in all seriousness that such performances as 46.2 sec for 400 metres (the then world record), 3 min 44.8 sec for 1,500 metres, 8 min 05.9 sec for 3,000 metres, 14 min 02.4 sec for 5,000 metres, and 29 min 17.7 sec for 10,000 metres would be the last word in human endeavour. The world records for these events, some 40 years later, stood at 43.8 sec; 3 min 32.2 sec; 7 min 39.6 sec; 13 min 13 sec; and 27 min 30.8 sec respectively.

Current world records in the field events also appeared utterly unrealistic in the 1930s. Hamilton boldly predicted a 6 ft 11¼ in high jump, 15 ft 1 in pole vault, 27 ft 4¾ in long jump, 54 ft 0¼ in triple jump, 57 ft 0 in shot put, 182 ft 1 in discus throw, 200 ft 8 in hammer throw and 256 ft 10 in javelin throw. Compare those with the 7 ft 6½ in, 18 ft 5¾ in, 29 ft 2½ in, 57 ft 2¾ in, 71 ft 7 in, 230 ft 11 in, 250 ft 8 in, and 308 ft 8 in, respectively, that have already been accomplished.

Why such dramatic progress? Harder and more scientific training is one reason. Among others are improved track surfaces and, in specific cases like the glass fibre pole and aerodynamic javelin, the advent of revolutionary new equipment. Weight training has been the major cause of the extraordinary explosion in the throwing events. There are also psychological reasons. When one man finally breaks through a seemingly impassable barrier others will follow. The four-minute mile and seven-foot high jump, for example, withstood the assault of generations of athletes, but since Roger Bannister (1954) and Charles Duman (1956) respectively showed the way, such performances have become commonplace.

One of the most fascinating, if ultimately profitless, speculations by athletics fans is in comparing athletes from different eras. Would Bob Hayes have beaten Jesse Owens in the 100 metres? How would Cornelius Warmerdam, who completely dominated vaulting in his day, have fared with a glass pole? Who would have won in a 10,000-metres race featuring Ron Clarke, Emil Zatopek, and Paavo Nurmi? Statistics suggest that Clarke would have finished a full lap ahead of Zatopek and 2½ laps clear of Nurmi. But merely comparing times, and ignoring such factors as the training methods—and competitive standards—of the day is certainly unfair. The only reasonable method of comparison is to assess a man's degree of superiority over his contemporaries, and to measure the duration of his records. On that basis, Zatopek and Nurmi would show up very well indeed. But now, what of athletic prowess in the future? Facilities will continue to improve, training will become even more scientific in its approach, and therefore the speculator will argue that records in all spheres of athletics will continue to be broken. Yet until the scientists produce something extraordinary that will turn the ordinary human into a superman, there must be some limit to the amount of physical effort of which any man or woman is capable.

Just how close we might be to the day when the ultimate is reached is yet another argument for the speculators.

Australian Rules Football

Australian rules football is virtually unknown outside Australia. Even there, this fast-moving, rugged spectacle is the major winter sport of only four States—Victoria, South Australia, Western Australia, and Tasmania. And yet 'rules' rates as a sporting phenomenon at any level. It is played, watched, and reported with all the fanatical dedication and emotional involvement of cricket in the West Indies, rugby union in New Zealand, and the bullfight in Spain.

The game is played on the largest field—twice the area of a soccer pitch—and by the biggest teams—18 men a side—known to football.

Variously described as 'a game for super-athletes' and 'ballet with blood', Australian rules has enormous crowd appeal. Bigger football audiences have been recorded at Hampden Park and in some of the huge stadiums of South America. But these have been in densely settled areas, and usually at international matches. On a *per capita* basis, no sporting event can pack them in like a simple club match in Melbourne.

Melbourne, with its environs, has a population of over 2 million. On any winter Saturday, about one person in every 16 watches matches in the Victorian Football League, the top club competition. Replays of the day's games—probably uniquely in the world of sport—push other programmes out of Saturday's early-evening TV time. And the remarkable feature of this interest is that these are not contests between states or even cities, but between 11 Melbourne suburban sides and one from the nearby country centre of Geelong.

For matches between their state teams and Victoria (usually the strongest state), Perth and Adelaide muster one in every five and one in every eight of the respective populations.

In Melbourne, football mania reaches epidemic proportions in September, when the finals series closes the season. The finals, played between the top four clubs on the VFL league table, attract an average attendance of 90,000. The 1968 Grand Final was watched by 116,800.

Before seat reservation sales were introduced in 1957, big crowds camped outside the ground up to a week before the gates opened. Even now, when all tickets are sold weeks before the Grand Final, people sleep outside the ground in makeshift shelters to get the best standing positions when the gates open.

Supporters identify strongly with their clubs. They not only wear clothing in club colours, but carry rugs, cushions, vacuum flasks, and carrier bags in club colours. In Melbourne it is possible for the loyal club fan to buy mats, bath towels, bed spreads, and even gas cookers and refrigerators in his club's colours.

What is it about Australian rules that induces such fanaticism? It is not a single aspect of the game, although the grace and agility of men *marking*, or catching, the ball high above an opponent give rules its most distinctive and dramatic quality. But the deft ball-handling at top speed, the long kicking—goals are frequently scored from 60-yard kicks—and the fierce physical clashes all make their contribution to the quickening of the pulse rate. It is this mixture of grace, skill, and rugged aggression that gives Australian rules such a strong and passionate following.

Development of the game

Gold brought Australia its biggest 19th-century influx of immigrants. It also brought the first crude form of Australian rules to the vast continent. Diggers on the goldfields of Ballarat and Bendigo were reported in the newspapers of the 1850s playing a game that appeared to be 'a conglomeration of many sports, including football, wrestling, and general rough house'. Because Irishmen outnumbered other nationalities on the diggings, the new game had a strong flavour of Gaelic football; because law and order was rudimentary and unwelcome, it had few rules; and because space was unlimited, play was unconfined by boundaries.

The first 'organized' game was held in Melbourne in 1858, between Scotch College and Melbourne Grammar School. In the manner of Shrovetide matches still played today between villages in the English Midlands and North, the goals were set a quarter of a mile apart and there were 40 players on each side. After three weeks of wrestling, jostling, scrummaging, kicking the ball and running with it, the game was abandoned without a result.

The father of Australian rules was H. C. A. Harrison, who with his cousin, T. W. Wills, a former

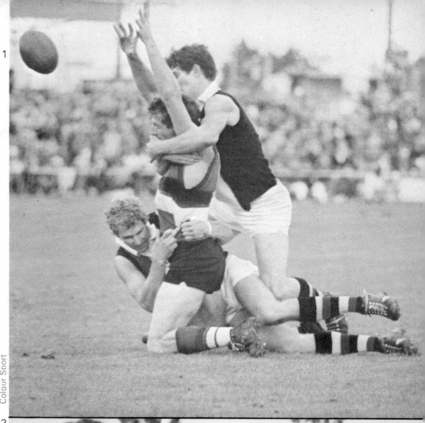

1 The rules say no contact above the shoulder or below the hips. St Kilda full-back Bob Murray (on ground) goes to one extreme while ruckman Stephen Roberts goes to the other. Footscray rover Ricky Spargo, attempting a mark, is the unfortunate victim.
2 Len Thompson, Collingwood's 6 ft 7 in ruckman, puts his whole body behind a downfield kick. Carlton's John Nicholls tries to put him off balance while team-mate Ricky McLean watches the ball's progress. **3** Where it all happens—a view of Claremont Sports Pavilion in Perth.

Colour Sport

Melbourne Herald

Colour Sport

student of Rugby School, England, drew up the first code of rules. The new sport borrowed liberally from rugby (the shape of the ball, body contact), Gaelic football (the kicking and marking), and soccer (the positional names). The mixture, and the passing of time, produced a distinctive and highly individual code.

Victoria has dominated 'rules'. Its comparatively big population supplies a greater depth of talent and provides its top clubs with the money to buy the best available players from other states. But the standard of play and administration has improved markedly in Western Australia and South Australia, and only their smaller population prevents them bridging the gap.

Australian rules is a semi-professional sport. Match payments to players are officially limited and transfer fees forbidden —a rule which was blithely ignored for 40 years. To stop un-official buying of players, the Victorian Football League introduced zoning of the whole state in 1968, allotting a specific area to each league club. In city areas, this enforced residential tie to one club had been a rule in Victoria, South Australia, and Western Australia for many years. Each state league has paid officers to administer the game. But policy

decisions on all vital issues are in the hands of delegates appointed by the clubs, an unwieldy and inefficient method hampered by intense club interest.

Interstate games are an annual event. They are popular in all states except Victoria, where fanatical club loyalty and this state's historic domination of the games has diminished local interest. The game flourishes at all levels—senior, junior, and schools. Well-established age-group com-petitions exist for boys as young as 14 years, and under-12 and even under-10 teams are not unheard of.

'Rules' is easily the most popular winter sport taught in schools in the 'southern states'. But observers have noted a slowing in attendance growth in the 1960s, attributable to the huge post-war influx of European immigrants whose football interests centre on soccer.

Attempts were made in the 1960s to 'sell' Australian rules overseas. Exhibition games were staged in Tokyo, Honolulu, San Francisco, and Bucharest. In 1967 and 1968 a team of 'rules' players toured Ireland. Several Gaelic football matches were played against leading Irish teams, includ-ing the All-Ireland champions. And despite the handicap of never having played the game before, the Australians were unbeaten.

How the Game is Played

Australian rules has been described as a team game played by 18 individuals. It is certainly true that it lacks the strong tactical emphasis and team disciplines of soccer and rugby, relying heavily on the impromptu co-operation of individual players. But it has its strategies which, while flexible, are basic.

Most important is the cooperation between ruckmen and rovers, who play the essential role in moving the ball away from 'set' positions. Opposing ruckmen, giants of up to 6 ft 7 in and 16 stone, contest the many centre bounces and boundary throw-ins. The strength to withstand heavy buffeting, the ability to manoeuvre in the air and a high degree of skill at 'palming' or deflecting the ball to the waiting rover are essential.

Since World War II, a new 'trick' has been added, perfected by the great West Australian 'Polly' Farmer. The ruckman leaps high to gain control of the ball in the air, brings it down to the ground and flashes it clear of the pack to a team mate.

The punch or hand pass is a distinctive feature, the ball being held flat on the palm of one hand and struck sharply with the clenched fist of the other. It is also an alternative to the kick in one of the most important tactics of Australian rules—the 'play on' game. In this move a player, running clear with the ball, draws an opponent towards him, leaving a team mate unmarked. He punches the ball to him and, still running down field, collects the return pass. This, with its many variations, has added considerably to the game's non-stop, fast-moving tempo, and is the major difference between the way 'rules' is played today and how it was played before and just after World War II.

To cope with this strong emphasis on pace, the dual purpose ruck-rover has evolved. As the name suggests he is a compromise between the towering ruckman and the small, nippy rover. Invariably a strongly built player with fine ball-handling skill, he must have the balance and accelera-tion to stage quick breakaways, combined with the muscular strength and power to burst through packs with the ball when the occasion demands.

A general increase in the size of the participants is another modern trend. This applies particularly across the centre, where the wingers and the centreman have taken on an increasingly important role in moving the ball from the centre bounce into attack. The wings, formerly the exclusive province of the small, clever player, are being taken over by rangy, fast-moving men prepared to sacrifice some ground-level possession for the benefits gained from winning the ball in the air.

The centreman has always been a vital member of a team. Today, with increased congestion at the centre bounce, he must add great physical strength to his traditional brilliance, have blistering pace and the stamina to range constantly over a wide area without tiring and, even more important, have the capacity to 'read the play' and think quickly.

Melbourne Herald

Hawthorn full-forward Peter Hudson kicks his sixteenth goal of the match to break his club's record for goals kicked in one match. 2 A little too close for comfort for Footscray ruckman Barry Round. Melbourne's Max Walker punches the ball away, preventing either Round or Footscray captain and coach, Ted Whitten, from marking the ball. 3 A Carlton player turns his back as Barry Round leaps higher than a team-mate to mark the ball. 4 As team-mates and opposing players close in, St Kilda's Kevin Neale (No. 18) wins the ball in a spectacular duel with Geelong's star ruckman, John Newman.

Rules of the Game

At first sight, 'rules' seems to the uninitiated a complete misnomer—the game appears to have none. There is no off side; violent physical clashes occur while the umpire—he is not a 'referee'—looks on unmoved; the ball can be passed forward or in any other direction; and the knock-on occurs regularly. The rules of the game, however, are myriad and often distinctive.

The ball can be kicked, *palmed,* or punched, but never thrown. A player may run with it, but must touch it to the ground or bounce it every 10 yards. When in possession of the ball, a player may be vigorously body-charged from the front or either side by an opponent using the shoulder, chest, hip, hand, or arm. Contact must not be made above the shoulder, below the hips, or in the back. But the man with the ball may be tackled from behind and held about the waist, by the jersey—called a 'guernsey'—or by the arm. When so tackled he must get rid of the ball by kicking or punching it. It must not be deliberately dropped or bounced. A player cannot be tripped, stiff-armed, or flying tackled, rugby-style. Players may *shepherd* a team-mate who is carrying the ball, by spreading their arms out (they are not allowed to hold an opponent) or by pushing or shouldering an opponent in the chest, provided that he is within 5 yards of the ball.

For a breach of any rule, a free kick is awarded on the spot. If a man is tackled or felled after disposing of the ball, the umpire may award a free kick downfield, where the ball landed. The free-kick spot is marked by an opposition player and the ball kicked over him. A free kick is also awarded for a mark.

The game is played on the world's largest sports arena. Exact dimensions of the oval field are not laid down, but suggested limits are 150 to 200 yards by 120 to 170 yards. Many major fields, such as Subiaco Oval (Western Australia), Adelaide Oval (South Australia), and the Melbourne Cricket Ground (Victoria), exceed these limits.

Teams comprise 18 players. While field placings are highly flexible, the players are matched man-to-man in five lines across the field and spaced between one goal and the other. Thus both centremen are opposed in approximately the middle of the arena, the wingers 'mind' each other, the full-back plays alongside the opposing full-forward, and so on. Exceptions are the two ruckmen, or followers, and the rover. As their titles imply, they have free-ranging assignments which demand they follow the ball to every part of the field.

Each team is allowed two reserves, or substitutes, called the 19th and 20th men, who may be used as replacements at any stage of the game. Once a player has been replaced he cannot resume playing.

Injuries are frequent, but they are seldom allowed to cause delays. Each team has several trainers who are permitted to attend injured players while the game goes on around them.

The central umpire controls play on the field, and the boundary umpires and goal umpires are responsible to him. He has sole discretion over free kicks. The two boundary umpires patrol the field's perimeter, signalling when the ball goes out of play. They run the ball back to the centre after a goal is scored and, when it goes out of play, throw it in—backwards.

The umpire starts play at the beginning of each period, or after a goal is scored, by bouncing the ball high in the air, aiming to get a straight high bounce.

A match is divided into four periods, called quarters, of 25 minutes each. Independent time-keepers off field sound a siren or ring a bell to start and end each quarter. The teams change ends for each quarter, kicking to and defending each goal in turn. The interval between the first and second quarters (quarter-time) is 3 minutes; that between the second and third quarters (half-time), 20 minutes; and that between the last two quarters (three-quarter time), 5 minutes.

The ball is a flattened ellipse, similar in shape to a rugby ball, though slimmer through the circumference and with less pointed ends.

Other than shin guards, players wear no protective gear or padding.

Scoring is by a system of *goals* and *behinds.* The scoring area is marked at each end of the playing area by four posts. The two central posts, often as high as 50 ft and set 21 ft apart, are known as *goal posts.* These are flanked by a shorter post on either side, known as *behind posts.* There is no cross-bar.

When the ball passes at any height between the major posts a goal is registered, as long as the ball has been kicked cleanly and not touched in progress. A behind is scored when the ball goes between the goal and behind posts or is touched on its way through the two goal posts. A goal is worth six points, a behind only one. The game is won by the side scoring the highest aggregate of points, not necessarily the one kicking most goals.

A goal umpire standing between the posts judges the score and signals it by waving flags—two for a goal, one for a behind. After a behind, the ball is kicked back into play by the full-back from a 10-yard zone in front of goal. The winning team gets four match points, the loser none; points are shared for a draw. Scoring is high—tallies in the 50s, 60s and 70s are normal—and, hence, draws are rare.

Australian rules has no order-off rule, but all five umpires have power to report players for serious offences. Independent tribunals hear evidence from umpires, players, and witnesses. Guilty players receive match suspensions, never direct financial penalties.

Syndication International

Central Press

Associated Press

1 Airborne, every muscle straining, Eddie Choong attacks the shuttlecock in typical style. With his lightning reflexes and marvellous agility, the Malayan champion carried all before him in the mid-1950s.
2 The 1967 All-England Championships, and the shuttle is just a blur as South Africa's Rennie de Toit tries to follow its flight off the racket of Thailand's Sila Ulao.
3 All-England doubles champions from 1967 to 1969, Erland Kops, (left) and Henning Borch of Denmark attack in the 1968 final against the Malaysian pair Tan Yee Khan, (left) and Ng Boon Bee, who were champions in 1965 and 1966. Kops was also singles champion seven times. Malaysians and Danes dominated the men's events until the late 1960s.

Badminton

A fast and physically demanding game, badminton requires lightness of foot, power of smash, a supple wrist action, lightning reflexes, and the utmost delicacy of touch. A top-class badminton player may be able to smash the 'shuttle' into his opponent's court at more than 100 mph, and in the next moment, with a barely perceptible change of action, send it gently floating across the net so that it seems to hover and drop almost vertically on the other side.

The singles game demands sound stamina. Two well-matched players may find themselves engaged in seemingly endless, strength-sapping rallies as they manoeuvre each other about the court. Speed is vital in the doubles game, where both sides strive to attack. Partners play side by side, covering equal ground, or one up at the net and one behind. The woman in mixed doubles usually plays at the net, taking anything short, while the man keeps up a barrage of low shots from the back or centre of the court.

There are international team competitions for both men (the Thomas Cup) and women (the Uber Cup), and badminton was included for the first time in the Commonwealth Games in 1966. But there are no official world championships for individual play. After World War II, the All-England Badminton Championships began to emulate the Wimbledon championships in tennis by being recognized as virtually the world championships. Leading players from South-East Asia, the Far East, Scandinavia, and the United States compete for the unofficial world titles.

The Danes have a fine record in the All-England Championships, particularly in men's badminton, where they have shared the post-war honours with Malaysia and Indonesia. Ladies' badminton was dominated for many years by the United States, in the person of Mrs Hashman (Judy Devlin), and to a lesser extent Margaret Varner. Yet the cradle of the game is England, and even today the measurements of the court all over the world are in feet and inches.

Where badminton is played.
Badminton is played both indoors and outdoors. For the outdoor game, particularly prevalent in the Asian countries, a heavier shuttlecock is used.

In Malaysia, Singapore, and Indonesia, badminton is the national sport, and the facilities for the game are exceptional. Denmark, Japan, and the United States are also leading badminton countries.

Badminton is a popular game in clubs. And halls used mainly for other purposes—in churches or schools—are often hired for a few evenings a week. In countries such as Britain, where space is at a premium, the halls used by small clubs often fall short of the ideal. The usual deficiency is lack of height, particularly important for the singles game. And sometimes, if the hall is too small, the back boundary lines may be painted up the walls!

Development of the game.
A form of badminton was mentioned as early as the 12th century, and the game's forbear, battledore and shuttlecock, was played in England 200 years ago. It is

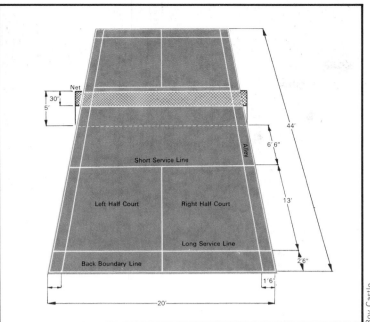

Court diagram labels:
Net
30″
5′
44′
Short Service Line
Alley
6′6″
Left Half Court
Right Half Court
13′
Long Service Line
2′6″
Back Boundary Line
1′6″
20′

Central Press

Roy Castle

Central Press

1 Mrs Judy Hashman was the leading woman badminton player from the mid-1950s to the late 1960s. She won her first All-England titles in 1954 as Miss Judy Devlin, and won a total of 17 singles and ladies' doubles titles in a period of 14 years. 2 Women's badminton is strong in Japan and Britain, and girls from these countries fought out the final of the All-England doubles in 1969. The British pair Mrs P. E. Whetnall, (left) and Miss M. B. Boxall beat T. Takehashi and H. Amano in straight sets. 3 First rounds of the All-England Badminton Championships. In the absence of world championships, winners of All-England titles are regarded as unofficial world champions. 4 Mrs Eva Twedburg of Sweden won the ladies singles title at the 1968 championships.

Associated Press

Keystone

Central Press

world sporting honours, and Indonesia and Thailand grew strong. Denmark has held her place among the leading nations. But England suffered a decline in men's badminton after World War II.

The All-England Championships were transferred in 1947 from the Royal Horticultural Hall, Westminster—which held a few hundred people—to the vast arenas of Harringay, the Empress Hall, and finally the Empire Pool, Wembley. While losing the intimate atmosphere of the smaller hall, the new venues were capable of accommodating thousands of spectators, and the world's best players began to compete.

The legendary David Freeman of the United States paid only one visit to the All-England Championships, winning the singles in 1949, the year he retired—after being undefeated in major singles since the age of 18, in 1939. Regarded by many as the greatest singles player of all time, he was renowned for his remarkable accuracy. This, allied to a perfect competitive temperament, made him virtually unbeatable. The next year, at Wembley, the Malayans began their domination of the men's game. Wong Peng Soon, generally regarded as the unofficial world champion of the 1950s, won three titles in a row and went back in 1955 for a fourth. The immensely popular Eddie Choong won four singles titles and three doubles titles (with his brother David) from 1951 to 1957. Tremendously fast about the court, and with an ability to make seemingly impossible returns, the Choong brothers were a vivid contrast—in both style and physique—to the Danes, who began their period of supremacy in the late 1950s. In 10 years, from 1958, Erland Kops won the singles titles seven times. And Finn Kobberö, while never

generally accepted that the name was derived from Badminton, the seat of the Duke of Beaufort, where the Duke's guests amused themselves at the game in the 1870s. Badminton was introduced to India, where the first rules were drawn up in 1877.
The court at one time was shaped like an hour-glass.

To cope with the game's administration in England, the Badminton Association was formed in 1893. This body organized the first All-England Champion-

ships in 1899. During the 1920s and 1930s, the game's popularity spread to the rest of Europe, to Canada, and on to the United States. In 1934 the International Badminton Federation was formed to administer the game on an international scale.

To add impetus to the game internationally, the Thomas Cup contest was inaugurated in 1948-49. The trophy, for men's international team competition, was donated by Sir George Thomas, All-England singles champion

from 1920-23, and a winner of more than 90 national titles between 1903 and 1929. And in 1956 Betty Uber, a leading British player of the 1930s and 40s, presented the Uber Cup for ladies' international competition.

Malaya's victory in the inaugural Thomas Cup contest was their first international success in any sport. Badminton became their chief game. Other Asian countries, doubtless inspired by their neighbour's triumph, followed suit in their search for

Chief coach to the Badminton Association of England, Ken Crossley demonstrates some of the strokes and techniques.
1 The backhand 'dink'. The player dashes to the net and taps the shuttle just inside his opponent's forecourt.
2 The service. This may be a low service, pushed rather than hit, or a flick over the receiver. **3** The backhand drive. The stroke is played so the shuttle crosses the net in a flat trajectory.
4 The round-the-head stroke which is unique to badminton.
5 The forehand smash. The player is balanced so he gets his body behind the stroke.
6 The backhand grip with the thumb acting as a splint.
7 The forehand grip, in which the racquet is held in a way resembling a loose handshake.

Colour Sport

Rules and equipment

The badminton court (44 ft by 20 ft for doubles; 44 ft by 17 ft for singles) should have about 3 ft clearance at the side and 6 ft at the ends, and air space of at least 25 to 30 ft above it. The singles game excludes the 'tram-line' area, but the two service courts are larger in singles than in doubles, extending from the short service line to the back boundary line. The top of the 2 ft 6 in net is 5 ft from the floor at the centre (5 ft 1 in at the posts).

The shuttlecock, 'bird', or 'shuttle' is made from goose feathers inserted into a kid-covered cork base. The slightest imperfection will affect its behaviour. Shuttles are graded by weight, for use in varying atmospheric conditions, and experts in important matches can be seen to discard shuttle after defective shuttle. But that is a luxury the average player cannot afford. A plastic shuttle responds less well to some of the delicate shots, but is much cheaper and has proved the salvation of many a small club.

Rackets are light, usually from 4 oz to 5 oz. The wooden racket has largely been replaced by the steel-shafted or all-steel racket, some of the latest ones weighing less than 4 oz.

A match is decided by the best of three games. Each game runs to 15 points (sometimes 21) or, in ladies' singles, 11 points. Scoring points depends on winning the right to serve. If the server wins a rally he scores a point. If he loses a rally his opponent gains service, but does not score a point.

A feature of badminton scoring is known as 'setting'. If the score is 13-all, the player or side that reached 13 points first can opt either to play the normal 15 points, or to 'set to 5', playing up to 18. Again, at 14-all (whether or not 13-all was reached) the first side to arrive at 14 may accept or ignore the option to 'set to 3' and play up to 17 points. In ladies' singles, at 9-all the option is to set to 3, and at 10-all to 2. The winner of a game has first service in the next.

At the start of a match the players toss for service or choice of ends. Serving is diagonal and begins in the right-hand court, but alternates from right to left at each new rally until service is lost. Then the opponent begins by serving from the right-hand court. In doubles games, each pair has two chances to serve. When the serving side has lost a rally, service passes from one partner to the other. Only when the second partner in turn has lost a rally is service given to the other side, and they serve from the right-hand court again. At the start of a doubles game, however, the side serving first have only one service.

The service itself must be made with the feet stationary inside the serving court, and with a part of both feet touching the ground. No preliminary feints or baulks are allowed. The shuttlecock must be struck below the level of the waist, with an underarm stroke, i.e. with the head of the racket below the hand at the point of impact. The player receiving service must also remain within the confines of his service court, with his feet stationary on the ground.

Play continues until the shuttle goes out of play by failing to clear the net, by hitting the ground, by touching the body of a player, or by hitting anything outside the court. A shuttle falling on a boundary line is deemed 'in'. It is a fault to hit the shuttle twice in succession or successively by partners, to obstruct an opponent, to touch the net with one's racket or person, or to hit the shuttle before it has crossed the net. The shuttle may not be 'slung' (held on the racket). It is no longer a fault if the shuttle is struck by the frame of the racket. Called 'wood' shots, these were made illegal in 1949, but the International Badminton Federation reversed the law in 1963.

How to play

One of the delights of playing badminton is the immense variety of shots possible from a particular position. A player may have a choice of playing a smash, a drop shot to either side of the court, or a 'clear' anywhere to the back of the court—and he can leave his decision to the last possible moment. He has immense opportunities for disguising his shots, and for varying the type of shot used in any particular situation.

The vital technique to be learnt in badminton is the wrist action. Most shots are played with a supple movement of the wrist, which is particularly important for deception—a major facet of the game. A player may shape up for a smash but do a drop shot instead. He may delay his shot until his opponent is committed in one direction, and with a last-minute flick send it the other way.

The most important tactical consideration, particularly in the doubles game, is attack, and the main attacking stroke is the **forehand smash.** The object is to hit the shuttle down from a high position, as steeply as possible over the net. The action for this stroke, as with all the overhead forehand strokes, is very similar to throwing a ball. The shuttle is met slightly in front of the line of the body, and the weight transferred from the back to the front foot.

The **overhead drop shot** is a deceptive shot, disguised as a smash. It is used especially in singles, where it is an advantage to draw the opponent into the forecourt. For the drop shot, a smash is prepared for, but the impact is checked so that the shuttle drops closer to the net.

The **forehand clear** is a defensive stroke. It too, begins like a smash, but contact is made directly above the body or just behind it. The shuttle travels high and deep, forcing the opponent onto the back line. By checking the racket swing, a slow drop shot can be made instead.

The **overhead backhand** strokes have the same characteristics as those of the forehand. For power, timing becomes even more important, and the shot should be taken as high and as early as possible, with the back turned to the net. Few players have mastered the **backhand smash,** but the **backhand clear** is an essential stroke to a singles player. The **backhand drop** is a slow deceptive shot, the player shaping up for a clear.

A stroke peculiar to badminton is the **round-the-head.** As its name implies, the shuttle is contacted on the backhand side of the body, but from a forehand stance, by bringing the racket across the top of the head. It is an effective alternative to a backhand shot, particularly to the smash.

Underarm strokes are used where the shuttle is hit from a low position. Mostly defensive, they can either be cleared, high and deep, to the back of the opposing court, or, if tactically possible, struck gently forwards just high enough to cross the net and fall into the forecourt.

Midway between the overhead and the underarm strokes comes the **drive.** Played with a flat trajectory, it is the basic stroke used by the man in mixed doubles. Chiefly from a mid-court position, the shot is played at approximately shoulder height with a sideways throwing action. Whether on the forehand or the backhand, the wrist leads into the shot and it is the snap of the wrist that speeds the shuttle just over the top of the net. Taken early, it is often effective against a weak smash.

There are various types of **service**—the **low, high, flick,** and **drive** services. The basic service is the **low,** which just passes the top of the net. To obtain this accuracy, the shuttle is 'pushed' rather than hit. Unlike most other strokes in badminton, it helps to keep a firm wrist for this service. The service, necessarily slower and more arched than other shots, can be the most vulnerable shot in the game.

ALL-ENGLAND BADMINTON CHAMPIONSHIPS

Winners since 1947

	MEN'S SINGLES	MEN'S DOUBLES
1947	Conny Jepsen (Sweden)	Tage Madsen & Paul Holm (Denmark)
1948	Jorn Skaarup (Denmark)	Preben Dabelsteen & Borge Frederiksen (Denmark)
1949	D. G. Freeman (USA)	Oio Teik Hock & Teoh Seng Khoon (Malaya)
1950	Wong Peng Soon (Malaya)	Preben Dabelsteen & Jorn Skaarup (Denmark)
1951	Wong Peng Soon (Malaya)	E. L. Choong & E. B. Choong (Malaya)
1952*	Wong Peng Soon (Malaya)	E. L. Choong & E. B. Choong (Malaya)
1953	E. B. Choong (Malaya)	E. L. Choong & E. B. Choong (Malaya)
1954	E. B. Choong (Malaya)	Ooi Teik Hock & Ong Poh Lim (Malaya)
1955	Wong Peng Soon (Malaya)	F. Kobbero & J. Hammergaard Hansen (Denmark)
1956	E. B. Choong (Malaya)	F. Kobbero & J. Hammergaard Hansen (Denmark)
1957*	E. B. Choong (Malaya)	J. C. Alston (USA) & H. A. Heah (Malaya)
1958	E. Kops (Denmark)	E. Kops & P. E. Nielsen (Denmark)
1959	Tan Joe Hok (Indonesia)	Lim Say Hup & Teh Kew San (Malaya)
1960	E. Kops (Denmark)	F. Kobbero & P. E. Nielsen (Denmark)
1961	E. Kops (Denmark)	F. Kobbero & J. Hammergaard Hansen (Denmark)
1962*	E. Kops (Denmark)	F. Kobbero & J. Hammergaard Hansen (Denmark)
1963	E. Kops (Denmark)	F. Kobbero & J. Hammergaard Hansen (Denmark)
1964	K. A. Nielson (Denmark)	F. Kobbero & J. Hammergaard Hansen (Denmark)
1965	E. Kops (Denmark)	Ng Boon Bee & Tan Yee Khan (Malaysia)
1966	Tan Aik Huang (Malaysia)	Ng Boon Bee & Tan Yee Khan (Malaysia)
1967	E. Kops (Denmark)	H. Borch & E. Kops (Denmark)
1968	R. Hartono (Indonesia)	H. Borch & E. Kops (Denmark)
1969	R. Hartono (Indonesia)	H. Borch & E. Kops (Denmark)
1970	R. Hartono (Indonesia)	T. Bacher & R. Petersen (Denmark)
1971	R. Hartono (Indonesia)	P. Gunalan & Ng Boon Bee (Malaysia)
1972	R. Hartono (Indonesia)	Ade Chandra & Christian (Indonesia)
1973	R. Hartano (Indonesia)	Ade Chandra & Christian (Indonesia)
1974	R. Hartano (Indonesia)	Tjun Tjun & J. Wahudi (Indonesia)

	LADIES' SINGLES	LADIES' DOUBLES	MIXED DOUBLES
1947	Miss Marie Ussing† (Denmark)	Miss K. Thorndahl & Miss T. Olsen† (Denmark)	P. Holm & Miss T. Olsen (Denmark)
1948	Miss Kirsten Thorndahl† (Denmark)	Miss K. Thorndahl & Mrs G. Ahm (Denmark)	J. Skaarup & Miss K. Thorndahl (Denmark)
1949	Miss A. Schiott Jacobsen (Denmark)	Mrs H. S. Uber & Miss Q. M. Allen† (GB)	Clinton Stephens & Mrs Stephens (USA)
1950	Mrs G. Ahm (Denmark)	Miss K. Thorndahl & Mrs G. Ahm† (Denmark)	P. Holm & Mrs G. Ahm (Denmark)
1951	Miss A. Schiott Jacobsen (Denmark)	Miss K. Thorndahl & Mrs G. Ahm (Denmark)	P. Holm & Mrs G. Ahm (Denmark)
1952	Mrs G. Ahm (Denmark)	Miss A. Jacobsen & Mrs G. Ahm (Denmark)	P. Holm & Mrs G. Ahm (Denmark)
1953	Miss Marie Ussing (Denmark)	Miss I. L. Cooley† & Miss J. R. White† (GB)	E. L. Choong (Malaya) & Miss J. R. White (GB)
1954	Miss J. Devlin† (USA)	Miss S. Devlin† & Miss J. Devlin (USA)	J. R. Best & Miss I. L. Cooley (GB)
1955	Miss M. Varner (USA)	Miss I. L. Cooley & Miss J. R. White (GB)	F. Kobbero & Miss K. Thorndahl (Denmark)
1956	Miss M. Varner (USA)	Miss S. Devlin & Miss J. Devlin (USA)	A. D. Jordan & Mrs E. J. Timperley (GB)
1957	Miss J. Devlin (USA)	Mrs A. Hammergaard Hansen & Mrs K. Granlund (Denmark)	F. Kobbero & Mrs K. Granlund (Denmark)
1958	Miss J. Devlin (USA)	Miss M. Varner (USA) & Miss H. M. Ward (GB)	A. D. Jordan & Mrs E. J. Timperley (GB)
1959	Miss H. M. Ward (GB)	Mrs W. C. E. Rogers† & Mrs E. J. Timperley† (GB)	P. E. Nielsen & Mrs I. B. Hansen (Denmark)
1960*	Miss J. Devlin (USA)	Miss S. Devlin & Miss J. Devlin (USA)	F. Kobbero & Mrs K. Granlund† (Denmark)
1961	Mrs G. C. K. Hashman† (USA)	Mrs G. C. K. Hashman (USA) & Mrs F. W. Peard† (Ireland)	F. Kobbero & Mrs K. Granlund (Denmark)
1962	Mrs G. C. K. Hashman (USA)	Mrs G. C. K. Hashman (USA) & Mrs T. Holst-Christensen (Denmark)	F. Kobbero & Miss U. Rasmussen (Denmark)
1963*	Mrs G. C. K. Hashman (USA)	Mrs G. C. K. Hashman (USA) & Mrs F. W. Peard (Ireland)	F. Kobbero & Miss U. Rasmussen (Denmark)
1964	Mrs G. C. K. Hashman (USA)	Mrs K. Jorgensen & Miss U. Rasmussen† (Denmark)	A. D. Jordan & Miss H. J. Pritchard (GB)
1965	Mrs U. H. Smith (GB)	Mrs K. Jorgensen & Mrs U. Strand† (Denmark)	F. Kobbero & Mrs U. Strand (Denmark)
1966	Mrs G. C. K. Hashman (USA)	Mrs G. C. K. Hashman (USA) & Mrs F. W. Peard (Ireland)	F. Kobbero & Mrs U. Strand (Denmark)
1967	Mrs G. C. K. Hashman (USA)	Miss I. Rietveld (Netherlands) & Mrs U. Strand (Denmark)	S. Andersen & Mrs U. Strand (Denmark)
1968	Mrs E. Twedburg (Sweden)	Miss Minarni & Miss R. Koestijah (Indonesia)	A. D. Jordan & Miss S. D. Pound† (GB)
1969	Miss H. Yuki (Japan)	Miss M. B. Boxall & Mrs P. E. Whetnall† (GB)	R. J. Mills & Miss G. M. Perrin (GB)
1970	Miss E. Takenaka (Japan)	Miss M. Boxall & Mrs P. Whetnall (GB)	P. Walsoe & Mrs P. Molgaard Hansen (Denmark)
1971	Mrs E. Twedberg (Sweden)	Miss N. Takagi & Miss H. Yuki (Japan)	S. Pri & Mrs U. Strand (Denmark)
1972	Mrs N. Nakayama (Japan)	Miss M. Aizawa & Miss E. Takenaka (Japan)	S. Pri & Mrs U. Strand (Denmark)
1973	Miss M. Beck (GB)	Miss M. Aizawa & Miss E. Takenaka (Japan)	D. Talbot & Miss M. Gilks (GB)
1974	Miss H. Yuki (Japan)	Miss M. Beck & Mrs M. Gilks (GB)	J. Eddy & Mrs P. Whetnall (GB)

*Trophy won outright. †Ladies listed under both maiden and married names.

Mrs. Nylen nee Miss M. Ussing; Mrs. K. Granlund nee Miss K. Thorndahl; Mrs. G. C. K. Hashman nee Miss J. Devlin; Mrs. G. Ahm nee Miss T. Olsen; Mrs. F. G. Webber nee Miss Q. M. Allen; Mrs. W. C. E. Rogers nee Miss I. L. Cooley; Mrs. E. J. Timperley nee Miss J. R. White; Mrs. F. W. Peard nee Miss S. Devlin; Mrs. U. Strand nee Miss U. Rasmussen; Mrs. P. E. Whetnall nee Miss S. D. Pound.

5

achieving a singles win, took the doubles seven times—six times with Jorgen Hammergaard Hansen. Both tall men, Kobberö and Hammergaard Hansen, whose backhand smash was a formidable weapon, formed an almost invincible combination in Europe.

In the Thomas Cup, the Danes invariably won the European Zone. But they just as regularly succumbed to one of the Asian countries in the inter-zone ties. Malaya won the first three contests for the Thomas Cup, and Indonesia took over the trophy and world dominance in 1957-58. The Danes came closest in 1963-64, when they beat both Malaysia and Thailand on the way to the Challenge Tie, which they lost 5-4 to Indonesia.

In women's competition, the Danes provided seven winners of the All-England singles from 1947. Then, in 1954, began the reign of the Americans, when Judy Devlin took the first of her 10 singles titles. Margaret Varner, who represented the United States at tennis and squash as well as badminton, won the title in 1955 and 1956. But Judy Devlin, who became Mrs Hashman, reigned supreme until the late 1960s. Apart from her singles triumphs, she won the ladies' doubles seven times—six of these in partnership with her sister Sue. Britain provided the singles champions in 1959 (Heather Ward) and 1965 (Ursula Smith).

Britain has had more success in the doubles. Iris Rogers and June Timperley, against the normal trend of ladies' doubles tactics, frequently adopted the mixed doubles techniques of one up at the net (Timperley) and the other, Rogers, playing a man's game at the back of the court. As Misses Cooley and White, they first won the title in 1953, following this with two very good victories in 1955 and 1959.

Tony Jordan, whose forte was mixed doubles, won that title four times, with three different partners, the last in 1968. And Britain took two titles in 1969—the mixed doubles and the ladies' doubles.

6

7

Balloning

Straight up into the blue, like a cork bobbing through water, the balloon rises; then it sweeps silently across the wide expanse of sky at the speed and mercy of the wind. How far will it go? Where will it land? Nobody knows. This barely controlled mystery of the trip, where the elements are still largely in command, is part of the fascination of balloning.

Man has always envied the birds their freedom in air, and his many attempts to get both feet off the ground record the transformation of a dream into reality. The first manned flight was actually made by Philâtre de Rozier, a young Frenchman, in 1784, who swayed gently over Paris in a balloon. Since then, man has been balloning continuously, and today the sport is enjoying a revival, due largely to the application of modern techniques to the original methods.

Although privately owned balloons do exist, most enthusiasts are members of clubs. There were four such clubs in Britain in the late 1960s, and many more in France and Germany. Depending on the size of the envelope, balloons commonly carry from one to four people.

Every year there are a number of balloon meets and international races in Europe, the most famous of the latter being the race over the Alps from Mürren in Switzerland into Austria. Through the Fédération Aéronautique Internationale, the international body controlling all forms of aviation sport, national clubs superintend attempts on various records. For record attempts balloons are classified according to capacity, from A1, which covers all craft with a capacity of less than 250 cubic metres, to A10 for 4,000 cubic metres and over. This refers to hydrogen balloons only. Hot-air balloons, bearing the prefix AX, are similarly classified.

Records are set for duration, distance, and altitude in each category. The sport has altered surprisingly little over the years. The absolute duration record of 87 hours, for example, was set up as long ago as 1913 by the German, H. Kaulen. Two illustrious names occur in the record lists of the smallest classes: D. Piccard, whose uncle, with his astonishing trips into the stratosphere, was the world's leading balloonist in the 1930s, and A. Dolfuss, a Frenchman with more than 50 years' balloning experience behind him.

Thirteen of the remaining 24 records are held by Russians, set up just before World War II, since when their interest in the sport seems virtually to have ceased.

Flame rises high into the centre of a hot-air balloon. The flame—from burning propane gas—may rise as high as six feet.

J. Allan Cash

Baseball

Baseball is more than just a game in America; it is an institution. A major-league baseball game is sport, drama, picnic, and circus all rolled into one. The hot dog is as much a part of the game as the home run.

The whole atmosphere of baseball is electric, because all operations are conducted at high speed. Surprise, uncertainty, are keynotes of play. One hit might change the whole trend of a game, because a 'home run' with men on the bases can transform a deficit into a winning lead.

As a box-office attraction, baseball was strongly challenged in the mid-1960s by American football. But by the beginning of the 1970s there were signs that crowds would be bigger than ever before. And as a participant sport, baseball is second to none. Almost from the day the major-league clubs begin spring training in Florida or Arizona in mid-February, right up to the conclusion of the World Series in October, there is no more common sight in the United States than boys of all ages throwing, hitting, or catching a baseball.

Baseball is played throughout the world, and is strong in Australia, Japan, and Mexico. But no country can dispute the right of the Americans to call the finals of their domestic competition the World Series. For in no other country can baseball draw on more than a hundred years of development, refinement, and sophistication.

Origins of baseball. When was baseball first played? Americans pride themselves that the game is essentially of American origin, as it was declared to be by a special commission in 1905 appointed in the United States solely to investigate that very question.

The appointment of this commission was an outcome of British claims that baseball was only an adaptation of the old English game of rounders. The commissioners were all leading baseball personalities of their day. After sifting all the available evidence, their finding was that in 1839 Abner Doubleday, then a young cadet at West Point and later a distinguished general in the US Army, laid out the first diamond-shaped pitch and, instructing Cooperstown, NY, lads in primitive rules to govern their pitching, batting, fielding, and running, started an original game which he called baseball.

Evidence since brought to light makes it clear that the 'diamond' and the three-strike-out rule, at least, were borrowed from—or at any rate were similar to—certain of the laws laid down for the playing of rounders in a publication known as the *Boy's Own Book*. It was published in England in 1829 and shortly afterwards reprinted in Boston, Massachusetts. In fact, the American writer Oliver Wendell Holmes claimed to have played baseball at Harvard University in 1829. The Doubleday legend, however, had sufficient authenticity for the Baseball Hall of Fame to be located at Cooperstown, and baseball celebrated its 100th anniversary there in 1939.

Development of baseball. Credit for organizing the first formal team in the United States belongs to Alexander Joy Cartwright, Jr. In 1845 he founded the New York Knickerbockers, who played their first opponents, the New York Nine, the following year—and lost 23-1! That game was played at Hoboken, New Jersey.

By 1858 so many teams were playing that a meeting was called to establish a league. As a result, the National Association of Base Ball Players was founded with 25 member clubs. For the league's opening game between New York and Brooklyn clubs (later to become the Giants and the Dodgers) on July 20, 1858, an admission fee of 50 cents was charged, although all players were amateurs. The game attracted a crowd of around 1,500.

In 1867 there were so many clubs that 500 delegates attended a big conference convened at Philadelphia for the purpose of making certain reforms. In the same year a development occurred that has had, perhaps, the most important effect of all on the technique of the game—the discovery of how to make the ball swerve by imparting finger-spin.

One year after that came another significant development, the formation of the first all-professional club (the Cincinnati Red Stockings, formerly a powerful amateur team).

Between the foundation of the National League in 1876 and the arrival of the American League in 1901 there were a number of other short-lived groupings (such as the American Association and the Union Association). But in 1905 the World Series, as it is known today, was permanently established as an annual knock-out competition between the winners of the two major leagues. And major-league baseball has been thriving and progressing ever since.

In 1914 a third league, the Federal League, threatened to upset the balance, but it survived only two years. Then in 1919 came what could have proved a disaster. The World Series that year was contested between the Chicago White Sox of the American League and the Cincinnati Reds from the National League. The Reds won the series 5-3, but afterwards it was discovered that eight of the White Sox, soon to be scorned as the 'Black Sox', had been bribed by gamblers to lose. All eight players were banned from baseball for life, but public

1

2

Five of the 'Greatest Players Ever' team, chosen at pro baseball's centennial dinner in 1969: **1** Babe Ruth's spectacular slugging in the 1920s captured the imagination of the public and brought a new dimension to the sport. Ruth hit 714 home runs in his career—nearly 200 more than the next man. **2** 'The Georgia Peach', Ty Cobb set many records, including lifetime runs scored and bases stolen. **3** Joe DiMaggio won worldwide fame when he married Marilyn Monroe. He was a national hero in his own right, in a career lasting from 1936 to 1952 with the New York Yankees. A brilliant outfielder, he set a record by hitting safely in 56 consecutive games. **4** Known as 'The Iron Horse', Lou Gehrig played 2,130 consecutive games for the Yankees in 14 seasons. **5** Second baseman Rogers Hornsby set a major-league record in 1924 with a .424 batting average.

5

3

4

U.P.I.

U.P.I.

U.P.I.

confidence in the sport was badly shaken.

The following year, however, two men emerged who were to make an indelible mark on baseball and set it on new roads to success. One was Judge Kenesaw Mountain Landis, who was appointed the game's first commissioner, with extensive powers for the betterment of the game. And the other was George Herman (Babe) Ruth.

Ruth had made his major-league debut as a pitcher with the Boston Red Sox in 1914. But by 1920 he had converted to being a specialist batter, and moved from Boston to the New York Yankees for $125,000 plus a $350,000 loan. That was a lot of money at the time, but he proved to be worth every penny.

Ruth changed the pattern of baseball with his long hitting. Until 'the Babe' came along with his 42-oz bat, most batters punched hits through or over the infield. Ruth clouted them right out of the parks, and in doing so captured the imagination of the American sporting public. New stadiums were built to accommodate soaring attendances, and Yankee Stadium to this day is

known as 'The House that Ruth Built'.

In 1927 Ruth hit 60 home runs —a mark that stood until Roger Maris (also of the Yankees) belted 61 (in more games) in 1961. By the end of his career Ruth had powered the ball out of the ground 730 times for the all-time record.

After Ruth's arrival in New York, the Yankees dominated the American League until the mid-1960s. Between 1921 and 1964 they won the 'pennant' 29 times No team has had such an ex-

tended period of rule in the National League, although the St Louis Cardinals, the Dodgers (first of Brooklyn and later of Los Angeles), and the Giants (of New York and later San Francisco) have shared the honours most frequently.

In the early 1950s the first shift of franchises took place. In the American League, the St Louis Browns became the Baltimore Orioles, and the Philadelphia Athletics moved to Kansas City.

Over in the National League, the Boston Braves had been the

1 'The Splendid Splinter', Ted Williams of the Boston Red Sox led the American League in 1941 with a .406 batting average, the last major leaguer to hit more than .400. In 1958 he won his sixth American League batting championship at the age of 40, and retired two years later with a lifetime batting average of .344.
2 Maury Wills, one of the fastest men in baseball, slides across the plate to score for the Los Angeles

BASEBALL

Year	Winners	Runners-up	Score*	Year	Winners	Runners-up	Score*
1903	Boston (AL)	Pittsburgh (NL)	5-3	1941	New York (AL)	Brooklyn (NL)	4-1
1904	No games played			1942	St Louis (NL)	New York (AL)	4-1
1905	New York (NL)	Philadelphia (AL)	4-1	1943	New York (AL)	St Louis (NL)	4-1
1906	Chicago (AL)	Chicago (NL)	4-2	1944	St Louis (NL)	St Louis (AL)	4-2
1907	Chicago (NL)	Detroit (AL)	4-0†	1945	Detroit (AL)	Chicago (NL)	4-3
1908	Chicago (NL)	Detroit (AL)	4-1	1946	St Louis (NL)	Boston (AL)	4-3
1909	Pittsburgh (NL)	Detroit (AL)	4-3	1947	New York (AL)	Brooklyn (NL)	4-3
1910	Philadelphia (AL)	Chicago (NL)	4-1	1948	Cleveland (AL)	Boston (NL)	4-2
1911	Philadelphia (AL)	New York (NL)	4-2	1949	New York (AL)	Brooklyn (NL)	4-1
1912	Boston (AL)	New York (NL)	4-3†	1950	New York (AL)	Philadelphia (NL)	4-0
1913	Philadelphia (AL)	New York (NL)	4-1	1951	New York (AL)	New York (NL)	4-2
1914	Boston (NL)	Philadelphia (AL)	4-0	1952	New York (AL)	Brooklyn (NL)	4-3
1915	Boston (AL)	Philadelphia (NL)	4-1	1953	New York (AL)	Brooklyn (NL)	4-2
1916	Boston (AL)	Brooklyn (NL)	4-1	1954	New York (NL)	Cleveland (AL)	4-0
1917	Chicago (AL)	New York (NL)	4-2	1955	Brooklyn (NL)	New York (AL)	4-3
1918	Boston (AL)	Chicago (NL)	4-2	1956	New York (AL)	Brooklyn (NL)	4-3
1919	Cincinnati (NL)	Chicago (AL)	5-3	1957	Milwaukee (NL)	New York (AL)	4-3
1920	Cleveland (AL)	Brooklyn (NL)	5-2	1958	New York (AL)	Milwaukee (NL)	4-3
1921	New York (NL)	New York (AL)	5-3	1959	Los Angeles (NL)	Chicago (AL)	4-2
1922	New York (NL)	New York (AL)	4-0†	1960	Pittsburgh (NL)	New York (AL)	4-3
1923	New York (AL)	New York (NL)	4-2	1961	New York (AL)	Cincinnati (NL)	4-1
1924	Washington (AL)	New York (NL)	4-3	1962	New York (AL)	San Francisco (NL)	4-3
1925	Pittsburgh (NL)	Washington (AL)	4-3	1963	Los Angeles (NL)	New York (AL)	4-0
1926	St Louis (NL)	New York (AL)	4-3	1964	St Louis (NL)	New York (AL)	4-3
1927	New York (AL)	Pittsburgh (NL)	4-0	1965	Los Angeles (NL)	Minnesota (AL)	4-3
1928	New York (AL)	St Louis (NL)	4-0	1966	Baltimore (AL)	Los Angeles (NL)	4-0
1929	Philadelphia (AL)	Chicago (NL)	4-1	1967	St Louis (NL)	Boston (AL)	4-3
1930	Philadelphia (AL)	St Louis (NL)	4-2	1968	Detroit (AL)	St Louis (NL)	4-3
1931	St Louis (NL)	Philadelphia (AL)	4-3	1969	New York (NL)	Baltimore (AL)	4-1
1932	New York (AL)	Chicago (NL)	4-0	1970	Baltimore (AL)	Cincinnati (NL)	4-1
1933	New York (NL)	Washington (AL)	4-1	1971	Baltimore (AL)	Pittsburgh (NL)	4-3
1934	St Louis (NL)	Detroit (AL)	4-3	1972	Oakland (AL)	Cincinnati (NL)	4-3
1935	Detroit (AL)	Chicago (NL)	4-2	1973	Oakland (AL)	New York (NL)	4-3
1936	New York (AL)	New York (NL)	4-2				
1937	New York (AL)	New York (NL)	4-1				
1938	New York (AL)	Chicago (NL)	4-0				
1939	New York (AL)	Cincinnati (NL)	4-0				
1940	Cincinnati (NL)	Detroit (AL)	4-3				

AL = American League; NL = National League
*The series is played over seven games, the first team to win four games being the winner. In 1903 and 1919-21, the series was played on a five games out of nine basis.
†Series included one drawn game.

U.P.I.

Dodgers in the game that clinched the 1959 World Series against the Chicago White Sox. Wills set the record for stolen bases with 104 in the 1962 season. No pitcher could relax with Wills on base. 3 The Pittsburgh Pirates shortstop, ball still in hand, is sent flying by sliding Yankees base-runner. 4 Stan 'the Man' Musial of the St Louis Cardinals shows some of the power that gained him National League records for hits and runs batted in.

first wanderers, moving to Milwaukee, and subsequently to Atlanta. But 1958 was the most significant year for moves. Previously, all major-league clubs had been limited to the eastern half of the country. Now, with easy air transportation, the two New York franchises in the National League transferred to the Pacific Coast.

The next year the two clubs— the Los Angeles Dodgers and the San Francisco Giants—met in a play-off to decide which should meet the Chicago White Sox in the World Series. The Los Angeles Dodgers won and went on to beat the White Sox 4-2, and set a new attendance record of 420,784 for the six World Series games.

The Baseball Hall of Fame was established in 1936. Players are elected to it by a special committee. There are two types of admission —one for players whose careers ended before the Hall's inception, and another for players who have recently hung up their 'cleats' for the last time. Famous managers and officials of the major leagues are also eligible.

Naturally enough, Babe Ruth was the number one candidate for the Hall of Fame, but he has some very distinguished company: Ty Cobb of the Detroit Tigers who had a lifetime batting average of .367 and led the American League in batting for 12 seasons; Stan Musial, who played in 100 or more games for 21 seasons with the St Louis Cardinals; Jimmy Foxx, Ted Williams, and Mel Ott, all of whom scored over 500 home runs in their careers; and Denton Young, a pitcher who won a record 511 games in his lifetime.

Players regarded as certain Hall of Fame members, but still playing or too recently retired for enshrinement, include Mickey Mantle (Yankees), Willie Mays (Giants) and Henry Aaron (Atlanta Braves).

At a celebratory dinner to mark professional baseball's 100th anniversay in 1969, a 'Greatest Players Ever' team was selected by the votes of nationwide writers and broadcasters. The 10 players chosen (two pitchers were named) were as follows: *Outfielders*, Babe Ruth, Joe DiMaggio, Ty Cobb; *first baseman*, Lou Gehrig; *second baseman*, Rogers Hornsby; *third baseman*, Harold (Pie) Traynor; *shortstop*, John (Honus) Wagner; *catcher*, Mickey Cochrane; *pitchers*, Walter Johnson (right-handed), Robert (Lefty) Grove (left-handed).

Baseball today in America. The baseball season in America starts to become news round about February, when the major-league teams go into training camps established in the warm climate of the southern states. From April onwards there are daily matches in the numerous leagues throughout the country, but the most intense national interest focuses on the doings of the 24 teams operating in the two chief competitions. The climax is reached when the winners of the National and American leagues are known, for they will then meet for the best of seven matches, played alternately 'home' and 'away', in the World Series. In 1969 the two leagues were each split into East and West divisions with six teams in each.

The title 'World Series' has drawn sarcastic comments from foreigners on the score that it is anything but that. The interest of Americans, however, could hardly be greater were the competition as international as the Davis Cup. Americans of all classes are reared on baseball. From the time he is eight, it is possible for an American boy to play organized baseball outside school or college. Progressing through farm leagues, little leagues, Babe Ruth leagues, and pony leagues, he can play legion baseball to the age of 18. And by this time any player of talent is likely to be of considerable interest to the 'scouts' of

In 1874 two teams of ball players, representing Boston and Philadelphia, toured England with a view to establishing professional baseball there. This prompted the following letter, which appeared in *Punch* (August 29, 1874) and was reproduced in *The Field* (July 11, 1936):

BASEBALL IN THE VERNACULAR

Worlton nr. Ipsidge, Suffolk.
August 1874.

Dear oad Poonch,

What fules you Lundoners be! You'r allus ridy to swaller any thing a furrenner hoads afore yar jaw. The newest thing I see in the peapers is that the hool country be a gooin to luze thar wits about the game o' baseball.

I m night furty year oad, and I ha' plaed base ball, man and boy, for more un thirtty-five year, as any o' yar folks up there could hev sen if tha'd come up to our village – or fur the matter o' that, to furty other villages herabouts – any evenin' a summer time. I'll try and tell yow the wai we plae base ball.

We make the base at the oad Church wall, and chuze sides, then we toss for In or Out; them ut git out stop outside the base-bounds, and hev to field, same as in cricket, and them ut get in stop in and take ball. Then the pitcher puts his men in the field where he chuzes, and then delivers the ball to fust man in base. If he doan't hit it wi his stick or his hand, and the ketcher behind him ketch it, he is out, and a dead man for t'innings, but if he hit, he must run like t'oad 'un to fust bounds, which in our place is t'corner o' public-house wall (the Feathers), and if the next man hit the ball, the fust man runs nation hard to 'tother end o' public-house wall, and the second man runs to where he left, and so on, to as many bounds but one, as there are fellows to the innard side. If the field men ketch the ball, the fellar ut struck it is out, same as in cricket.

Blarm me if I doant think them Yankees hev ben down here and larnt the game, jest to gull yow Cockneys wi', or else some Suffolk emmergrunts ha' goon and larnt them Merricans the game, and thay're a lettin' yow hev it second-hand. Carn't yow get 'em to come and plae agin our village? – I think thar'd git that match.

Yours to command,   Cow-parstur farm,
SAML. PLANT.   Worlton, Near Ipsidge, Suffolk.

professional clubs.

The actual mechanics of throwing and hitting have been carried nearer to perfection on the baseball diamond than anywhere else. Whereas in cricket the dice seems loaded to the advantage of the man with the bat, the reverse is true in baseball. One pitcher may dominate a game so completely that the other side fails to score a single run. An observer fresh to the game might well wonder that the batter manages to hit the ball at all, because the ball is thrown (not bowled) at him at tremendous speed from a short distance (60 ft 6 in), and is loaded by the pitcher with spin that may cause it to rise, drop, swing in, or swing out. But pitching is a strength-sapping occupation, and in the major leagues, with their daily matches, a pitcher might play in only one of every three or four games. Often the strength of a side will depend largely on who happens to be pitching, and the club's overall strength on the number of top-class pitchers available.

The aspect of baseball most likely to be appreciated by people used to cricket is the brilliant throwing of the fielders, developed in long hours of practice under skilled coaches. The catching is exceedingly sure, though the baseball player does have one aid that the cricketer does not— a padded glove worn on one hand.

To the uninitiated, the strangest aspect is the role of manager and coach. In American major-league baseball, much of the spontaneity of individual action has been taken out of the game. Often the manager indicates to the batter whether he is to swing, or withhold his attempt to hit the next pitch. The base coaches tell runners whether or not to run or to steal a base. And even the catcher indicates, by a pre-arranged series of finger signals, what type of pitch the pitcher should make next. Detecting, translating, and frustrating the opposing side's signals has by some coaches been brought to a fine art. Each player on the fielding side knows from the signals just what is likely to happen and is therefore on the alert for developments.

The two 12-team major leagues in the United States attract more than 25 million fans each season. There are those, as in every sport, who think that baseball 'isn't what it used to be'. But certainly the players are not likely to agree. Superstars such as Mantle, Mays, and Carl Yastrzemski are merely some of the first to command salaries in excess of $100,000 a year. Only a flourishing sport can afford such luxuries.

Baseball round the world. The game has expanded greatly outside the United States. With the admission of the Montreal Expos to the US National League in 1969, Canada now has top-class pro baseball. During the winter, large numbers of major-league players of Latin-American origin

Australian News and Information Service

Syndication International

U.P.I.

1

2

3

1 Baseball in Australia is played during the winter months, when it does not clash with cricket. But public support is meagre because of competition from the various football codes.
2 The Duke of York (later King George VI) greets the New York Giants baseball team at Stamford Bridge in October 1924, where they played an exhibition game with the Chicago White Sox.
3 Roger Maris of the St Louis Cardinals lets this one go. In 1961, with the New York Yankees, he set a major-league record of 61 home runs in a season, beating Babe Ruth's 34-year-old record on the last day of the season.
4 Los Angeles Dodgers pitcher Sandy Koufax in action against the Minnesota Twins during the 1965 World Series. The Dodgers won, and Koufax climaxed a brilliant season in which he broke the major-league record for strikeouts with a total of 382. He received the 'best pitcher' award for the third time, pitched a 'perfect game' (no batter reached first base). That was his fourth no-hitter, another major-league record. Koufax retired in 1966, with arthritis in his pitching arm.
5 Star outfielder and batter Carl Yastrzemski of the Boston Red Sox at bat in the 1967 World Series against the St Louis Cardinals.

4

return home and help raise the standards of play in places such as Puerto Rico, Venezuela, and Mexico.

Crack American teams touring various parts of the world at intervals since the turn of the century have helped to establish the sport internationally. Several American players with experience in the two major leagues are contracted to professional teams in Japan. And there, at least, baseball seems likely to become as much the national game as it is in the United States. Visiting American teams introduced baseball into Australia in the late 19th century. There is an interstate carnival series, first held in 1934, and, despite the deep-rooted traditions of cricket, baseball is flourishing there as a winter sport. Several star cricketers in Australia and South Africa have also excelled at baseball. Among others, Australian Test cricketers Norman O'Neill and Bill Lawry, and Berry Versfeld of Natal were offered trials with American major-league clubs. Baseball also has a footing in Europe, with the European Baseball Championship, inaugurated in 1954.

In 1936 an International Baseball Association was founded at the time of the Olympic Games. The first executive secretary-treasurer was Frank Matsumata, a Japanese sports leader, with Dinty Dennis, an American sports writer as his assistant secretary. At that Berlin meeting 17 nations registered as foundation members.

U.P.I.

5

U.P.I.

How the Game is Played

Compared with the relatively uncomplicated game of rounders, baseball, particularly as played professionally in the United States, is a complex sport. It is played between two teams of nine players each, and the objective of each team is to score more runs than their opponents.

The playing field consists of an *infield* and *outfield*. The infield, from which comes the name *diamond,* is 90 ft square. The outfield varies in size, but the nearest boundary must be a minimum of 250 ft from the apex of the diamond. In the United States at pro level there is a minimum distance of 325 ft for fields constructed after 1958.

At each corner of the infield are the *bases*—first, second, third, and home. To score a run, a player must complete the circuit of the bases, touching each in turn. First, second and third bases are marked by canvas bags, 15 in. square, anchored in position. Home base, over which the batter stands to hit the ball, is a five-sided rubber plate.

Extensions of the lines from home base to first and third bases are known as the *foul lines.* Any ball hit within the 90-degree angle enclosed by these lines is in *fair territory.* The first-base line is known as the *right field foul line,* and the third-base line as the *left field foul line.* Outside these lines is *foul territory.*

The baseball bat is a smooth, rounded stick with a diameter of not more than $2\frac{3}{4}$ in. at its thickest part, and not more than 42 in. long. The handle, for up to 18 in. from the end, may be covered or treated with any material to improve the grip.

The ball is thrown to the batter by a member of the opposing side, known as the pitcher. He stands on a raised earthen mound and must have one foot in contact with the pitcher's plate (or rubber) as he throws the ball. The rubber is $60\frac{1}{2}$ ft from the rear point of home plate.

The baseball itself is a sphere formed by yarn wound round a small core of rubber or cork, and is covered by two strips of white horsehide tightly stitched together. It weights between 5 and $5\frac{1}{4}$ oz and has a circumference of between 9 and $9\frac{1}{4}$ in.

A baseball game consists of nine innings. (Extra innings are played if the score is tied at the end of the regulation innings.) One inning is the portion of a game within which each team has a turn at bat. Each team's time at bat is regarded as a half-inning. Though there are nine players to a team, only three need be put out for the half-inning to end.

Although each team may have a captain, his is almost nominal leadership. The manager of a team produces all strategy and policy, decides his team's batting order, and introduces substitute players during the course of a game.

There is no toss of a coin to decide which team bats first. That privilege is always accorded the visiting team.

Each member of the fielding team may wear a leather glove or mitt on one hand. Right-handed fielders wear this on the left hand. The catcher, who squats behind the batter and home plate, is the only fielder who wears additional protection. This consists of a chest protector, knee-and-shin guards, and a face mask.

In addition to the pitcher and catcher, four other players are positioned in the infield. They are the first baseman, second baseman, third baseman, and shortstop. The shortstop occupies the gap between second and third base, as the second baseman rarely holds to his bag; he is positioned closer to first base.

In the outfield are the right fielder, who occupies the territory around the right-field foul line, the centre fielder, and the left fielder.

There are four umpires. The plate umpire has the most onerous and hazardous duties. He stands immediately behind the catcher and home plate and he decides whether the pitcher has thrown a strike or a ball. Because he is in the line of fire, he also wears a face mask and chest protector. The other three umpires are positioned close to the other three bases, and their chief function is to determine whether a runner reaches the bag safely.

After the plate umpire calls 'play', the pitcher delivers the ball to the batter. The batter stands in the area known as the *batter's box,* immediately beside the home plate, with his bat over the plate itself.

The pitcher's objective is to throw the ball over the plate, which is 17 in. wide, and within the *strike zone,* which extends from the top of the batter's shoulders to his knees when he adopts his normal stance.

A *strike* is called if the pitcher fulfils these requirements and throws the pitch past the batter. It is also a strike if the batter swings at the pitch and misses, or if he hits it into foul territory. If the pitch is low, high, or wide of the strike zone, the umpire indicates it is a *ball.* If the batter sustains three strikes he is given out, and the pitcher is credited with a strikeout. When the batter has two strikes on him, however, he cannot be struck out by hitting the pitch into foul territory. He may 'foul off' any number of pitches. If the pitcher delivers four *balls,* the batter is awarded a *base on balls*—he draws a free 'walk' to first base.

The batter's objective is to hit the pitch into fair territory and away from a fielder. Once he hits into fair territory, he *must* drop his bat and run for first base. If he thinks it safe, he may try to advance further—to second or third base. A one-base hit is called a *single,* a two-base hit a *double,* and if he reaches third he has hit a *triple.* If he reaches home base (or if he hits the ball fair, and out of the playing area) he is credited with a *run.* At the same time, any member of his team who is already on a base ahead of him (a *base runner*) can score a run by reaching home base. A *grand-slam homer,* counting four runs, comes when the batter himself, plus three team-mates already on bases, all succeed in completing the circuit to reach home base.

If the batter hits a *fly ball* (a ball hit in the air) into fair territory and it is caught by a fielder, the batter is out. He is also out if the ball drops to the ground, but the fielder throws it in to the base for which the runner is trying before he reaches his objective.

When a runner *must* run, it is known as a *force play.* A batter who hits the ball into fair territory must run. A player on first base must, obviously, run when the batter does. A player on second base does not have to run on if first base is unoccupied, nor does a player on third base if second base is unoccupied. When the bases are 'loaded' (players on all three bases), they all have to run. To put a man out on a force play, a fielder has just to catch the ball while keeping one foot on the bag. Or, if he does not have a foot on the bag, he can *tag* the runner, by touching him with the ball.

A base runner may advance only if the hit is fair. When a fly ball is caught, all runners must return to the bases they occupied previously. It is possible to advance to a vacant base or to score from third base, however, if the runner holds to his bag until after the catch has been made (*tagging up*).

A base runner may also advance when the batter does not hit the pitch. If he reaches the base successfully it is called a *steal* or a *stolen base.* But he can be put out if he fails to reach his objective ahead of the catcher's throw.

When three men on the batting team have been put out by the fielding team, the half-inning is closed and the other team takes bat.

If the team that batted second is leading after the first half of the ninth inning it does not need to bat again, having won the game.

It is possible for the pitcher to put out the opposition with only three pitches if all three are hit as fly balls and are caught. On the other hand, it is also possible for all nine men in a team to bat in their half of the inning, provided they are hitting the ball well. They will continue to bat in turn until the fielding team achieves three put-outs.

It is possible for the fielding side to achieve two or three put-outs on one play, however. Suppose there are runners already on first and second bases. The batter hits a fair ball on one bounce directly to the third baseman. The latter fields the ball and steps on the bag to put out the runner advancing from second base. Then he throws over to the second baseman, who is now standing on his bag. That eliminates the runner forced off first base; and the second baseman's throw to first base can still be in time to put out the batter. *Triple plays* of that nature are relatively infrequent. But *double plays,* where two men are put out, occur almost every game.

Substitutes are allowed at any stage of a game. Most often a pitcher will be taken out of the game if he is allowing too many hits. His place is taken by a relief pitcher, who will have been warming up by throwing in advance of the event. Each team has a number of such relievers in a special enclosure known as the *bullpen.*

A substitute known as a *pinch hitter* may also be introduced in place of a batter. And sometimes, in the later stages of a game, when a slow-of-foot batter reaches base, he is replaced by a *pinch runner.*

Records — batting

Home runs:	Season	60	Babe Ruth (154 games)	1927
		61	Roger Maris (162 games)	1961
	Career	714	Babe Ruth	1914-35
Hits:	Season	257	George Sisler	1920
	Career 4,191		Ty Cobb	1905-28
Runs batted in:	Season	190	H. Wilson	1930
	Career 2,209		Babe Ruth	1914-35
Runs scored:	Season	177	Babe Ruth	1921
	Career 2,244		Ty Cobb	1905-28
Batting average:	Season	.424	Rogers Hornsby	1924
	Career	.367	Ty Cobb	1905-28
Bases stolen:	Season	96	Ty Cobb (154 games)	1915
		104	Maury Wills (162 games)	1962
	Career	892	Ty Cobb	1905-28
Strikeouts:	Season	382	Sandy Koufax	1965
	Career 3,508		Walter Johnson	1907-27
Wins:	Season	41	Jack Chesbro	1904
	Career	511	Cy Young	1890-1911
	Career 715+		Henry Aaron	1954-

UPI

1 The crowd is on its feet as a runner makes for home base. The catcher, mask discarded, awaits the throw. Coaches and players watch from the 'dugout', and the umpire, in black, stands impassively behind home plate.
2 Mickey Mantle at bat for the New York Yankees in the 1964 World Series against the St Louis Cardinals. The most exciting player since Babe Ruth, Mantle was a brilliant outfielder and could hit the ball out of the park both right-handed and left-handed. **3** A relief pitcher is driven to the mound from the 'bullpen' in a motorized cart. Relief pitchers warm up in the bullpen during the game. If a pitcher begins to lose control, he is hastily replaced. A pitcher 'wins' a game if his side takes the lead while he is still in the game, and keeps the lead to win the game. He loses a game if his side falls behind while he is pitching, and stays behind.
4 Yankee Stadium, known as 'The House that Ruth Built' because it was Babe Ruth's hitting that drew the crowds that made it possible.

Associated Press

Glossary of terms

Balk One of the several illegal acts by the pitcher with one or more runners on base. It entitles all runners to advance one base.

Ball A pitch that does not enter the strike zone in flight and is not struck at by the batter.

Base on Balls The 'walk' to first base granted to a batter who receives four pitches outside the strike zone.

Batter's box The area within which the batter must stand while at bat.

Battery The combination of pitcher and catcher.

Batting average The proportion of a batter's hits to the number of times he bats. It is always shown to three decimal places.

Bench, or dugout The seating facilities reserved for players when they are not actively engaged on the playing field.

Bunt A batted ball, not swung at, which is tapped within the infield.

Double play The putting out of two players as the result of continuous action.

Earned run average Average number of runs a pitcher allows his opponents to score per nine innings.

Error A mistake made by a fielder on a play that should have resulted in an out.

Fair ball A ball that is struck within the 90-degree angle between home base and first and third bases.

Fielder's choice The decision by a fielder to throw to a base other than first in order to put out a preceding runner.

Force play This occurs when a runner loses his right to occupy a base because the batter has become a runner.

Foul ball A ball struck within the playing field, but outside the 90-degree angle encompassed by first and third bases.

Hit, or base hit Any hit that allows the batter to advance at least to first base.

Home plate A five-sided slab of whitened rubber set in the ground, with the point at the intersection of the lines extending from home base to first and third bases. This is *home base*—the point of completion of a run.

Home run A ball struck fairly which enables the batter to complete the circuit of the bases on the one hit.

Infield fly A ball struck in the air within the infield must be caught by a fielder and not allowed to drop in order to achieve a double play on runners already on base.

No-hitter A game in which one pitcher prevents the opposing side from making a safe hit.

Obstruction An illegal act by a fielder who, while not in possession of the ball nor in the act of fielding it, impedes the progress of a runner.

Rubber The usual description of the pitcher's plate, a rectangular slab of whitened rubber (24 in. by 6 in.) set on the pitcher's mound and 60½ ft away from the rear point of home plate.

Run The score made by a player who, advancing from batter to runner, touches first, second, third, and home bases in that order without being put out.

Rundown This occurs when a runner is caught between bases by players of the defensive team.

Runs batted in (rbi) Runs credited to a batter, including his own runs and those scored by his side as a result of his hits, bases on balls, or even when he is hit by a pitched ball.

Sacrifice This occurs when a team has one or more runners on base and less than two men out. The batter hits a deep fly ball to the outfield, knowing it is likely to be caught, but giving at least one runner the chance to advance a base by tagging up while the ball is being returned to the infield.

Safe The umpire's ruling that a runner has reached the base for which he was trying.

Squeeze play The situation when a team with a runner on third base attempts to bring home that runner by means of a bunt.

Stolen base An advance from one base to another by a runner when no hit has been made.

Strike Called by the umpire when a legal pitch is struck at by the batter and missed; when it is not struck at, but passes through the strike zone; when the ball is fouled by a batter who has less than two strikes already; or when the ball is bunted foul.

Strike zone The area over home plate between the top of the batter's shoulders and his knees when he assumes his normal stance.

Switch hitter A player able to bat right- or left-handed.

Tag The action of a fielder in putting out a runner by touching a base with his foot while holding the ball in his hand, or by touching the runner with ball, or with his hand or glove, while holding the ball firmly in the same hand.

Tagging up A base runner holding to the bag until a fly ball is caught.

Triple play The putting out of three players as the result of continuous action.

Wild pitch A pitch so high, low, or wide of the plate that it cannot be handled by the catcher.

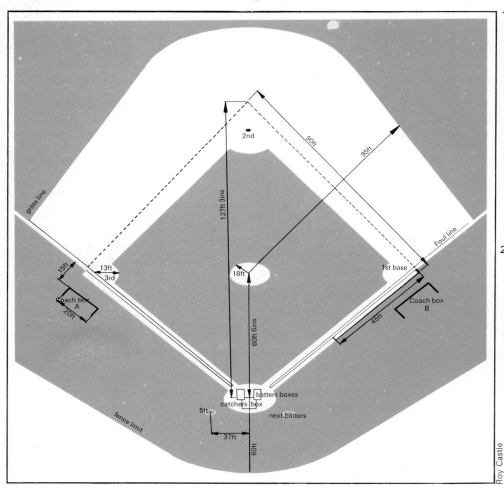

Roy Castle

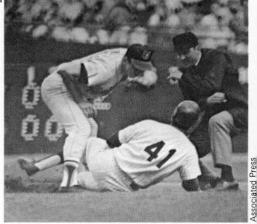

Associated Press

U.P.I.

The baseball field has an infield and an outfield. The main part of the infield is the diamond, which is bounded by home plate and first, second, and third bases. The runners move round the bases in an anti-clockwise direction. Outside the field, in foul territory, are the coaches' boxes and the 'on-deck circles' (for the batter coming in next).

1 Down, but not out—a runner slides in at second base and the umpire prepares to signal a safe arrival. **2** Canadian capers at third base—a Montreal Expo, in sky blue uniform, slides in.

Basketball

Unlike many other sports, basketball did not 'just happen'. Nor did it evolve from an earlier game. It was invented in 1891 by Dr James Naismith at Springfield College, Massachusetts, USA—and might easily have been 'boxball' instead.

Now so popular that it rivals soccer as the world's most widely played team sport, basketball was invented because the students at Springfield complained of a dull physical education programme that consisted mainly of physical exercises by numbers. Naismith chose a game for indoors, so that it could be played both at night and during the winter, when outdoor recreation was often impossible.

The game he devised had 13 rules. It was played with a soccer ball in a gym with a balcony around it. Originally, Naismith had intended to tie a cardboard box to the balcony at each end of the gym, and the main idea of the game was to throw the ball into the box, or goal. Unable to find any boxes, he used peach baskets instead; so the game became 'basketball'.

By coincidence, the height of the balcony to which the baskets were nailed was exactly 10 feet, and that has remained the height of the basket ever since. And the backboard behind the basket also became a part of the game by chance. As the game grew in popularity, fans used to sit in the balcony, watching. It became common practice for some fans to reach down and push away the opposition's shots. To counteract this, someone thought of erecting boards behind the baskets to protect them. The pieces of wood just happened to be 6 ft by 4 ft—a size that has proved satisfactory enough to be retained.

Naismith's teams had nine players, and teams often varied from five to nine players. But by 1897, the five-man team had become established. Players could move only in certain zones and only specified members of each team could shoot.

Dr Naismith had a good reason for keeping the players in certain zones. He wanted a game that relied on skill alone, not on physical contact. The emphasis was primarily on dribbling and passing, and scores were nearly always low. Shots were taken strictly with both hands, there were few long shots, and there was a jump at the centre of the court after every goal.

It did not take long for basketball to catch on away from Springfield. At that time, the college was the only establishment in the United States that had a course especially for YMCA directors. These men were early fans of the

Transworld

The side dribble—an effective way of retaining possession.

new sport and propagated it not only across the United States but also overseas.

Basketball soon became one of the leading spectator sports in the United States, and it was there that the present game developed. Several radical changes took place in the 1930s. By that time, basketball's popularity had a firm hold on almost all parts of the United States, but many people thought the game moved too slowly.

The jump following a goal was eliminated. Instead, the team that had been scored against took possession and threw the ball in from the end line beneath the basket. The style of play that had been prevalent—clever passing, quick dribbling, and the two-handed set shot—suddenly became outmoded by the one-handed jump shot, which could be made either from the set position or on the run.

The jump shot was originally popularized by Hank Luisetti, a Stanford University star of the mid-1930s. This shot has now become routine from junior schools to the professional levels.

Inevitably, the game is tremendously sophisticated at the highest level. And although the sport is not intended to include excessive bodily contact, more is permitted at higher scales of ability until basketball becomes a fairly tough affair in the professional ranks.

Probably the greatest ambassadors for basketball have been the Harlem Globetrotters who, as their name suggests, have performed in almost all corners of the globe. Organized in 1927 by the late Abe Saperstein, this team of Negro players travel with their own opposing team, and their play is merely for exhibition and not competition. But their ability to do everything but make the ball talk has played a major part in arousing interest in the game throughout the world.

Professional basketball. Although the Harlem Globetrotters are professionals, the top teams of professional basketball are found in the United States' National Basketball Association (NBA). The NBA came into existence in 1949 with the merger of the Basketball Association of America and the National Basketball League. The 14 teams in the NBA are divided into an Eastern and a Western Division, and the four teams finishing highest in each division during the season play in an elimination tournament each spring to decide the NBA champion. As the NBA features almost all the greatest players in the United States (and therefore the world), the eventual winners may accurately be called the world champions.

In the early days of the NBA, the Minneapolis Lakers, with the league's first superstar, George Mikan, dominated the championship. But thanks to Bill Russell, straight from the 1956 US Olympic squad, and the inspired coaching of Arnold (Red) Auerbach, the Boston Celtics won the play-off championship 11 times in 13 seasons during the late 1950s and the 1960s. Russell succeeded Auerbach as coach, to become the first Negro mentor of a major-league sports team in the United States.

One of the most remarkable players in the NBA has been Wilt (the Stilt) Chamberlain. This 7 ft 1 in, 250-plus pounds giant once scored 100 points in a game against the New York Knickerbockers. That same 1961-62 season, he averaged 50 points a game for the Philadelphia Warriors.

In an American sports editors' poll for the all-time NBA team, Bob Cousey, former star guard for the Boston Celtics, headed the list followed by Russell, Mikan, Elgin Baylor, Chamberlain, and the 'Big O', Oscar Robertson.

A new star appeared on the NBA horizon when Lew Alcindor signed a million-dollar contract to play for the Milwaukee Bucks during the 1969-70 season. The 7 ft 1½ in Alcindor was voted an All-America selection in each of his years at the University of California at Los Angeles.

College and high school basketball. Since the early 1920s, high schools in the United States have held end-of-season tournaments that have drawn capacity crowds. And colleges in the Midwest, such as the University of Minnesota, University of Illinois, Michigan State, and Ohio State, regularly attract crowds of over 15,000 to their games.

Most of the top collegiate players are guaranteed a career in professional basketball after graduation, and the collegiate standards are so high that many players step right into the professional game without much difficulty. Players are drafted in a system similar to that in American football—the team at the bottom of the NBA has first choice of the college stars. This maintains a more or less even standard in the professional game.

College teams play in *conferences*—competitions based on geographical location. Leading conferences include the Big Ten, the Big Eight, the Southwest Conference, the Southeast Conference, and the Ivy League Conference. Each year, the National Collegiate Athletic Association (NCAA) holds a tournament in which teams from the major conferences play off for the NCAA championship. And each year, the coaches of the NBA and their talent scouts select, by voting, an All-America team of the best college players.

There are approximately 22,000 high schools, 900 universities, and 500 two-year junior schools in the United States, all with one or more basketball teams. And in addition to these, there are innumerable other amateur teams playing in organized leagues.

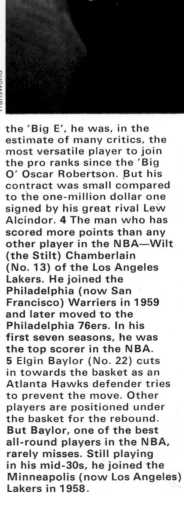

1 At 6 ft 9 in, Bill Russell is not the tallest basketball player, but the Celtic centre ranks as one of the greatest. As player-coach of the Boston Celtics, Russell took them to yet another NBA championship in 1969. But several months later, he astounded the club and the basketball world by announcing his retirement.
2 New York Knickerbockers' Bill Bradley waits as Jerry West prepares to throw a two-handed overhead pass to a Los Angeles Lakers team-mate. The pass is thrown quickly and is difficult to intercept. It is a useful pass to a player who is breaking in to the basket, and can be used effectively by either tall or short men.
3 Elvin Hayes in an attentive mood. One of the leading college players while he was at the University of Houston, Hayes preferred a $440,000 contract with the professional San Diego Rockets to a place in the United States Olympic team and the subsequent gold medal. Known to the fans as the 'Big E', he was, in the estimate of many critics, the most versatile player to join the pro ranks since the 'Big O' Oscar Robertson. But his contract was small compared to the one-million dollar one signed by his great rival Lew Alcindor. 4 The man who has scored more points than any other player in the NBA—Wilt (the Stilt) Chamberlain (No. 13) of the Los Angeles Lakers. He joined the Philadelphia (now San Francisco) Warriers in 1959 and later moved to the Philadelphia 76ers. In his first seven seasons, he was the top scorer in the NBA.
5 Elgin Baylor (No. 22) cuts in towards the basket as an Atlanta Hawks defender tries to prevent the move. Other players are positioned under the basket for the rebound. But Baylor, one of the best all-round players in the NBA, rarely misses. Still playing in his mid-30s, he joined the Minneapolis (now Los Angeles) Lakers in 1958.

How the game is played

The purpose of basketball is to score by throwing the ball into the basket being defended by one's opponents. It is one of the idiosyncrasies of basketball that the goal a team is *attacking* is called its own basket or goal, whereas in the football codes or in hockey a team's goal is the one it *defends*. The opposition tries to keep the attacking team from scoring by defending the basket. The ball may be thrown, deflected by hand, rolled, or dribbled in any direction subject to the restrictions of the rules.

A team comprises a *centre,* who is usually the tallest player, two *forwards,* and two *guards.* As, the names suggest, the forwards play close to their own basket to shoot and collect the ball when it rebounds from the backboard. The guards prevent the opposition from scoring, collect rebounds, and take the ball down the court for the centre and forwards. The centre stays near the basket or along the free-throw lane when his team is attacking and concentrates on shooting and collecting rebounds. On defence, he returns to assist the guards. But within this framework there is infinite flexibility, depending on the physical make-up and skills of a team and its opposition.

When a goal is scored, any player throws the ball up court from the end-line. If a player puts the ball out over the sideline, the opposition take a throw-in.

Two of the main styles of offensive play are the *fast break* and the *pattern offence.*

The *fast break,* or *free-lance* style is a helter-skelter type of offence. The ball is grabbed by any player as it rebounds off the backboard, and he passes it to one of his guards or forwards as quickly as possible. The idea is to give the opposition little or no time to regroup and set its defence. As a result, the fast-breaking team may have as many as three or four players going against two defenders. And a team that plays this style may possibly get many more shots than its opponents during a game.

A player scores two points each time he throws the ball through the basket from anywhere on the court. This is a *field goal.* If, however, he scores from a free throw (from the free-throw line), awarded as the result of an infringement by an opponent, he scores only one point.

Although some forms of physical contact often enter the game, strictly a player is not allowed to hold, push, barge into, or impede the progress of an opponent. Pushing and elbowing are also infringements that draw a *personal foul.* If two players commit an infringement at the same time, each draws a personal foul but neither is awarded a free throw. Instead, play is resumed by a jump ball.

A player also infringes by committing a *technical foul.* This can occur when a player deliberately delays the game, leaves or enters the court without permission, or is guilty of unsporting conduct. In such a case, the opposition receives two free throws.

If a player *travels* with the ball or does a *double dribble,* the opposing team gains possession. A player travels by either running or walking with the ball without dribbling it. Double dribbling is using both hands to bounce the ball or ceasing to dribble, holding the ball, and then dribbling again.

George Kalinsky/Transworld

George Kalinsky/Transworld

International basketball. Basketball is played in more than 130 countries, and has had Olympic status since 1936. Until 1972, the United States reigned supreme as Olympic champions, but at Munich that year, in the dying minutes of the final—and amidst considerable confusion and brawling—the Soviet Union defeated the Americans by a single point. It was one of the greatest upsets in Olympic history, for though the Russians, on overall Olympic performances ranked second to the United States, they were not favoured to wrest the title from the Americans.

Although an amateur sport, basketball rates as a major sport in Italy, France, Brazil, Mexico, and Yugoslavia, as well as, of course, the Soviet Union and the United States. And at club level, the game has an enormous following throughout the world.

In Britain, however, basketball has not enjoyed quite the same success it has in other European countries, although there is a large and enthusiastic following at club level. One of the reasons for

the games' failure to grip the public imagination in Britain is the great popularity of soccer. But thanks to the introduction of the game as part of the physical education programme in the schools, the standard of the game is improving all the time.

In many South-East Asian countries, basketball is the national sport. Although these countries do not have the tall men who dominate American basketball, their best players have great speed, ball control and positional play, and their game is fast and entertaining.

Australian basketball has improved rapidly, and its popularity has increased with Australia's improved performances in international competition.

Unlike Australia, New Zealand has yet to send a team to the Olympic Games, but the game enjoys a limited popularity in both islands. Basketball in New Zealand has similar problems to that in Britain—lack of facilities and the predominance in the winter sporting scene of another sport, rugby union.

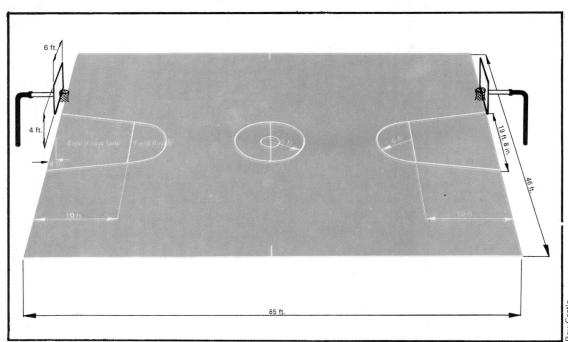

Roy Castle

1 Both teams await the result of a jump shot. Although the white team has four players on attack and all the blue team are defending, each team is prepared to change roles if the shot misses. No. 51 is well-positioned to go up for the rebound and deflect the ball to a team-mate standing on the edge of the 'key'. The white guard, No. 24, is ready to rush back on defence to stop a possible fast break.

2 Earl Monroe calls the play for a pattern offence and his Baltimore Bullets team-mates run to their set positions. A brilliant ball-player, Monroe has shown that a basketballer does not have to be tall to be great. Tall, that is by NBA standards.

Right. University basketball in the USA is a breeding ground for future stars. Here, an inter-collegiate match is played beneath the floodlights at Denver, Colorado.

Barnaby's

George Kalinsky/Transworld

Rules of the Game

Basketball is played by two teams of five players each, and a team may have up to seven substitutes. The playing court is a rectangular surface measuring 85 ft by 46 ft. These dimensions are marked by sidelines and end lines. The court is divided into two halves by the halfway line. All lines on the court are 2 in. wide.

The centre circle consists of a concentric ring at a radius of 6 ft from the centre of the halfway line.

At each end of the court a free-throw lane is marked. It is a rectangle 12 ft wide and extending 19 ft from the end-line. A semi-circle with a radius of 6 ft is drawn from the centre of the free-throw lane giving the lane some resemblance to a keyhole. Hence it is normally referred to as the 'key'. No player is allowed to remain in the key for more than 3 sec when his team has possession of the ball. The free-throw line, which is parallel to the end line, is 15 ft from the plane of the face of the backboard.

The backboard and the basket are suspended over the court. Although the original backboards were of wood, some are now constructed of unbreakable glass. And, instead of peach baskets, the basket consists of a metal ring, with an inside diameter of 18 in. from which hangs a net of approximately 15 in. in length. It is designed to check the ball momentarily as it passes through the basket.

Each basket ring is securely attached to the backboard with its upper edge 10 ft above and parallel to the floor. The nearest point of the inside edge of the ring must be 6 in. from the face of the board.

The basketball is spherical, with leather or composition covering, and is approximately 30 in. in circumference. It weighs between 20 and 22 oz, and when dropped from a height of 6 ft the pressure inside should cause it to bounce a little over 4 ft.

The players, whose dress consists of shorts, sleeveless shirts, and rubber-soled canvas shoes, are controlled by a referee, who is the senior official, and an umpire. The score, the number of fouls, and the time are kept by one scorer.

The length of a game varies according to the class of competition. At international and Olympic level the game consists of two 20-minute halves. But American professional leagues play 12-minute quarters, with a half-time intermission, and American schools play four 8-minute periods.

Another major difference between the American professional leagues and international and college basketball is on 'stalling'. The professionals have a 24-second rule which limits the time either team may retain possession of the ball before taking a shot at the basket. The limit in international amateur basketball is 30 sec. But at collegiate level almost indefinite stalling can take place.

The *pattern offence*, however, is just as popular. Players using this style are taught specific plays and run to certain spots knowing they will receive the ball there. Each play is usually called out verbally or indicated by a prearranged hand signal. Set options are available if the plan seems unlikely to succeed.

On defence, many teams base their play on a *zone defence*. Basically, this means that all five players concentrate on the defensive aspect of the game, retreating under the basket to keep their opponents from positioning for a shot, and retaining possession of the ball for long periods. At collegiate level in the United States, where there are no time limits on possession, a poor team can sometimes beat a better one by means of a zone defence.

Because this style does not lend itself to entertaining basketball, it is banned in American professional leagues. There, *man-to-man defence* (one man marking one man) is essential. If an offensive player shows any signs of beating his marker the defensive players switch positions, ensuring that no offensive player is allowed to break completely free from defensive attention.

U.P.I.

Billiards

One day, it is said, Louis XIV of France was ordered by his doctors to play billiards, or die. The emperor chose wisely, lived another 50 years, and became quite a good billiards player. In addition to its therapeutic value, billiards is probably the most scientific of all games and some form of it is played in every civilized part of the world.

Although snooker players outnumber them by five to one, there are more than 600,000 regular billiards players in Britain. There is a substantial following in Australia, New Zealand, South Africa, India, Pakistan, Ceylon, Malta, and Burma—all of which have been represented in the World Amateur Billiards Championship.

Origins of billiards

Nobody knows for certain who invented billiards, or when or where. The name comes from a Norman French word, *billart*, meaning 'playing cue', and the game was probably first played in England and France in the 1300s. Charles Cotton, author of *The Compleat Gamester* (1674), was the first historian of billiards. But before that Spenser and Shakespeare had both referred to the game.

The first known owner of a billiards table was Mary, Queen of Scots, who reportedly was heartbroken at being parted from hers in 1576. At the end of the 1700s the first billiards room, run by Abraham Carter, flourished in London at the Piazza, Covent Garden. In the early 1800s the game attracted big gamblers like wasps to the jam pot, and by 1855 the first reports of public matches began to be published. Two well-known professionals, Jonathan Kentfield and Jack Carr, from Brighton and Bath respectively, each claimed to be the champion. Carr died on the eve of a deciding match, so Kentfield assumed the title.

Kentfield formed a business association with John Thurston, founder of the renowned billiards equipment firm. Together they improved the tables, introducing, among other things, rubber cushions to replace the old stuffed ones.

As the game grew in popularity, Kentfield was eventually challenged by John Roberts the Elder, who won the championship by default in 1849 and remained undisputed champion for 21 years. He was eventually beaten by Willie Cook in the first official championship in 1870. That year marked the beginning of modern billiards.

Development of billiards

Family honour was avenged by John Roberts Jr who succeeded Cook as champion and dominated the scene through his skill, personality, and organizing ability for the next twenty-odd years. By 1885 Roberts was so much better than any of his rivals that he re-

fused to waste his time by taking part in any more championship matches. He was never beaten again on level terms except by the American Frank Ives, in a hotchpotch Anglo-American version of the game. Standards of play improved steadily, and W. J. Peall made a break of 3,304, including 3,174 by means of successively potting the red from its spot. To prevent even bigger breaks being made by this boringly repetitive method, a rule was introduced stipulating that the red be placed on the centre spot after being potted twice in succession from the top spot.

This limitation inspired players to master top of the table play, a most attractive method of break-building which involves great artistry in keeping the object-white within a few inches of the spot in order to prolong lengthy sequences of pots and cannons.

This sensible rule was brought in by the Billiards Association, a professional body founded in 1885. In 1908, the Billiards Control Club, in which amateur interests were prominent, was founded. For a time, the two bodies went their separate ways until they amalgamated in 1919 to make the Billiards Association and Control Council the sole governing body.

Meanwhile, a new generation of players had arisen after the turn of the century. They included H. W. Stevenson, whose break of 1,061 in 1912 was the first thousand to be made without highly concentrated repetitive sequences. Other players of this calibre included Charles Dawson, Melbourne Inman, Tom Reece, Claude Falkiner, and Willie Smith.

In 1907, Reece compiled a break of 499,135 by means of the *cradle* or *anchor cannon*, a sequence in which all three balls were grouped in the jaws of one corner pocket. But official recognition was withheld because the press and public were not present throughout the period. The break took 85 hours 49 minutes. In the same year, Willie Cook made a break of 42,746 by the same means, but it was not until the exploitation of *nursery cannons* by Walter Lindrum and others in the late 1920s

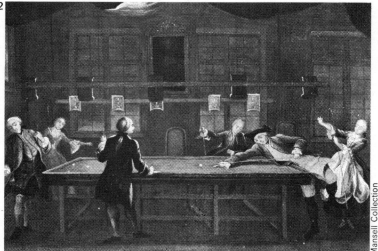

'Let's to billiards', cried Cleopatra in Shakespeare's play, but while the game has a long history, it does not date back to ancient Egypt.
1 The game's angles appear to have fascinated these players in a French variation of the game played in the 1690s.
2 English country house billiards in the 1730s.
3 J. Thurston's billiard room off the Strand was a popular meeting place for enthusiasts in Regency London.
4 The Bethlehem Hospital, better known as Bedlam, was infamous for the brutal treatment of its lunatic inmates. One place that was calm was the billiards room.

Equipment and Rules

A full-sized billiards table measures 12 ft. by 6 ft. 1½ in. and stands between 2 ft. 9½ in. and 2 ft. 10½ in. from the floor. The wooden framework of the table is traditionally supported by eight table legs, although certain tables of modern design stand on a central rectangular base proportionate to the table's playing area but giving an overhang on each side. This wooden framework supports a slate bed (in five sections), which is covered by a green woollen cloth called *baize*. The baize has a strong nap running from the baulk end of the table.

Rubber cushions backed by wooden cushion rails form a continuous boundary to the playing area and provide a natural angle from which the balls can rebound. The cushions, which are also cloth-covered, project two inches over the edge of the bed of the table. Thus, the playing area of a table is 11 ft. 8 in. by 5 ft. 9½ in. Each end of the six cushion sections (the length of cushion extending from one pocket to another) is shaped to help access to the pockets.

Pockets are 3½ in. wide at the fall of the slate, but the ease of access depends more on the way the pocket entrances are shaped than on the size of the pocket openings. Once inside the pockets, balls fall into strong, closely knit string containers or, more usually, an end-stopped retaining rail from which they can easily be retrieved and replaced on the table.

All official matches are played with composition (crystalate) balls that measure $2\frac{1}{16}$ in. in diameter, and which must be of equal weight. Two of the balls are white (the *cue-balls*) and the third red. One of the white balls carries two black spots on it to distinguish it from the other. It is referred to as *spot*, while the other is *plain*. Cues usually about 4 ft. 10 in. in length and tapering from the butt end, are commonly made of ash or maple, although a tubular aluminium cue is becoming increasingly popular. They weigh about 16 to 18 oz., but some may be as light as 15 oz. or as heavy as 21 oz.

A leather tip, 10-12 mm in diameter, is glued to the narrower end of the cue for the purpose of striking the cue-ball. To be effective, the tip must be treated every few shots with a cube of billiards chalk that enables the tip to 'grip' the ball it strikes. This makes for accuracy and a wide variety of spin effects.

Because of the area of the table, players cannot reach to play certain shots. In those cases they use a *rest*—a long rod with a steel X at one end that makes an artificial bridge for the cue.

English billiards is an indoor game played with three balls (two white and a red) and a cue on a rectangular table, with 6 pockets.

There are other versions of billiards, notably the *carom* game, widely played on smaller, pocketless tables in Europe and the United States. This itself has a number of variants, the most popular of which, in America, is *three cushion*. But these versions are not played on English billiards tables and, as such, are not controlled by the Billiards Association and Control Council, the world governing body.

The object of the game is to score more points than your opponent. This may involve a prearranged target of anything from 100 to 1,000 points, or a specific time, say, 2 hours.

At the start of a game, the red ball is placed on the spot nearest the top cushion. The first player (choice of ball having been determined by lot or *stringing*) places his white ball in the D. He must play the red with his first shot. If he misses, his opponent scores the appropriate penalty points.

When the first player fails to score, the second player plays from the D at either the red or the first player's ball, provided the white is not directly in baulk.

Points are scored in four ways: *pots*, *in-offs*, *cannons*, and *penalties*. A sequence of point-scoring strokes by any combination of the first three methods is called a *break*.

A *pot* occurs when the striker drives his white against one of the other balls in such a way that the object-ball is pocketed. If the object-white is potted it counts 2 points, but the ball remains in the pocket until the break ends. If the red is potted it counts 3 points and is replaced on the top spot. If the red is potted five times in succession it is replaced on the centre spot, but returns to the top spot when it is potted again.

An *in-off* occurs when the striker's ball strikes either the red or object-white before entering a pocket. An in-off red counts 3 points, an in-off white 2.

A *cannon* occurs when the striker's ball contacts both red and object-white on the same stroke, and counts 2 points.

If a player misses both balls, by accident or design, his opponent is credited with 1 point. When the striker's ball enters a pocket without contacting another ball, his opponent receives 3 points.

Glossary of Terms

Cannon A scoring shot in which the cue-ball strikes both white and red ball.

Coup Striking the cue-ball into a pocket without contacting another ball.

Cue-ball The ball that is struck with the cue.

Full-ball shot A contact in which the cue-tip, the centre of the cue-ball, and the centre of the object-ball form a straight line.

Half-ball shot A contact in which half the cue-ball covers half the object-ball at the moment of impact.

Hazard A pot, in-off, or combination of the two.

In hand The situation in which a player, having scored an in-off, can place the cue-ball by hand in the D for his next shot.

In-off A scoring shot in which the cue-ball enters a pocket after contacting an object-ball; archaically called a *losing hazard*.

Long in-off An in-off played into a top pocket when the cue-ball is in hand; archaically called a *long loser*.

Miss A failure to strike any object-ball.

Natural angle Any angle which

the cue-ball may take after striking an object-ball at medium pace without receiving any spin, side, screw, or stun.

Nursery cannons A series of cannons made by keeping the balls close together.

Pot A scoring shot in which the cue-ball sends an object-ball into a pocket; archaically called a *winning hazard*.

Safe position A situation in which a scoring stroke looks very unlikely.

Screw The art of applying reverse spin.

Swing The wide arc followed by the cue-ball after hitting an object-ball hard at about half-ball; the shot is usually employed to widen the angle taken by the cue-ball to achieve an in-off or cannon.

Stringing A method of deciding which player shall begin the game or have choice of ball. Each player plays a white from the baulk line to the top cushion to bring it back as near as possible to the baulk cushion. The player whose ball finishes nearer the baulk cushion has the choice.

Stun A shot in which the cue-ball is stopped dead at or near the point where it hits the object-ball.

Techniques

If you are right-handed, grasp the cue with your right-hand two or three inches from the butt end and rest the other end of the cue, five or six inches from the tip, in a groove formed by the thumb and first fingers of your left hand. Stand sideways on to the table rather like a boxer faces his opponent. Your front (left) leg should be bent and your rear (right) leg should be straight. Stretch out your left arm almost straight and keep your right arm from wrist to elbow perpendicular to the cue. Bend your back and push your near leg far enough back for the cue to brush your chin lightly as you address the ball. The whole stance should be firm but comfortable. (Left-handed players should read left for right, and vice versa.)

After regular practice you should be able to hit the object-ball smack in the centre every time. Then you can start on some of the more advanced skills—*side, screw,* and *stun*.

Side, or sidespin, is applied by striking the cue-ball to the right or left of centre. The use of right-hand side spins the cue-ball to the right so that, on contacting the right-hand part of the object-ball, it will take a wider angle to the right and, when it strikes a cushion, take a wider angle off it. The use of side in this way, to widen the angle taken by the cue-ball, is known as *running side*. But if you apply right-hand side to the left-hand part of the object-ball you will narrow the angle taken by the cue-ball. This is known as *check side*.

Screw is the art of applying reverse spin. To do so, strike the cue-ball well below centre so that it skids towards the object-ball rotating backwards. On contact, this spin will cause the cue-ball to spring back, either straight or at an angle, instead of running 'through' the object-ball in the normal way.

Stun, a stroke in which you strike the cue-ball a fraction below centre, is used to stop a ball dead at or near the point at which it hits the object-ball.

that a rule was passed limiting consecutive ball-to-ball cannons to 25. Later the rule was amended to make the number 35.

Just as this limitation was necessary in order to preserve a balance between all parts of the game, so did the supreme in-off play of Australian George Gray presage some limitation of consecutive in-offs. In 1910 Gray went to England and made 23 breaks of more than 1,000 by consecutive in-offs from the red ball mostly into the middle pockets, but also into the top pockets when the red finished short of a position from which it was possible to play an in-off at a natural angle into the middle.

This sequence remains an integral part of championship billiards today, but to prevent excessive repetition, consecutive in-offs were limited first to 25 and then to 15. Since a similar limitation applies to pots and to combinations of pot and in-off sequences, a cannon must, in effect, be played at least once every sixteen shots.

Artificial limitations also proved necessary in the case of nursery cannons, which were fully exploited by the Australian Walter Lindrum and hardly less so by the New Zealander Clark McConachy. Joe Davis, Tom Newman and other English players also fell into this category.

Lindrum unanimously regarded as the finest player in the history of billiards, still holds the official world record break with a 4,137 made in 1932. This break included 1,295 nursery canons. In 1933, Lindrum took the balls two-and-a-half times round the table in making 529 consecutive cannons —a performance of supreme skill, but for the average spectator one

that bored him stiff.

While acknowledging the effectiveness of nursery cannons, fans preferred the greater variety of the all-round game epitomized by the British player Willie Smith, whose 2,743 in 1928 still stands as a record for a break made without the aid of nursery cannons.

Ironically, the mastery of top players ruined the game as a public spectacle. Perfection became boring, and there was no professional championship between 1934, when Lindrum won it, and 1951, when McConachy beat the young Englishman John Barrie.

The decline of top billiards coincided with the rise of snooker, which began to attract all the leading professionals. At the same time, billiards continued to be widely played by amateurs, and top amateur standards rose to impressive heights, particularly with such players as the Australian Bob Marshall, the Indian Wilson Jones, and the Englishman Leslie Driffield.

There are now signs of a professional revival. The British snooker expert Rex Williams travelled to New Zealand in 1968 and beat the veteran McConachy for his world title. Driffield, with no new worlds to conquer as an amateur, turned professional with a view to challenging Williams.

Countries affiliated to the BACC hold annual championships, and the amateur championships are held every other year.

1 Eight times English amateur champion Leslie Driffield won two world titles. 2 Twice world amateur champion, twice Empire champion, Australian Bob Marshall won his national championship 18 times.

Bowls

Bowls has the biggest player-participation of all games in three major sports-playing countries in the world—Britain, Australia, and South Africa. Once saddled with a 'cloth cap, old man's game' image, it is now recognized as a highly skilled game demanding an early start if success is to be achieved.

Bowls is one of the few games at which an octogenarian can compete on reasonably level terms with a man a quarter of his age. But despite its immense popularity as a participant sport, bowls receives little national newspaper coverage and is more or less ignored by television and radio.

As a result, even the world champion – British schoolmaster David Bryant—is virtually anonymous compared with quite moderate footballers, tennis players, cricketers, athletes, and others who are featured regularly on television and in the press. Yet when South African golfing ace Gary Player watched Bryant during the world championships,

he concluded that the accuracy achieved by Bryant was even greater than that of top-class golfers—himself included.

The game today

Bowls is an amateur sport except in some variations, such as crown green bowls, which is played mainly in the Midlands and North of England. The main difference between the two codes is that crown green bowls is played on a green that is 9 inches higher at the centre than at the ends. Flat green bowls, as it is sometimes called to differentiate it from the crown green game, is played both outdoors and indoors and is governed by the International Bowling Board (IBB). In the late 1960s there were 18 countries affiliated to this world governing body.

For an outdoor game, bowls has a remarkable space-utilization factor—championship bowls need as little as 16 square yards per player as against the 200 per player in tennis doubles or the 400 in soccer. Nevertheless the cost of maintaining a green in first-class condition makes the sport expensive unless subsidized. In Britain,

industrial and commercial clubs are providing an increasing number of bowling greens. British tax laws encourage industrial companies to provide sports facilities, and many organizations have responded with magnificent centres. Watneys, the brewers, are in the van of these, and they have provided the facilities for, and virtually sponsored, the English championships since 1958.

Indoor bowls in Britain is booming and by the end of the 1960s there were about a hundred fully fledged indoor halls in the country. The idea has also spread to Australia and, surprisingly, to Switzerland, where a retired Englishman adapted a hall previously used for curling—a game derived from bowls—to the lawn game. Indoor bowls is almost identical with the outdoor game, except that it is played on carpets.

It is also immensely popular in New Zealand, although here they

play a miniature version on rinks shorter than the standard outdoor greens and with special miniature bowls.

Most men and women are taught to play bowls by parents or friends, the instruction usually consisting of a few demonstrations and then an injunction to 'now have a go yourself'. Indeed, it was long held that there were as many individual styles of delivery as there are of walking, and that it was not possible to teach bowls in the way that, say, tennis or golf is taught. That theory has now been largely refuted. In Australia there are many professional teachers, and in England the Central Council for Physical Recreation, in association with county bowling associations, now promotes extensive 'Bowls for Beginners' courses each summer. And a few schools have adopted bowls to cater for pupils not suitable physically or temperamentally to

David Rhys Jones in action during the English Bowling Association's pairs championships at Mortlake, Surrey. A champion at 26 in what is generally regarded as an old man's game, Rhys Jones won his fifth EBA title in 1969.

traditional school games such as cricket, soccer, and rugby.

Competitions

The first ever world championships were held in October 1966 at New South Wales Leagues Club at Kyeemagh, on the outskirts of Sydney. All 16 countries then affiliated to the IBB entered. England, with David Bryant, won the singles, Australia the doubles and triples, and New Zealand the fours.

Because bowls, other than crown green, is not a popular spectator sport except in South Africa, financing any truly international event is an almost insurmountable problem, and the staging of a second world championship series did not take place until 1972, at Worthing, England.

The British Commonwealth Games bring together many of the great exponents of the game, although South Africa, Rhodesia, and the United States are not eligible. The United States, seeking to spread the international competitive spirit, is promoting an annual Masters Tournament in memory of Walt Disney, of film cartoon fame, who was himself a bowler of much enthusiasm and no little skill.

Australia and South Africa play regular test matches, and these have proved so successful and financially viable that the women followed suit in November 1969. It has also become an Australian custom to invite one or two overseas players to compete in selected Masters Tournaments, a habit that is slowly spreading.

Each major country affiliated to the IBB promotes its own national championships and of these England has by far the largest entry—in 1969 the total was nearly 70,000 men and 24,000 women. In addition to the national championships, open tournaments, regional events, district competitions, club championships, international, county, and district team championships proliferate so profusely that many bowlers are on the green nearly every summer day or evening.

Origins of the game

Games of the bowls type were played in some of the earliest civilizations. Sir Flinders Petrie, a world authority on Egyptology, discovered implements for playing a game remarkably similar to bowls when examining the grave of a child authentically dated 5200 B.C. And there are many ancient vases, markers, plaques, and the like to show that the game was played in many lands at least from that date onwards.

The earliest known green in England is at Southampton, where play began in 1299 and where a special commemorative game is staged annually. A manuscript in the Royal Library at Windsor contains a drawing captioned in old English: 'XIII Century Game of Bowles'. The drawing depicts a game in which bowls are being directed towards a cone, and suggests that 'bowles' was still a target game.

No one is quite sure how 'bias' was introduced into the game, but the most popular theory is that it happened in the reign of Henry VIII during a game at Goole in Yorkshire. One of the players, Charles Brandon, delivered his bowl with such force that it split in half after cannoning into an oppo-

nent's bowl. Not one to be thwarted easily, Brandon is reputed to have run to the nearest house, borrowed a saw, and cut off the decorative top of the stair bannister. Returning to the green, he delivered this improvised bowl, which, because of the flat surface where the saw had cut, was unbalanced. So instead of running in a straight line, it curled round at the end of its travel. This enabled Brandon, sometimes known as the Duke of Suffolk, to curve subsequent deliveries round other bowls. In this way, he was able to reach the target where, previously, there would not have been a path. Delighted, he rewarded the owner of the house with £5.

Soon, other bowlers flattened one side of their spheres, and the bias—the essential characteristic of the modern game—came into being.

Originally, all bowls were manufactured, or 'turned', from a special wood called lignum-vitae, introduced into Europe from the island of San Domingo in 1508. Diameters were strictly related to weight, and these dimensions were governed by the density of the wood. In the early 1900s, experiments began on hardened rubber bowls, and these became extremely popular in Australia between 1918 and 1924. At the same time, sets of bowls made from vulcanite and ebonite were produced. But all suffered from disadvantages of one kind or another, and it was not

Mansell Collection

High Commissioner for New Zealand

1 An international bowls match at London's Crystal Palace in 1901—in blazer and cap, the ubiquitous Dr W. G. Grace, who influenced the development of bowls as he had that of cricket. He was a prime mover in the founding of the English Bowling Association in 1903 and was their first president. Stepping onto the mat is John Young of the Australian touring team, and to his left the waistcoated J. W. Dingles from New Zealand. The Australian side were the first to tour England under the aegis of the Imperial Bowling Association. The New Zealand team arrived a few days later for a separate tour. 2 The serenely beautiful bowling green in Government Gardens, Rotorua, New Zealand.

until 1931 that the first completely satisfactory set of composition bowls was produced. Made from a moulding compound perfected by a Dr Lang, an Australian, it was produced by William David Hensell, whose company subsequently produced and sold well over two million sets of perfectly matched bowls. Later, other plastic compounds were developed and used in the manufacture of 'woods', but the Hensell product remained the most commonly used.

The most famous exponent of bowls must surely be Sir Francis Drake, whose refusal to join in battle with the Spanish Armada until he had finished his game must rank as one of the great apocryphal tales in history. And in another way, Dr W. G. Grace, of cricketing immortality, also fills a unique spot in bowls history. For it was his passion for all-the-year-round exercise that largely resulted in bowls becoming an indoor game as well as an outdoor one.

Big names in bowls

Bowls has its personalities—its champions and great characters—as much as any other sport. There is still talk of the skill of Jimmy Carruthers, the winner of the first English singles championship, in 1905. David Bryant won a record eight English championships while still in his thirties, and his friend and partner, David Rhys Jones, won his fifth English championship in 1969 when only 26.

C. M. Jones

Syndication International

Australian News and Information Bureau

3 'The Crab': a characteristic study of Sid Drysdale, who earned his nickname in Australia at the 1962 British Commonwealth Games. A great favourite with the spectators because of his antics on the green, he skipped the English fours to a gold medal at Perth. **4** A tense moment in the Scottish Ladies' Bowling Championship, at Queen's Park Bowling Club, Glasgow. The women take the game just as seriously as the men, and play bowls as a recreation as well as a competitive sport. Women's bowls flourishes in many countries, but particularly in Australia, New Zealand, and South Africa. **5** The bowling greens of the New South Wales Leagues Club at Kyeemagh, a suburb of Sydney on the

shores of Botany Bay. The magnificent club-house in the background is typical of Australian club-houses, with their modern auditoriums and facilities for other sporting activities and recreation. Kyeemagh was the scene of the first world bowls championships, held in 1966. Australia won both the doubles and the triples, and New Zealand won the fours. David Bryant of England won the singles, so becoming the first world bowls champion. The Leonard Trophy, which is a team award given for the best overall performance in the championships, went to Australia.
No firm date was set for the next world championships because of the difficulty in finding support for bowls on such a scale.

BOWLS

World Championships
1966 Kyeemagh, NSW

Event	Winners	Country
Singles	D. Bryant	England
Doubles	A. Palm	Australia
	G. Kelly	
Triples	D. Collins	Australia
	A. Johnson	
	J. Dobbie	
Fours	N. Lash	New Zealand
	R. Buchan	
	G. Jolly	
	W. O'Neill	

Leonard Trophy (team award) won by Australia

1972 Worthing, England

Event	Winners	Country
Singles	M. Evans	Wales
Doubles	C. Delgado	Hong Kong
	E. Liddell	
Triples	R. Folkins	USA
	C. Forrester	
	W. Miller	
Fours	E. Hayward	England
	C. Stroud	
	N. King	
	P. Line	

Leonard trophy won by Scotland

British Commonwealth Games

Year	Winner	Country
Singles		
1930	R. G. Colquhoun	England
1934	R. Sprot	Scotland
1938	H. Harvey	South Africa
1950	J. Pirret	New Zealand
1954	R. Hodges	Southern Rhodesia
1958	P. Danilowitz	South Africa
1962	D. Bryant	England
1966	Event not held	
1970	D. Bryant	England
1974	D. Bryant	England
Doubles		
1930	T. G. Hills	England
	G. W. A. Wright	
1934	T. G. Hills	England
	G. W. A. Wright	
1938	L. L. Macey	New Zealand
	W. Denison	
1950	R. Henry	New Zealand
	E. P. Exelby	
1954	W. Ramsbotham	Northern Ireland
	P. Watson	
1958	J. M. Morris	New Zealand
	R. E. Pilkington	
1962	R. McDonald	New Zealand
	H. Robson	
1966	Event not held	
1970	N. King	England
	P. Line	
1974	J. Christie	Scotland
	A. McIntosh	
Fours		
1930	England	
1934	England	
1938	New Zealand	
1950	South Africa	
1954	South Africa	
1958	England	
1962	England	
1966	Event not held	
1970	Hong Kong	
1974	New Zealand	

Keystone

Australian News and Information Bureau

1 A breathtaking setting for bowls at Cape Town, in South Africa. Bowls is a popular spectator sport in South Africa, as well as being one of the leading participant sports for both men and women. The South African national championships regularly attract crowds of several thousand paying spectators. In the Empire Games the South Africans were usually among the medals until they became ineligible in 1962. With no indoor bowls in South Africa, the players do not get the amount of practice enjoyed, say, by bowlers in the British Isles. **2** Players watch as the distance between the jack and a bowl is measured. Measurement is necessary when bowls from opposing players or teams are a similar distance from the jack at the completion of an end. It is a common sight in top-class bowls.

How the game is played

Stripped of all technicalities, the object of the game is to deliver one's bowls closer to the jack (the small white target ball) than the opponent's balls. Each one finishing nearer to it than the best of the opponent's is called a *shot* and scores a point.

Bowls is played between two men or women (singles), two a side (doubles), three a side (triples), or four a side (fours or rinks). The green on which any major international event takes place normally measures from 40 to 44 yards in length and is usually square, the width being divided into six playing areas called *rinks*. The green is surrounded by a ditch, which, for international play, is from 8 to 15 inches wide and 4 to 8 inches deep. This is bounded by a bank 9 or more inches high and not more than 35 degrees from the vertical.

In singles, each player delivers four bowls, alternating with his opponent. The first player to reach 21 (31 in Australian domestic events) is the winner. When each man has delivered all his bowls, the 'end' is changed, and the bowls are delivered back down the green.

In pairs (four bowls per man) and fours (two bowls), the side leading after 21 ends is the winner, extra ends being played as necessary if the score is tied. In triples, each player delivers three bowls per end, and the match is decided over 18 ends.

To start a game, after the initial trial end, the jack is bowled from a mat by the player or the side playing first, and it must travel at least 25 yards from the mat and come to rest at least 2 yards from the ditch. In delivering a bowl, a player must have the whole of one foot either on the mat or directly above it.

If a bowl travels at least 15 yards from the mat and remains within the confines of the rink, it is termed a *live* bowl, and is in play. Otherwise it is declared *dead,* and is placed on the bank. A bowl that touches the jack in its initial run is called a *toucher,* and marked with chalk. It remains live even when in the ditch. If a jack is knocked into the ditch, it too remains live so long as it is still within the lateral confines of the rink. But if it goes out of bounds, the end has to be replayed. A player may strike his own bowls and his opponent's with a bowl, and even drive them into the ditch. Non-touchers that rebound from the bank or from a toucher or the jack in the ditch are declared dead and are removed to the bank.

Shots are counted at the completion of an end, and no measurements may be made until the end is completed. In singles, a marker is responsible for measuring any shots in doubt. During an end he stands behind the jack and to one side. His duties include chalking touchers; checking distances of jack and bowls from the boundaries of the rink where necessary, and indicating to a player, when requested, the distance of any bowl from the jack or from another bowl, or which bowl he thinks is standing shot (lying nearest to the jack). In cases of dispute, an umpire gives a final ruling.

John Lloyd

C. M. Jones

Australian News and Information Bureau

The bowls and the green

The maximum and minimum diameters and weights of bowls, as laid down by the IBB, range from $4\frac{3}{4}$ to $5\frac{1}{8}$ inches and 3 lb to 3 lb 8 oz. (The British Isles Bowls Council observes the IBB rule in competitions outside Britain, but in domestic championships retains the old 'weight for size rule' in which the $5\frac{1}{8}$-inch bowl weighs 3 lb 8 oz and $4\frac{3}{4}$-inch one only 3 lb).

The use of plastic removes the imposed relationship between size and weight and, theoretically, there is no reason why the smallest-diameter bowl should not weigh the maximum permitted 3 lb 8 oz. Thus bowlers with small hands are no longer handicapped because they cannot use full-weight bowls. It is thought that weight is important to a bowl's stability, but there are other factors which render the whole subject of a bowl's behaviour one of great mathematical complexity. Suffice to say that composition bowls have virtually ousted lignum vitae, except in places where the turf is especially heavy. There is a widely held belief that because wood is 'live' it rides heavy turf better than 'dead' plastic.

The permissible degree of bias is set by comparison with a master bowl held by each official tester, so that all bowls used in competitions have to be approved and stamped by one of these official testers every 10 years.

A true surface is vital if full use is to be made of bias; a bowl hurtling through the air is not affected by bias to anything like the same degree.

The amount a biased bowl curves depends on the relationship between the forward force given by the deliverer and the side pull imposed by the imbalance, the bias. The slower the forward movement, the more effective is the bias. Thus it is normally the aim to make bowling greens as smooth and resistance-free as possible. This lengthens the time the bowl runs and so allows it to curve more sharply. The faster the green, the longer this 'trickling' period lasts. It has become customary to measure the speed of greens in the number of seconds it takes a bowl to come to a stop near to a mark or jack 30 yards down the green.

The greens at Kyeemagh, Australia, during the world championships were timed around 16 seconds. In Britain, greens are much heavier and a bowl comes to rest 30 yards away in an average of 12 seconds. On greens in the south during the summer, the run may be extended by a couple of seconds, while in the north 10-second greens are common.

Greens as slow as the latter afford limited opportunity for exploiting bias, and so the game tends to have less variety. However, Scotland won the British International Team Championship for the fifth year running in 1969, so there seems little reason to question the skills of bowlers raised on heavy, slow greens.

1 A Kent player shows his team-mate the correct line in a match against the touring Australian side in 1969. **2** The outstanding player of the 1960s, world champion David Bryant, pipe in mouth, is as formidable on the carpet as he is on grass. He dominated British indoor bowling in the 1960s. **3** South African star 'Snowy' Walker, checking his card, won his national singles championships four times, and an Empire gold medal in fours.

Percy Baker, in a long and illustrious career, won the English singles a record four times. And Glyn Bosisto dominated Australian bowling for many years, winning four Australian singles championships. These careers were paralleled in South Africa by Norman 'Snowy' Walker. Four times South African champion and a firm believer in physical fitness, Walker uses maximum-bias bowls, and is exceptionally skilled in 'drawing' his bowls close in to the jack. Delivered with such exact delicacy, his bowl sometimes turns through 180 degrees, and travels its last inch or so backwards towards him!

In the United States one of the three top players, left-hander Ezra Wyeth, is a university professor from Queensland. His other claim to fame is the regularity with which he used to dismiss Don Bradman in their State cricketing days. Regarded by many as the world's greatest skip (short for skipper, or rink director in Australia) is Harry Reston, a demonstrative Scot whose enthusiastic leaps, runs, and general cavorting at the world championships made him a favourite with the spectators. But perhaps the most colourful character in the game was Sid Drysdale, skip of the gold-medal-winning English four in the 1962 Commonwealth Games, at Perth. Nicknamed 'The Crab' in Australia because of his curious squatting stance as he watched the play, he habitually danced cheerfully up the green after his wood. His hilarious antics caused one onlooker in Perth to remark that he paid half his entry fee to see the bowls and half to watch Sid.

Central Press

1

Technique

The basic shot in bowls is the *draw*. Most shots are scored by *drawing* one's bowls nearer to the jack than the opponent's. All else being equal, this is normally achieved by the player with the smoothest, most rhythmical, and regular delivery.

So it is vital to learn, develop, and master a delivery which sends the bowl up the green with the accuracy of a machine and on a completely even keel; that is, with the flattened side of the bowl at 90 degrees to the green. Spin should be avoided, unless it be a slight top-spin, which makes the bowl rotate slightly forwards at the top. This adds slight 'run' to the bowl, so allowing the bias additional time in which to work.

And the delivery must be so fixedly grooved that it is capable of sending bowl after bowl along a precise, predetermined line. In developing a delivery, it is advisable to master line first and then to develop that sensitivity of touch which governs length. Any bowl in a more or less straight line with the jack is a potential scorer.

The *drive* or *firing shot* is a forceful delivery designed to break up the head—the cluster of 'live' woods round the jack—and perhaps force the jack into the ditch. It is sometimes frowned upon—unjustifiably—as being crude and even unsporting, but it is a difficult shot to master, and played correctly is an essential part of a bowler's armoury.

The *trail* is another difficult shot to perfect. It is used to move, or trail, the jack to a new, advantageous, position. Other shots include the *wick*, which is a shot off another bowl; the *yard-on shot*, used to push out an opponent's bowl and the *block*, or *guard*, shot, a delivery stopped short to protect a position and block an opponent's line.

C. M. Jones

Glossary of Terms

Backhand The delivery which, in the case of a right-handed bowler, sends a bowl towards the jack along a line running diagonally to the left from the mat.

Bias The inbalance in a bowl caused by its special shape and which results in the bowl running a curved course.

Bumper A bowl delivered in the air instead of right down on the green's surface. A common fault in aged bowlers or those with poor techniques.

Cannoning The action of a bowl glancing off one bowl onto another.

Dead Bowl A bowl out of play.

Dead End An end deemed not to have been played. It is normally caused by the jack being driven beyond the boundaries of the rink, the end then being replayed in its entirety.

Draw The effect of bias upon a bowl. The path that a bowl should take when approaching the jack and allowing for the effect of bias.

Draw Shot Delivering a bowl so that it comes to rest immediately adjacent to the jack.

Drive or **Firing Shot** A bowl delivered forcefully with the object of breaking up the head, forcing the jack into the ditch, or clearing the way to the jack for subsequent deliveries.

End The completion of all deliveries from all the players in one direction on a rink. At the completion of an end, a count of shots is taken, and then an end is begun in the opposite direction.

Firm Shot A stronger delivery than a draw shot, but less forceful than a drive.

Forehand The delivery by a right-handed player of his bowl towards the jack along a line running diagonally to the right from the mat.

Head The jack and all the 'live' bowls that have been delivered at any given moment during an end.

Heavy A bowl delivered with too much force and which overruns its objective.

Jack (Colloquially 'kitty' or 'cot') the small white ball used as the target. It is unbiased and 2½ inches in diameter, and weighs from 8 to 10 oz.

Jack-high A bowl level with the jack.

Land The amount of green taken to allow the bowl to finish in the desired position after allowing for the curve caused by bias.

Lead The first player in a pair, triple, or four. The leads, bowling alternately, play their bowls before the other players.

Live Bowl Any delivered bowl forming part of the head within the confines of the rink, or any bowl in the ditch which has been chalked as a *toucher*.

Port A narrow gap between bowls through which to draw the shot.

Resting Out Delivering a bowl that pushes out an opponent's from an advantageous position.

Skip The last man in a pair, triple, or four; called the rink director in Australia. He is normally the man who decides the tactics.

Short A bowl that does not reach the jack or other specified objective.

Toucher A bowl that touches the jack during its initial run, whether or not it cannons into other bowls en route. Touchers are chalked and remain effective even when in the ditch. Non-touchers going into the ditch are ineffective (dead), and are placed on the bank until the commencement of the next end.

Trailing An expression used when a delivered bowl moves the jack to a new position, usually adjacent to one or more of one's own bowls.

Wicking Glancing a bowl off another to change its direction.

Yard-on Shot A delivery intended to push out an opponent's bowl lying near the jack or to trail the jack away from it

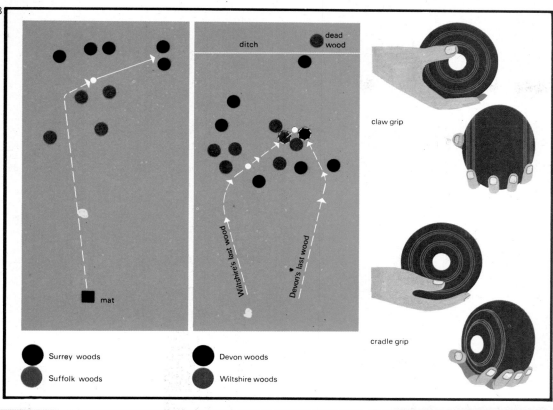

| Surrey woods | Devon woods |
| Suffolk woods | Wiltshire woods |

claw grip

cradle grip

Roy Castle

1 One of the youngest players at the EBA championships.
2 English international Paddy Orr in waterproof outfit. Rain stops play at bowls only if the green becomes flooded.
3 The diagrams show two of the commonest grips and (by kind permission of C. M. Jones, from his book *Winning Bowls*) two examples of what can be accomplished in bowls by the leading players. *Left,* The shot of a lifetime: Ernie Lake, skipping for Surrey in a Middleton Cup match, faced a seemingly hopeless position. But he wobbled his wood so that it curved round sharply about 18 inches from the jack, trailing it past his opponent's woods onto two of his own. *Right,* Another Middleton Cup match. Wiltshire skip Ernie Pullen trailed the jack with his last wood to leave a winning position. But Devon skip Harold Shapland had the perfect reply, a full-length draw through a narrow gap to nestle his wood against the jack. **4** A typical English green, on the sea front at Weymouth. **5** Bowling the jack.

John Lloyd

1 The bourgeoisie gamble on a fight in a fives court in the early 19th century. **2** The famous 'Ring' in Blackfriars Road.

Boxing

Everybody loves a fight. The aggressive instinct is very close to the surface in man, and when this instinct can be satisfied vicariously, with no danger or discomfort to himself, he is usually prepared to pay for the privilege. Thousands will flock to watch two evenly matched contestants punch it out, and the prospect lures millions more to their radios and television sets. The arc-lights of the ring accentuate the colour and showmanship of combat, the speed of attack, the science of defence, the knock-down and the count-out. All these give boxing, amateur and professional, a fascination all its own.

The magnetism of boxing lies in its unpredictability. It is difficult to forecast the winner from a well-matched pair. Even when a man is favourite to win on current form, there are a number of hazards to upset the forecast. The referee may err in his judgement; one man may accidentally commit a foul and be disqualified; a cut eye or other physical damage can stop the fight; one man may fall out of the ring and be unable to get back in time; another may feel that he has had enough and quit. In fact, anything can happen.

Boxing as a form of entertainment began in the early 1700s in village fairgrounds. At one time men were prepared, for a few guineas thrown into the ring, to battle on until one contestant dropped unconscious. Today a boxer who is any good can command a guaranteed sum running into thousands of pounds for a single bout, plus more money from film, radio, and television rights.

Boxing has its greatest hold in sports-loving countries and those that breed fighting men. The best and most determined performers come from the underprivileged races; they are known as the 'hungry' fighters. The sport reached its peak at the time of the industrial depression in the 1920s and 1930s, and its decline began with the growth of the welfare state. Some of the greatest champions were Jewish, Italian, and Irish. Britain's best came from the mining areas of Wales, the ports of Liverpool, Newcastle, and Glasgow, and the East End of London. Sheer want, plus the basic urge to conquer, inspires a youth to fight.

Most boxers begin as amateurs. They fight for the joy of it, and are rewarded for their achievements with a silver trophy or the honour of representing their country at international matches and championships. They can begin as schoolboys and progress in stages until they become stars

Boxing Facts

Shortest bouts

The shortest world title fight took place on April 6, 1914, when Al McCoy ko'd George Chip in 45 sec to win the middleweight title in New York. For comparison, the Cassius Clay-Sonny Liston fight at Lewiston, Maine, on May 25, 1965, lasted 1 min 57 sec, including the count.

Al Couture ko'd Ralph Walton in 10½ sec (including count) at Lewiston, Maine, on September 26, 1946.

Teddy Barker beat Bob Roberts in 10 sec at Maesteg, Wales, on September 2, 1957. The referee stopped the fight.

World champions

Joe Louis (USA) was the longest reigning world champion, holding the heavyweight championship for 11 years, 8 months. Eugène Criqui (France) held the official world featherweight championship for only 55 days, from June 2 to July 26, 1923.

The youngest world champion was Tom 'Pedlar' Palmer of England who won the world bantamweight title when he was 19 years and 6 days old, on November 26, 1895.

The boxer to win a world title the most often is 'Sugar' Ray Robinson, who won the middleweight championship five times from 1951 to 1958.

The only man to hold three world championships at the same time is Henry Armstrong (USA) who held the world featherweight, lightweight, and welterweight titles from October to December, 1938.

Olympic Games

In Olympic Games Laszlo Papp of Hungary won three gold medals in middleweight (1948) and light-middleweight (1952 and 1956) divisions.

O. L. Kirk of the USA won the bantamweight and featherweight titles at the St Louis Olympic celebrations in 1904.

Crowds

The largest amount of gate money paid for a world title fight was the $2,658,660 paid for the Jack Dempsey-Gene Tunney fight on 22 September, 1927, at Soldier Field, Chicago, USA. The highest paying attendance for any boxing match is 120,757 who saw the Dempsey-Tunney fight on September 23, 1926, at the Sesquicentennial Stadium, Philadelphia, USA.

World heavyweight champion Muhammad Ali (Cassius Clay) surveys his damage to British title-holder Henry Cooper's left eye in their 1966 meeting for the world crown at Highbury. The same ill-luck had plagued Cooper in 1963.

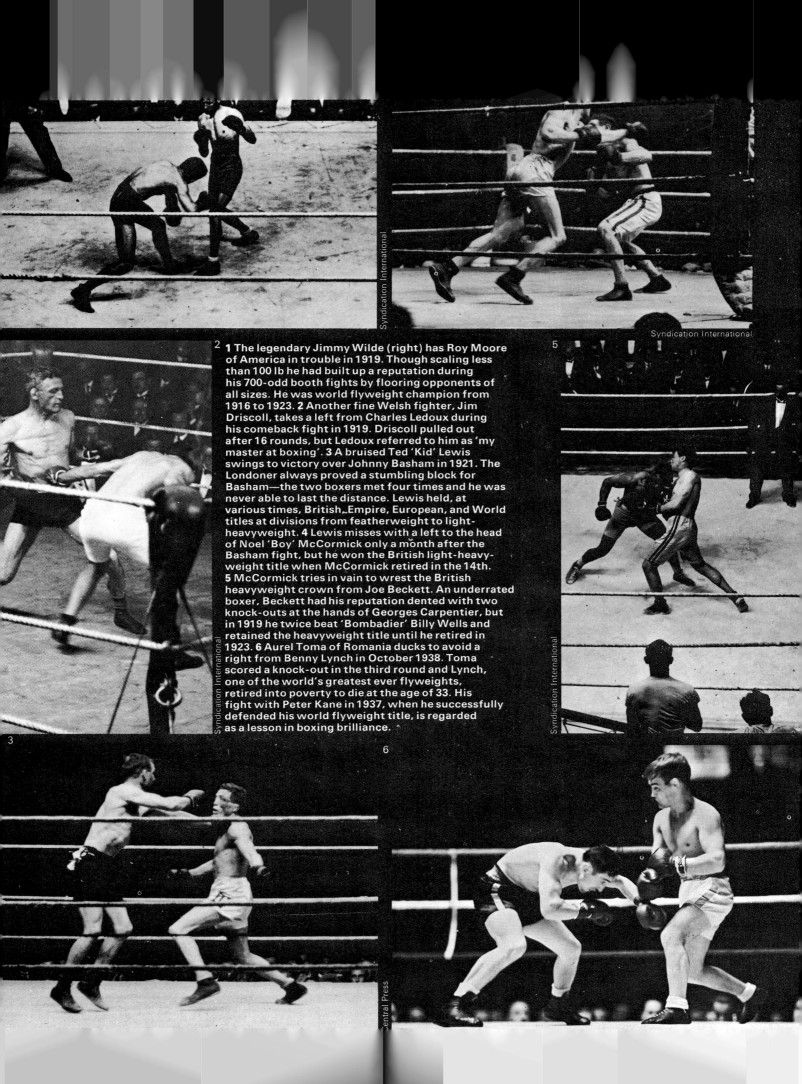

Syndication International

1 The legendary Jimmy Wilde (right) has Roy Moore of America in trouble in 1919. Though scaling less than 100 lb he had built up a reputation during his 700-odd booth fights by flooring opponents of all sizes. He was world flyweight champion from 1916 to 1923. **2** Another fine Welsh fighter, Jim Driscoll, takes a left from Charles Ledoux during his comeback fight in 1919. Driscoll pulled out after 16 rounds, but Ledoux referred to him as 'my master at boxing'. **3** A bruised Ted 'Kid' Lewis swings to victory over Johnny Basham in 1921. The Londoner always proved a stumbling block for Basham—the two boxers met four times and he was never able to last the distance. Lewis held, at various times, British, Empire, European, and World titles at divisions from featherweight to light-heavyweight. **4** Lewis misses with a left to the head of Noel 'Boy' McCormick only a month after the Basham fight, but he won the British light-heavy-weight title when McCormick retired in the 14th. **5** McCormick tries in vain to wrest the British heavyweight crown from Joe Beckett. An underrated boxer, Beckett had his reputation dented with two knock-outs at the hands of Georges Carpentier, but in 1919 he twice beat 'Bombadier' Billy Wells and retained the heavyweight title until he retired in 1923. **6** Aurel Toma of Romania ducks to avoid a right from Benny Lynch in October 1938. Toma scored a knock-out in the third round and Lynch, one of the world's greatest ever flyweights, retired into poverty to die at the age of 33. His fight with Peter Kane in 1937, when he successfully defended his world flyweight title, is regarded as a lesson in boxing brilliance.

of their clubs. Bouts are limited to three rounds, and each round lasts two or three minutes, according to the age and ability of the boxers. No boxer may be granted a licence to box professionally until he is 18—if he is attached to a club—but of course, a boy can take up professional boxing without ever having been an amateur.

Amateur boxers always wear vests and carry an identifying red or blue sash. There are three judges in amateur boxing, with a referee who takes no part in the decision, but is there solely to be in charge of the contest. In professional boxing the referee always gives the verdict, although in countries other than Britain two judges join the referee in providing a majority verdict. Amateurs are usually controlled by their trainers; professionals by managers, who are entitled to a percentage of their earnings.

Amateur boxing

Amateur boxers are, of course, unpaid, and while most of the governing bodies of amateur boxing throughout the world are strict about this, some interpret amateur status more liberally than others and supply ample expenses or provide leading exponents with sponsored jobs that give them unlimited time off for their sport.

Britain's Amateur Boxing Association (ABA), formed in 1880, embraces a number of regional associations. The annual champions of these associations are brought together for the ABA championships each year. The ABA also selects teams for international matches, the Commonwealth and the Olympic Games, held every four years, and the European Championships, held every two years.

In Britain, an amateur can begin in his schooldays, and progress through schoolboys, boys' clubs, youth, and junior titles before entering for the ABA titles. Most other countries have similar facilities.

In most European countries, amateurs and professionals are controlled by the same body and are permitted to train together and even appear in the same tournaments. In Russia and its allied countries, there are no professional boxers, as such, and the amateur sport is state-controlled. In America, amateur boxing is governed by the American Athletic Union, but there are annual Golden Gloves and Diamond Gloves eliminating tournaments, usually sponsored by newspapers. In these, an amateur can win a city title, inter-city title, or state title, and go on to become a national champion and be selected to represent his country at the Olympic Games.

In the European Championships and the Olympic Games, referees are neutral and bouts restricted to three rounds, each of three minutes duration. A stand-

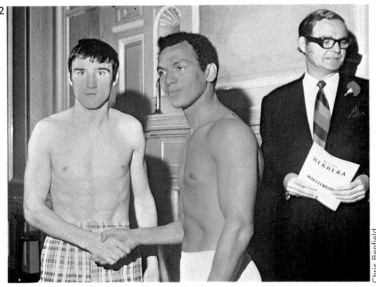

(photo credit: H. W. Neale)

(photo credit: Chris Benfield)

1 Punch and parry during an amateur bout. Amateur boxers wear vests, and red or blue sashes for identification.

2 Jimmy Revie and Miguel Herrera pose at the weigh-in before their professional featherweight contest.

ing count of 'eight' operates if a boxer is put down or is in serious trouble. The verdict is given by the majority scoring of three judges, so that there is bound to be a winner, either by a unanimous or a split verdict.

In Britain, an amateur boxer is given a medical card that is brought up to date each time he engages in a contest. Without this card he is unable to box, and should he apply to become a professional, his amateur body reports on his medical history and active record. These are carefully studied before he is issued with a professional licence. There is a close working agreement between the ABA and the British Boxing Board of Control in the change-over of boxers from amateur to professional status—the amateur side of the sport being virtually the nursery for the paid ranks.

Control

In all countries that practise professional boxing, with the exception of the United States, there is one controlling body. In Europe the boxing nations are

governed by the European Boxing Union. Each of the Commonwealth countries governs its own professional boxing, but there is a Commonwealth committee that controls the championships.

In America a complex situation inhibits a unanimous voice in world championships. The New York State laws do not allow allegiance to any other controlling body, as far as boxing is concerned, but the New York State Athletic Commission permits its boxing commission to have a working arrangement with the British Boxing Board of Control and also the World Boxing Council (WBC), set up in 1963. And there is also, in the United States, the World Boxing Association (formerly the National Boxing Association), which from time to time sets up its own champions, but which does not have the widespread authority of the WBC.

Affiliated to the WBC is the Continental European Boxing Union, the British Boxing Board of Control (with its Commonwealth committee), the North American Boxing

Federation, Central and South, the Oriental and Pan Pacific Federations, and the African Boxing Federation. On the other hand, included among those states affiliated to the WBA are a number that have very little or no professional boxing.

In professional championship contests, the boxers fight for a purse submitted by a promoter and accepted by the controlling body. The purse is split 60-40, with the larger portion going to the champion. If a vacant title is contested, the purse is divided equally. In former days all purses were split 60-40, the major share going to the winner, unless a previous arrangement had been made at the signing of contracts. Nowadays boxers—as already mentioned—fight for a guaranteed sum, win, lose, or draw, plus a percentage of film, radio, and television rights. From his guaranteed purse the boxer pays his manager a fixed percentage after training and travelling expenses have been deducted. If the boxers agree to back themselves, or if they have backers prepared to put up a side-stake, the money is held by the controlling body until after the contest has been decided.

The duties of a manager, in addition to looking after his boxer's welfare, include accepting matches on his behalf that aid his advancement and earning capacity. There is a boxing adage that a match well made is a match half won, and a good manager sees that all the engagements he arranges for his boxer are well made. Naturally it is the prime purpose of a manager to make his boxer into a box-office draw, while the promoter, whose main object is to show a profit, hopes to present to the public matches that will stir them. If he can match two men of equal interest to the fight fan, this contest is called a 'natural'. To attract a full house a promoter need not necessarily stage a championship fight—a match between two ambitious men of equal merit and colourful contrasting styles can also command a capacity attendance.

History of boxing

Men have fought or sparred with their fists ever since they learned to stand on their feet. As a competitive sport boxing had its origin in ancient Greece, both Homer and Virgil making references to notable contests. In Roman amphitheatres men fought without weapons, but their hands were encased in a brutal iron guard known as the *caestus*, forerunner of the illegal knuckle-duster. Boxing was one of the sports at the original Olympic Games and there is no doubt that it spread throughout Europe, being taken up as a sport and public entertainment in those countries where athletic competition is popular.

1 Present-day boxers owe much to the Marquess of Queensberry. In the 1860s, together with John Graham Chambers, he drew up a set of rules for boxing, known now as the Queensberry Rules. With some modifications, they still apply.

2 The Queensberry Rules were not the first, however. Over a hundred years before these rules were drawn up, Jack Broughton, one of the greatest of the bare-knuckle fighters, wrote a set of rules and introduced the use of gloves, or 'mufflers' as they were then known. In 1810, what is considered to be the first world championship was held. The contestants were **3** Tom Molineux and **4** Tom Cribb. They fought twice with Cribb winning both times. Molineux, a freed American slave, was unlucky to lose the first contest though. There are varying reports on why Cribb, who was being soundly beaten by the negro, won. Some

say that Molineux stumbled over Cribb into a ring post and fractured his skull. Others suggest Cribb recovered as the bout went on towards the 39th round and finally won. The second fight, however, did not last anywhere near as long and was easily won by Cribb.

5 By modern standards, Daniel Mendoza was only a middleweight but by combining agile footwork with a good straight left he was able to beat fighters much bigger than himself. Mendoza was champion of England but lost his title to 'Gentleman' John Jackson in 1795. Later, he set up a boxing school for young noblemen.

6 Another great Champion of England who was a middleweight was Tom Sayers. In 1860, Sayers fought the American John C. Heenan, who was about 3 stone heavier. The fight ended in a draw after 42 rounds. After this fight, Sayers retired as the undefeated champion.

Mansell Collection

Radio Times Hulton Picture Library

Radio Times Hulton Picture Library

Boxing found a ready home in England where sport of any kind was a national recreation and where participation was more important than victory. Boxing became a feature of the travelling fairs that provided regular entertainment for the towns and country villages. The early boxer was a tough character, prepared to take on all-comers and, apart from using his fists, he was generally an adept at *singlesticks* (fencing), broad-swords, cudgels, and other forms of martial arts. Those who were pugilistically inclined, particularly the gentry, loved to encourage contests between their servants and tradesmen. One of the earliest references to a boxing match, between a footman and a butcher, was published in the *Protestant Mercury* in 1681.

In 1719 James Figg (or Fig) opened an arena for boxing in London. It is the first record we have of a permanent public place for boxing. Exhibitions of manly sports were provided there and lessons given in the art of self-defence. Figg, a fairground product of outstanding ability, was the earliest professional fighter and promoter. His card, drawn for him by William Hogarth, advertised his unique business. In 1723, by order of George I, a games ring was formed in Hyde Park, London, where impromptu contests took place for the amusement of the public. Men went into the 'ring' to compete, and it is thought that from this the place for boxing became known as the *ring*, even when it became a roped square.

1 John L. Sullivan, 'the Boston Strong Boy', who rivals Jack Dempsey as the most idolized fighter in American ring history. He won his country's heavyweight championship when he knocked out Paddy Ryan after 10½ minutes of a bare-knuckle contest at Mississippi City in 1882. He had two bouts with the British champion, Charlie Mitchell, but one was broken up by the police and the other abandoned as a draw after 39 rounds. Sullivan is nevertheless seen as the world champion by most boxing historians. 2 James J. Corbett—called 'Gentleman Jim' because of his fair methods of fighting—knocked out Sullivan in the 21st round at New Orleans in 1892, though the champion had not fought for over three years and had been acting. Corbett retained his unofficial world title until 1897. 3 A cheeky Corbett in an unusually friendly clinch with Bob Fitzsimmons during their fight at Carson City in March 1897. Fitzsimmons knocked out the champion in the 14th and kept the title until he was floored by James J. Jeffries in 1899.

Another version claims that when a fight took place a ring was formed by the spectators to contain the contestants.

Figg was followed by his pupil John Broughton (1704-1789) who set up his own establishment in the same area, but with many improvements. The new place was less rowdy, with the result that he attracted wealthy patrons such as the Prince of Wales, son of George II. When George Stevenson, a Yorkshire coachman, died after being beaten in the ring by Broughton, it led to Broughton's drawing up a set of rules in 1743 devised to prevent further deaths in the prize ring. These form the basis of today's rules. Another of Broughton's innovations was the use of 'mufflers' or gloves, by his aristocratic pupils, in order to prevent facial damage. When Broughton was beaten for the championship by Jack Slack in 1750, the Duke of Cumberland,

who had backed the loser heavily, complained that he had been cheated and used his influence to outlaw prize fighting.

The sport continued sporadically throughout the country, contests taking place in secret, usually in the open in out-of-the-way places, and very often broken up by the police. It was not until the coming of such characters as Richard Humphries, the Gentleman Boxer, who was active from 1784-1790; Daniel Mendoza, The Jew (1764-1836), and Gentleman John Jackson (1769-1845) that prize-fighting once more won the patronage of the young bloods of the day who called themselves the Corinthians. Mendoza introduced speed into the sport and wrote one of the first books on boxing, while Jackson had an academy in Bond Street where the poet Byron was one of his most ardent pupils. But prize-fighting was still illegal, and the contestants and

the organizers could be arrested and fined, or even imprisoned for causing a breach of the peace.

In 1814 the Pugilistic Club was formed in an effort to control prize-fighting, and in 1838 Broughton's Rules were continually amplified and amended until 1860, when they became known as the London Prize Ring Rules. These were adopted in both England and America, where the sport was becoming established. When Jackson retired in 1795 he was followed by a galaxy of champions: Jem Belcher, Hen Pearce, John Gully, and Tom Cribb. Cribb fought the first recorded contest with a negro— Tom Molineux, an American freed slave. It was the golden age of the prize ring, with more science creeping in with each succeeding champion. In 1821 George IV ordered Jackson to form a bodyguard of champions to attend his coronation and help to keep order.

Cribb was succeeded by his adopted son, Tom Spring, who was acknowledged champion in 1824, but from then on the prize ring declined and fell into disrepute because of the increase in 'fixed' fights and the hooligans who attended them. Once again boxing was outlawed, even up to the time of that epic international battle between Tom Sayers of England and John C. Heenan of America, which was fought at Farnborough in Hampshire in 1860, and ended in a 'draw' when the mob broke into the ring during the 42nd round and put an end to the whole proceedings.

Jim Jeffries returned to the ring after six years of retirement in an attempt to regain the world heavyweight title for the white man. He met the legendary Jack Johnson in a famous fight at Reno, Nevada, in 1910. **1** The two men size each other up in the early stages of the fight. **2** Jeffries lands a straight left. **3** The challenger goes down for the first time in his life. He was knocked out by Johnson in round 15 —the only defeat he sustained in his career. **4** Johnson had won the title from Tommy Burns in Sydney on Boxing Day 1908, when the police saved the Canadian from further punishment in the 14th. The negro retained his crown until 1915 when, past his best, he was worn down by the giant Jess Willard (6 ft 6¼ in) and ko'd in the 26th round.
5 William 'Iron' Hague (left), British heavyweight champion, was beaten by the renowned Sam Langford at the National Sporting Club in 1909.
6 Georges Carpentier floors Joe Beckett. The Frenchman won various titles, including world, at almost every weight.

1

2

3

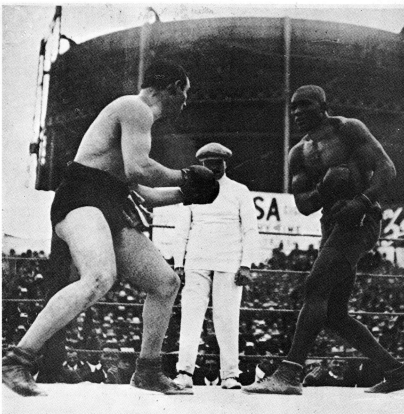
4

Syndication International

5

6

Associated Press

In 1865, the Marquess of Queensberry drew up his famous rules designed solely for glove-fighting, which by that time was fast becoming popular. Gradually bare-knuckle fighting faded into obscurity, with some of its last exponents, such as Jem Mace and Charley Mitchell, fighting in both styles. Mace went to America in 1870 and beat Tom Allen for the championship of the world, then went on to New Zealand and Australia where he set up a boxing school from which emerged some of the great fighters of the early 1900s.

From Australasia, men such as Bob Fitzsimmons and Peter Jackson took scientific boxing into America, where it continued to flourish and produced the finest fighters the world has ever known. The last championship fight with bare fists was fought in America in 1889 between Jake Kilrain and John L. Sullivan, affectionately known as The Boston Strong Boy. The first championship fight with gloves (1892) saw Sullivan defeated by James J. Corbett (Gentleman Jim), a San Francisco bank clerk who coolly outboxed the more robust title-holder.

In England, glove-fighting became popular and tournaments took place regularly at sporting clubs, in the bar parlours of pubs, and at music halls. In London's West End the Pelican Club held sway for a time as a sponsor of boxing, but the club was eventually dissolved, whereupon the National Sporting Club (NSC) came into being in 1891 with its headquarters in Covent Garden market. From there it ruled boxing in Britain with an iron hand, introducing its own set of rules, based on the Queensberry Rules. For nearly 20 years its power went unchallenged, and fighters would willingly box for nothing for the privilege of appearing at 'the club'. Its select membership wore dress suits to watch the boxing, and the ordinary public were not admitted. Whenever there was a big fight, hundreds would wait in the street outside just to hear the result.

In 1909 the eight class weights were officially established. Lord Lonsdale, the club's president, gave his name to the challenge belts that have been in circulation ever since. Before that, championships were fought at all sorts of odd weights, usually at the poundage that best suited the man who styled himself champion and there were only three recognized classes—heavy, middle, and light. But the NSC extended the range, bringing in fly, bantam, and featherweight divisions before the lightweight class, welter between light and middle, and light-heavy (or cruiser) between middle and heavy. The first contest for a Lonsdale Belt took place on November 8, 1909, when Freddie Welsh took the British light-weight title from Johnny Summers.

The power of the NSC began to diminish in the years just before World War I. Boxing enjoyed a remarkable boom wherever it was practised, and commercially minded promoters multiplied—men eager to foster the fast-growing public interest in

Syndication International

Associated Press

Syndication International

London Express News and Feature Services

the sport. Such men could hire large arenas and consequently offer huge purses, far beyond anything the club could provide. The NSC continued until it lost its Covent Garden home in 1929. Since then it has kept going but in a subdued capacity, having handed over its former power to the British Boxing Board of Control (BBB of C). That body was first formed in 1918, and reconstituted in 1929, since when it has issued its own Lonsdale Belts and rules and regulations. Prior to 1929 the police could warn a boxer in his dressing-room that if a fatal accident occurred to his opponent in the ring, he would be charged with manslaughter, because boxing was still regarded as illegal. But with the formation of the Board of Control the responsibility shifted from the law to the controlling body.

In the early 1900s, boxing spread rapidly throughout most of Europe. France was specially gifted with fighters such as Georges Carpentier, Charles Ledoux, Eugène Criqui, and many subsequent world champions. In America, boxing became an industry with a wealth of talent,

Keystone

4 but even this pales alongside the amount that Muhammad Ali and Joe Frazier received for their 1971 world heavyweight title fight. The purse was $2,500,000—for each fighter.

There has been, and still is, particularly in America, a seamier side to boxing, which by its very nature directly involves only two men—with many others financially interested. In the bad days of the prize ring, fixed fights abounded, and later there were a number of suspicious incidents, in spite of the efforts of the National Sporting Club to keep the game clean. Nowadays, in Britain and the rest of Europe at least, there is barely a breath of suspicion, such is the strict control of the sport. But in America, particularly in the 1930s, boxing came under the influence of gangsters. The lack of a single ruling body in that country, with each state organizing its own government of the sport, has encouraged its exploitation and abuse.

Incidents have occurred where a boxer has been counted-out according to prearranged plans, and a referee has been bribed to name the wrong man as the winner. But there have been many more perfectly innocent occasions when an honest referee has made an error of judgment, or a boxer, highly fancied to win, has suffered sensational defeat. One of the most controversial boxing events of all time was the famous 'long count' in the seventh round of the second Dempsey-Tunney fight, when Tunney was put down and badly hurt. Because Dempsey delayed in going to a neutral corner, the champion gained a breathing space that amounted to 14 seconds, according to ringside stop-watches, and got up to win on points.

Allegations of doping have also been made. Jim Jeffries claimed that his food had been tampered with before his epic contest with Jack Johnson in 1910, and in more recent times, Ezzard Charles maintained that he had been given a doped orange to suck between rounds during his title bout with Jersey Joe Walcott. But nowadays there is always the danger of a boxer taking drugs voluntarily in order to boost his morale and performance, although it is extremely difficult to prove such cases.

Whenever there has been any doubt about behaviour of the boxing fraternity, retribution by fines, suspension, or withdrawal of licence has been swift; and it is all accepted as part and parcel of the colourful showmanship of the sport. Even the disgruntled fans who leave a hall vowing that they are finished with boxing for ever are always the first to clamour for tickets when the next attractive bout is advertised. And in boxing, the attractive bout between promising discoveries is never far away.

---

particularly among the negroes. The first Negro to win the heavyweight championship of the world was Jack Johnson, who beat Tommy Burns at Sydney on Boxing Day, 1908. He has been succeeded by many notable Negro champions at all weights, including Joe Louis, Jersey Joe Walcott, Floyd Patterson, Sonny Liston, Cassius Clay (now Muhammad Ali) and Sugar Ray Robinson.

Bob Fitzsimmons, James J. Jeffries, and Tommy Burns followed Corbett, and a 'white hope' era began in an effort to try and find someone to dispose of the arrogant Johnson. He kept them waiting for seven years, until he was 37, before falling victim to a giant cowboy, Jess Willard, who in turn was pounded to defeat in three rounds by the dynamic Jack Dempsey. Dempsey was a colourful fighter who attracted fight fans as no one had before him. His possibilities were seen by Tex Rickard, a western gambler, who matched him with Carpentier to produce the first million-dollar gate in 1921. More vast audiences watched Dempsey fight the Argentine Luis Firpo, and the American Gene Tunney. Dempsey lost to Tunney in Philadelphia in 1926 before a crowd of 120,757, and again a year later in Chicago before 104,943 fans.

Since those days boxers' earnings have increased astronomically with film, radio, and television fees. Joe Louis is believed to have earned a total of $4,684,297;

1 A guarded Floyd Patterson. When he knocked out Archie Moore for the vacant world heavyweight title in 1956 he became, at 21, the youngest ever fighter to hold it. Four years later he was the first man to regain that honour by flooring Ingemar Johansson. **2** Johnny Pritchett, British middleweight champion (right), won the vacant British Empire title at Belle Vue in 1967 when Milo Calhoun retired in the eighth. **3** Walter McGowan covers up against Salvatore Burruni. He robbed the Italian of the world flyweight title in 1966. **4** An anxious moment for Clay as Sonny Liston lunges—Clay won both their fights.

BOXING (Weight divisions recognized by world boxing authorities)			
Weight	WBC	EBU	ABA
	under	under	under
Fly	8 st	51 kg (8 st 4 oz)	8 st
Bantam	8 st 6 lb	54 kg (8 st 7 lb)	8 st 7 lb
Feather	9 st	57 kg (8 st 13½ lb)	9 st
Junior Light	9 st 4 lb	—	—
Light	9 st 9 lb	60 kg (9 st 6 lb)	9 st 7 lb
Junior or Light-welter*	10 st	63.5 kg (10 st)	10 st
Welter	10 st 7 lb	67 kg (10 st 7 lb 9 oz)	10 st 8 lb
Junior or Light-middle†	11 st	71 kg (11 st 2 lb)	11 st 2 lb
Middle	11 st 6 lb	75 kg (11 st 11 lb)	11 st 11 lb
Light-heavy	12 st 7 lb	81 kg (12 st 10 lb)	12 st 10 lb
Heavy	over 12 st 7 lb	over 81 kg	over 12 st 10 lb

Abbreviations: WBC – World Boxing Council
EBU – European Boxing Union
ABA – Amateur Boxing Association
Note: the British Boxing Board of Control recognizes all the classes listed under WBC except for Light-middle.
* Termed Super Lightweight by the EBU
† Termed Super Welterweight by the EBU

BOXING—facts and figures		
World heavyweight champions		
Tallest		
Jess Willard	USA	6 ft 6¼ in
Shortest		
Tommy Burns	Canada	5 ft 7 in
Heaviest		
Primo Carnera	Italy	19 st 11 lb
Lightest		
Bob Fitzsimmons	England	12 st 4 lb
Oldest		
Jersey Joe Walcott	USA	37 yrs 5 mths
Youngest		
Floyd Patterson	USA	21 yrs 10 mths
Highest pay for one fight		
Muhammad Ali/ Joe Frazier	USA	$2,500,000

Rules of boxing

All professional contests must be decided in a three-roped ring with the ropes joined in the centre on each side. The ring must not measure less than 14 ft. square or more than 20 ft. square, with a minimum of 18 inches of ring floor outside the ropes. The floor must be covered with a canvas sheet over a layer of felt, and tethered securely. Corner posts must be padded. In amateur boxing the measurements of the ring must not be less than 12 ft. square nor more than 16 ft. square.

Professional boxers in the ring wear a pair of trunks (under which there must be a regulation protector), socks, and boxing boots. They must be bare from the waist upwards. Before entering the ring a boxer's hands are bandaged with not more than 12 feet of 2-in. soft bandage for all weights, and/or 9 feet of 1-in. zinc oxide plaster tape for weights up to and including middleweights, and 11 ft. of similar tape for light-heavy and heavyweights. In all cases these lengths are for each hand and the tape must not be applied over the knuckles. The bandaged hands are inspected before the contest and, in the case of the British Boxing Board of Control, rubber-stamped by the tournament inspector if they have his approval. The gloves must weigh not less than 6 oz each for flyweights to welterweights, and 8 oz each for middleweights to heavyweights. These are supplied by the promoter and must not be used more than once in each tournament. In the case of a championship contest the gloves are supplied by the controlling body. The boxer usually comes into the ring for a preliminary bout wearing his gloves, but in the case of a title fight the gloves are fitted in the ring. The boxer wears a dressing-robe that generally carries his name, or initials, and place of origin. Often he wears his initials on the left leg of his boxing trunks.

The number of rounds to be fought varies with the contest. Novices are restricted at first to six two-minute and later to six three-minute rounds. They are then upgraded to 8- and 10-round contests, while eliminating championship fights can be extended to 12 rounds, and title bouts must not be less than 15. In some continental countries title fights are contested over 12 rounds, while in the Far East the championship distance is 10 rounds. The universal rest period between each round is one minute.

The timekeeper sits at the ringside with two stop watches that show the seconds clearly. One of these he holds in his hand to use when a knock-down occurs. He starts this watch as soon as a boxer goes down and counts the seconds audibly, at the same time beating with his hand. The referee crouches over the fallen boxer and calls out the count in unison with the timekeeper until 'ten' and 'out' are called. The other watch keeps the time of the rounds and the intervals.

Apart from controlling the contest and seeing that both men box according to the rules, the referee controls the corners of both men and looks after their welfare. He must not let a defenceless boxer take punches or allow a boxer to suffer unnecessary punishment. He must visit a distressed boxer in his corner between the rounds to make sure that he is fit to continue, and check facial damage, especially cuts round the eyes. If necessary, he may stop the bout to examine an injury. It is also his duty to caution a boxer in his corner if he has been guilty of infringing the rules.

There is no such term as 'knock-out' in professional boxing—it is purely a journalistic term. A man can be counted or knocked 'out of time', the time being the 10 seconds allowed for his recovery from a knock-down. The American term 'technical knock-out' is the verdict on a fighter who has been stopped inside the scheduled distance and is unable to continue.

A boxer can be disqualified for hitting below the belt (an imaginary line drawn across the top of the hips); using the 'pivot' blow or back-hander; hitting on the back of the head or base of the neck (rabbit punch); kidney punching; hitting with the open glove, the inside or butt of the hand, or with the wrist or elbow; for holding, butting, or careless use of the head, shouldering, wrestling, or roughing. Other things that merit disqualification are not trying; persistently ducking below the waistline; failing to 'break' out of a clinch when ordered to do so, or failure to step back from a 'break', or striking an opponent after the command to 'break'; deliberately striking an opponent when he is going down or on the floor; or any act of conduct that the referee considers foul.

When a knock-down occurs, the referee orders the standing boxer to go to a neutral corner where he must remain until told to 'box on'. A neutral corner is one not occupied by either boxer during the intervals between rounds. A boxer can win a contest on a points decision; on the stoppage of the contest by the referee; on the disqualification of his opponent; on the inability of his opponent to continue, or by reason of his opponent being counted out. If a knock-down occurs and the end of the round comes during the count, the timekeeper must continue counting to 'ten' and 'out', when the fight is automatically ended if the fallen boxer is still down. The count is stopped if the boxer rises unaided before its completion.

A standing count, used in amateur boxing and also in professional boxing in places other than Britain, is an enforced rest following a knock-down. The referee counts until the boxer rises, then continues the count until 'eight' is reached before allowing the men to 'box on'. The referee may compel a standing count if a boxer is dazed following a hard punch. A 'no foul' rule, which means that a boxer cannot be disqualified for breaking the rules, exists in some states in America, but not elsewhere. Boxers fighting under this rule are equipped with a foul-proof protector, although they can still win on a foul if they are hit below the belt—even if not incapacitated.

The referee must keep a score-card, which he brings up to date during the interval between the rounds. Points are awarded for attack with direct clean hits to the front or sides of the head or body; for defence, guarding against or the avoidance of punches; for showing initiative, and for style. In Britain a maximum of 5 points per man is awarded for each round, with $4\frac{3}{4}$ points for the man outpointed, and $4\frac{1}{2}$ points if the margin is very wide with one man taking heavy and continuous punishment or sustaining a knock-down or knock-downs. In Europe and America the maximum points for each round are 20, with no fractions, and this method scoring is also used in amateur boxing throughout the world.

The referee speaks to the boxers if minor infringements are committed during the course of a round, but if there is a flagrant breach of the rules he stops the fight and severely warns the offender. A persistent offender is disqualified after a final warning. In such cases, a boxer's purse is withheld by the promoter, except for bare travelling expenses, and the matter reported to the controlling board.

The promoter must supply an official second for each corner to look after any boxer without a trainer, to assist as required, and to see that there is clean water available for the boxer's use. Usually a boxer is accompanied into the ring by his manager and/or trainer, who act as his seconds. Their duty is to care for the boxer between rounds and advise him on tactics.

The chief second is permitted to take into his corner the following equipment: white petroleum jelly, sterile cotton wool, sterile gauze in sealed packets, surgical spirit (not methylated), swab sticks, solution of adrenalin 1/1000 (for the staunching of cuts), blunt-edged surgical scissors (for cutting off bandages), and an ice-bag. No stimulants may be used other than cold water sprinkled on the body or swilled in the mouth. Alcohol, smelling salts, or ammoniated liniments are strictly taboo.

An official known as the 'whip' obtains the full programme from the promoter and sees that each boxer is available in the dressing-room in good time before the start of the tournament. He makes sure that the fighters are properly dressed for the ring and are equipped with two pairs of trunks in contrasting colours in case the opponent chooses a similar colour. He must have the first pair of boxers ready at starting time and a second pair gloved up prepared to enter the ring should the preceding bout end quickly. He assists the Board of Control inspector and the official doctors at all times. The master of ceremonies or announcer acquaints himself with the full programme, knows the substitutes, and has the exact weight of each boxer marked on his programme. He also ascertains from the referee the official verdict and publicly announces the points-scoring.

A promoter must deposit with the controlling body a bond to cover the maximum cost of any programme he proposes to stage, this amount being held to ensure that the boxers receive the guaranteed payments for their services. A promoter must supply efficient stewarding for his hall, the official seconds, the whip, and the announcer, and pay for the services of the referee, timekeeper, and doctors who are appointed by the controlling body. A promoter may make his own matches or appoint a matchmaker, but all contests must be notified to the controlling body at least a week before the date of the tournament. To finance the control and administration of the sport, promoters pay a tax proportionate to the money involved, and each boxer pays tax on his earnings over a stated amount (in Britain it is 5 per cent on a purse of £500 or more). The promoter is also required to hold a weighing-in ceremony at midday on the day of the tournament, at which each boxer must be weighed and his weight publicly announced. Each also has a medical examination by an official doctor to ensure his physical fitness.

In general the rules and regulations of the British Boxing Board of Control are basically those of boxing throughout the world. The principal variations are in the scoring of points, the number of weight divisions, and the fixed poundages of the various weight classes. The rules that govern boxing originated in the London Prize Ring Rules, which were modified by the Marquess of Queensberry, brought up to date by the National Sporting Club of London, and subsequently altered and embellished by the various controlling bodies throughout the world to suit local conditions and national traits. But fundamentally the differences are so slight that it is possible for a boxer to fight anywhere in the world without any major change in procedure.

Chris Benfield

Chris Benfield

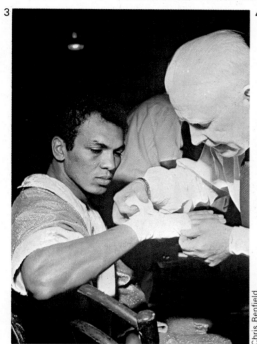

Chris Benfield

Chris Benfield

Chris Benfield

Weekend Telegraph

Chris Benfield

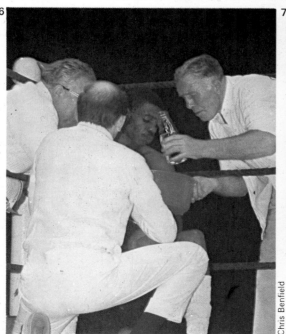

Weekend Telegraph

1 Boxers spar in preparation for a forthcoming encounter. Headguards and protectors are worn in training to prevent possible injury. **2** American heavyweight Phil Smith looks on as a second begins to tape his bandaged hands. Not more than 12 feet of 2-inch soft bandage is permitted. **3** Tape is applied over the bandage, but must not go over the knuckles. The bandaged hands are inspected by an official before the contest starts.

4 Although boxers sometimes enter the ring wearing their gloves, they must be fitted in the ring for title fights.

5 The boxers gloved and ready for the bout, the MC introduces them to the audience.

6 Between rounds, a boxer is given attention and advice. The seconds are usually the boxer's manager and trainer.

7 Down but not out, a boxer takes advantage of the count to clear his head.

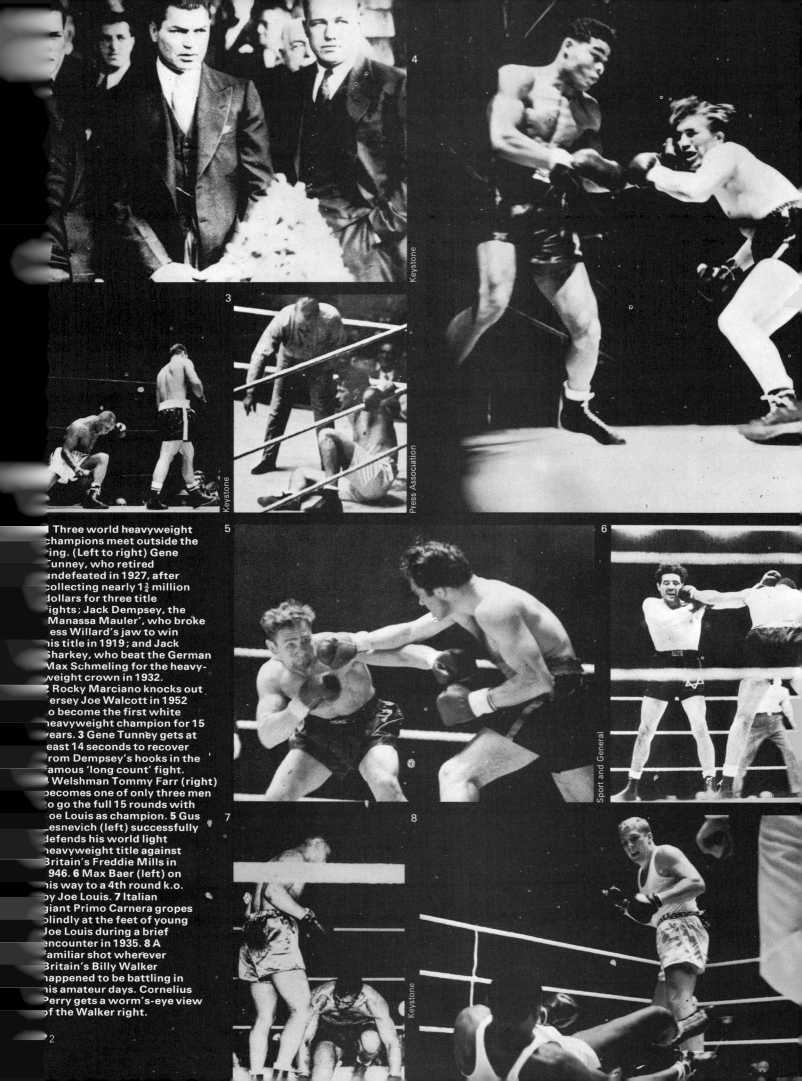

Keystone

Keystone

Press Association

Sport and General

Keystone

1 Three world heavyweight champions meet outside the ring. (Left to right) Gene Tunney, who retired undefeated in 1927, after collecting nearly 1¾ million dollars for three title fights; Jack Dempsey, the 'Manassa Mauler', who broke Jess Willard's jaw to win his title in 1919; and Jack Sharkey, who beat the German Max Schmeling for the heavyweight crown in 1932. **2** Rocky Marciano knocks out Jersey Joe Walcott in 1952 to become the first white heavyweight champion for 15 years. **3** Gene Tunney gets at least 14 seconds to recover from Dempsey's hooks in the famous 'long count' fight. **4** Welshman Tommy Farr (right) becomes one of only three men to go the full 15 rounds with Joe Louis as champion. **5** Gus Lesnevich (left) successfully defends his world light heavyweight title against Britain's Freddie Mills in 1946. **6** Max Baer (left) on his way to a 4th round k.o. by Joe Louis. **7** Italian giant Primo Carnera gropes blindly at the feet of young Joe Louis during a brief encounter in 1935. **8** A familiar shot wherever Britain's Billy Walker happened to be battling in his amateur days. Cornelius Perry gets a worm's-eye view of the Walker right.

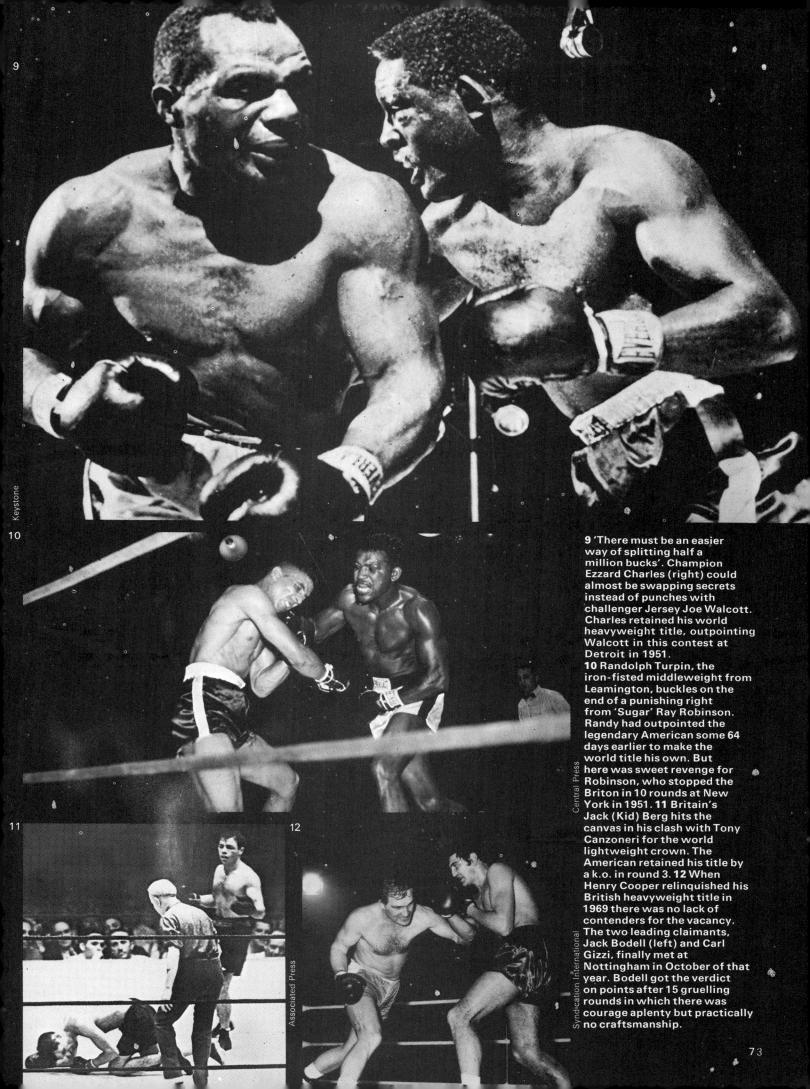

9

Keystone

10

Central Press

11 12

Associated Press

Syndication International

9 'There must be an easier way of splitting half a million bucks'. Champion Ezzard Charles (right) could almost be swapping secrets instead of punches with challenger Jersey Joe Walcott. Charles retained his world heavyweight title, outpointing Walcott in this contest at Detroit in 1951.
10 Randolph Turpin, the iron-fisted middleweight from Leamington, buckles on the end of a punishing right from 'Sugar' Ray Robinson. Randy had outpointed the legendary American some 64 days earlier to make the world title his own. But here was sweet revenge for Robinson, who stopped the Briton in 10 rounds at New York in 1951. 11 Britain's Jack (Kid) Berg hits the canvas in his clash with Tony Canzoneri for the world lightweight crown. The American retained his title by a k.o. in round 3. 12 When Henry Cooper relinquished his British heavyweight title in 1969 there was no lack of contenders for the vacancy. The two leading claimants, Jack Bodell (left) and Carl Gizzi, finally met at Nottingham in October of that year. Bodell got the verdict on points after 15 gruelling rounds in which there was courage aplenty but practically no craftsmanship.

Technique and training

Boxing is primarily the art of self-defence, so the stance of a boxer is based on defence more than attack. The classic stance is with the left hand extended to keep an opponent at a safe distance and to protect the face, while the right hand is kept back as a guard for the other side of the head, and also used as a potential striker. The original stance, of course, was perfected in the days before the proliferation of left-handers and before the age of speed. The new era introduced the 'southpaw' or right-foot-foremost boxer and the two-fisted fighter who regards attack as the best form of defence. But basically boxers use the original stance—left foot forward, right foot 18 inches behind, with the heel in line with the left arm, the toes of both feet pointing slightly to the right, the weight on the ball of the right foot, and the knee slightly bent. The hands should be held well up with the elbows tucked in; the left hand is slightly extended and the right poised to strike.

Correct hitting uses the knuckle part of the hand. It is far more effective, scores points, and avoids damage. A fist is made by clenching the hand so that the back and after part of the fingers make a square, the fore part of the fingers being tucked underneath to form a box—hence the term *boxing*. The thumb is laid along the fingernails to protect it from injury.

A right-handed boxer moves by gliding his left foot forward, the right foot following but keeping its rear position. To retreat, he draws his right foot back, the left foot following in a straight line in order to preserve balance.

The left hand does most of the attacking, travelling straight from the shoulder with a slight turn of the body to impart power. It can be driven at the head through an opponent's guard and, provided it is well-timed and strikes the target just before the full extension of the arm, its effect can be both damaging and demoralizing. It also has maximum points-scoring value. It is equally effective driven below the opponent's guard to the *solar plexus* (the nerve centre at the central point just below the ribs).

The right hand, used to ward off an attacking left, is also used as a cross-counter blow, being driven over and across an opponent's left lead to strike his head, and is principally aimed at the jaw. The right hand is particularly dangerous when aimed under an opponent's left lead to strike his body just below the heart—a weakening and stamina-draining blow when it connects with full bodyweight and power.

Such are the principal long-range hits, but at shorter range the hooks and uppercuts do the most damage. The *hook* is a lead shortened to a jab, with the wrist turned on impact to give extra striking power. It is not a blow struck with a bent arm. Left and right hooks are equally effective, although many left-foot-foremost boxers perfect the left hook to great advantage, while southpaws do the same with the right. Hooks, like all other blows, are useless, both as points-scoring or damaging blows, unless they are struck with the knuckle part of the glove.

The *swing,* from either hand, describes itself. It is a difficult blow to use against an alert opponent, because it advertises itself in advance. The swing is generally used as a deterrent under pressure or when both boxers decided to exchange punches, regardless of defence.

The *uppercut,* left or right, is most effective to head and body. It is delivered in an upward swinging movement, with the fingers and thumb on top of the hand at the point of impact. It is a very damaging blow, under the heart, to the solar plexus, or to the point of the chin, but it has to be timed to perfection to gain its full value. Some American boxers cultivate a swinging uppercut called the *bolo,* which starts from the region of the hips.

Infighting, while not so spectacular, can be a valuable means of weakening an opponent. Here, both fists are used to pound the body simultaneously, working up through a rival's defence to attack the head. Short hooks and uppercuts can prove damaging but, of course, such spells are brief because any boxer so attacked will naturally hold or go into a clinch, whereupon the referee can order a 'break'.

The *break* requires both boxers to step back and push themselves away from each other. One must come out of a clinch (holding grapple) fully defended, even though a 'clean break' is ordered by the rules and no blow should be struck before the referee calls 'box on' or signals for the fight to be resumed. An alert boxer can dart forward and strike a damaging blow if his opponent is not fully on guard.

If a boxer is put down by a blow, he should try to get to one knee and take the utmost advantage of the count by watching his corner and getting a signal from his chief second on when to rise. Some boxers, after getting up from a knock-down, immediately launch an attack to prevent their opponent from adding to his advantage, but the orthodox plan is to go on the defensive by using the ring,

Striking part of glove

Lace always tied on back of glove

Bar for grip

Elastic lace cover

Chris Benfield

Syndication International

Syndication International

2 ducking, dodging and stalling, if necessary, until the effects of the knock-down blow have worn off.

Although points are earned for attack, it is possible for a boxer to attack in every round and yet lose the contest because his opponent has used the outer perimeter of the ring and let him run onto his defensive punches, jabs, hooks, and uppercuts. The primary object is, of course, to out-think your opponent, to frustrate his efforts and beat him to the punch. 'Be first' is a maxim impressed on boxers from the start.

The most vulnerable physical targets are the temples, the edges of the jawbone beneath the ear, the point of the chin, the nerve centre directly beneath the nose, the solar plexus, the region under or over the heart, and below the ribs to the front and side of the body.

Contests between a good defensive boxer and a strong attacking fighter usually produce the most attractive bouts for the connoisseur of boxing, but the average fight fan prefers a match in which both performers exploit the big punch. For this reason, heavyweights usually command the largest audiences.

In addition to the medical examinations immediately before and after a contest, a professional boxer must also undergo a strict medical examination once a year when his boxing licence comes up for renewal. All boxers are compelled to allow a clear four days between contests and, if a knock-out or injury causes a contest to be stopped, at least 21 days must elapse before the victim's next fight.

Professional boxers keep in strict training during the recognized season from September to May, and in light training during the summer, unless an engagement is booked. Matches, unless they involve championships, are usually made a pound or two over the boxer's best fighting weight. For example, a featherweight who can make the class limit of 9 st when at his fighting peak will take non-title contests at 9 st 2 lb. As soon as he is

notified of an engagement, the boxer reports to the gymnasium where his manager or trainer first weighs him to see how much training he will need to meet the required weight. If he is very much over-weight, he is given plenty of roadwork—five miles each morning—followed by work in the gym (wearing a sweat suit), ball and bag punching, ground exercises, skipping, shadow boxing, and sparring. Roadwork is essential for a boxer whose main strength is in his legs.

The *punchball* (an inflated ball suspended under a platform) helps him to perfect his timing and speed, and co-ordination of hand and eye.

The *punchbag* (a hard-stuffed canvas sack) is used for developing hard punching and correct hitting. *Ground exercises* are for suppleness and muscular conditioning; *skipping* is essential for footwork, balance, and stamina-building; *shadow-boxing* (fighting an imaginary opponent) induces quick thinking and perception; and *sparring* (usually with a sparring partner of similar build and style to the prospective opponent) brings the boxer to fighting pitch. The trainer makes sure that his charge does not over-train or go stale by stopping training the day before the date of the contest if the boxer is considered to be at his peak.

When a boxer is trying to get down to the right weight he modifies his diet. Fat-producing and starchy foods are eliminated and liquid is cut down to a minimum. The boxer has a light breakfast after his roadwork, a substantial meal following his midday training, and a light supper. He is usually in bed by 10 p.m. at the latest, and up at 6 a.m. to go on the road.

On the day of the fight he eats little or nothing before going on the scales at the midday weigh-in, and then has a substantial meal—with nothing more until after the bout. Before leaving for the arena he will rest and sleep.

Training methods have hardly varied from the earliest days of boxing, except for the use of more modern equipment and the speeding-up of exercises. At one time boxers sparred without any head protection, but the head-guard was subsequently introduced to prevent cuts and abrasions. The bandaging of hands for protection is a more modern practice, but hands that are too tightly bound can be injured, especially if the boxer hits incorrectly. In prize-ring days and in the early years of glove-fighting when hands were not bandaged, boxers relied on 'pickling' their hands in a brine solution—in order to toughen the skin.

1 The 6-oz gloves used by professional boxers. 2 Johnny Caldwell (left) smothers a right uppercut from Alphonse Halimi. 3 A right cross from Cassius Clay in his quick victory over Britain's Brian London. 4 Johnny Pritchett about to throw a left hook, after cornering Milo Calhoun. 5 Shadow-boxing in front of a mirror sharpens a boxer's reflexes and helps his footwork; the exercise can also be carried out without the mirror. He practises correct hitting on the punchbag.

Syndication International

Chris Benfield

Canoeing

Canoeing is the collective name given to a variety of sports practised in many countries throughout the world. From hunting seal by kayak to shooting by canoe the rapids of a mountain river, from gliding at high speed across the smooth waters of a lake in a purpose-built racing kayak to a leisurely canoe camping trip—all this comes in the canoeing category.

Although canoeing goes back hundreds of years to the Eskimos who developed the kayak, the Red Indians who developed the Canadian canoe, and the South Sea Islanders with their outrigger canoes, it did not develop as a competitive sport comprising many branches until the mid 1800s. Sprint racing, slalom, down-river, long-distance, and even sailing are all facets of the sport open to the enthusiast. But whatever he chooses, he will find that the type of boat used, the equipment required, and the water course allotted are unique to each branch.

Sprint racing
A race of pure speed, sprint racing is held on flat water over 500, 1,000, and 10,000 metres, and is contended in both kayaks and Canadian canoes, although in Britain the latter went into a period of decline in the 1960s. There are classes for singles and pairs for both types of canoe, and kayaks also have a class for fours.

The boats used in sprint racing have become highly specialized, with little consideration given to

anything other than speed. Kayaks, unlike the Canadian canoes, are fitted with a rudder, and continual developments are being made. Paddles, too, have become refined, and the best blades are now spoon shaped and have a hollow shaft.

The ideal racing conditions are on windless, still water, man-made courses which have such a depth that there is no 'bottom drag' effect, in which the disturbance of the water under the surface reflects off the bottom and slows up the passage of the boat. The course at Xochimilco, scene of the 1968 Olympic regatta, was almost perfect in this respect, but such courses are sparse.

Sprint racing has been a regular event in the Olympic Games since 1936 when, at the request of the Germans, it obtained Olympic recognition. The sport is par-

1 Flying paddles send water spraying at the start of the men's kayak doubles class of a long distance race on the River Tay in Scotland.
2 A 1,000 metres K-4 event (four men in a kayak) on the Thames at Pangbourne. Sprints are always contested on flat-water courses.

ticularly strong in Eastern Europe, Germany, Russia, and Scandinavia, and one of the outstanding exponents was Sweden's Gert Fredriksson who won six Olympic gold medals in a career that embraced four Olympics.

Slalom
Akin to the slalom of alpine ski racing, canoe slalom is an exacting test of skills and speed. Slalom canoes are made of glass fibre, and are designed for manoeuvrability as well as for speed.

They are completely closed in except for a small hole in which the canoeist sits, if it is a kayak, or kneels, if it is the Canadian type. Foot-rests, knee grips, and a bucket seat are securely fitted to the boat so that the competitor is able to achieve maximum control. A spray deck is attached to make the boat watertight, and should the canoe capsize, the canoeist can right without its filling with water by levering on the surface of the water with the paddle.

Kayaks and Canadian canoes are given different classifications for competition slalom and are listed: kayak singles, for men and women, K1; Canadian singles, for men, C1; and Canadian men's and mixed doubles, C2. Courses which are held on rough water consist of up to 30 pairs of poles, called gates, which are suspended vertically over a suitable stretch of river up to half a mile long. The gates are positioned in a set sequence designed to form a smooth-running path down the river, and negotiating these provides the competitor with an excellent test of his ability to manoeuvre his boat in rough, heavy water. His task is made no easier by the rule preventing competitors from practising on the course before the event.

Each competitor makes two timed runs down the course, and penalties are incurred for touching or wrongly negotiating the gates. The penalty points are added to the time in seconds, and range from 10 to 100 per gate; 10 if one pole is touched inside the gate, 20 if both poles are touched; 50 if the bow or body passes outside the gate, or if a forward gate is negotiated in reverse or vice versa, and 100 if the gate is missed altogether.

In addition to the individual classes, there are team events in each class, and in these, three boats form a team and descend the course together, the time of the first to start and the last to finish being taken. The same rules apply except that one gate is designated the team gate, and the team must pass through it within 15 seconds of each other or incur a 50-second penalty.

Though the best slalom courses are found on mountain rivers, good courses can also be set below suitable weirs. The rivers are graded I to VI according to their degree of difficulty, and top competitions are held on grade IV to V water. Leading competitors come from East Germany, West Germany, Czechoslovakia, Austria, France, and Britain, and they meet every two years to contest the world championships.

Down-river
Down-river racing is a speed contest, held on a course 6 to 10 kilometres long and on grade III to V water. Competitors start at one minute intervals and, in contrast to slalom, are allowed to practise on the course before racing. The classes are the same as

for the slalom, but the boats are **2** specially designed for speed and have little turning ability.

Down-river races are normally held in conjunction with slalom events, and the biannual world championships are held a few days after the slalom championships, usually on the same river, or a nearby venue.

Long-distance

Held over courses of 10 to 25 miles, long-distance races can take the canoeist over flat water, grade I to III river descents, or tidal water and may include portages round locks and weirs. Normally, classes are held for kayaks only, and the main classes use boats similar in design to those used for sprint racing, except that they are made of glass fibre for added strength. Other classes are also held for open kayak singles and doubles.

There is a mass start for each class, and these often provide a **4** thrilling spectacle as competitors fight fiercely for a good start. Once the race is under way, competitors are allowed to wash hang —that is, follow in the wash or bow wave of an opponent's canoe.

As yet, there are no world championships in this event, and top paddlers focus their main attentions on the Sella race in northern Spain and the Liffey Descent in Ireland. The first Sella race was held in 1930, but it was not until 1951 that it became international. Since then, it has become the main event in this branch of canoeing, of which the British, Spanish, Irish, West Germans, and Scandi-

1 The East German Merkel brothers were three times world champions in the C-2 slalom in the 1960s.
2 Dam-fed slalom courses such as this artificial stream at Lipno in Czechoslovakia are rare. The dam provides a steady spate of tumbling water. Many mountain streams are too remote to attract big crowds for even the most important events, and these man-made river beds bring canoeing to the public.
3 The sluice is opened and a swirling stream covers the rocky bed. Here the Czech team passes through a gate in the kayak team event.
4 Pauline Squires was British K-1 champion in 1968 and '69.

navians are the leading exponents.

The toughest canoe race in the world, although not strictly a long-distance race, is that held in England from Devizes in Wiltshire to Westminster in London. This marathon, for doubles only, started in 1950 and takes place during Easter each year. It includes canal, river, and tidal water over its 125-mile course, and there are 77 portages. All crews carry a specified minimum camping and survival kit, and a crack senior crew, paddling non-stop, has done the race in 20 hours. Junior crews, on the other hand, enjoy three nights rest during the race. One of the hazards expected in this race is exhaustion, but as Easter weather in England is inclement, cold and frostbite are added problems.

Cricket

How a game such as cricket, which depends so much on good weather conditions, came to be born and developed in England is a mystery that troubles people more than ever today when it is played so widely elsewhere in more reliable climates. The solution, no doubt, is that it arose from man's natural instinct to play with a ball and to hit it with a stick. It developed in the south of England in the 17th and 18th centuries because, before the development of the United States, Australia, and Africa, that was one of relatively few areas where society was sufficiently educated and disciplined to organize the playing of a game that required special rules and skills. And there were also the wealthy patrons available in England to give the game the encouragement it needed.

Cricket at Mary-le-Bone Fields in the days when batsmen used curved bats and the bowlers had only two stumps at which to aim. If the ball passed between them, the batsman was not out.

In the time of Edward I, references were made to 'creag', which may have been cricket. Around 1550, a more certain record suggests that cricket was played at the Free School of Guildford in some form. But most of the reliable early references to cricket come from the late 17th century. There is, for example, a record of a party of British sailors going ashore near Aleppo in 1676 and playing a game of cricket. At this time, too, the game was undoubtedly taking a hold in Kent, Sussex, and Hampshire.

In 1719, the first county match took place between Kent and London in Lamb's Conduit Fields,

By the beginning of the 19th century, three stumps had become a permanent feature of the game, although the use of pads did not become widespread until several decades later.

probably on the edge of what is now Bloomsbury. In 1744, the earliest known Laws of Cricket were drawn up, though these were probably a consolidated version of earlier rules. Already matches were being played for large sums of money, and these must have needed sets of rules. In the same year, a match was played between Kent and England that is historic because it is the first for which a complete score-card survives.

The game already had many important patrons. One of them, Frederick Louis, Prince of Wales, son of George II and father of George III, was said to have died prematurely in 1751 because of a

blow received while playing cricket the previous year.

Kent were the early champions, but in the second half of the 18th century cricket was developed to a remarkable extent in the small Hampshire village of Hambledon, a few miles north of Portsmouth. The inspiration of the Hambledon Club was Richard Nyren, the landlord of the Bat and Ball Inn and the exploits of the club on the nearby Broadhalfpenny Down are recorded for posterity through the writing of his son, John Nyren. The era of Hambledon's greatness lasted for barely 35 years, and when Richard Nyren moved to London in 1791, it soon ended. But in those years this little village team, recruited mainly from local players, could take on the rest of England without fear. What is thought to be the first recorded century was made by a Hambledon man, John Small, who scored 135 against Surrey on Broadhalf-

Lancashire's Ken Shuttleworth
is airborne as he comes in to
bowl.

penny Down in 1775.

In the second half of the 18th century the White Conduit Club was formed, playing its matches in the White Conduit Fields in Islington. Out of this was to come the Marylebone Cricket Club and Lord's Cricket Ground.

A Yorkshireman in the service of the Earl of Winchelsea, Thomas Lord was a ground bowler at the White Conduit Club. Though not an outstanding cricketer, he was a competent businessman, and when the White Conduit Fields were threatened by building, he was asked by the Earl and Charles Lennox, later the fourth Duke of Richmond, to start a new ground. Wealthy members of the club would support him in the venture.

Lord accordingly chose a piece of ground on what is now Dorset Square, and the first match was played there in 1787. Twice he was forced by the expansion of London to take up his turf and move it, first about 1,000 yards north, and then, when it was decided by parliament to cut the new Regent's Canal through the ground, to the present site where the first match was played in 1815. The White Conduit Club had dissolved and re-emerged as the Marylebone Cricket Club in 1787, and MCC took on the responsibility for the Laws that it still holds today, playing a big part in the game's administration.

By the middle of the 19th century, county clubs were being formed, and the All-England XI were taking famous players to all parts of the country. Soon Dr W. G. Grace became a great national figure. And from 1859, English teams began to journey abroad to play in distant lands where the game was taking root. The first Test match was played between England and Australia in the season of 1876-77 in Melbourne.

Cricket by then had changed in most basic features from the origins of a century before to a pattern that is easily recognizable today. Although the pitches were becoming less rough, the length of the pitch seems to have been unchanged since 1744, when it was settled as the length of an agricultural chain, 22 yards. In 1774 the bat was restricted to not wider than $4\frac{1}{4}$ inches, which is the limit today, though the length was not limited to 38 inches until much later and the shape had changed considerably. In the early days some bats might have weighed 4 lb, but the average now is between 2 lb 4 oz and 2 lb 6 oz. There has never been a limit on weight. The weight of the ball, agreed in 1774 as between $5\frac{1}{2}$ and $5\frac{3}{4}$ ounces, has not changed either. Its size was specified for the first time in 1838 as between 9 and $9\frac{1}{4}$ inches in diameter.

The over originally consisted of four balls. In the 1880s it was increased to five in England and six in Australia. England adopted the six-ball over in 1900, and after World War I Australia changed to eight balls. Other countries have experimented with this from time to time, though the only trial that the eight-ball over has been given in England, in the 1939 season, has not been repeated.

The technique of batting has developed in relation to the pitches used and to the bowling which it was required to meet, and it has been in the method of bowling that one of the main changes from the early days has taken place. Bowling originally was under-arm but changed, through a long period of controversy, to round-arm, which was officially recognized in 1835. This was a stepping-stone to the present over-arm bowling which, again after much controversy, was legalized in 1864.

The number of players comprising a side seems to have been accepted as 11, often 12, from an early period, but without any rigid insistence on this. Indeed, as many as 22 local players might take the field against a strong side such as the All-England XI. Not until 1884 was the number specified officially as 11.

Changes have been made to the wicket in the passing years. Since 1931 it has been $28\frac{1}{2}$ in high and 9 in wide. In 1774 there were only two stumps and the dimensions were 22 in and 6 in. A third stump was introduced in 1776, and in four stages the wicket grew to its present size though the 1931 increase of $1\frac{1}{2}$ inches in height and 1 inch in width was the first change for 108 years.

Nowadays, the law that most often comes under consideration when it is thought that a change

1 A print of the Grand Jubilee match played at Lord's between the North and South of England in 1837 to commemorate the 50th anniversary of the MCC.
2 Cricket in the colonies. In 18th century Australia, the matches were usually played on Saturdays, and teams would often ride miles for a game.
3 The scorecard of the 1882 Test, played at the Oval. It was after this match, won by Australia by seven runs, that the Ashes came into being.
4 'Rain stopped play'—words familiar to cricket lovers in all parts of the world. And even if it hails, as it did during the Lord's Test between Australia and England in 1968, the wicket is well protected by covers. The spectators are not always quite so lucky.
5 Trent Bridge, 1926, and a capacity crowd watches the start of the first Test between England and Australia.

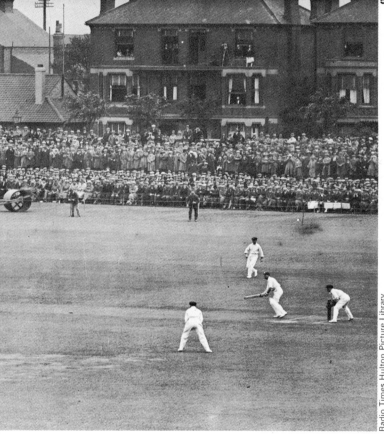

4 have been repeated changes, especially since World War II, in what are known as playing conditions, such as the hours of play and the scoring of points in competitions.

Cricket is a game that is easily understood in the bare fact that the side that scores the most runs wins. But it has so many aspects to it and such subtleties that, however long one studies, there is always something new to learn. Its variety is one of the great virtues. The most influential factor in every cricket match is the pitch, and on whether it is hard or soft, well-grassed or bare, dry or damp will depend the quality and tempo of the cricket played.

Tactics and strategy vary from age to age and from country to country. One weapon at the disposal of a captain is the *declaration*, which was first authorized in 1889 and which is usually employed to close an **5** innings when a captain considers that his side has made enough runs and is out of reach of the opposition. It has been used to get the other side in to bat when the pitch is giving help to bowlers, and in the modern game it is frequently used as an enticement, giving the opposition a faint chance of victory if they are prepared to take risks. The declaring captain hopes that in taking risks they will lose wickets that they would probably not have lost if they had been batting circumspectly.

The captain of the side batting first in a match may also have to decide whether or not to enforce the *follow-on*—that is, whether to ask his opponents to bat again at once if they are a specified number of runs behind on first innings. The figure is 100 runs in a two-day match, a 150 in a three-day match, and 200 in a five-day Test or a match exceeding three days.

The selection of the team is often a difficult one, which, in the case of bowlers, may be partly influenced by the type of pitch expected. Five batsmen, five bowlers, and a wicket-keeper are roughly what are required. But unless the batsmen and bowlers are especially proficient in their own speciality, the strength of the side will probably depend on how well some of the bowlers and the wicket-keeper can bat.

The standard time of play in first-class cricket is six hours per day, divided roughly into three periods of two hours each with a lunch interval of 40 minutes and a tea interval of 20 minutes. In some countries that have warmer climates and an early sunset, only five hours a day may be played, in which case the match probably extends over an extra day. In the English county championship and in the Currie Cup in South Africa, the match lasts three days; Sheffield Shield matches in Australia last four. The duration of Test matches is usually, but not necessarily, 30 hours or five days. Some countries, such as Pakistan

and New Zealand in 1969, arrange between themselves to play four days. It can also be decided by agreement to play an extra day if the series is still undecided when the last Test is due to begin.

As touring teams went overseas and the population of countries such as Australia and South Africa increased, the game developed quickly, helped by favourable weather conditions. Mostly the 'missionary work' was done by the Royal Navy or the British Army, but it was soon being played in the early settlements in Australia. It was natural that in the days of the British Raj the game should blossom in India and what is now Pakistan. Indians and Pakistanis have a natural aptitude and a specially quick eye that helps them to excel in some departments of the game, though not in fast bowling for which by diet and physique they are usually ill-equipped. The warm dry winter of the Indian sub-continent provides the ideal weather for cricket. When the game was brought to the West Indies, the inhabitants were found to have some of the greatest natural talent for cricket in the world.

Of the larger countries developed under British influence, Canada alone does not play regular first-class cricket, though it maintains a good standard that has been helped by an influx of West Indians since World War II. The game there, however, has never become established as in the Test-playing countries, perhaps because of a non-cricketing American and French-Canadian influence and perhaps because of the shortness of the summer in some areas.

There are now nearly 20 countries who are members or associate members of the International Cricket Conference. They include Denmark, where the game was established partly through the visits of Danes to England and through Danish enthusiasm for cricket. In the Netherlands, too, the game has a strong hold, and close contacts are maintained at club level with English cricket. Perhaps the greatest day for Dutch cricket was in 1964 when, in a one-day match at The Hague, the Australians were beaten by three wickets in the last over.

British residents established cricket in Argentina and Brazil, and MCC teams pay visits there and to other South American countries, as they do to East Africa and countries such as Malaysia and Hong Kong in the Far East. Ceylon is included in the itineraries of most English and Australian teams on their way to or from each other's countries. The game is played enthusiastically in Fiji, though Indians, Europeans, and part-Europeans tend to be more successful there nowadays than the flamboyant native Fijians.

In all the main cricket-playing countries there is a central ad-

might be needed is the one concerning lbw (leg before wicket). But in fact there have been only two changes in it since the lbw law was first formulated in 1774. There had been some mention previously of 'standing unfair to strike', but in 1774 the batsman was firmly adjudged to be out if he 'puts his leg before the wicket with a design to stop the ball and actually prevents the ball from hitting the wicket'. In 1788 the reference to 'design' was omitted and it was stipulated that the ball had to be pitched between wicket and wicket.

This remained the law until 1937 and there are many who would like to return to it. In 1969 it was agreed that several variations might be tried as an experiment in different countries, and it is interesting that 'intent'—the 'design' dropped in 1788—was suggested again. In 1972 the law was amended to include batsmen making no attempt to play with the bat a ball which, would have hit the stumps.

Whereas the Laws are changed very seldom, and then after long and searching experiment, there

Sport & General

Radio Times Hulton Picture Library

ministrative body. MCC shouldered this responsibility in England in the past, but from 1969 it has been taken over by a Cricket Council under which are the Test, and County Cricket Board, looking after first-class cricket, and the National Cricket Association, handling cricket at all other levels.

In Australia the parent body is the Board of Control, in South Africa the South African Cricket Association. However, the counties in England and the States, provinces, and islands elsewhere all have autonomous associations. It is these that produce and develop the players who ultimately represent their country.

Each country has a principal domestic competition. In England it is the County Championship, to which have been added—the Gillette Cup, the John Player League, and the Benson & Hedges Cup. In Australia it is the Sheffield Shield, in South Africa the Currie Cup, in New Zealand the Plunket Shield, in West Indies the Shell Shield, in India the Ranji Trophy, and in Pakistan the Quaid-e-Azam and Ayub Trophies. English cricket differs in one big respect from the others. Its championship is contested by 17 counties, whereas the Sheffield Shield has only five states. The competitions of other countries have not many more contestants.

In some of these countries, notably India and Pakistan, there are still relatively few counter-attractions to cricket and, irrespective of the quality of the play, matches are watched by large crowds because it is an occasion. The game is booming in South Africa, helped by success on the field and the new interest being shown in it by the Afrikaans-speaking population. In New Zealand it is over-shadowed by rugby football, at which New Zealanders are pre-eminent. But in the late 1960s and 1970s, New Zealand teams were good enough to win Test matches against the West Indies, Australia, Pakistan and India.

In the Test-playing countries, the matting pitches on which cricket used to be played have now been superseded by grass, but the pitches in India and Pakistan tend to be slower than those elsewhere. Australian and West Indian pitches on their hard grounds are usually faster than average, with a steeper bounce of the ball. English pitches, because of the vagaries of the English climate, have a unique variety.

Cricket has become so much a part of the English way of life—cricket expressions such as a 'sticky wicket' or 'hit for six' are often used in non-sporting contexts—that from time to time its issues are exposed to the glare of publicity in a way that no other sporting events are. The England captaincy, especially overseas, and indeed the Test captaincy of any

country, is a position of responsibility requiring a man who is not only a tactician and leader on the field but a diplomat and speech-maker off it. A change in the England captaincy, such as that in 1967 when Colin Cowdrey took MCC to West Indies instead of Brian Close, is a matter hotly disputed by people who may never have watched a cricket match at all. In years to come, the classic case may prove to have been that of Basil d'Oliveira in 1968, with its many political implications. Other incidents have taken on gigantic proportions, such as the body line controversy on the England tour of Australia in 1932-33. And in 1955-56 a practical joke on an umpire in Pakistan expanded into an international incident and led to correspondence between the president of Pakistan and Field-Marshal Lord Alexander, then President of MCC.

An increasing threat to the conduct of matches has come with declining standards of public behaviour. In 1954 a Test match in what was then British Guiana between West Indies and England was interrupted by a riot. And on each of the two subsequent MCC tours to West Indies a riot stopped play, once in Trinidad and once in Jamaica. In 1969 the MCC visit to Pakistan coincided with a period of public unrest. The Test matches were frequently interrupted and the last was abandoned on the third day. Later in 1969 a Test match between India and New Zealand at Hyderabad was stopped by riots. In almost all these cases the cause of the disorder had little to do with the cricket. The disturbances were made at cricket matches because they provided an opportunity for an excited crowd to assemble and express themselves against authority.

Press coverage of cricket has grown enormously with the years, though with the closing of some newspapers since the mid-1950s there has been some reduction in the number of cricket writers who accompany touring teams. But whereas it was only one or two in 1930, it had grown to around 20 in the years after World War II. And besides these, there may be nearly 100 journalists of some sort covering a Test match in their own country.

With the growth of television coverage and the ball-by-ball radio commentaries, a new public has been drawn to cricket. The crowds on the ground often do not reflect the great interest that may be taken in a match, but in England, though not elsewhere, television fees are large enough to cover the money lost at the gate through the decision of would-be spectators to watch at home.

Right, **The field placings. A fielder moves about as his captain directs him, and the positions vary frequently.**

Whether or not it is sensible and economically sound to allow cricket to be televised frequently has not become as big a question as seemed likely in the early days of television. It has been considered by cricket administrators that television would on balance do more good than harm because it would bring the game to people who might otherwise have had no opportunity to become interested in it. If the television companies were refused permission to screen cricket, they would almost certainly televise some other sport which, especially in doubtful weather, might become an equally strong counter-attraction to attendance at cricket grounds.

In the 1960s sponsorship became a big factor in the financial side of cricket, especially in England. Industrial firms, partly out of goodwill and interest in the game and partly out of a desire to keep their name before the public, donated large sums for the organizing of competitions, such as the Gillette Cup and the John Player League, or for prizes to individual players. It was a sign of cricket's continued importance in the English way of life that commercial firms should associate themselves with it in this way. The game, it could be said, was back where it started in the early days of patronage. Only now the patrons were not landed gentry but businessmen. They have breathed new life into a game which, with all its ups and downs, is an integral part of the British sporting scene.

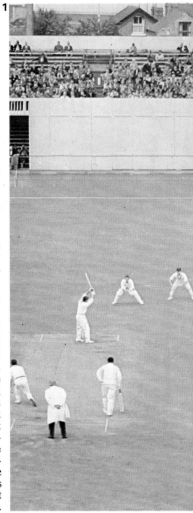

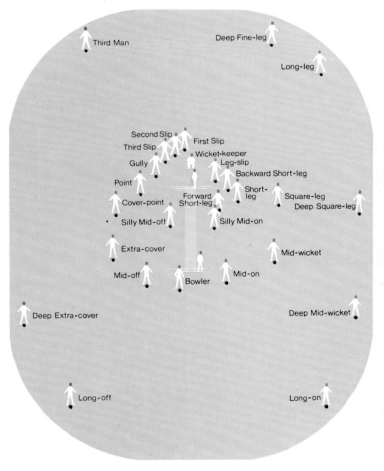

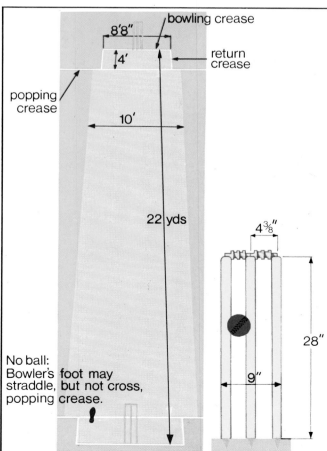

1 A Test match in progress at Trent Bridge. For enthusiasts, the Tests are the highlight of the season, and many young cricketers hope to represent their country in a Test some day. **2** Many, however, never advance past cricket on the village green. Yet such is the game's appeal that it can be enjoyed at all levels. **3** 'Big Doug' Goodwin (left) and Alex O'Riordan played an important part in Ireland's surprise victory in 1969 over the touring West Indians in a one day match in Tyrone. Goodwin, the Irish captain, took 5-6, and O'Riordan 4-18 to dismiss the tourists for 25. **4** Australia's Ian Johnson and England's Peter May await the result of the toss—a preliminary to every cricket match.

bowling crease

8'8"

4'

return crease

popping crease

10'

22 yds

No ball: Bowler's foot may straddle, but not cross, popping crease.

4⅜"

28"

9"

Below. The lbw law. Batsmen must make a genuine attempt to play with the bat a ball pitched outside off-stump.

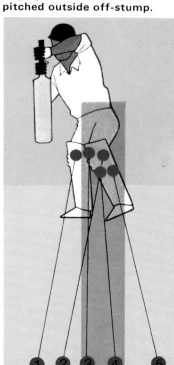

① ② ③ ④ ⑤

1,5–not out
2,3,4–out, lbw

Barnaby's

Barnaby's

Syndication International

Radio Times Hulton Picture Library

Roy Castle

Glossary of Terms

Bowled A batsman is out bowled if the ball hits the wicket and dislodges a bail, even if the ball has come off his body or bat.

Bump Ball A ball that is hit hard into the ground and rises so that, when fielded, it seems like a catch.

Bye(s) Extra(s) scored when the ball passes the wicket untouched by bat or person and the batsman runs or the ball reaches the boundary.

Draw A match in which no decision is reached.

Extras Runs not scored by the batsman. See also *byes, leg-byes, no-balls, and wides.*

Handled ball A batsman is out *handled ball* if he touches the ball with his hands while it is in play. He may, however, touch it if the fielding side give him permission to do so.

Hat-trick A bowler achieves a hat-trick if he dismisses three batsmen with consecutive deliveries, either in the same over or at the end of one and the beginning of another over. The wickets must be taken in the same match.

Hit the ball twice Unless he is doing so to defend his wicket, a batsman is out if he hits the ball twice. The bowler is not credited with the wicket.

Hit wicket A batsman is out *hit wicket* if a bail is dislodged by his bat, body, or cap while he is in the act of making his stroke.

Leg before wicket (lbw) A batsman is out lbw if the ball hits the batsman and the umpire considers that it was pitched on a straight line between the wickets or on the off side and would have hit the wicket.

Leg-byes Runs scored as extras when the ball goes off any part of a batsman except his hands or bat, but only when he is playing a stroke.

Leg side, or **on side** The side of the field (in front and behind the stumps) behind the batsman as he takes up his stance.

Maiden over An over in which no runs are scored by the batsmen.

No-ball Called when either umpire considers the bowler's delivery is not fair. A batsman can score runs off a no-ball, but he cannot be bowled, caught, stumped, or out lbw (he may be run out). If no runs are scored, one no-ball is added to the extras. And as a no-ball is not a legal delivery, the bowler is given an extra delivery in the over for every no-ball.

Off side The side of the field in front of the batsman as he takes up his stance.

Over the wicket A method of delivery in which the bowler, delivers the ball with the hand nearer the stumps.

Overthrow A throw from a fielder that travels past the wicket-keeper or fielder at either set of stumps and allows the batsmen further runs.

Played on Term used when a batsman hits the ball onto his own wicket. The dismissal, however, is recorded as 'bowled'.

Popping crease The line 4 feet in

front of the wicket (a) on or behind which the batsman must ground his bat to avoid being stumped or run out and (b) on or behind which the bowler must ground his leading foot.

Return crease A line running at right-angles from the popping crease (to an undetermined length behind the bowling crease) inside of which the bowler must ground his back foot at the moment of delivery.

Round the wicket A method of delivery in which the bowler delivers the ball with the hand farther from the stumps.

Run out A method of dismissing a batsman. The batsman is run out if a fielder breaks the wicket while the batsman is out of his ground—i.e. between the two popping creases. When both batsman are out of their ground, the one nearer the broken wicket is out.

Short run A batsman is said to have run short if he fails to ground his bat over the popping crease while running. Short runs are not counted.

Stumped A batsman is out stumped if, having played at the ball, he is out of his ground when the wicket-keeper breaks the wicket with the ball or with the hand holding the ball, or if the ball rebounds off the wicket-keeper onto the stumps and removes the bails.

Tie A completed match that ends with an equal total of runs scored by both sides.

Twelfth man The emergency fielder. He may not bat or bowl, and if he makes a catch it is credited to 'sub' (substitute).

Wide A wide is bowled if the umpire considers the ball was too high over or wide of the stumps for the batsman to reach from his normal batting position.

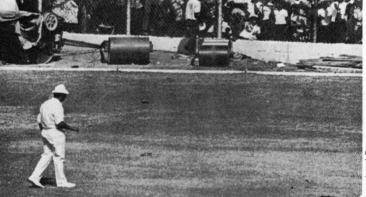

1 A lighter moment for England captain Colin Cowdrey as he takes part in a benefit match, for Kent team-mate Alan Dixon, against an England Ladies' XI. **2** Cowdrey pleads with spectators to stop throwing bottles onto the field during the second Test between England and West Indies in 1967-68. The declining standards of public behaviour have become an increasing threat to the game. **3** What crowds love—a batsman willing to hit the ball hard.

Syndication International

Associated Press

Radio Times Hulton Picture Library

Noeline Kelly

Syndication International

Croquet

Croquet, that 'queen of games' has been the subject of more misconception than almost any other game. Table tennis lived down its 'ping pong' image, and badminton survived the 'battledore and shuttlecock' era; but croquet, in the minds of millions, still conjures up a picture of elderly ladies and gentlemen coaxing balls through hoops in a leisurely manner, on the restful, tree-shaded lawn of the vicarage garden.

It is certainly a picture of what croquet *is not*. The game today consists of relentless efficiency, careful plotting and planning for several moves ahead, and unremitting concentration and discipline—with a vocabulary peculiarly its own.

The striking of the ball with a mallet is not the spontaneous act of a polo or hockey player. It is an operation that has to be carried out with precision and finesse and might be compared to the delicate touch required of the billiards player. But a billiards player could be flattered by the comparison. He, when trying to persuade a ball to go into the pocket, has, for certain shots, something like one-and-a-half inches to spare. A croquet player, faced with such latitude when aiming to shoot a ball through a hoop, would think he was at the entrance of a railway tunnel.

Croquet players can allow no margin for error. The balls are $3\frac{5}{8}$ inches in diameter, and the hoops have uprights measuring $3\frac{3}{4}$ inches apart at the insides. Attempting to force the ball through on its own

1 Croquet essentials: mallet; red, yellow, blue, and black balls; hoops, of which there are six; and a lawn that ideally should be smooth as a bowling green. **2** Play in progress at the Croquet Association's Centenary All England tournament final at Hurlingham in July 1967. **3** Mrs C. Watkins of Hastings, North Island, plays the opening stroke in the 1956 test match between England and New Zealand at Roehampton.

Central Press

momentum is of no avail. Such a stroke, even if absolutely accurate, is no guarantee that the ball will be set up for the next shot nor that it will land for a strategic deployment.

Like the billiards player, the croquet player works out a series of *breaks*. Opponents stand or sit off the lawn while a break is in progress, and, as with chess, plan their own campaigns. Perhaps because croquet calls for so much consistency and anticipation, it exercises a strong appeal for generals, admirals, and other service personnel of exalted rank. Classics masters, bridge internationals, chess solons, and distinguished golfers and hockey players are among today's champions.

Croquet enjoys another distinction. It is the one serious ball game in which men and women compete against each other, with no holds barred, on level terms. Rifle shooting, a few forms of

motor racing, and the Olympic grades of equestrianism are the only other well-known sports participated in at international level that can claim a similar distinction.

Development of Croquet

Croquet is of French ancestry. It first reached England via Ireland, in the 1850s, but did not attain international level until 1925. Croquet was taken to America when it was the fashionable pastime in the 1870s. Eventually clay courts were used, making for greater speed. Games' manufacturers in 1899 decided on a game with four composition balls and rubber-faced mallets. The new game, to distinguish it from the old, was called *roque* by the simple expedient of topping and tailing *croquet*.

The English game has changed substantially through the years as the demands for a more intellectual attitude have been felt, and precision has now become paramount. Hoops were originally 4 inches wide. The balls used to be played in sequence, the next ball to play being 'put out of the game' at the end of a turn. The ability of players to make a break from the first hoop to the peg in one turn, leaving their opponents a shot of some 30 yards to hit before they took their partner ball round to finish the game with a maximum score, led to the innovation of *lifts*, in order to give a more equal opportunity to both players.

Croquet in England has had an open championship since 1867—and 'open' in the croquet sense really means what it says. Nobody is barred—amateur or professional, male or female, old or young.

The women's championship inaugurated in 1869, was a trailblazer of its kind. It preceded lawn tennis (Wimbledon) by 15 years and golf by 24, and was the first to attain its centenary.

In 1925, Sir Macpherson Robertson donated a shield that bears his name to be played for by Britain and Australia. Britain was the first winner. In 1935 New Zealand joined in to make it a triangular series. At the end of 1969 the trophy was in possession of Britain, who had retained it in Australia earlier that year and were acclaimed world champions.

The game flourishes in many parts of the Commonwealth, particularly in Australia and New Zealand. Australia, with about 10,000 active croquet players, has an association in each of the six states. Each of them is represented in test matches. Adelaide and Melbourne were the test cities when Britain and New Zealand were the visitors competing in the 1969 series. The triangular test schedule in the post-war period has been a six-yearly one, but the increasing popularity of the game and the facility of air travel are strong arguments for reducing the interval between tests to four or five years.

Among the 5,000 or so players in New Zealand, women form the majority. Test grounds are located at Auckland, Wellington, and Dunedin.

The king of the croquet world in the 1960s, John William Solomon, started playing the game at the age of 16 in 1948. An executive in the tobacco business, he has been open champion a record 10 times since 1953. Since the introduction in 1964 of the lowest playing handicap at minus 5, Solomon has been on that mark.

Patrick Cotter, senior classics master at St Paul's School, in London, a bridge international and scratch golfer, is another minus-5 handicap player. Three times open champion, Cotter partnered Solomon in the doubles, and they dominated that department at championship level 11 times from 1954 to 1969.

Dorothy D. Steel, known always as 'Deedee', won the open championship four times—in 1925, 1933, 1935, and 1936, and made the final on 10 occasions. The Bedford player also won the women's title 15 times, including a record 8 times in a row from 1932. Miss Steel added five doubles and seven mixed doubles championships for good measure.

Court and Equipment

The field of play, called a *court*, is a lawn ideally (but seldom kept) as smooth as a bowling green. A full-size court measures 35 yards by 28 yards, far larger than a tennis court, but smaller lawns may be used provided that the proportions remain the same. The four boundaries of the court are called *south*, *west*, *north*, and *east*. A flag stands in each corner of the court,

and a yard from each flag along the boundary a small peg is placed to mark the *yard-line*, an imaginary line running round the court one yard inside the boundary. The western half of the south yard-line and the eastern half of the north yard-line are called *baulk-lines*.

There are six hoops of round iron, square-topped, and standing 12 inches out of the ground. The space between the inside edges of the uprights is 3¾ in. There are also four clips, coloured to correspond to the colours of the balls, which are attached to the hoops to indicate which hoop that particular ball has to pass through next. The first and last hoops are distinguished by being painted blue and red respectively.

Four balls of different colours are always used—red and yellow play against blue and black. They weigh 1 lb each, are made of composition, and have a diameter of 3⅝ inches. This allows an overall clearance within the hoop of an eighth of an inch. Mallets vary in weight, size, shape, and material, according to individual preference.

1 G. N. Aspinall, one of croquet's great players, won the open singles trophy at Hurlingham in 1969. He is about to croquet yellow with the black ball, using a full roll in a crouching position. Note the hands low down on the shaft and well positioned to gain extra power. 2 The peg, which must be struck by both balls (red and yellow or blue and black) before a game is won. The peg stands 18 in. high and has a detachable top to hold the clips.
3 Diagram of a full-sized croquet court with its six hoops, which must be run once in each direction, and the final peg. 4 The redoubtable Patrick Cotter in action, three times open singles champion. Not surprisingly when teamed up with world champion John Solomon they produced a practically unbeatable doubles combination.
5 In this cannon position red is about to croquet blue and then will roquet yellow.

H. W. Neale

Noeline Kelly

How the Game is Played

In a singles game each player has two balls. The object of the game is to knock the balls through the six hoops in turn twice—once in each direction. On the outward round the hoops are numbered 1 to 6 and on the way back 1-back, 2-back, 3-back, 4-back, *penultimate*, and *rover*. When rover has been negotiated the balls have to hit a wooden peg, 1½ inches in diameter and standing 18 inches out of the ground in the centre of the court.

The first player (or, in doubles, team) to score all 12 hoops and hit the peg with each ball is the winner. A point is scored for each hoop and the peg—making 26 in all for the two balls. In Britain a result is announced as the difference between the full score and that of the loser. If, for example, the loser scored only 10 points, the result would be +16 for the winner, and —16 for the loser. In Australia and New Zealand the more conventional result of 26-10 is preferred.

Play begins from either baulk, and the player whose turn it is (settled by tossing a coin) is called the *striker* and his opponent the *outplayer*. The striker may hit only one of his balls with the mallet during a turn. The players basically play alternate turns, each turn consisting of one stroke, but there are various ways of extending a turn so that it is possible for a striker to monopolize the play with a continuous series of strokes and turns while the outplayer looks on helplessly.

There are basically two kinds of shots in croquet—the *one-ball* shot and the *two-ball* shot. The only way the striker can continue his turn before his opponent takes over is by *running* (knocking one of his balls through) the correct hoop. But he can earn bonus shots (which must be played immediately on their being earned) by making a *roquet*. He does this when his ball hits any of the other three balls on the court. By making a roquet he earns two extra shots. His ball becomes dead—*in hand* is the term—and he must place it so that it touches the roqueted ball. He then strikes his own ball with the mallet in such a way that both balls move. This is known as a *croquet* stroke, and the opponent's ball may be *croqueted* to any part of the court that the striker wishes. If either ball goes off the court on this stroke the turn ends.

When the striker's ball has come to rest he takes the second of his two bonus strokes—the *continuation* stroke. With this he can try either to run the hoop or to roquet another ball. If he succeeds in running the hoop he gets another stroke and the process starts again. If, instead of trying for the hoop, he goes for another roquet, he is now restricted to two possible targets only, because he is not allowed to roquet the same ball more than once in any one turn. If he fails to run the hoop or make a roquet his turn comes to an end.

A player is not forced to play his balls in any particular order. If he is on red and yellow, for instance, he can play red first and then yellow, or he can concentrate on one colour exclusively for the whole of the round if he wishes. The skills of the game, apart from the very obvious one in attempting to run the hoops, lie in using the roquet and the croquet to position one's balls to the best advantage, and to the detriment of the opponent. By continually croqueting balls to the next hoop but one the striker will always have a ball awaiting him at each hoop, so that an all-round break can be made. In this way croquet players can plan their campaigns several moves ahead.

Colour Sport

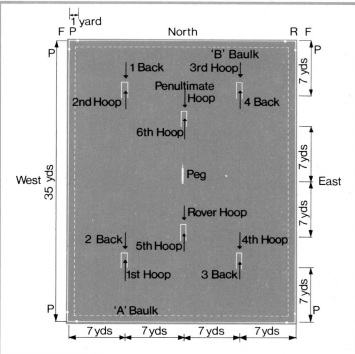

Eric Jewell

Gerry Cranham/Transworld

H. W. Neale

Colour Sport

CROQUET

The MacRobertson International Shield

Year	Winners	Venue
1925	Great Britain	England
1928	Australia	Australia
1935	Australia	Australia
1937	Great Britain	England
1950	New Zealand	New Zealand
1956	Great Britain	England
1963	Great Britain	New Zealand
1969	Great Britain	Australia

The Croquet Championship
(first held in 1867)

Year	Winner
1946	D. J. V. Hamilton-Miller
1947	H. O. Hicks
1948	H. O. Hicks
1949	H. O. Hicks
1950	H. O. Hicks
1951	G. L. Reckitt
1952	H. O. Hicks
1953	J. W. Solomon
1954	A. G. F. Ross (New Zealand)
1955	E. P. C. Cotter
1956	J. W. Solomon
1957	Dr W. R. D. Wright
1958	E. P. C. Cotter
1959	J. W. Solomon
1960	Mrs E. Rotherham
1961	J. W. Solomon
1962	E. P. C. Cotter
1963	J. W. Solomon
1964	J. W. Solomon
1965	J. W. Solomon
1966	J. W. Solomon
1967	J. W. Solomon
1968	J. W. Solomon
1969	G. N. Aspinall
1970	K. F. Wylie
1971	K. F. Wylie
1972	B. G. Neal
1973	B. G. Neal

The President's Cup
(first held in 1934)

Year	Winner
1946	D. J. V. Hamilton-Miller (after a tie with E. L. Ward Petley)
1947	H. O. Hicks
1948	H. O. Hicks
1949	E. P. C. Cotter
1950	E. P. C. Cotter
1951	H. O. Hicks
1952	E. P. C. Cotter (after a tie with J. W. Solomon)
1953	E. P. C. Cotter (after a tie with J. W. Solomon)
1954	H. O. Hicks
1955	J. W. Solomon
1956	E. P. C. Cotter (after a tie with J. W. Solomon)
1957	J. W. Solomon
1958	J. W. Solomon
1959	J. W. Solomon
1960	E. P. C. Cotter
1961	H. O. Hicks
1962	J. W. Solomon
1963	J. W. Solomon
1964	J. W. Solomon
1965	J. P. R. Bolton
1966	Dr W. P. Ormerod
1967	K. F. Wylie
1968	J. W. Solomon
1969	G. N. Aspinall
1970	G. N. Aspinall
1971	J. W. Solomon
1972	W. de B. Prichard
1973	G. N. Aspinall

1 Studying the line before attempting to run a hoop with the red. The clearance between the ball and the uprights in some competitions can be as little as $\frac{1}{16}$ in., so that anything over a foot away can be considered a long shot! 2 Patrick Cotter playing in the 1969 open championship at Hurlingham which he won with his partner John Solomon. 3 King of the croquet court John William Solomon weighs up the situation at Hurlingham. His opponent has just broken down at the third hoop after being all set for a triple peel.

Glossary of Terms

Baulk Lines The western half of the south yard-line and its complement—the eastern half of the north yard-line, known respectively as *A-baulk* and *B-baulk*.

Bisque An extra turn given in handicap play. The turn may be taken at any stage of the game. The difference in handicap between any two players determines the number of *bisques* that the weaker player receives. Handicaps range from 16 to −5 (the best).

Break A *turn* in which more than one hoop is scored.

Cannon A *croquet* shot in which the ball about to be croqueted is touching a third ball, which is roqueted immediately by striker's ball.

Clips Coloured markers that are attached to the hoops to show which one is to be run next by a particular ball. On the outward course the clips are attached to the crowns of the hoops—on the return journey to an up-right.

Continuation Stroke The stroke that follows the *croquet* stroke.

Corner To *corner* is to play a ball into one of the corners on purpose, as a defensive move.

Croquet A player *takes croquet* by placing his ball in contact with the *roqueted* ball and playing his ball so that both balls move. If either ball goes off on this stroke the turn ends.

Cut-Rush A *rush* played in such a way that the rushed ball is sent off at an angle to the stroke.

Four-Ball Break A *break* involving all four balls.

Free-Shot A long shot that can be attempted with little risk.

Half-Bisque A *bisque* in which no points can be scored.

Hammer Shot A shot in which the mallet is played down onto the ball —generally in a situation where the mallet's swing is impeded by another ball or a hoop.

Leave The position of the balls after a *break*.

Lift A free shot played from the baulk-line at certain stages of the game at championship class.

Make a Hoop To *score* a hoop in its correct order.

Outplayer The striker's opponent.

Pass-Roll A *croquet* shot in which the back ball (the striker's ball) travels farther than the front ball (the croqueted ball).

Peel Any ball other than the striker's ball that is made to run its own hoop is said to be *peeled*.

Peg-Out When a ball scores the peg point it is said to be *pegged out*.

Penultimate The last hoop but one.

Pull A term describing the tendency for the front ball to come round towards the angle of the back ball in a split croquet shot.

Qualifying Shot The shot with which a *turn* opens.

Roll A *croquet* shot in which the angle of split is small and the balls travel about the same distance.

Roquet When the striker's ball hits any other ball that it has not already contacted during that *turn*, it *roquets* that ball.

Rover The last hoop. Also a ball that has made the last hoop.

Run a Hoop To play a ball through its own hoop; same as to *make a hoop*.

Rush When the striker attempts to *roquet* a ball to a predetermined spot, he plays a *rush* shot.

Scatter A shot that separates balls that are too close together.

Single Peel A *break* in which a ball is *peeled* through the *rover* hoop in its correct order and *pegged out*.

Split Shot A *croquet shot* in which the back ball and the *croqueted* ball travel away from each other at an angle.

Take-Off A *split shot* played so wide that the *croqueted* ball hardly moves.

Three-Ball Break A *break* involving only three balls.

Triple Peel A break in which the striker, while making the hoops for one of his balls, peels another (normally his partner's) through the last three hoops and pegs out—very expert play.

Turn A shot or series of shots in which no hoop is scored.

Two-Ball Break A *break* involving only two balls.

Two-Ball Shots *Croquet* shots.

Yard-Line An imaginary line running round the court one yard inside the boundary line.

Yard-Line Area The area between the *yard-line* and the boundary. If the ball finishes up in this area it must be placed on the *yard-line* before the next stroke is played, except for the striker's ball after a croquet stroke or after running a hoop.

3

J. W. Solomon

A crowded start to the 1967 senior international cross-country championship, held at Barry in Wales.

H. W. Neale

Cross-Country Running

Despite lack of success in the Olympic arena, Great Britain produces a great depth of middle- and long-distance runners. Cross-country running is the basis of this aspect of British athletics, for the track runners' winter training consists largely of cross-country or road running competitions. The names of successful track artists reads like a cross-country 'Who's Who', from the first winner of the international championship, Alf Shrubb, and France's immortal Jean Bouin, to the great names of

modern distance running—1964 Olympic steeplechase champion Gaston Roelants, and the 5,000 metres gold-medallist in 1968, Mohamed Gammoudi.

Like rugby football, Eton and Rugby fives, and racquets, cross-country running originated in the English public schools. At Rugby, the Crick Run was founded in 1837, and there is some evidence that Shrewsbury had held cross-country races at an even earlier date. Set runs were held weekly during the Christmas term at

Shrewsbury, amid great ceremony. A 'Huntsman' would appear dressed in a black cap with a scarlet jersey and stockings. The 'Gentlemen of the Runs' would follow the first division of the pack, running coatless and carrying a bludgeon to ward off the town 'toughs' who delighted in stoning the boys. They would be pursued by the second division, clad in mortar board and gown. The idea of these runs spread to other schools: Rugby had the Crick and Barby Hill runs, Bradfield a run through the Pang Valley, and Sedburgh a run of 10 to 12 miles over the Yorkshire

moors.

This sort of activity soon extended beyond the public schools. In 1867 a few members of the Thames Rowing Club held cross-country steeplechases to keep fit in the winter months. This idea came from one Walter Rye who later became the founder of the Thames Hare and Hounds Club, the first of its kind. Many of these early races were 'paper-chases'—a 'hare' would lay a trail of scraps of paper and be pursued by 'hounds'. Thames's first race, held at Roehampton, was of this type.

In 1870 enough clubs existed for

inter-club contests to take place. The first was a match between the Thames Hare and Hounds and the Gentlemen of Hampstead. Sufficient interest was aroused in the sport for a national cross-country-championship to be held in 1876. The race was held in Epping Forest, but all the 32 runners took the wrong course and the race was declared void. Nevertheless, the event was staged annually thereafter. A nationwide authority, the English Cross-Country Union, was founded in 1883 with the same Mr Walter Rye as president. In that year, 91 men entered for the English championship.

Inevitably, with the growing interest in sport, international competitions were started. The first was in March 1898 when England met France at Ville d'Avray near Paris. The race was run over 9 miles, and the English team of eight men occupied the first eight places. Five years later, in 1903, the first home international cross-country championship was held at Hamilton Park racecourse in Scotland. England won, beating the teams of Ireland, Scotland, and Wales. That year the International Cross-Country Union was founded, and since then the popularity and influence of the sport have grown steadily.

England has always been a stronghold of the sport, and from

1 Alfred Shrubb won the first two international cross-country championships in 1903 and 1904. The outstanding runner of his day—he held world records at 2, 3, 6, and 10 miles, and one hour—he was subsequently banned from amateur sports in 1904.
2 Jack Holden wins the first of his four international titles at Caerleon in 1933.
3 On flat courses artificial obstacles such as hurdles sap a competitor's energy as much as mud and hills.
4 Alain Mimoun trails Basil Heatley of Britain in the annual 12-km San Sebastian cross-country race in 1959. Mimoun won in 38 min 38.2 sec with Heatley in fourth place.
5 Belgium's versatile Gaston Roelants wins his third international title in 1969 at Clydebank from a distant Dick Taylor of England.
6 Bespectacled Doris Brown seemed unbeatable at women's cross-country in the 1960s. She was also one of the best female 800 metres and mile runners of the period.
7 Maureen Dickson (USA) leads the field in the women's international race in 1969. Winner Doris Brown lurks in third place behind New Zealand's Millie Sampson.

Associated Press

Radio Times Hulton Picture Library

H. W. Neale

Associated Press

Ed Lacey
H. W. Neale
Ed Lacey

7 the 33 participants in the second national championship in 1877, the number of runners grew to over 1,000 in 1969—all competing in the same race. Although the championship acts as a trial for the 'international', each place from first to last is important to the runners—who come from over 100 different clubs. This 1,000 man race is not the only championship held: the scope of the national championship was widened in 1946 with the introduction of a youth (16-18 years old) championship, and a junior (18-21) race was added in 1948.

Outside the British Isles the sport is well supported. Cross-country is a standard winter activity in France and Belgium, and rather surprisingly in Spain where up to 50,000 spectators have attended some events.

Cross-country is less popular outside Europe. The United States season is short—only two months —and the competitions are mainly inter-collegiate. The courses as well as the organization are different from those in Europe. The races are normally about 4 miles long compared with the 9 miles or so of the English championship.

In Australia and New Zealand, cross-country is a minor adjunct of track and field activities. The Australian season is very short, and running over the country is

CROSS-COUNTRY RUNNING

The International Cross-Country Championship

Year	Individual	Team
1903	Alfred Shrubb (England)	England
1904	Alfred Shrubb (England)	England
1905	A. Aldridge (England)	England
1906	C. J. Straw (England)	England
1907	A. Underwood (England)	England
1908	Arthur Robertson (England)	England
1909	A. E. Wood (England)	England
1910	A. E. Wood (England)	England
1911	Jean Bouin (France)	England
1912	Jean Bouin (France)	England
1913	Jean Bouin (France)	England
1914	A. H. Nicholls (England)	England
1920	James Wilson (Scotland)	England
1921	W. Freeman (England)	England
1922	Joseph Guillemot (France)	France
1923	C. E. Blewitt (England)	France
1924	W. M. Cotterell (England)	England
1925	Jack Webster (England)	England
1926	Ernest Harper (England)	France
1927	L. Payne (England)	France
1928	H. Eckersley (England)	France
1929	W. M. Cotterell (England)	France
1930	Tom Evenson (England)	England
1931	T. F. Smythe (Ireland)	England
1932	Tom Evenson (England)	England
1933	Jack Holden (England)	England
1934	Jack Holden (England)	England
1935	Jack Holden (England)	England
1936	William Eaton (England)	England
1937	J. C. Flockhart (Scotland)	England
1938	Jack Emery (England)	England
1939	Jack Holden (England)	France
1946	Raphael Pujazon (France)	France
1947	Raphael Pujazon (France)	France
1948	J. Doms (Belgium)	Belgium
1949	Alain Mimoun (France)	France
1950	Lucien Theys (Belgium)	France
1951	Geoffrey Saunders (England)	England
1952	Alain Mimoun (France)	France
1953	Franjo Milhalic (Yugoslavia)	England
1954	Alain Mimoun (France)	England
1955	Frank Sando (England)	England
1956	Alain Mimoun (France)	France
1957	Frank Sando (England)	Belgium
1958	Stan Eldon (England)	England
1959	Fred Norris (England)	England
1960	Rhadi ben Abdesselem (Morocco)	England
1961	Basil Heatley (England)	Belgium
1962	Gaston Roelants (Belgium)	England
1963	Roy Fowler (England)	Belgium
1964	Francisco Arizmendi (Spain)	England
1965	Jean-Claude Fayolle (France)	England
1966	Ben Assou El Ghazi (Morocco)	England
1967	Gaston Roelants (Belgium)	England
1968	Mohamed Gammoudi (Tunisia)	England
1969	Gaston Roelants (Belgium)	England
1970	Mike Tagg (England)	England
1971	Dave Bedford (England)	England
1972	Gaston Roelants (Belgium)	England
1973	Pekka Paivarinta (Finland)	Belgium
1974	Erik De Beck (Belgium)	Belgium

Olympic Games—Individual

1912	(8,000 metres)	Hannes Kohlemainen (Finland)
1920	(10,000 metres)	Paavo Nurmi (Finland)
1924	(10,650 metres)	Paavo Nurmi (Finland)

Olympic Games—Team

1912	(8,000 metres)	Sweden
1920	(10,000 metres)	Finland
1924	(10,650 metres)	Finland

not regarded as an end in itself as it is in Europe. Even so, many of Australia's best runners, including Ron Clarke, run in cross-country events.

New Zealand has a long tradition of cross-country running, but has failed to produce a star runner in this sphere to rank with a man such as England's Jack Holden, four times winner of the international championship. New Zealand's strength lies in very strong team efforts, and the Kiwis excelled in the 1973 international championship when their team ran into third place, and Rod Dixon took third place ahead of the Finn, Kantanen, and Belgium's Gaston Roelants. Regular exponents of the art of cross-country in New Zealand have been Mike Ryan, bronze medal winner in the 1966 Commonwealth Games and 1968 Olympic Games marathons, and Dick Taylor, the 10,000 metres gold medallist at the 1974 Commonwealth Games.

British runners like their courses long and arduous, ideally simulating rural conditions with deep mud, hills, and water. The English championship is run over 9 miles, compared with the international's 7½. European races, on the other hand, tend to be rather shorter, flatter, and strewn with artificial obstacles. They are about 4 or 5 miles early in the season and become longer as the season progresses. The European attitude to the British type of cross-country course is best summed up by the French description of heavy mud as 'le cross Anglais'.

The main international competition in cross-country is the annual International Cross-Country Championship. Because this has always been held in Europe or North Africa, very few teams from far afield have taken part. France first entered the contest in 1907, and in 1922 became the first nation to defeat England in the event. Belgium entered in 1923, and in 1929 there was a massive influx of teams from Spain, Italy, Switzerland and Luxembourg. The Dutch first appeared in 1950, Yugoslavia in 1953 and Portugal in 1955. In the 1960s entries expanded to include teams from New Zealand, South Africa, and the United States, as well as north African nations. Invitations were sent to the eastern European nations to enter teams in the 1970 race, but they were already regular contestants in a 'communist' race promoted annually by the French newspaper *L'Humanité*.

Despite the tough, gruelling nature of the sport, women have not been deterred from holding contests. In 1931 an unofficial international event was held at Douai, in France, where an English team competed against France and Belgium. Gladys Lunn, the world 880 yards record holder from England, was the winner. An official women's international championship was first held in 1967 over a 4-mile course. Ameri-

can runners have excelled in this contest, Doris Brown winning the event in 1967, 1968, and 1969, and the United States team taking the team awards in 1968 and 1969.

For a sport with a wide following in Europe, cross-country running is a conspicuous absentee from the Olympic calendar. In fact, races were included in the 1912, 1920, and 1924 Games, but the race at Paris in 1924 was a débâcle and cross-country has since been excluded. The distance had been 8,000 metres in 1912 and 1920. In 1924, on a day of nearly tropical heat, the runners set out to travel 10,000 metres through the Paris streets and parks. Paavo Nurmi retained the title he had won in 1920, but behind him the race developed into a farce. Britain's Ernest Harper finished fourth and collapsed on the finishing line, while others had to receive medical attention.

Despite the lack of a truly international event with all the kudos that winning it may carry, European athletes make every effort to win at cross-country. The names of the winners of the international championship include many of the greatest names in athletics. The winner of the first two, in 1903 and 1904, was Alf Shrubb, who was also a multiple English champion and world record holder. The Frenchman Jean Bouin took the title in 1911, 1912, and 1913, and he also won a silver in the 1912 Olympic 5,000 metres and held world records for 10,000 metres and one hour. In the 1960s the winners have included Gaston Roelants of Belgium, and Mohamed Gammoudi. The most convincing victor was perhaps England's Jack Holden in 1934—he won by 56 seconds and 400 yards. By way of a contrast, in 1965 Jean-Claude Fayolle of France and Mel Batty of England raced neck and neck to the finish; Fayolle got the decision but both runners were credited with the same time. But perhaps the greatest champion of them all over the country was the 1956 Olympic marathon champion Alain Mimoun. He ran for France 11 times in the international championship between 1949 and 1964, winning it four times to equal Jack Holden's record.

The achievements of such men over the country and on the track go a long way towards disproving the theory held by some coaches that cross-country is an unambitious form of athletics that instills in runners an escapist attitude, so that they forget their Olympic ambitions. Such criticism may be valid in some cases, but with the value of off-season racing and participation in an activity that closely resembles the Swedish form of *fartlek* (speed-play) training, there can be little doubt that track stars over the longer distances find it an ideal way of maintaining fitness and speed during the close season.

1 Early in the 1969 International Cross-Country Championship held at Clydebank, England's Tim Johnson led the field, closely followed by the Spaniard, Mariano Haro. Two New Zealanders and two Englishmen make up the leading bunch. 2 England's strength at cross-country is based on a high level of participation at all standards. *Opposite page:* The 1967 senior National Championship field gets under way at Norwich; with most of the gruelling course still to be run, the strain of this gruelling event is etched on the faces of all the runners.

Curling

'The Roaring Game' as curling is called, is aptly named. It is indeed a riproaring game—the deep, reverberating roar of the stones as they glide over the ice mingling with the shouts of 'soop! soop!' from players and onlookers. The skill and subtlety attached to the method and moment of delivering the stone and the technique of sooping (sweeping ahead of the stone with brooms), together with the varying tactics and strategy, provide a constant fascination which never wanes for the player and has attracted as many as 25,000 spectators to a Canadian national championship final.

Although there is some doubt as to whether curling originated in Scotland or the Netherlands about 400 years ago, the sport owes its development to Scotland, where it has progressed and prospered since the early 1600s.

The international administrative body is the Royal Caledonian Curling Club, with permanent headquarters in Edinburgh. It was inaugurated in July 1838 as the Grand Caledonian Curling Club. Four years later, the royal prefix was granted following a special exhibition of the game before Queen Victoria and Prince Albert— on the polished floor of the Palace of Scone's spacious drawing-room! The Prince Consort was at the time presented with a pair of curling stones. He consented to become a patron of the club and has been succeeded in this office by subsequent monarchs.

The world championship, contested originally for the Scotch Cup and later for the Silver Broom, was inaugurated in 1959 and won six times by Canada before the United States and Scottish teams were successful. The most prominent teams in the 1960s were the Canadian quartets skipped by Ernie Richardson and Ron Northcott, and the Scottish four led by Chuck Hay.

Curling schools have opened in Switzerland on almost as large a scale as the country's well-organized ski-teaching system. The game attracts more than 2,000 women curlers in Scotland. South of the border, the sports's expansion has been severely limited because of the great hold that skating maintains on England's 21 indoor ice rinks. Even an ardent infiltration at Richmond, in Surrey, is restricted to a few hours' playing time per week. The converse situation exists at most of Scotland's 16 rinks, where few managements can afford to take much appreciable time from curling to satisfy the skaters' demands.

There are more than half a million curlers in Canada, compared with 25,000 in Scotland, the game's early pacemaker. Apart from its great hold in Switzerland, curling also flourishes in the United States, Sweden, Norway, West Germany, France, Italy, and New Zealand.

In many respects curling resembles bowls, the fundamental difference being that, instead of rolling woods on grass, polished, disc-shaped granite stones are propelled across a sheet of ice 14 feet wide and 138 feet long.

The stones, which have smoothly curved edges, do not need to be picked up from the ice during the course of a game, which is just as well because many of them weigh the maximum 44 pounds. They are limited to 36 inches in circumference, and their minimum height is one-eighth of their circumference.

One 'sole' of the stone is usually designed for use on hard ice and the other for a softer surface, a metal handle by which it is set in motion being detachable and interchangeable according to which sole is used. Stones used to be named after the regions in which they were quarried, hence such colourful nomenclatures as Ailsa Craigs, Carsphairn Reds, Crawfordjohns, and Burnocks. Ailsas are still quarried from Ailsa Craig in the Firth of Clyde.

Many curling terms are similar to those in bowls. The playing area is called a *rink*, and it has a fixed *tee* (a jack in bowls) at each end. Circles round each tee, used as guides, are called the *house*. The outside one has a diameter of 12 feet.

Each curling team—also, somewhat confusingly, termed a *rink*—consists of four players who each use two stones, playing them alternately with those of an opponent. Thus, with eight players—four on each side—16 stones are delivered in each end or *head*. All matches, under the jurisdiction of an umpire, comprise an agreed number of heads or period of time.

The stones are played from a point called the *hack* or *crampit*, on

1 Curling under cover in Scotland's great winter sports centre at Aviemore. 2 Outdoors, the Bernese Alps provide a magnificent backdrop for the game at Mürren 3 A woman competitor delivers her first stone on a Swiss rink. 4 Britain beats Sweden to win the curling title in the 1924 Winter Olympics at Chamonix. 5 To cries of 'soop! soop!' a sweeper gains those last few vital inches. 6 Layout of a full-sized curling rink with dimensions.

Keystone

Barnaby's

Glossary of Terms

Burnt A burnt stone is one that is touched by the broom while sweeping; it must be removed.

Crampit A narrow sheet of metal, about 4 ft. long, fixed to the ice on a line called the *foot-score*. The player delivers the stone from the crampit. See *Hack*.

End An end is completed when all the stones have been played; sometimes known as a *head*.

Foot-score A line, 12 ft. behind each tee, on which the *crampit* or *hack* is situated.

Hack A variation of the *crampit*, consisting of a metal ridge on which a player places the sole of his foot when delivering the stone.

Head Another word for *end*.

Hog Any stone that fails to cross the *hog-score* is called a *hog*, and is removed.

Hog-score A line 21 ft. from the *tee*.

House The circles forming the curling target, in the centre of which is the *tee*.

Rink The playing area; also the curling team of four players.

Skip The captain of a team.

Sole The 'top' and 'bottom' surfaces of the stone. These vary according to the nature of the rink.

Soop A variant of 'sweep'—the shouted instruction to the sweepers by players and spectators.

Tee The target for the stones, corresponding to the jack in bowls.

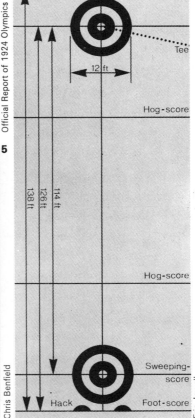

a line known as the *foot-score*, situated 12 feet behind each tee. After delivering his stone, a player must not slide past the *hog-score*, a line 21 feet from the tee at his end. Any stone not passing the *hog-score* at the other end is termed a *hog* and removed, as is any stone that rolls over or comes to rest on its side or top. When an end of 16 stones has been played, a point is scored for each stone lying nearer the tee than an opposing stone. The equivalent of bias in bowls is achieved by the turn or twist to right or left given to the handle at the moment of delivery. The stone rotates during its journey and curls (hence 'curling') to the right or left as it finally slows to a halt.

One of the major differences from bowls is the way in which the course and speed of a curling-stone may be influenced *after* it has left the player's hand. Because particles of ice-dust and, if outdoors, snow-flakes can slow up the stone, two players are authorized by their team captain (the all-important *skip* whose orders in this game are absolute law) to sweep rapidly and skilfully with special brooms just ahead of the moving stone—but without touching it—in order to adjust its pace and direction as required. This is known as *sooping*, and to the uninitiated it is perhaps the most curious spectacle of curling. In certain conditions sooping can add three yards or more to a stone's distance. The skip directs operations from the outer ring, and another player in the team temporarily takes over the skip's duties when he plays his own stones.

No special clothing is required except for footwear, which can have rubber or slippery soles, according to the amount of 'slide' employed by each curler, and must be free of spikes or other contrivances that could damage the ice surface.

Characteristic appendages include a multitude of badges adorning lapels and breast pockets; in Switzerland and Scandinavia, colourful bobbles are attached to the stone handles to denote which side they represent; and, in Scotland and elsewhere, the Balmoral or Kilmarnock bonnet with a gay toorie.

So popular has the game become that when the Austrians stage the winter Olympic Games in 1976, they will, in all likelihood, exercise the host nation's traditional right to introduce a demonstration sport and insist on curling which was included in the 1924, 1932, 1936, and 1948 Games.

In 1924, three countries contested the curling demonstration, and the event was won by a British team led by T. S. Aikman, with Sweden runners-up. The more widely practiced rules of Scottish origin were used, and again in 1932 when only the Americans and Canadians took part. But in 1936 the German style of curling was demonstrated.

Cycling

The fascination of cycle racing is that it's a sport of so many worlds and so many moods. It takes place indoors in the smokey velodromes and in the thin air of the mountain summits, in the summer heat of Tasmania and the frost of a January hillside in the north of England. At one end of the social and financial spectrum it's a young lad on a second-hand bike riding alone through an Essex lane, straining to shave a couple of seconds off his personal best in the club '25'. At the other it's Eddy Merckx, the Belgian prodigy, surrounded by fans wherever he goes, asking, and getting, £1000 for appearing in a one-day race in a French provincial town. Yet if these two ever met, which isn't likely, they would recognize something of themselves in each other—the 'bikey's' true frustration and delight in trying to make the wheels spin a little faster. And that is why these three snapshots belong in the same album. . . .

The Col du Galibier, a barren mountain rising 8,800 ft. in the Alps, reopened only three weeks before when the snow ploughs got through. Yet today it's as crowded with life as a colony of gannets. Ten thousand people must have left their cars on lower roads and climbed to the summit. And waiting for the Tour de France to arrive, they have carved out the names of their heroes—Poulidor, Gimondi, Pingeon—in the snow. But it is none of these who comes into sight first at the sharp hairpin bend, but a little Spaniard, Julio Jimenez, a slight, almost frail-looking figure with a lined face and thinning hair. Up and up he dances on the pedals, cheered every inch of the way. Jimenez has arrived once more to claim

his Kingdom of the Mountains and its richest prize.

The Sportpaleis at Antwerp, a circus filled with the blue haze from Belgian cigars. In the centre of the wooden track, the more affluent spectators tuck into their chicken dinners, the rest drink their spilling lager at wooden trestles. On a rostrum a Tyrolean band plays in its coloured braces. In the roof an acrobat swings

from a trapeze. What's all this got to do with cycling? At the Six Day race a great deal. A 'Six' is a non-stop variety show; there must never be a dull moment. Yet it's the cyclists who get the star billing, brilliant entertainers who handle their bikes superbly on the crowded track, swoop excitingly from the end banking, and give a grandstand finish to every sprint.

At 5 a.m., when at last the

Six Day riders call it a night, the English cyclists are just setting off on their favourite sport, the time trial. In the cold dawn light the riders come up, one by one, to a chalk mark drawn in a lane somewhere to the west of Reading. And at one-minute intervals they swing away, alone and unpaced, to cover 50 miles. There are no visible rivals to beat, only the hands of the stopwatch and the temptation to ease up. There will be no crowds at the finish, only club-mates and family. And the prizes—six guineas to be shared among the first three—will scarcely pay for the petrol to take the rider home. Yet that deters no one. On some Sunday mornings in summer there may be over 300 time-trial meetings taking place throughout the country.

These three different forms of cycling, and many more, have developed within a century—and often for what seem quite incidental reasons.

How cycling began

Cycle racing is as old as the bicycle. From 1818, when Baron Drais devised his foot-propelled hobby horse, every inventor wanted to put his machine through its paces against other types of 'velocipede'—the name still used by the French though generally in its shortened form, 'velo'. Competition took over as the mother of invention. In 1839 cranks to drive the rear wheel were introduced, and in 1850 treadles to drive the front. And these developments were followed in 1865 by the first French 'boneshaker', with pedals mounted directly on the axle of a front wheel which was slightly larger than the back.

Over the next 20 years the size of the front wheel was steadily increased so that faster speeds could be reached with the same number of turns of the pedal. So

THE ROVER SAFETY BICYCLE (PATENTED).

Safer than any Tricycle, faster and easier than any Bicycle ever made. Fitted with handles to turn for convenience in storing or shipping. Far and away the best hill-climber in the market.

MANUFACTURED BY

STARLEY & SUTTON,

METEOR WORKS, WEST ORCHARD, COVENTRY, ENGLAND.

Price Lists of " Meteor," " Rover," " Despatch," and " Sociable" Bicycles and Tricycles, and the "Coventry Chair," Illustrated, free on application.

Three cycling snapshots . . .
1 Eddy Merckx, one of the highest-paid athletes in the world, wears the leader's *maillot jaune* in the 1969 Tour de France . . .
2 A lonely start for an early morning time-triallist in an

English country lane . . .
3 Britain's second post-war six-day race was held at Earls Court in 1967.
4 An ancestor of the modern cycle—the 'Hobby 'or 'Dandy' horse invented by Charles, Baron Drais, in 1818, was

the rage of its time.
5 F. J. Osmond won the 1, 5, 25, and 50 miles championships of Britain in 1890 riding a penny-farthing.
6 An advertisement for the 'Rover Safety Bicycle' which appeared in January 1885.

7 In the late 19th century, paced record attempts were a popular feature of cycling. Here a Dunlop 'quintuplet' is in action, attired in the company's colours—as early as this, commercialism had entered the sport of cycling.

the *ordinary*, as it is properly **2** called, took on its famous penny-farthing shape. At the same time, efforts were made to lighten the machine. Solid rubber tyres replaced iron-clad wheels, and wire spokes and tubular frames were brought in. The Rudge racing ordinary of 1884 might have looked a bit grotesque with its front wheel standing 58 inches high and the saddle perched above it, but the whole thing weighed only 21½ lb.

The ordinary was fast; on one of these lofty machines in 1882 H. L. Cortis became the first man to cycle 20 miles in an hour. But it was also precarious. So the next stage of development was directed towards the 'safety' bicycle, with wheels of almost equal size, a chain drive to the rear wheel and a diamond-shaped frame. The most successful of these was John Kemp Starley's Rover Safety Bicycle produced in Coventry from 1885.

The ordinary had already given birth to cycle racing and record making, which had been governed since 1878 by the world's first cycling body, the National Cyclists' Union (now replaced by the British Cycling Federation). And as late as 1891 the first six-day cycle race to be held in New York was ridden on high-wheelers. But it was the safety bike that transformed the scene, producing the great cycling boom of the 1880s and 1890s. It also set a pattern in cycle design which, with the refinement of pneumatic tyres from 1888 and variable-speed gears the following year, remained basically unchanged until the Moulton mini-bike appeared three-quarters of a century later.

Road and track

Early races were run on the roads,

Derek J. White

1 Sunday morning and a club goes out on a road race. For the club cyclist, just as for the world-class professional, there is a constant challenge to record faster times. **2** Sixty-one-year-old G. A. Jessop takes part in a 100-mile time trial.

despite the ruts and pot-holes that made them unsuitable for fast riding. But when the cycling craze developed, promoters were quick to build tracks of grass, gravel, and — later — concrete where they could stage amateur and professional events. Bicycles were still the fastest racing vehicles available. Hard as it may be to imagine nowadays, spectators were excited by their sheer speed. Particularly popular were record attempts in which individual riders were paced by tandems, triplets, and even eight-man 'octets', and in paced races it became common to cover 29-30 miles in an hour. In fact in an American stunt in 1899, Charles 'Mile-a-Minute' Murphy covered a mile in 57 4/5 seconds riding behind a locomotive on a board

track laid down between the lines.

America and Australia were as keen on the sport as the continental countries at that time, but England was indisputably the leader. In London in 1892 the first world governing body, the International Cycling Association, was set up by eight founding nations: England, Belgium, Denmark, Germany, France, the Netherlands, the United States, and Canada. But there was some discontent with British dominance of the sport, and in 1900 France took the lead in forming a new world authority, the Union Cycliste Internationale (UCI), to which Britain had later to apply for membership.

By then the British boom was over. Rival manufacturers had fought each other to a standstill.

Many tracks were closed, and racing on the public roads had been outlawed. However, a peculiarly British form of the game was developing—the time trial. This was devised by F.T. Bidlake in 1889-90 to avoid trouble with the police. Since the riders set off at intervals there was no congestion. Events were held on lonely stretches of the road in the early hours. No publicity or professionalism was permitted. And even up to World War II an 'inconspicuous clothing rule' was enforced, which required riders to dress in black.

The time trial transformed the character of British cycle sport. On the debit side, it became fanatically discreet and amateur, largely cut off from the more flamboyant happenings on the continent and even the mainstream of British sport. But to its credit it developed a strong and highly sociable club life, avoiding the excesses of professionalism, among them the fashion for taking artificial stimulants.

Track racing continued on a small scale, producing three world champions, Reg Harris, Cyril Peacock, and Norman Sheil, in the 1940s and 1950s. Massed-start racing was revived after the war, and a small professional class grew up in the mid-1960s. But the most popular cycling activity in Britain is still the time trial, 'the secret game'

Professionalism

On the continent, cycling went on developing through the already established pattern of track and road racing. It became the accepted national summer sport of France, Belgium, and the Netherlands, gained ground in Italy, Spain, Germany, and Scandinavia, and attracted vast audiences. In France some of the great classic races such as the Bordeaux-Paris, Paris-Roubaix, and Paris-Tours were established before the turn of the century. The Tour de France was founded in 1903, and the tours of Belgium, Italy, the Netherlands, and Germany before World War I. And this enabled a strong professional class to build up under the sponsorship of cycle manufacturers.

The cycle industry was badly hit after World War II, however. With the increase in car ownership, cycling declined sharply as a recreation and a mode of travel. Yet as a sport it still commanded a loyal following, and an Italian professional, Fiorenzi Magni, thought of a way of using this interest for wider publicity purposes. He persuaded firms that had no connection with cycling to sponsor teams as a means of keeping their names in front of the public. And he, swarthy and balding, led the way by riding with the somewhat incongruous product name *Nivea* on his racing jersey. This saved the day for the professionals, and explains why today they ride as

1 The sun beats down on a small group of Australian cyclists racing in the 1967 Melbourne to Warrnambool road race. Such gruelling races are an integral part of the Australian cycling scene. 2 Reg Harris (left) was one of England's finest post-war cyclists. He won the 1947 world amateur sprint title, and took the professional title in 1949, 1950, 1951 and 1954. 3 The great Australian cyclists Russell Mockridge (front) and Lionel Cox. Between them, they won three golds and a silver at the 1952 Olympics. Mockridge won the 1,000 metres time trial and the 2,000 metres tandem with Cox, who was second in the 1,000 metres sprint. 4 Big names of professional cycling during the 1969 Tour de France. *From left to right;* Pingeon, Poulidor, Zimmerman, Merckx (the eventual winner), Van den Bosche, and Gutty. Pingeon was second and Poulidor third.

Melbourne Herald

Popperfoto

Melbourne Herald

virtual sandwich-board men for cigar, petrol, vermouth, and kitchen equipment firms rather than for the makers of bicycles and accessories. Cycling is still a precarious career, but the big names such as Eddy Merckx, Raymond Poulidor, and Jan Janssen are among the highest-paid sportsmen in the world.

Major events

For the professional roadmen, training starts at special centres set up by their trade teams in February. They ease into the season with one-day races along the mild Mediterranean coast, and then open up in earnest with the classics of spring and early summer. Some of these are stage races such as the Paris-Nice, 'the race to the sun', others are continuous marathons such as the Paris-Roubaix, 'the Hell of the North', over the cobblestones of northern France. Then come the great national tours which reach their climax with the Tour de France in the latter part of June. This is the great showpiece of pro-

Colour Sport

fessional racing, the 3,000-mile three-week circuit of the plains and mountains where reputations are made and lost. At the end of the tour the trade teams disband and the riders follow the schedule arranged by their agents, which takes them to a series of minor but well-paid one-day stands.

The season for the amateur roadmen is less formal, but is also made up of short races, usually in the rider's home country, and major international tours. The chief of these are the Peace Race, which links Warsaw, Prague, and East Berlin, the Tour de l'Avenir, a miniature version of the Tour de France, and the British Milk Race. This Tour of England and Wales, which began in 1951 and has been sponsored by the Milk Marketing Board since 1958, now attracts a first-class entry, especially from the countries of eastern Europe, for its fortnight's racing.

The British amateur trackmen occupy less of the limelight, though they have their big summer meet-

London Express News and Feature Services

ings at Herne Hill, at Fallowfield in Manchester, and at Leicester, the centre for the 1970 world championships. The professionals, on the other hand, nowadays ride mainly indoors. Their activities are based on the winter velodromes of Belgium, Germany, and Switzerland, and on the six-day racing circus. This opens in London in September, moves on through the major cities of western Europe into the New Year, and for some riders finishes in Melbourne, Adelaide, and Montreal months later.

The one meeting place for all these classes is the annual world championships. The amateurs and professionals have sometimes been separated—between Antwerp and Brno (Czechoslovakia) in 1969, for instance—but there is usually a continuous programme of mixed racing. Most of the prizes since the war have gone to riders from the continental countries where the

sport is strongest. But there have been some notable exceptions. Up to 1969, Beryl Burton of Yorkshire had won five world pursuit championships and two road championships. Other post-war British golds are: Reg Harris, amateur sprint 1947, professional sprint 1949-50-51-54; Cyril Peacock, amateur sprint 1954; Norman Sheil, amateur pursuit 1955 and 1958; Tom Simpson, professional road race 1965; Graham Webb, amateur road race 1967; Hugh Porter, professional pursuit 1968, 1970, 1972, and 1973, and professional sprint 1972. For Australia, gold medals were won by Sid Patterson, amateur sprint 1949, amateur pursuit 1950, professional pursuit 1952-1953; and by Graham French, motor-paced 100-km race 1956.

Cycling was included in the first Olympic Games, and in 15 other Games up to Munich. There have been no British gold medals since

the war, though Reg Harris won two silvers—in the sprint and tandem—when the Olympic torch was picked up again in London, 1948. In the team pursuit, however, British riders won the bronze in three successive Games: 1948-52-56. The best Australian result was at Helsinki in 1952 when Russell Mockridge won the 1-km time trial, and the 2-km tandem race with his fellow countryman Lionel Cox. The Robinson-Shardelow team took the silver in the tandem for South Africa that year, and Australia's Ian Browne and Anthony Marchant the gold in Melbourne four years later.

But the attraction of cycling is not confined to medal-winning. It continues to be a major pastime for amateurs of all ages and in most countries.

The drug problem

Cycle racing was hit more severely than most sports by a series of

Cycle racing takes a variety of forms on road and track . . .
1 Close finishes are typical in track sprint races. Riders jockey for position and try to 'slipstream' behind an often reluctant leader, then pounce in the final stretch.
2 Beryl Burton was twice the world women's road race champion, and five times the track pursuit champion.
3 A devil-take-the-hindmost race at London's Herne Hill track in 1968. At regular intervals the last man is eliminated until only one man—the winner—is left.
4 A Madison relay in six-day cycling: six-day ace Peter Post 'throws' his team-mate Patrick Sercu into the race.
5 Riders come down a hill and cross a ford in Westerdale, Yorkshire, on a stage of the 1969 Tour of Britain.

Glossary of Terms

Bidon Water bottle, generally of plastic, carried by the rider.

Coureur Racing cyclist, or rider.

Criterium Circuit race round the closed streets of a town or over the roads linking a group of villages. Criteriums are usually held in the latter half of the continental season after the Tour de France is over.

Demi-fond Literally, *middle-distance;* used in a special sense it refers to a motor-paced event on the track.

Devil-take-the-hindmost Popular track event in which at regular intervals—perhaps every 3, 5, or 10 laps—the last man to cross the finishing line drops out. The elimination race continues until there are only two riders left to contest the final sprint.

Domestique In road racing, the supporting rider whose job it is to devote himself to his leader's interests—to the extent of giving up his wheel if the leader punctures, marking opponents, and carrying water for him—rather than trying to win on his own account.

General classification In stage races, the overall ranking of the competitors based on the *time* they have taken to cover the distance so far. The list is published separately from the results of the day's stage.

King of the Mountains Title often awarded, both in one-day and in stage races, to the rider who wins most points in certain designated hill climbs along the way.

Lanterne rouge Booby prize, literally a *red lantern* in most cases, which goes to the last man overall in a stage race; the term also applies to the rider himself. There is some prestige attached to the prize since it shows the rider's perseverence even when he has no hope of winning the race.

Madison relay Type of relay race devised for two-man teams during the Six Day events at Madison Square Garden, New York. Both men in the team are on the track at the same time, but only one is in the race. This man, after riding flat out for anything from one lap to three laps, will relay his partner into the race with a shove on the rump or a hand sling. He will then rest by slowly circling the outside of the track until the moment comes to take over again in another relay change.

Maillot jaune Yellow jersey worn by the race leader in the Tour de France and some other stage races; also refers to the leader himself.

Musette Light satchel in which the rider picks up his rations while passing through a feeding station.

Omnium Track contest made up of a series of different types of race (sprint, devil, motor-paced, etc). Points are awarded for places in each, and the winner is the rider with most points overall.

Peloton Main bunch of riders in a road race.

Points classification In stage races, the overall ranking of the competitors according to their finishing *positions* in the stages regardless of the time factor. Various methods are used to award points. Sometimes the stage winner gets one point, the second man two, and so on—the rider who has collected the least points being, therefore, the leader. Or 15 points are given for first place, 14 for second, and so on down to 15th place, in which case the rider with the most points wins. The points contest favours the specialist sprinter, and the prize is usually equal in value and prestige to that of the King of the Mountains.

Point-to-point Track event rather like a 'devil' in reverse. At regular intervals of so many laps, the riders crossing the line are awarded points according to their placings; the eventual winner is the man who collects most points irrespective of where he finishes in the final sprint.

Prime Intermediate prize awarded to the first rider to pass a particular point in a race; this may be a mountain summit, a town boundary or landmark, or the finishing line after so many laps of the track.

Stayer Rider who specializes in motor-paced events on the track.

4

Colour Sport

5

Roy Castle

scandals and tragedies over the use of forbidden stimulants—in particular drugs of the amphetamine group—during the late sixties. The habit of taking drugs to boost the rider's physical performance was more deeply rooted among the professionals, but it also spread to the amateurs. In the amateur Tour of Britain of 1965, for instance, three Spanish riders, including the race leader, Luis Santamarina, and one Briton, were disqualified just before the start of the final stage when positive results from the dope tests came through to the organizers. Although this was the first detected case in 13 years of the British tour, such upsets were comparatively frequent on the continent. And while the fans tended to shrug them off, among sportsmen generally these disclosures did a great deal of damage to the reputation of cycle racing.

What aggravated the problem was the stubbornness of many professionals, who refused to see any danger in dope-taking, and the weakness of organizers and ruling bodies who often side-stepped the issue. Some top riders argued that stimulants were essential in relieving the hardships of their profession, and that taken prudently under medical supervision they would cause no ill-effects. In 1966 the first five men to finish in the professional world road race championships at the Nurburgring—Rudi Altig, Jacques Anquetil, Raymond Poulidor, Gianni Motta, and Jean Stablinski—refused to take a dope test. They were suspended . . . only to be absolved by the UCI a few months later.

Matters came to a head in 1967 with the death of the much-admired Tom Simpson on Mont Ventoux during the Tour de France, and the coroner's verdict that the taking of stimulants had been a contributory cause of his collapse. Even then many riders failed to learn their lesson, for in the world track championships that followed two months later at Amsterdam, a dozen competitors either failed to pass the dope tests or refused to take them. But official reaction against drugs was hardening. The 1968 Tour de France was billed as the 'Tour of Health'. Strict regulations were laid down, daily tests were carried out, and when two French riders were penalized there was no question that the controls were being exercised impartially.

Not that this was the end of the problem. In 1969 came another shock when Eddy Merckx, the most powerful rider of the day, was dismissed from the Tour of Italy after a positive result in the dope test. His suspension was lifted after a spectator admitted to having sabotaged Merckx's chances by handing him a doped drink, but in November that year the UCI, meeting in Geneva, continued its war on drugs. It issued the following scale of penalties:

Amateur. Disqualification plus one month's suspension from racing at the first offence, three months' at the second, a year's at the third, and life suspension at the fourth.

Professional. First offence, fine of 1,000 Swiss francs plus a suspended sentence of one month's disqualification from racing. Second offence, disqualification and three month's suspension. Third offence, disqualification and suspension for life.

In each case refusing to take a dope test is as much an offence as failing to pass it.

These measures may prove effective if the medical controls are stringently enforced. But the best hope of ending the drug menace is that a generation of professionals who formed the doping habit will give way to younger riders who have never taken it up. The greatest incentive to take drugs has always been that someone else was doing so and gaining an unfair advantage.

1

Above, **Walter Godefroot of Belgium, paced by a Derny moped in the final stages of the '69 Bordeaux-Paris race, which he won.**

Cyclo-Cross

Cyclo-cross is to cycle racing what cross-country running is to the track. It is the winter sport of cycling, an exciting and rugged form of cross-country racing in which the competitors ride when they can, and when the going becomes too tough they lift their bikes on their shoulders and run. The course of a race is normally about 12 to 15 miles long, and includes some combination of rough and smooth going, field and woodland, flat stretches and hills, and whatever the weather throws up in the way of mud, rain, snow, or ice. The course is planned so as to include many obstacles such as walls, fences, stiles, fallen trees, and streams, and if the landscape does not provide these hazards, then the organizers will build their own.

Although most cyclo-cross races consist of so many laps of a half-mile to two-mile circuit, there are also point-to-point events. One of

events each season, which showed that the interest-level in Britain was fast approaching that of Belgium, the stronghold of the sport, where some 200 races are annually promoted. In addition there were 80 junior and schoolboy events, and in 1969 the national championship of the Scout Movement, in only its second year, attracted nearly 200 entries.

The growth in popularity brought specialists into the game, men who reversed the old order by racing on the roads in summer to keep in training for cyclo-cross. A professional class grew up in the sixties and competition became much keener, though there is still more friendliness and humour in cyclo-cross than in most branches of cycle sport—a rider cannot rest on his dignity when he is wallowing in the mud.

With specialization went a good deal of technical development. Although the bikes had to put up with a lot of hard wear and needed frames of high-grade steel, they

the most formidable of these is the annual Three Peaks race in Yorkshire where the competitors have to scale in turn the Pen-Y-Ghent, Ingleborough, and Whernside mountains, each of them over 2,250 ft. above sea level. Mountain rescue teams often have to go out and round up the stragglers.

The precise origins of this predominantly European sport are lost, though it is thought to have been influenced by military exercises in France around the turn of the century. By the mid-twenties unofficial world championships had begun on the continent and the first primitive British event had been held—a Cyclists v Harriers challenge race at Walsall in 1921. Until World War II, however, and even for a decade afterwards, cyclo-cross remained a light-hearted form of competition that road-race cyclists entered simply as a means of keeping fit during the close season.

In 1954, when the British Cyclo-Cross Association was formed, there were only half a dozen established events, of which the best known was the Bagshot Scramble held on Bagshot Heath. But within 15 years there were 180

shed five or six pounds in weight through the sixties with the use of aluminium alloy in the handlebars, brakes, and pedals. A custom-made cyclo-cross bike, which can cost over £80, today weighs a little over 20 lb. It has five or six nylon gears, with special guards to prevent the chain wheel gathering mud, 16-oz tubular tyres with deep treads (against the 8-oz ones conventionally used on the road), double toe-clips on the pedals, a plastic saddle that will not absorb rainwater, and some kind of carrying handle. The riders wear running spikes and football studs in their shoes.

The tactics of the sport are comparatively simple. From a massed

1 A wintry mass start in a cyclo-cross event at London's Shirley Hills course.
2 The snow thaws and riders have to contend with floods.
3 Artificial obstacles break the riders' rhythm and make the race a true test of handling and manoeuvrability.
4 Belgium's Robert Vermeire leads John Atkins in the 1969 Smirnoff scramble at Harlow, eventually won by Atkins.

start the ambitious rider tries to get clear early on so that he is first over the initial obstacles and can set the pace on the narrow sections where it is difficult to overtake. On a fast dry course a certain amount of tactical teamwork is possible, the riders from one team taking turns to attack and try to tire out an opponent. But over muddy, slippery ground and on the hills, it is every man for himself. A good deal of skill in bike handling is involved, but it has to be combined with some acrobatic agility in crossing the hurdles and both speed and stamina on foot. The worse the conditions the more advantage the light, wiry man tends to have over heavier rivals.

It may seem surprising that in a sport so full of unexpected problems some riders should be so consistently successful. In fact during the first nine years of the official world championships, which began in 1950, there were only three different title holders. A Frenchman, André Dufraisse, was winner five times in succession. And in the period of 11 years, 1958-68, Rolf Wolfshohl of Germany was only twice missing from the first three places; he won three gold medals, four silver, and two bronze. Consistency even seems to run in families, for in 1968 when the Belgian Eric de Vlaeminck took his second world title in the professional class, his younger brother, Roger, won the amateur gold medal.

The outstanding British cyclo-cross rider, John Atkins (born 1942) of Coventry, won five national championships as an amateur and another when he turned professional for the 1968-69 season. His fifth place in the 1968 world championships in Luxembourg was the best ever by a British rider. With a height of 5 ft. 7 in. and weight of less than 10 stone, Atkins's greatest attribute is his light-footed nimbleness in vaulting

1 Cyclo-cross specialist John Atkins tries his luck in the water at Enfield. Though not outstanding on the road, he ranked as one of Britain's best men over the country in the 1960s and 1970s, and reigned supreme as British champion.
2 A pale English sun shines on the colourful backs of a cycle-cross field. Clear, cold weather makes the courses fast, conditions in which team tactics make the race more exciting then ever for riders and spectators alike.
3 Keith Mernickle negotiates one of the many stony gullies of the Shirley Hills course. He is one of Britain's best professional exponents of this ever-growing sport.

CYCLO-CROSS

World Championships*

Year	Winner (nationality)	Venue
1950	Jean Robic (France)	Paris
1951	Roger Rondeaux (France)	Luxembourg
1952	Roger Rondeaux (France)	Geneva
1953	Roger Rondeaux (France)	Onate
1954	Andre Dufraisse (France)	Crenna
1955	Andre Dufraisse (France)	Saarbrucken
1956	Andre Dufraisse (France)	Luxembourg
1957	Andre Dufraisse (France)	Edelaerb
1958	Andre Dufraisse (France)	Limoges
1959	Renato Longo (Italy)	Geneva
1960	Rolf Wolfshohl (Germany)	Tolosa
1961	Rolf Wolfshohl (Germany)	Hanover
1962	Renato Longo (Italy)	Esch-sur-Alzette
1963	Rolf Wolfshohl (Germany)	Calais
1964	Renato Longo (Italy)	Overboelare
1965	Renato Longo (Italy)	Cavaria
1966	Eric de Vlaeminck (Belgium)	Beasain
Professional		
1967	Renato Longo (Italy)	Zurich
1968	Eric de Vlaeminck (Belgium)	Luxembourg
1969	Eric de Vlaeminck (Belgium)	Stuttgart
1968-1973	Eric de Vlaeminck (Belgium)	
1974	Albert Van Damme (Belgium)	
Amateur		
1967	Michel Pelchat (France)	Zurich
1968	Roger de Vlaeminck (Belgium)	Luxembourg
1969	Rene Declercq (Belgium)	Stuttgart
1970	Robert Vermiere (Belgium)	
1971	Robert Vermiere (Belgium)	
1972	Norbert de Deckere (Belgium)	
1973	Klaus-Peter Thaler (West Germany)	
1974	Robert Vermiere (Belgium)	

* Held as an Open championship from 1950 to 1966

over the obstacles and jogging uphill over really rough country. Unlike Wolfshohl and Eric de Vlaeminck, who are all-rounders, Atkins is very much a specialist who has never been able to reproduce such commanding form in road races.

Although cyclo-cross is the most recent addition to cycle sport, it is also the fastest-growing. It has the advantage of being spectacular and sometimes amusing to watch. It is fun to take part in—even for quite ordinary performers there is some stoical satisfaction to be gained simply by finishing the course—and for a number of good reasons it is being encouraged by schools and youth organizations. While there are frequent spills, they are rarely serious; the riders usually fall harmlessly on soft ground. And of course there is no danger or inconvenience from other traffic. As more private cars take over the public roads, so more cyclists are likely to take to the fields and hills.

Diving

In modern international sport, there are few pursuits requiring more skill or more courage than diving. In its present-day concept, diving demands a mixture of dramatic acrobatics, concentration and consistency, elegance and *élan*, plus almost blind courage of a high order.

Divers are expected to perform intricate somersaulting and twisting movements from whip-lash springboards or 35-foot-high platforms. To miss hitting the diving board while in the middle of a complicated feat of agility is enough in itself, but to it must be added the ability to plummet through the air with graceful ease and make a perpendicular entry into the water.

Though diving is a water sport, the only part water plays is in providing the landing area; soft, blue, and inviting in the eyes of the inexperienced, but hard and unfriendly to the diver hurtling to break its surface at more than 30 miles an hour.

Fortunately for the competitors these days there are people who understand the demands of their sport. There are deep diving pits, often separate from the swimming pool, with specially designed boards and stages. There are detailed safety regulations governing the depth of water under and around the boards. And there are highly knowledgeable and specialized coaches to teach their craft.

This was not so at the end of the 19th century, when diving first became a competitive sport. Then, divers were expected to compete in water areas quite unsuited to diving, without being able to see the bottom or any hidden dangers, and in shallow pools that these days would not be sanctioned.

The first divers were, indeed, a heroic breed, and from their early beginnings the most sophisticated developments have come about.

Diving facilities

The tools of the divers' trade—the boards—had none of the modern advantages. Even in 1920 the only technical requirement of an international springboard was that it should be 'a little springy', while the 10-metre highboard, which had to be a minimum of 15 feet long, could be narrow and perched on a rickety wooden staging that would shake and shudder with the wind and the action of the divers.

The springboards of the 1970s are sophisticated descendants of the early wooden plank boards, made of thin wooden core, surfaced with glass-fibre, or fabricated totally in light alloys. These are mounted on precision moveable fulcrums, and measurement requirements are laid down to centimetres.

The usual international pool complex has 1 and 3-metre springboards and 5, 7½ and 10-metre firm highboards. There are regulations covering the siting of the boards, how far they must be from the back and side walls of the pool and from each other.

Most important are the regulations dealing with the minimum depths of water around and in front of the boards. These are:

Springboard

1-metre	3-metre
3.40 m	3.80 m
(11 ft. 2 in.)	(12 ft. 6 in.)

Highboard

5-metre	10-metre
3.80 m	4.50 m
(12 ft. 6 in.)	(14 ft. 9 in.)

For smaller baths with low firm platforms, the minimum depth is 3.40 metres for the 1 and 3-metre boards, though many older baths have nowhere near this depth yet still have diving boards.

The springboard must be at least 4.8 metres long and 0.5 metres wide, and covered along the whole length with rough coconut matting unless it has a non-slip surface.

The highboard must be rigid and covered with a resilient hardwood surface, although the staging may be of concrete or other like material. The 5-metre board must be 1.5 metres wide and 6.0 metres long, and the 10-metre board 2.0 metres wide and 6.0 metres long.

History

Like swimming, diving goes back so far into the history of mankind that it is impossible to say when man first entered the water headfirst. Certainly, the Pacific Islanders were fearless divers, as Lady Brassey tells in the *Badminton Book of Swimming*, published in London in 1894.

Writing of a voyage in the ship *Sunbeam* to Hawaii, she said: 'We found half the population of Hilo putting on a show for us, taking headers and footers (jumps) and siders (twists) from the cliffs up to 25 feet. Then came the special display in which two natives were to jump from a precipice 100 feet high into the river below, clearing on their way down a rock at 80 feet which projected some 20 feet from the face of the cliff.

'Two men, tall, strong and sinewy, appeared against the skyline far above us, their long hair bound back by wreathes of leaves and flowers with other garlands round their waists. Then they disappeared from sight to take their runs, reappearing with bounds from the edge of the rock, turning over in mid-air and disappearing feet first into the water. Another

Pat Besford

Radio Times Hulton Picture Library

1 Albert Dickin , three times England's plain diving champion, winning the title in the harbour at Plymouth Hoe in 1926.
2 Greta Johansson, Olympic plain high diving champion in 1912, diving at Highgate Ponds, in London, the headquarters of the Highgate Diving Club until shortly before World War II.

Photographic Library of Australia

Courtesy of the Amateur Swimming Association

native, who a year before had broken several ribs and spent six months in hospital, did a standing turn over dive from the projecting rock and added a twist on the way down.'

The islanders who 'turned over' were doing what came naturally to them, but their dives, in fact, were the forerunners of the forward somersault and its later developments up to the 3½ somersault. The daring one who twisted as well as somersaulted, unknowingly, was setting a pattern for the combined multi-movement dives of the modern era, such as the forward 2½ somersault with two twists and the forward 1½ somersault with three twists, two of the most difficult in the international list.

Diving of a sort, too, was known in London in 1871 when a Mr J. B. Johnson, a noted swimmer, caused a sensation by diving from London Bridge in an exhibition mock rescue of his brother Peter, who was an equally good swimmer. Later, in the United States, bridge jumping became a favourite pastime of the courageous.

Competitively, the first head-into-the-water championship was for *plunging*, staged by the Amateur Swimming Association of England in 1883 and won by T. H. Clarke. This was not diving in the true sense, for the main aim, having plunged in, was to float forwards on the surface for as far and as long as breath and momentum would allow. Mr Clarke managed to achieve 63 ft. 2 in.

Diving proper followed inevitably, with Scotland showing the way in 1889 with their Graceful Diving championship, won in the first year by J. Milne of the Northern Glasgow Club. In 1895, the

Courtesy of the Amateur Swimming Association

1 Richmond Eve, Australia's only Olympic diving medallist, won the plain diving event at the Paris Olympics in 1924.
2 H. E. Pott, from London's Otter SC, was the English champion in 1909, 1910, and 1911. The temporary scaffolding stage he dives from was a typical feature of early diving.
3 A swallow dive from Arvid Spangberg in the 1908 Games. He took the bronze medal in the fancy high diving, an event in which Swedish competitors occupied the first three places.

Royal Life Saving Society held their first National Graceful Diving competition for men, open to all amateurs in the world. H. S. Martin of the London St James's club was the winner for the first two years, followed by a Belgian, V. Sonnemans, of Brussels, and later by assorted visitors from Scandinavia, including Hjalmar Johansson of Sweden, the 1908 Olympic champion who, in fact, won this British event five times.

Johansson was also the first winner of the High Fancy Diving championship, instituted by the Amateur Diving Association—

later to become part of the ASA in 1903. The ASA High Diving championship followed in 1907 and the first major competition for women, the King's Cup, organized by the RLSS, took place in 1911.

The Olympic Games
Diving came into the Olympic programme at the St Louis Games in 1904 when the competition for men, with dives from both highboard and springboard, was won by Dr George Sheldon of the United States.

There were separate competitions from these two boards at the 1908 Olympics in London. Ger-

many had an almost clean sweep of the medals in the springboard, which was won narrowly by 18-year-old Albert Zürner from Kurt Behrens, with Gottlob Walz tieing America's George Gaidzik for third—the only official tie for a diving medal in any Games.

The Swedes, with the advantage of magnificent facilities at home, were supreme in the highboard, taking the title through Hjalmar Johansson, then 35 years old, who had been Swedish champion continually since 1897, except for the two years he spent in London. And they won the silver and bronze through Karl Malmstrom and Arvid Spangberg.

By 1912, at the Stockholm Games, there were three diving events for men, while women made their first appearance in the pool with a plain high diving contest (as well as freestyle swimming races).

Germany won all three medals on the springboard, Sweden and Germany shared the fancy high diving medals, while Sweden had a clean sweep of the honours in their speciality, the new plain high diving event. The first lady champion was also a Swede, Greta Johansson—no relation to Hjalmar. Her team-mate Lisa Regnell took the silver and Belle White, Britain's first diving medallist, the bronze.

The achievement of Miss White, then 18, who started diving at 10 years of age and gave displays in Paris at 14, was a great effort considering the difficulties the London girl had in obtaining training on 5 and 10-metre boards. Her only local highboard facilities were in the men's pool at the Highgate Ponds, to which women were admitted, as a concession, on

one day a week. Much of her other training had to be from the tiny platforms attached to unsteady ladders, rising from the end of seaside piers at Brighton and Clacton. So, the year before the Stockholm Games, she went to Sweden for two months to train from their fine wooden platforms. Essentially a firm-board competitor, Miss White's record is remarkable. She competed in four Olympics (1912-1928), won the first European highboard title in 1927 at the age of 33, and gained numerous national championship medals.

The American stranglehold on Olympic diving began in earnest in the 1920 Antwerp Games. They won all six springboard medals (a women's event was instituted that year) and the gold and bronze in the men's highboard. Only in the plain diving field did Scandinavia and Britain still reign supreme. The Swedish men repeated their 1912 feat of taking gold, silver, and bronze. In the women's, Stefani Fryland-Clausen won Denmark's sole diving gold, Eileen Armstrong became Britain's only diving silver medal winner, and Sweden's Eva Ollivier was third.

By 1928, the Olympic diving programme had been reduced to four events—highboard and springboard for men and women—and these are the ones that have been held ever since.

Olympic medals

Since diving was included in the Olympics (1904), the United States have won 101 of the 167 medals awarded up to and in-cluding the 1972 Olympics. These include all the golds in the men's springboard from 1920 to 1968; all the silvers except in 1968 and 1972; and 9 of the 12 bronzes. America's men have been first in 9 of the 12 highboard contests (including double golds by Sammy Lee in 1948 and 1952 and by Robert Webster in 1960 and 1964) and 14 of the other 24 medals.

The girls from the United States made a clean sweep of the springboard medals between 1920 and 1948 (18 in all). They were first and second in the highboard from 1924 to 1956. Among these winners were Dorothy Poynton in 1932 and 1936 (the latter year as Mrs Poynton-Hill), Vicky Draves who won both the springboard and the highboard in 1948, and the redoubtable Mrs McCormick who won the highboard and springboard in 1956 and 1960 to become the most bemedalled diving girl of the Olympics with four golds. And they had the youngest champion of all, Marjorie Gestring, who won the 1936 springboard in Berlin at the age of 13.

Germany and Sweden have each won 20, most of these between 1904 and 1924. Germany's total includes the three golds and one silver effort of Ingrid Krämer (later Mrs Engel-Krämer), who was first in both her events in 1960 and retained her springboard crown in 1964 when she was also second from the highboard.

The remaining 32 diving medals are shared among 12 nations. Mexico's six include four by Joaquim Capilla who, on the

1 Clarence Pinkston of the United States winning his heat of the springboard diving at the Paris Olympics in 1924. He was third in the final, and he won the fancy high diving event.
2 Victoria Draves did the diving 'double' at the 1948 Games, winning both highboard and springboard competitions.
3 Dr Sammy Lee, one of diving's 'greats', winces as he enters feet first during the highboard event at the 1948 Olympics. He went on to win the title and take a bronze in the springboard diving, and he retained his title at Helsinki in 1952.

highboard, was third in 1948, second in 1952, and champion, at last, in 1956, the year when he also took a springboard bronze.

Italy's four all belong to Klaus Dibiasi (second in the highboard 1964, and first in 1968 and 1972, and second springboard 1968). Britain's five, none of them gold, include both springboard bronzes in 1960 through Brian Phelps and Elizabeth Ferris. Denmark claim one winner in Miss Fryland (plain high diving 1920) and a bronze. The other golds went to Australia's Richmond Eve (plain high diving 1924) and little Milena Duchkova of Czechoslovakia, the highboard heroine of Mexico City in 1968, who decisively beat her Russian rival in an emotive confrontation. Russia, despite a fair record in Europe, did not produce their first Olympic winner until Vasin won the men's springboard in 1972,

Central Press

U P I

though their women have won two silvers and two bronzes since 1960. Egypt (2), Canada and France (1) complete the line-up.

Other major competitions

With the introduction of European championships in 1926 and the Empire and Commonwealth Games in 1930, there were new, and welcome, competitive opportunities for non-Americans. Two teams emerged as top nations —Germany, with 16 of 42 European titles, and England, with 16 out of 32 Empire and Commonwealth golds.

In Europe, three men have won titles at successive championships. Two were Germans, Hans Luber (highboard in 1926 and 1927) and Ewald Riebschläger (springboard 1927 and 1931). The third was Britain's Brian Phelps, who, in 1958, became the youngest champion when he won the highboard

1 A graceful reverse dive by Britain's Liz Ferris that helped her to the springboard bronze in the 1960 Olympics.
2 Bob Webster goes into a forward 1½ somersault from the 10 metre board at Tokyo, where he retained his title.
3 Pat McCormick was the most successful female diver in history, with four Olympic golds to her credit.
4 Mexico's Joaquin Capilla was Latin-America's answer to United States domination in diving. Only once an Olympic winner (highboard in 1956) he also won three place medals.
5 Scotland's Peter Heatly amassed five Commonwealth Games medals—two highboard golds (1950 and 1958) and a bronze in 1954, a springboard silver in 1950, and the gold at Vancouver in 1954.

with consummate ease, diving from the 10-metre board seven times his own height and beating, at the age of 14, men old enough to be his father. Phelps retained his crown in 1962 but had to be content with a silver in 1966, bowing out with honour to Klaus Dibiasi.

In women's diving France had two golden years—1947 and 1950. Mady Moreau topped the springboard and Nicole Pelissard the highboard on both occasions. The first double winner had been Germany's Olga Jensch-Jordan (springboard 1931 and 1934) with Betty Slade gaining Britain's only gold in 1938 at the Empire Pool, Wembley, after a near disaster. She crashed badly on her second dive and lost vital marks, yet pulled back miraculously to beat the much favoured German Gerda Daumerlang by 1.32 points.

England, in winning 33 per cent

of the Empire and Commonwealth gold medals, claim four champions out of twelve in each of the four events. Most successful was Brian Phelps, highboard and springboard champion in 1962 and 1966 and highboard silver medallist in 1958. Scotland's Peter Heatly, Vice-Chairman of the Organizing Committee for the 1970 Commonwealth Games in Edinburgh, also won five, a gold for highboard and a springboard silver in 1950, a springboard gold and a highboard bronze in 1954, and a highboard gold in 1958, in beating Phelps by 3.3 points.

Edna Child of England took both her events in 1950, as did Charmian Welsh, also England, in 1958, and Australia's Sue Knight in 1962. Kathy Rowlatt (springboard) and Joy Newman (highboard) completed a clean sweep of the titles for England in 1966.

Organization

The supreme governing body for swimming, which includes diving, water polo, and synchronized swimming, is the Fédération Internationale de Natation Amateur (FINA), founded in London in 1908. FINA delegate diving responsibility to their sub-committee, the International Diving Committee.

This committee frame all diving laws, approve the addition of new dives to the international tariff, appoint officials to control the Olympic diving competitions, and approve the specifications for all diving equipment.

The Ligue Européenne de Natation (European Swimming League) have a similar diving sub-committee to organize their activities, as do all the National Swimming Federations of the countries practising this sport seriously.

There is no standardization of ages for junior competitions. For the European Youth championships, held every two years, competitors may not be more than 15. For the ASA events, a junior is one who is under 17 on 31 December in the year of the championship.

A diving competition

To organize a diving event is a complicated process and the compiling of the judges' points, awarded for each dive, requires accurate mathematical calculations. In fact, at the 1964 Olympic Games, a computer was used.

In charge is a referee, who is the final arbiter on everything. He announces the name of the competitor and the dive to be performed, gives a signal (usually a whistle) for the dive to commence, another signal for the judges to display their marks, which he then announces for the recorders (sometimes called secretaries) to enter on the recording sheets.

The judges, normally five, though for major events such as the Olympics there are seven, mark each dive up to 10 based on the following standard.

	Points
Completely failed	0
Unsatisfactory	$\frac{1}{2}$—2
Deficient	$2\frac{1}{2}$—$4\frac{1}{2}$
Satisfactory	5—6
Good	$6\frac{1}{2}$—8
Very good	$8\frac{1}{2}$—10

The highest and lowest marks are then eliminated. This leaves five scores in an Olympic-type event (or three in a lesser event), and these marks are added together by the two recording officials. For example: $(6\frac{1}{2})$, $6\frac{1}{2}$, 7, 7, 7, $7\frac{1}{2}$, $(7\frac{1}{2})$ = 35 points.

In awarding their marks, the judges ignore the difficulty of the dive, concentrating solely on their impression of the diver's movement from the start of the run, or the standing take-off, the technique and grace of the flight through the air, and the entry—perpendicular is the ideal—into the water.

The evaluation of the dive on its comparative difficulty is made through the international tariff tables, which state a degree of difficulty of each dive. And the aggregate of the judges' marks is multiplied by this tariff figure. With the tariff figures ranging from 1.2 to 3.0, it is easy to see how degree of difficulty rating materially affects the final mark entered on each competitor's recording sheet. For example, taking the 35 points earned by the mythical diver above on two different dives from the 3-metre springboard: a forward dive (straight), with a tariff of 1.6, would score 56.00 points; and a forward $3\frac{1}{2}$ somersault (tucked), with a tariff of 2.7, would score 94.50 points.

At the end of the competition the aggregate of the judges' marks, multiplied by the appropriate tariff values, is the final score for the diver. But in competitions in which there are five scoring judges (after taking off the top and bottom marks), the grand total is reduced to a three-judge level by dividing these points by five and then multiplying by three. This is done to have a world-wide standardization of scores, there being more events in which there are three scoring judges than five.

This elaborate system is not necessary for lesser events in which the referee, judges (and there may be as few as three), or recorder may carry out more than one function.

The diving authorities have settled on this process after much trial and error, in an effort to get as fair a result as possible in a sport that is always open to doubt and difficulty because the result depends upon personal opinion (that of the judges) and not point of fact.

There was a time, from 1904 up to 1920, when the judges' place marks, and not the points given for the dives, determined the result. Now, with the scores taken down to two decimal points, diving is as fair as it is humanly possible to be.

Coaching

In this highly individualistic sport with so many facets, it is not surprising that the task of the coach is a demanding one. Each dive by each diver in a squad has to be watched and corrected. And as one practice can take two hours or more, it is tiring work.

In most countries, there are external problems, too, such as a shortage of deep pools with good boards in which the divers can train without worrying about swimmers underneath them.

Separate pits are the answer, but there are not so many of these. If a diver does crash onto a swimmer, the force can break limbs.

Technique

The style and standards of diving

3

4

Courtesy of the Amateur Swimming Association

5

Associated Press

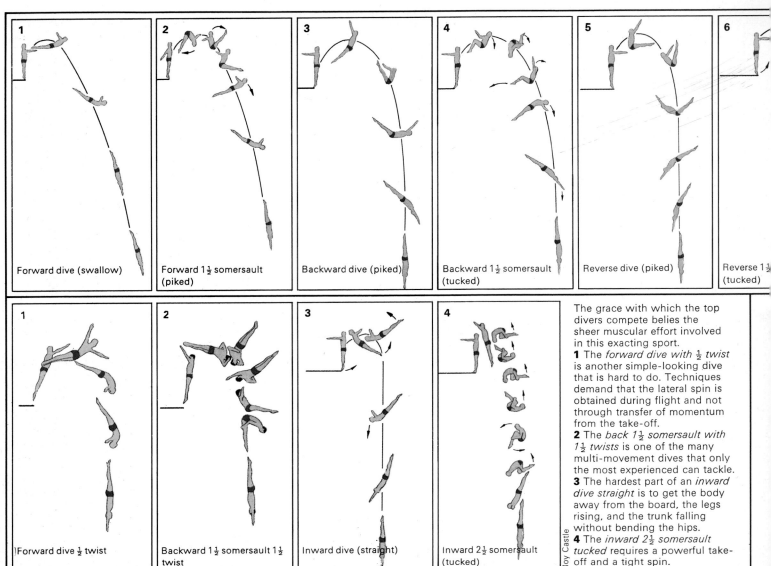

1 Forward dive (swallow)

2 Forward 1½ somersault (piked)

3 Backward dive (piked)

4 Backward 1½ somersault (tucked)

5 Reverse dive (piked)

6 Reverse 1½ (tucked)

1 Forward dive ½ twist

2 Backward 1½ somersault 1½ twist

3 Inward dive (straight)

4 Inward 2½ somersault (tucked)

The grace with which the top divers compete belies the sheer muscular effort involved in this exacting sport.

1 The *forward dive with ½ twist* is another simple-looking dive that is hard to do. Techniques demand that the lateral spin is obtained during flight and not through transfer of momentum from the take-off.

2 The *back 1½ somersault with 1½ twists* is one of the many multi-movement dives that only the most experienced can tackle.

3 The hardest part of an *inward dive straight* is to get the body away from the board, the legs rising, and the trunk falling without bending the hips.

4 The *inward 2½ somersault tucked* requires a powerful take-off and a tight spin.

Roy Castle

International Diving Competition Tests

In all major national and international events (including the European championships and the Commonwealth Games) the Olympic tests for diving are used.

SPRINGBOARD (3 METRES)

Men: Five required dives (forward, back, reverse, and inward dives, and forward dive ½ twist) and six voluntary dives selected from the five groups, making a total of 11 dives.

Women: Five required dives (as for a men's event) and five voluntary dives, making a total of 10 dives.

HIGHBOARD (5, 7½ or 10 METRES)*

Men: Six dives with a combined degree of difficulty not exceeding 11.2, and four voluntary dives without limit. In each section each dive must be selected from a different group. Total, 10 dives.

Women: Four required dives (forward, back, reverse, and inward) and four voluntary dives selected from four groups, making a total of 8 dives.

In selecting dives for the second section of their competitions, divers may not repeat any dives they have performed in the first section, even in a different body position.

In major competitions with big entries, all competitors perform all but the last three dives of their test. The best 12 compete in a final round consisting of their last three dives.

This system, with small variations, has been used for most of the diving era, but different ways have been used to determine the winner. In the 1908 Olympic Games, for example, the divers went through heats, semi-finals, and finals, on lines similar to swimming races, performing the whole of their diving test in each round.

*Because of the higher tariff values of dives from the 10-metre board, all leading competitors use only the top platform.

have become progressively more elegant and difficult as techniques and facilities have improved. On the old thick plank springboard (though it had little or no spring) a running dive called for a sharp sprint along the board and a one-foot take-off rather like the long-jump athlete in action. But on the sensitive, flexible, slender modern board the approach is absolutely different. The diver walks smoothly and unhurriedly, does a controlled hurdle step (as though there is an obstacle across the board to clear), and lands with both feet on the end in order to depress the board and then take advantage of the recoil to obtain maximum lift into the dive.

Natural and graceful body lines are the modern way to earn high marks from the judges. This was not so in the early 1900s, when the demands were for force and energy, with chest well expanded and the back hollowed.

Many of the old dives not only looked unnatural but were contrary to body mechanics, like some of the dives performed up to 1920 in which the arms had to be pressed to the sides throughout.

One of these was the ordinary header forward (arms by sides) in which the diver literally did take off head first, somehow, without the directional help of his arms, managed to get his feet moving upwards behind him fast enough to turn his body 180°, and go straight into the water literally headfirst.

A more dangerous exercise it is hard to imagine. Without the protection of arms above the head, the diver could very easily crack his skull on the bottom, especially in the old shallow baths, often with only 5 ft. 6 in. of water.

The importance of the arms in controlling the flight was appreciated to a high degree by the Swedes in the early years of this century, and they pioneered the swallow, still one of the key dives.

The swallow, which is the only version of the plain dive used in modern competition, was known then as the 'Swedish swallow'. It was a variation of the original 'English header' plain dive in which the arms were swung above the head on take off and kept in this position until entry into the water, giving no possibility of correcting errors in flight.

In the Swedish swallow, the

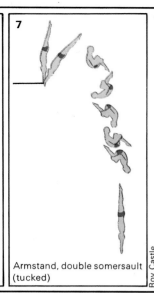

7

Armstand, double somersault (tucked)

Roy Castle

1 The *swallow* is one of the most graceful dives, yet its simplicity is deceptive, for it is most difficult to perform correctly. Well-placed arms, no hollow in the back, and a vertical entry earn good marks.

2 The *forward 1½ somersault*, in the open pike position, is used particularly from the 10 metre platform. From the spring-board it is usually performed in the closed position with hands on shins and a tight body fold.

3 The diver pushes vigorously upwards and outwards in the *backward dive piked*, lifting his legs strongly into the pike position. The legs are stretched upwards as the shoulders and head pull back for entry.

4 The *backward 2½ somersault with tuck* requires even greater momentum from the board and stretch on entry to check the spin.

5, 6 Momentum and correct angle of take-off are even more important in reverse movements, in which the hands reach upwards and the shoulders are pressed back as the chest rises. If the take-off is done correctly in the *reverse dive piked* (**5**) or *reverse 1½ somersault tucked* (**6**), the diver need have no fear of hitting the board as he turns into his backward movement.

7 The key to the *armstand and double somersault* is the initial hand-balance. The diver must do this consistently and surely, and show a steady balance before pushing away with his hands into his double somersault.

Keystone

Top Right: Brian Phelps, highboard champion of Europe in 1958 (when he was only 14 years old) and again in 1962, and four times a Commonwealth champion, demonstrates the armstand position.
Above: Wales's Mandi Haswell floats gracefully down from the 10 metre board during the 1966 Commonwealth Games in Jamaica.

arms were swung up and out almost to shoulder level, then closed to the above-the-head position before entering the water. This arms-wide technique allowed the diver to correct any small errors in take-off, and the final, closing movement of his arms enabled him to realign his dive to make the ideal of a perpendicular entry. So, if the dive was a little flat, the arms would be closed below the face and the head lowered into them; by closing behind the head a dive that was going over could be checked. Modifications of this technique are used to adjust and control head-first entry dives to this day.

What the early divers did not know was how to avoid knocks and bruises sustained on hitting the water, especially from high boards. The speed and force of their entries sent their hands and wrists crashing against each other, against their upper arms and shoulders and even their heads. They often landed painfully on their chests. Flat dives meant a stinging stomach, and dives that were 'over' caused hurtful landings on the back.

Now, divers lock their shoulders and arms by overlapping their hands and gripping their thumbs. This way, they punch through the surface of the water and soften their head-first entries.

The most difficult early dives were the 1½ somersault forward and inward and the straight dive with one twist. Now, with multi-spinning, multi-twisting, and combinations of both, the modern competitor requires a high level of understanding of body mechanics to activate and then check his aerial acrobatics and yet plunge arrow-like into the water.

It takes courage to be a diver. But those who start never want to stop. Standing on the 10-metre board, looking down on the pigmy-like people below, then soaring as free as a bird, is to a diver as exciting as flying.

Dressage

The art of improving one's horse beyond the stage of plain usefulness, dressage can transform a plain horse into an attractive one. Derived from the French *dresser*, meaning 'to teach' or 'school' (an animal), the word, however, implies more than teaching fundamental obedience, and the whole idea of the art is to make the horse more amenable, easier to control, more graceful in its bearing, and better in its looks. The horse is trained to execute certain movements with extreme precision and smoothness, and an animal trained to perfection in advanced dressage is a revelation to all and a joy to watch.

In its competitive form, dressage is seen in two spheres—first as a test in itself and secondly as one of the three sections of horse trials or three-day events. As an individual test, dressage has exercises for various standards, with the grand prix the ultimate goal of its advanced form. The grand prix test is used in the dressage competition at the Olympic Games, into which it was introduced in 1912. The grand prix includes the following classical exercises: *passage* (an elevated slow trot), *piaffe* (an elevated marking time at the trot), canter changes of leg at every stride, changes of direction on two tracks at the canter, and pirouette. The test is a demanding one, and it is not unusual for a horse to have at least five years' training before it has achieved a standard suitable for grand prix dressage. In the Olympic three-day event, the dressage test is of a medium standard and takes place on the first day of the competition. It is second in importance to the speed and endurance section that follows on the second day, the full points ratio for the event being: dressage 3, speed and endurance 12, and show-jumping 2.

The modern principles of dressage are laid down by the Fédération Equestre Internationale (FEI) to which all equestrian nations of any moment belong. Its prescriptions on matters of dressage are based on the traditions and practices of the world's most famous equestrian institutes such as the French Cavalry School at Saumur, the Spanish Riding School of Vienna, the German Cavalry School of Hanover, and the cavalry schools of Sweden and of Switzerland, both famous for the riders they have produced. The theory of modern dressage, and much of its practice, finds its roots in the schools of the 17th and 18th centuries, which produced their most famous exponent in F.R. de la Guérinière, author of *Ecole de Cavalarie*.

The Spanish Riding School of

Fox Photos

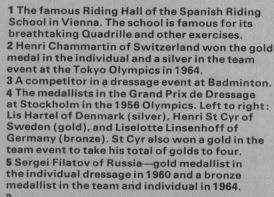

1 The famous Riding Hall of the Spanish Riding School in Vienna. The school is famous for its breathtaking Quadrille and other exercises.
2 Henri Chammartin of Switzerland won the gold medal in the individual and a silver in the team event at the Tokyo Olympics in 1964.
3 A competitor in a dressage event at Badminton.
4 The medallists in the Grand Prix de Dressage at Stockholm in the 1956 Olympics. Left to right: Lis Hartel of Denmark (silver), Henri St Cyr of Sweden (gold), and Liselotte Linsenhoff of Germany (bronze). St Cyr also won a gold in the team event to take his total of golds to four.
5 Sergei Filatov of Russia—gold medallist in the individual dressage in 1960 and a bronze medallist in the team and individual in 1964.

Keystone

Vienna is known all over the world for its displays of *haute école* in the exquisitely beautiful and famous Riding Hall that was completed in 1735. Founded in the late 16th century to teach the art of horsemanship in its highest forms, this school of classical riding uses only Lippizaner stallions, descendants of the original Spanish horses, and the introduction of Arab blood has resulted in a horse of spectacular presence and temperament. A rider serves an apprenticeship of 10 to 15 years before becoming a finished Bereiter, specializing in 'airs above the ground', the *courbette* (the execution of several jumps on the hind legs without the forelegs touching the ground), *capriole* (leaping into the air off all four legs and kicking out with hind legs in mid-air), *levade* (holding a raised position on the hind legs), and other exercises.

The type of horse used in dressage varies according to the standard to be ultimately obtained, but for many the English thoroughbred, endowed with the necessary calm temperament, would be the ideal. The requisites for a suitable dressage horse are intelligence and elegance coupled with straight movement, a well 'let-down' hind leg, and a strong but supple back. All horses will improve physically as their dressage training progresses, but just as some human beings are more athletic than others, so some horses are more suited to excel in this art than their fellows. However, every horse needs a modicum of dressage to be really effective for any purpose beyond the stage of plain utility, and some require a great deal. The top-class showjumper, the three-day event horse, the show hack, the police horse, and the troop horse are all subject to dressage training to a greater or lesser degree.

In the majority of Olympic Games, the European countries have proved outstanding in the dressage events. Germany, Russia, Sweden, Switzerland, and France have provided many medal-winning teams and they have also produced some of the great individual dressage medallists. Swedish horsemen took the first three places at the 1912 Olympics and repeated this performance at the first post-war Olympics, in 1920—a feat that had not been equalled 50 years later. Until 1928, the individual was the only class in the Games, but teams were included from 1928, although there was no team event in 1960.

And it is a Swedish rider, Henri St Cyr, who has won more Olympic dressage gold medals, four, than any other competitor. This figure would have been five had the Swedish team not been disqualified after winning the team event in 1948 because one of their team was ineligible under FEI rules. St Cyr won golds in the individual and team events in 1952, and again in 1956 when both he and the Swedish team retained their titles.

After winning a bronze at Mexico City in 1968, Switzerland's Henri Chammartin had won five medals—a gold, two silver, and two bronze—in an Olympic career that began in 1952 and was highlighted when he won the individual event on Woermann in 1964. That same year, a strong German team including Josef Neckermann and Harry Boldt, who was runner-up in the individual, won the team event. Neckermann won his second gold as a member of the West German team in 1968, the year that Ivan Kizimov won the individual and collected a silver in the team event. Kizimov's victory showed that earlier Russian successes—an individual gold by Sergei Filatov in 1960 and two bronze medals in 1964—had not been a flash in the pan and that the Russians were a force to be reckoned with in future dressage grands prix.

Keystone

DRESSAGE Olympic Champions		
Year	Individual	Team
1912	Carl Bonde (Sweden)	not held
1920	Janne Lundblad (Sweden)	not held
1924	Ernst Linder (Sweden)	not held
1928	Carl von Langen (Germany)	Germany
1932	Francois Lesage (France)	France
1936	Heinrich Pollay (Germany)	Germany
1948	Hans Moser (Switzerland)	France
1952	Henri St Cyr (Sweden)	Sweden
1956	Henri St Cyr (Sweden)	Sweden
1960	Sergey Filatov (USSR)	not held
1964	Henri Chammartin (Switzerland)	Germany
1968	Ivan Kizimov (USSR)	W. Germany
1972	Liselott Lisenhoff (W. Germany)	USSR

Picturepoint

Keystone

Fell Running

Fell running is a sport confined to the highland areas of Britain—the mountains of Scotland, the Lake District, the fells of north Yorkshire and Lancashire, and the upland areas of Northumberland. As an organized sport, it is relatively new, and still does not have a governing body.

In its simplest form, fell running consists of racing from one prominent point to another, either on an 'out-and-home' or a circular route. The runners are free to take their own paths across country, and in bad weather they often have to navigate using map and compass, as clouds and mist may obscure the landscape in the hills. The challenge is not only presented by the weather: the runs take place over some of the most rugged countryside in Britain.

Though essentially a form of cross-country running, fell running is a sport apart. A run may be up to 20 miles long, and one recognized run—the 'Lake District Four Three-Thousander'—is 40 miles long. Speeds too are different: anything over 5 mph may be considered very good going. Beginners can tackle events as short as 1½ miles, and build up to the longer distances.

While the shorter races are arduous and keenly contested, the classics of fell running are the longer events. Pride of place is

1 Fell runners set off in the 1969 Three Peaks race, won by Mike Davis (right). The 22-mile run is the nearest approach to a national fell running championship. 2 Weary runners ascend the Malvern Hills in the 1970 Worcestershire Beacon race.

taken by the Ben Nevis race—the toughest and most dangerous. The 12-mile course from Fort William climbs the 4,406-foot mountain, the highest in Britain, and then back again. The first recorded run was made in 1895 by William Swan of Fort William who negotiated the tricky mountainside in 2 hr 41 min. In 1964, Peter Hall of Barrow won the race in 1 hr 38 min 56 sec, a record for the course. At least one fatality has been recorded in this race.

But the run that carries the title of the 'Fell Runners' National' is the Three Peaks race. Held annually in north-west Yorkshire since 1954, the race includes three well-known peaks in the area—Ingleborough (2,373 ft.), Pen-y-Ghent (2,273 ft.), and Whernside (2,419 ft.). The record for this 22-mile race, 2 hr 40 min 34 sec, was set in 1968 by Mike Davies of Reading, who won the race four times in succession and, in 1965, became the first 'southerner' to win.

Other major races include: in the Lake District, the Ennersdale Horseshoe (23 miles) and the Vaux Mountain trial (15-20 miles); in Lancashire, the Three Towers race (18 miles); and in Northumberland, the Chevy Chase, a run of 17 miles over the Cheviot Hills. In parts of England where strictly there are no 'fells', similar races are held. Two prominent ones are the Ten Tors race on Dartmoor and the Beacon race in Worcestershire.

Mike Davies' wins in the Three Peaks are really an exception to the general trend, that the best fell runners are local men. Peter Watson of Bramley was possibly the most consistent fell runner of the 1960s, with seven victories in each of two short distance runs, the Harden Moss (2½ miles) and the Bursall 'Classic' (1¾ miles). In the long runs, the man bidding for the title of 'King of the Fells' was Colin Robinson of Rochdale who in 1969 won the Three Peaks, the Rossendale Fells run (9 miles), and the Three Towers race (a run inaugurated in 1969 and held near Bury).

The fell runner, with only map, compass, and *cagoule* (the all-embracing cape of the fellsman) to aid his own wits, is a strange figure in the moorland landscape. To climb from sunny valleys up into the cloud-shrouded summits for mile after mile and finish the course is his satisfaction: to win is merely a bonus.

Fencing

The skilful use of swords according to set rules and movements, fencing has a long and fascinating history and owes much to the traditions of chivalry. It has developed through the centuries to become a modern and athletic sport that is widely practised throughout the world.

The growth of interest in the sport reflects its many advantages. And they are not just advantages that the specialists benefit from. Fencing provides the enthusiast with concentrated exercise in a short space of time, no matter what the weather, and it is an ideal sport especially for those who live in towns. Nor does it require a large venue—any resonably large room will do—or expensive apparatus. And any multiple of two can practise together.

One of the great advantages of fencing is that it develops balance, poise, and muscular control combined with a high degree of co-ordination of mind and body. A bout in a club brings a wonderful sense of relaxation and freshness to both mind and body because it is so concentrated that it is impossible to fence and think of anything else. It provides a medium for quick thinking, speed, and finesse, and, since there is no advantage to be gained from mere brute strength, differences of physical attributes such as height or strength are largely levelled off. Consequently, boys and girls can fence together at foil on far more level terms than is possible at most other active sports.

But fencing is a difficult art to master and much time must be devoted to learning it and gaining competitive experience. Once a sound technique has been acquired, though, the enthusiast will have a sport that will fascinate him all his active life. For though it provides complete physical exercise, fencing does not put excessive strain on heart and lungs. It can be started at an early age and be continued practically all the fencer's life.

Because the sport is such an art, it cannot be learnt from a book but requires constant lessons from a competent master or coach. And only when the technique has been perfected will the mind be free during a bout to analyse the opponent's game and to devise the tactics required to outwit him. This necessity for the fencer to be thinking all the time has led to fencing being described as a game of chess played at lightning speed.

But it is not difficult to learn fencing, and it is a cheap participant sport once the initial equipment—foil, glove, jacket, and mask—has been acquired. Not excessively expensive, these items last for many years. And provided adequate protective clothing is worn at all times, there is no danger in the sport.

1 With the cessation of duelling in Britain in the early 19th century fencing became mostly a provincial amusement with backsword, single stick, and quarter staff. 2 An artist's impression of a 16th century fencing bout.

The three weapons

Modern fencing is practised with three weapons—the foil, the épée, and the sabre.

A light weapon with a tapering quadrangular blade and a small, bell-shaped guard, the *foil* was evolved as the practice weapon for the short court sword of the 17th and 18th centuries. It has never been a duelling weapon. Valid hits with the foil are made with the point only on the trunk of the body. Hits that arrive on the head, arms, or legs are not counted as good.

Foil fencing is governed by somewhat complex rules and conventions based on the principle that the initial attack has the right of way until it is parried. Once it has been parried, the right of way passes to the opponent's *riposte* (the offensive movement made by a fencer after he has successfully parried an attack). If the riposte is parried, the right of way reverts to the original attacker for his counter-riposte and so on through the series of movements that build up a fencing *phrase*. There is an exception, however. If an attack is made slowly or with a bent arm, the opponent may score a stop hit, which, to be valid, must arrive a *period of fencing time* before the attack.

e planche, Le Contre Coup du Cavé par une demie volte, En opposant La main gau
foldiert Einfach.

Leon Paul Equipment

Derek J. White

Left, The weapons (left to right), the sabre, the épée, the French foil and the Italian foil. The épée is a French épée. The Italian épée differs in that it has a cross-bar fixed to the inner edges of the guard, similar to the Italian foil. But though the cross-bar gives more strength in holding and manipulating the weapon, it does limit finger play.
Above, A foilist dressed for a bout. Hits on the metallic over-jacket she wears are registered by a coloured light on the electrical apparatus.

Cushion Guard Forte Foible

Pommel Button

Handle

Mounting Blade

All weapons consist of a blade and mounting. The mounting consists of the guard within which there is a small cushion to protect the fingers, a handle or grip through which the *tang* of the blade passes, and a pommel or locking nut screwed to the end of the tang. The strongest half of the blade, nearest the guard, is called the *forte* and the remainder is called the *foible*. There are a number of different designs of mountings including the plain French grip, the Italian weapon with cross bar, and the orthopaedic grips moulded to the shape of the hand.

Leon Paul Equipment

The *épée* is the duelling sword. It is the same length as the foil but differs from it in that it has a triangular, stiffer, fluted blade and a larger bell guard.

While foil fencing was becoming increasingly conventional, duelling was still going on, and the complex movements learnt in the schools were of little avail in a duel where the essential requirement was to hit without being hit. So in the mid-19th century, the *épée de combat* was established to enable duellists to

practise in the schools. It has since become a competition weapon in its own right and is fenced as near to the conditions of a duel as the wearing of protective clothing allows.

A hit made with the point is valid if it arrives on any part of the opponent or his equipment, but there are no conventions as to the right of attack as there are at foil. If both combatants are hit, advantage to one is given only if there is an appreciable difference of time between the arrival of the

hits. If no such difference exists, a hit is scored against each on the principle that in a duel both would be wounded—or dead.

Foil and épée competitions are now judged with an electric apparatus that registers the arrival of hits. At foil, the fencers wear a metallic overjacket that exactly covers the target (trunk). Hits arriving thereon are recorded by a coloured light. Hits that arrive off the target are shown by a white light. But the apparatus cannot differentiate between the order in

which hits — attack, riposte, remise, etc—arrive. Therefore a president or referee is still required to analyse the phrase, which is stopped after every hit, and award hits according to the rules and conventions of foil fencing.

But at épée, the apparatus is the complete judge. If a hit arrives more than 1/25 of a second before the opponent's hit, the apparatus records only the first hit. If less than this time interval exists between two hits,

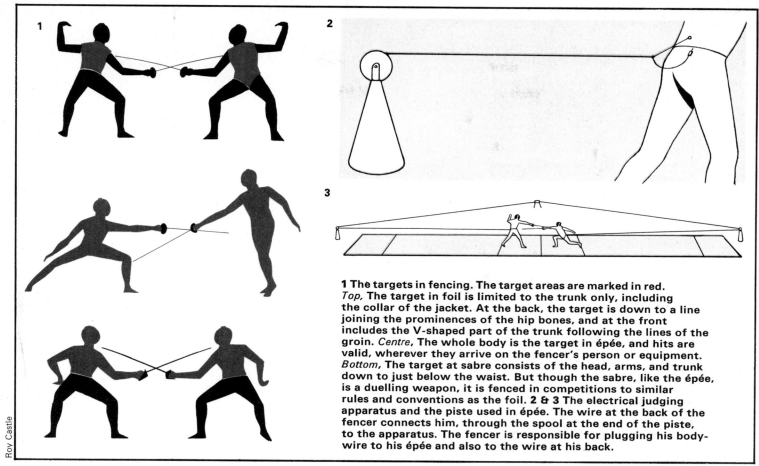

Roy Castle

1 The targets in fencing. The target areas are marked in red. *Top,* The target in foil is limited to the trunk only, including the collar of the jacket. At the back, the target is down to a line joining the prominences of the hip bones, and at the front includes the V-shaped part of the trunk following the lines of the groin. *Centre,* The whole body is the target in épée, and hits are valid, wherever they arrive on the fencer's person or equipment. *Bottom,* The target at sabre consists of the head, arms, and trunk down to just below the waist. But though the sabre, like the épée, is a duelling weapon, it is fenced in competitions to similar rules and conventions as the foil. **2 & 3** The electrical judging apparatus and the piste used in épée. The wire at the back of the fencer connects him, through the spool at the end of the piste, to the apparatus. The fencer is responsible for plugging his body-wire to his épée and also to the wire at his back.

the apparatus records a *double hit*.

The last of the three swords, the *sabre*, is the cut-and-thrust weapon. It continues the tradition of the backsword of Elizabethan times, the heavy cavalry sabre, and the naval cutlass. The light duelling sabre now universally used was developed by the Italians during the last quarter of the 19th century. It has a flattened V-shaped blade and a half-circular guard to protect the swordhand from cuts. Hits may be made with the whole of the front edge, with the back edge nearest the point (both are known as *cuts*), or with the point.

But even though the sabre is a duelling weapon, sabre fencing is governed by rules and conventions similar to those used for the foil. There is not, however, electric judging apparatus for sabre. Bouts are judged by a jury comprising a president, who directs the bout, and four judges, who observe the arrival of hits.

At all weapons, a fencing bout normally lasts until one contestant has scored five hits (best of nine hits) for men and four hits (best of seven) for women. There is, however, a time limit— 6 minutes of actual fencing for five hits and 5 minutes for four hits. Competitors are warned when one minute remains.

Because the foil is the lightest weapon, the body movements, footwork, finger play, and 'feel' of the blade are most easily learnt with it. In fact, all fencing movements can be made with the foil.

And the rules and conventions applicable at foil also teach appreciation of fencing time, distance, and phrasing. Once the basic technique has been acquired with the foil, a fencer may find that, because of his build or temperament, the épée or sabre suit him better. It is easy to adapt the techniques learnt with the foil to the other weapons. The reverse, however, is much more difficult.

History of fencing

Swords were used by man long before history was recorded; many examples date from the Bronze Age when they were in current use. And all the ancient peoples such as the Persians, Babylonians, Egyptians, Greeks, and Romans practised swordsmanship for both single combat and war. Yet there is also evidence that even in those times, fencing was a sport or pastime as well.

There is, for example, a record of a fencing match depicted in a relief carving in the temple of Madinet-Habu, near Luxor in upper Egypt, built by Ramases III about 1190 BC. This is clearly some form of fencing bout and not a duel because the swords have the points covered and the fencers are wearing padded masks tied to their wigs. And there are spectators and judges, with feathered wands. The score is being kept on a papyrus, and an inscription records one contestant as saying: 'On guard and admire what my valiant hand shall do.'

During the Middle Ages, the general use of armour until the

16th century necessitated the use of heavy and clumsy weapons such as the battle-axe, the mace, or the long two-handed sword to bludgeon the well protected opponent. Sheer strength rather than skill and speed were the order of the day.

Curiously enough, swordsmanship was developed as an art by the invention of gunpowder in the 1300s. In the following century, the general use of gunpowder led to the gradual disuse of full armour in war, and skill with the sword became of paramount importance. This led to the rapid transformation of swords to lighter and more easily handled weapons. Guilds of fencing masters were soon established all over Europe to develop the essential skills in swordsmanship. One of the first, and perhaps the most famous, was the Marxbrüder of Frankfurt. However, each country soon established its own distinctive style and methods.

This early fencing was somewhat rough and included many wrestling tricks. The guilds developed various fencing techniques that were sold to pupils for enormous sums. Assiduously practised in great secrecy, they were undoubtedly successful when suddenly produced in a duel, and brought great renown to the master concerned. Examples of such moves are the *Coup de Jarnac,* a cut inside the knee, and the *Botte de Nevers,* a stop hit between the eyes.

The Italians are said to have

first discovered the skilful use of the point that soon superseded the exclusive use of the edge of the sword. And by the end of the 16th century, the rapier was established throughout Europe, wrestling tricks were mostly abandoned, the lunge was discovered, and true fencing emerged.

The rapier was a long, beautifully balanced weapon, but its length and weight confined its use mostly to aggresive thrusts and to keeping the opponent at a distance. Defence was generally accomplished by parrying with the left hand armed with a dagger or protected by a gauntlet or cloak. Attacks were also avoided by ducking (*passata sotto*) or by sidestepping (*in quartata*). And even when the rapier gradually became shorter and lighter, rapier fencing remained a two-handed game, the combatants standing almost facing each other and circling round like boxers to gain advantage of light or ground.

The 17th century, however, saw a revolution in swords and swordmanship. Brought about largely by a radical change of fashion in dress, this was to bring fencing closer to the modern art.

At the court of Louis XIV of France, dress became more elaborate than ever before—silk breeches and stockings, brocaded coats, lace ruffles, and *peruques* were the required dress. Every gentleman had to wear a sword at all times, but with this new elegance, the long, trailing rapier could no longer be tolerated. A light, short court sword was dictated by fashion and the French soon set the tone throughout Europe as the Italians had done earlier. The skilful use of the light court sword soon became an indispensable accomplishment for every gentleman.

This sword at last enabled the fencers to make all attacking and defensive movements with one weapon wielded with one hand. The left hand was no longer armed with a dagger and hits were made mostly with the point. Swift and subtle swordplay became a reality. But fencing with light weapons at close quarters brought a new hazard—the risk of injury to the eyes. It was, therefore, necessary to regulate practice with the light court sword, or its practice weapon the foil, by the imposition of rules and conventions. Thus valid hits were restricted to those that arrived on the breast. And a fencer who initiated an attack had the right to complete the movement unless it was deflected or parried before his opponent could, in his turn, attack or riposte. Fencing became complex and formalized.

About 1780, the French master La Boessière 'invented' the mask, and its use increased the possibilities of swift and more complex movements. It was, however, necessary to maintain the rules and conventions in order to prevent a bout with the foils degenerating into a brawl of simultaneous movements. The rules and conventions developed a *conversation* with the foils, forming a fencing phrase, and these govern fencing today.

In Britain, swordsmanship was practised from the earliest times, but in 1285 Edward I issued a statute prohibiting the teaching of fencing or the holding of tournaments within the precincts of the City of London. And for a long time, fencing schools were regarded as places that encouraged duelling, brawling, and ruffianism.

This attitude continued until Henry VIII, a great lover of swordplay, recognized the value of fencing by granting letters patent to a Corporation of Masters of Defence some time before 1540. The Corporation received great privileges, including a coat of arms and the lucrative monopoly of teaching fencing in the King's realm. It is claimed that this was the first governing body established for any sport in Britain. And it was because the first fencing organization in Britain had been established by a Tudor king that, in 1902, Edward VII granted the Amateur Fencing Association the right to adopt the Tudor rose as the badge for British fencers of international rank.

From the 16th century until mid-Georgian days, prize fights were immensely popular tests of swordsmanship. A stage would be set up in a hall or public garden,

and the masters of the period would fight with a variety of weapons, often with 'sharps', until the winner emerged. He was the one who finally 'held the stage', or defeated all his opponents either in single combat or in a melée. But towards the end of the 18th century, James Figg, champion of the Corporation of Masters of Defence and the first British boxing champion, introduced fisticuff fights into the prize-fight arena. These became so popular that they eventually ousted fencing.

With the virtual cessation of duelling in Britain in the first quarter of the 19th century, fencing became mostly a provincial amusement with backsword, single stick, and quarter staff. Only a few masters, such as the famous Angelos, and a few clubs such as the London Fencing Club, founded in 1848, kept fencing alive. However, when the Army Physical Training School was established in 1861, following a study of physical training in the French and Prussian armies, fencing was included in the curriculum. This led to a revival of interest in fencing fostered by Captain Alfred Hutton, who wrote a number of books on the subject and gave displays.

In 1895, a fencing branch of the Amateur Gymnastic Association was formed, and the following year it changed its name to the Amateur Gymnastic and Fencing Association. Amateur foil and sabre championships were inaugurated in 1898, and four years later the fencing clubs broke away to form the Amateur Fencing Association with Captain Hutton as president.

Up to 1914, though, fencing in Britain was restricted to a few London clubs and *salles*, the larger universities, some public schools, and the armed services. But between the wars fencing spread to many provincial towns and became a more popular sport in every sense. World War II arrested all activity, but since then, the sport has increased in popularity throughout the United Kingdom and the Commonwealth.

Fencing was first included in the British Commonwealth Games in 1950 at Auckland, where the British Empire and Commonwealth Fencing Federation was founded to co-ordinate and develop the sport in the Commonwealth. Founded by Great Britain, Australia, and New Zealand, the Federation later included Canada, Hong Kong, Rhodesia, Singapore, and South Africa. The success of the Federation is reflected in the flourishing associations in these countries and the constantly improving standard of their fencers in both national and international competition, such as the Olympics, the Commonwealth Games, and the world championships. But European fencers still dominate the international scene.

Roland Leach

118

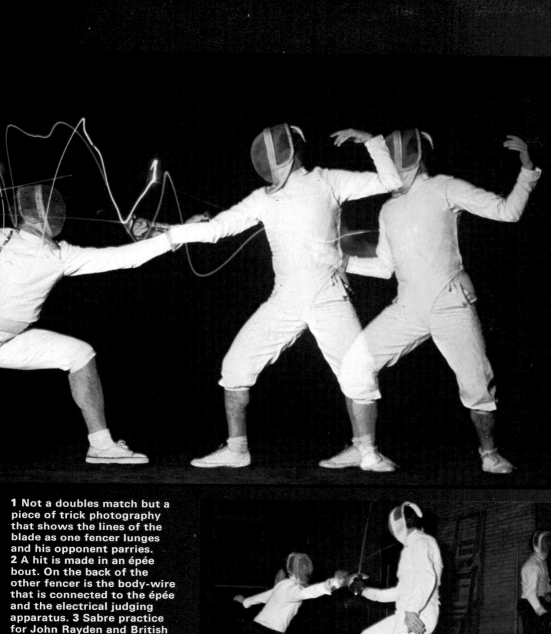

1 Not a doubles match but a piece of trick photography that shows the lines of the blade as one fencer lunges and his opponent parries. 2 A hit is made in an épée bout. On the back of the other fencer is the body-wire that is connected to the épée and the electrical judging apparatus. 3 Sabre practice for John Rayden and British Olympic fencer Sandy Leckie. The sabre continues the tradition of the Elizabethan backsword, the heavy cavalry sabre, and the naval cutlass. 4 A foil bout is watched by the jury at the 1968 Olympic Games at Mexico City.

Glossary of Terms

Balestra A short jump forward from the soles of both feet, usually followed by a lunge.

Barrage A tie or fight-off.

Bind A preparation of attack that carries the opponent's blade in a diagonal from a high to a low line or vice versa.

Ceding parry A parry formed by giving way to an opponent who is taking the blade. It is used against a *prise de fer.*

Circular (or counter) parry A parry made by describing a circle with the blade, which gathers the attacking blade and returns it to the original line of engagement.

Coquille The bell-shaped guard of an épée or foil.

Coulé A straight thrust that keeps contact with an opponent's blade.

Envelopment A preparation of attack in which the fencer takes his opponent's blade and describes a circle to return to the line of engagement without losing contact of the blades.

Fencing time The time needed to make one simple fencing movement.

Flèche A running attack depending on speed and surprise.

Froissement A preparation of attack made by deflecting an opponent's blade with a strong, sharp grazing movement along it.

High lines The parts of a fencer's target that his opponent can see above his sword hand when he is on guard.

Hit When contact is made with point or edge on an opponent.

Inside lines The parts of the target farthest from the sword arm.

Line of engagement The position of the fencer's sword hand in relation to his target.

Low lines The parts of the target below the fencer's sword hand when he is on guard.

On guard The position adopted by a fencer when prepared for a bout.

Outside lines The parts of the target nearest the sword arm.

Parry A defensive action in which the fencer deflects the attacking blade with his own blade.

Phrase A sequence of fencing movements leading up to a hit.

Pressure A preparation of attack made by pressing on the opponent's blade.

Prise de fer A preparation of attack in which an opponent's blade is taken and dominated until the attack is completed.

Prises de fer include the envelopment, bind, or *croisé.*

Redoublement A renewed attack, made while still on the lunge, that includes one or more blade movements.

Remise A renewed attack, while still on the lunge, made by replacing the point on the target in the same line without withdrawing the arm.

Reprise A renewed attack that is preceded by a return to guard forward or backward.

Riposte An offensive movement made after a successful parry.

Stop hit A counter-offensive action made on an opponent's attack.

Daily Telegraph

H. W. Neale

3

4

London Express News and Feature Services

Figure Skating

There are few sports in which the majority of supporters watch only one half of a championship, yet such is the case with figure skating. The spectacular appeal of freestyle jumps and spins magnetizes millions of fascinated televiewers and capacity stadium crowds, who clap in time to the music in support of their favourite. But the compulsory figures that precede all this usually take place at a comparatively deserted rink in a hushed atmosphere of almost cathedral-like dignity, when a sudden burst of laughter would seem quite out of place.

Many a past champion, notably American Dick Button and Parisienne Jacqueline du Bief, has said that figures, which must be learnt as the solid basis of technique, should not be part of a championship at all and that free-skating should be the sole criterion for the judges. The controversy continues, but the fact remains that figure skating championships are divided into two distinct sections, each worth 50 per cent of the maximum possible marks.

The first section, *compulsory skating*, requires solo competitors to trace with their skates on the ice up to six specific figures drawn from an internationally recognized schedule, and requires pair skaters to perform a series of prescribed movements. The second section, *free-skating*, provides up to five minutes for men and pairs, and four minutes for women, to skate a freestyle performance of their own creation.

The figures
The compulsory figures are started from a stationary 'rest' position and are composed of a prescribed pattern in the form of either a two-lobe or a three-lobe 'eight'. Each figure is skated three times, each tracing an indention on the ice. The figures vary greatly in degree of difficulty and are drawn to suit the standard of the event.

The judges are concerned not only with the merits of the tracings but also with the skater's control, posture, and balance. Other aspects of the skater's performance taken into account are the positions of hands, fingers, and non-skating foot, and the judges also look for a smooth, steady speed and a change from one foot to the other by a single stroke from the skate edge and not from the toe.

When the skater completes a figure, the judges converge on the tracing, sometimes even getting down on their hands and knees to examine the pattern left by the sharp edge of the skate. The print on the ice is of prime concern, followed closely by carriage and flow of movement.

A bulge in a circle, a 'flatting' of the skate, or an improper change from one blade edge to the other will cost tenths of points. Points up to a maximum of six are awarded by each judge for each figure and these marks are subsequently multiplied by a factor, according to the recognized standard of the figure.

The free-skating
The climax of the figure skating

Techniques

The jumps

The art of jumping is dependent on the strength of spring, the timing of the take-off, and the control of the landing.

For the *three jump*, a half-turn in mid-air, the skater takes off from the forward outside edge of one skate and lands on the back outside edge of the other. In the *loop jump*, however, he takes off from a back outside edge and, after a full revolution in the air, lands on the same edge of the same foot. This jump is especially important as it forms the basis of several more advanced jumps.

The *spreadeagle jump*, which is started from the spreadeagle position—feet well apart and toes turned outwards—is executed on either the inner or the outer edges. It is effected by holding the original position until the last moment, when the heels are pulled closer together and a half-turn or full-turn is made in mid-air while the spread position is retained. The *split jump* adopts the split position and is begun with a back-edge take-off (inner or outer) and finishes with a forward landing on two feet.

Although most jumps entail counter-clockwise rotation in the air, a notable exception is the difficult *lutz jump* featuring a reverse, clockwise rotation. The lutz take off is from a back outer edge and the landing is on the outside back edge of the opposite foot to that used in the take-off. The almost full turn in the air is accomplished in the simple *salchow jump*. This spectacular jump starts from a back inside edge and ends with the skater landing on the back outside of the other skate. The *axel jump*, one and a half turns, requires extra rotation in the air and is, in fact, a three jump combined with and continued into a loop jump.

There are other variations of these jumps, and also more advanced jumps such as the double or triple salchow, loop land lutz, the names indicating the number of mid-air rotations involved. The doubles and triples call for greater height so that the turns can be completed.

The spins

A good spin is executed on one spot without any 'travel'.

The single *flat-foot spin* is performed on the flat of the skate with balance centred over the ball of the foot. The single *toe-spin* is similarly performed except that the weight is on the toe-point.

In the *sit spin*, the skater starts off with a standing spin and then sinks on the skating knee in a sitting position with the free leg extended forward. The *camel spin*, is performed with the torso and free leg parallel to the skating surface and with the back arched.

More advanced are the *change-foot spins*, which lead to the skater jumping from one spin to another. But perhaps the most impressive of all is the *cross-foot spin*. Performed on the flat of both skate blades with the legs in a crossed position, toes together and heels apart, this spin is often used to conclude a performance because of the dramatic effect its speedy rotation gives.

As an advanced freestyle repertoire is enhanced by a combination of jumps and spins, many variations such as the *flying sit spin* and the *flying camel* have been evolved.

Proficiency Tests

Ambitious figure and pair skaters improve their technical standards by taking graduated proficiency tests, very simple ones at first, progressively winning bronze, silver, and gold medals. The highest test passed determines what class of competition the skater is qualified to enter.

1 America's Peggy Fleming won the women's world championship from 1966 to 1968 and an Olympic gold at Grenoble in 1968. **2** Gabriele Seyfert was second to Peggy Fleming at Grenoble, but in 1969, with her rival turning pro, she established herself as the leading female amateur by winning the world title, which she retained in 1970. **3** Norway's Sonja Henie won three Olympic and 10 consecutive world titles. **4** Dick Button makes a spectacular jump at St Moritz where, in 1948, he won the first of his two Olympic gold medals.

ICE FIGURE SKATING
Pairs' World Championships

Year	Winners	Country	Venue
1908	Heinrich Burger & Anna Hubler	Germany	St. Petersburg
1909	James Johnson & Phyllis Johnson	Great Britain	Stockholm
1910	Heinrich Burger & Anna Hubler	Germany	Berlin
1911	Walter Jakobsson & Ludowika Eilers	Finland	Vienna
1912	James Johnson & Phyllis Johnson	Great Britain	Manchester
1913	Karl Mejstrik & Ludowika Eilers	Austria	Stockholm
1914	Walter Jakobsson & Ludowika Jakobsson	Finland	St. Moritz
1922	Alfred Berger & Helene Engelmann	Austria	Davos
1923	Walter Jakobsson & Ludowika Jakobsson	Austria	Oslo
1924	Alfred Berger & Helene Engelmann	Austria	Manchester
1925	Ludwig Wrede & Herma Jaross-Szabo	Austria	Vienna
1926	Pierre Brunet & Andree Joly	France	Berlin
1927	Ludwig Wrede & Herma Jaross-Szabo	Austria	Vienna
1928	Pierre Brunet & Andree Joly	France	London
1929	Otto Kaiser & Lily Scholz	Austria	Budapest
1930	Pierre Brunet & Andree Brunet	France	New York
1931	Laszlo Szollas & Emilie Rotter	Hungary	Berlin
1932	Pierre Brunet & Andree Brunet	France	Montreal
1933	Laszlo Szollas & Emilie Rotter	Hungary	Stockholm
1934	Laszlo Szollas & Emilie Rotter	Hungary	Helsinki
1935	Laszlo Szollas & Emilie Rotter	Hungary	Budapest
1936	Ernst Baier & Maxi Herber	Germany	Paris
1937	Ernst Baier & Maxi Herber	Germany	London
1938	Ernst Baier & Maxi Herber	Germany	Berlin
1939	Ernst Baier & Maxi Herber	Germany	Budapest
1947	Pierre Baugniet & Micheline Lannoy	Belgium	Stockholm
1948	Pierre Baugniet & Micheline Lannoy	Belgium	Davos
1949	Ede Kraly & Andrea Kekessy	Hungary	Paris
1950	Peter Kennedy & Karol Kennedy	USA	London
1951	Paul Falk & Ria Baran	Germany	Milan
1952	Paul Falk & Ria Falk	Germany	Paris
1953	John Nicks & Jennifer Nicks	Great Britain	Davos
1954	Norris Bowden & Frances Dafoe	Canada	Oslo
1955	Norris Bowden & Frances Dafoe	Canada	Vienna
1956	Kurt Oppelt & Sissy Schwarz	Austria	Garmisch
1957	Robert Paul & Barbara Wagner	Canada	Colorado Springs
1958	Robert Paul & Barbara Wagner	Canada	Paris
1959	Robert Paul & Barbara Wagner	Canada	Colorado Springs
1960	Robert Paul & Barbara Wagner	Canada	Vancouver
1962	Otto Jelinek & Maria Jelinek	Canada	Prague
1963	Hans-Jurgen Baumler & Marika Kilius	W Germany	Cortina
1964	Hans-Jurgen Baumler & Marika Kilius	W Germany	Dortmund
1965	Oleg Protopopov & Ludmilla Belousova	USSR	Colorado Springs
1966	Oleg Protopopov & Ludmilla Belousova	USSR	Davos
1967	Oleg Protopopov & Ludmilla Belousova	USSR	Vienna
1968	Oleg Protopopov & Ludmilla Belousova	USSR	Geneva
1969	Alek Ulanov & Irena Rodnina	USSR	Colorado Springs
1970	Alek Ulanov & Irena Rodnina	USSR	Ljubljana
1971	Alexsei Ulanov & Irena Rodnina	USSR	Lyon
1972	Alexsei Ulanov & Irena Rodnina	USSR	Calgary
1973	Alexander Zaitsev & Irina Rodnina	USSR	Bratislava
1974	Alexander Zaitsev & Irina Rodnina	USSR	Munich

4

Keystone

ICE FIGURE SKATING Olympic Games

Year	Venue	Men's Champion	Country	Women's Champion	Country	Pairs Champions	Country
1908	London	Ulrich Salchow	Sweden	Madge Syers	Great Britain	Heinrich Burger & Anna Hubler	Germany
1920	Antwerp	Gillis Grafstrom	Sweden	Madga Julin-Mauroy	Sweden	Walter Jakobsson & Ludowika Jakobsson	Finland
1924	Chamonix	Gillis Grafstrom	Sweden	Herma Plank-Szabo	Austria	Alfred Berger & Helene Engelmann	Austria
1928	St Moritz	Gillis Grafstrom	Sweden	Sonja Henie	Norway	Pierre Brunet & Andree Joly	France
1932	Lake Placid	Karl Schafer	Austria	Sonja Henie	Norway	Pierre Brunet & Andree Brunet	France
1936	Garmisch	Karl Schafer	Austria	Sonja Henie	Norway	Ernst Baier & Maxi Herber	Germany
1948	St Moritz	Richard Button	USA	Barbara Ann Scott	Canada	Pierre Baugniet & Micheline Lannoy	Belgium
1952	Oslo	Richard Button	USA	Jeanette Altwegg	Great Britain	Paul Falk & Ria Falk	Germany
1956	Cortina	Hayes Jenkins	USA	Tenley Albright	USA	Kurt Oppelt & Sissy Schwarz	Austria
1960	Squaw Valley	David Jenkins	USA	Carol Heiss	USA	Robert Paul & Barbara Wagner	Canada
1964	Innsbruck	Manfred Schnelldorfer	Germany	Sjoukje Dijkstra	Holland	Oleg Protopopov & Ludmilla Belousova	USSR
1968	Grenoble	Wolfgang Schwarz	Austria	Peggy Fleming	USA	Oleg Protopopov & Ludmilla Belousova	USSR
1972	Sapporo	Ondrej Nepela	Czechoslovakia	Beatrix Schuba	Austria	Alexei Ulanov & Irena Rodnina	USSR

competition is the free-skating, in which the precise edges and turns learnt in figures are combined to create intricate footwork embellished with jumps and spins. The performer is in no way restricted in what is attempted, how he performs, or the sequence. This, by far the more theatrical part of the contest, is naturally what most onlookers more readily appreciate.

The permitted freedom in free-skating is influenced by the need to incorporate as many difficult movements as possible within the time allotted so that the highest possible marks can be gained. These are awarded in two sets, one assessing technical merit, the other artistic impression. Scoring is again graded up to a maximum six for each, and the totals are multiplied by a factor to ensure an aggregate parity with the marks awarded for figures.

The judges have to assess the variation of contents, degree of difficulty, and manner of performance. They must decide, for example, whether speed was gathered without visible effort, whether the skater mixed in original footwork on toes and edges, and whether the transitions and changes in tempo were smooth. Then, too, the skater must always be in the proper position, with toes pointed and back straight, and make intelligent use of the entire ice area. His performance should give the feeling of being planned and skated to the music, rather than of being a set show where the music is only incidental.

When a free-skating programme is devised, jumps and spins should be varied and spaced between spirals and linking steps. Spirals simulate moving statues—while various body postures are held one-foot glides in forward or backward direction. Holding the position unwaveringly is the hallmark of a good spiral, and the ability to control spirals provides a sound basis for a freestyle repertoire.

Each figure-skating blade, being hollow-ground, has two edges, inner and outer, and nearly all movements in this sport should be performed on an edge. Skating on an edge entails a lean of the body over the appropriate edge to cause a forward or backward movement in a curve. The sense of balance is comparable to that of a cyclist's lean as he turns a corner.

Pair skating
Ice pair skating competitions are also divided into compulsory and

1

U.P.I.

ICE FIGURE SKATING Men's World Championships

Year	Winner	Country	Venue	Year	Winner	Country	Venue
1896	Gilbert Fuchs	Germany	St Petersburg	1947	Hans Gerschwiler	Switzerland	Stockholm
1897	Gustav Hugel	Austria	Stockholm	1948	Richard Button	USA	Davos
1898	Henning Grenander	Sweden	London	1949	Richard Button	USA	Paris
1899	Gustav Hugel	Austria	Davos	1950	Richard Button	USA	London
1900	Gustav Hugel	Austria	Davos	1951	Richard Button	USA	Milan
1901	Ulrich Salchow	Sweden	Stockholm	1952	Richard Button	USA	Paris
1902	Ulrich Salchow	Sweden	London	1953	Hayes Jenkins	USA	Davos
1903	Ulrich Salchow	Sweden	St Petersburg	1954	Hayes Jenkins	USA	Oslo
1904	Ulrich Salchow	Sweden	Berlin	1955	Hayes Jenkins	USA	Vienna
1905	Ulrich Salchow	Sweden	Stockholm	1956	Hayes Jenkins	USA	Garmisch
1906	Gilbert Fuchs	Germany	Munich	1957	David Jenkins	USA	Colorado Springs
1907	Ulrich Salchow	Sweden	Vienna	1958	David Jenkins	USA	Paris
1908	Ulrich Salchow	Sweden	Troppau	1959	David Jenkins	USA	Colorado Springs
1909	Ulrich Salchow	Sweden	Stockholm	1960	Alain Giletti	France	Vancouver
1910	Ulrich Salchow	Sweden	Davos	1962	Donald Jackson	Canada	Prague
1911	Ulrich Salchow	Sweden	Berlin	1963	Donald McPherson	Canada	Cortina
1912	Fritz Kachler	Austria	Manchester	1964	Manfred Schnelldorfer	West Germany	Dortmund
1913	Fritz Kachler	Austria	Vienna	1965	Alain Calmat	France	Colorado Springs
1914	Gosta Sandahl	Sweden	Helsinki	1966	Emmerich Danzer	Austria	Davos
1922	Gillis Grafstrom	Sweden	Stockholm	1967	Emmerich Danzer	Austria	Vienna
1923	Fritz Kachler	Austria	Vienna	1968	Emmerich Danzer	Austria	Geneva
1924	Gillis Grafstrom	Sweden	Manchester	1969	Tim Wood	USA	Colorado Springs
1925	Willy Bockl	Austria	Vienna	1970	Tim Wood	USA	Ljubljana
1926	Willy Bockl	Austria	Berlin	1971	Ondrej Nepela	Czechoslovakia	Lyon
1927	Willy Bockl	Austria	Davos	1972	Ondrej Nepela	Czechoslovakia	Calgary
1928	Willy Bockl	Austria	Berlin	1973	Ondrej Nepela	Czechoslovakia	Bratislava
1929	Gillis Grafstrom	Sweden	London	1974	Jan Hoffman	East Germany	Munich
1930	Karl Schafer	Austria	New York				
1931	Karl Schafer	Austria	Berlin				
1932	Karl Schafer	Austria	Montreal				
1933	Karl Schafer	Austria	Zurich				
1934	Karl Schafer	Austria	Stockholm				
1935	Karl Schafer	Austria	Budapest				
1936	Karl Schafer	Austria	Paris				
1937	Felix Kaspar	Austria	Vienna				
1938	Felix Kaspar	Austria	Berlin				
1939	Graham Sharp	Great Britain	Budapest				

ICE FIGURE SKATING Women's World Championships

Year	Winner	Country	Venue
1906	Madge Syers	Great Britain	Davos
1907	Madge Syers	Great Britain	Vienna
1908	Lily Kronberger	Hungary	Troppau
1909	Lily Kronberger	Hungary	Budapest
1910	Lily Kronberger	Hungary	Berlin
1911	Lily Kronberger	Hungary	Vienna
1912	Meray Horvath	Hungary	Davos
1913	Meray Horvath	Hungary	Stockholm
1914	Meray Horvath	Hungary	St Moritz
1922	Herma Plank-Szabo	Austria	Stockholm
1923	Herma Plank-Szabo	Austria	Vienna
1924	Herma Plank-Szabo	Austria	Oslo
1925	Herma Jaross-Szabo	Austria	Davos
1926	Herma Jaross-Szabo	Austria	Stockholm
1927	Sonja Henie	Norway	Oslo
1928	Sonja Henie	Norway	London
1929	Sonja Henie	Norway	Budapest
1930	Sonja Henie	Norway	New York
1931	Sonja Henie	Norway	Berlin
1932	Sonja Henie	Norway	Montreal
1933	Sonja Henie	Norway	Stockholm
1934	Sonja Henie	Norway	Oslo
1935	Sonja Henie	Norway	Vienna
1936	Sonja Henie	Norway	Paris
1937	Cecilia Colledge	Great Britain	London
1938	Megan Taylor	Great Britain	Stockholm
1939	Megan Taylor	Great Britain	Prague
1947	Barbara Ann Scott	Canada	Stockholm
1948	Barbara Ann Scott	Canada	Davos
1949	Aja Vrzanova	Czechoslovakia	Paris

Year	Winner	Country	Venue
1950	Aja Vrzanova	Czechoslovakia	London
1951	Jeanette Altwegg	Great Britain	Milan
1952	Jacqueline du Bief	France	Paris
1953	Tenley Albright	USA	Davos
1954	Gundi Busch	Germany	Oslo
1955	Tenley Albright	USA	Vienna
1956	Carol Heiss	USA	Garmisch
1957	Carol Heiss	USA	Colorado Springs
1958	Carol Heiss	USA	Paris
1959	Carol Heiss	USA	Colorado Springs
1960	Carol Heiss	USA	Vancouver
1962	Sjoukje Dijkstra	Holland	Prague
1963	Sjoukje Dijkstra	Holland	Cortina
1964	Sjoukje Dijkstra	Holland	Dortmund
1965	Petra Burka	Canada	Colorado Springs
1966	Peggy Fleming	USA	Davos
1967	Peggy Fleming	USA	Vienna
1968	Peggy Fleming	USA	Geneva
1969	Gabriele Seyfert	East Germany	Colorado Springs
1970	Gabriele Seyfert	East Germany	Ljubljana
1971	Beatrix Schuba	Austria	Lyon
1972	Beatrix Schuba	Austria	Calgary
1973	Karen Magnussen	Canada	Bratislava
1974	Christine Errath	East Germany	Munich

In the second half of the 1960s, Russia dominated pair skating. 1 Ludmilla and Oleg Protopopov—perhaps the sport's greatest exponents. 2 A spectacular lift by Ludmilla Smirnova and Andrei Suraikin, who were second in the 1970 world championships to fellow Russians Alek Ulanov and Irena Rodnina (3).

Ed Lacey

Syndication International

freestyle sections. For the former, pairs are required to skate specified movements, their skill in performing them being worth a quarter of the contest's total marks.

In the freestyle, competitors are unrestricted within the limits of regulations demanding that the two partners must perform movements giving a homogenous impression. And although both partners need not always perform the same movements as each other and may separate from time to time, they must give an overall impression of unison and harmonious composition. *Shadow skating* is the term generally applied to those parts of the pairs programme in which both skaters perform with unity of movement but while separated.

Pair skating essentially requires teamwork in every sense. Ideally, the man should be slightly taller, and the couple should match in ability and appearance to pleasing effect. Each partner must learn to understand the other so that they can anticipate and match each other's every step.

Among the favourite specialized pair-skating highlights, as distinct from synchronized solo shadow movements, are the death spiral, the lasso lift, the overhead axel lift, the split lutz lift, and the catch-waist camel spin (see *Techniques*).

The *death spiral* is the popular name given to a movement in which the man swings his partner round at very great speed while retaining virtually the same pose. The girl apparently risks 'death' by arching backwards as she revolves round her partner and, in the process, sometimes touches her hair on the ice. The styles can be varied with one- or two-handed holds in various grips.

In the single *lasso lift*, from a side-by-side, hand-to-hand position, the lady is lifted overhead in an outside forward take-off, turning one and a half rotations with the man's arms stretched upwards and with the lady's legs in split position. The man remains forward to complete a backward landing on the right outside edge.

In the spectacular *axel lift*, the girl is turned one and a half times completely over her partner's head and the man rotates beneath the girl throughout the movement.

History

Administratively at least, one man stands out as the leading pioneer of figure skating—H. E. Vandervell. As well as inventing the bracket, counter, and rocker figures, this Englishman is also credited with instigating the whole idea of proficiency tests, and it was his original conception of a graduated system of figure tests that was subsequently improved upon and universally adopted by the International Skating Union.

In Vandervell's era, freestyle technique was completely subordinated by an enthusiasm for figures, a restrained and dignified science in an age of somewhat unwieldy Victorian dress. But in the late 19th century, the English and freer Viennese styles became separately recognized until the latter eventually dominated and was established as the international style adopted for all major championships.

Gaelic Football

Played almost exclusively in Ireland, Gaelic football is a fast, tough, thrilling game that combines elements of soccer and rugby. But the game it most resembles is Australian rules football; except that the Irish version uses a round ball. The two games have much in common, including the high catching, the punched passes, and the spectacular long kicks at goal.

Although football of one kind or another has been played in Ireland for close on a thousand years, Gaelic football as it is known today was not formalized until the late 19th century. The exact origins of the game as a separate sport are unknown, but it was popular in Dublin in 1527. The actual rules regarding playing the ball were very like the modern ones, but the teams and the playing area were different. Games might be played between two teams of up to 100 players and from parishes often as much as 10 miles apart; the game would start midway between the parishes, and the first team to get the ball over the boundary of their rivals' parish was declared the winner. It was a rough and often bloody pursuit, but an integral part of the Irish culture. Traditional dancing and poetry readings would often precede the combat.

Gaelic football, like other Irish sports such as hurling, handball, and rounders, declined during the hard times of the 19th century and games hitherto unknown in the Emerald Isle—lawn tennis, cricket, and polo—took their place.

But Ireland's traditions gradually began to recover from the disastrous years of the famine, sport included. The idea of reviving the typically Irish games was conceived by one Michael Cusack of Clare. Aided by Maurice Davin of Carrick, he dispatched a call to people in various walks of Irish life to meet at Hayes Hotel, Thurles, on November 1, 1884. The meeting elected a committee of seven with the responsibility of establishing the Gaelic Athletic Association, under the patronage of the Most Rev Dr Croke, Archbishop of Cashel, and the approval of Michael Davitt (on ticket-of-leave from an English jail where he had been released after serving 7 years of a 15-year sentence for sending firearms to Ireland), and Charles Stewart Parnell, the MP for Wicklow.

A hard and difficult road lay ahead for those pioneers and their successors. In those troubled times it seemed as if the new body must fail. But somehow it survived and grew in strength until it

Top, **A goalmouth scramble during the 1966 All-Ireland semi-final between Down and Meath (green). Down's 'keeper Patsy McAlinden fists the ball clear to break down a Meath attack.** *Left*, **Meath's defence watch helplessly as a Down shot goes over the bar for one point. The game was played, like all finals nowadays, at Croke Park, Dublin.**

Fionnbar Callanan

became one of the greatest sporting associations in the world, recognised and obeyed by all who play Gaelic games throughout the 32 counties of Eire and Northern Ireland. The constitution of the GAA comprises clubs, county boards, provincial councils in Ulster, Munster, Leinster, and Connaught, and the central council. The annual congress, held every Easter Sunday, is the final voice in all matters.

The county boards arrange tournaments and championships for the clubs in their own areas, and an All-Ireland club championship is to be established. The four provincial councils are responsible for the Provincial Championships. These are the preliminaries for the All-Ireland championship—the principal competition of the Association for which each county enters teams selected from the clubs in their area.

The highlight of the Gaelic football season is the All-Ireland final for the Sam Maguire trophy. Held at Dublin's Croke Park on the fourth Sunday of September, it is a unique occasion for all Irishmen, a day when the Emerald Isle is agog with excitement. The arena is packed to capacity—90,556 watched the Down v Offaly final in 1961—and millions see the game on television or listen on radio.

The king-pins of Munster, Kerry have dominated the series since its inception in 1887. By 1969 they had won the Sam Maguire on 21 occasions. A great deal of the credit for their 1969 win went to their mid-fielder Mick O'Connell—a stalwart of

many hard-fought battles. Dan O'Keeffe appeared in 10 finals and won 7 winners medals for Kerry.

Although Dublin have not won since 1963, they are in second place to Kerry with an aggregate of 17 title wins. And like the Kingdom of Kerry, the names of their stars would fill a book. Such greats of the past as Freeney, Ferguson, and Kevin Heffernan are often recalled as the capital searches for their successors.

But the 1960s belonged to Galway and to Down. Down, the county of the Mountains of Mourne, astounded the whole island when, in 1960, they beat Kerry and became the first county to take the title over the border into Northern Ireland. In Joe Lennon they can boast one of the great thinkers of the game.

Galway's tally of three successive title wins in 1964, 1965, and 1966 was one of the best performances since separation. Only two teams have won four times in a row—Kerry (1928-1931) and Wexford, 1915 to 1918. Those who helped Galway stand supreme in the 1960s were such players as Enda Colleran, Noel Tierney, John Donnellan, Cyril Dunne, and Matty McDonough.

In 80 years, Gaelic football developed from being a minority sport played and remembered only by Celtic purists into one of the great spectator sports of the whole of Ireland. Although it has not caught on in the rest of the world, its future in the land of its origin seems secure as an expression of the united Ireland for which its rejuvenators dreamed and sometimes died.

GAELIC FOOTBALL

All-Ireland Championship
(instituted 1887)

1950	Mayo	1970	Kerry
1951	Mayo	1971	Offaly
1952	Cavan	1972	Offaly
1953	Kerry	1973	Cork
1954	Meath		
1955	Kerry		
1956	Galway		
1957	Louth		
1958	Dublin		
1959	Kerry		
1960	Down		
1961	Down		
1962	Kerry		
1963	Dublin		
1964	Galway		
1965	Galway		
1966	Galway		
1967	Meath		
1968	Down		
1969	Kerry		

Left, **Mick O'Connell of Kerry pumps the ball upfield. Although the ball may be carried, it must be passed by either kicking or fisting, but only the goalkeeper is permitted to pick up the ball off the ground.** *Above,* **High jumping and stern physical contact are salient features of a game peculiar to Ireland. It includes some elements of Australian Rules, rugby, and soccer, but it has never caught on outside its birthplace. It does, however, like rugby union unite the two parts of a divided island. The All-Ireland final for the Sam Maguire trophy has attracted 90,000 spectators to Croke Park.**

How the Game is played

Body contact abounds in Gaelic football, which is a hard game at all levels. The pace of the game requires that the participants possess a high degree of skill, strength, and stamina. High jumping, catching, and long kicking are the main features of the game which is played at a fast pace throughout. The ball may be caught when it is off the ground, but it may not be thrown. Goals, therefore are scored by kicking or fisting the ball between the posts. Likewise, all passes must be kicked or fisted. When the ball is on the ground it may be kicked or scooped up into the hands with the foot, but only the goalkeeper may pick the ball up off the ground.

The pitch is between 140 and 160 yards long, and between 84 and 100 yards wide. It is marked with side lines, goal lines, and lines across the pitch at 14 yards, 21 yards, 50 yards, and half way. In front of the goal is the penalty area, called the 'parallelogram', which is 15 yards wide and extends 5 yards into the field. The goal posts are 21 feet apart and 16 feet high, and the bar below which is the goal net, is 8 feet from the ground. Goals (worth 3 points) are scored by playing the ball into the goal net and one point is scored by playing the ball over the bar and between the uprights (like a goal in rugby).

Teams consist of 15 players with 3 substitutes allowed, and they play for two 30-minute halves. But the All-Ireland semi-finals and final last 80 minutes in all.

The game starts with the referee throwing the ball in, and thereafter the game progresses in accordance with the handling rules until a goal is scored. When one side puts the ball over the side lines a free kick is awarded to the opposition. If the attacking side play the ball over the end line play is resumed with the ball being kicked out from goal. If the last person to play the ball was a member of the defending side a free kick on the 50 yards line, known as a 'fifty', is awarded.

Golf

Politicians and statesmen play golf; comedians, golfing addicts themselves, make jokes about it; millions enjoy just watching it, and because they do, a small group of professionals make millions of dollars from it. It has been called many things, both by exasperated devotees and by their wives, yet the definition that is the first rule of the game makes it seem almost dull in comparison with some other games: 'The game of golf consists in playing a ball from the teeing ground into the hole by successive strokes in accordance with the rules'. It hardly does justice to a sport that is royal, ancient, and modern. One that goes back 600 years in British history, has, since its earliest days, appealed as much to dustmen as to dukes, and has spread throughout the world.

This sport, which satisfies what must, somewhat incredibly, be one of man's basic urges—to knock a ball in a particular direction with a stick—has developed until it has become the most commercialized outdoor activity in the world. In 1970, prize money on the American professional circuit—the world's biggest—had climbed to $6 million; the production of equipment and accessories had reached the proportions of a major industry. And even though the rules limit the number of clubs a player may carry on a round to 14, the manufacturers still produce an infinite variety of clubs within that range.

Television too plays an important part in the golfing industry. For while there is a limit to the number of spectators that can find a place on a championship course, millions can watch the great championships live on television. This mass exposure has greatly raised the prestige of the sport's leading personalities. And at the same time, golf has spread outwards and become far more international in character. Both in the professional and in the amateur game, international competitions have sprung up to supplement the old traditional contests between nations, such as the Walker and the Ryder Cup matches. The modern professional has become a jet traveller with the chance of making money at any of half-a-dozen tournament circuits around the world. And in the amateur game, a dazzling programme of world events awaits the top performers who reach international standard and can afford to devote time to golf.

Yet the true heart of golf does not lie in these much publicized advances in the game. That heart beats as surely in the humble courses lying in the shadow of slag-heaps in the North of England or in rough areas hewn out of jungle as it does in the luxurious country-club atmosphere or on the great championship links of the world. The essence of the game can easily be found in playing a few holes on a solitary course in the quiet of evening. The holes may even be played alone, for it is a main feature of the game—and one that is true of hardly any other sport—that it is not necessarily dependent on the performance or interplay of an opponent for its enjoyment. It is possible for any player to match his skill against either a known standard of play for the course or his own previous performances. On a smaller, but no less genuine scale, the humble player can experience all the emotions of the game—the pleasure of a well-hit stroke; the frustration of missing a short putt; the humility after a poor stroke; and the tension as a crisis approaches. They are common feelings for the game that provide a bond that overcomes every national frontier and unites the giants with the rabbits all over the world.

Many attempts have been made to establish the origins of golf, and one scholar has seen a link between it and a game called *paganica* that was introduced into Britain by Roman legionaries. A later development of this was *cambuca*, which was played in the 14th century with a bent stick and a wooden ball. The word golf itself suggests that the sport was introduced to Britain from Holland or the Low Countries, and it probably derives from the German *kolbe* meaning club, the Dutch form of which is *kolf*. Early Dutch prints show players engaged in some sport with curved sticks and a round ball directed towards a hole.

The first official evidence that golf was played in Britain, however, comes from Scotland where, in 1457, a statute prohibited the exercise of golf on the grounds that it was interfering with the practice of archery. In 1471, the Scottish Parliament decreed against football and golf, and twenty years later it was ordained 'that in na place of the realme there be usit futteballis, golfe, or other sik unprofitabele sportis for the common gude of the realme...' For such steps to be taken, the game must therefore have had a firm foothold in Scotland as early as the beginning of the 15th century.

And by the end of the century, ministers of religion were no more successful in keeping their parishioners away from the public links on Sunday than their 20th-century successors. The records of Edinburgh Town Council show many instances of the conflict between conscience and love of the game. In 1604, for example, Robert Robertson and others were convicted 'of profaning the Lord's Sabbath, by absenting themselves from hearing of the Word, and playing at the Gowf on the North

Through his personality and temperament, Arnold Palmer did more than any golfer to popularize the game in the 1960s.

Fred Kaplan/Black Star

The golfer with no weakness—
Jack Nicklaus allies drives
of tremendous length with a
short game that has rarely
been surpassed.

Inch, Perth, *in time of preaching*'. Robertson, the ringleader, was fined and with others ordered 'to compear the next Sabbath into the place of public repentance, in presence of the whole congregation'. It was tough in those days to be a good Presbyterian and a keen week-end golfer.

By this time though, golf, historically speaking, was becoming reasonably established. James IV and James V of Scotland both played in East Lothian, and Mary Queen of Scots is reported to have played at St Andrews shortly after the murder of Darnley. Her son, James I of England, took the game south and it was played for a time at Blackheath. Charles I and Charles II were both partial to it, and an old print shows Charles I receiving news of the Irish rebellion while he was playing golf at Leith, with the messenger on his knees on the fairway and his horse cropping grass in the rough.

Origins of the game
For centuries after the game was first played in Scotland, it remained a classless, unorganized sport with no code of rules and no clubhouses. In England though, it quite failed to capture the imagination, Royal Blackheath remaining an outpost of the game, an appendage of the Royal court. On the one hand the game was kept alive by the nobility with their private courses. But on the other, the humblest club-maker's apprentice could go freely to the links at St Andrews or Leith without paying a green fee. And in such circumstances, it is not surprising that few names have come down to us as giants of the game. One exception, however, is William St Clair of Roselin, who was brought to life by the pen of Sir Walter Scott. A man of formidable appearance 'built for the business of war or the chase', he serves as a link with the next stage of the game, for he was one of the early captains of the first known golf club to be formed—that of the Honourable Company of Edinburgh Golfers in 1744. At this time, the Honourable Company was operating over five holes at Leith, and it later moved to Musselburgh before becoming established at Muirfield. Before that date, as Mr Robert Browning, one of the game's most distinguished historians, said: 'courses were purely natural; the only green-keepers were the rabbits'.

The formation of this and other clubs arose from the decision to offer a prize for annual competition, and as such a competition required organizing, the group developed into a club. And from this club came the first code of rules, 13 in number and wonderfully simple by modern standards.

In the early 19th century, there was a steady growth in the number of clubs, and then, slowly at first, the idea took up in England, where

Scotland's Prestwick club, original hosts of the Open championship, contributed greatly to the spread of the game.

But there were other changes and developments taking place in the game, and one of them featured the composition of the ball. It has been suggested that the earliest golf balls were made of solid boxwood, but the ball that was in use for several centuries after the game arrived in Scotland was made of leather and stuffed with feathers. Then about the middle of the 19th century, an employee in a company manufacturing cables insulated with gutta-percha applied this substance to a new golf ball and tried it out at Royal Blackheath. It had both its advantages and disadvantages. For one thing, until some form of marking of the surface of the ball was introduced—the equivalent to the modern dimpling—the ball flew badly and it made the game hard work. In addition, its unyielding solidity frequently imparted an unpleasant jar to the arm if the shot were mis-hit. But the ball was cheaper and indestructible, and as clubs could be adapted to its use, with an increasing emphasis on iron clubs, it was accepted. Public competitions at this time took the form mainly of challenge matches, often over 72 or even 144 holes, between the giants of the day for a modest prize. The undisputed champion was Allan Robertson, victor of many such matches. And it was after his death that the Prestwick club, perhaps intending to find his successor, decided in 1860 to hold an open championship—the first of its kind in the world. The trophy was a challenge belt in red morocco, to become the property of anyone winning it three times, and it was won in 1860 by Willie Park who headed the other seven competitors with a score of 174 for 36 holes.

A new era
Although it was some years before the entry increased noticeably—it did not reach three figures until 1901—a new era had begun. Golf, for the first time, was to have a show window as its best players came to be known more widely, and golf, in a literal sense, was on the move. In its early years, the championship was highlighted by the rivalry between the first winner and old Tom Morris of St Andrews. And then towards the end of the 1860s there arose a greater player than either of them, the latter's son, Young Tom Morris. A golfer of genius, he won the belt outright, won it a fourth time in 1872, and died at the age of 24, inconsolable after the death of his young wife in childbirth.

Golf now entered a period of stability in preparation for the great explosion of events about the turn of the century. In the 1880s and 1890s, English golf began to make up for the slow start that had

left it far behind Scotland. The year 1894 saw the first victory in an Open championship of that great figure from Westward Ho!, John Henry Taylor, who with Harry Vardon and James Braid made up the 'Great Triumvirate' that dominated British golf for the next 20 years. That year, the prize money totalled £100, with £30 to the winner. In 1946 the total had risen to £1,000, and 25 years later it had gone up to £40,000, most of that increase occurring in the last decade.

In 1902, a new ball—the Haskell, made of rubber strips wound round a rubber core—was introduced from America. Its qualities were hotly debated before the Open championship, with most of the big names, including the Triumvirate, opposed to it. But Sandy Herd was converted to its use after a round with the famous amateur John Ball, and when he won his only Open with it, the old 'guttie' ball was dead.

About this time also, the game was spreading to the United States. Traces of its being played there can be found as far back as the 18th century—in the *Georgia Gazette* of 1796 mention is made of the Savannah Golf Club. But the first sustained wave of enthusiasm begins only in the 1880s and is once again attributable to Scottish influence. In 1887, a Mr Lockhart returned to New York from his native Dunfermline with a supply of clubs and balls and was, in the same year, arrested for hitting a golf ball about on the sheep pasture in Central Park.

But other Scots rallied to the cause and helped to form the first recognized club, the St Andrews golf club of Yonkers, outside New York. Another early club was Shinnecock Hills formed in 1891. The game received a boost from the immigration around the turn of the century of experienced players and craftsmen from Carnoustie and other Scottish cities. And then in 1900 the great Vardon went over and won the American Open. Three years later, the Oxford and Cambridge Golfing Society sent over the first international team to compete in the United States, beginning a rivalry that has grown ever since.

During the first half of the 20th century, America exercised a growing influence on the game throughout the world. They were not always the first to spread the gospel, for in many countries this had been done by British colonials. Royal Calcutta, for example, was founded in 1829, Royal Hong Kong in 1889, and even the French club at Pau, the oldest in Europe outside Scotland, was started in 1854 thanks to Scottish officers who had stayed on after convalescing from the Peninsular War. But once the Americans had become fired with enthusiasm, it was inevitable that by sheer weight of numbers and with their vigour and financial backing they

should come to dominate the game, not only in the skill of their greatest players—Jones, Hogan, Palmer, Nicklaus—but in their attitude towards the game and in fashioning its equipment.

Britain stood out for a time against the centre-shafted putter with which Walter Travis won their Amateur championship in 1904, and were also slow to accept the steel-shafted club of American design, an innovation which, by giving increased length and by reducing the effects of a bad shot, revolutionized the game almost as much as the rubber-cored ball had done. But as the factory bench turning out graded sets of 14 matched clubs took over from the craftsmen, so the game became more and more of a science and British and world golfers were forced to follow American trends and developments.

Development of the game
Other directions in which American influence is felt today are in slowness of play, the watering of fairways and greens so that a high pitch shot can be played to the flag instead of the running shot needed for dry ground, and the predominance of stroke-play over match-play. Yet in spite of the difference between golf in America and Britain, the governing bodies of the two countries work together and as far as possible determine a common policy.

Whereas the Royal and Ancient Golf Club evolved naturally as the headquarters of the game after its foundation in 1754, other governing bodies were formed much later. Its counterpart in America, the United States Golf Association, was formed in 1894 at a meeting called between five clubs, and it now has a large headquarters in New York and 20 sub-committees to deal with the needs of about nine million golfers in their country alone. The R and A in Britain controls the rules of the game and of amateur status, as well as those championships entrusted to it; and the national unions of the four home countries, the Professional Golfer's Association, and the Ladies' Golf Union all look to it for guidance.

The spread of golf has been rapid in the old Commonwealth countries, such as South Africa, New Zealand, and Australia, and has been encouraged by such world-wide competitions as the world team championships for men and women, and by the Commonwealth tournament, first held to commemorate the bi-centenary of the Royal and Ancient club. Circuits are now established in South Africa, Australasia, and the Far East and these annually attract many of the world's finest golfers. But the size of the American prize list is still the most powerful magnet. Ambitious young men from every country know it is there that they must

1 An early 19th century print of golfer and caddie at Royal Blackheath, the club that was an outpost of the game in England until the latter part of the century. 2 Mary Queen of Scots played golf at St Andrews in 1563. 3 'Old' Tom Morris, the grand old man of golf who won four of the first eight British Open championships when Prestwick, his club for many years, was the regular venue. His son succeeded him to the title in 1868, and won the championship three years in a row. 4 Bobby Jones, the great American amateur who between 1923 and 1930 won the British Open 3 times, the US Open 4 times, and the US Amateur championship 5 times. He later became the driving force behind the course in Augusta, Georgia, which is the home of the American Masters. 5 Bobby Locke of South Africa drives from the 16th tee at Royal Lytham in 1952 when he won his third British Open. 6 Walter Hagen, winner of a record five American PGA titles in the 1920s. 7 Ben Hogan won the Open, American Open, and Master's in 1953.

L.E.A.

Topix

Fox Photos

Syndication International

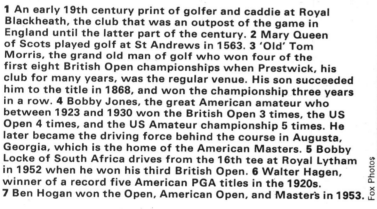

Keystone

try themselves out, for it is there that the best golf is played. It is a tough school, though, and all but the strongest go to the wall.

The advent of television on a big scale—TV cameras standing on lorries were being tried out as early as 1939 at a golf tournament outside London—gave added impetus to the sponsors who were ready to pour money into golf tournaments. Through the medium of television, no figure has done more to popularize the game than Arnold Palmer. By the colour of his personality he has become a household name to thousands of people all over the world who have never and may never play golf. The game has made Palmer a millionaire, and it has given players such as Peter Thomson, Bill Casper, Gary Player, and Lee Trevino a way of life far beyond the imagination of the early professionals. Perhaps only one player has rivalled Palmer's popularity in the 1960s— Jack Nicklaus. While still in his twenties he won all the major tournaments in the world.

But the televising of championships is an expensive, complicated process, and TV companies have gone in for the staged match between two or three players, or more easily manageable spectacles such as 'par-three golf', 'two-shot golf', or 'target golf' to a series of greens at varying ranges with the flagstick as the bull's-eye and the green marked with concentric white circles with varying points values. But the normal tournament remains a stroke-play event in which every shot played over the four rounds counts. Both television and professionals prefer this kind of play, which is a surer test of ability and is certain to finish on the last green, to match-play, the traditional form of settling amateur championships. In this, the result depends on the winning of a greater number of holes and not on the total number of strokes taken in a complete round. It is the form in which the traditional matches between Britain and the United States—the Walker Cup for amateurs, the Ryder Cup for professionals, and the Curtis Cup for women—are decided. But among professionals, it is kept alive only by one or two events, including the British match-play championship and the Piccadilly world match-play.

It is possible that the years ahead may well see the co-ordination of the existing tournament circuits round the world so that a professional can always be seeking his fortune somewhere. It is a lucrative game, well worth the necessary effort.

But, as the rewards become bigger, there may well be a tendency for players to travel less. For the world professional, golf is a hard grind, far removed from the relaxing game that it was intended to be and that most amateurs find it.

6

Leb (signature)

Mary Evans (vertical credit)

Amateur Golf

For the most part, amateurs represent that section of the iceberg of golf that lies below the surface. They are as old as the game itself, and the most famous star of the professional game recognizes that in the last analysis he owes his livelihood to the great army of week-end golfers, most of them duffers compared with himself. But without the demand for the game, for goods, instruction, and courses, there would be no purpose in the professional game. For once the amateur loses his taste for the game, the demand for the spectacular side of it would cease to exist.

The first landmark in the organization of the amateur game was the action taken by the Prestwick club, who in 1857 invited a number of Scottish clubs and Blackheath from England to St Andrews to take part in a knock-out foursomes competition. The trophy, a silver claret jug, was won by the Blackheath pair. The next year, the idea of club foursomes was abandoned in favour of an individual contest, but this attempt to start an amateur championship came to nothing, and the championship proper dates from 1885 when the Royal Liverpool club issued an open invitation. The history of that club is closely intertwined with the history of amateur golf, for it was there that the English championship was inaugurated in 1926 and it was also the venue of the first international match between England and Scotland and later between Great Britain and the United States. It was also the home of some of the greatest amateurs of the times, notably John Ball, whose eight Amateur championship victories spanned a quarter of a century, his last one coming in 1912. Other distinguished members of the club were Harold Hilton, who, in addition to winning the Amateur four times, won the Open twice and the US Amateur once, and Jack Graham.

After World War I, three outstanding golfers, Roger Wethered, Cyril Tolley, and Ernest Holderness, bestrode the scene. As in the professional field though, the scene became increasingly dominated by the Americans who went over to play in the Walker Cup matches between the two countries. This was especially so after World War II, but British golfers, Joe Carr and Michael Bonallack, checked this tendency, Bonallack winning four championships in the 1960s.

As the game became more international, so the number of world-wide fixtures increased. The United States and Britain had been contesting the Walker Cup since 1922. but after World War II, a number of international events emerged, among them the world team championship for the Eisenhower Trophy; the Commonwealth tournament, inaugurated in 1954 to mark the bicentenary of the founding of the Royal and Ancient club; the European team championship; and the match between Great Britain and the Continent of Europe for the St Andrews trophy. Competition for places in these teams is strong, but the time taken in justifying selection and then in taking part in these events is raising increasing difficulties for amateurs, who are drawn more and more from the ranks of those who find it difficult to take a lot of time off their work.

And the rules of amateur status are more strictly observed in golf than in many other sports. The prize an amateur may take is limited to £50 in value, and the expenses he may allow others to pay are clearly defined. The result is that more and more young amateurs are obliged to turn professional, and the incentive becomes all the greater when they see young men, such as Bobby Cole and Bernard Gallacher so quickly making a success of their careers. But if the question of amateur status may eventually raise difficulties, in other respects the amateur scene encourages every kind of young player. Amateur golf gives the appearance of being ordered without being regimented, and in many parts of the world the young player of promise is encouraged from the start.

1 Jack Nicklaus in a studious mood on the green. One of the game's longest drivers, he is also one of golf's leading money-winners and is, along with Gary Player, Gene Sarazen, and Ben Hogan, the only golfer to have won all four major titles—the British and American Opens, the Masters, and the American PGA.
2 Even the best miss them. Gary Player shows just how he feels after missing a vital putt in the 1968 British Open. 3 And some of them, like 'Arnie', wind up in the strangest places.
4 But when the putt goes down, every player from the pro, like Brian Barnes, to the weekend golfer is well entitled to jump for joy.
5 A fan finds two periscopes better than one. But many golf fans never even see their heroes live. Extensive television coverage brings all the major tournaments into their sitting room.
6 John Ball, the leading amateur golfer before World War I, won the British amateur championship eight times. 7 Peter Townsend, one of many amateurs to turn professional and seek fame in America. 8 Michael Bonallack—four times British amateur champion in the 1960s.

7

8

Transworld (vertical credit)

H. W. Neale (vertical credit)

Women's Golf

Apart from the general belief that Mary Queen of Scots knocked a golf ball about in the grounds of Seton Castle shortly after Lord Darnley's death, evidence is almost non-existent about the early days of women's golf. The fisher-girls of Musselburgh used to compete for prizes at golf, but otherwise little seems to have happened before 1880 beyond a little gentle putting.

But for all the awkwardness of their clothing the women were not to be denied. The St Andrews Ladies Club, the largest and probably the oldest in Britain, had 500 members on its lists in 1888, and even in the respectable seaside resort of Eastbourne the ladies' club numbered 100. In view of this, it is not so surprising to find the formation of the Ladies Golf Union and of their championship, in 1893. This event grew steadily in popularity among the higher levels of society between then and 1914, though it remains a wonder that women's clothing, which hardly moved with the times, allowed them to play at all. Miss Enid Wilson, herself three times winner of the Ladies' Championship in the 1930s, has written of this earlier era; 'The tempo of those days was leisurely, and those ladies who took their golf seriously enough to enter for competitions conducted their championships on a country-house party basis. Everyone knew everyone else and after a day in the open air, they indulged in musical evenings together.

In the 1920s, two great golfers, Miss Joyce Wethered, as she then was, and Miss Cecil Leitch, brought a new atmosphere to women's golf and set new standards of play. Women's golf naturally lacks the power of men's, for they are generally much weaker in hand and wrist, but these two brought a power that had not been seen before. Miss Wethered in particular was a supreme stylist, who won the Ladies Open Championships on four occasions and the English Ladies Championship five times.

In the early 1930s two international matches were inaugurated —the Vagliano Trophy, an annual encounter between Britain and France, which was later turned into a Continental team, and the Curtis Cup match between Britain and the United States. This followed the pattern set by the men, but in all other respects the women went their own way, devising their own handicap system and perpetuating the principle already adopted in such women's clubs as Formby and the Wirral of having their own clubhouse and course.

In the years before World War II, a young girl, Miss Pam Barton, came to the fore and earned the unique distinction of holding the British and American championships. Miss Barton was

a great believer in practice, and she might have had an important influence on the game had she not been killed on active service in the war. The outstanding figure in post-war golf was the American Babe Zaharias. She was a world-class athlete, who could hit the ball great distances, and in her free swing and uninhibited manner the emancipation of women's golf was fully expressed. After winning the 1947 Open, she returned to America where she turned professional, going on to become perhaps the greatest woman golfer.

America offers more opportunities than elsewhere for a woman to turn professional. Some clubs have women attached to their staff; there are other teaching posts; and the women's professional circuit, though modest compared with the men's, has gradually been built up to a point where the leading performers can make a worthwhile living. But they have to work hard for a comparatively small return, and the number of young women amateurs turning professional is nowhere near as great as that of men. Elsewhere, though, sponsors have not been prepared to put up money for the handful of women professionals to compete for, and the few who have crossed the line have done so in connection with their work.

Associated Press

H. W. Neale

Heather & Pine International

Ed Lacey

1 For most of the 19th century, women's golf was restricted to gentle putting, the awkwardness of the ladies' clothing itself prohibiting anything more vigorous. **2** Pam Barton was one of the all-time great women golfers, and before her untimely death in 1943 won the British Open twice and the American Women's Amateur championship. **3** After World War II, the American Babe Zaharias dominated women's golf, both as a professional and an amateur. **4** A well bunkered 11th green at Worthing Hill Barn Golf Club in Sussex illustrates the problems golfers face on courses all over the world. And it does not matter whether the golfer is a leading professional or a weekend duffer, he still has to clear those bunkers in order to get to the green.
5 Water hazards, such as this one at Augusta, Georgia, home of the US Masters, are a feature of American courses. In Britain, it is the 'rough' that provides golfers with a challenge.
6 A guide to Royal Birkdale during the 1968 Alcan.

Courses

Although it was not always so, most golf courses usually consist of one circuit of 18 holes; there are, however, still a number of 9-hole courses and even some with anything from 8 to 16. Not that this is in any way odd. For when golf began, there was no set number of holes. The players gathered together at the start and played to as many holes as the land seemed to offer naturally. This varied from place to place, and it was not until much later that 18 holes became the standard the world over.

Because of the primitive equipment used in the early days, courses were quite short, but today, with more sophisticated clubs featuring steel or aluminium shafts and balls that are complicated products of the rubber industry, courses have to be around the 6,000-yard mark for the 18 holes. In fact, many are much longer, and for championships the standard is over 7,000 yards—a figure that is by no means a maximum.

One of the unique pleasures of golf is that, although a course may have been prepared for a championship and its stars, it is possible for a club member to go out immediately afterwards and tread where the great have trodden. This pleasure, however, is denied to followers of many other sports. Only in his dreams does the football fan play at Wembley or the cricketer at Lord's.

Some of the finest courses in the world are found in Great Britain, where the climate results in the growth of the finest golfing grass and nature has provided seaside linksland that is the envy of the world. The Lancashire coast and parts of Scotland boast splendid courses that have tested, and often beaten, some of the world's greatest players. Australia has also produced a number of first-class courses, but these have been modelled on American, rather than British, lines.

America, without Britain's advantages in types of grass, has done away with the sort of punitive rough that is a feature of British courses and has concentrated largely on sand and water hazards. The tee shot has to be carefully placed, not to avoid the rough, but to set up the second shot to the green. The Americans have also tried to eliminate entirely the luck of the bounce, which can play a large part in the British game, and in this they have largely succeeded.

The American pattern is being followed in those countries that are not blessed with a British climate. In the hotter parts of Europe, such as Spain and Portugal, and in Malaysia and the Far East, courses, including the fairways, are kept alive by constant watering. It is in these newer golfing countries that the newer aspects of golf course design can be seen. Many clubs have three or four nine-hole loops that start and finish by the clubhouse, and even these loops have more than one starting point to ease the pressure at weekends. The fairways are wide and the rough sparse so that time is not wasted in looking for balls. The whole emphasis is on getting people round the course without undue delay.

Golf course architecture. One of the tests of good golf architecture is that the result should give the appearance of being entirely natural, of having grown that way without the benefit of man. Of the earlier generation of architects, Willie Park (Sunningdale Old) was an outstanding artist and Sunningdale also provides an example in the New Course of the work of another master, H. S. Colt. In the United States many fine courses were built by expatriate Scots, notably Donald Ross (Pinehurst) and Dr Alister Mackenzie (Augusta National, in collaboration with Bobby Jones).

One exception to the generalization that great architects are notable for the unobtrusiveness of their work is the American Robert Trent Jones, one of the busiest and most successful practitioners. He stamps his signature unmistakably on his work, with raised and extravagantly sculptured greens, eccentrically shaped bunkers, and the liberal use of artificial water hazards.

He sculpts the landscape, making full use of earth-moving machinery to build mountains if he feels them to be necessary. At Baltusrol, New Jersey, the members complained that the short fourth hole, involving a long carry over an artificial pond, was excessively difficult after he had redesigned it for the 1954 US Open. Trent Jones returned to the club, placed a ball onto the tee and struck it over the pond, onto the green, and right into the cup for a hole in one. Pausing only to remark, 'I think that answers your criticism, gentlemen', he strode from the scene.

1

Equipment Lillywhites/Photo Alan Duns

2

Equipment Lillywhites/Photo Alan Duns

The grip

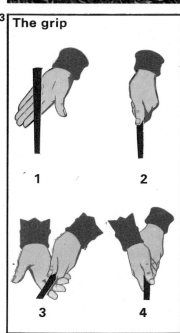

1   **2**

3   **4**

Roy Castle

Opposite page, **Equipment** proves an irresistible fascination for most golfers and they read every golf book out and endlessly debate the pros and cons of various items. One of the current controversies centres on the merits of the British ball, foreground, left, and larger American one, right. **1** The four woods and **2** some of the many putters available. Putting is a matter of touch and confidence and the search for consistency brings out some curiously shaped clubs. **3** In order to play any shot correctly, the golfer needs the correct grip. Simply, this is the one that allows him to hit the ball where he wants it to go and most golfers use the 'V' grip. The drawings show the various stages used in taking up the grip which was originated by the great Harry Vardon and is usually known as the Vardon Grip.

Equipment

The basic items of golf equipment are clubs and balls. Both vary enormously in price, but most are efficient enough for the golfer who plays for pleasure. The rules of golf prohibit the introduction of gimmicks such as variably angled club faces and the croquet-style putter, so all clubs are basically variations on a well-defined theme. There are few differences in the quality of clubs of various prices that will substantially affect their playability. The main difference is in the quality of the shaft.

The rules of golf limit the number of clubs a player may carry on any round to 14, but a set sufficient for normal play will include only 8—numbers 2 and 4 woods, 3, 5, 7, and 9 irons, a wedge, and a putter. Such a set enables the golfer to play the ball in almost any predicament. The tournament professional no doubt, requires the full range, but his technique has been refined to an enormous extent.

The length of the club shaft may vary with the player's physique, and also with the club used. The longest shaft is found on the No. 1 wood, and the length decreases progressively through the low irons (2, 3, and 4), the medium irons (5, 6, and 7), the short irons (8 and 9), the wedge, and the putter. The degree of loft of the club face also varies progressively from about 11° on the driver to 59° on the sand wedge. The weight of the club, like the length of the shaft, is a matter for individual preference. The 'feel' of a club is more important than its weight, although most men use heavier clubs than women do.

Two types of golf ball are in general use. The traditional British ball with a minimum diameter of 1.62 inches and maximum weight of 1.52 ounces, and the bigger American ball (minimum diameter of 1.68 inches) coexist uneasily in the golf world. It is generally considered that the American ball induces a higher standard of play, although many British professionals have had difficulty in adapting to its behaviour in flight. For the everyday golfer, however, there will be little substantial diference, as the aerodynamic idiosyncrasies of the ball are more likely to originate in the way the ball is hit than in its actual construction. Modern golf balls are hard and elastic, and this quality is a result of their composition: the core is a small sac filled with liquid silicone or a similar substance, and this is surrounded with tightly wound rubber threads, and the whole is covered with a thin rubber or plastic case. Balls are normally white, though the game's fanatics use dark balls when they are playing in snow!

A third practical item of equipment is the tee, a small plastic or wooden support on which the ball is placed prior to playing it from the teeing ground (also known as the tee). It is brightly coloured so that it can be easily recovered after the ball is played.

All these items are carried round the course in a large, waterproof bag, but as a round may take some time to play, many golfers carry the bags on a two-wheeled trolley, known as a caddie-cart. On some courses small electrically powered cars are available for the less energetic player.

Almost every player wears spiked shoes to give him better purchase during the swing and the right-hander will wear a glove on his left hand to give him a better grip. The weight of the bag is increased by markers, which indicate the position of the ball on the green when it is lifted for cleaning, and by a miscellaneous assortment of towels, rags, rule books, and bad weather equipment.

Techniques

The techniques of golf are at once basic and elusively subtle. They are basic in that all one has to do is to stand still and hit a stationary ball in a chosen direction. An apparently simple task, yet as soon as you attempt it you realise how incredibly difficult it really is. There are in fact so many variables involved that some people play the game all their adult life and never even approach perfection, which, in golfing terms, can be defined as the ability to play a course in par figures. To make things easier the different clubs have been designed to fit particular situations in which a golfer may find himself, but essentially the flight of the ball in the air or its path along the ground depends directly on the manner in which it is struck.

There are three main types of shot in golf, just as there are three main types of club. There are the strokes used with the woods and long irons, the short irons and wedge, and putting. The angle of the club face and the length of its shaft determine the distance and path of the ball, but the success of any shot depends directly on the correct actions of the player himself.

The drive is the basic golf shot, and its execution can be dramatic in the case of Jack Nicklaus or traumatic in the case of the nervous weekender who fluffs it on the first tee outside the clubhouse bar. The first essential of any successful shot is the grip. There is no one correct way to grip a golf club, but certain elements apply to all golfers. The illustrations show the placings of the hands on the shaft which have, in general produced the best results for the greatest number of people.

The hands should be in such a position that if the fingers are opened the palms of the hands are directly opposed to each other. Basically, the 'V' formed between the forefinger and thumb of each hand should (in the case of a righthanded player) point to a spot somewhere between the chin and the right shoulder.

Two basic faults—the slice and the hook—often arise through an incorrect grip. For the right-hander, if the ball swings from left to right in the air it has been sliced. In other words it has been hit with the club face 'open'. If it is the grip that is at fault both hands should be moved to the right on the shaft, as a unit. If the ball is hooked—from right to left in the air for the right-hander—then the reverse remedy applies. If the ball flies straight—in any direction—through the air, then the grip is satisfactory. By intelligent experiment, every golfer can quickly find his own perfect grip. If the ball is flying straight but not in the intended direction then the player must look for some other fault in his technique.

The angle of the club face at the moment of impact determines the character of the ball's flight. The actual direction of flight is dependent on the direction of the swing, while the distance the ball travels depends on the speed of the club head at the moment of impact. The easiest way to achieve the 'perfect' swing path is for the golfer to stand with the feet, hips, and shoulders all parallel to the intended path of the ball. If the body is placed in this position and the club is correctly gripped and swung the ball should travel in the intended direction. In taking his stance, the golfer places the clubhead behind the ball, aiming at the target, and then adjusts his grip and feet position so that he can reach the ball comfortably. For the long-shafted woods, he will stand farthest away, and get progressively nearer the ball when playing with the higher irons. When, at last, he reaches the green and plays with the putter, he will stand with his head directly over the ball. If he stands too far from the ball, the chances are he will 'top' it, and the ball will be hit into the ground. If he stands too near, he will get underneath it and the club will probably dig deep into the earth, and the ball will fly into the air much higher than intended and land short.

The purpose of the swing is to return the clubhead to the ball at point of impact in exactly the same position that it was in at time of address. The backswing is the source of power in the golf shot. It is the coiling of the body spring, that governs the position from which the club can be swung into the back of the ball to project it straight to the target. In order to achieve a square hit into the back of the ball it is necessary to maintain the direction of the swing and the angle of the club's approach to the ball.

Above all, the backswing is one smooth movement of shoulders, arms, and club into the preparatory position. Then comes the moment of truth—the downswing. The purpose of the downswing is to release the power that has been built up in the backswing but at the same time the golfer must maintain the plane and direction of the swing. At all times during the downswing the golfer must keep his eyes on the ball, and as the spring of the body is uncoiled the rotational effect of the swing forces the body round. Thus, in the case of a right-handed golfer, the body is twisted to the right, and the whole combination of torso, arms, and legs, untwists to the left. This action will force the head to turn after the ball has been struck, and the right foot to rotate on its toes. The left foot is kept firmly on the ground. A combination of hand, body, and eye makes for a successful shot.

As the length of the shaft decreases, so less body movement is used and more wristiness comes into the stroke. The legs will also be bent more, especially on difficult lies in the rough or in bunkers. Approach shots are normally played with the higher numbered irons, so that the ball descends almost vertically onto the green and does not run beyond it. With these shorter shots better players are able to put extra 'back-spin' on the ball so that it stops almost dead on the green or even runs backwards.

More words have been written on the art and problems of putting than on any other feature of the golf game. Equally, there are probably as many theories on successful putting as there are golfers, so it is impossible to generalize. To see equally proficient golfers using quite disparate techniques on the green, and for all their practice missing the most simple of putts, is one of the everlasting mysteries of golf. Some grip the top of the putter, others grip it halfway down the shaft. Some even place one hand at the top of the club and the other near the bottom, or putt with their hands the wrong way round—that is a right-hander putting with his right hand at the top of the shaft, a sort of 'backhand'. But in putting the composition of the green plays a larger part than the course otherwise plays in the approach shots. Course architects introduce subtle slopes and runs into the green that can add many shots to the careless or luckless player's score. The well-holed long putt in excess of 25 yards is a sight more dramatic than the longest drive.

Golfers must, therefore, master a considerable number of skills if they are to reach the top. As well as the physical art of hitting the ball true, they must be able to judge distances accurately and master the quite considerable physical and mental demands of playing two full 18-hole rounds a day in tournaments.

Equipment Lillywhites/Photo Alan Duns

1 The irons from 3 to 9 and two wedges (far right). The angle of the face, or 'loft', of irons determines the length of the shot. As is illustrated in 2, the length the ball is hit decreases as the higher-numbered irons are used. Clubs with more loft are used for approach shots and the wedges are used for high, short pitches and for getting out of bunkers. The distances given in 2 are approximately those that the average golfer should reach. 3 The short chip to the green. 4 Blasting out of a bunker. The wrists are kept firm throughout the shot. 5 Bob Charles lives up to the axiom that good golfers take turf with their irons. 6 Gary Player plays a delicate chip to the green, allowing the ball to land short and run up to the hole. 7 The basic swing is applicable to most shots.

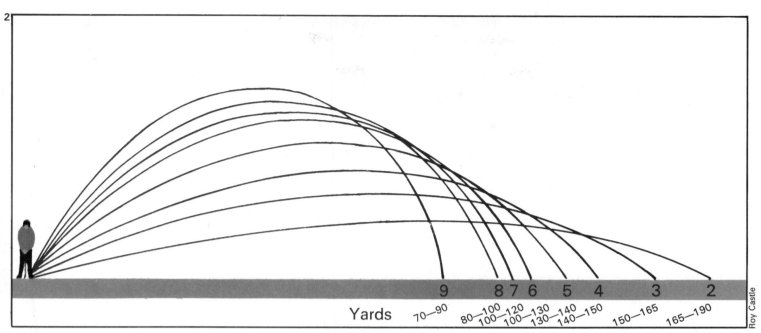

2

9 8 7 6 5 4 3 2

Yards 70—90 80—100 100—120 100—130 130—140 140—150 150—165 165—190

Roy Castle

5

Colour Sport

6

Colour Sport

Roy Castle

Greyhound Racing

The stands are jam-packed. The six Greyhound Derby finalists, muscles rippling lazily under light-weight racing jackets, complete their parade on the green track. The multi-coloured totalisator-board flashes the latest betting figures; the bookmakers in the forecourts bawl the last-minute odds, which are frantically signalled across the stadium by white-gloved tic-tac men. Bowler-hatted kennel lads carefully place the dogs into the starting box, and the stadium lights dim, leaving the grass of the racetrack a green oval ribbon under blazing overhead lamps. The 35,000 crowd is silent for an eternal second, and then the dummy hare wobbles to a start. As it picks up speed, the crowd erupts into the famous Derby roar, which mounts to a crescendo when the hare flashes past the starting box. Up spring the traps, and out streak the six champion greyhounds in hot pursuit of the hare and a £10,000 pay-off for the winner. Four incident-packed bends and 28½ seconds later, the top classic event in British greyhound racing is over for another year. The winner, who may have cost £50 as a pup, or £3,000 as a grown dog, returns to the presentation dais to wag his tail while the gold and blue jacket of honour is fitted, and the cups are presented to owner and trainer.

To greyhound racing enthusiasts the world over, the scene is similar. It could, for example, have been the National Greyhound Sprint Championship in Sydney, Australia, or the American Derby at Taunton, in the United States. Ireland, Spain, the Canary Islands, New Zealand, Indonesia, Macao (China), and Italy all have greyhound racing. So, too, do Norway, Sweden, Denmark, Germany, Finland, the Netherlands, and Switzerland, though betting is not permitted in these countries.

The greyhound's ancestry can be traced back several thousands of years. It is mentioned in the Bible and was prized by Greeks, Egyptians, Assyrians, and Persians as a hunting dog. And it was because it was a hunter that the dog received its name, from the Icelandic *greyhundr—grey* meaning *dog, hundr* meaning *hunter.* In fact, greyhounds are never grey but brindled, blue, black, fawn, or white.

As opposed to hounds, who hunt by scent, greyhounds chase by sight, and the first recorded instance of a dummy hare being used to entice the greyhounds to race was in 1876, at the Welsh Harp in Hendon, North London. The hare was dragged along by a rope attached to a windlass, but the venture never really caught on and died a natural death. One reason may have been that,

because a straight course was used, the fastest dog invariably won. But with the advent of a circular track in America in the early 20th century, greyhound racing soon came into its own.

The American founder of greyhound racing, Owen Patrick Smith, spent years attempting to develop an artificial lure suitable for an oval or circular track, and in 1919 his experiments paid off when the first important meeting using his device, at Emeryville, California, was a success. The new sport spread overseas, England holding its first greyhound meeting in 1926 and Australia following a year later—the year Owen Smith died, having already patented 53 dog-track devices and organized the International Greyhound Racing Association.

The racing

Modern greyhound races are divided into graded and open events, ranging from 230-yard sprints to 1,200-yard marathons. Up to six greyhounds may run in a British or Irish race; eight is the usual number in America and Australia. British greyhounds usually race on grass, but America and Australia favour a sand track.

Graded races are for greyhounds attached to the track where the races are held. The local manager selects the runners for each race and grades them according to ability, his theoretical objective being a dead-heat between all runners. Registered wide runners may be placed in outside trap positions and a draw is made for the other placings. Though these races carry only modest prize money, they are the sport's mainstay.

Any approved runner, including the best graded runners and greyhounds trained in private kennels, can enter for *open* races. Entry fees are charged and prize money can be lucrative for prestige events which draw big crowds. And as wide runners are not seeded, the draw plays an important part. *Handicaps*, in which faster runners are penalized by having to start behind slower rivals, are particularly popular in Scotland and the North of England but are rarely used elsewhere. But *hurdle*

1 Greyhounds at the 'off' bound from their traps in pursuit of a dummy hare that they can never quite catch.
2 Cornering at almost 40 mph places an enormous pressure on a dog's fragile legs and is a common cause of injury. Inexperienced runners tend to run wide on corners where clever dogs can gain lengths.
3 The electrically operated dummy hare is run along either the inside or the outside of the track.
4 Greyhounds take a corner beneath the totalisator betting indicator which records pre-race price fluctuations for each runner.

races are popular, especially in Britain. They present a thrilling spectacle, and greyhounds who lose interest on the flat often take a new lease of life over the jumps.

Most American racetracks subscribe to an automatic grading system which moves dogs to a higher grade when they win and to a lower grade when they finish out of the prize money (first four) thrice running. The grade of the race is indicated in the track programme, and racing forms have a barometer of each dog's ability.

Because of Britain's strict quarantine laws, international racing there has been thwarted. However, Anglo-Irish international races have taken place in both countries and teams from Britain and Ireland are sent to race permanently in America and also in Spain.

Before a race, runners are fitted with light muzzles and wear coloured jackets denoting the starting-traps number. After a veterinary examination and identity check in the paddock, the runners parade on the track for public inspection and are then put in the respective compartments of the starting traps, which have a grilled front. The dummy hare—usually skins stretched over a frame—has a bobbing movement and is electrically operated. It passes the box at speed, tripping a mechanism that automatically opens the front grill to release the greyhounds who have already been alerted by first the noise and then the sight of the lure. During the race, the hare must not be too close to the runners, for this causes checking, or too far ahead, as the dogs will lose sight of it.

Once the race is under way, many factors come into account. Speed is vital, but courage and trackcraft count for a lot. The ability to negotiate the bends and the luck of the trap draw can make or mar chances. For example, a wide runner drawn in trap one could badly bump itself and others when swinging out on the critical first bend, where a clash of racing styles can cause major mishaps before the field spreads out. Around the second bend and along the back straight speed nullifies earlier set-backs, though a back-straight specialist may encounter trouble entering the third bend where front runners may start to fade. The clever dog, however, can slip through if openings are presented, and on the last bend, where the leaders may be tiring and challengers looming up, railing ability can gain yards as opponents swing wide.

Once the race is over, the hare is slowed to a halt round the next two bends and covered with a metal lid. An old skin is often thrown to appease the dogs, who are collected by their handlers and returned to the racing kennels or paraded for presentation.

Development of the sport

Britain and Ireland. When an American, Charles Munn, showed pictures of the embryonic American sport to Brigadier-General A. C. Critchley, a Canadian living in England, 'Critch' immediately saw its immense possibilities. A company called the Greyhound Racing Association (GRA) was formed, and a track built at Belle Vue, Manchester. Greyhounds recruited from coursing kennels were trained to pursue the dummy hare. And on July 24, 1926, 1,700 people saw Mistley, a dog with half a tail, win the first race ever held in Britain on a circular track.

The GRA introduced greyhound racing to London, and White City opened in 1927. Tracks mushroomed all over the country, particularly on waste grounds in the metropolitan areas, and some raced seven days a week. But many managements were less than satisfactory. There were doping scandals, dogs were switched, and razor gangs and protection racketeers harassed the bookmakers. All of which gave ammunition to the anti-gambling elements, headed by the Church.

Promoters acted swiftly. The best-run tracks banded together in alliance as the National Greyhound Racing Society, from which developed a governing body, the National Greyhound Racing Club, in 1928. Rules were drawn up and all members of the NGRS accepted the Club as having complete control over the sport. Stewards administered the new rules, officials were licensed, malpractices stamped out, and gradually public confidence in the sport was restored.

But 1928 saw the sport suffer a major set-back on the betting front. Racing had first operated with a monopoly for bookmakers and then came the introduction of the mechanical totalisator. The Racecourse Betting Act of 1928 legalized gambling for the first time, making the new 'tote' legal on horse-race courses. It did not, however, mention greyhound racing. But despite this, totes were installed at tracks all over the country, encroaching on the bookmakers' business. Antagonized by this, they brought a case against one track, and after they eventually won it on appeal and another case was won in Scotland, the greyhound tote seemed doomed and the future of the sport looked grim. Public sympathy for a greyhound tote made the government promise new legislation though, and in 1934 the Betting and Lotteries Act legally recognized greyhound racing and its tote.

The totalisator made greyhound racing phenomenally popular, and by 1938 the annual attendance had reached 25 million. There was a boom after World War II and the 1946 Derby final drew a crowd of 58,000. Record wagering on the tote produced inflated profits for shareholders in the public companies that promoted the various tracks, and greyhound shares reached a new high on the stock exchange. The boom did not pass unnoticed by the government, and a resultant betting tax on greyhounds (but not on horses) started a slow decline that was accelerated by the advent of television and the legalizing of betting shops. By the end of the 1960s, attendances were below 10 million and the future of the sport was clouded by mounting pressures of takeover bids from property developers as the land value of greyhound tracks appreciated.

Though many champions have been bred in Britain—Derby winners Trev's Perfection, Narrogar Ann, and Ford Spartan, to name a few—Ireland is where most English owners seek potential stars. Because breeders have always carefully retained their best bitches for breeding and so many Irish stud dogs, such as Tanist, have dominated breeding lines, Ireland has produced some of the best blood lines. In addition, it is generally thought to be more suitable for rearing greyhounds, who thrive on being allowed to roam free all day in open country.

The most renowned of all British greyhounds came from Ireland—Mick the Miller. By 1970, he was still the only greyhound ever to have won the Derby twice, and the publicity he received when the sport was young has done much for the Irish breeders, who frequently receive five-figure sums from English owners seeking a Derby winner.

The United States. Though America was the sport's birthplace, few of the 160-odd tracks constructed between 1920 and 1930 are still in operation. Most states that legalized totalisator betting limited it to days only, thus prohibiting wagering at night when the greyhounds, which had difficulty competing with horse racing during the day, might run.

However, although the sport is legal in only seven states, it ranks as the seventh largest spectator sport in America. And in Florida, where it is the state's largest spectator sport, it attracts more than four million people a year to 17 tracks. The most important races in the United States are the US $125,000 Flagler International and the American Derby over 660 yards. Both are open to greyhounds from any tracks in America or other countries.

The American-bred greyhound is a great sprinter, but it cannot match the Irish-bred dogs for stamina. Most of the country's breeders are found in the states of Kansas, Texas, Oklahoma, Nebraska, Missouri, and Arkansas, and some greyhounds come from Canada and Australia.

1 Weighing the dog before the race. Too great a variation from its last weight means withdrawal. 2 Belle Vue track at Manchester, scene of the first greyhound meeting in England. 3 Eight American greyhounds lunge towards the hare on Florida's Daytona Beach track. American races usually involve eight or nine dogs. 4 Hurdle races can produce even more spectacular spills than flat events.

Australia. Greyhounds have been part of Australia since its discovery in 1770 by Captain Cook, who carried greyhounds on the *Endeavour*. Live hare coursing as a sport first started in the New South Wales country town of Orange in 1897, the first event—the NSW Waterloo Cup—being won by a bitch with the unlikely name of Bunny. Live hare coursing is now banned in every state, but all states run mechanical-hare greyhound racing.

The first of these meetings was held at the Harold Park track in Sydney on a May night in 1927, and a week later the first daylight meeting was held. Twelve days later bookmakers took part for

Transworld

3

Ray Green

4

Fox Photos

2

Radio Times Hulton Picture Library

the first time in a greyhound meeting. Church opposition, however, helped persuade the government to ban night meetings after only six months, and eventually the ban was extended to all meetings. It was 1931 before it was rescinded, and night meetings are still illegal in Queensland.

Since the introduction of the TAB—Australia's off-course tote—greyhound racing has enjoyed unprecedented popularity, and in New South Wales alone there are an average of five meetings a day with prize money for the year well in excess of $A1¼ million. The richest race is the National Greyhound Sprint Championship, which had its first running in 1969, carrying $A21,000 prize money. The fastest dogs from each state, selected after elimination races, run in the finals in Sydney. Other important races include the Wentworth Park (Sydney) Derby and the Australian Greyhound Cup.

Australia has produced some of the world's fastest greyhounds, and their times, usually set on hard-packed damp sand tracks, have startled overseas observers. The finest effort by one of these champions was at Harold Park in 1944, when Chief Havoc attempted to set six different track records from 440 yards to 880 yards. Over 17,000 people saw him break five and equal the sixth. Another leading greyhound was Zoom Top, Australia's top prizewinner with almost $A60,000 when she retired in 1970. A consistent performer, she won races in four different states from 310 yards to 870 yards against the best greyhounds from every part of Australia, and ran record times on 16 occasions.

Doping

Since the start of the sport, a constant battle has been fought against dopers, and trainers are constantly on the alert against the doping menace. Today, however, doping attempts are rare. And even if the security barrier is ever breached, the modern chromatography unit is the ultimate safeguard. This mini-laboratory, installed at many courses, is used for tests of the greyhounds when they arrive at the track. Traces of dope can be detected in 60 minutes after tests on urine samples. Should a test be positive, the greyhound is withdrawn from the meeting and a full inquiry by stewards and security officers is held.

Greyhounds can also be made to run slower by being fed a heavy meal before racing, though this method would soon be detected as every dog is officially weighed before the start. Other frauds have involved 'ringing' the slang term for switching a runner with a faster, and almost identical dog. Not uncommon in the sports' early days, the practice was effectively stamped out by the introduction of greyhound identity books, which contain details of

ownership, breeding, and the complete markings and colours of the dog right down to its toe nails.

An Australian greyhound, however, did not even give officials the opportunity of testing it. Part-owners both doped the dog without telling the other. One used caffeine and the other amphetamine—a combination that did not have the desired effect. The dog collapsed and died before it reached the start.

Betting

British racegoers have a choice—they may place their bets with bookmakers or on the tote. In most other countries, tote betting is the only legal form. Nerve centre of the tote is the control room at each track, where all bets are recorded. The betting is shown on public indicators so that the punters can see how the odds are progressing. Win, place, and forecast—naming the first and second dogs in correct order—are operated. Some tracks have accumulator pools—requiring, say, correct forecasts for three or four races—and these can produce dividends of several thousand pounds.

In Britain, off-course betting operates on starting price returns from the track. In the 1960s, in order to increase attendances at the track, promoters refused to allow infringement of their tote dividend copyright. This change also had the effect of preventing a certain type of betting coup—rigging the tote. This was done by investing large amounts on the tote on outsiders at tracks with weak attendances, in order to extend the price of the favourite, which could be heavily backed in betting shops.

The classic case of such a coup occurred at Dagenham, in Essex, in 1964. A brilliant plan involving a team of 90 people queueing at 31 tote windows produced the amazing result of just one winning forecast ticket worth £987 11s 9d—representing odds of nearly 9,875-1. Delaying tactics by the team kept the tote windows clear of other punters, while money was poured on combinations involving the rank outsiders. One ticket only was purchased on each of the favourite combinations, and the result went according to plan. Meanwhile collaborators were placing bets on the favourite combinations at betting shops around the country. It was never discovered how much was laid, but every £100 invested off the course on the winning combination would win nearly a million pounds. In the event, the bookmakers refused to pay up, and it was only after several court cases that the Dagenham track paid out on the winning ticket two years later.

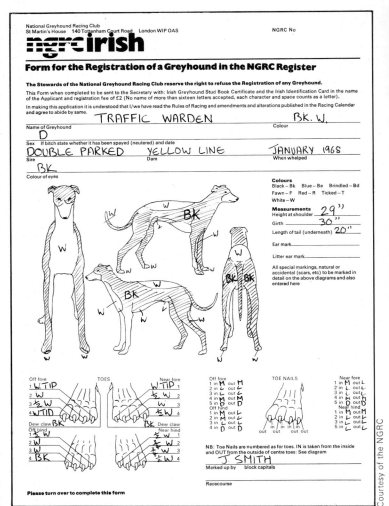

Above, **Modern greyhound racing authorities such as Britain's National Greyhound Racing Club require a complete description of every racing dog. Attention to minor details like toe nail patterns has eliminated betting coups based on 'ringing'—the illegal replacement of a runner by a dog that closely resembles it.** Below, **A vet gives runners their compulsory examination before the race—another of the measures that have restored public confidence in a sport rocked in its early days by scandals and doping.**

Courtesy of the NGRC

Sunday Times

Gymnastics

When the gymnastics competitions at the Tokyo Olympic Games in 1964 were relayed by television into millions of homes all round the world, most of the viewers were watching and marvelling at a sport that was to them completely new. The television commentators realized they knew little or nothing about it: the Press reported it incorrectly. Only since the early 1960s has the mystery which seemed to surround gymnastics been clarified, and it is now recognized all over the world as a sport for everyone.

All schoolchildren are taught sports and games as part of their general education, but in English-speaking countries gymnastics as an extension of physical exercises never became a major sport as it did in other parts of the world. Possibly, the emphasis on individual perfection was thought alien to a society in which team effort was considered of paramount importance. But then, the rise of team games — soccer, cricket, rugby, and so on—was a phenomenon of English life in the 18th and 19th centuries. On the continent of Europe, however, gymnastics flourished, particularly in Germany and the Scandinavian countries. Indeed, the Germans and the Scandinavians laid the foundations of modern gymnastics, but their lead was whittled away, and after the 1940s the sport was dominated by the Russians, the Japanese, the Czechs, and, more recently, the East Germans.

The Russians entered the Olympics for the first time since 1912 at Helsinki in 1952. To everyone's surprise—except their own—the Soviet male gymnasts won five of the eight gold medals at stake, and their women won four out of six. Four years later at Melbourne the men improved to seven golds, and the women to five. Boris Shakhlin and Larissa Latynina won the first of their many Olympic titles in 1956, and they were to remain two of the world's greatest gymnasts for a decade.

The most significant feature of the Russian domination, especially among the women performers, was the new enlightened style they had developed. Gymnastics had always been an exciting and skilful sport, but the Russians added another quality—beauty. This new blending of art and science was in no small way the cause of the great rise in the popularity of the sport.

But the Russians did not go unchallenged. In 1952 a Japanese men's team made their Olympic debut, and finished fifth out of 23 teams. Four years later they had closed the gap and overtaken the western European nations, finishing second to Russia in the team competition. Japan's first individual gold medal came from Takashi Ono, who won the

Chris Benfield

Yvonne Muggeridge, one of Great Britain's top female gymnasts, prepares to dismount from the asymmetrical bars.

horizontal bar at Melbourne in 1956, while in 1960 the Russians had to concede first place in the team competition to Japan.

The Japanese were anxious to excel at their own Olympic Games held in Tokyo in 1964, not least in gymnastics. They retained their team title, with Russia again second, and won four of the seven individual gold medals. Only Boris Shakhlin, on the horizontal bar, won an individual title for the USSR. At the next Olympic Games, at Mexico City in 1968, the Japanese men increased their lead

over the Russians in the team competition, and their tally of individual wins increased to five. The Russians had only one victor, Mikhail Voronin, who won both the horizontal bar and the vault.

The Japanese women had been making great strides forward, too. In Tokyo their team closed up into third place, behind Russia and Czechoslovakia, and were placed fourth in Mexico City. But it was the rapid resurgence of the Czechoslovakian women's gymnastics team led by Vera Caslavska that was the real threat to the Russians.

In Tokyo she dethroned the immortal Latynina as the most successful woman gymnast of the Games, while the Czech team came within one mark of winning the team title. In Mexico City it was again Caslavska who was the undisputed queen of the gymnastic events, while the gap between the two teams was closed—marginally —with the Russians winning with 382.85 points to the Czechs' 382.20.

In the leading gymnastic countries, the sport is very popular. Many of the traditional homes of

GYMNASTICS Olympic and World Champions—Men

Year	Team	Combined Exercises	Horizontal Bar	Parallel Bars	Pommel Horse	Rings	Vault	Floor Exercises
1896*	Germany[1]	not held	Hermann Weingartner (Ger)	Alfred Flatow (Ger)	Louis Zutter (Swi)	Jean Mitropoulos (Gre)	Karl Schumann (Ger)	not held
1900*	not held	S. Sandras (Fra)	not held	not held	not held	not held	not held	not held
1904*	USA[2]	Adolf Spinnler (Ger)	Anton Heida (USA) & E. A. Hennig (USA) tied[3]	George Eyser (USA)[4]	Anton Heida (USA)	Hermann Glass (USA)	Anton Heida (USA) & George Eyser (USA) tied	not held
1908*	Sweden[5]	A. Braglia (Ita)	not held	not held	not held	not held	not held	not held
1912*	[6]	A. Braglia (Ita)	not held	not held	not held	not held	not held	not held
1920*	[7]	G. Zampori (Ita)	not held	not held	not held	not held	not held	not held
1924*	Italy	Leon Stukelj (Yug)	Leon Stukelj (Yug)	August Guttinger (Swi)	Josef Wilhelm (Swi)[8]	Francesco Martino (Ita)[9]	Frank Kriz (USA)	not held
1928*	Switzerland	Georges Miez (Swi)	Georges Miez (Swi)	Ladislav Vache (Cze)	Hermann Hanggi (Swi)	Leon Stukelj (Yug)	Eugen Mack (Swi)	not held
1932*	Italy	Romeo Neri (Ita)	Dallas Bixler (USA)	Romeo Neri (Ita)	Istvan Pelle (Hun)	George Gulack (USA)	Savino Guglielmetti (Ita)	Istvan Pelle (Hun)[10]
1936*	Germany	Karl Schwarzmann (Ger)	Aleksanteri Saarvala (Fin)	Konrad Frey (Ger)	Konrad Frey (Ger)	Alois Hudec (Cze)	Karl Schwarzmann (Ger)	Georges Miez (Swi)
1948*	Finland	Vikko Huhtanen (Fin)	Josef Stalder (Swi)	Michael Reusch (Swi)	Paavo Aaltonen, Veikko Huhtanen, & Heikki Savolainen (all Fin)	Karl Frei (Swi)	Paavo Aaltonen (Fin)	Ferenc Pataki (Hun)
1950†	Switzerland	Walter Lehmann (Swi)	Paavo Aaltonen (Fin)	Hans Eugster (Swi)	Josef Stalder (Swi)	Walter Lehmann (Swi)	Ernst Gebendinger (Swi)	Josef Stalder (Swi)
1952*	USSR	Viktor Chukarin (USSR)	Jack Gunthard (Swi)	Hans Evester (Swi)	Viktor Chukarin (USSR)	Grant Shaginyan (USSR)	Viktor Chukarin (USSR)	Karl Thoresson (Swe)
1954†	USSR	Valentin Muratov (USSR) & Victor Chukarin (USSR) tied	Valentin Muratov (USSR)	Viktor Chukarin (USSR)	Grant Shaginyan (USSR)	Albert Azaryan (USSR)	Leo Sotornik (Cze)	Valentin Muratov (USSR) & Masao Takemato (Jpn) tied
1956*	USSR	Viktor Chukarin (USSR)	Takashi Ono (Jpn)	Viktor Chukarin (USSR)	Boris Shakhlin (USSR)	Albert Azaryan (USSR)	Helmuth Bantz (Ger) & Valentin Muratov (USSR) tied	Valentin Muratov (USSR)
1958†	USSR	Boris Shakhlin (USSR)	Boris Shakhlin (USSR)	Boris Shakhlin (USSR)	Boris Shakhlin (USSR)	Albert Azaryan (USSR)	Yuri Titov (USSR)	Masao Takemato (Jpn)
1960*	Japan	Boris Shakhlin (USSR)	Takashi Ono (Jpn)	Boris Shakhlin (USSR)	Boris Shakhlin (USSR) & Eugen Ekman (Fin) tied	Albert Azaryan (USSR)	Nobuyuki Aihara (Jpn)	Takashi Ono (Jpn) & Boris Shakhlin (USSR) tied
1962†	Japan	Yuri Titov (USSR)	Takashi Ono (Jpn)	Miroslav Cerar (Yug)	Miroslav Cerar (Yug)	Yuri Titov (USSR)	Premysel Krbec (Cze)	Nobuyuki Aihara (Jpn) & Yokio Endo (Jpn) tied
1964*	Japan	Yukio Endo (Jpn)	Boris Shakhlin (USSR)	Yukio Endo (Jpn)	Miroslav Cerar (Yug)	Takaji Hayata (Jpn)	Haruhiro Yamashita (Jpn)	Franco Menichelli (Ita)
1966†	Japan	Mikhail Voronin (USSR)	Akinari Nakayama (Jpn)	Serg Diamidov (USSR)	Miroslav Cerar (Yug)	Mikhail Voronin (USSR)	Haruhio Matsuda (Jpn)	Akinari Nakayama (Jpn)
1968*	Japan	Sawao Kato (Jpn)	Mikhail Voronin (USSR) & Akinari Nakayama (Jpn) tied	Akinari Nakayama (Jpn)	Miroslav Cerar (Yug)	Akinari Nakayama (Jpn)	Mikhail Voronin (USSR)	Sawao Kato (Jpn)
1970†	Japan	Eizo Kenmotsu (Jpn)	Eizo Kenmotsu (Jpn)	Akinori Nakayama (Jpn)	Miroslav Cerar (Yug)	Akinori Nakayama (Jpn)	Mitsuo Tsukuhara (Jpn)	Akinori Nakayama (Jpn)
1972*	Japan	Sawao Kato (Jpn)	Mitsuo Tsukahara (Jpn)	Sawao Kato (Jpn)	Victor Klimenko (USSR)	Akinori Nakayama (Jpn)	Klaus Koeste (EG)	Nicolai Andrianov (USSR)

*Olympic Games †World Championships (venues: 1950, Basle; 1954, Rome; 1958, Moscow; 1962, Prague; 1966, Dortmund)
[1] Germany won two team events, on parallel bars and the horizontal bar.
[2] Team event comprised horizontal bar, parallel bars, pommel horse, shot put, 100 yards sprint, and long jump.
[3] Also won club swinging competition. [4] Also won a rope climbing competition.
[5] This was a Swedish gymnastics team event, with up to 60 men in a team.
[6] Team competition (Swedish gymnastics) won by Sweden; Team competition (special conditions) won by Italy; Team competition (free choice) won by Norway. [7] Team competition (European system) won by Italy; Team competition (Swedish system) won by Sweden; Team competition (special conditions) won by Denmark. [8] There was also a 'side horse' competition won by J. Seguin (France).
[9] There was also a rope climbing event won by B. Supcik (Czechoslovakia).
[10] There were also competitions in Club Swinging won by G. Roth (USA), Rope Climbing won by R. Bass (USA), and Tumbling won by R. Wolfe (USA).
National abbreviations have been used as follows: Ger=Germany; Swi=Switzerland; Gre=Greece; Fra=France; Ita=Italy; Yug=Yugoslavia; Cze=Czechoslovakia; Hun=Hungary; Fin=Finland; Swe=Sweden; Jpn=Japan.

Romano Cagnoni/Report

Tony Duffy

1 Yuri Titov was one of the world's best ever performers on the rings. He won world titles in the vault in 1958, and the rings and combined exercises in 1962. This photograph shows the great strength needed to excel in the rings event.
2 The 1960 Olympic gymnastic events were held in the historic Terme di Caracalla, a former Roman bath. As at most major meetings, a number of events are taking place together and the teams will move on to the next apparatus simultaneously.
3 A Japanese girl gymnast on the asymmetrical bars at the 1968 Olympic Games. Her trainer stands by to guide and assist her through the routine.
4 One of East Germany's outstanding young gymnasts, Erica Zuchold, was sixth on the beam at the 1968 Games.
5 A feature of European gymnastics is the mass display, such as this one at the 1965 Gymnaestrada in Vienna.
6 Danish gymnasts compete in the 1908 Olympic team event—a Swedish gymnastics contest for teams of up to 60 people.
7 An unbalanced and ungainly dismount from the pommel horse—a legacy of Roman martial dismounting exercises.

j&f   Holland   System Reuther

Popperfoto

Radio Times Hulton Picture Library

Alan E. Burrows

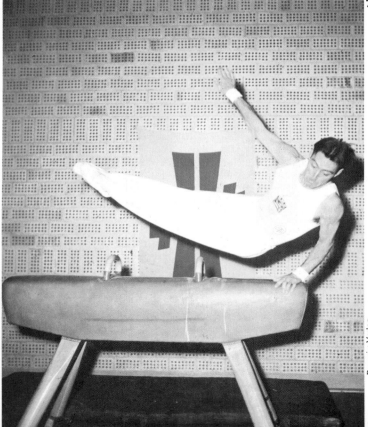

Bavaria-Verlag

Morley L. Pecker

2 the sport—Germany, Sweden, and Switzerland—hold regular large gymnastic festivals. The greatest of these are the famous Czech Spartakiade and the International festival, the Gymnaestrada. The Spartakiade is an almost incredible feat of organization, with 30,000 gymnasts regularly taking part in the giant Stradov Stadium before capacity audiences of 200,000 people. It is essentially a domestic event, but the Gymnaestrada is by contrast a worldwide international event, and it says much for the spirit of the sport and the international body, the Fédération Internationale de Gymnastique, that such universal participation and friendship is to be found at these 'Olympics without medals'. Only one country, China, does not take part.

Development of gymnastics

6 The idea of the Gymnaestrada was conceived after World War II, and replaced the less successful Lingiard which was intended to perpetuate the memory of Pehr Henrik Ling, the acknowledged father of Swedish gymnastics who lived from 1776 to 1839. But although gymnastics is considered to be a sport that has developed in the last 200 years, it does have strong links with the very earliest days of mankind. Over 2,000 years before the ancient Greeks gave the world the word 'gymnastics' and its various derivatives, the Chinese were indulging in a highly organized form of mass exercises based on religious rituals. Centuries later, the Indians and Persians had adopted similar practices.

7 Gymnastics reached a level of development unknown before or since with the successive flowering of the Greek and Roman civilizations. Aristotle, the Greek philosopher, wrote: 'Gymnastics is not just an art, but it is also a science, an anthropological science with a social purpose'. Significantly, he considered gymnastics as first and foremost an art. Galen, the famous physician and a disciple of Hippocrates, produced some of the earliest treatises on gymnastics, showing a profound knowledge and remarkable foresight. Many of his theories are as sound today as when they were written.

The Romans adopted the Greek ideas of physical culture, but they also developed them into a part of the military training of the time. They originated the exercise now known as the vault—they built wooden dummy horses on which to practise mounting, dismounting, and feats of dexterity.

The abolition of the ancient Olympic Games by the Roman emperor Theodosius I in about A.D. 393 led to a decline in all sports for their own sakes. That, and the fall of the Roman Empire and the consequent decline in the martial arts, led to a similar falling away of interest in sport.

In the 19th century there was a

Central Press

revival in interest in all sports especially the ancient ones. The first popular treatise on gymnastics, *Gymnastics for Youth*, was published by Guts Muth (1759-1839), and his work was translated and published all over Europe, where it had a great influence on the sport in its formative years. But two men, Pehr Ling and Johan Ludwig Jahn, were the real instigators of the sport. Ling provided a basis of physical education which many countries followed, while Jahn developed the system of gymnastics on which the modern sport is based.

Jahn's *Turnvereine*, or Gym Club, idea spread throughout Europe, and even to the United States where the German word 'turners' is often used in preference to the English 'gymnasts'. For some years there was an intensive debate concerning the relative merits of Swedish and German interpretations of gymnastics, the Swedish style based on a series of rhythmic exercises, and the German on apparatus work of a formal nature stressing muscular strength and power.

Inevitably, the sport spread to Britain, and the Army Gymnastic Staff (later to be known as the Army Physical Training Corps) was formed in 1860, with the Amateur Gymnastic Association being founded in 1888. The sport flourished, although only one Olympic medal was gained in the years before World War I, by S. W. Tysall, who came second overall at the 1908 Games in London to the legendary Alberto Braglia of Italy.

After World War I, gymnastics in Britain declined partly because of its German origins, but mainly because it was in disfavour with the education authorities. Apparatus was banned, and in some cases destroyed, and the teaching of apparatus gymnastics was forbidden. The advent of television following World War II together with government aid to assist with administration and coaching have helped to popularize and stabilize the sport in Britain. Meanwhile, gymnastics has always been a popular sport in the lands of its origin and although it has spread to almost every country, the honours in Olympic competitions have remained confined to a few proficient countries.

Competitions

Gymnastics as a sport is flexible, and the lower standard contests may consist of as few as one or two exercises. Vaulting and agility are the two most common of these. Competitions are also graded to accommodate all levels of competitor, from school standard up to international. At national and international level a men's competition consists of six exercises: floor exercises, vault, pommel horse, parallel bars, hori-

1 Takashi Ono, one of Japan's greatest gymnasts, finishes his horizontal bar routine with a straddle dismount at the Rome Olympics in 1960. **2** British international Diana Lodge exhibits good balance on the beam. **3** 'Incomparable' was the only way to describe Vera Caslavska as she put on a superb display to win four golds at the 1968 Olympics.

GYMNASTICS Olympic and World Champions—Women

Year	Team	Combined Exercises	Beam	Asymmetrical Bars	Vault	Floor Exercises
1928*	Netherlands	not held	not held	not held	not held	not held
1936*	Germany	not held	not held	not held	not held	not held
1948*	Czechoslovakia	not held	not held	not held	not held	not held
1950†	Sweden	Helena Rakoczy (Pol)	Helena Rakoczy (Pol)	Kolar (Aut) & Anna Petterson (Swe) tied[1]	Helena Rakoczy (Pol)	Helena Rakoczy (Pol)
1952*	USSR	Maria Gorokhovskaya (USSR)	Nina Bocharyova (USSR)	Margit Korondi (Hun)	Yekaterina Kalinchuk (USSR)	Agnes Keleti (Hun)
1954†	USSR	Galina Roudiko (USSR)	Keiko Tanaka (Jpn)	Agnes Keleti (Hun)	Tamara Manina (USSR) & Anna Petterson (Swe) tied	Tamara Manina (USSR)
1956*	USSR	Larissa Latynina (USSR)	Agnes Keleti (Hun)	Agnes Keleti (Hun)	Larissa Latynina (USSR)	Larissa Latynina (USSR) & Agnes Keleti (Hun) tied
1958†	USSR	Larissa Latynina (USSR)	Larissa Latynina (USSR)	Larissa Latynina (USSR)	Larissa Latynina (USSR)	Eva Bosakova (Cze)
1960*	USSR	Larissa Latynina (USSR)	Eva Bosakova (Cze)	Polina Astakhova (USSR)	Margarita Nikolayeva (USSR)	Larissa Latynina (USSR)
1962†	USSR	Larissa Latynina (USSR)	Eva Bosakova (Cze)	Irina Peruschina (USSR)	Vera Caslavska (Cze)	Larissa Latynina (USSR)
1964*	USSR	Vera Caslavska (Cze)	Vera Caslavska (Cze)	Polina Astakhova (USSR)	Vera Caslavska (Cze)	Larissa Latynina (USSR)
1966†	Czechoslovakia	Vera Caslavska (Cze)	Natalia Kuchinskaya (USSR)	Natalia Kuchinskaya (USSR)	Vera Caslavska (Cze)	Natalia Kuchinskaya (USSR)
1968*	USSR	Vera Caslavska (Cze)	Natalia Kuchinskaya (USSR)	Vera Caslavska (Cze)	Vera Caslavska (Cze)	Larissa Petrik (USSR) & Vera Caslavska (Cze) tied
1970†	USSR	Ludmila Tourischeva (USSR)	Erika Zuchold (EG)	Karin Janz (EG)	Erika Zuchold (EG)	Ludmila Tourischeva (USSR)
1972*	USSR	Ludmila Tourischeva (USSR)	Olga Korbut (USSR)	Karin Janz (EG)	Karin Janz (EG)	Olga Korbut (USSR)

*Olympic Games †World Championships
[1]Prior to 1950 the rings were used in all women's events. After 1950 they were replaced by the asymmetrical bars. 1950 was a transitional year when the gymnast could choose to perform on either.
Pol=Poland; Aut=Austria; Swe=Sweden; Hun=Hungary; Cze=Czechoslovakia; Jpn=Japan.

zontal bars, and rings. Women's competitions are limited to four exercises: floor exercises, vault, beam, and asymmetrical bars (also called parallel bars). Both men and women perform two sections —one compulsory and one voluntary—on each item of apparatus. Four judges mark each performance out of 10. The highest and lowest marks are discarded, and the average of the remaining two is the accepted score.

As in any sport requiring judging, the skill and integrity of the judges needs to be of a very high order, and the code book issued by the international body contains a vast wealth of information for the judges' guidance. In brief, each judge looks for the following qualities in a performance: correction of execution, difficulty of execution, and general appeal and aesthetic quality, meaning continuity of movement, balance, poise, sureness, co-ordination, and a wide range of component movements. In the case of the compulsory exercises, the judge must also understand each exercise perfectly, and severely penalize any deviation from it.

The marks thus gained are added together and give the overall result of the combined exercises and the team competition. The best six in each section go forward to fight for the prizes awarded for performances on each separate apparatus.

International championships
There are three main events in the international gymnastics calendar —the Olympic Games, the world championships held every four years midway between the Olympics, and the European Championships held in uneven years. In addition, there is the Gymnaestrada, which is non-competitive and held every four years. The world and Olympic events are combined team and individual championships. Each team has six members and each competitor performs compulsory and voluntary exercises. In the European Championships, there are only individual events: three men and two women from each country perform the voluntary exercises.

The world and Olympic championships are both amazing feats of organization. The competitions last for five days, and nearly 300 men and women from about 30 countries usually take part. Contests begin at 8 o'clock in the morning and go on until late in the evening. All events take place simultaneously, with men and women performing on alternate days. At prearranged times, all groups move on to the next piece of apparatus.

On the last day the pressure on the organizers eases somewhat, as the six top scorers in each event in the combined section fight out the awards given for each separate exercise, performing the voluntary exercise only. It is therefore possible for a man to win eight gold medals and a woman six in an Olympic Games or world championship competition—one for each apparatus, one for the combined, and one for the team event.

No gymnast has ever made such a clean sweep of the awards. The person who has come closest to doing so is the Russian woman Larissa Latynina, who won five out of six golds at the 1958 world championships, while her compatriot Boris Shakhlin won five out of a possible eight at the same competition to become the most successful man. Miss Latynina also won all five titles contested at the 1957 European Championships, a feat accomplished twice by Czechoslovakia's Vera Caslav-

having won 9 Olympic titles and 15 gold medals in world and European championships. Vera Caslavska was only slightly less successful—she won 7 Olympic titles and 14 other major events.

The leading men cannot compare with Miss Latynina and Miss Caslavska in terms of medal totals. The two most successful men in Olympic Games are both Russians, Boris Shakhlin and Viktor Chukarin, who won seven gold medals each in the 1950s and 1960s. The Russians have been forced to give way to the highly successful Japanese in the 1960s. It is the Japanese teamwork that makes them so dominant, though each member of their team is capable of winning major titles. But one must not forget the contributions made to the sport by such gymnasts as Miroslav Cerar, the shy and unassuming Yugoslav who introduced a new style into the pommel horse exercise and won the Olympic title in 1964 and 1968. Franco Menichelli revived memories of Italian greatness in the 1920s and

A spectacular dismount from Serg Diamidov, world parallel bars champion in 1966.

ska, in 1965 and 1967.

Universally regarded among the all-time greats, these two women elevated their sport to heights hitherto unknown. Their styles were flawless, and are studied and copied by their successors. Latynina, who achieved most of her victories after the birth of a daughter, eventually retired at the age of 32 with nearly 20 years of competitive gymnastics behind her,

1930s when he won the Olympic floor exercises in 1964 with a remarkably individualistic display.

Menichelli's Tokyo success emphasized the way in which gymnastics is always developing, becoming more skilful, more challenging and more exciting, but always retaining the essential aesthetic quality which prompted the Greeks, 2,000 years ago, to elevate gymnastics to an art.

Hockey

Among the fastest ball games in the world, hockey at its best is a magnificent spectacle combining skill and speed. To have watched the great Indian sides of the 1920s and 1930s was to have been held spellbound by the supreme mastery of their stickwork over the ball.

One reason for the Indians' success is the fact that they have always been able to play on flat and hard pitches, whereas many countries, especially the British ones, still regard the game as a winter sport. Consequently they are playing when grounds are at their worst and the players' skills suffer.

For many years, men's hockey has to live with the unfortunate stigma that it was a girls' game, even though there is a noticeable difference in the style of play. The pattern of women's hockey is open and elegant, while that of men's is more physical. In addition, the best male players have developed a mastery of the ball that women have not been able to equal. And even though hockey is one of the few team sports at which both sexes can play together the two codes have

tended to keep well apart, except in some European countries.

One of the last truly amateur sports and extremely proud of its status, hockey is noted for the fine spirit that prevails at all levels of the game both on and off the field. If one criticism could have been made of the game though, it is that in the past it preferred to remain insular and isolated. But there is now a new progressive spirit emerging, and at the beginning of the 1970s the game was in the process of rapid expansion, with 60 countries affiliated to the men's international federation and 30 to the equivalent women's body.

Development of the game

Though present-day hockey is often thought to have descended from the Irish version, hurling, which was being played as early as 1272 BC, archaeological evidence suggests that the game, or at least a form of it, is older than that. On a wall in Tomb No. 16 at Beni-Hassan in the Nile Valley, there are drawings of six sports, and one of these depicts two men standing square to each other holding sticks with crooked ends, between which is a hoop or ball. Historians agree that the object is most likely a ball, as the artist

One of the last truly amateur sports, hockey has remained essentially a participant rather than a spectator sport.

could not have coloured it in and still shown the bent ends of the sticks—a drawing technicality emphasized by the other pictures.

Before the end of the pre-Christian era, stick and ball games were being played in many parts of the world, as pictorial references show. It would seem that most of the ancient civilizations had their own versions, and as the world became more civilized so too did the versions. Yet even in comparatively modern times they were often discouraged and sometimes even banned as being too rough and dangerous.

It is not known exactly how the name 'hockey' originated, although there are several possible explanations. It may well have been an abbreviation of *Camogie* (*caman* is Gaelic for bent stick), or it may be a derivation from the Old French *hocquet*, meaning a shepherd's crook. There is an isolated entry on *hockie* in the Galway Statutes of 1527, but it was not until 1838 that *hawkey* was recorded as a game. In 1853, however, Lord Lytton, an English novellist, wrote of 'hockey . . . that old fashioned game'.

Hockey as it is known today

was founded in England. The Blackheath club in South London claims to be the oldest hockey club in the world, and as evidence can produce a minute book with an entry: '1861—Blackheath Football and Hockey Club'. But their game was rough and ready: the ball was a solid cube of pure rubber with rounded corners, the ground was at least 200 yards long, and everyone charged after the ball together. In the west side of London, however, a more sophisticated version developed, and it is to there that the modern game must be attributed. It seems to have caught on initially as an alternative to soccer for cricketers seeking a winter sport. And the Teddington club introduced such niceties as standard rules, umpires, a limited playing area, and curbs on the dangerous use of the stick.

More and more cricket clubs started hockey sections with their own variations, and it was apparent that one set of rules was needed. Consequently, the representatives of the clubs met in the Holborn Restaurant in London on January 18, 1886, and the national body, the Hockey Association, was

formed. Hockey, as an organized **1**
sport, was launched.

Organization

The game spread from England, and today it is played regularly in over 70 countries by men, women, and children of all races. In 1900, the British set up the International Hockey Board to control the rules of the game throughout the world, but they failed to realize the need for an international body to control all the aspects of a rapidly expanding game. And when it was learnt that the International Olympic Committee had decided to drop the game from the 1924 Paris Olympics, seven European countries—Austria, Belgium, Czechoslovakia, France, Hungary, Spain, and Switzerland—formed the Fédération Internationale de Hockey (FIH). Subsequently, British influence on the game dwindled, and the FIH grew steadily in size, scope, and stature. It ensured the return of hockey to the Olympic programme in 1928, and it has never been omitted since.

The progress of the FIH was due mainly to a series of dedicated European officials, and perhaps none has done more to ensure the game's development than René Frank of Belgium, who was elected president in 1966. A member for more than 20 years, he has helped the Fédération grow from a body controlling hockey in 21 countries to one with 60 member nations. And such is the strength of the FIH that even the Rules Board, the

last bastion of British control over the men's game, is in danger of being absorbed within the FIH framework.

The FIH, however, has no direct control over the organization of hockey within its affiliated nations. That is entirely the responsibility of the national associations. In most countries, it is generally the club system that forms the base. These clubs, like the national associations themselves, are run entirely by amateur officials.

An ambitious player usually graduates from his club first XI through county, state, or division side to international level, though some European countries have introduced national teams at several age levels, and junior (under 22) and school internationals are becoming firmly established. The game is being accepted more and more in schools, especially those with restricted recreation areas and pupils of both sexes, and this is one of the reasons the game is making such rapid strides.

A great deal of men's hockey is competitive, with league and cup competitions, although in England hockey officials have not always accepted the need for such a stimulus. Competitive hockey has brought with it a much greater desire to succeed, and it has also led to the emergence of a relatively new but important figure within the sport—the coach.

Though the sport is still predominantly a winter sport, it is increasingly being played in the summer, when conditions are much better. Some continental countries are unable to play in the thick of winter and so have developed a highly sophisticated game on indoor courts. The small playing areas and hard surfaces demand increased skill, and this has led to a vast improvement in the standard of European hockey.

1 The drawing in Tomb No. 16 at Beni-Hassan that suggests a type of hockey was being played as long ago as 2000 BC. **2** The Teddington XI of 1904. In the four seasons up to 1904 they lost just 22 of their 188 games and in that period provided more internationals than any other side—a proud achievement for the club that gave hockey the round ball. *Below*, Lord's, the headquarters of cricket, is the scene of a 1967 pre-Olympic tournament match between Britain and India.

Rules and equipment

As in soccer, the object in hockey is to score goals, and, just as in soccer, the game is played by teams of 11 a side. Each player carries a stick, which must have a flat face on its front side only and a curved end. The head of the stick (the part below the top of the splice) must be of wood, and not have any sharp edges or splinters. The majority of male players now use the Indian-headed stick with a short 'toe', but a great many women still use the old English stick. The main thing, however, is to have a stick that feels right. Handle grips come in three sizes—thick, medium, and thin—and there are four kinds of grips—towel, tape, rubber, or leather.

The ball can be played only with the flat side of the stick, but it is permitted to turn the stick over, which is known as *reverse stick*. No part of the stick may be raised above the shoulder when striking the ball, and the ball may not be undercut or hit in any way as to make it dangerous. It is, however, permissible to play the ball in the air.

Morley L. Pecker

Reverse stick play is used by a player as he is tackled.

The ball, like a cricket ball, is made of leather but is white, weighing between $5\frac{1}{2}$ and $5\frac{3}{4}$ ounces with a circumference of between 8 and $9\frac{1}{4}$ inches.

The goalkeeper is permitted to wear pads and other protective clothing, including gloves, and he usually has a heavier boot than the other players. Canvas boots were once popular but are not really suitable for modern hockey. If the ground is hard, a gym shoe with a serrated sole is ideal, but on wet ground good studs are needed. Certain types of studded cross-country shoes are ideal.

The game is played over two 35-minute periods and is controlled by two umpires who discharge their duties on opposite side-lines, each umpire taking one half of the ground for the whole game. They are permitted to go onto the field.

The ground is rectangular, 100 yards long and between 55 and 60 yards wide. In the centre of the goal-lines are the goals—two perpendicular posts 4 yards apart joined by a horizontal cross-bar 7 feet above the ground. Both the posts and the cross-bar must be 2 inches wide. In front of each goal is the *striking circle,* bounded by a line, 4 yards long, parallel to and 16 yards from the front of each goal and continuing to the goal-line by quarter circles. For a goal to be scored, the ball must have been played by an attacker within the circle, and the ball must pass completely over the goal-line. Twenty-five yards from each goal and parallel to the goal-line is the *twenty-five.*

The game is started with a *bully*. Two players, one from each side, face each other at the centre of the centre-line and tap the ground and each other's stick above the ball three times before either may play the ball. The remainder of the players must be behind the ball and no closer than 5 yards. If play stops for injury, the game is restarted by a bully on a spot chosen by the umpire. In the striking circle, however, a bully must not be taken within 5 yards of the goal-line. A centre bully is used to restart the game after a goal and to start the second period.

Once play is under way, the ball must be hit with the stick and may not be stopped intentionally by any part of the body, except with the hand when it must be stopped absolutely dead. The goalkeeper, however, may kick the ball or stop it with any part of his body, but only within his own circle. A player may not run between an opponent and the ball or place himself or his stick in any way that can obstruct an opponent. Nor may he attack from an opponent's left unless his stick touches the ball before he touches the stick or person of his opponent. He may not charge, kick, shove, trip, strike at, or hold an opponent.

Again as in soccer, hockey has an *offside* rule, and a player is offside if, at the moment the ball is hit by a member of his own team there are fewer than three (as opposed to soccer's two) opponents between him and the goal-line. A player is not offside, though, if he is in his own half of the field, is not influencing play, or if the striker is nearer the opponent's goal-line than he is. If a player is offside, he is penalized and a *free hit* is given to the opposite side.

Free hits are also awarded for any other breaches of the rules that occur outside the striking circle. As the rules do not stipulate that the whistle must blow before the free hit is taken, there is an obvious advantage in taking the hit as quickly as possible before players can mark each other. However, no other player may be within 5 yards of the ball, which must first be motionless. It may be hit, or pushed, along the ground.

If an umpire is satisfied that an offence committed by a defender in his own '25' was deliberate, he may award a *penalty corner*. Inside the circle, there are individual laws for both attackers and defenders. If an attacker commits an offence, a free hit is awarded to the defending team, and is taken within 16 yards from the goal-line in line with the spot where the offence occurred. If a defender offends, either a *penalty corner* or a *penalty stroke* is given.

As well as being awarded for a deliberate offence by a defender in his own '25', a penalty corner is given when a defender intentionally puts the ball out of play. It is taken as for a *corner,* except that the striker can hit-in from any spot on the defenders' goal-line 10 yards or more from the goal-post.

The penalty stroke is awarded as a penalty against a defending team that makes an intentional foul in the circle to prevent a goal being scored, or an unintentional foul in the circle that would probably prevent a goal being scored. The stroke—a push, flick, or scoop—is taken from a central spot 8 yards from the goal. The player may take just one stride forward before playing the ball, and the goalkeeper must stand still on the goal-line until the ball has been played. All the other players must remain on the far side of the 25-yard line until the penalty is taken.

The *corner (long),* is awarded when a defender unintentionally sends the ball over the goal-line from within his own '25'. An attacking player hits or pushes the ball into play from a spot on the defenders' goal-line, or on the side-line within 3 yards of the corner flag on the side of the pitch that the ball went out of play. No attacker may stand inside the circle before the ball is struck, and no more than six defenders may be behind the goal-line; the remainder must go beyond the centre-line.

If the ball is hit behind the goal-line by an attacker, or unintentionally by a defender from more than 25 yards away from the goal-line, the game is restarted by a free hit 16 yards from, and in line with, the point where the ball crossed the line. If the ball crosses the side-lines, play recommences with a *push-in*. The stick and ball must be in contact before the stroke is made, and the ball must travel along the ground.

Women's hockey

The rules for women's hockey are basically the same as for men's, but there are some disparities between the two codes. Women play with a 15-yard circle as opposed to the 16-yard in men's hockey, although the larger size has been experimented with. When the ball goes out of play over the side-line, play is restarted by a roll-in with the hand (a move now obsolete in men's hockey) and consequently the pitch for women's hockey is still marked with a line 5 yards inside the side-lines. At corners, five defenders go past the 25-yard line but not to the centre-line.

A special feature of hockey is the bully that starts play.

Ed Lacey

1 Officials check players'
equipment before an India v
New Zealand international.
The regulations with regard
to the stick are most strict,
and any stick that does not
comply with them is forbidden.
Umpires are also within their
rights to prevent any player
wearing boots or clothing
that might be dangerous.

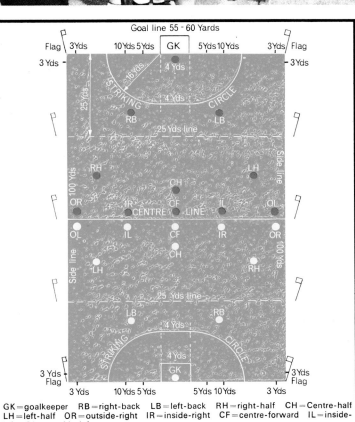

Goal line 55 - 60 Yards

GK=goalkeeper   RB=right-back   LB=left-back   RH=right-half   CH=Centre-half
LH=left-half   OR=outside-right   IR=inside-right   CF=centre-forward   IL=inside-
left   OL=outside-left

2 The ground is 100 yards in
length and between 55 and 60
yards wide. Until 1970, when
the push-in replaced the roll-
in in men's hockey, there was
also a dotted line marked 7
yards inside the side-line
behind which all other players
had to stand until the ball
was rolled back into play.
3 As well as gloves and pads,
some goalkeepers also wear
masks for extra protection.
4 East Germany (blue) score
against Great Britain from a
penalty corner during one of
the 1968 Olympic matches.

International men's hockey

The first men's international hockey match was played between Wales and Ireland in 1895, and soon after this the Home Countries were playing each other regularly. Yet even as means of transport improved, hockey on a truly international scale developed rather slowly, and it was only in the second half of the 20th century that the number of internationals played increased dramatically. From an average of 20 a year in the late 1940s, the figure spiralled to nearly eight times that number by 1970. But as the number has increased, so the nature of the game has changed. For many years it was extremely friendly, but with each successive Olympic Games it has become more and more competitive.

Apart from the Olympics, there are several major continental tournaments, such as the Asian Championships, Pan American Games, and (East) African Championships. An inaugural European Cup competition was scheduled for September 1970, and a World Cup to be played on a four-yearly basis from 1971.

Though the British played such an important part in the game's history and though their hockey is still of a good quality and highly respected, they are no longer the masters of the game. That accolade rightly belongs to the Indians. Hockey was introduced to the sub-continent by British servicemen in the early 1900s, and the Indians soon proved to have a natural aptitude for the game, which flourished in almost perfect conditions. They won the Olympic hockey tournament at their first attempt, in 1928, and have only three times lost their crown—to Pakistan (1960 and 1968) and West Germany (1972). In 1932 the classy Indians gave such a magnificent performance that they were considered to have produced the outstanding exhibition of skill in the whole Games.

They have produced a steady stream of players with fantastic skill, but none is as revered as Dhyan Chand, a centre-forward whose wizardry and goal-scoring ability captured the imagination of the public wherever he played. His appeal was such that it was not rare for crowds of 20,000 to watch him weaving his magic patterns.

Apart from India, there are eight other countries who can claim to have fielded national teams of a consistently high standard since World War II—Pakistan, Australia, Germany, Great Britain, Kenya, the Netherlands, New Zealand, and Spain. And not far behind these are Belgium, France, Japan, and South Africa.

Chris Benfield

Morley L. Pecker

Das Sportbild von Schirner

Hockey Facts and Figures

Attendance: The largest recorded crowd at a hockey match was 60,707 at the England v Wales women's international played at Wembley on March 8, 1969.

Teams: No less than 290 teams took part in a 7-a-side tournament in Argentina in November 1965.

Longest Game: The longest recorded match took place between the Netherlands and Spain at the 1968 Olympic Games in Mexico. It lasted 145 minutes and the final score was 1-0 to the Netherlands.

Highest scores: The highest score in a full international is India's 24-1 defeat of the United States in the 1932 Olympic Games at Los Angeles. In the same match Rup Singh established an individual international scoring record with 10 goals.

The post-World War II international record is India's 16-0 victory over the United States in the 1956 Olympic Games at Melbourne.

In women's international hockey the highest score is England's 23-0 defeat of France at Merton in Surrey in 1923.

Olympic Games: India have won the Olympic hockey tournament seven times in ten attempts. The only other winners have been England, Great Britain, Pakistan and West Germany.

Excluding final pools played on a league basis, only eight teams have reached Olympic finals: Australia, England, Germany, Great Britain, India, Ireland, the Netherlands, and Pakistan.

Only three players, all Indians, have won three Olympic gold medals: Dhyan Chand, Randhir Gentle, and Richard Allen.

Techniques and tactics

The first essential of hockey is ball control, for without it the other qualities of a good player are fairly useless. Both hands should be grasped firmly on the stick whenever the ball is played, the left hand above the right. When making a hit, the hands should be close together, and at all times the eyes should be on the ball. For other strokes, such as the push, flick, or scoop, the left hand should hold the stick firmly near its top and the right hand should be moved to a comfortable position farther down. The feet should always be astride so that the player is well balanced and the body weight can be transferred easily.

Other skills that must be mastered quickly are passing, trapping a ball, stopping the ball with the hand, tackling and dribbling, and the use of the stick in a reversed position.

Hockey has tended to adhere strictly to the 5-3-2-1 formation of five forwards, three half-backs, two backs, and a goalkeeper. But because the three-man offside rule still exists, many teams play with one back to prevent the opposition throwing attackers too far forward. The other back is invariably included in the half-back line, helping to form a strong wall of defenders farther up the field and giving a bigger springboard for attack. Some teams, though, are content to place their wall of defenders with only the goalkeeper behind them and use link men to harry the opposition's inside forwards.

In the past, there has been a noticeable contrast between Asian and European hockey styles; the Asians being renowned for their close passing and zone marking, the Europeans for their rugged hit-and-run type of game. But the development of hockey tactics after the 1950s has led to a rapid closing of the gap between the styles, and many teams now employ man-for-man marking—tactics that have been criticized as being ultra-defensive and that are possibly the major reason for the levelling out of world standards.

1 Indian hockey wizard Dhyan Chand in the 1936 Olympics at which he won his third hockey gold medal. Chand was to hockey what Don Bradman was to cricket and Pelé to soccer. **2** The Indians' skills develop under almost perfect conditions. **3** Umpires caution Indian and Spanish players after continual dirty play. As the game has become more competitive, such incidents have become more frequent. **4** The 1968 Olympic finalists Australia and Pakistan in a preliminary round tussle. **5** Pakistan attack the West German goal in a 1966 Test.

HOCKEY Olympic Finals

Year	Winner	Runners-up	Score
1908	England	Ireland	8-1
1920	Great Britain	Denmark	*
1928	India	Netherlands	3-0
1932	India	Japan	†
1936	India	Germany	8-1
1948	India	Great Britain	4-0
1952	India	Netherlands	6-1
1956	India	Pakistan	1-0
1960	Pakistan	India	1-0
1964	India	Pakistan	1-0
1968	Pakistan	Australia	2-1
1972	West Germany	Pakistan	2-1

*In final pool Great Britain beat Denmark 5-1 and Belgium 12-1, and Denmark beat Belgium 5-2.
†In final pool India beat Japan 11-1 and the United States 24-1, and Japan beat the United States 9-2.

HOCKEY Major International Men's Tournaments
(tournaments involving six or more countries)

Year	Venue	Winner	Runners-up	Countries competing
1925	Geneva	France	Belgium	7
1929	Barcelona	Germany	Netherlands	7
1935	Brussels	British	Germany	8
1950	Barcelona	Netherlands	Pakistan XI	7
1954	Brussels	West Germany	Belgium	10
1955	Warsaw	India	Poland	7
1957	Barcelona	Netherlands	Spain	6
1958	Amsterdam	West Germany	Netherlands	6
1958	Brussels	West Germany	Belgium	6
1962	Ahmedabad	India	West Germany	10
1962	Djakarta	Pakistan	India	9
1964	Barcelona	Spain	Belgium	8
1966	Cairo	Poland	East Germany	6
1966	Bangkok	India	Pakistan	8
1967	Madrid	India	Spain	8
1967	Winnipeg	Argentina	Trinidad	8
1967	Poznan	East Germany	France	6
1968	Lahore	Pakistan	Kenya	7
1969	Lahore	Pakistan	Pakistan 'B'	10
1970	Bombay	West Germany	Netherlands	7

5

Morley L. Pecker

Horse Racing

Horse racing is as popular today throughout the world as it has ever been. Well over a quarter of a million spectators packed Epsom Downs to see the brilliant Nijinsky speed to victory in the 1970 Derby—proof that top-class racing will always draw the crowds. And although not every meeting can boast a Derby winner, let alone a Derby, racing continues to thrive thanks largely to man's gambling instinct, with millions of pounds wagered daily on horse races around the world.

Today the sport is more an international one than ever before. And Nijinsky is a perfect example —bred in Canada, owned by an American, Charles Engelhard, trained by an Irishman, Vincent O'Brien, and ridden by an Englishman, Lester Piggott.

In the 1960s racing thrived particularly in countries such as France and the United States, where betting is a totalisator monopoly. Cuts are taken from the pool for tax and improvements to racing, and the rest paid back as dividends. This simple formula has enabled France, whose betting turnover is estimated to be half that of Britain's, to plough back to racing about four times the amount Britain does.

with very few wins to their credit. More successful trainers can charge owners upwards of £20 a week per horse.

Nearly all trainers employ a number of apprentices who generally start work on leaving school. Hundreds of small boys start off thinking they will one day make it to the top as jockeys, but in reality the percentage of successful apprentices is very low.

In return for a small wage, the boys work an arduous week and are taught how to ride and look after horses. Their day starts soon after dawn when they are up early to ride out with the first string before breakfast. Later there will be another lot, and sometimes two, to be 'mucked out' and ridden before lunch.

A couple of hours off and then it's back to work, mucking out and grooming two and sometimes three horses for up to 2½ hours. It's no easy life for small boys, but there is always another young hopeful ready to take the place of any apprentice who finds the life too tough. If they shape well they may be given rides in public.

Lengths and conditions of apprenticeships vary from country to country. English apprentices can claim a 7 lb allowance until they have ridden 10 winners; a 5 lb allowance until they have ridden 50 winners; and a 3 lb allowance until they have ridden

A box of one's own and good company—pre-season pleasantries for horses that will soon be racing to earn their keep.

Horse racing is more an industry now than ever before, an industry that employs thousands of people in every racing country.

The cost of keeping a horse in training continues to rise at a sharp rate. Latest estimates put the bill for a year at something like £1,500 in England and a little more in France. One owner in four never has a winner, so it remains strictly a rich man's game.

In Britain there are some 700 licensed trainers. A remarkable number of trainers with large strings manage to keep going

75 winners. In contrast the American apprentice—called a 'bug', after the asterisk attached to his name in the racebook— starts with a 10 lb allowance and works his way down the allowance scale until, after he has ridden his 35th winner, he receives 3 lb for a year—if he continues to ride for his contracted employer. If he changes stables after his 35th winner he 'loses his bug' immediately. Under National Hunt rules riders are not apprenticed and can claim an allowance, regardless of age, until they have ridden 25 winners. On the flat

apprentices 'come out of their time', and lose the right to claim, on their 23rd birthdays.

A few races on the flat each year in most countries are confined to amateur riders, or 'bumpers' as they are rudely known. But amateurs come more into their own in jump racing. Women jockeys ride regularly in Britain and many European countries, while in the US and, to some extent, in Britain, they ride on level terms against male jockeys. The girls' fight to ride against men in the United States was a long and arduous one, which took in court actions and strikes by the male jockeys. The latter finally succumbed, and the success of

the lady riders could have far-reaching effects in the years to come.

Britain's conservative Jockey Club for long resisted the idea of allowing women trainers even when it was general knowledge that several women were training with success with the licence held by their stable's head man. It finally took a court action to make the Jockey Club change it's mind.

Increasing paper work is making the life of trainers ever more difficult. Entries, months and sometimes years in advance, have to be carefully logged, declarations and forfeits have to be made daily, transport arranged, jockeys booked, owners'

All over the world, the moment the racing fan's blood starts to stir—as they come round the last bend and head for home.

visits arranged, and numerous other matters dealt with. On top of this the trainer must watch his team on the gallops whenever possible before travelling to saddle runners often four or five days a week.

Jockeys, in contrast, earn their money in double quick time. In England they used to earn 10 per cent of the winning prize, but in the 1960s this was reduced to 7½ per cent, the difference of 2½ per cent rightly going to stable employees. Each race meeting is controlled by three or more stewards who are required to keep an eye on activities on and off the track during racing. Stewards have wide-ranging

powers, including the right to abandon or postpone meetings; leave out fences or hurdles if their retention would cause abandonment of racing; and hold inquiries into running.

The clerk-of-the-course, who is responsible to the stewards, is the man in charge of the day-to-day running of each track. He has to see that everything runs smoothly on race days, and the success or failure of a course rests on his shoulders.

The draw for each race is made at the declaration stage the day before racing. On some courses the draw makes very little difference, particularly in longer races. However, it can be all-important

in sprint races on awkward tracks with tight turns.

With the advent of starting stalls it has become possible to start horses in their correct positions. Sometimes, a team of strong—and necessarily agile—men push into the stalls the more reluctant horses. Horses that are extremely recalcitrant are blindfolded until they are persuaded to take their place.

Racing has certainly become more mechanized in the 20th century. Starting stalls, the photo-finish, and the camera patrol have all served to make the sport

fairer and more open. Once judges faced with a blanket finish suffered agonies about which horse had won—and often stories circulated suggesting that a financial interest helped sway their judgements. Now the photo-finish camera sorts out any close finishes and the judge has the relatively simple task of giving his verdict after studying the print. Dead heats are far less prevalent and no suspicion can be cast in the direction of the judge's box.

The camera patrol films running of races at crucial points and in the closing stages is a tremendous help to stewards in cases of objections or rough riding. It also helps to eliminate non-triers, for no jockey likes to be seen giving his mount an 'easy'.

The going, of course, is very much determined by the prevailing weather, but watering systems have improved all over the world since the war. Racecourses in France are a model for those who always wish to have good going. There is a saying that great horses should act on any ground, but in reality it is only natural that some should have their preferences. Many cannot act on firm ground while others are all at sea in heavy going.

One of the major factors in determining the value of a horse's performance is time, particularly in sprint races. Most advanced countries use electrical apparatus, although in this respect Britain lags behind and still uses hand timing on many courses.

Racing Round the World

Great Britain. The administration and control of racing in Great Britain lies in the hands of the Jockey Club, a body of roughly 100 men devoted to the maintenance and improvement of all aspects of the sport—flat racing and steeplechasing. The Horse-race Betting Levy Board, established in 1961, is the other powerful 'machine'. Its duty is to assess and collect monetary contributions from bookmakers and totalisator which go towards grants for improving racecourse amenities and prize money. Messrs Weatherby's, secretaries to the Jockey Club, handle entries, forfeits, and declarations, as well as licensing of trainers, jockeys, and stable employees.

The British pattern of racing, as far as the top events are concerned, has changed very little for 150 years. The Classic races for 3-year-olds—2,000 Guineas (instituted 1809), 1,000 Guineas (1814), Derby (1780), Oaks (1779), and St Leger (1776) —remain the great targets for every owner, trainer, breeder, and jockey in the country. And the prestige of an English Classic victory receives world-wide acknowledgement. Advances in prize money have provided for a series of five 'semi-classics' at weight-for-age, for 3-year-olds and upwards —the Coronation Cup ($1\frac{1}{2}$ miles, Epsom, June), Gold Cup ($2\frac{1}{2}$ miles, Ascot, June), Eclipse Stakes ($1\frac{1}{4}$ miles, Sandown Park, July), King George VI and Queen Elizabeth Stakes ($1\frac{1}{2}$ miles, Ascot, July), and Champion Stakes ($1\frac{1}{4}$ miles, Newmarket, October).

The racing calendar provides the biggest incentives for middle-distance horses. Three-year-olds and upwards have no £10,000 races open to them at less than a mile, while the Ascot Gold Cup offers the only purse in that range at or over 2 miles. This is a clear encouragement to British breeders to aim at the production of horses capable of staying a mile-and-a-half, in contrast to many other countries which have their racing geared to shorter distances.

There are, however, a number of valuable races for 2-year-olds, catering for those who show early development. Among the most important are: Gimcrack Stakes (York), Middle Park Stakes (Newmarket), and Cheveley Park Stakes (Newmarket), all at six furlongs; Champagne Stakes (Doncaster) and Dewhurst Stakes (Newmarket) at seven furlongs; Royal Lodge Stakes (Ascot) and Observer Gold Cup (Doncaster) at a mile.

Handicaps have made great advances in the post-war years, materially assisted by the growth of commercial sponsorship. Moderate horses now have far more chances to pay their way than at any other time, and some of the most important handicaps generally attract heavy ante-post betting, including the Lincoln, Ebor, Cambridgeshire, and Cesarewitch.

The combined effect of the legalization of betting shops, increased live television coverage of racing, and the imposition of the betting tax has been to reduce racecourse attendances in Britain to an all-time low. This is despite the imaginative introduction of the Racegoers' Club

1 A sight not often seen—ace jockey Lester Piggott takes a tumble. 2 A horse is broken in at Newmarket, the main centre of racing in Britain. 3 All part of a day's work for both smithy and horse. A loose shoe could severely handicap a runner. 4 Diverse styles in riding and headgear as these apprentices fight it out at Sandown Park. Riding in races, though, is just a small part of an apprentice's life. 5 A carnival atmosphere at an English racecourse. 6 Swimming pools are often used to ensure horses have sufficient exercise without risking injury training on hard surfaces. 7 They're off!

Popperfoto

Patrick Ward/Uniphoto

Sport & General

Fox Photos

Patrick Ward/Uniphoto

Australian News and Information Bureau

and strenuous efforts by the Betting Levy Board.

Ireland. Racing in Ireland comes under the jurisdiction of the Turf Club (flat racing) and the Irish National Hunt Steeplechase Committee (jumping), while the Racing Board collects and distributes a levy from tote and bookmakers. Thus the administration of racing is modelled closely on English lines. The pattern of racing too, is similar, though on a considerably smaller scale. Average prize money is generally a little below the English standard on the flat, but a shade higher over jumps.

The hub of Irish racing is The Curragh, in County Kildare, where all five Classics are staged.

These generally come slightly later than the English equivalents, which means that the Irish fields are often graced by the presence of English Classic winners. The oldest Irish Classic is the Derby, which dates from 1866. An earlier attempt to establish a counterpart of the Epsom Classic was made in 1817, with a race with the improbable name of the O'Darby Stakes, but it was discontinued after the following year. The Irish Oaks was instituted in 1895, the St Leger in 1916, the 2,000 Guineas in 1921, and the 1,000 Guineas in 1922.

The winning of an Irish Classic carried no worthwhile status until after World War II. Now the Derby and Oaks, their prizes

boosted by commercial sponsorship, are among the best contested races in Europe. The Derby, called the Irish Sweeps Derby since 1962, receives a grant of £30,000 from the Irish Hospitals Sweepstakes, entry fees and forfeits generally taking the winner's share of the purse over £50,000. Since 1963 the Oaks has been sponsored by the Guinness firm and the winner usually takes a prize in excess of £20,000.

The Dublin government provides incentives—principally in the form of tax relief—for those who invest capital in Irish breeding for the benefit of the industry. Overseas breeders—mainly English, American, French, and German—also make a great and

growing contribution to the Irish scene by establishing studs there and sending their horses to be trained.

The American influence has been particularly strong, with many millions of pounds worth of stock being imported. The successes of American-owned horses in Ireland such as Sir Ivor, Meadow Court, and Nijinsky, are bound to accelerate this transatlantic flow.

The vast improvement in the standard of the racing has not been matched by a corresponding increase in attendance figures, and commercial exigencies of the 1970s seem certain to result in the closure of some of the smaller tracks.

France. Racing in France—or at least in the Paris area—is the envy of the world. The high level of prize money, the quality of the horses, the cheap admission prices, the payments to breeders of winners; these factors confer benefits on all sections of the racing community. Visitors to France make justifiable complaints about the length of the pari-mutuel (totalisator) queues—there are no bookmakers—and the cost of refreshments, but its status as Europe's leading racing nation is scarcely in doubt. And, in the Prix de l'Arc de Triomphe, it stages the most important race in the world.

Scarcely a Sunday goes by between mid-March and the end of October without at least one major prize being contested at either Longchamp, Chantilly, Saint-Cloud, Maisons-Laffitte, or Deauville. International competition frequently adds spice to the proceedings. The reasons for the French pre-eminence are the centralization of racing and the *tiercé*, a tote pool which draws an enormous revenue from punters on a selected race each week in which the backer tries to nominate the first three horses.

The French Jockey Club, the Société d'Encouragement pour l'Amélioration des Races de Chevaux en France, was established in 1833. The French racing calendar lists 22 events as *Classiques*, the pattern of racing being in marked contrast to that of England. Its counterparts to the English Classics are the Poule d'Essai des Poulains (2,000 Guineas), Poule d'Essai des Pouliches (1,000 Guineas), Prix du Jockey-Club (Derby), Prix de Diane (Oaks), and Prix Royale Oak (St Leger). The first two and the last are run at Longchamp, the Derby and Oaks at Chantilly. In addition to these races, the leading prizes for staying 3-year-olds are the Grand Prix de Paris (colts and fillies) and the Prix Vermeille (fillies only).

The Prix de l'Arc de Triomphe, run on the first Sunday in October over Longchamp's mile-and-a-half, provides the greatest international confrontation in world racing. The great Italian colt Ribot won it twice; the memorable 1965 clash brought together five National Derby winners, those of France, England, Ireland, the United States, and Russia, victory going to France's Sea Bird II, winner of the English Derby. When Vaguely Noble won in 1968, the winner's prize was a world record £97,685.

United States. Many Europeans who go racing in the United States find the sport a bore. Almost all the tracks are the same, left-handed ovals roughly a mile in circumference; most of the

Top, Such is the popularity of horseracing that courses can be found in or near most major cities and towns. Some are located on rolling downs and some, like this one at Brighton, Sussex, are seaside courses. 1 A happy Lester Piggott on Humble Duty after the filly had given him his first win in the 1,000 Guineas—the only English Classic to have evaded him—in 1970. The previous day he had won the 2,000 Guineas on Nijinsky, the colt he rode to a Derby victory later in the season.
2 Sea Bird II receives some attention from a stable lad as he works out for the 1965 Derby. Favourite for the event, this French horse was regarded as the best winner of the decade.
3 After World War II, French horses tended to dominate horse-racing in Europe. Galcador's Epsom Derby victory in 1950 was the third French victory in the Classic in four years.
4 A string of horses under the direction of Harry Wragg, a famous English jockey before he became a successful trainer.

racing is on dirt; the horses are apparently run into the ground from the start; and the jockeys are insignificant automatons, who, the way races are run, are rarely called upon to show the slightest degree of horsemanship. For all that, the United States leads the world in breeding of fast horses, and its presentation of the sport to the public is also unsurpassed. Despite the counter-attractions of baseball and American football racing is the leading spectator sport.

There is no legalised bookmaking, all betting going through the pari-mutuel on the courses. An affluent society has ensured a plentiful supply of people with the time and money to go racing; the big business methods of companies controlling the tracks have given them the inclination. Not that everything in the garden is rosy—the 1960s have seen industrial action from pari-mutuel employees which brought racing to a halt at some tracks, and there have even been strikes by owners demanding higher prize money.

The American racing year makes no concession to the seasons, continuing on a January 1 to December 31 basis, with many of the major courses staging meetings of up to 10 weeks' duration. Training takes place at the tracks themselves, so that each stable has a circus-like existence. The overall arbiter of the turf is the New York Jockey Club, but each state that stages racing appoints its own racing commission, which may make its own regulations.

American racing puts a premium on speed. Time is regarded as all-important, and short distance races abound. The most coveted race in the calender is the Kentucky Derby (1¼ miles, Churchill Downs, Kentucky), which forms the first leg of the 3-year-olds' triple crown, completed by the Preakness States (9½ furlongs, Pimlico, Maryland) two weeks later, and the Belmont Stakes (1½ miles, Belmont Park, New York) three weeks after that. The top prestige event for 3-year-old fillies is the Coaching Club American Oaks (1¼ miles, Belmont Park).

Two-year-old racing is very richly endowed and the vast prize money available for juvenile races necessarily places an emphasis on sprint-bred horses. Horses often break down, the result of breeding from fast but unsound parental stock. But the current prosperity of American racing suggests that breeders can well afford to make frequent trips to purchase horses from the hardier European strains.

Italy. The amazing fact about the Italian racing and breeding industry is its high ratio of success to opportunity. The thoroughbred population is small, in comparison with those of France and Great Britain, yet its limited numbers have included such as Nearco, Ribot, Tenerani, Cavaliere d'Arpino, Donatello, Niccolo dell'-Arca, Marguerite Vernaut, and Molvedo—all performers of the highest international standard.

Federico Tesio, who died in 1953, was the architect of the Italian thoroughbred. Breeder, owner, and trainer extraordinary, he bought cheap fillies and mares in England and took them home to establish world-ranking families at Italy's long-time leading stud, the Razza Dormello-Olgiata. His genius as a breeder is unparalleled throughout the world.

Italy stages its counterparts to all the English Classics: Premio Parioli (2,000 Guineas) and Premio Regina Elena (1,000 Guineas), both at Rome over 1,600 metres, Derby Italiano at Milan over 2,400 metres, Oaks d'Italia at Rome over 2,200 metres, and St Leger Italiano at Milan over 2,800 metres.

Many of the top weight-for-age events, including the Classics, were thrown open to international competition in the 1960s after long periods confined to locally bred horses. As there has been no Italian super-champion to defend them, French and British raiders have met with considerable success. And increasing numbers of foreign-bred horses are being imported as yearlings to race on Italian tracks.

Australia. Australia was long regarded as one of racing's 'Cinderella' countries. Most of its horses were the products of inferior animals imported from England, leading many to the natural, but erroneous, assumption that those products were themselves inferior. Over the years there came isolated examples to show that this was not entirely the case. And more recently came incontrovertible proof that Australia is well and truly on the international racing map. Australian-breds are now being exported in increasing numbers, particularly to the United States. Prize money has risen sharply, thanks to increasing hand-outs from the states' off-course totalisator betting authorities.

Among the top Australian gallopers sent to America were Bernborough, Shannon, Royal Gem, Noholme, Pago Pago, and Tobin Bronze, all of whom made

1 American horses fight out the last few yards at Santa Anita on a dirt track typical of those in the United States. **2** Early morning exercise for a string from a Newmarket stable.

their presence felt in their new home. Australia is regarded as the land of stayers. Its calendar has always placed an emphasis on events that put a premium on stamina, including the Caulfield (1½ miles, Caulfield), Sydney (2 miles, Randwick), Adelaide (2 miles, Morphettville), and Melbourne (2 miles, Flemington) Cups. All these events are handicaps for three-year-olds and upwards, the category that provides the most popular races in Australia. The tight tracks, adjusted weights, and short straights almost invariably ensure a 'blanket' finish.

The various states have their own ruling bodies for the sport and each stages a 'Derby' after the Epsom pattern for 3-year-old colts and fillies at 1½ miles. The

Victorian is run at Flemington, the Australian Jockey Club (New South Wales) at Randwick, the South Australian at Morphettville, the Queensland at Eagle Farm, and the West Australian at Perth.

In addition to the big metropolitan meetings, a large number of clubs are licensed to hold fixtures in the country areas. For instance, while Victoria has four racecourses in the Melbourne area, there are no less than 70 country courses in the state. The standard of racing and attendance figures are immeasurably superior at the city meetings.

Other Countries. South Africa continues to import extensively, and its list of leading stallions generally consists solely of foreign horses. The country's sound economy has seen expansion on all racing fronts, with record stake money, record prices at yearling sales, and increased attendances. The 1960s have also brought a succession of brilliant home-bred horses, including Colorado King, Sea Cottage, Hawaii, and Home Guard.

South American countries, particularly Argentina and Brazil, have already made a notable impact on the United States, and the 1970s seem certain to see their influence extend throughout the world. Stallions and mares imported from Europe in the past have now accomplished their task in founding a native South American breed comparable with the best overseas. Among the best have been Nigromante, Argentine-bred sire of the top-class United States racer Candy Spots, and Emerson, undefeated in five starts in his native Brazil and a successful stallion in France.

The end of the 1970s may also see Japan as a world power in racing and breeding. Spending sprees in Europe and America have resulted in many top-class stallion prospects and well-bred mares making the Tokyo trip. Six Epsom Derby winners—Nimbus, Galcador, Lavandin, Hard Ridden, Parthia, and Larkspur—have been standing at stud there. There is tremendous popular support for racing in Japan—170,000 spectators witnessed the 1969 Tokyo Yushun Kyoso (Derby), and the tote turnover on the race was £6,576,000.

History of Racing

The precise origins of horse racing will never be determined. What can probably be safely said is that as soon as man learned to ride the horse, he had an inclination to race him. The earliest evidence of the sport in Britain dates from the years AD 206-210, when Roman soldiers stationed at Wetherby, in Yorkshire, are known to have staged races. Thereafter, references to racing are few and far between, but one notable account comes from the Venerable Bede (died 735) who related how a

3 party of horsemen came across a spacious plain that had been adapted to the purpose of a racecourse. There they determined 'to run and try who had the swiftest horse'.

The association of royalty and the nobility with the turf has always been its most priceless asset, starting on the day in 1377 when the Prince of Wales (later Richard II) rode in a match against the Earl of Arundel. Since then, racing has been the 'Sport of Kings'. Henry VIII played a significant part by prohibiting the export of horses and compelling owners of parks to keep brood mares not less than 13 hands high. He also established a stud at Eltham and imported high-quality horses from Italy and Spain. Early in Henry's reign, in 1511, came the first recorded instance of a race-meeting on the Roodee, at Chester, a fixture that has continued for over four and a half centuries. At that first meeting a prize of a silver bell, to the value of 3s. 4d. was given 'to whom shall runne best and furthest upon horseback'. Elizabeth I inherited her father's love of racing and maintained her stud at Greenwich. She and her court used to adjourn to the races at Croydon, establishing them as the height of fashion.

James I, first of the Stuart Kings of England, was responsible for the 'discovery' of Newmarket. He acquired a palace there and spent long periods in the vicinity, hunting and hawking. On March 19, 1619, he was present at a race on Newmarket heath, the earliest recorded instance of racing there.

One of the first acts of the Protectorate was to ban horse racing, though its purpose was probably more to prevent the risk of riotous assembly than to instil high moral feelings. Cromwell, indeed, is believed to have enjoyed racing—he kept a stud, whose manager, a man named Place, was the foremost breeder of the day and the owner of Place's White Turk, a celebrated stallion.

After the Restoration, Charles II resumed and revitalised racing. The Merry Monarch was pas-

1 The best place is in front as snow flies in a race at St Moritz in Switzerland.
2 Tanino Moutier wins the 1970 Japan Derby at Fuchu racecourse. Intensive buying and increasing crowds promise to make Japan one of horse-racing's major countries.
3 Flemington, venue of the Melbourne Cup, Australia's premier event. **4** Country meetings are a great favourite 'down under'. **5** A spectacular stand dominates a Venezuelan track. **6** A classic scene in English racing—the Derby field thunder round Tattenham Corner at Epsom.

Photographic Library of Australia

Australian News and Information Bureau

John Bulmer/Uniphoto

Daily Telegraph

sionately fond of Newmarket, where he spent far more time than was good for affairs of state, and he was never more at home than when riding his own horses in races over the heath. Charles acquired the nickname 'Old Rowley' after his favourite hack, a fact commemorated by the Rowley Mile, the course over which the 2,000 and 1,000 Guineas are contested. During Charles's reign, racing expanded and there are accounts of meetings at many venues, including The Curragh, in Ireland, and on the Isle of Man. The Isle of Man fixture was established by the Earl of Derby, then the King of Man, which has led some historians to suggest that there may have been a Derby Stakes on the Isle of Man a century before the founding of Epsom's great event.

Until Charles II's day, the story of English racing was the story of world racing. Then the sport began to go overseas. In 1665, Richard Nicolls, first Governor of New York, laid out New Market racecourse on Salisbury Plain, Long Island. As the governor had assumed control less than 12 months before, racing was clearly one of his priorities.

Back in England, when William III came to the throne he imported Eastern horses and encouraged his subjects to do likewise. Accordingly, one Captain Byerly brought home the Byerly Turk, the ancestor of Herod and head of a line which survives to this day. Queen Anne, it is said, personally selected Ascot as a site for a racecourse, and during her reign the Darley Arabian, male ancestor of the great Eclipse, was imported.

Racing was now beginning to make rapid strides. The year 1715 saw the birth of Flying Childers,

1 Ribot, champion in Europe in the 1950s. He later became a great sire and his stock won a record £121,288 in Britain and Ireland in 1963. 2 George I arrives at Newmarket in 1722. The sport in Britain has a long association with royalty.

the fastest horse of his day and the first racehorse to capture the public imagination. Twelve years later came the first *Racing Calendar*, originally produced by John Cheny, and the model for the world's racing annals.

In 1729 came the importation of the Godolphin Arabian, third of the great Eastern progenitors, and in the following year the first export of a 'thoroughbred' (the term was not then in use) stallion to America, when Bulle Rocke, a son of the Darley Arabian, left for Virginia. The Americans were now becoming very racing conscious and, although no documentary proof is available, it is said that in Charleston, South Carolina, a form of Jockey Club was established to run local racing in 1736.

The English Jockey Club was formed at some time between 1750 and 1752 simply as an association of gentlemen with the common interest of racing at heart. Soon it was to assume responsibility for the conduct of the sport at Newmarket and, eventually, throughout Britain. The first recorded steeplechase took place in 1752, the name deriving from the fact that the initial race, over $4\frac{1}{2}$ miles of hunting country, was run between Buttevant Church and St Leger Church, in Ireland.

By now, the British thoroughbred was becoming well established. Whereas the pure-bred Arab had always been regarded as the best racer, he was now being out-galloped consistently by the Arab-English blend. In a few years' time it was possible for the thoroughbred to give allowances of weight to the Arab and beat him hollow. The thoroughbred's superiority was beyond question.

The year 1758 brought the

2

birth of Herod, an outstanding racehorse, but an even more important stallion. Six years later came Eclipse, undefeated and unextended in his racing career and a brilliant stud success. Both Herod and Eclipse were bred by HRH the Duke of Cumberland, further evidence of royalty's contribution to the turf.

The vogue for long-distance races was now passing. Events of 4, 6, 8, and 12 miles had been common; many races had been run in three- or four punishing heats, often with 12 stone in the saddle. The thoroughbred's forte was speed, and though he could manage long distances, the feeling grew that it was not a pretty sight. Horses were also developing at a faster rate and they were ready to race earlier. In 1769 a 2-year-old raced for the first time, and won at Newmarket.

This example was not followed for a few years, but events for 3-year-olds took on rapidly. In 1776 a 2-mile sweepstakes for colts and fillies in this age group was staged at Doncaster and won by Lord Rockingham's Allabaculia. Two years later this race received the name 'The St Leger Stakes.' The first Oaks was run in 1779, for fillies over a mile and a half at Epsom, and the following year a mile event, christened 'The Derby Stakes', was launched at the same course.

By 1777 racing had spread to Jamaica. By the turn of the century, the sport was well established in many parts of the world and the importance of 3-year-old stakes was paramount. Of the 21 Derby winners between 1780 and 1800, eight were sent abroad as stallions, including six to America and one to Russia. Diomed, the first Derby winner, was sent to Virginia at the age of 21 for a paltry sum, but lived to sire the outstanding American racer Sir Archy (1805) and establish the great male line of Lexington, the leading American sire on 16 occasions.

The first handicap was run in 1785 and six years later came the first volume of the *General Stud Book*, which was to set a pattern soon to be copied universally.

At the start of the 19th century racing expanded rapidly in Europe, with France, Prussia, and Austria among the foremost new powers. In England, the sport of kings was fast becoming the sport of villains, too, and corrupt practices grew rife. Doping, ringing, crooked riding, and a general lax attitude by the stewards of meetings resulted in the sport losing public confidence. It was left to Lord George Bentinck (1802-48) to expose and eliminate these scandals.

France's Jockey Club was formed in 1833 and in a few years the country had its own Derby (1836) and Oaks (1843). By 1853, a French-bred filly was good enough to win the Goodwood Cup; a

dozen years later the French colt Gladiateur shattered British illusions by running away with the 2,000 Guineas, Derby, and St Leger. France had achieved parity with England.

1 An artist's impression of the running of the 1836 St Leger Stakes. The oldest of the English Classics, it was first run at Doncaster in 1776 as a 2-mile sweepstake for 3-year-old colts and fillies.
2 Women jockeys were allowed in Britain in 1972, and the following year the Jockey Club permitted them to apply for professional licences from 1975.

Meanwhile, racing had spread to Japan, where the first meeting was held at Yokohama in 1852. Progress had been swift in Australia, where a host of important prizes had been established, including, in 1861, the Melbourne Cup. The 1860s also brought the first Irish Derby (1866), the first German Derby (1869) and, in America, the first Belmont Stakes (1867). The Preakness Stakes was instituted in 1873, and, two years later, the Kentucky Derby. In 1876, the Epsom Derby went to a Hungarian-bred colt, Kisber, and the remainder of the decade belonged to another Hungarian, the filly Kincsem, who swept

unbeaten through 54 races all over Europe.

The United States, which had introduced pari-mutuel betting in the 1870s, made its presence felt in Europe in 1881, when American-breds won the Derby and St Leger (Iroquois) and Grand Prix de Paris (Foxhall). The 1880s also brought the births of two of the greatest horses in the history of the turf—St Simon (1881) and Ormonde (1883). Both were unbeaten. Thanks to a colony of English trainers and jockeys, the Italian Derby got under way in 1884. Two years later, perhaps the greatest English jockey, Fred Archer, committed suicide at the

age of 29. He rode 2,748 winners from 8,084 mounts. The 1890s were more notable for American jockeys: one, the Negro Isaac Murphy, died after a career in which he won on 44% of all his mounts, while another, Tod Sloan, revolutionized the English style of riding with his introduction of the 'crouch'. In 1890 the photo-finish camera was used for the first time, at Sheepshead Bay, Coney Island. Nearly half a century was to elapse before the innovation reached England.

Racing in America was now at a critical stage. Its growth rate had been rapid, so that by 1897 a total of 314 courses were running meetings. By 1908 the figure had dwindled to 25 and betting was declared illegal in New York. Suddenly, despairing American owners sent shiploads of their horses to England and France. There followed the controversial 'Jersey Act' (1913) laid down by the English Jockey Club, which in effect denied many of the imports the designation 'thorough-bred'. The 'act' was repealed in 1949, when the so-called 'half-breds' were carrying all before them in Europe.

In 1919 came the first appearance of Man o' War, reputedly

the best American-bred of all time. He was beaten only once in 21 starts. In 1920, France initiated the Prix de l'Arc de Triomphe, which was to become the world's most important race. The early 1920s saw the introduction of starting stalls in the United States and by 1930 they were in general use there. Only in 1967 did they become widely employed in England. Australasia produced a great champion in Phar Lap, who won 36 races worth over £66,000. Bred in New Zealand and trained in Australia, in 1932 he ventured to Mexico to win the Agua Caliente Handicap, then died of poisoning in California a few days later. Another star of the 1930s was the Italian Nearco, undefeated in 16 starts before going to England where he was a tremendous stud success. The 'film patrol' was first operated in California in 1936, 24 years before its introduction to England.

The 1940s and 1950s were dominated in Europe by the great stud and stable of French textile millionaire Marcel Boussac and in the United States by the products of Warren Wright's Calumet Farm. The former was represented by such as Djebel, Ardan,

1 The tape goes up and 184 legs jostle forward in this 1962 Newmarket race. By 1967 scenes like this had been largely eliminated by the use of starting stalls, although **2** some horses were reluctant to enter them.

The Horses
Racehorses are bred for one purpose only—to win races. But the sad fact is that the majority of horses in training never win a race of any description. Fillies who fail to make their mark on the racetracks often end up at stud, but colts who fail to show any form are likely to be castrated—an operation known as gelding. Castration in most cases quietens down a colt and makes him more interested in racing by taking his mind away from other matters. Only a few of the best colts end up in stud, where they serve a given number of mares each year (see article on BREEDING).

But all this is ignored when a new foal is born into the world. Then the sky is the limit, and until he has run hopes will be high that he could be a champion. Unless bred by one of the comparatively small minority of owner-breeders, the foal is likely to be sent to be sold as a yearling. At the sales will be hundreds of owners, trainers, breeders, and exporters on the look-out for bargains. The chances are that the yearling will be sold to go into training into a racing stable. There he will be broken in by an experienced stable hand. After being walked, trotted, and cantered on the end of a long rein, he will have a saddle placed lightly on his back for the first time.

Gradually he will become used to the strange feeling of the saddle, girths, reins, and the metal bit between his teeth. If he is broken properly he will show little resentment when a light lad will sit quietly on his back. After that initial experience he will be ridden out every day. As a 2-year-old he will be given fast work to see how he shapes. Finally comes his racecourse debut—the day that will decide his future.

Marsyas, and Coronation, while the latter had Whirlaway, Citation, Coaltown, and others. British racing in 1947 saw three landmarks—the first use of the photo-finish camera, the first evening meeting (at Hamilton Park) and the record total of 269 winners by 26-times champion jockey Gordon Richards—who, in 1953, became the first jockey to be knighted. The 1950s opened with the export to the United States of Nasrullah (a son of Nearco), who was to become five times champion American stallion and sire of Bold Ruler, the champion from 1963 to 1969 inclusive. In 1953, leading American jockey Willie Shoemaker booted home a world record 485 winners. Europe's best horse of the decade was Ribot, Italian-bred victor of all his 16 races, including two Prix de l'Arc de Triomphes. The champion of the 1960s was another 'Arc' hero, Sea Bird II, who later left to join Ribot at stud in Kentucky. Sea Bird's pedigree, comprising the best English, American, and French lines, exemplifies the truly international character racing and

breeding have now achieved. The speed and simplicity of long-distance travel in the 1970s will make it even more pronounced.

Betting
Racing could not survive without the betting industry, for it is the percentage of money channelled from betting that pays for course improvements, increased prize money, and many other essential facilities.

Britain is rare in having book-makers and totalisator betting both on and off the course. Most countries have no bookmakers at all. All betting is done through the totalisator (tote), which simply creams off a set percentage for the needs of racing, a further percentage for tax, and hands the rest out as dividends for winning tickets.

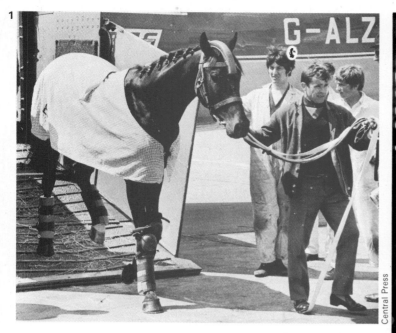

Central Press

Melbourne Herald

1 French colt Prince Regent flew to England for the 1969 Derby. Airports will probably welcome rising numbers of equine guests as air speeds and stakes rise in the 1970s. **2** A huge crowd watches the horses leave the mobile starting stalls in Australia's second-biggest race—the 1½-mile Caulfield Cup. **3** Any decision—even the right one—left the judge open to criticism in a finish as tight as this before the introduction of the infallible photo-finish camera.

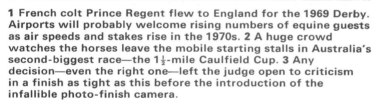

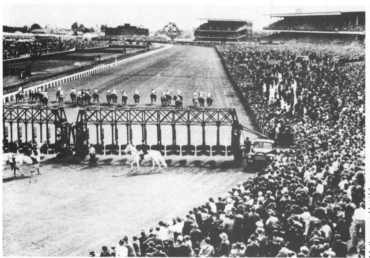

Racing Technical Services

Daily Telegraph

Jockeyship

Every jockey weighs out before each race and the first four home weigh in again. Jockeys go to the scales carrying their saddles, but their crash helmets are not included in the weights. Sometimes jockeys bring their poundage up to the correct mark by adding lead to their saddles.

Starting stalls are standard practice in many countries. Starting from the old-style barrier gate put a premium on jockeyship, but the stalls have virtually eliminated the unsatisfactory state of affairs of horses being left at the post.

Nearly all jockeys carry whips. The correct use is for encouragement rather than chastisement, because the majority of horses in training do their best without having to be reminded. Those who do not sometimes respond to the whip, but the more usual way of getting them to run well is to fit them with the form of a head cap known as blinkers. This hood effectively cuts out side vision and allows them to concentrate on what is in front of them.

Jockeys must have a knowledge of their own mount's style of running and should know what to expect from other runners in the race. A few horses like to go on in front on their own, but the majority prefer to settle in behind and come with a sustained run. Others have to be held up for a sharp late burst. Keeping a horse well-balanced throughout a race is all-important. The fashion nowadays is to ride with very short stirrups, but in the 19th century British jockeys rode in a stiff, upright position. Their complacence was shaken in the late 19th century when American riders introduced the now standard crouching style. British riders at first laughed at their American rivals. But after seeing how effective such men as Tod Sloan and the Reiff brothers were, they pulled up their stirrup leathers and imitated them.

Now they ride even shorter. French jockeys in particular ride as short as England's inimitable Lester Piggott, while the Australians ride a shade longer and give their mounts a little more rein.

Racing thrives in tote-monopolized France and the United States. And although bookmakers compete with the tote on Australian courses, the state-run off-course totalisator monopolies distributed $A120 million to various Australian racing bodies in the first eight years of their existence.

Certainly the money collected from British bookmakers bears no comparison with the annual rich haul from the tote in America and France. And the small percentage fed back from the British tote does little to offset the balance.

The small group of on-course bookmakers in England are more important than their numbers suggest, for they form the fulcrum of the betting market and determine the starting price (SP). Their betting fluctuations are transmitted to the some 15,000 betting shops that handle most of Britain's betting.

These shops offer many complicated forms of wager for the intrepid punter apart from the normal win and each-way bets. Some of the most popular are:
Double—a single bet naming two horses to win different races.
Treble—the same, but for three horses.
Accumulator—an extension of the treble involving four or more horses in different races.
Yankee—a bet on four selections in combination, making six doubles, four trebles, and an accumulator.
Heinz—as the name suggests, 57 bets on six selections, comprising 15 doubles, 20 trebles, 15 four-horse accumulators, 6 five-horse accumulators, and 1 six-horse accumulator.

Such betting possibilities, and even more complex ones, are all part of the service offered by British bookmakers, some of whom give a choice of tote or SP odds. And although it cannot be disputed that a tote monopoly would plough more money back into racing, the tote could not provide such a variety of betting for Britain's punters, who would resist any changes in their betting habits.

As well as operating on every British meeting, the tote provides an off-course credit betting service. The British tote offers much the same range of bets as the pari-mutuel systems of France and the United States. Apart from win and place betting, clients can select *forecasts*—the first two placegetters in correct order in a field of three to six runners—and *dual forecasts*—the first two placegetters in either order in larger fields. In Australia and the United States a dual forecast is known as a *quinella*. France provides an immensely popular treble forecast known as a *tiercé*, which offers the punter big dividends for picking the first three horses in the correct order, as well as a smaller return for

Fox Photos

Su Gooders/Fores Ltd.

1 The 'tote' board reflects the fluctuations in betting before a race begins and gives punters an indication on what horses the big money is going. **2** Match races, those between just two horses, were once popular with heavy betters. A famous match was that in York in 1851 between Derby winners Flying Dutchman (1849) and Voltigeur (1850) after the latter had inflicted on 'The Dutchman' his only defeat, in the 1850 Doncaster Cup. The race was held over two miles for a stake of 1,000 sovereigns, and saw Flying Dutchman gain his revenge. **3** Picnic races in Australia's 'outback' are more an occasion to get together than an opportunity for betting, though some private wagers often prove lucrative. **4** Tipsters are a common sight in England, but perhaps none has been as renowned as Ras 'Prince' Monolulu, whose flamboyant attire and cry 'I gotta horse' made him one of the turf's characters. **5** A tote maid at Randwick in Sydney takes a bet from Mrs George Moore, wife of the champion Australian jockey. **6** At Epsom, bets go to less attractive hands.

Odds

The odds displayed on bookmakers' boards fluctuate before the race according to the volume of betting. Heavy support for a horse shortens its price, and lengthens the odds of unfancied rivals. Both on- and off-course punters have the choice of accepting the current price offered or accepting 'starting price'—the last price offered by the leading bookmakers before the race begins. (Starting prices are returned by a team of trusted officials.) On-course punters 'shop around' the bookmakers' stands for the best odds—something they cannot do on the tote. Most horses start at odds 'against'—for example, 7-4. A winning bet at this price would return a profit of £7 for a £4 stake (minus any betting tax). But when punters back a horse heavily enough the bookmakers quote it at odds 'on'—which means that a winning bet returns a profit lower than the stake. A 7-4 on (or 4-7 against) winner would gain £4 on a £7 investment. Odds-on horses usually win, but they are by no means 'sure things', especially in distance races. The great Australian galloper Ajax is a case in point—he was once defeated at the prohibitive odds of 40-1 on.

Australian News and Information Bureau

Australian News and Information Bureau

Types of Races

The wide range of races run throughout the world can be classified according to prize-money conditions into sweepstakes, plates, purses, and matches. Within these categories are run selling, claiming, post, and overnight races, under weight-for-age or handicap conditions. Races may be confined to horses of a certain age, sex, performance, or parentage. Eligibility can even depend on the location of a horse's stable or the experience of his rider.

A *sweepstake* is a race in which the prize money (or a proportion of it) is made up of the entry fees, forfeits, or other subscriptions from the owners of the horses entered. In other words, all owners' contributions are lumped together and redistributed to the prize-getters. In addition, many sweepstakes carry added money, and sometimes trophies, from other sources.

A *plate* is a race for which prizes of a definite value are guaranteed by the race fund of the course staging the race. Thus, a plate of £300 guarantees that £300 will be paid out in prize money. If owners' contributions fall short of that sum, the race fund must pay the difference; if they exceed it, the surplus goes into the race fund.

A *purse* is a race for a prize to which owners make no contribution. These races are particularly common in the United States where the courses supply the prize money.

A *match* is a race between two horses only, the property of different owners, arranged on terms agreed by them. There may be no prize at all, or just a sidestake. Matches used to be the most common of all races; now they are extremely rare.

A *private sweepstake* is a race that has not been publicly advertised prior to the closing of entries and which carries no money, or other prize, added. This is merely an extension of the 'match' idea, involving more than two entries. Very few such races are now run.

Selling races cater for the lowest class of horse. The rules stipulate that the winner must be offered for auction after the race and that any other runner may be 'claimed'. Thus, if the race conditions state a runner is 'entered to be sold for £200', he will (a), if the winner, be submitted to auction, the bidding to start at £200, or (b), if a loser, be liable to compulsory sale to anyone paying £200 plus the value of the race to the stakeholder within 15 minutes of the jockey weighing in.

Claiming races, run in preference to 'sellers' in the United States and some other countries, involve any runner with a liability to be claimed for its entered price. But American rules state that claims must be made at least 15 minutes before the advertised time of the race.

Overnight races are races for which the entries close 72 hours or less before the advertised time for the first race of the day on which the race is to be run. Thus runners and (in the case of handicaps) weights become known only a very short time before the race.

Post races are races for which an owner need not declare the name of the horse to represent him until the eleventh hour—at the time when declaration of runners is normally made on the racecourse. All the owner is required to do in advance is to make his subscription. Such races are rarely run nowadays.

The basis of weighting horses is the weight-for-age scale first devised by Admiral Rous in 1850, and still operated, with some amendments and modifications, the world over. The scale provides for four different allowances for the various distances and times of the year. Most prestige events open to all age groups adhere strictly to the weight-for-age scale, while others provide for penalties for winners of valuable races and/or allowances for those without comparable good form.

Handicaps are races for which the weights are adjusted for the purpose of equalizing the chances of all the entries. They may vary in importance from a lowly selling hurdle race to a $100,000 sweepstake, of which there are several in the United States.

A number of races impose very definite restrictions on the type of horse which may run. Some specify as to sex, such as the 1,000 Guineas and Oaks, which are for fillies only; some admit only horses of certain age groups, such as the Classics for 3-year-olds; some are 'maiden' races, for horses which have never won; some are for the produce of stallions or mares that won over a certain distance; some even stipulate that entries must be trained at a specific training centre, or be ridden by apprentices who have not ridden more than a certain number of winners.

getting them right in any order.

A *tote double* and *treble* are run on selected races at every British meeting, and sometimes a *jackpot*, in which the investor has to pick all six winners. If the pool is not won it is carried forward to the next meeting. Similar tote jackpots are big money-spinners in New Zealand.

Doping

Doping has been a great potential threat to horse racing since the sport began. The authorities have taken stringent steps to stamp out the evil of 'nobbling', but it will always remain a danger.

Dopers of horses can be classified under two headings—those who administer a stimulant to make the animal go faster, and those who administer a depressant to slow the animal down.

Stopping a horse from winning is generally considered to be an easier task than making the animal go faster. A large bucket of water or a generous feed just before the race can do the trick without even resorting to drugs. Depressants have the effect of slowing a horse down and making it listless.

Such drugs also constitute a grave danger to jockeys riding horses that have been doped. Favourites are nearly always the target of the 'nobbler'. For, safe in the knowledge that the market leader has no chance, those in the know can back the other fancied runners without worry.

Doping animals to win is rather more difficult. The stimulants most used today are caffeine and amphetamine. George Lambton, a great English trainer in the early part of the century, carried out private tests on some of his less genuine horses and proved beyond doubt that given stimulants their racecourse performance improved out of all knowledge.

In Britain the problems of doping were thrashed out in the public eye in the 1960s. Three horse-doping gangs were sent to prison—in 1960, 1963, and 1966, and the trials and the subsequent increasing public disquiet at the rumoured large-scale doping activities led to action by the Jockey Club in the early sixties.

Trainers were strongly urged to use the protection of overnight racecourse stables to minimize the chances of their charges being doped. And, most important of all, a pilot scheme for the testing —'swabbing'—of horses was introduced in 1961. Now, at each

Glossary of Terms

Aged Of a horse six or more years old.

Apprentice Boy bound to a trainer for a certain period. He is taught to ride and look after horses. If good enough he is given rides in races and can claim weight allowances until he has ridden a certain number of winners or his apprenticeship is terminated.

Bay Lightish-brown horse common among thoroughbreds.

Bit The mouthpiece of the bridle. A horse 'on the bit' is being restrained by its jockey.

Blaze A patch of white spread over a horse's forehead.

Blinkers Two eye screens attached to the bridle or mask of an easily distracted horse. They limit sideways vision.

Brood mare A mare used at stud for breeding purposes.

Classic Definition of a classic differs in various countries. Broadly, Classics are the most important races in a country's racing calendar.

Clerk-of-the-course Official responsible for the running of a course.

Colt A male racehorse under five years old.

Dam A brood mare with offspring.

Distance A winning margin of 240 yards or more.

Foal A horse less than a year old. All horses' ages are calculated from a theoretical birthday of January 1 in the Northern Hemisphere, July 1 in South America, August 1 in Australasia and Southern Africa.

Field All the runners in a race.

Filly A female racehorse under five years old.

Gelding A horse that has been castrated and hence cannot be used for breeding purposes. An ungelded colt or horse is known as an *entire*.

Going State of ground when racing is held; can vary from hard to heavy.

Hand Distance of measurement for racehorses. Horses are measured from the ground to their withers, and a hand equals 4 inches.

Horse A male race horse five or more years old.

Leather Connects stirrup to saddle.

Maiden Horse that has never won a race under any rules.

Mare A female racehorse five or more years old.

Nursery A 2-year-old handicap.

Plate Racehorse's shoe. A horse with a loose shoe is said to have 'spread' or 'cast' a plate.

Scratch To withdraw an entry from a race before it begins.

Sire A stallion with offspring.

Snip Horse thought to be a certainty ('pea', 'bird' in Australia).

Stallion A horse at stud for breeding purposes.

Starter's orders Just before a race starts a flag is hoisted and the field comes under 'starters orders'. From that moment a horse cannot be withdrawn from the race.

Stirrups Supports for jockey's foot suspended by straps on either side of the saddle.

Thoroughbred A racehorse whose pedigree is recorded in the stud-book.

Trotted up Phrase used when a horse wins very easily.

Walk-over Occurs when just one horse is left in a race. The horse has only to be ridden past the judge's box.

Weighing room Central hub of a course where jockeys change and weigh out.

Yearling A horse between one and two years of age.

Canadian-bred, American-owned, Irish-trained Nijinsky wins the Derby with an English jockey.

Central Press

meeting, one or more horses is given a routine test and samples are taken of both saliva and urine. These are sent for expert examination to the Equine Research Station of the Animal Health Trust, at Newmarket, an establishment that has been a tremendous asset to the authorities in their bid to stamp out doping.

At the research station, precise techniques are used to ensure there is no confusion of the identities of horses' samples, and strict secrecy is maintained to ensure there is no tampering with the samples. If dope is found in urine or saliva, the case is handed over to a top-level security team.

The case of Hill House, 12 lengths winner of the 1967 Schweppes Hurdle at Newbury, in a field including some of the best hurdlers in Britain, was unique in the history of the British turf. The horse's trainer (Ryan Price) and jockey (Josh Gifford) were reported to the National Hunt Committee by the Newbury stewards, who considered there has been abnormal improvement in the horse's performance since it had finished fourth at Sandown a week earlier. Both men strongly denied allegations against them, but a dope test taken after the race proved positive and an amount of cortisone, several times more than is normal, was found to be in the horse.

Further tests seemed to prove, however, that Hill House produced the excessive cortisone himself. To settle the matter the horse was sent to the Equine Research Station. More tests there proved conclusively that the horse manufactured its own cortisone . . . and trainer and jockey were cleared.

Doping is a world-wide problem, and all leading racing countries counter it with dope tests. In the United States winners are swabbed, but Australian dope testing provisions vary—in major New South Wales centres winners and occasional well-backed failures are swabbed; in Melbourne and most other centres random checks are made. New Zealand, too, favours random checks.

Most Australian tests—and about 10,000 are made each year—are analysed by the Australian Jockey Club in its Sydney Laboratory—after Tokyo, the second biggest outside the United States. Tests analysed there show similar results to the rest of the world—about one test in 1,000 proves positive.

Swabbing, however, is no deterrent to 'nobblers' who aim at preventing a horse from running at all. In November 1969 Melbourne Cup favourite Big Philou took ill just before the start of the big race, and subsequent tests showed that he had been doped. His withdrawal cost Australian punters an estimated half-million dollars in ante-post bets.

Hurling

Reputed to rival ice hockey for speed, skill, and grace of movement, hurling is confined, in the main, to Ireland. If not as popular as Gaelic football, it nonetheless takes precedence over it in the aims of the Gaelic Athletic Association. And it contains as many thrills as Gaelic football; long solo runs on which players carry the ball perched on top of the hurley (stick); the clash of 'ash' as players fight furiously for possession; the plucking of the ball out of the air with one hand; and the first-time overhead striking of the ball with the hurley.

For anyone new to the game it is amazing that few injuries are sustained in hurling—a tribute to the skill and dexterity of the participants, all of whom are born to the game. For hurling skill is a quality difficult to acquire. The game itself is hard and exacting, and as well as the usual requirements of strength, stamina, and skill, it calls for near-perfect eye-sight. Indeed, if anything reduces hurling's appeal as a spectator sport, it is the difficulty of following the flight of the ball.

Deriving its name from *ioman*, meaning driving or urging, hurling is played by two teams, each comprising 15 players. The hurley is about 3 feet in length, and the leather ball weighs between $3\frac{1}{2}$ and $4\frac{1}{2}$ ounces, and has a circumference of between 9 and 10 inches. It has little hop or bounce, but travels 75 to 85 yards when struck by the hurley in a swinging movement, called a *puck*. Goals, worth three points, are scored by hitting the ball between the posts and under the cross-bar, and one point is scored if the ball goes over the bar.

The sport was always closely identified with the Irish spirit of self-government, and was outlawed by the statutes of Kilkenny and Galway in 1367 and 1527 and by local edicts from time to time. But these had no effect, and entire parishes used to play each other over an area embracing fields and roads alike. Wrestling matches would add to the excitement and enjoyment of the afternoon.

The number of participants was gradually reduced in time: 21-a-side, then 17-a-side, until the present format was introduced in 1913. And eventually the game was taken off the roadways into the fields and some sort of rules accepted. When the Gaelic Athletic Association (GAA) was founded in 1884, it brought about proper control and organization.

The main competition is the All-Ireland Championship for the McCarthy Cup, which is decided at Croke Park, Dublin, on the first Sunday of September each year. Munster and Leinster dominate the hurling scene, with the counties of Cork, Tipperary, Kilkenny, and Wexford ever to the fore.

And names such as Mick Mackey of Limerick, Christy Ring of Cork, John Doyle of Tipperary, the Rackards of Wexford, and Ollie Walsh and Eddie Keher are synonymous with all that is good in the game.

Syndication International

Despite its format, hurling results in few major injuries.

Hurling is played on a pitch not less than 140 yards or more than 160 yards long, and not less than 84 yards or more than 100 yards wide. In addition to the goal and side lines, lines are drawn across the pitch at intervals of 14 yards, 21 yards, and 70 yards. The goalposts are 16 ft. high and 21 ft. apart, with a crossbar 8 ft. from the ground. A penalty area of 15 by 5 yards is marked in front of each goal.

The referee starts proceedings by throwing the ball in, and play continues according to the rules. Free hits, or pucks, are awarded when the ball goes over the goal-line or sideline, or for breaches of the rules. The ball may be caught in the hand during flight, and may be lifted from the ground with the aid of the hurley, or kicked.

Ireland's principal hurling competition is the All-Ireland Championship for the McCarthy Cup. The eventual winners, Wexford, and Tipperary fight out the 1968 final. In the last ten years, Kilkenny has emerged as a team worthy of the Championship. Since 1963 they have appeared in eight finals, winning four and losing four. But Cork, Tipperary and Wexford are still teams to contend with. In 1973, though, a relatively unfancied team, Limerick, which had not reached the finals in over 20 years, came through to win the title.

Fionnbar Callanan

HURLING
All-Ireland Champions from 1950

	Winners	Runners-up
1950	Tipperary	Kilkenny
1951	Tipperary	Wexford
1952	Cork	Dublin
1953	Cork	Galway
1954	Cork	Wexford
1955	Wexford	Galway
1956	Wexford	Cork
1957	Kilkenny	Waterford
1958	Tipperary	Galway
1959	Waterford	Kilkenny
1960	Wexford	Tipperary
1961	Tipperary	Dublin
1962	Tipperary	Wexford
1963	Kilkenny	Waterford
1964	Tipperary	Kilkenny
1965	Tipperary	Wexford
1966	Cork	Kilkenny
1967	Kilkenny	Tipperary
1968	Wexford	Tipperary
1969	Kilkenny	Cork
1970	Cork	Wexford
1971	Tipperary	Kilkenny
1972	Kilkenny	Cork
1973	Limerick	Kilkenny

Ice Hockey

The world's fastest game—a claim made by more than one sport today. In the case of ice hockey, though, the claim is not easily disputed. Known simply as 'hockey' in North America, the game is played at a temper-testing pace that demands frantic substitutions every few minutes; heavily padded but phenomenally fast skaters flash across the ice scoring goals with shots often too quick for the eye to follow. And not only is the game fast, it is also exciting. The robust clashing of bodies, flashy stick-handling skill, and ability of players to 'turn on a sixpence' are features of this uncompromising game that repeatedly pulls spectators forward in their seats.

Claims to have been the sport's birthplace come from several Canadian cities, notably Kingston, Ontario, and Montreal. The pioneer players in Kingston were mainly Crimean War veterans in a Royal Canadian Rifles regi-ment who played a game with a puck, instead of a ball, on the frozen expanse of Kingston harbour in 1860. British troops also played at Halifax, in Nova Scotia, about this time, but it was not until 1879 that the first rules were formulated, by W. F. Rober-son and R. F. Smith, students at McGill University in Montreal. They added a few original ideas to what was basically a com-bination of field hockey and rugby regulations. A square puck was used, and each team had nine players. The following year the first recognised ice hockey team, the McGill University Hockey Club, was formed.

Leagues of all grades were soon thriving throughout Canada. There were nearly 100 clubs in Mon-treal alone when the game was first played in the United States in 1893, by Yale University in New Haven and Johns Hopkins University in Baltimore. That same year, Lord Stanley of Preston, then Governor-General of Canada, donated the Stanley Cup as a permanent senior trophy that was destined to become the sport's most famous prize. It was first won in 1894 on natural ice by a team representing Mon-treal Amateur Athletic Asso-ciation. When the Stanley Cup became the property of the professional league, the Allan Cup, which had been donated soon after the Stanley Cup, was raised to prominence and is now widely regarded as the most coveted amateur club trophy.

International Development

The United States Amateur Hockey League was founded in New York in 1896, and by the turn of the century the sport had spread to Europe. A Cana-dian demonstration popularised the game in Great Britain suf-ficiently to inspire a five-team league competition in 1903. Five years later, in 1908, the Inter-national Ice Hockey Federation (IIHF) was formed, with Belgium, Bohemia, France, Great Britain, and Switzerland founder mem-bers. The first European cham-pionship was held in 1901 at Les Avants in the Swiss Alps and was won by Great Britain. Yet it was not until four years later that the British Ice Hockey Federation was inaugurated.

Ice hockey mushroomed in Britain as more electrically-frozen rinks were built, and the nation's best years dated from 1934, when the Empire Pool, Wembley, came into being. Brighton Sports Stadium, London's Empress Hall, and Harringay Arena followed Wembley's lead to promote a British pre-war big-rink era bolstered by Canadian talent. And an international club tourna-ment was held between four London sides—Wembley Lions, Richmond Hawks, Streatham, and Wembley Canadians—and six European teams—Berlin, Français Volants, Milan, Munich,

A far cry from today's game— ladies playing hockey on the ice at Wimbledon, London, in the late 19th century.

Right. **Bobby Orr of the Boston Bruins—one of the greats of professional ice hockey.**

Su Gooders/Guildhall

Radio Times Hulton Picture Library

Prague, and Stade Français.

The ice hockey tournament in the 1936 Winter Olympics at Garmisch provided one of the great surprises of that or any other Games when Carl Erhardt led Britain to a historic defeat of Canada—a victory that also won Britain the world championship. Until then, the Canadians had won every Olympic tournament, and had lost their world title only once, in 1933 to the United States. But World War II curtailed this promising forward surge in Britain. After the war, teams and talent faded considerably with the acute shortage of large ice arenas with worthwhile spectator accommodation. Elsewhere, though, the game began to expand.

There are now thousands of teams throughout North America, taking part in league competitions comparable in diversity with those of soccer in Britain. And by the late 1960s, the approximate number of players registered in Canada was 230,000, and 48,000 in the United States. The Soviet Union, however, has at least 300,000 registered players, while there are 140,000 in Sweden, 77,000 in Czechoslovakia, and 40,000 in Finland. Outside Europe and North America, the sport has grown in proportion to the limited ice acreage available.

In post-war years, more than 20 nations have contested the Olympic and annual world and European championships, decided concurrently and organized primarily by the IIHF president, J. F. Ahearne, whose astute negotiation of television rights has provided much of the teams' travelling expenses. World championship tournaments are divided into three groups of six or more teams, each group being decided on a league points basis. The top team in Group A takes the world title, and the highest-placed European team the European title. Interest in the other groups is boosted by the annual promotion and relegation of top and bottom teams.

Until 1956, the Canadians' general supremacy among amateurs was never seriously questioned. But that year at Cortina, the Russians won the Olympic tournament and afterwards domi-

nated the world championships with teams noted for great skating skill. Their success was based on a combination of quick manoeuvrability and a well-drilled technique of keeping possession until the right scoring chance came. They were also able to keep their leading players in the amateur ranks, not losing them to the professional game as other countries do, and in 1968 nine of their players became the first in the sport to win second Olympic gold medals.

As in other winter sports, however, the amateur-professional problem has threatened ice hockey. In 1969, the IIHF had opened the way to 'open' championships by allowing professionals to compete with amateurs in future world championships. A maximum of nine professionals per team was agreed upon. But this progress received a setback when Avery Brundage, president of the International Olympic Committee, warned that such mixing could jeopardize the acceptance of future Olympic entries. As a result, Canada refused to participate in the 1970 world championships, and no nation included a registered professional.

National Hockey League of North America (NHL)

The sport's major professional competition, contested among the foremost clubs in the United States and Canada, the NHL was inaugurated in its present form at Montreal in November 1917. A National Hockey League had been organized previously, in 1908, as a professional major circuit, but it was disbanded at the end of the 1916-17 season. The new league had four clubs—the Montreal Wanderers, Montreal Canadiens, Ottawa Senators, and Toronto Arenas—with the first championship won by the Arenas, the original name of the club that became famous as the Toronto Maple Leafs.

From 1943, the league settled to a regular contest between the 'big six' teams—the Boston Bruins, Chigago Black Hawks, Detroit Red Wings, Montreal Canadiens, New York Rangers, and Toronto Maple Leafs—the champions winning the Prince of Wales Trophy and the four

1 Ice hockey was extremely popular in Britain in the 1930s, but after World War II, lack of interest soon resulted in decreasing attendances, and what had once been a flourishing sport withered, while it began to expand rapidly wherever else in the world it was played. **2 & 3** World and Olympic champions Russia (red) in action against West Germany (white) and Sweden (yellow) at the 1968 Winter Olympics. They won all but one of their seven games to retain their Olympic and world titles.

4 The Czechs, silver medallists and the only team to beat the Russians at Grenoble, go wild with joy as they beat them again, this time in the 1969 world championships at Stockholm. But the 4-3 defeat did not prevent Russia winning her seventh consecutive world championship. 5 Canada's Morris Mott gets the worst of a goalmouth clash with a Russian defender. Until the rise of the Russians in the mid-1950s, Canada was rarely challenged as the leading amateur ice hockey nation.

Equipment

Sticks, made entirely of wood, are limited to a handle length of 53 inches and a blade length of $14\frac{1}{2}$ inches, except in the case of goalkeepers who may use heavier and wider sticks. The angle between the blade and the handle varies, and blades are shaped to a player's individual needs. The puck is circular, made of solid vulcanized rubber 3 inches in diameter, 1 inch thick, and weighing about $5\frac{1}{2}$ ounces.

Boots have lower ankle supports than those used for figure skating, and important features of the ice hockey boot are reinforced caps at toe and heel, moulded arch supports, and tendon protectors. The skate blade is only $\frac{1}{16}$ of an inch wide and is reinforced with hollow tubing for greater strength and lighter weight. The goalkeeper's more specialized skate is wider and less high, affording easier balance. Extra stanchions are fitted to prevent the puck from passing underneath his boots.

Apparel is highly specialized to cater for the player's protective needs. All players wear knee-pads, shin-guards, elbow-pads, shoulder-guards, thick gauntlet-type gloves, and long stockings that fit over the knee-pads. Helmets, though optional, are a wise precaution to minimize possible head injuries. For special protection, goalkeepers wear extra-large leather leg-guards, chest protectors, and extra-padded gloves (a different type for holding the stick from the one on the catching hand). Some goalkeepers also wear face-masks to avoid possible cuts from skates or sticks after falling on the ice or from a flying puck.

London Express News & Feature Service
London Express News & Feature Service
London Express News & Feature Service
Fox Photos

leading teams contesting the Stanley Cup. Inevitably, though, spiralling support demanded expansion, and in the 1967-68 season the league was doubled in size to 12 clubs. The six new teams—the Los Angeles Kings, Minnesota North Stars, Oakland Seals, Philadelphia Flyers, Pittsburgh Penguins, and St Louis Blues—have all since competed in a West Division while the old clubs make up an East Division.

The expansion proved a quick success. Each team plays a 74-game schedule, 10 games against each of the others in its own division and 4 against each of the clubs in the other division. At the end of the NHL matches, the top four in each division compete in two separate play-off series, the winners of each finally meeting in a best-of-seven-matches contest for the Stanley Cup.

The average spectator accommodation at the 12 participating rinks is around 15,000, and many games draw capacity attendances. The rules of professional hockey are basically similar to those in the amateur sport, with only slight variations in interpretation. One difference is in the control of the game: professional hockey is controlled by a referee and two linesmen instead of two referees.

NHL All-Time Greats
Beliveau, Jean (1931-). A centreman of great natural ability with a keen sense of anticipation and accurate marksmanship, Jean Beliveau joined the Montreal Canadiens in 1953, having already been a crowd-drawing amateur star at 20 with the Quebec Aces. Heavily built and 6 ft. 3 in. tall, he was nonetheless a gracefully moving forward and, calm-tempered, he seldom retaliated in rough play. He won the Hart Trophy twice (1956 and 1964), the Art Ross Trophy in 1956, and the Conn Smythe Trophy in 1965.
Durnan, Bill (1922-). One of the safest goalkeepers the game has known, Bill Durnan was with the Montreal Canadiens from 1943 until 1950, when a deep head gash from another player's skate prompted a premature retirement. Ambidextrous, he had a rare ability to catch and block shots with either hand, which he used with spectacular effect almost as much as he used his stick and pads. Six feet tall, he used his height to full advantage, and his winning of the Vezina Trophy in six of his seven NHL seasons is significant testimony to his outstanding technique. In the 1948-49 season, he achieved 10 shut-outs, including a record run of four games without conceding a goal. He totalled 34 shut-out games during his NHL career, and in that time played 901 games, letting through an average of only 2.35 goals a game.
Harvey, Doug (1924-). A cool, subtle defenceman who made 432

assists in 1,043 games, Doug Harvey played for the Montreal Canadiens from 1948 to 1961, and ended his career with a brief spell for the New York Rangers. He won the Jane Norris Trophy for seven of its first nine years.
Howe, Gordie (1926-). Often described as the best all-round exponent the sport has seen, Gordie Howe first played for the Detroit Red Wings in 1946, and by 1967 he had played in the NHL longer than anyone else—21 seasons, a remarkable figure when it is considered the average NHL career is less than seven seasons. This outstanding 6-foot right-winger achieved the NHL record for the most goals scored, most

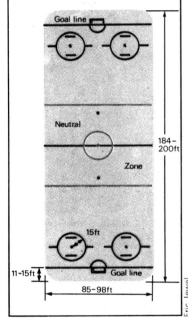

Eric Jewel

assists, most points, and most games played. By 1968, he had scored 743 goals—678 in league matches and 65 in Stanley Cup play-offs. He won the Art Ross Trophy a record six times (1951, 1952, 1953, 1954, 1957, and 1963); the Hart Trophy a record six times (1952, 1953, 1957, 1958, 1960, and 1963); and also the Lester Patrick Trophy in 1967.
Hull, Bobby (1939-). A muscular, fast-moving winger, the Chicago Black Hawks' Bobby Hull, with probably the hardest shot in ice hockey—one was timed at 116.3 mph—could skate over 28 mph while retaining full control of the puck. He became the first NHL player to score 50 goals in a season more than once (50 in 1961-62, 54 in 1965-66, 52 in 1966-67, 58 in 1968-69), and in 1965-66 he set the NHL seasonal point-scoring record of 97, with 54 goals and 43 assists. He won the Art Ross Trophy three times (1960, 1962 and 1966), the Hart Trophy twice (1965 and 1966), and the Lady Byng Memorial Trophy in 1965.
Johnson, Ching (1897-). Ching Johnson joined the New York Rangers in 1926 for their in-

Paul Berman

How the game is played
Ice hockey is a six-a-side game, the normal line-up being the goal-keeper, two defencemen, and three forwards. Substitutes are allowed at any time, such is the fast, energy-sapping speed at which the game is played. A team usually carries between 11 and 18 players.

A game is divided into three periods, each of 20 minutes actual playing time. The time is taken by stopwatch only while the puck is in play. Play is started at the beginning of each period and after a goal has been scored by a 'face-off' in the centre of the rink. The referee drops the puck between the sticks of the opposing centremen, who try to hit it to a team-mate. At other times in the game, play is restarted by a face-off on the nearest face-off spot to the point at which play stopped. The puck becomes dead only when hit over the barrier or when the whistle blows for an infringement.

A goal can be scored only by propelling the ball from the stick, not by kicking or throwing nor when an attacking player is in the goal crease. Goal judges signify a score by switching on a red light behind the goal concerned—a necessary procedure, as spectators, not to mention the goalkeeper, rarely see the puck as it flashes in for a goal.

The playing area is divided into three zones—defence, neutral (centre), and attacking—by two blue lines. Only three players may be in their own defence zone when the puck is outside it, and a player may enter the attacking zone only in line with or behind the puck or puck-possessor. To adhere to the onside rule, a player may pass only to a colleague in the same zone, or, if he is in his defence zone, to anyone in his own half. After an offside pass, the puck is brought back to the circle nearest where the pass was made, for a face-off.

Players are penalized for rough play by being sent off the ice for two or more minutes, according to the severity of the offence, and generally no substitution is allowed for a penalized player. The term of suspension is served in a penalty box, known colloquially as the 'sin bin'. Minor penalties of 2 minutes are imposed for charging, elbowing, tripping, body-checking, high stick, or deliberately shooting out of the rink. More severe penalties of 5 or 10 minutes, or suspension for the rest of the game, are imposed according to the seriousness of the offence. A goalkeeper's minor penalty is served by a team colleague.
The playing area. Ideally, the ice rink should be 200 ft. long and 85 ft. wide. It is surrounded by barrier boards which are curved at each of the four corners and must be between 3 ft. 4 in. and 4 ft. high. 11 to 15 ft. from the end of the rink are red goal lines, in the centre of which are the goals, 4 ft. high and 6 ft. wide with nets not less than 2 ft. deep at the base.

Two blue lines divide the rink equally into three zones, and a centre red line is equidistant between them. The centre of the rink is marked by a blue spot surrounded by a blue circle of 15 ft. radius. In each half, there are two red face-off spots in red circles of similar circumference to the centre circle. They are marked 15 ft. from the goal-line, and are midway between each goal-post and the barrier. On each side of these four spots are red lines 2 ft. long, parallel to the goal-lines behind which the two players in the face-off stand, and other red lines, 3 ft. long, extend from the outer edge of the circle, indicating where other players must stand. In the centre zone, there are two red spots, 5 ft. from each blue line and midway between the side barriers. In the NHL, however, there are four spots in the centre zone, 5 ft. from the blue lines and in line with the red spots in the end zones. The creases in front of the goals also vary under the different rules: they are indicated by 6-ft.-radius semicircles under IIHF rules and by 8 ft. by 4 ft. rectangles under NHL rules.

augural season, and stayed as a defenceman for 12 seasons during which time he was frequently voted one of the most successful defencemen in the NHL. A difficult player to pass in his own defence zone, he was more adventurous than most in moving forward with the puck. Like many defencemen of his day, he often played a full match without being substituted.

Morenz, Howie (1902-1937). A fast-moving centreman, Howie Morenz played for the Montreal Canadiens for 10 seasons from 1923. And after brief spells with the Chicago Black Hawks and New York Rangers he returned to the Canadiens for a final season. His career came to a tragic end in January 1937, when he was badly injured in a game against Chicago and died several weeks later. He was renowned for his clever stick handling and as a marksman who outwitted defenders by skilful feinting before he shot. A versatile player whose ability in defending and distributing was also outstanding, Morenz scored 270 career goals at a time when players averaged fewer than 50 games a season.

Orr, Bobby (1948-). Seldom had so young a player looked so certain to become a star of distinction as Bobby Orr. A defenceman of rare natural ability and considerable potential, he played four seasons for Oshawa Generals of Ontario before graduating to the Boston Bruins as soon as he reached the eligibility age of 18, in 1966. Winner of the Calder Trophy in 1967, he gained the James Norris Trophy in 1968 and looked likely to merit the award many more times. In 1970, Orr scored the winning goal in the Stanley Cup after 40 seconds of 'sudden death' overtime to clinch Boston's four straight wins in the final series against the St Louis Blues. During that season, he won the NHL awards as the highest scorer, top defenceman, and most valuable player.

Richard, Maurice (1921-). With a scoring ability second only to Gordie Howe, Maurice Richard amassed 626 goals for the Montreal Canadiens from 1942 to 1961. And in the winter of 1944-45 he became the first NHL player to score 50 goals in a season. An uncompromising winger who excited with his constant sense of urgency, he had a particularly fast and low left-handed shot. His forte was shooting, and his assists were less frequent.

Sawchuk, Terry (1929-). One of the game's nomads, Terry Sawchuk joined the Detroit Red Wings in 1950, was transferred to the Boston Bruins in 1955 but returned to Detroit two years later. In 1964 he moved to the Toronto Maple Leafs and to the Los Angeles Kings in 1967. A goalkeeper who specialised in shut-outs, Sawchuk won the Calder Trophy in 1951 with 11 shut-outs in his first NHL season. and in 1967 achieved a record hundredth for the NHL. He inspired the now-normal crouching stance, goalies before him having usually stood straight. In a career that stretched over almost two decades, he won the Vezina Trophy four times (1952, 1953, 1955, and finally, as joint holder, in 1965).

Shore, Eddie (1902-). One of the most frequently injured players in ice hockey, Eddie Shore was a fearless, long-striding defenceman with a useful turn of speed that enabled him to burst suddenly into the attack, a move that frequently brought him as many points as his forwards. His career tally of 105 goals and 178 assists was remarkable for a regular defenceman. Four times winner of the Hart Trophy (1933, 1935, 1936, 1938), he played for the Boston Bruins for 14 seasons from 1926, and afterwards made a brief return to the game with the New York Americans in 1940.

Glossary of Terms

Assist Individual point-scoring credit to the player who makes the final pass to the goalscorer.

Board-checking Deliberately pushing a player onto the barrier boards.

Body-checking Throwing oneself in front of an opponent to block his progress.

Face-off Method of starting or restarting play, when the referee drops the puck on the ice between two opposing players.

High-sticking Illegal carrying of the stick above shoulder level.

Hooking Illegally using the blade of a stick to hook an opponent from behind.

Offside Offside occurs when an attacking player precedes the puck into the attacking zone or when the puck travels untouched over more than one line. The position of a player is taken from his skate, and not from the stick.

Penalty shot A clear shot at goal, awarded if an attacking player is tripped or pulled down when he is in a scoring position in front of the goal. Only the goalkeeper is allowed to defend, and no goal can be scored from a rebound.

Power play Sustained attack by one team, particularly when the opposition is numerically below strength.

Shut-out Goalkeeper's achievement of not conceding a goal throughout a match or period.

Sin bin Colloquial term for the penalty box in which a term of suspension is served.

Stick-handling Retaining possession of the puck while in motion. The equivalent of dribbling in soccer, it is achieved by flicking the puck alternately with each side of the blade. Among the well-known players with a rare ability to control the puck, were Bobby Hull, of the Chicago Black Hawks, and Howie Morenz.

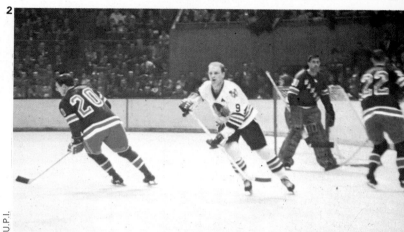

Associated Press

U.P.I.

Fox Photos

1 A brilliant save by New York Rangers 'Gump' Worsley from a low drive by Claude Provost of the Montreal Canadiens.
2 Chicago Black Hawks winger Bobby Hull (9) set an NHL point-scoring record in 1965-66 and was the first player to score 50 goals in a season more than once. **3** The Montreal Canadiens and the Toronto Maple Leafs clash in a Stanley Cup encounter.

NHL AWARDS TO PLAYERS

Hart Trophy: Player adjudged to be the most valuable to his team.
Vezina Trophy: Goalkeeper of the team conceding fewest goals.
Art Ross Trophy: Top points scorer at the end of a regular NHL season.
Calder Trophy: Most proficient player in his first season.
Lady Byng Trophy: Player exhibiting best type of sportsmanship combined with high playing standard.
James Norris Trophy: Defenceman demonstrating greatest all-round ability.
Conn Smythe Trophy: Most valuable player for his team in Stanley Cup matches.
Lester Patrick Trophy: Outstanding service to hockey in the United States.

Judo

Judo is a thrilling, violent, combat sport which originated in the Oriental world as a method of self-defence and grew into a world-wide sport that received Olympic recognition in 1964. Skill, stamina, fighting spirit, and the use of one's strength against an opponent's weakest point are essential qualities for the *judoka*, a judo exponent. Training is extremely tiring, involving long hours of *randori* (free practice) in which a *judoka* tries to throw his opponent but which lacks the intensity of *shiai* (competition). On a less vigorous level judo has become extremely popular outside the competitive field, and women, children, and older men all find that they benefit from the sport, which can be adjusted to suit everybody's needs. Many people practise *kata*, the formal movements of judo which give the sport an aesthetic quality that is sometimes lacking in the rough-and-tumble of the contests.

The origins of judo are not clear. Ju-jitsu, a method of unarmed combat, is believed to have been introduced into Japan by a Chinese monk, Chin Genpin. Various schools of ju-jitsu developed, and in the era of Japanese chivalry the young samurai (knights) were instructed in the art. But with the ordinance of 1871 which forbade the samurai to carry swords, ju-jitsu fell into disrepute as the experts used its devastating methods on ordinary members of the public. The skills of unarmed combat were saved by the founder of judo, Dr Jigoro

1 Former British team captain Ray Ross demonstrates the acrobatic rolling break-fall which judo fighters use to cushion their fall. The arm hits the ground first and the fighter tucks in his head, wrapping himself in a ball. As he somersaults over he beats the mat with his other arm. This break-fall is used against some of judo's most violent throws, including *tomoe-nage* (stomach throw) and *seio-nage* (shoulder throw).
2 *Sono-mama* (do not move). When judo fighters are grappling near the edge of the contest area a referee will often call *sono-mama* to prevent one man escaping from a hold by crawling out of the area. Assisted by the two judges he will drag the pair to the centre of the mat where they continue fighting.
3 The famous All Japan championships were inaugurated in 1948, although there were similar age-group competitions before World War II. The All Japans are open championships, with no weight category, and as a result—although men of all sizes and weights are theoretically equal—a big man has invariably won the title, the victor's average weight since 1948 being 15 stone. The championships are the highlight of the Japanese judo calendar, and the participants qualify through a series of regional eliminations. The early rounds provide much of the most exciting judo, and once the pressure increases in the final stages the fighters become less adventurous and more wary in this knock-out contest.

1-3 *O-soto-gari* ('major outer reaping throw'). Syd Hoare, Britain's middleweight representative at the Tokyo Olympics, drives junior international Terry Garrett into the mat with his favourite technique. **1** Hoare pulls his opponent off balance with a vicious tug from his left hand. Hoare's right hand grasps Garrett's lapel and assists in the drive backwards. **2** Catching Garrett's right leg with the back of his own thigh, Hoare sweeps him onto the mat while continuing the pull. Hoare completes the throw (**3**) causing both of Garrett's legs to leave the ground.

4-6 *Harai-goshi* (sweeping hip throw). European light-heavyweight bronze medallist Ray Ross throws British international middleweight Dave Starbrook. **4** Ross pulls his opponent forward using a hard tug with his right hand (Ross is left-handed). **5** Continuing the pull, Ross moves in sideways, sweeping his left leg backwards and catching his opponent just above the knee. **6** The completion of the throw, just before the spreadeagled Starbrook hits the mat. Often a judo fighter will use a *makikomi* (winding) technique to pin his opponent as he plunges to the mat.

7-9 *Morote-seio-nage* (shoulder throw). Tony Sweeney (4th Dan, Britain's heavyweight entrant at the Tokyo Olympic Games) hurls British light-heavyweight Tim Bishop to the mat. **7** Sweeney pulls Bishop off balance holding his opponent's right sleeve and left lapel. The pull had to be fast and strong to get the opponent rocking forward onto his toes. **8** Sweeney has bent his knees so as to get under Bishop's centre of gravity, at the same time continuing his powerful pull. **9** Sweeney wheels him over his back and throws him to the ground.

Kano, who studied at a number of ju-jitsu schools and welded the best methods of each into a new school which he called 'Kodokan Judo'.

Shortly after its foundation in 1882, the Kodokan won a series of contests against the other leading methods of unarmed combat, and from that time the future of judo was assured.

Although Jigoro Kano realized the need for expansion, judo developed slowly. He visited Europe in 1889, when Yukio Tani, a leading ju-jitsu exponent, made his first appearance in Britain. Another of Kano's leading pupils, Y. Yamashita, began instructing in America in 1902, and during his stay instructed the President, Theodore Roosevelt. Three years later, the Paris police were taught judo, and

in Britain Tani became an amazing success in the music halls—where professional wrestling was enjoying its golden era—by defeating most of the leading fighters of the day.

However, the first club in Europe was not founded until 1918, by Gunji Koizumi, who opened the famous Budokwai in Westminster (later moving to South Kensington). Yukio Tani was the first instructor at the club, and was a tireless teacher. Once a pupil gasped when Tani was holding him on the ground, 'How do I get out of this?' Tani replied, 'You learn by suffering'. Another of Kano's pupils, Shinzo Takagaki, took judo to Australia in 1928 and Africa in 1931. Despite the growing popularity of judo in Japan and elsewhere, it was still thought of as a number

of self-defence moves rather than a sport in its own right, and it was not until the end of World War II that it blossomed into a competitive form. The European Judo Union was established in 1948, the same year as the British Judo Association, and the International Judo Federation was founded three years later.

The European championships were first held in 1951, and have been, except for 1956, an annual event ever since. Increasing numbers of Europeans go to Japan for tuition—one of the first was Britain's Trevor Leggett, a 7th Dan, in the late 1930s—and the gap between Japan and the rest of the world began to narrow.

Japan, who had held the famous All Japan championships since 1948, realized the need for world championships, and the first of

these were held at Tokyo in 1956. Only open events were held, and at the first two meetings, in 1956 and 1958, the championship went to Japanese experts. But at Paris in 1961, the Orientals suffered a humiliating reverse when the giant Dutchman, Anton Geesink, beat the three Japanese entrants in successive rounds for the championship.

Until Geesink's arrival, it was thought that weight categories were unecessary in competitions, as the sport had always claimed that it was possible for a big skilled *judoka* to be beaten by an equally skilful smaller man. The trouble was that Geesink was not only big—he stood 6 ft. 6 in. tall and weighed 18 stone—but was also tremendously skilful.

At the request of the Japanese hosts, judo was first included in the Olympic programme at Tokyo in 1964. The Japanese showed they were still the outstanding nation by winning the three weight-category events, the lightweight, middleweight, and heavyweight. The middleweight class gold medal was won by a man who was, pound for pound, perhaps the finest judo fighter in history, Isao Okano, who won the All Japan titles in 1967 and 1969 beating vastly heavier men on both occasions. Geesink, however, took the Open title, and confirmed himself as the world's best exponent a year later when he won the world heavyweight title in Rio de Janeiro.

In 1967 new weight divisions were introduced. The lightweight class was for men under 9 st 12 lb, welterweight 9 st 12 lb to 11 stone, middleweight 11 stone to 12 st 8 lb, light-heavyweight 12 st 8 lb to 14 st 9 lb, and heavyweight over 14 st 9 lb.

However, the Open category, which anyone can enter, is still retained but it is inevitably won by a heavyweight.

In 1969 the Japanese won all six divisions at the world championships in Mexico City and thus proved that they were still the dominant force in the sport. With 8 million participants, intense rivalry between the universities, and deep-rooted tradition and pride, they have a leadership in numbers and strength that is almost impossible to overhaul.

Only Geesink and another Dutchman, the massively built Wilhelm Ruska who won the world title in 1967, have taken world titles away from them.

The main opposition to the Japanese comes from the USSR, a country with 140,000 fighters. Their interest in sambo—a sport

Tomoe-nage (stomach throw) is a spectacular sacrifice throw often used in international competitions. The judo fighter drops to the mat, planting a foot in his opponent's stomach and then spinning him over his head. The opponent does a rolling break-fall to prevent injury.

somewhere between judo and wrestling—has produced an unusual style, and most of the Russian judo stars have graduated through sambo. The United States, with 250,000 contestants, West Germany, and France, also provide a number of leading competitors, while Korea gives the Japanese their biggest problem in the East.

Britain were at first a leading European power, winning the European team title in 1958, 1959, and 1960.

Their lead was soon overhauled, but Brian Jacks became the first Briton to win a European weight category when in 1970 he took the middleweight gold.

Glossary of Terms

Japanese terms are still used in most countries.

Ashiwaza Technique of foot throws.
Chui Warning for an infringement.
Dan Degree.
Dojo Judo practice hall.
Gyaku Reverse—applied to locks, holds, etc.
Ippon One point.
Jigotai Defensive posture.
Judogi Judo costume, loose fitting trousers and jacket without buttons. The jacket is fastened with a belt to assist in identification.
Jodoka Person who practises judo.
Ju-no-kata Demonstration of judo principles in slow motion.
Kaeshiwaza Counter-attack techniques.

Kata A series of pre-arranged movements. Now performed as a training method and for demonstrations.
Katsu A method of resuscitation.
Koshiwaza Techniques of hip throws.
Kyu Pupil degree.
Newaza Groundwork.
Osaekomiwaza Holding techniques.
Randori Free practice.
Sensei Teacher.
Shiai Contest.
Shihan Master.
Sutemiwaza Sacrifice throws.
Shimewaza Strangulation techniques.
Tachizawa Throwing techniques.
Ukemi Breakfalls.
Waza Technique.

Daily Telegraph Magazine

How to play

The object of a judo competition is to throw one's opponent cleanly, hold him immobile on his back for 30 seconds, forcing him to submit through the pressure of an armlock or stranglehold, or—more usual in top-class competitions—to gain a decision given by two judges and a referee. Only one point—an *ippon*—is needed to decide a contest, because the theory is that in early times a single clean throw, a stranglehold, or a hold-down could disable a person. The two judges sit at two diagonally opposite corners of the mat, and the referee conducts the contest from the mat itself.

The fighters approach one another, and after a ceremonial bow they take hold of each other by the jacket. They are permitted to grab at the legs or hold the belt to assist with throws. *Newaza* (groundwork) is resorted to when the competitors fight on the ground. Some competitors specialize in this aspect of the sport and lure their opponents onto the ground and use their strength there.

Most international contests are won on a decision in which a number of knock-downs are counted by the judges. But a *waza-ari* (almost a point) can be scored which overrules a knock-down. In the event of an equal number of knock-downs and no score on the ground, the contestant who has done most attacking gets the decision. A *chui* (warning) for an infringement can also decide a close contest when a *waza-ari* or an *ippon* have not been awarded.

When practising, judo experts attempt to be more free than in contests. *Randori* forms the basis of training, but techniques are improved with frequent practice of movements or parts of movements. Weight training and running are part of the training of more ambitious competitors.

Because judo throws are violent, a system of breakfalls has been evolved which allows the expert to soften his own fall. He relaxes and hits the mat with an outstretched arm to prevent any serious damage.

Despite its violent nature, judo is a very formal sport. Competitors bow to each other before and after each match, even in training. The instructor is always respected, and people in the higher grades are always honoured. Black belts assist *kyu* (pupil) grades in their training, as they were once beginners themselves. There are other traditions, but the philosophy behind judo is not emphasized as much as it once was, as judo becomes more of a sport and less a martial art.

Grades

The judo grading system enables an individual's skill and experience to be ascertained. Grades are divided into Dan (degree) and Kyu (pupil) sections. A beginner wears a white belt, and after examinations goes through the following stages:

5th	Kyu	Yellow belt	Japan: White belt
4th	Kyu	Orange belt	
3rd	Kyu	Green belt	
2nd	Kyu	Blue belt	Japan: Brown belt
1st	Kyu	Brown belt	
1st	Dan	Black belt	
2nd	Dan	Black belt	
3rd	Dan	Black belt	
4th	Dan	Black belt	
5th	Dan	Black belt	
6th	Dan	Red and white belt	
7th	Dan	Red and white belt	
8th	Dan	Red and white belt	
9th	Dan	Red belt	
10th	Dan	Red belt	
11th	Dan	Red belt	
12th	Dan	White belt	

Grades are given according to fighting ability—a contestant has an increasing number of fights as he gains experience—and also on technical knowledge. Above 5th Dan, grades are given for the *judoka's* contribution to the sport and not on fighting ability. Thus the top international fighters are usually 4th or 5th Dans. Theoretically, it is possible for a person to reach the 12th Dan and receive the White Belt—having done the complete circle in judo—but this honour has never been bestowed. The highest grade ever awarded by the Technical Panel of the Kodokan, the centre of the sport, is the 10th Dan.

With the spread of judo, gradings have become less significant, but they are still useful for estimating the level a person has reached in the sport. Downgradings are given only in the event of misconduct. In the late 1960s, the British Judo Association introduced a points system to bring them into line with the rest of Europe and Japan. This enabled a *judoka* to accumulate points from gradings in major contests for promotion to the next grade. But the Kyu gradings are still given at regular three-monthly contests.

Karate

The most devastating and lethal method of unarmed combat yet devised is karate, a Japanese word meaning literally 'empty handed'. The karate expert is proficient at striking an opponent with his hands, legs, and elbows, and even his head. He can produce combinations of blows with amazing dexterity and speed, or demonstrate his power by breaking boards, tiles, rocks, or blocks of ice. And a *karateka* (karate exponent) is better equipped for a real fight than a boxer, a wrestler, or a judoka.

Such values have brought karate tremendous popularity—in America it has overhauled judo in the number of participants. But the sport suffers from a lack of organization, while the contests, though exciting, are somewhat unsatisfactory, because real blows cannot be landed.

Although karate was developed in the Orient, particularly in Japan, it probably originated in Greece where the Olympic Games included an event called the *pankration*. This 'sport' was a combination of wrestling and fist-fighting in which the participants were allowed to use punches, kicks, throws, or holds. It was so keenly contested that the loser invariably ended up maimed or dead.

Pankration as a sport gradually lost popularity and divided into two streams in Europe—the striking techniques of boxing and the grappling skills of wrestling. But the other skills involved spread into Asia, probably with the invasion of India by Alexander the Great in the fourth century BC. An Indian Buddhist monk, Daruma Taishi, is accepted as the man who took the techniques into China where they became diffused with other fighting arts.

As a result of trade between China and the Japanese island of Okinawa, karate arrived in Japan in about 1600. But it was not until 300 years later that karate as it is known today was developed. The man chiefly responsible was Funakoshi Gichin, whom all schools and styles recognize as the father of the sport. Born in Okinawa in 1869, he studied karate from the age of 11, and introduced it to Japan after World War I. It aroused tremendous interest, and was watched by the founder of judo, Jigoro Kano, who insisted that Funakoshi give a demonstration at the Kodokan.

Funakoshi remained in Japan, and in 1936 founded the Shotokan, a training hall, which was to become the name of the principal style of karate. The Japan Karate Association—the organizing body for shotokan—was established in 1955 with Funakoshi as chief instructor.

One of the problems of karate has been the diversification of styles. Some of Funakoshi's followers felt they could adapt the original style and improve it as a fighting sport. Each school of thought varies its emphasis, and sometimes has its own techniques and methods of grading. The relations between the schools are usually strained, but in some countries some kind of harmony has been achieved. All the major styles in Japan are represented on the FAJKO (Federation of All Japan

1 Hirinori Ohtsuka (8th Dan), the founder of the *Wado-ryu* style, in a demonstration in London in 1970.
2 Keinosuke Inoeda, the 1963 All Japan champion, counters a knife attack with *Yoko-geri-kekomi* (side thrust kick).
3 Pauline Laville, Britain's first female black belt *karateka*, launches *Yoko-geri-kekomi* at her instructor at the Budokwai in London.
4 Two contestants in the 1970 GB-Japanese Universities goodwill match at close quarters.

Ed Lacey

Karate Organisation), which was founded in 1965 and has been granted government recognition.

There are five major schools of karate. The chief of them is, of course, the *shotokan*, controlled by the Japan Karate Association. This 'orthodox' style lies somewhere between the light-moving *shito-ryu* and the powerful *goju-ryu* styles. Shito-ryu itself gets its name from its leading instructors, Itosu and Higaonna, and its methods are based on speed and mobility. Goju-ryu is derived from the Japanese words *goken* (strong fist) and *juken* (soft fist). The training involved in this school is extremely rugged and is frequently practised oudoors in all weathers. *Wado-ryu* is a style similar to shotokan, but involving less use of the hips. The name means 'way of peace'. But possibly the most spectacular type of karate is *kyoku-shinkai*, founded by Korean-born Mas Oyama, one of the most famous figures in karate, in 1923. The style is based on tremendous strength, and was popularized by Oyama's ceaseless exhibitions. He used to smash 30 roofing tiles with a single blow, and has defeated 52 bulls in combat! He killed three outright with his bare hands and feet, and broke the horns off the others.

The first European country in which karate became popular was France. But it spread to Britain, and by 1968 there were 250 karate clubs there. The chief styles in Europe are shotokan and wado-ryu. But the highest graded judoka in Britain—Steve Arneil (5th Dan), who trained for many years in Japan—took up the kyokushinkai school of karate.

Tony Duffy

Ed Lacey

How to play

Grading All schools of karate have a different method of grading. But they are all based on the judo principles of Kyu (pupil) and Dan (degree) grades. The lower levels are judged more on the precision of their techniques than on fighting ability, but as a student advances he has to take part in free-sparring.

Kumite (sparring) As a karate blow can be extremely dangerous, punches and kicks have to be 'pulled' in contests. The object is to pierce an opponent's guard, and before hitting him withdraw the blow. A match is adjudicated by a referee and four judges, one judge sitting in each corner of the 9-metre-square contest area. If a judge sees an *ippon* (point) or *waza-ari* (almost a point) he blows a whistle and shows with a flag who he thinks has scored. If the referee agrees, he declares the point. Just one point—which in real life might have been a fatal or a disabling blow—is needed for victory.

Kata (forms) Contests are also held in *kata*—a series of regularized movements where competitors are marked on the precision of their movements and correct posture. The preliminary rounds are conducted on a knock-out basis. In the final pool, seven judges officiate with numbered cards. The highest and lowest scores are discarded and the remaining five aggregated. The individual with the highest score is the winner.

Training All styles of karate are based on hard and regular training. There are three main training methods: basic techniques, kata, and kumite, and sessions usually last a minimum of one hour. Some styles, notably shotokan, restrict jiyu-kumite (free sparring) until the 3rd Kyu is reached, usually after two years' hard training. This is because the less experienced karateka lacks control, and can also ruin his style by sparring too early. Basic techniques, including combinations of kicks and punches, are repeated time and again in a bid to reach perfection, while kata helps to brush up the basic movements. The breaking of boards and rocks is done in training only to give the pupil some idea of the power he has acquired.

Motor-Cycling

From man's instinct for competition, one might think the first motorcycle race took place soon after the second machine was built. Perhaps something of the sort did happen, but the first 'official' contests were not held until almost 20 years after Gottlieb Daimler produced the first motor-cycle in Germany in 1886.

The engine of Daimler's wooden-framed machine produced only half a brake-horse-power, so its racing potential could hardly have impressed its rider, Wilhelm Mayback, the pioneer who went on to develop Mercedes cars. But speed rose, and motorized sport became the rage as engineers discovered the secrets of producing increased power. Mile-a-minute performance was feasible by 1900.

Racing found its beginning on the Continent, notably in France, where enthusiasts were not held back by the 4, 12, and later 20 mph limits which applied in Britain. Moreover, there were no problems in Europe over the closure of roads for sport—a concession never permitted in England.

Trans-continental, inter-city races for both cars and motorcycles had begun in 1897, but these tragically dangerous contests came to an end in 1903 when the Paris-Madrid event was stopped at Bordeaux after a series of fatal accidents. The popularity of these marathon races over open roads caused most of the trouble—in 1903 three million frenzied spectators were said to line the dust-hazed roads, totally free of safety precautions as the speeding vehicles shot past. The tragic race did, however, confirm the potential of the two-wheeled machines. The French ace, Bucquet, winner of an earlier Paris-Vienna epic, led at Bordeaux at an average speed of almost 40 mph.

The ill-fated marathons were followed in 1904 by a race for motor-cycles only, on closed roads. Organized by the Auto-cycle Club de France, it was called the International Cup Race and intended as a prestige event for teams of three riders representing Austria, Denmark, France, Germany, and Great Britain. For some reason, the continental riders did not welcome the British entry and made their antipathy clear by committing acts of sabotage. It was all part of the game, apparently, to delay the opposition by scattering nails on the road as they approached. The harassed British team were forced to retire. Everything about the race was highly suspect. Even the organizers were accused of cheating and the outcry against them caused the results to be declared void and never issued to the public. This fiasco led to the formation of the

Fédération Internationale des Clubs Motorcyclistes as the governing body for member nations in 1905. Ireland had established the first such national organization with the formation of the Motor Cycle Union of Ireland in 1901. The Auto-Cycle Club (ACC), the two-wheeler offshoot of the Royal Automobile Club, was set up a year later.

With order established, the 1905 International, held once more in France, proved more satisfactory, although the event still suffered from British discontent. Their team had returned home in 1904 determined to redeem themselves. The expedition had not been entirely wasted, for, disregarding the poor sportsmanship, they realized that British machines were inferior to those of the Austrians and French for racing on the roads of the time. Still unable to gain the support of Parliament, the self-governed Isle of Man offered assistance by agreeing to close a section of road, and a 15.8-mile circuit was selected starting from Tynwald Green, the ancient seat of Manx rule at St John. Staged as an eliminating event for the 1905 'International', the Manx rehearsal was a great success. The winner, J. S. Campbell (Ariel), averaged over 40 mph for the 175-mile distance. In France, however, the British team's new-won confidence was shattered. Their machines proved inadequate and all retired. Of 12 starters, only 3 finished, victory going to the Austrian C. V. Wondrick on a twin-cylinder Laurin-Klement—an Austro-Hungarian firm which, with boundary changes after the 1914-18 war, later became famous as the Czechoslovakian Skoda company. Wondrick's speed was a record 54.5 mph.

British resentment was directed against the machine specification limiting the weight to 110 pounds. This, they said, was dangerous, as it encouraged the use of big engines in unnecessarily light frames. They claimed the main object of racing was the development of better touring motorcycles and therefore should be aimed at improving design. They would not agree to produce machines solely for racing. The organizers refused to ease the rules—presumably because they were more concerned with the success of racing and the greater excitement the special machines produced. The 1906 race in Austria proved to be the last, for although Britain gained some success with Harry Collier (Matchless) finishing third, both sides remained adamant and the race was never held again. Ignominious as they were, however, the International Cup Races nonetheless stand as the first official events in the history of the sport.

The British riders returned home determined to establish road racing, but found the Westminster

Parliament was unbending on road closure. Luckily, the Manx authority did not hold this view. Appreciating the great success of the International rehearsals, they invited the ACC—later the Auto Cycle Union (ACU)—to establish an annual meeting on the island. From this, in 1907, the famous Tourist Trophy Races were born. Curiously enough, this coincided with a loss of interest on the Continent, where, apart from odd races in France, no racing was held until after World War I.

So the home of motor-cycling moved to Britain, for apart from the introduction of the 'TT' for road racing, 1907 also brought the

opening of the 2.75-mile motor racing track at Brooklands, where flat-out speed could be maintained for as long as the rider wished. With this testing-ground available, the development of British machines streaked ahead. No longer were manufacturers restricted to creating machines along fairly sober lines for use on the banked, but short, cycle racing tracks such as that at Canning Town, London. It was at Canning Town in 1907 that Charlie Collier (Harry's brother, and winner of the first TT) covered 51 miles in 60 minutes to establish the first world's one-hour record. It was a remarkable achievement, for the

Daily Telegraph Magazine

track measured only one-third of a mile. Bert Colver (Matchless) bettered this at the White City Stadium, London, with 52.93 miles in the hour during a race which formed part of the 1908 Olympic Games.

Charlie Collier had meanwhile built a new 1000 cc machine to take advantage of the potential offered at Brooklands, and the same year raised the record to almost 70 miles in the hour—a record that stood until 1920.

As these 'touring' machines improved, so came the need for more demanding races. After Charlie Collier won the 1910 TT at 50.63 mph, the St John circuit was de-clared too fast and dangerous, and the more demanding 'Mountain' course adopted for the race in 1911. The Isle of Man government was delighted to agree, for as a tourist attraction the TT races had become world famous.

Foreign manufacturers could also see the great value of the TT. In 1911, the island was invaded by the American Indians (machines manufactured at Milwaukee), and they took the first three places in the Senior (500 cc) race. The winner was British rider Oscar Godfrey at 47.63 mph. This defeat revitalized British manufacturers, who, riding the rising tide of motor-cycle enthusiasm, after World War I, developed their machines to such a peak that they dominated racing and the industry. Such famous names as AJS, Brough Superior, Cotton, Norton, Rudge, Triumph, and Velocette all contributed to the 'roaring twenties'. Even the newly established grands prix of European countries were dominated by British teams.

Indeed, not only did Britain produce dominant machines, she also appeared to breed superior riders. The reason for this possibly stemmed, paradoxically, from those early days when riders had difficulty finding venues where they enjoyed the sport. Under the juris-

1 The danger and excitement of two-wheel racing draw big crowds all over the world.
2 Three production machines angle for position in a 1968 '500-miler' race. 3 1970 125cc racers rocket around Brands Hatch at speeds that would have amazed—and beaten—riders of machines four times their capacity 30 years earlier.
4 World 250 champion Rodney Gould corners his Yamaha in the 1970 Hutchinson 100 at Brands Hatch. The Japanese company's fine 125 and 250 cc racers have been the mounts of six road-racing world champions since 1964.

Brian A. Holder

Wilmik

Wilmik

Radio Times Hulton Picture Library

English ace Oscar Godfrey with his Indian motor-cycle at Brooklands in 1911. Godfrey spearheaded the American company's successful British invasion that year, winning the Isle of Man Senior TT at an average 47.63 mph. Indians finished 1, 2, 3 in the classic—a success that spurred British manufacturers such as Norton on to greater efforts.

diction of the ACU, clubs sprang up to organize localized events on private land. By this means, dozens of events, catering for all forms of sport—trials, scrambles, grass-tracks, sand-tracks, speedway, hill-climbs, sprinting, record-breaking, and road racing, were held every weekend throughout the summer. No other country adopted motor-cycle sport on such a scale as Britain, where the opportunity to improve progressively from novice to star rider has always existed. This opportunity to compete still gives British riders an edge on their foreign counterparts.

Modern competition demands complete concentration for success and is best achieved by specializing in one form of activity. But this was not always the case. The sporting clubman almost invariably owned just one machine —it was all he could afford—and it would serve for everyday transport and provide sport at weekends. He would ride the machine to the meeting—grass-track, scramble, trial, or whatever it might be—strip off the road equipment, compete in the event, rebuild the bike, and motor home . . . all being well. The system produced some aces of astonishing versatility—during the 1930s, for example, riders such as George Rowley, Allan Jefferies, Jack Williams, and Len Heath were 'works' riders in trials, scrambles, and racing. And after the war, Geoff Duke paved the way to his world championship winning road races of the 1950s with successes in major trials and scrambles for BSA and Norton. Not all riders found their only interest in racing. Reliability runs were very popular from the beginning. Hubert Egerton, of Norwich, made the first-ever Land's End to John O'Groats run in August 1900.

The desolate Yorkshire moors also attracted pioneer motor-cyclists and saw the still-existant Scott Trial established in 1914. This event, ostensibly a rough-country race with the addition of observed tests to prove riding skill, was the forerunner of modern scrambling and moto-cross.

Complacency from the long years of virtually unchallenged dominance finally caught up with the British sport and industry in the 1950s, with European and later, Japanese works machines sweeping to a series of victories. English manufacturers could scarcely complain, however, for the first sign of renewed foreign challenge had appeared as early as the late 1920s. Pietro Gherzi on a Moto Guzzi challenged for the 250 TT in 1926. It was a first-time effort by the all-Italian team and they won—only to be excluded for using an unspecified sparking plug.

The German BMW factory gained its strength by regularly successful attacks on the world speed record, beginning in 1929 when Ernst Henne achieved 134.5

mph on a 740 cc supercharged twin. Admittedly, Joe Wright regained some glory for Britain with his superb 150 mph run on a 1000 cc JAP at Cork, Ireland, the following year, but thereafter Henne and BMW raised it stage-by-stage to 169 mph in 1936. A private effort by Britain's Eric Fernihough shaved this with 169.5 mph on a 1000 cc Brough Superior, only to lose it to Italy's Piero Taruffi on a 500 supercharged, four-cylinder Gilera-Rondine at 170.5 mph. Henne and the government-backed BMW were having

none of that. They wheeled out a 500 to set 173.5 mph at Munich in November 1937—a speed which stood until 1951.

The development of the German and Italian record machines was a prelude to a new era of racing. It was inaugurated by Irish ace Stanley Woods, who won the 250 and 500 TTs for Moto Guzzi in 1935. While British manufacturers were content to rely upon unsupercharged, single-cylinder engines, their continental counterparts were taking full advantage of the FICM rules allowing multi-cylinders,

Brian A. Holder

It might not look fun, but trials-riding events such as the Scottish Six-Day Trial are among the most popular of all motor-cycle sports.

Trials-riding

Trials-riding holds little of the glamour of racing, but it is a sport demanding the most delicate touch and sensitive balance with a motor-cycle. Many top scramblers and road-racers have acquired their basic skill by competing in trials, for it is a sport demanding courage, concentration, lightning reactions, and firm control by a rider in unity with his machine.

The term 'trials-riding' does little, however, to describe this sport. Events are held over rough country, where deliberate hazards are arranged to test riding skill. The riders have to remain poised on their motor-cycles while attempting near-vertical climbs or drops, or riding through sand, mud, or over rocks made treacherously slippery from slime, or even submerged by water. The task is made no easier by having to follow a narrow, predetermined path featuring sharp bends at the most awkward points. The object is to negotiate these 'sections' without penalty. Penalties are incurred for stopping or for touching the ground to maintain balance or forward movement.

Trials machines are basically similar to normal road machines, with adaptations for the type of terrain encountered. They have a high build to clear jutting obstacles, and the engine provides low-speed pulling power. Comparatively simple designs, they are inexpensive to buy and maintain. As a result, trials-riding is the most popular of competitive sports among motor-cycle clubmen. There are some 5,000 active participants in Great Britain, and the sport has become increasingly popular in Europe and the United States.

The ultimate trial event is the International Six Day Trial, held annually in countries of nations belonging to the FIM. In this event, at least 200 miles is covered each day. The world's outstanding trials-rider, Ulster-born Sammy Miller, won five gold medals at this 'Olympics of motor-cycling'.

Grass-track racing

Once a training school for road-racers, modern grass-track racing closely resembles professional speedway events. Many top speedway stars have cut their teeth on the sport's tight, bumpy, grass circuits.

World War II left England virtually without smooth road-racing circuits, so prospective grand prix drivers turned to grass-track racing as the only way to gain experience. Competition became so keen that the 1-mile Brands Hatch grass circuit became the Mecca of motor-cycle racing in the south-east of England until it gave way to asphalt in 1949. Those years saw a significant technical development that affected the whole field of motor-cycle design.

In 1947 a team of Irish riders challenged the locals at Brands Hatch with unusual machines fitted with spring suspension for the rear wheel. Ever since the early days of grass-track racing in the late 1920s, it had been an item of faith that all-rigid assemblies were better able to deal with the nasty bumps of the grass circuits. The Irish team changed all that, racing away to an easy win on their smooth-handling machines, while the local lads bounced about in futile pursuit. The rear-springing conversion fitted to the Irish machines was the creation of Rex McCandless, who developed his concepts further with his revolutionary 'featherbed' road-racing frame for Norton in 1950. His grass-track innovation contributed greatly to the development of the modern spring-frame for road-racing machines.

But as more road-racing circuits became available, the style of grass-track racing began to change. The biggest single factor behind this was the scarcity of available land. The long circuits, with left- and right-hand bends and gradients, gave way to short, speedway-style ovals. These shorter circuits ($\frac{1}{4}$ to $\frac{1}{2}$ mile) demanded development of entirely new machines, and a type of bike similar to speedway machines became essential for success.

Grass-tracks still have bumps, and machines retain rear suspension, but in all other respects there is no longer any similarity to road racing or touring machines. The style of riding is similar to speedway, with the left leg and foot being used as an essential pivot in the sliding method of cornering.

Speedway ace Ivan Mauger is also an accomplished devotee of the grass-track. Here he leads Gottfried Schwarze and John Britcher at Lydden Hill.

superchargers, and streamlining. Only the outbreak of war stopped world supremacy changing hands sooner, for in 1939 BMW won the Senior TT. This also marked the first time a non-British rider won the race, with George Meier, a German soldier, setting a new record of 89.38 mph. The same year the Ulster Grand Prix went to an Italian, Dorino Serafini, on a Gilera. At 97.85 mph it was the fastest road race in the world.

As in other fields, Britain was slow to see the threat, although AJS and Velocette had begun to develop new machines to counter the challenge. In fact, Walter Rusk on a four-cylinder, supercharged AJS, had led the 1939 Ulster race with a lap record of 100.03 mph before retiring with steering trouble. The stage was set, then, for exciting competition in 1940, but meanwhile more pressing problems than beating opponents by racing intervened for five years.

Sadly, the 'super-projects' of 1939 were never developed after the war. Presumably to prevent victories by the erstwhile enemy, the Fédération Internationale Motorcycliste (FIM) banned superchargers with the resumption of racing in 1946—a move that gave a new lease of life to the pre-war British machines. Harold Daniell won the 1947 Senior TT on the 1938 model 500 Norton, and Bob Foster gained the 350 race for Velocette at 80.31 mph. The first new machine to appear after the war was a 500 twin-cylinder AJS. Intended for supercharging, it was modified to run atmospherically. On it Les Graham gained the first 500 world championship in 1949.

To cope with this threat—and an impending one from the Italian factories—Norton chose to rely on their single-cylinder engine

Radio Times Hulton Picture Library

Geoff Duke—the man who revolutionized motor-cycle racing—has one eye on Artie Bell as he wins the 1950 TT.

mounted in an entirely new frame that, combined with revolutionary rear springing, brought a new concept to steering. What it lacked in top speed, the new Norton regained with super-fast cornering. In Geoff Duke, Norton had a rider to match their bikes' superlative handling, but even he was unable to prevent Italy's Umberto Masetti on a new Gilera 'four' taking the

Wilmik

Keystone

Keystone

Daily Telegraph Magazine

Brian A. Holder

1

2

3

4

1950 world title.

Duke brought a completely new approach to racing in style and technique. Not for him were the cumbersome, heavy leather jackets, trousers, and boots riders wore for protection. He devised clothing equally adequate but much lighter—skin-fitting one-piece leather overalls which cut wind resistance to a minimum and so provided more speed. Duke also showed how to lay flat on a machine to make it still faster.

With his 1950 experience behind him, Duke proved unbeatable in 1951 and gained both the 350 and

1 Bob McIntyre leads John Surtees in the sensational 1957 TT in which the Scot's 500 Gilera four times lapped the IOM circuit at more than 100 mph. **2** Mike Hailwood presses Gary Hocking hard in the 1962 350 TT. Hocking led from the first lap, but Hailwood finally caught him and won by 5.6 sec. Both rode MV Agustas. **3** Centripetal force poses more problems for two wheels than four. Phil Read's mastery of it gives him the lead in the 1967 German GP. **4** Rising star Giacomo Agostini (6) was a leading attraction at the 1967 Isle of Man TT races. **5** British television has brought mud into the home with its winter coverage of scrambling, a fast-growing sport that developed in England in the 1920s as a racing version of trials competition. Most scrambling riders still acquire their skills in trials, which give them the delicate touch and balance they need to race over mud, snow, sleet, and ice. **6** Balance is just as vital in sidecar racing, a sport that demands complete understanding between driver and passenger. Here Georg Auerbacher and Herrmann Hahn combine to keep their BMW on the Brands Hatch track.

500 cc world titles for Norton. Gilera however, knew they had potentially the greatest machine, and they wanted the greatest rider. They got him when Duke joined them in 1953. This 'defection' spelt the end to Britain's half-century lead in motor-cycling. Other top British riders joined foreign teams as first Velocette, then AJS and Norton, withdrew factory support in 1954.

There was also a new threat from Italy. MV Agusta had enlisted the Gilera designer, Remor, to provide them with a similar prestige projectile, and Moto Guzzi were developing a machine with no less than eight cylinders. As a result, the Italian factories, together with NSU of Germany in the 125 and 250 cc classes, gained total control of the world championships after 1952. The Italian companies' task was made easier by the breathtaking skills great English riders John Surtees and Mike Hailwood—together with Rhodesia's Gary Hocking—brought to their powerful machines.

Never highly competitive before 1939, NSU came into calculations by breaking the BMW world speed record in 1951 at 180 mph. This was broken by New Zealander Russell Wright on a 1000 cc Vincent HRD with 185 mph in 1955, but Wilhelm Herz then regained it for NSU in 1956, first by achieving 189 mph on a 350 cc machine and then by breaking 200 mph for the first time by a motor-cycle, with 210 mph on a 500 twin. NSU then embarked on a racing programme, no expense spared, which gave them untroubled wins in the 125 and 250 cc classes between 1952 and 1955. They then chose to withdraw in the same way as Mercedes did from motor racing—unbeaten.

Other manufacturers, however, began to find the cost of producing such super-machines prohibitive. Their development no longer aided that of touring machines, and racing success was doing little to aid sales. At the end of 1957 every

world manufacturer then racing withdrew their support from the circuits.

Reflecting the attitude of the FICM at the time of the International Cup Race troubles in 1906, the FIM did nothing to modify the rules to allow racing to continue at world-title level more economically for manufacturers. World-title racing continued under existing regulations, although only MV Agusta decided to carry on. With no factory opposition against them, MV gained every 125, 250, 350, and 500 cc world championship during 1958, 1959, and 1960.

At the same time, the Japanese manufacturer Honda conceived the notion of capturing world markets for motor-cycles on a scale never before dreamed of. The quickest way to gain prestige, Honda decided, was by racing for world success.

The first racing Hondas that appeared at the TT in 1959 were clearly based on the earlier all-conquering 125 cc NSUs. While they did not have the performance of the German machines, they were reliable and won the team prize by finishing 6th, 7th, and 11th. Honda returned to Europe with entirely new machines in 1960—125 cc twins and 250 four-cylinders. After a year, their performances prompted MV to withdraw from these classes, allowing Honda to take over unopposed.

Honda were soon joined by Suzuki and Yamaha, and between them these Japanese factories took development of small-capacity machines far beyond anything imagined possible. Honda built 50 cc twins capable of over 120 mph at 20,000 rpm, five-cylinder 125s, and six-cylinder 250s and 350s. They finally produced a 500 developing over 110 bhp.

The Isle of Man TT results reflected the technical boom. The circuit was first lapped at 100 mph in 1957 by Bob McIntyre on a 500 Gilera. Phil Read set the first 100 mph lap by a 250 in 1965, and team-mate Bill Ivy achieved a remarkable 100.32 mph on a 125

in 1968.

With no tangible opposition, MV Agusta continued to dominate the 500 cc class—their 1970 win was their thirteenth in succession—and the fifth in a row for their star rider, Giacomo Agostini. The original four-cylinder machine was superseded by a lighter, better-handling three-cylinder version and these attributes had been sufficient to keep it ahead of the 500 Honda challenge in 1966 and 1967.

At this stage, even the Japanese chose to pull out. Not perhaps so much because of the enormous cost, but because they had gained their objective—world markets. Motor-cycle racing to manufacturers is business, not sport.

Motor-cycle racing is now being aimed back towards its original concept. Manufacturers are keen to race to help development of better road machines. With this in mind, races for production machines are gradually reappearing, and in 1970 the FIM agreed to consider the introduction of a world title class in 1971.

There can be no doubt that racing 'improves the breed'. At the production machine race in 1969, Malcolm Uphill on a road-going 650 cc Triumph, complete with silencers and lights, lapped at 100.37 mph—faster than all the super-expensive works specials of just a decade previously.

WORLD ROAD RACING CHAMPIONSHIPS—50 cc

Year	Champion (country)	Motor-cycle
1962	E. Degner (Germany)	Suzuki
1963	H. Anderson (NZ)	Suzuki
1964	H. Anderson (NZ)	Suzuki
1965	R. Bryans (Ireland)	Honda
1966	H. Anscheidt (Germany)	Suzuki
1967	H. Anscheidt (Germany)	Suzuki
1968	H. Anscheidt (Germany)	Suzuki
1969	A. Nieto (Spain)	Derbi
1970	A. Nieto (Spain)	Derbi
1971	J. de Vries (Netherlands)	Kreidler
1972	A. Nieto (Spain)	Derbi
1973	J. de Vries (Netherlands)	Kreidler

WORLD ROAD RACING CHAMPIONSHIPS

Year	125 cc Champion (country)	Motor-cycle	250 cc Champion (country)	Motor-cycle	350 cc Champion (country)	Motor-cycle	500 cc Champion (country)	Motor-cycle
1949	N. Pagani (Italy)	Mondial	B. Ruffo (Italy)	Moto Guzzi	F. Frith (GB)	Velocette	L. Graham (GB)	AJS
1950	B. Ruffo (Italy)	Mondial	D. Ambrosini (Italy)	Benelli	R. Foster (GB)	Velocette	U. Masetti (Italy)	Gilera
1951	C. Ubialli (Italy)	Mondial	B. Ruffo (Italy)	Moto Guzzi	G. Duke (GB)	Norton	G. Duke (GB)	Norton
1952	C. Sandford (GB)	MV Agusta	E. Lorenzetti (Italy)	Moto Guzzi	G. Duke (GB)	Norton	U. Masetti (Italy)	Gilera
1953	W. Haas (Germany)	NSU	W. Haas (Germany)	NSU	F. Anderson (GB)	Moto Guzzi	G. Duke (GB)	Gilera
1954	R. Hollaus (Germany)	NSU	W. Haas (Germany)	NSU	F. Anderson (GB)	Moto Guzzi	G. Duke (GB)	Gilera
1955	C. Ubialli (Italy)	MV Agusta	H. Muller (Germany)	NSU	W. Lomas (GB)	Moto Guzzi	G. Duke (GB)	Gilera
1956	C. Ubialli (Italy)	MV Agusta	C. Ubialli (Italy)	MV Agusta	W. Lomas (GB)	Moto Guzzi	J. Surtees (GB)	MV Agusta
1957	T. Provini (Italy)	Mondial	C. Sandford (GB)	Mondial	K. Campbell (Australia)	Moto Guzzi	L. Liberati (Italy)	Gilera
1958	C. Ubialli (Italy)	MV Agusta	T. Provini (Italy)	MV Agusta	J. Surtees (GB)	MV Agusta	J. Surtees (GB)	MV Agusta
1959	C. Ubialli (Italy)	MV Agusta	C. Ubialli (Italy)	MV Agusta	J. Surtees (GB)	MV Agusta	J. Surtees (GB)	MV Agusta
1960	C. Ubialli (Italy)	MV Agusta	C. Ubialli (Italy)	MV Agusta	J. Surtees (GB)	MV Agusta	J. Surtees (GB)	MV Agusta
1961	T. Phillis (Australia)	Honda	M. Hailwood (GB)	Honda	G. Hocking (Rhodesia)	MV Agusta	G. Hocking (Rhodesia)	MV Agusta
1962	L. Taveri (Switzerland)	Honda	J. Redman (Rhodesia)	Honda	J. Redman (Rhodesia)	Honda	M. Hailwood (GB)	MV Agusta
1963	H. Anderson (NZ)	Suzuki	J. Redman (Rhodesia)	Honda	J. Redman (Rhodesia)	Honda	M. Hailwood (GB)	MV Agusta
1964	L. Taveri (Switzerland)	Honda	P. Read (GB)	Yamaha	J. Redman (Rhodesia)	Honda	M. Hailwood (GB)	MV Agusta
1965	H. Anderson (NZ)	Suzuki	P. Read (GB)	Yamaha	J. Redman (Rhodesia)	Honda	M. Hailwood (GB)	MV Agusta
1966	L. Taveri (Switzerland)	Honda	M. Hailwood (GB)	Honda	M. Hailwood (GB)	Honda	G. Agostini (Italy)	MV Agusta
1967	W. Ivy (GB)	Yamaha	M. Hailwood (GB)	Honda	M. Hailwood (GB)	Honda	G. Agostini (Italy)	MV Agusta
1968	P. Read (GB)	Yamaha	P. Read (GB)	Yamaha	G. Agostini (Italy)	MV Agusta	G. Agostini (Italy)	MV Agusta
1969	D. Simmonds (GB)	Kawasaki	K. Carruthers (Australia)	Benelli	G. Agostini (Italy)	MV Agusta	G. Agostini (Italy)	MV Agusta
1970	D. Braun (Germany)	Suzuki	R. Gould (GB)	Yamaha	G. Agostini (Italy)	MV Agusta	G. Agostini (Italy)	MV Agusta
1971	A. Nieto (Spain)	Derbi	P. Read (GB)	Yamaha	G. Agostini (Italy)	MV Agusta	G. Agostini (Italy)	MV Agusta
1972	A. Nieto (Spain)	Derbi	J. Saarinen (Finland)	Yamaha	G. Agostini (Italy)	MV Agusta	G. Agostini (Italy)	MV Agusta
1973	K. Andersson (Sweden)	Yamaha	D. Braun (W. Germany)	Yamaha	G. Agostini (Italy)	MV Agusta	P. Read (GB)	MV Agusta

Motor-Racing

Every year, about 120,000 people turn up to watch the British Grand Prix. In Germany, about 300,000 spectators witness the German Grand Prix. And over 80,000 make the annual pilgrimage to Monza to watch the Italian event. Each June, at least half-a-million fans converge on Le Mans in France to see the famous 24-hour race, and in the United States the Indianapolis 500 attracts crowds of 350,000. There are many theories about why people enjoy motor races like these. The most obvious encompass such facets as the colour, the excitement, and the glamour of observing top drivers in action. The public of just about every nation under the sun relish this raucous atmosphere compounded of sight, sound, and smell. But there is more to it than this. One idea is that human beings are basically bloodthirsty, and that they go there hoping for a crop of crashes. A more likely notion, put forward by a psychologist, is that they like to see such considerable skill being employed, obtaining a kind of comfort out of watching drivers go to the limits and survive.

Whatever the truth, motor racing has become one of the world's most popular spectator sports. Grand prix drivers could now be said to belong to a branch of show business. Their pay is in the same class, and a reigning world champion may earn £50,000 a year—possibly much more. Few people will deny that such men deserve every penny. They belong to an occupation that demands total dedication. Stirling Moss once remarked that he had given motor racing 'all but my life'. Sometimes the sport requires that as well. In the 1970 season, three stars of the grand prix circus were killed in action. One of them, Jochen Rindt, became the first man to win the World Drivers' Championship posthumously.

Every motor racing circuit in Britain displays a notice warning the public that 'Motor Racing is Dangerous'. It is, yet it is also a strangely compulsive occupation. When a driver is lying in hospital, recovering from a crash, he usually spends little time thinking about how lucky he is to have survived. Instead he concentrates on getting back into the cockpit as soon as possible.

Types of Motor Racing

Sixteen or, perhaps, 20 drivers from all over the world compete annually for the World Drivers' Championship—the highest accolade the sport has to offer. The

Drivers wait patiently for the moment when they will have only themselves and the track to contend with.

cars used in this contest are, or should be, the fastest vehicles in the world. In terms of quality, nothing comes higher. But in terms of quantity they represent only the smallest fragment of a sport that takes many forms—all governed by one factor, speed.

Sometimes, a driver races against a pack of others. Sometimes, he competes against a stop-watch. The longest race in Europe is the Le Mans 24-hour event, in which the winning car covers well over 1,000 miles. The shortest is a drag event, in which remarkably powerful oddities called dragsters take off in a smoke screen of scorched rubber, travel flat out for a ¼-mile, and then—with the aid of parachutes—stop.

Whether the contest for the world land-speed record can be called a race is doubtful. If it can be, it is certainly the sport's fastest, for in October 1970 the record was pushed up to 622 mph and enthusiasts began to consider the possibility of man breaking through the sound barrier (765 mph) on land.

Getting into motor racing is not difficult. An enthusiast simply needs to join a club. Soon he will discover what his particular *métier* is, and the level of his talent. He may have a skill for blazing up a hill against a stop-watch. He may have an aptitude for autocross—that rumbustious stampede across country. He may have a talent for driving a Mini to its limits around a circuit, or his particular style may be more suited to sports car events. Usually motor racing has something to satisfy the talents and ambitions of almost every enthusiast.

Indeed, for the enthusiast there is a gamut of motor racing activities to cater for his, or her, tastes. One branch of motor racing–rallying–which almost rivals Grand Prix racing in skills and excitement, is open to anybody with the flair and determination to succeed. And for the less ambitious there is always the fascinating sport of karting.

Getting into motor racing may not be difficult: getting to the top is. It requires an enormous amount of skill, absolute dedication, and a certain amount of luck. Even when they reach the top, many drivers find it just as difficult to stay there. Because, unlike the amateur, very few of them own their cars, they have little control over their destinies. If they cease to win events, or to be well placed, they may suddenly find themselves unwanted. For the politics of the

Any type of car can be raced, and most of them have been. The thoroughbreds of the circuits gain most of the glory, but humbler machines (1) have their races and fans. This hill-climbing Ford Anglia is racing a stop-watch—a far less expensive activity than modern sports-car racing. 2 This Porsche 910 and its harrying Chevrons show just how specialized sports-car racing has become. Unlike their counterparts of 20 years ago, they have little in common with road cars. 3 Single-seater racing is the most expensive form of all. Even a car as tiny as this Formula Three Lotus-Ford relies on sponsors for its existence. 4 Increased power and handling qualities make the modern production saloon more exciting to race and watch. The large and varied fields add to the spectacle, danger and rewards.

Wilmik

1 Autocross, an invention of the early 1960s. The more modest autocross races offer cheap, exciting competition on dusty or muddy circuits.

game are as tough as its conditions.

Modern types of circuit racing fall into three groups: for single seaters, for sports cars and sports prototypes, and for saloon cars. Many leading drivers have excelled in all three of them. In sports-prototype racing Jacky Ickx and Jochen Rindt, for example, both won the Le Mans 24-hour race, and both of them went on to conquer in the world of Formula One—the absolute in single-seater racing. Mario Andretti won a unique single-seater classic—the 1969 Indianapolis 500. Two years earlier, he had made a name for himself in sports-prototype racing

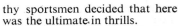

Picturepoint

2 Dragster racers come up with some ingenious technical solutions to the problem of increasing straight-line acceleration. These powerful 200 mph-plus projectiles are followed with fervour in the United States. 3 Stock car racers—the crowd-drawing 'dodgems' of the dirt-track.

by winning the Sebring 12 hours. Stirling Moss won almost every major event in the book; Jim Clark was a wizard with saloon cars as well as single-seaters, and Phil Hill, Lorenzo Bandini, Dan Gurney, Pedro Rodriguez, Bruce McLaren, and Chris Amon are some of the Formula One aces who have won at Le Mans.

Yesterday and Today

Once the motor car arrived, it was not very long before somebody had the idea of using it for racing. The manufacturers, particularly on the Continent, decided that it would be an excellent way of publicizing their products. Weal-

Syndication International

thy sportsmen decided that here was the ultimate in thrills.

Because the car had been designed to run on roads, they seemed to be the logical places over which to race them. At first France had the monopoly. In July 1894, a collection of 'horseless carriages' set off uncertainly from Paris on a road race that was to take them to Rouen. The vehicles entered ranged from a Panhard, which won the event at an average speed of 10.7 mph, to a steam omnibus, which never reached its destination.

The following year, the enthusiasts became more ambitious. They motored from Paris to Bordeaux and back. The winner used a Peugeot, though the most deserving entrant was undoubtedly Emile Levassor of the Panhard and Levassor factory. Ignoring the option to use relief drivers, he travelled non-stop for 48¾ hours over the 732 miles of the course. He was first across the finishing line—only to learn that he had been disqualified on a technicality.

Road races began to creep beyond the frontiers of France. There was a race to Amsterdam and back, to Vienna, and to Berlin. These early motor races offered hazards in addition to the normal ones of high-speed travel. Little or no attempt was made to control the spectators, who, in many cases, had never seen a motor car before. Entirely unable to appreciate its speed, they saw nothing wrong in crowding onto the road in front of it. And as the roads themselves were little more than rutted lanes covered with dust, the entire cavalcade of competitors usually sped along through a thick artificial fog. The only driver who could really see where he was going was the leader.

The first leg of the proposed Paris-Madrid race of 1903 was as far as Bordeaux. Cars were now capable of travelling at 80 mph, yet the precautions taken were negligible. Level crossings that should have been open were closed. Cattle wandered across the road, and so did dogs, cats, hens, children, and adults. Inevitably there were accidents—far to many of them. Drivers, mechanics, and spectators were killed. As soon as the French and Spanish authorities heard the sickening story, they put an immediate ban on all motor racing. The few cars to reach Bordeaux were ignominiously drawn by horses to the station—and sent home by train.

If governments on the Continent had at first been tolerant of the new sport, the politicians at Westminster would have nothing to do with it. From the very start, racing was banned on the roads of England, Scotland, and Wales. The ruling factions in Ireland and the Isle of Man were more open minded. Scenting, perhaps, increased tourist revenue, they gave their consent. On the mainland, however, racing had to be done on private land. Land was forthcoming—the enterprising H. F. Locke King conceived the idea of building a track on his Surrey estate on which British car makers could test their products. Work on the circuit, to be called Brooklands, began in 1906. The first meeting was held there the following year.

An air of amiable eccentricity surrounded the early events at Brooklands. Almost as if trying to prove that the automobile had not yet ousted the horse, drivers were required to wear colours—just like jockeys. The values of the prizes were expressed in sovereigns, and a member of the Jockey Club was appointed as official starter. It was all good sport, but the 2¾-mile enclosed concrete track bore little resemblance to the big road circuits on which major events in Europe were held. The

known as the Association Internationale des Automobiles Clubs Reconnus, and assumed international responsibility for motor sport. In 1946, it changed its name to the more simple Fédération Internationale de l'Automobile.

In 1906, France became the

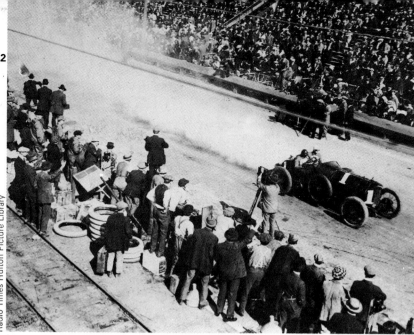

1 A 70 hp Mons, one of the entrants in the abortive Paris-Madrid race of 1903. **2** The new sport cast a spell on the New World too, and a packed Santa Monica crowd saw an Issotta start the 1914 Vanderbilt Cup. **3** Lagonda leads Bugatti in the 1928 Tourist Trophy on the famous Ards road circuit near Belfast. **4** Nuvolari and Auto-Union. The German racers of the 1930s launched a Nazi-backed blitzkrieg on Europe's races.

Radio Times Hulton Picture Library

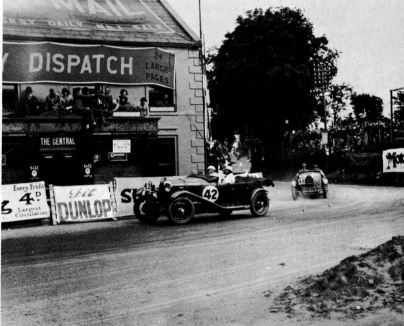

Radio Times Hulton Picture Library

result was that, owing to government apathy on the one hand and a marked lack of interest by most of the motor industry on the other, Britain's emergence as a power in grand prix motor racing took the better part of 60 years.

When, in 1903, the Gordon Bennett Race had to be held in Britain, it took place on a triangular circuit of closed roads in Ireland. And when, in 1905, a race for touring cars called the Tourist Trophy was devised, the Isle of Man played host.

Meanwhile, the pattern of motor racing was beginning to assume something approaching its modern shape. The first national automobile club to be founded was, understandably, the French, but other nations soon formed their own. After the Gordon Bennett race in Germany in 1904, the six national clubs concerned with the events met at Hamburg, and decided to co-ordinate their efforts. Soon afterwards, seven more clubs joined the alliance, which became

Sport & General

scene of the first grand prix, held on a road circuit at Le Mans. The winner was Louis Renault's personal mechanic, a Romanian named Szisz. By then, racing cars had developed into huge, thunderous machines that had drawn farther and farther away from the types of cars that ordinary people used. Enthusiasts insisted that one of the objects of the sport was 'to improve the breed'. As far back as 1904, a number of critics were suggesting that the sport should take this responsibility more seriously. What was the object, they argued, of organizing races for monsters which most people neither wanted nor could afford? Surely a better idea would be to arrange events for vehicles that had something in common with the family car. Nothing could stop the growth of the giants; but, under the leadership of a paper called *L'Auto*, a new class of motor sport was established—*voiturette* racing. To all intents and purposes, it marked the birth of production car events—and, therefore, of sports car racing.

Initially, the *Coupe des Voiturettes* was organized as a reliability trial. Competitors had to cover 125 miles a day over a period of six days. They had to keep up a steady average of not less than $15\frac{1}{2}$ mph, and the whole event culminated in a race over about 160 miles. The event opened up the sport to less powerful vehicles, and was soon followed by other touring car races: the *Kaiser Preis*

1 The stylish Nino Farina won the 1950 British Grand Prix for Alfa Romeo. 2 Juan Fangio's Mercedes—a grand prix car in sports clothing—leads Mike Hawthorn's Jaguar in the 1955 U.K. Tourist Trophy. Mercedes finished 1, 2, 3.

(as its name suggested, the Kaiser presented the cup) in Germany, the Targa Florio (first held in 1906) in Sicily, and the Tourist Trophy races on the Isle of Man.

The first competitors were a mixture of wealthy sportsmen, car manufacturers, and a handful of drivers employed by them. In the early events, they took their mechanics in the cars with them. Mechanics found it a somewhat dangerous undertaking, and they were eventually barred from grand prix events in 1925—though, for the next two years, it remained obligatory to have a mechanic's seat in the car.

Over the years, the trend of motor racing has been towards greater professionalism. In Britain, owing to the reluctance of all British car makers except Bentley to take the sport seriously, amateurism survived for much longer than anywhere else. Between the wars, drivers such as Sir Henry Birkin, Lord Howe, Richard Seaman, and other wealthy individuals took part in grands prix—usually, for want of anything better, in the cockpits of foreign cars.

On the Continent, Rudolf Car-

acciola, Tazio Nuvolari, Hermann Lang, Berndt Rosemeyer, Louis Chiron, Achille Varzi, and others, became the forerunners of the completely professional ace. Certainly, in grand prix racing, Britain might be accounted a failure. In other types of event, however, the country was more successful. Soon after the Le Mans 24-Hour Race had been introduced, Bentleys established their sports-car over-lordship. And British drivers established 23 new land-speed records between 1922 and 1947.

Until British constructors finally made it in grand prix racing at the end of the 1950s, the race-winning cars invariably bore the names of well known production makes such as Alfa Romeo, Mercedes, Bugatti, and Ferrari. At the start of the 1970s, the only competitive non-British cars in the grand prix circus were the Ferrari and the Matra. All the others were the output of relatively small factories. Lotus has become a big name in the production car industry, but only after the factory made its name with racing cars. Brabham, McLaren, BRM, and March have little or no connection with the normal industry. These companies illustrate the fact that the modern grand prix car is a highly specialized vehicle, useless for any other purpose.

No modern major team manager could support his team off prize money. For this reason, a system of sponsorship has sprung up. Behind every grand prix marque stands a sponsor—sometimes several. Oil and tyre companies are the major sponsors, but a number of less obvious industries—such as the makers of cigarettes, toiletries, and tea—contribute as well.

Drivers are employed by the teams for which they drive. Their contracts come up for review annually. With the cars becoming increasingly powerful, many of them prefer to limit their commitments to Formula One and Formula Two events, and to cut out saloon and sports car racing. It would, indeed, be virtually impossible to find a great all-rounder involved in the sport—such as Stirling Moss.

Even in sports car racing, which began with touring cars and was a comparatively tame imitation of grands prix, the emphasis has turned increasingly to specialization. In an event such as the Le Mans 24-Hour Race, or the 1,000 km at Brands Hatch, you may find a production car—such as a specially tuned MGB—taking part, but it will certainly not be an outright winner. That distinction will probably belong to one of the enormously powerful Porsche or Ferrari prototypes. Porsche insist that these cars serve a valuable purpose as tools of research. But, on the surface at any rate, it is difficult·to see how they relate to ordinary road cars.

Organization

The organization of modern motor sport is not unlike that of the United Nations. The world authority is the Fédèration Internationale de l'Automobile, which has its headquarters in Paris. The FIA is concerned with nearly all aspects of motoring, and is divided into two groups. One, which is composed of four committees, deals with touring matters. The other has two committees and is responsible for sport. The committees in question are the International Sporting Commission (more commonly known as the CSI) and the International Karting Commission.

Members of the FIA are the national automobile clubs such as the RAC in Britain and the Automobile Club von Deutschland in Germany. Each club sends two delegates to its meetings. Just as the FIA lays down the policy and writes the regulations for international events, so do the national clubs perform a similar task for national fixtures. If, after an international race or rally, a competitor wishes to lodge an appeal, he is heard, first of all, by his national club. But if he is dissatisfied with the verdict, he can ultimately have the matter taken up with the FIA. This is very seldom done, for the process is a long one.

The FIA provides a number of motor racing championships which are competed for, internationally, every year. In 1950, at the instigation of the Italian delegate, the World Drivers' Championship was introduced. Eight years later, a constructors championship was inaugurated. Generally, the winner of the latter is the team that builds the former's car. Also in the world of single-seater racing, there is a European Trophy for Formula Two drivers, and a European Cup for Formula Three.

In sports car racing, there is an international championship for constructors, but nothing for the drivers. There is a European championship for touring cars, another one for hill-climbs, plus an international championship for the manufacturers of rally cars, and a European championship for rally drivers.

Scoring in all cases is on a points system. For the World Driver's Championship, 15 grands prix have been selected as qualifying races, and a driver's best nine races count, though these figures are liable to periodic change. For the Manufacturers' World Championship, points are awarded on a similar basis, with all selected races counting, and the manufacturer's best placing in each race taken.

At intervals of five years, the FIA reviews the specifications for cars competing in Formula One. Under the formula in force in 1970, engines must not exceed 3 litres, or $1\frac{1}{2}$ litres in the improbable event of their being supercharged. They can use any type of oil they

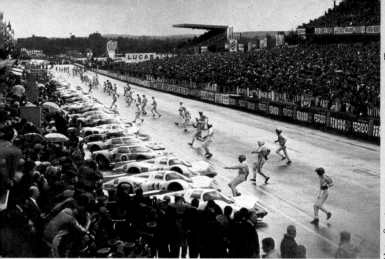

Four scenes from modern sports car life.
3 Why hurry? 24 hours still to go at Le Mans.
The traditional sprint start was dropped in
1970. 4 The German factory of Porsche took the
1970 manufacturers' title. This 917 won the Spa
1,000 km race. 5 Pit preparations for the 1970
Targa Florio, one of the sport's oldest races.
Porsche proved their reliability by winning
this car-devouring romp over bad Sicilian
roads. 6 Another Porsche victory—Jo Siffert is
well clear in the Austrian Grand Prix. 7 Ice
driving, a popular Scandinavian sport, has
developed the skills of many top drivers.
8 Fans crowd the strange machines that will
fight out a 1968 grand prix. The next year a
rash of aerofoils made the cars even odder.

like; but ordinary pump petrol,
the kind that any car burns, must
be used.

A Grand Prix Meeting

There was a time when any town
in Europe that needed to attract
tourists staged a grand prix. The
result was that these events pro-
liferated at such a rate that things
got out of hand. Leading teams
could not possibly take part in all
of them, and the scene was set for
a general cheapening of what
should have been the highest pinnacle of the sport. In 1933, the
international body governing
motor sport stepped in. The rules
for that year contained a paragraph
stating that the title could be
applied only to 'events of first importance and when the words are
accompanied by the name of the
country in which the race takes
place. The race may only be
organized by the appropriate
national club.'

To qualify for inclusion in the
world championship contest, a
grand prix must be approved by the
FIA. The race distance must be at
least 300 kilometres, but not more
than 500, and the event must last
for at least two hours.

The task of organizing a grand
prix begins soon after the previous
one is over. It is usually carried out
jointly by the national club and
the owners of the circuit. All told,
about 1,000 people are involved in
the running of the event, of which
about half are actually concerned
with the conduct of the race.

There have to be several doctors on hand—at one grand prix, there were 33 of them, reinforced by 15 medical students from a hospital's motor club. Also present is the grand prix hospital unit—a massive vehicle equipped in the manner of a small hospital.

During the race, a doctor is stationed on every corner in company with two flag marshals, an observer, and someone responsible for fire fighting. These units keep in touch with race headquarters by means of field telephones. All the marshals are volunteers recruited from car clubs. On the Continent, policemen control the crowds and keep them out of prohibited areas. In Britain, the authority is in the hands of the race officials.

Also employed are something like nine timekeepers, four commentators, and seven scrutineers (who are responsible for ensuring that the cars are in a safe condition and comply with the regulations).

The commander-in-chief of the exercise is the clerk of the course, who has it in his power to stop the race. This happened once in Britain, when a sudden cloudburst made the going exceptionally dangerous, and the timekeepers were unable to see the cars and their numbers to distinguish the leaders. But such occasions are rare. Even after the fearful accident at Le Mans, when over 80 people were killed, the race continued.

The grand prix circus arrives at the circuit about three days before the event, and there are two days set aside for practice. In 1933, the Monaco Grand Prix distinguished itself by becoming the first in which positions at the start were determined by the drivers' times in practice. All grands prix now use this method. The driver who does best in practice earns the 'pole position', which usually puts him on the inside for the first corner—the most advantageous place.

The Grand Prix Driver

Materially, a grand prix driver adds up to one all-enveloping helmet, one set of flame-proof overalls, a pair of light shoes, and a pair of driving gloves. Most drivers wear long woollen underwear and woollen socks as an extra precaution. Although flame-proof overalls do not burn, they will smoulder, and in intense heat char and disintegrate. Wool, which itself does not burn, provides an added layer of protection.

Inside all this there is a strangely anonymous man. All that can be seen of him during the race is his head sticking up above the cockpit. It seems as if he is part of the car, and this is little short of the truth, for during a race most drivers see their cars as extensions of themselves—not only of their limbs, but, also, of their personalities.

Research on the question of what makes a grand prix drive different from other mortals has shown that his intelligence is above average, and compares favourably with that of university graduates. His judgement is good. He has an above-average assessment of his own capabilities, and an amazingly

Glossary of Terms and Racing Slang

Back marker A driver at the back of the field who is likely to be lapped.
Blip up Revving the engine quickly, dabbing at the throttle.
Blow up Engine failure.
Brew up To catch fire.
Chicane A man-made corner at a point where the circuit authorities wish to reduce the speed of the cars.
Come-in signal Normally an arrow, which tells the driver that he should visit the pits on his next lap. Given by the pit crew—as opposed to *black flag*, which is given by the officials.
Dice Close racing between two or more cars.
Drift A cornering technique in which the wheels become unstuck and the car is driven through the bend on the throttle.
Dummy grid An assembly area before the proper grid. The cars move forward from the dummy grid to the proper grid for the start of the race.
Formula Specifications for a class of racing car.
Formule libre A free formula in which anything goes.
Full bore Flat out.
Full chat Flat out.
Go into the country or farming Leave the circuit.
Hairy Wild.
Limit Speed at which loss of control is imminent.

Lose it Lose control of the car.
Monocoque A system of car construction—evolved in the aviation industry—that dispenses with chassis or tubular frame construction. Instead, the car's body strength comes from the combination of the body's components themselves. All grand prix cars now are monocoque designs.
Oversteer When the back of the car tries to overtake the front.
Pole position Best place at the front of the starting grid, awarded to driver with fastest practice times.
Run out of road To use up all the road and leave the circuit.
Shunt An accident involving damage to the car.
Spin (spin off) To lose control of the car and revolve.
Squirt A short, sharp burst of speed.
Starting grid An assembly of cars, in the order of their practice times, immediately before the start of the race.
Ten-tenths Driving on the limit.
The ton 100 mph.
Understeer When the front tyres become unresponsive to the steering owing to loss of adhesion.
Unstick To lose adhesion.
Use up the road To drift from the inside to the outside of a corner.
Wash out To lose control of the front end of the car.

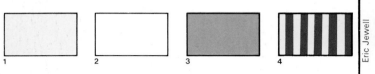

Motor Sport

Eric Jewell

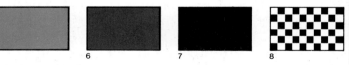

Flag Signals

The race is started usually by the clerk of the course, who gives the signal by dropping the national flag of the host nation quickly downwards. Once a driver is out on the circuit, the only means of communicating with him is by visual signals. Every team has its own code of pit signals that show the driver his position in the race, how many seconds he is behind the man in front, and how many separate him from the man behind. Race control sends its messages to drivers via marshals stationed at various points along the track. They communicate by means of an international code of motor racing signals, using the following flags:

1 Yellow flag *Stationary:* indicates danger and that there must be no overtaking. *Waved:* the danger is greater and drivers must be prepared to stop.
2 White flag A service car (such as an ambulance) is on the circuit.
3 Blue flag *Stationary:* indicates to the driver that another competitor is following close behind him. *Waved:* that another competitor is trying to overtake him.
4 Yellow flag with red stripes *Stationary:* there is oil on the road ahead. *Waved:* there is oil in the immediate vicinity.
5 Green flag The road is now clear.
6 Red flag All cars must stop at once. Use of this flag is exclusive to the clerk of the course.
7 Black flag (this flag always carries a white number). The car bearing the number indicated must stop at its refuelling pit.
8 Black and white chequered flag Signals the end of the race. After nightfall, these cloth flags are often replaced by solid panels with luminescent paint.

Eric Jewell

Geoffrey Goddard

1 The Castrol-BRM of Pedro Rodriguez at Riverside, a round in the rich North American Can-Am series for sports cars. 2 Winner and a former World champion Graham Hill uses his Lotus-Ford's aerofoil and all the road in the 1969 Dutch Grand Prix. Jo Siffert (Lotus-Ford) is in pursuit. 3 Colin Vandervell celebrates a Formula Ford win at Crystal Palace in a Merlyn. 4 This Lotus-Ford would like to fly, but aerofoils keep it firmly on the ground. 5 The racing car is a potential pyre. Jackie Stewart wears flame-resistant clothing in this Formula Two cockpit. 6 Jack Oliver and Jacky Ickx escaped from this smash in the 1970 Spanish Grand Prix, although Ickx suffered minor burns.

accurate awareness of his own performance. He is at his best when under pressure. Under normal conditions, his ability to carry out a set task is neither more nor less than average. But under stress the relative speed and quality of his work improves remarkably. The pressure his profession exerts on him is shown by the fact that, during the minute before a major race, the rate of his heart beat goes up to about 150 per minute. And during the race itself, it increases still further to something between 180 and 210 per minute.

The basic requirements of a grand prix driver are concentration, fast reactions, and dedication. But the extent to which they are present are so far above normal that it is not unreasonable to describe the drivers as 'supermen'.

Grand prix drivers who have won world championship points become known as 'graded drivers' —a distinction that shows they are at the very top of their profession. Graded drivers may not take part in Formula Three races, nor are they able to compete for the European Formula Two championship (though there is no objection to their taking part in Formula Two events).

They belong to an organization founded in 1961 and known as the Grand Prix Drivers Association (GPDA). This, they stress, is not a trade union. It does not negotiate starting money or contracts. Its main concern is safety. Before every grand prix, two of its members walk round the course, noting any features that might be dangerous, or points where, in their opinion, barriers ought to be erected. In 1969, the GPDA was responsible for the cancellation of the Belgian Grand Prix—because, the members believed, its safety had not been brought into line with the needs of increasingly powerful cars. In 1970, again at their instigation, the German Grand Prix was shifted from Nurburgring to Hockenheim for the same reason.

Wives of racing drivers belong to an association known as the Dog House Owners' Club, which is primarily concerned with raising money for charity, and making awards to the dependents of drivers who have been injured in races.

The grand prix driver has good cause to be worried about safety.

His occupation is one of the most hazardous in the world, and it is only by skill and a responsible attitude that he can hope to survive. Sometimes, even this is not enough. World champions Alberto Ascari, Jim Clark, and Jochen Rindt all died in the cockpit of a racing car. Since 1966, top drivers Lorenzo Bandini, Bob Anderson, Mike Spence, Ludovico Scarfiotti, Bruce McLaren, and Piers Courage have been killed while practising, testing, or racing. Not that the story is one of unremitting gloom. At the end of 1970, 44-year-old Jack Brabham joined the ranks of aces such as Nuvolari and Fangio who have retired healthy in both body and bank balance. His most serious injury in 23 years of racing occurred in 1969 . . . a broken ankle.

MANUFACTURERS' WORLD CHAMPIONSHIP			
Year	Car	Year	Car
1958	Vanwall	1971	Tyrrell
1959	Cooper	1972	John Player Special
1960	Cooper		
1961	Ferrari	1973	John Player Special
1962	BRM		
1963	Lotus		
1964	Ferrari		
1965	Lotus		
1966	Brabham		
1967	Brabham		
1968	Lotus		
1969	Matra		
1970	Lotus		

Mountaineering

Man's quest for the ultimate is nowhere better expressed than in climbing mountains. Despite the dangers inherent in the sport, and the fact that most of the 'big' mountains have now been climbed, the urge to climb remains as vital as it was 200 years ago when the pioneers first strove to climb the great peaks.

As the number of virgin peaks dwindles, mountaineers' aspirations change. The ambitious find their métier in harder, more demanding routes. Yet merely being on a mountain has its fascination. The exposure to danger, the elements, or hostile terrain, the confrontation with nature at its most savage, and the sense of achievement after a difficult climb give mountaineering its special attraction.

An integral part of the sport is, of course, danger. At its most adventurous, mountaineering consists of putting oneself into carefully calculated situations of risk. This lure attracts thousands of climbers—and kills hundreds—every year.

Men have always climbed mountains, but the true origins of the modern sport date from the late 18th century, when a series of attempts on Mont Blanc culminated in its ascent by Balmat and Paccard in 1786. By the mid-19th century, many of the easier Alpine peaks had been climbed by scientists, aesthetes, and travellers, but mountaineering had still not emerged as a sport.

The Alps

Sir Alfred Wills' ascent of the Wetterhorn in 1854, with his guides, signalled the beginning of the 'Golden Age' of Alpine climbing. Victorian gentlemen founded the Alpine Club in 1857, and soon a spirit of competition crept in.

Ascents of many difficult Alpine peaks were made, including Edward Whymper's epic on the Matterhorn during which four of the party of seven were killed. As virgin summits grew scarcer, new routes were explored—the unclimbed ridges and faces of the mountains. Climbers began to appreciate the difficulties of steep rock, and as a result the allied sport of rock climbing became popular. The *piton* was developed, though deplored by the British, and accepted by the other Europeans. And by the early 20th century the German and Italian schools dominated the climbing scene. The leisurely Swiss, British, and French contrasted with the competitive and aggressive German, Austrian, and Italian climbers, who, scorning guides, vigorously attacked the great unclimbed rock and ice faces. By the 1930s only the notorious Eigerwand (the Eiger's north wall) had withstood the onslaught. Team after team tried to climb it—though few returned. But in 1938 an Austro-German group emerged triumphant at the top after three gruelling days on the face. It was one of the finest achievements in mountaineering.

After World War II, climbing in the Alps recovered its popularity. Later, solo climbs became more and more fashionable, and the Italian Walter Bonatti's ascent of the smooth rock pillar on the south-west face of the Petit Dru was outstanding. Improvements in equipment made winter climbing a reality. The most outstanding example of winter climbing was the 1966 ascent of the Eigerwand

Keystone

Mount Everest Foundation

by a party of German, British, and American climbers.

The Himalayas

Although expeditions were being mounted in the Himalayas towards the end of the 19th century, it was not until after World War II that climbers began to cope with the Himalayan scale and altitude. Parties were bigger, stronger, better-equipped—and more successful. Annapurna (26,504 ft.) was climbed by a French team in 1950, and Everest (29,028 ft.) by Edmund Hillary and Sherpa Tenzing in 1953. During the following decade most of the great Himalayan peaks were climbed, mainly by large, chauvinistically inspired expeditions. But some outstanding ascents were made by small parties. Broad Peak (26,400 ft.) was climbed by four Austrians in 1957, and small British and French teams independently climbed Mustagh Tower, a relatively small but very difficult peak. Strong, ambitious parties attempted the harder peaks as climbers began to respect technical difficulty rather than sheer height.

1 Gustave Doré's impression of the Matterhorn tragedy of 1865. Four of Whymper's party of seven were killed.
2 Tenzing stands on Everest's summit after his and Hillary's climb in 1953.
3 A typical ice face. Dougal Haston during the first winter ascent of the Aig d'Argentière in the Alps.
4 A Scottish ice climb. One climber leads a steep, difficult ice pitch in the Cairngorms. **5** In Patagonia. Descending fixed ropes during the first ascent of the Fortress, by a British team in 1968.
Below. one of the famous Alpine climbs—the Eiger's North Wall (in shadow).

Sunday Times

Camera Press

MOUNTAINEERING A selection of important climbs

Year	Climb	Accomplished by	Remarks
1786	Mont Blanc	Balmat & Paccard	The first important Alpine climb
1854	Wetterhorn	Sir Alfred Wills & party	The start of the 'Golden Age' of Alpine climbing
1865	Matterhorn	Whymper, Hudson & party	The first ascent of this peak. Four men were killed on the descent
1897	Aconcagua	M. Zurbriggen	At 22,835 ft, the highest peak in the Andes
1907	Trisul	T. Longstaff & party	The first important Himalayan ascent (23,360 ft)
1910	Mt McKinley	Anderson & Taylor	At 20,320 ft, the highest peak in North America
1931	Matterhorn (North face)	T. & F. Schmid	One of the great, hitherto unclimbed, faces
1938	Eiger (North face)	Heckmair, Vörg, Harrer & Kasparek	The most important pre-1939 Alpine route
1950	Annapurna	Herzog & Lachenal	The first 8,000-metre peak climbed (26,504 ft)
1952	Fitzroy	Magnone & Terray	A very difficult climb in the Patagonian Andes. One of the finest climbs ever
1953	Everest	Hillary & Tenzing	29,028ft—The world's highest point, at that time wrongly measured as 29,002ft
1953	Nanga Parbat	H. Buhl	A remarkable solo climb to the summit
1955	Petit Dru (South West pillar)	Bonatti—solo	Perhaps the most outstanding piece of Alpine climbing ever
1959	Cerro Torre	Maestri & Egger	A disputed ascent of Patagonia's most difficult peak. Egger killed on the descent
1961	Eiger (North face)	Kinshofer, Mannhardt, Almberger & Hiebeler	The first winter ascent of this dangerous rock wall
1963	Everest (West ridge)	Unsoeld & Hornbein	
1964	El Capitan (North American wall)	Robbins, Pratt, Frost & Chouinard	Perhaps the hardest rock climb in the world
1968	Mt Communism (South face)	A Russian party	A dangerous wall on a 24,000 ft peak
1970	Annapurna (South face)	Whillans & Haston	
1970	Nanga Parbat (Rupal face)	R. & G. Messner	G. Messner died on the descent

Daily Telegraph Magazine

To climb difficult routes with any confidence, the climber must carry a large assortment of equipment with him . . .
1 300-ft split colour rope.
2 Canvas snow gaiters.
3 North Wall hammer.
4 Ice axe. **5** Piton hammer.
6 Waterproof anorak. **7** Slings fitted with nuts for jamming in cracks. **8** Crash helmet.
9 Webbing slings. **10** Pied d'elephant. **11** Climbing boots.
12 Ten-point crampons.
13 Climbing breeches. **14** Ice screws. **15** Snow goggles with nose protection piece.
16 Karabiners. **17** Various rock pitons. **18** Special wire slings for protection on rock climbs.

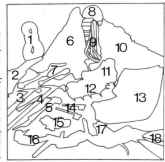

Christopher Smedley/Pindisports

Eric Jewell

Glossary of Terms

Artificial Climbing Climbing with the aid of pitons, bolts, etc.
Belay A form of anchor to secure the climber to the mountain. Each climber anchors himself in this way while the other climbs. The rope is paid out and in event of a fall one of the team is always secure.
Bergschrund A large crevasse separating the upper slopes of a glacier from the steeper rocks or ice above.
Couloir A gully or furrow in a mountain side, whether of rock, ice, or snow.
Crampon A metal frame with spikes which fits onto the soles of boots. For use on hard snow or ice.
Direttisima A route up a mountain which keeps to a direct line with no deviations.
Etriers Rope stirrups that are clipped to pitons for the climber to stand or sit in.
Good Style Climbing a route in the best possible way, eliminating aid, fixed ropes, bivouacs, large support teams, etc.
Grading Systems A system of numerals or words that indicate the difficulty of a climb, thereby enabling a climber to assess in advance whether he is likely to succeed.
Jumar A device that can be fixed to a climbing rope and will move freely up the rope and lock when weight is applied. It allows a fixed rope to be climbed without undue effort.
Karabiner A large metal spring-loaded clip, which can be fixed to the rope or a piton.
North Wall Hammer A short axe incorporating features of the ice-axe and piton hammer, especially designed for use on difficult mixed routes.
Rappel, Abseil, or Rope Down A technique for sliding down a double rope. Steep sections of the descent can be negotiated and the rope retrieved by pulling one end.
Running Belay A method used as the climber progresses; he safeguards his advance by fixing pitons or slings to the mountain. These are joined to the climbing rope with karabiners, allowing it to run freely, but acting as a sort of pulley and cutting down the effective distance of any fall.
Verglas A thin coating of ice over rock.

Gasherbrum 4, Jannu, Nuptse, and new routes on Everest and Nanga Parbat typified this phase of development.

Political difficulties rendered Himalayan climbing impossible in the mid-1960s. In 1968, however, Nepal was opened again to climbers, and since then expeditions have abounded. Two years later, face climbs as hard as those in the Alps were being attempted. And the successes on Annapurna (South Face) and the Rupal flank of Nanga Parbat show that Himalayan climbing is following a pattern similar to that of the Alps in the 19th century.

The Andes
The classic Alpine pattern of development has also been followed in the South American Andes, though here it is more advanced than in the Himalayas. Aconcagua (22,835 ft.), the continent's highest peak, was first conquered in 1897, and Huascaran (22,205 ft.), the highest Peruvian mountain in 1932.

But it is the unique climatic conditions in Patagonia in the south of the continent that attract men to this part of the world. The small, very difficult peaks are subject to appalling weather almost continuously. Fast, dramatic, ascents, such as Magnone and Terray's success on Fitzroy in 1952, are necessary. Patagonia's most difficult peak—Cerro Torre—was still, in 1970, awaiting an undisputed ascent and remained one of mountaineering's 'big prizes'.

Mountaineering Equipment
A modern climber needs a full range of equipment to embark on big climbs with confidence. His clothing must be warm and light, and may consist of a tough pair of breeches, a warm shirt, gloves, sweaters, anorak, *cagoule* (waterproof smock), heavy, well-designed boots, gaiters, crash-helmet and snow goggles. If a bivouac is necessary, he will also carry long woollen underwear, a *duvet* (quilted jacket), a *pied d'elephant* (short sleeping bag), cooking equipment, and a tent sac to cover both himself and any companion in the event of a storm. Food will be light, energy-giving, and tasty. Liquid foods and drinks are more important than solids in most cases.

Specialized climbing equipment will include a rope (usually about 300 ft. long), crampons, an ice-axe and/or a North Wall hammer, a selection of slings, pitons, and ice screws, and a piton hammer. In addition, a head torch will be required because many climbs begin and end in the dark. On pure rock climbs, the ice gear can be dispensed with and replaced by a greater selection of slings and pitons. Variations in clothing and equipment will depend on the climate. On pure ice climbs, however, the alpinist will need a selection of screws, stakes, and deadmen (belay plates). He will also need ice daggers and North Wall hammers according to personal taste.

If fixed ropes are being used on a big mountain the climber will carry large amounts of rope, and an armoury of belaying devices. He will also carry mountain tents or bivouac boxes to establish camps as he progresses.

The Rest of the World
In North America, New Zealand, Japan, Russia, eastern Europe, and elsewhere, independent schools of climbing owing little to Alpine traditions have arisen. Russian mountaineers have made remarkable face climbs in the Pamirs. Discipline and supreme fitness, rather than exceptional skill, account for their achievements. Similarly, Japanese climbers have doggedly attacked the Himalayas and Alps with remarkable results. New Zealanders, home-trained, are very proficient on ice.

The most potent non-European school of climbing is the American. Despite the enormous potential of the Rockies, the Americans were slow to emerge. Alaska's huge, difficult peaks were developed gradually in the 20th century. Several post-World War II ascents by Europeans—notably of McKinley's south face in 1961 and Mount Huntington in 1964—appeared to stimulate the Americans. Hard routes on McKinley, Huntingdon, and Mount Logan's phenomenal Hummingbird Ridge are the cream of such efforts. Farther south, in California, the sheer rock walls of the Yosemite Valley have given rise to new techniques which have had a great influence on climbing.

Mountaineering is not, of course, confined to the highest or most difficult mountains. Exploratory climbing in Antarctica, Greenland, and Africa will probably give way, in time, to recreational or sporting climbing. But the easier climbs rapidly pall, at least for the experts, and instead of simply aiming for new peaks, the experienced mountaineer places more and more emphasis on the challenge of the difficult and arduous routes.

The drama of mountaineering . .
Mick Burke ferries a load up a
fixed rope on the ascent of the
10,000-ft south face of Annapurna I, a 26,504-ft Himalayan
peak.

Netball

An amateur game for women and girls of all ages, netball is played seven-a-side in or out of doors. An extremely fast game that takes place within a small area, it demands from its players unwavering concentration and lightning decisions. Speed and accuracy in passing are essential, for a player may not hold the ball for more than three seconds, may not run with the ball, and must not throw the ball over a complete third of the court without its being touched by a player in that section. Such restrictive rules, however, have made team work the life blood of the sport, for no individual, however brilliant, can do more than her share in the game, and one weak link can neutralize the team's effort.

Netball might well be called the granddaughter of American basketball. Four years after Dr James Naismith originated basketball in 1891 at Springfield College, Massachusetts, a fellow-American, Dr Toles, introduced the game to Britain. It was by then sweeping America, and Americans posted abroad were taking it to Europe and the Far East.

The turning point in Britain came in 1900-01 when the Ling Association, appreciating the game's potential, drew up rules for women and named their game *netball*. The title still distinguishes the game from American basketball, although it was not until 1970 that Australia and New Zealand adopted the term, having previously used the name basketball.

Netball, or basketball, was introduced into New Zealand by the Rev. Jamieson in 1906, and their association was founded in 1924, two years before the All-England Netball Association was established. Australia, where the game was being played in the late 19th century, constituted their association in 1927.

International Netball

More than most games, netball has succeeded in bringing together women and girls from all walks of life, and both domestically and internationally it continues to expand in numbers and standards. This progress has been more pronounced since the inauguration of the world championship in 1960. That year, netball was established internationally when the All-England Association called a conference in Ceylon where delegates from Australia, Ceylon, England, New Zealand, South Africa, and the West Indies formed the International Federation of Women's Basketball and Netball Associations, and made an international code of rules and plans for a four-yearly world championship. The word *basketball* was included in deference to Australia and New Zealand, until both countries agreed to aid the distinction from the American game by changing their associations' titles.

The first world championship was at Eastbourne, England, in August 1963, with 11 countries competing. Each country played all the others, and Australia, with a last-second goal over New Zealand, emerged undefeated. The positions were reversed, however, at Perth, Western Australia, in 1967 when New Zealand captured the title undefeated, including in their run a 6-goal victory over Australia.

Considering the size of New Zealand's netball-playing population, their world championship displays are excellent. The country, which is to be host to the 1975 world championship, had well over 4,000 teams representing at least 29,500 individuals at the beginning of the 1970s compared with 70,000 known players in Australia. And it has been estimated that in England there are nearly one million players.

In South Africa, netball was played widely in girls' schools before World War II, but since then has grown increasingly stronger—an advance reflected in their third place in the Perth world championship.

Another area where the standard of netball is ever-improving is the West Indies, where the game was given a big impetus when Jamaica were allotted the 1971 world championship. Jamaica and Trinidad and Tobago withdrew from the West Indies Netball Board to form independent associations when they gained political independence in 1962, and the West Indies board now covers the remaining islands.

Partly as a result of British colonization or emigration, netball is also played in Ceylon, Singapore, Hong Kong, the Bahamas, Guyana, Papua-New Guinea, Kenya, Zambia, and Uganda, all of which have their own governing bodies.

NETBALL World Championships		
1963—Eastbourne (11 countries)		
1st	Australia	20 points
2nd	New Zealand	18 points
3rd	England	16 points
1967—Perth (8 countries)		
1st	New Zealand	14 points
2nd	Australia	12 points
3rd	South Africa	10 points
1971—Kingston		
1st	Australia	16 points
2nd	New Zealand	14 points
3rd	England	12 points

1

Wilmik

2 1 Players break position after a centre pass in a match between the 1970 New Zealand tourists and an England team at Crystal Palace. The England goalkeeper has her arms outstretched to block the NZ shooter. Such blocking was banned in 1971.
2 An incident from the same tournament in which world champions New Zealand played teams from the England squad. The tourists won both their matches, but the English performances showed the value of a national squad system.
3 An England shot evades a high leap by a Jamaican defender.

A diagram of a netball court with players in their marking positions for a centre pass by the blue team. The positions are as follows: GK=goal keeper, GD=goal defence, WD=wing defence, C=centre, WA=wing attack, GA=goal attack, GS=goal shooter. Players are permitted to enter only certain zones of the court, and should a player move into any area other than that shown below, she is off-side. The playing areas for each player in the blue team are: goal shooter **1 & 2**; goal attack **1, 2 & 3**; wing attack **2 & 3**; centre **2, 3 & 4**; wing defence **3 & 4**; goal defence **3, 4 & 5**; goal keeper **4 & 5**. The converse applies to the red team. Goals can be scored by either the goal shooter or the goal attack, who must be inside the shooting circle.

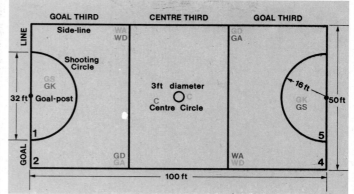

Eric Jewel

Rules and How the Game is Played

The rules of netball have evolved from constant revision. The game is played on a court, preferably hard-surfaced, 100 ft. long by 50 ft. wide, which is divided equally into three zones. There is a 3-foot diameter centre circle in the centre third, and in each goal third a 16-foot radius semicircle around the goals.

At the top of the goalposts, 10 ft. above the ground and projecting 6 inches horizontally, is a metal ring 15 inches in diameter with a net open at both ends. For a goal, the ball (a soccer ball size 5 or a basketball between 27 and 28 inches in circumference), must pass through the ring into the net, shot by either the goal attack or the goal shooter or deflected off a defending player.

Each team consists of seven players: goal keeper, goal defence, wing defence, centre, wing attack, goal attack, and goal shooter. Players are restricted to certain areas of the court, and should a player go out of bounds she is ruled offside and a free pass is given to the opposing team.

Matches are of 15-minute quarters, with 3-minute intervals after the first and third quarters and a 10-minute break at half-time. Teams change ends after each quarter. In certain circumstances, a game may consist of two 20-minute halves.

Play starts and restarts after a goal or an interval with a centre pass taken alternately by opposing centres. The centre pass must be caught or touched by another player in or landing in the centre third, and each player must then pass the ball within a maximum three seconds. Footwork rules are most precise, limiting the player in possession to movement with one foot only while pivoting on the other foot, although the pivotal foot may be lifted as long as the ball is released before it lands again. The ball must not be passed over a complete third without being touched by another player, and must not be deliberately kicked, rolled or punched. Players must avoid bodily contact, and must not obstruct play by being closer than 3 feet to the player with the ball.

The game is controlled by two umpires, each looking after half the court and one whole side-line. There are no clothing restrictions, except on footwear: spiked shoes are prohibited.

First-class netball requires exceptional muscle control in twisting and jumping, and stopping dead to avoid offside, illegal foot movements, or bumping. With scoring the object, speed and accuracy of passing are essential, and for the two concerned with shooting, accurate aim and judgement are additionally vital.

Wilmik

Tony Duffy

Polo

Played by only a small number anywhere in the world, polo has, owing partly to royal interest in the sport, received more publicity than most other minority sports. Consequently there are few who do not have a basic concept of the game, which is played between two mounted teams of four players on a grass ground, 300 yards long by 200 yards wide. Goals are scored by striking the 3 inch diameter white-painted bamboo ball with a mallet-shaped stick between goal posts which are set 24 feet apart.

The word *polo* is derived from the Tibetan *pulu*, meaning a ball, although the game itself probably originated in ancient Persia where it was known as *changar* (a mallet). It developed its present character in India under the British Raj, and was introduced into England by cavalry officers in 1868. The strokes, tactics, and style of play were further developed by John Watson, who came to be known as the 'Father of English polo'. The grounds were then all in the London area—Hurlingham, Ranelagh, and Roehampton—and it soon became a highly fashionable game, an integral feature of the 'season'.

It was first played in the United States in 1883, Meadow Brook being the American polo headquarters, and the first match for the Anglo-American Westchester trophy was contested in 1886. This competition, however, was discontinued after 1939. On the continent, polo was never played on as large a scale as in England and the United States, but in South America, the Argentines, with their wealth, their natural facility for ball games, and their ranch ponies (*criollos*), soon came through as undisputed leaders of the polo world. By 1970, there were about 3,000 players in Argentina, 1,000 in the United States, and 400 in Britain, and the world's leading handicap players —Francisco and Gaston Dorignac, J. C. Harriot, and Horatio Heguy—all came from Argentina.

In 1899, the English imposed a pony height limit of 14.2 hands. But in 1916, when polo had fallen into abeyance in Europe, the Americans abolished this rule, other countries conformed, and the average height went up to 15.0-15.3 hands. In 1909, the American handicapping system was also adopted internationally. It rates players from -2 to 10 goals, but it is no indication of goal-scoring capacity: it is simply a yardstick to indicate a player's status in the polo world and his value to his team. The term *High Goal polo* means that the aggregate handicap of each team entered in a particular championship is 19 or more.

The successful polo player is invariably a natural ball-game player and not necessarily a high-class horseman. It is harder to teach a non-ball-game player to

Ed Lacey

hit a ball from horseback that it **2** is to teach any ball-game player to ride well enough to play polo. Beginners spend many hours at individual training, first practising the strokes from a wooden horse in a polo pit and then with stick and ball on a quiet pony.

Also important is the choice and training of a polo pony. He must be ready to pit his weight against another pony, he must not flinch at the swinging stick or the dazzling ball, and he must possess a good temperament, the best sign of which is a kind, alert eye. As well as these qualities, he requires the conformation that provides speed, stamina, and agility—a well sloped shoulder set on a straight humerus, a deep heart, well rounded loins, a deep stifle, and a long sloping pastern. Useful ponies can scarcely be bought for **3** less than £500, though, and as the minimum price per year of keeping a pony is £300, polo is essentially an expensive sport.

1 Swinging sticks and more-than-occasional jostling are all part of a polo pony's life: but his training ensures that he does not flinch.
2 Making the best use of pony and person to mount an attack. The successful polo player is not necessarily a first-class horseman, but he should be a natural ball-game player.
3 A match in progress at the Hurlingham ground, one of the early centres of English polo.
4 A diagram of the field. The area between lines A and B is the safety zone, but it is not always indicated.

How the Game is Played

Because polo is played at a more or less continuous gallop, it is necessary to change and rest ponies, and therefore the game is divided into periods, or 'chukkas,' of 7½ minutes duration. The big tournament matches are now divided into six chukkas and the smaller contests into four. There are four players in a team, these being numbered 1 and 2 (forwards), 3, and back. Three is usually the strongest player and pivot of the team. The back's duty is mainly defence and marking the opposing No. 1. The opposing 2 and 3 also mark each other, but the positions are not rigid, and the essence of good polo is flexibility in changing positions as the game dictates.

At the start of the game, the two teams line up in the middle of the ground, each team being on its own side of the halfway line, numbers 1, 2, 3, and back facing their respective opponents. The umpire then bowls the ball underhand between the opposing ranks. A goal is scored when the ball passes between the posts and over and clear of the goal line. Teams change ends after each goal. There is no 'off-side' rule, and 'riding off' an opponents is all part of the game, but owing to the hazards inherent in a fast-galloping stick-and-ball duel, penalties are stringently enforced for bumping, zigzagging, and 'crossing' (riding across another player's right of way). These normally take the form of free hits, 60, 40 or 30 yards from the goal-line of the side fouling.

When the ball goes over the side lines, a fresh ball is thrown in by one of the two umpires, who keep a number of spare balls in their saddle holsters. When the ball is hit over the goal-line by the attacking team it is hit in, by the defending back or 3, from the point where it crossed the line. If it is hit behind by a defender the attacking side is awarded a free hit from 60 yards out from a point opposite where the ball went over the line. A bell is sounded at the start and finish of each chukka, but play is continued until the ball is hit behind or over the side lines or, in the opinion of the umpires, lies in a neutral position. If the game ends in a draw, additonal chukkas are played until one more goal is scored.

Power Boat Racing

Although extremely expensive in some classes, power boat racing has achieved enormous popularity on both sides of the Atlantic. The sport falls into two natural divisions, depending on whether the racing is carried out on an inland lake or on the sea. The former is known variously as circuit racing, runabout racing, or sportsboat racing, and the latter as offshore racing (Eastern Hemisphere) or ocean racing (Western Hemisphere).

Power boat racing has had a rather chequered history and for a number of years its growth was spasmodic. Both world wars completely disrupted its progress, and it was not until the 1960s that it settled down into its two distinct divisions. Now, all aspects of power boat racing are universally governed by the Belgium-domiciled Union Internationale Motonautique.

Early records refer to a motorboat race across the English Channel that took place in the early 1900s and was won at around 16 knots. But it was not until after World War I that power boat racing emerged from the realms of 'gimmickry' and became a sport that an ever-increasing band of enthusiasts began to take seriously. Early development during the 1920s was confined to inland waters, with special emphasis being laid on hydroplanes (boats whose hull shape is specifically designed to give them some aerodynamic lift, and thus increase their speed). These 'circuit' races were of limited length and duration, and it was not until 1930 that the first long distance power boat race,

over 100 miles, took place in Britain. This same event—the course was laid in Poole harbour —also gave an early hint of the future possibilities that lay in racing at sea. Modern day 'offshore' racing drivers would consider Poole harbour a pretty tame racing venue, but in certain conditions of wind and tide it provided some exciting racing.

No less than 32 boats came to the starting line for this sensational event, which was won by Viscount Kingsborough in a clinker-built motor dinghy powered by a 32 hp Johnson engine at an average speed of just under 20 knots. This 100-mile endurance race at Poole continued for a further four years, but after 1934 it lapsed through lack of support, and attention reverted to the inland circuits until all power boat racing came to a standstill at the outbreak of World War II.

After the war, power boat racing, like many other sports, took some time to find its feet again, and it was not until the mid-1950s that it began to take on a recognizable, organized form— again on the inland lakes. Then, in 1959, something happened that was to revolutionize the sport. An ocean power boat race from Florida to the Bahamas was organized, and this concept of long-distance racing at sea captured the imagination of Sir Max Aitken, who became determined that a similar kind of marathon event should take place in Great Britain. Subsequently, in 1961, his newspaper, the *Daily Express*, sponsored the first of a series of annual races from Cowes to Torquay. This event was for large, fast cruisers and was subdivided into two classes by length of boat —Class I (28-45 ft.) and Class II (20-28 ft.) Since 1968, it has involved the round trip from

1

Gerry Cranham

Cowes to Torquay and back to Cowes non-stop, and is now accepted as the greatest offshore power boat race in the world, regularly attracting an entry of over 50 boats. Speeds in offshore races vary with sea conditions, but, in general, they have increased considerably since the first race. Tommy Sopwith, who won the first Cowes-Torquay race at 22 knots, repeated his performance in 1968 at 33 knots (for the double trip) and in 1970 won at just over 50 knots. In calm conditions in 1969, the American Don Aranow clocked an average of a fraction under 60 knots.

Races of a similar calibre to the *Daily Express* event are now run all around the European seaboard and in the United States, and are spreading to South Africa, South America, and Australia. A world championship series is held each year under the auspices of the UIM, but regrettably, if somewhat inevitably, it is open only to the very rich. A suitable boat costs around £20,000, and maintenance and transport costs account for at least a similar amount each year.

The thrills of offshore power boat racing are still available to those of more modest means, however. In 1962, a few owners of small open runabouts, hitherto restricted to the inland circuits, decided that anything the sea-going cruisers could do, they could do better. A small but intrepid band set off from Putney in the early dawn to race down the Thames estuary, across the Channel to Calais and back again, all in one day—a distance of 220 nautical miles. Thereafter the 'Putney to Calais', like the 'Cowes to Torquay', became an annual event and led to the formation of a third offshore class, Class III (for boats of 14 ft. upwards in length). This is still a British 'national' class and does not have international recognition, but there have been similar developments in other countries.

It quickly transpired that Class III would be a development class, and as both boats and engines became more sophisticated, so the cost of competing began to escalate. To keep the offshore side of the sport within the means of as many boat owners as possible, the Royal Yachting Association (British national authority for power boat racing since 1964) introduced a new national class—Class IV, which is for standard production boats of a minimum length of 12 ft. Anyone who owns a standard runabout or ski boat sensibly fitted out for use at sea can start Class IV racing for an additional outlay of about £20.

The 'circuit' side of the sport continued to grow steadily throughout the 1960s, but although these inland races have spectator appeal, which the offshore races lack, it is the offshore side of the sport that seems to hold most attraction for competitors. This may be due to what has been described as the 'double jeopardy' aspect of offshore racing. The driver not only has to face all the other competitors; he has the additional thrill of pitting himself and his craft against the unpredictable 'cruel sea' as well.

1 Hydroplaning on a Middlesex lake—one side of power-boat racing, a sport that won many converts throughout the world in the 1960s. 2 Power-boats burst down the Thames towards the open sea and Calais at the start of the 1970 Putney-Calais-Putney race that attracts smaller craft that serve as test-beds for 3 the large, fast, and expensive cruisers that fight out such long-distance classics as the Cowes-Torquay-Cowes event.

Colour Sport

Daily Telegraph Magazine

Rally Driving

According to most dictionaries, a rally is a sort of coming-together. Therefore a motor rally should be a gathering of cars. This may be true of what happens before the start of a rally, or at the finish, but while a rally is in progress, 'going-apart' might be a better way of describing what happens, for in no other sport are the contestants scattered so widely over the countryside as in rallying.

To the outsider, a rally driver must be a strange creature. What sane person would voluntarily deprive himself of basic comforts for days and nights on end, cram himself, his partner and a few essentials into the cockpit of a motor car, and spend the whole time driving over some of the wildest roads imaginable in some of the most atrocious conditions? Is the sport really some quaint manifestation of mechanized masochism? Rally enthusiasts say not; to them it is one of the most virile, demanding activities of modern times, immensely satisfying to its participants and highly rewarding as a technical test-bed to the industry that provides them with their motor cars.

Car manufacturers can advertise, but rally enthusiasts find it more difficult to describe the excitement and exhilaration they experience standing, say, beside an undulating gravel track in the wilds of Wales watching the world's leading rally drivers push their cars along at 110 mph where normal men would venture at no more than 15; to watch them slew their cars sideways so that they slow for a corner without having to use the brakes and at the same set the cars up facing the right direction to accelerate away.

The Beginnings

Almost as soon as the motor car first appeared, sporting gentlemen realized its potential as a provider of competitive pleasure, and the most obvious of these—the race—was with us. There were races from point to point and then around a defined circuit, but it was not long before a group of motoring sportsmen became somewhat blasé about a contest of speed from A to B. They wanted something more; something that was tougher, physically strenuous, mentally exerting, and appealed to their sense of fun.

The first rallies were no more than social runs, with the accent on getting there at all rather than in any particular fashion. Obstacles were introduced, driving tests had to be undertaken, mountains crossed, ice and snow negotiated, and fog penetrated. Natural hazards were more or less gathered together as much as possible, and it became the rule that rallies were run at times when local conditions were at their most severe. It is no coincidence that

the Monte Carlo Rally takes place in January, the RAC Rally in November, and the East African Safari at a time when the rainy season is just about under way.

Modern rallying is largely a post-war development. European rallies of the 1920s and 1930s were leisurely jaunts vastly different from today's hard-fought events.

Today

A motor rally is not a race, and its followers are not motorized hooligans using public highways as race tracks. All too often the sport is decried by public opinion as a result of confusion between one form of sport and another. Basically, a rally is a competition between pairs of people, each pair using a motor car to get from one place to another in a given time and using a given route. The cars do not race against each other, for they set off separately, usually at intervals of one minute. When they are on public roads, competitors have to observe normal road traffic law. Indeed, there is a rule which forbids the setting of any average speed in excess of 30 mph, except on motorways when the average is allowed to be up to 50. And, there are additional rules that go beyond the limits of the statute book to ensure that everyday road users are not inconvenienced by the passage of a rally. These rules have been formulated in Britain by the Royal Automobile Club (RAC), governing body for all motor sports in Britain and to which all leading motor clubs are affiliated. In other countries there are similar governing bodies and similar rules, the whole under the direction of the Paris-based Federation Internationale de l'Automobile.

Rallying is largely a European phenomenon, although European competitors make frequent forays on the fast, tough rallies of Australia. A form of rallying exists in America, but European enthusiasts regard it as little more than a mathematical puzzle that places little pressure on men or machines. Competitors on the largely European circuit aim for an international manufacturers' and a European drivers' championship. (The manufacturers' title changed its name from European to International when the East African Safari Rally was added to the list of qualifying events in 1969). The manufacturers' championship is the most important. Its list of qualifying events is, strangely, quite different from that of the drivers' championship, which is regarded by many as a vague, over-regulated series.

Navigation

It is all very well to drive a motor car at speed and in safety; its crew must also ensure that it is being driven in the right direction. That is why competitors always

1 The tranquility of a Kenyan village is rudely interrupted as a Citroen DS 19 takes a trial run over a stage of the East African Safari Rally.
2 A combination of heat, dust, mud, and torrential downpours that turns streams into rivers makes the African event the hardest to stay in, let alone win. 3 & 4 Marathon rallies came into being in the late 1960s, with both amateurs and professionals leaving London on the first two 'big ones':
3 a 1970 World Cup rally Porsche in Italy with a long way to go to Mexico City, and
4 London-Sydney winner Cowan in Australia's outback.

work in pairs—one man to drive, the other to navigate. On smaller events each sticks to his job, but on longer ones they must change roles, sometimes leaving both jobs to one man while the other sleeps. In these cases they become 'co-drivers' rather than 'driver' and 'navigator'.

The main navigational instrument in Britain is the inch-to-a-mile Ordnance Survey map. These charts are so detailed that as the competitors drive along the navigator can read the map to the driver, warning him of bends, hills, bridges, fords, and all manner of other hazards as they come up. The combination of a one-inch map and a skilled navigator behind it has often been referred to as 'rallyman's radar', and this description is not far from the truth. In any condition, it is of great help to know the degree of severity of the next bend to come up; when foggy it becomes vital.

Route cards for British events take the form of series of numbers called map references. These are really map co-ordinates based on Britain's national grid. When competitors arrive at the start of a rally, they sign on, collect their route cards, and retire to the seclusion of their own motor cars (or hotel rooms if they are sufficiently affluent and there is a hotel handy) to plot the route on their maps. A simple enough task, usually involving anything up to a hundred pairs of co-ordinates with as many minutes in which to do the work. Another type of rally allows no time at all before the start for plotting; the navigator has to do this on the move.

Other forms of navigation are also used on some of the smaller rallies, such as following a series of spot heights on the map, using compass bearings, or even latitude and longitude co-ordinates. These are regarded as the province of those who enjoy short, relatively slow rallies for amusement only, although any experienced co-driver will be *au fait* with all the tricks which any rally organizer may serve up.

When professional drivers go rallying, they are well paid for their skills by the manufacturers

who employ them, and know they must give of their best in return. When they know in advance where the special stages will be they spend days, sometimes weeks, practising those stages. It is impossible to commit to memory every single twist and corner of anything up to 50 special stages each between 5 and 25 miles long. So the pace notes become substitutes for the navigator's map in club rallies—a more sophisticated kind of 'rallyman's radar'. Each bend, gradient, surface, straight, crest, camber, and the various other important features along the whole length of a stage is committed to paper in a

2

3

Keystone

Colin Taylor Productions

sort of shorthand easy to understand and quick to read. 'Maximum speed', for example, becomes 'flat'. The code is full of such monosyllables, and it has been so perfected by British rally crews that many foreign drivers and co-drivers now use the English language for their notes—they find it easier and quicker to speak.

Navigators often use the 'Tulip' system in preference to unreliable maps. Invented by the organizers of the Netherlands' Tulip Rally, it consists of diagrams of important road junctions joined by very accurate measurements of the distance between them. Even

in rallies of a different type many teams prefer to build up in practice their own version of this simple code.

During the heat of a rally, the co-driver sits with his eyes moving rapidly between the road and the notes, on which he keeps his place with a finger. He then reads the notes to the driver, adjusting his speed of delivery to the speed at which the car is being driven over the road. Thus the driver, knowing exactly what is around each bend, can drive at virtually undiminished speed even in thick fog—knowing, of course, that the road is closed to all other traffic. To eliminate the need to shout above

engine and road noise, driver and co-driver usually have 'intercom' sets built into their crash helmets.

Organizing a Route

Racing is banned from the public roads of Britain; rallying is not. But to safeguard the public (and the competitors) there is a statutory instrument called the Motor Vehicles (Competitions and Trials) Regulations that sets out comprehensive requirements which must be followed by anyone who wants to organize a rally using public roads. These came into force in the mid-1960s—and have made rally organization most complex. They weeded out

the casual organizer, who paid little heed to the safety of other road users and the privacy of country dwellers. Every rally must be properly approved by the central organizing body well in advance of its date. Most organizers go even further by arranging that their asssitants call on every householder along the proposed route to warn them of the passage of the rally and to discuss any peculiar local problems, such as the passage of cattle along a particular road at milking time, the presence of an invalid who should not be disturbed, or a ford which is particulary prone to flooding during

3

1 2

Central Press

Few sports can offer such diverse conditions and events as modern motor rallying. Conditions range from **1** The French *pave* of the Monte Carlo Rally to **2** dusty, dangerous roads 10,000 feet up on the Peruvian 'route of the Incas'. **3** Not all hazards are natural ones—this control point loomed up too fast for a Ford Escort TC at the end of a special stage in the Welsh mountains during the 1970 RAC Rally of Great Britain. **4** A competitor in Portugal's TAP Rally adds some more rubber to a special section designed to test driving skills. **5** Such tests are unnecessary in the famous Scandinavian snow rallies. Northern drivers who complete their apprenticeship on these treacherous roads supply most of the sport's professional drivers.

5

Fotosports International

Colin Taylor Productions

heavy rain. All are taken into account by rally organizers keen to provide their competitors with the best and toughest possible competition without causing inconvenience to those who live along the chosen route.

Obviously, the best roads for rallying are in country areas where the population is at its lowest. Thus in Britain certain parts of the country, including Mid-Wales, the West Country, the Lake District, the Yorkshire Moors, and parts of Scotland are more suitable than anywhere else. Perhaps Wales comes out on top of the list, for there the terrain is at its best, and equally important, the populace is generally keen on the sport and offers every encouragement to its participants.

As the motor car became faster, safer, stronger, and more sophisticated, and rally crews more experienced and skilful, it became more and more difficult to provide a competitive rally on public roads without breaking the law. In some parts of Britain it is still possible to run a tough rally without falling foul of the authorities, but for the larger national, and certainly the international events, organizers took their routes onto private land where the normal rules do not apply.

Nearly all the world's international rallies were doing this at the start of the 1970s. One notable exception is the East African Safari, which takes in only public roads and has no special stages. It does not need them—average speeds as high as 100 mph can be set when road conditions allow it. Usually, however, the route on public roads is no more than a gentle run to take competitors from one 'special stage' to another.

Special Stages
These special stages are the sections on private land. They can be anything from 1 to 20 miles long and can vary from smooth tarmac to loose gravel, slippery mud, hard rock, or even sandy dirt. They all have one thing in common; they provide the most testing form of driving competition imaginable. In Britain, each special stage has a target time, and every competitor is penalized for each second he takes in excess of that target. It is very rare that a target is reached, for the schedules are such that flat-out driving, at speeds often well in excess of 100 mph, are demanded on the most atrocious of surfaces, with trees, fences, and other natural hazards whistling past the windows in a blur. Small wonder that rallying not only improves driving skill but also provides car manufacturers with such a wealth of information about the capabilities of their cars.

In Britain, most special stages are run on the roads of the State Forests. The Forestry Commission is reasonably tolerant towards

the rally fraternity, and their local officials help organizers when they go out selecting their routes. The rally organizer makes a payment to cover the cost of repair to any roads which are damaged by the passing of cars at high speed. Apart from the Isle of Man and Ulster, where it is permitted to run special stages on public roads closed to all other traffic, rally routes are kept more or less secret until the day of the event. This prevents competitors practising or making notes about the difficult bends, the jumps, and the danger spots.

In many other countries, private roads are not as abundant. However, many public roads on the Continent are just as testing and it is on these that special stages are held. As in Ulster and the Isle of Man, organizers must tell the public long in advance which roads will be closed. This has led to a striking feature of modern-day rallying—practising (or 'recceing', as most rally people call it) and the making of 'pace notes'.

How Manufacturers Benefit
Today's sophisticated suspension layouts owe much to lessons learned in rallying, and tyre-tread design and the ingredients of the rubber compounds have their origins in experiments carried out in conjunction with rally drivers and teams competing all over the world. Instrumentation, body strength, rear-axle design, engine mountings, windscreen glass—all have benefited from the vast proving ground provided by the sport of rallying. It is more than a sport; it is almost an integral part of the motor industry, for many car and component manufacturers go beyond using it for testing and use their success stories as a basis for publicity and advertising. The manufacturer of the car that wins

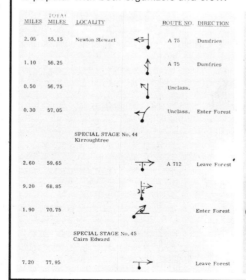

A section of a crew's route card for the 1967 Monte Carlo Rally, recording five control-point checks.

the East African Safari certainly has reason to boast, and who can blame him for doing so?

Climbing the Rally Ladder
Rallying is a hard, satisfying, exciting sport. It is not a breeding ground for 'road-hogs', for its followers tend to look after their own and anyone with anti-social tendencies is quickly found out and made to mend his ways. Its skills are not easily acquired. One rally does not make a top driver, and those who aspire to the higher levels must start at the bottom— in Britain, for example, by competing regularly in the many small rallies run every weekend. Higher up the scale there is a series of some 15 of the country's top restricted rallies grouped together into a championship by *Motoring News*. And higher still there are

some half-dozen international events based on special stages. Only then can one aim at the pinnacles of the sport—the RAC Rally, the Acropolis, the Rally of the Thousand Lakes, even the East African Safari.

It would seem to have been a help to have learned to drive on Scandinavian roads. Drivers from Finland and Sweden tended at times to dominate the sport in the 1960s, and drivers such as Salstrom and Waldegard from Sweden and Finland's Lampinen, Makinen, Aaltonen, and Mikkola seem set to carry on the tradition in the 1970s. Not that they will have everything their own way—they will have to overcome challenges from southern drivers of the calibre of Roger Clark (England), Jean-Luc Therier (France), and Sandro Munari (Italy).

The 'Tulip' version of part of a rally route. This simple code, showing the major route deviations and the distance between them, is popular with both organizers and crew.

Given a chance, crews build up 'pace notes' in practice to cope with the pitfalls of the special stages. The navigator translates them over the car's intercom to the driver.

MILES	TOTAL MILES	LOCALITY		ROUTE NO.	DIRECTION
2.05	55.15	Newton Stewart		A 75	Dumfries
1.10	56.25			A 75	Dumfries
0.50	56.75			Unclass.	
0.30	57.05			Unclass.	Enter Forest
		SPECIAL STAGE No. 44 Kirroughtree			
2.60	59.65			A 712	Leave Forest
9.20	68.85				
1.90	70.75				Enter Forest
		SPECIAL STAGE No. 45 Cairn Edward			
7.20	77.95				Leave Forest

209

Rowing

'Rowing', Lord Mancroft once said, 'is a sport the French rightly reserved for their convicts and the Romans for their slaves'. Be that as it may, the popularity of this most demanding of all sports has steadily increased in modern times, and 50 national associations were affiliated to the international governing body, the Federation Internationale des Societes d'Aviron (FISA), by 1970.

References to rowing as a sport, as distinct from an enforced occupation, go back thousands of years—there is a description of a boat race by Virgil in the *Aeneid*—but in its modern form the sport first developed in England in the late 18th and early 19th centuries.

From medieval days the River Thames had been a flourishing highway for state barges and professional watermen, and races among these were frequent. In 1715 Thomas Doggett, an Irish comedian, instituted a sculling race for apprentice watermen, and the annual race for 'Doggett's Coat and Badge' is now the oldest existing rowing or sculling race in the world.

In 1775 the first regatta was held on the Thames and amateur enthusiasts began to take up the sport. Within 20 years Eton College boys had begun to row and there were several amateur clubs in existence, although the oldest surviving club, Leander, was founded about 1818. The Westminster School 'Water Ledger' dates from 1813 and the earliest record of college racing is at Oxford in 1815, Cambridge following suit some ten years later.

The first Oxford and Cambridge Boat Race at Henley in 1829 attracted enormous public interest and this race probably did more to establish rowing than any other single event in its history. As a direct result of the interest aroused by the Boat Race, Henley Regatta was instituted in 1839 and received a royal charter from Prince Albert in 1851.

By then, other countries had begun to take up the sport. In the United States, ferrymen from New York City raced and defeated crews from Long Island and Staten Island, in 1811 and 1813, and in 1824 they defeated a crew of Thames watermen from a British frigate, the *Hussar*. The first amateur clubs in the United States were in New York, but the oldest rowing club still in existence is the Detroit Boat Club, which dates from 1839. The Harvard-Yale Boat Race was inaugurated in 1852, 20 years before the first amateur regatta was held.

In Australia, rowing started in Tasmania about 1830, the Royal Hobart Regatta dating from 1838. In 1832 there was an amateur sculling race in Sydney, and records indicate that the sport must have been fairly well established by then. The oldest Australian club still active is the Melbourne University Boat Club, founded in 1859. In 1863 Melbourne and Sydney Universities raced each other in fours, and there were also some inter-state contests during the next few years. The first official inter-state eight-oared championship, however, was not held until 1878.

On the continent of Europe, rowing spread quickly during the mid-19th century, initially as a result of British influence. In 1842 an Englishman at St Petersburg introduced the amateur sport to Russia and the first important rowing club there was the English Arrow Boat Club, founded by English oarsmen in St Petersburg in 1864.

Germany, the Netherlands, Belgium, Italy, France, and Switzerland all took to the sport readily, and in 1892 the international federation was formed, with the first European Championships being held in 1893. Rowing was included unofficially in the 1900 and 1904 Olympics and was officially introduced for the 1908 Games.

Boats and Oars

Rowing events are held for eights, fours, and pairs; sculling events for single, double, and quadruple scullers. In the first half of the 19th century six-oared craft were common, and there were also ten- and twelve-oared craft, but these gradually went out of fashion.

Fours and pairs can be with or without a coxwain but, because of their length, eights always carry a cox. In sculling, only quadruple scullers carry one, but these can often be coxless. In a coxless boat, one of the oarsmen steers with a pivoting shoe to which the rudder-lines are attached.

Rowing in coxless boats developed in England and the North American continent earlier than on the continent of Europe. At Henley, a coxless pairs event was put on the programme as early as 1845, but it was not until W. B. Woodgate persuaded the cox of his college four to jump overboard at the start at Henley in 1868, winning the race but being disqualified for his pains, that coxless fours events were introduced to Henley. And it was not until the 1920s that coxless pairs and fours were included in the European championships.

At the beginning of the 19th century, rowing boats were used as much for pleasure boating as for racing and they were widely and solidly built. Gradually, however, modifications and technical improvements led to long, slender

Cambridge train on the Thames tideway for the 1968 Boat Race—a sporting event which, with 20 million televiewers, has become almost a part of the British way of life.

hulls of very light construction. Modern eights are between 55 and 60 feet long but are only 24 inches at their widest beam, while cold-moulding and other modern methods of construction mean that the weight can be kept down to below 240 lb—about a sixth of the total weight of a heavy crew.

Fours and pairs are correspondingly shorter, slimmer, and lighter, while sculling boats are very finely built, sometimes being known as 'toothpicks'. 'Small boats' are very difficult to balance and the smaller the boat, the greater the skill needed to get the best from them.

The first innovation in the evolution of the modern racing boat came in 1841, with the replacement of the old clinker hull construction of overlapping planks by smooth skins, which reduced weight and friction. Then, three years later, a major development came with the introduction of outriggers by Clasper, the Newcastle boat-builder. This in turn led to a drastic reduction in the beam and weight without losing the leverage of the oars.

Keelless boats were built in 1856 and an American, J. C. Babcock, introduced sliding seats the following year. This enabled the oarsman to reach a stronger position at each end of the stroke and had a profound influence on rowing technique. Slides reached English rowing some years later, in 1871.

Oars are long but surprisingly light, being hollowed out inside the shaft (or loom), which is reinforced down the back. A modern 12½-foot oar, which is a popular length for international class rowing, can be as little as 8 lb in weight. In rowing an oarsman holds one oar with two hands; a sculler holds a smaller oar, or scull, in each hand, and thus a scull is correspondingly shorter and lighter, with a smaller blade area. In the 1960s blades generally became shorter and wider as a result of the successes of the West German crews, who introduced this type of blade, known colloquially as a 'spade' blade, in the late 1950s.

There are no restrictions to the dimensions of boats and oars, though at novice level certain types of restricted boats are used for some events. These, being wider and flatter, are easier for beginners to handle.

Technique
Rowing flourishes wherever there are suitable stretches of water, but technique varies to some extent according to the types of boat used and the water on which they are employed. There is a Coast Rowing Association in Britain, for instance, and coastal clubs use short, broad boats that require a different technique from the one needed to move faster, slimmer boats on quiet inland rivers and lakes.

Ed Lacey

Glossary of Terms

Best boat A light racing boat with a smooth skin.

Blade The part of the oar that obtains resistance in the water.

Bow The front end of a boat; or the oarsman rowing nearest the bow.

Bowside The side of the boat in which the bow oarsman's oar is placed, usually starboard; or the oarsmen whose oars are on that side.

Bumping race Traditional form of racing, usually lasting four days, at Oxford and Cambridge and occasionally elsewhere, in which the crews start in line ahead and attempt to bump the crew in front and so start in a higher position on the following day.

Button A collar round the shaft of an oar to prevent it from slipping out of the rowlock.

Canvas The bow and stern sections of racing boats are covered with thin linen. A verdict of 'a canvas' at a regatta indicates that this is the winning margin.

Carvel boat A method of constructing a best boat with a smooth skin.

Catch a crab To turn the blade of the oar while it is still in the water.

Clinker boat A heavy boat with a hull of overlapping planks, primarily for novices.

Coxswain or cox The steersman of a boat that is not steered by one of the oarsmen.

Double A boat for two scullers, as distinct from oarsmen.

Fin A small metal protrusion under the hull of a best boat to help steering and balance.

Head of the River The crew finishing first in a bumping race or a timed head of the river race.

Novice An oarsman who has never won an open race.

Paddle To row at less than full pressure.

Pinch the boat To take the beginning at such an acute angle to the boat that the pressure is inwards rather than forwards; an inefficient action.

Puddle The swirl of water left by a blade after a stroke.

Rate of striking The number of strokes rowed per minute.

Recovery The part of the stroke after the finish when the oarsman reverses his movements and starts forward for the next stroke.

Rigger The usual term for an outrigger, which is a metal stay or stays protruding from the side of a boat and which supports the rowlock.

Rowlock Support for the oar, acting as a fulcrum.

Rudder A wooden or metal flap, attached either to the stern or to the fin, by which the boat is steered.

Run The way in which a boat travels during and between the strokes.

Shell A racing boat of carvel construction.

Skiff A term usually applied to a type of heavy, clinker-built sculling boat used in a special type of sculling called skiff racing.

Sky To raise the blade too high off the water before the beginning.

Slice To put the blade too deeply into the water.

Slide The seat on which an oarsman or sculler rows, or the runners on which it travels.

Stakeboat A moored boat from which the stern of a boat is held prior to the start of a race.

Stern The rear part of a boat.

Stroke The complete cycle of the rowing action; or the oarsman rowing in the seat nearest to the stern of the boat, who sets the rate of striking and the rhythm for the crew.

Strokeside The side of the boat on which stroke's oar is placed, usually port, except in coastal crews; or those oarsmen who row on that side.

Swivel A moving rowlock that swings freely from a vertical pin, and the usual type in racing boats.

Tank An indoor pool with a fixed boat and shaved-down blades for winter training and for coaching purposes.

Tub A wide, heavy boat for teaching novices.

Turns The acts of squaring and feathering the blade.

Wash out To tear the blade out of the water before the finish.

2 Nevertheless, the basic problems remain the same for all oarsmen and the differences are of emphasis rather than principle. An oarsman has to get hold of a solid 'chunk' of water on the end of his blade and, by means of this resistance, apply maximum possible pressure with the oar against the rowing pin—the vertical pin holding the rowlock on the outrigger. Between the strokes he must do as little as possible to interfere with the run of the boat.

The coach's problem is to find the optimum length of stroke and the optimum number of strokes per minute, as well as the correct size of blade, length of oar, and leverage to produce maximum pace in his crew. These factors, affected by the size, experience, and skill of the oarsmen and the length of course to be rowed, will vary from crew to crew.

1 This print purports to show Cambridge's first ever racing eight. Whatever its identity, it shows how far construction techniques—and dress—have progressed since the early days of organized rowing.
2 One of a family of Thames watermen, Edwin Phelps, after winning Doggett's Coat and Badge in 1938. This event has been in existence since 1715.
3 A sculling event for women. Women's rowing, though not part of the Olympic Games, is included in the European and world championship meetings.
4 The cox and the stroke—the two most important men in a racing eight. The cox's traditional megaphone has been superseded by more sophisticated equipment.
5 Switzerland's double sculls pair of Martin Studach (bow) and Melchior Burgin win the 1967 Silver Goblets at Henley.
6 Coxed fours, with coxes in the bows, at Henley regatta.

5 In a racing boat, an oarsman sits on a sliding seat that enables him to use his weight and leg-drive to maximum advantage. The power of the stroke comes from the legs, so a hard leg-drive, coupled with a firm draw from the arms, is essential.

Control of the slide is also vital, especially when coming forward for a stroke. If a crew hurry forward, they are likely to hit the stops on the runners and check the run of the boat, and this alone can add up to half a length or more over a full course—perhaps the difference between victory and defeat. At the beginning of the stroke, when the blade enters the water, it is important to avoid driving with the legs before the blade goes fully in because this also checks the boat and dissipates the leg-drive, leading to a loss of power.

Between the strokes the blade is turned flat, or 'feathered', to reduce wind resistance and to

avoid hitting waves, and then 'squared' again just before the next stroke is begun. These movements must be smoothly and neatly carried out to avoid inaccurate bladework. If an oarsman feathers his blade while it is still in the water it will get caught and the oarsman will be knocked over by the momentum of the boat as the oar handle hits his chest. 'Catching a crab', as it is known, is the most dangerous fault in rowing and almost invariably leads to a race being lost.

For a beginner the first problem is to balance his boat and oar, and many coaches believe that this is best learnt in a single sculler, where nobody is interfering with the control of the boat. Much of this is instinctive, and when he has learnt to balance a sculling boat, the novice is more likely to be able to adjust to other oarsmen in a crew without upsetting his own rowing. Taught in this way, a novice can learn very quickly, and the technique, being an almost identical sequence of movements constantly repeated, is not really difficult to acquire. An outstanding success story in this respect was that of the 1956 University of British Columbia coxless four that won the Olympic gold medal at Melbourne: no member of the crew had rowed for longer than nine months.

Technique is just one of the problems in boat racing. Another is fitness. Rowing is one of the most exhausting of sports, bringing virtually every muscle in the body into play during each stroke. The only consolation the oarsman has is that he is sitting down. Nevertheless, in a top-class crew each man is pulling approximately 100 lb every stroke at a rate of something like 30 or 40 to a minute for 6 to 8 minutes, so strength and

exceptional powers of endurance are needed. A long distance event such as the Boat Race, which lasts for 20 minutes, and in which the rate of striking and work-load are less, is less exhausting than a race over the international championship distance of 2,000 metres—though a losing Boat Race crew might tend to disagree.

The ideal oarsman is tall, with good lung capacity and low pulse rate. Height and weight are very important: top-class international crews often average well over 14½ stone. Because of this, many countries have lightweight events and championships in order that lighter men may compete successfully in the sport.

Rules of Boat Racing
Rules for international championships and regattas are laid down by the International Federation,

and though in some countries the national associations race under their own laws, these differ only marginally from the international ones. In Britain the rules of the Amateur Rowing Association were brought into line with FISA in 1971, but both the Boat Race and Henley Royal Regatta are held under their own regulations.

There are two main types of open events: head of the river races and regattas. The former are processional races decided on times, the fastest crew winning the event. Introduced in England in 1926 and now found all over the world, they are generally held in the autumn or late winter. In the spring and summer, regattas are held every weekend at various centres throughout the world. Rowing and sculling events for different classes of boat and status of oarsmen are put on, and over a hundred races may take place in one day.

for juniors, but there is a minimum weight—40 kilograms for junior coxes and 50 for seniors. A certain amount of dead-weight may be carried to bring coxes up to the necessary minimum.

The rules of boat racing are comparatively simple. No crew may receive extraneous assistance from the bank or other boats, either verbally or materially. A crew must stay on their own 'station' and can be disqualified for 'washing' or interfering with another crew in any way if they leave their own lane. 'Washing' means either making the opposing crew row in the wake left by the leading boat or in the 'puddles' caused by the blades. A crew can also be disqualified for a foul out of their station if any part of the boat or oars touches the opponents' boat or oars. A crew·may appeal for a foul but not for interference: that is entirely at the discretion of the umpire, who usually follows the race in a motorboat and has sole jurisdiction over the race from start to finish.

If the course is too narrow to allow for launches, umpires may be stationed at intervals along the side of the course, each being responsible for his section of the race. At some continental regattas the umpire drives along the side of ·the course in a car. Only umpires registered by the national or international associations may officiate at regattas.

International Rowing

Throughout the 1800s the highest standard of rowing was to be found in England, but by the turn of the century foreign crews, particularly from Belgium, were beginning to challenge that supremacy. In 1897 Belgian crews won all four events then con-

Swinging in unison: one of the most exhilarating sights in sport is a race for eights. In the 1960s, the Ratzeburg club from West Germany were a new force in the world.
1 Ratzeburg (third from top) won this 1962 world championship final at Lucerne.
2 Ratzeburg beat Vesper of the United States in the 1965 Grand Challenge Cup final.
3 Head of the river races attract enormous entries.
4 Another view of Henley.
5 Oxford lead Cambridge in their 111th race, in 1965.

For international championships, the 'repechage' system is employed, whereby the losing crews in the first round race again for a second chance to qualify, this ensuring that the best crews reach the finals.

Regatta courses vary in length according to the water available, but international championship distances are standard: 2,000 metres for men, 1,500 for boys and 1,000 for women. The longest race in Europe is the 31-mile Boston Marathon in Lincolnshire.

The status of oarsmen and scullers is determined first by age and then by wins. Under FISA rules, an oarsman may compete as a junior up to end of the year in which he becomes 18, after which he is a senior. A senior who has won six races in his grade becomes an 'elite' oarsman, the top category. Sculling and rowing status are separate and wins in one do not affect status in the other. There are also subdivisions for women, veterans, and lightweight oarsmen.

Coxes do not have a status, except that of the age restriction

Geoffrey Page

Central Press

4 tested in the European championships, and they won the eights title 12 times between 1897 and 1910.

British crews, however, did not compete in the championships at that time, so that it was a considerable blow to British pride in 1906 when a Belgian eight, rowing in an unorthodox style, became the first foreign crew to carry off the premier Henley eight-oared event, the Grand Challenge Cup, and followed this up with wins in 1907 and 1909. Prestige was slightly recovered when a veteran Leander eight defeated the Belgians in the 1908 Olympic final.

But British confidence was shaken and an indication of the international rise of another country, the United States, came when the Harvard second eight won the Grand in 1914. By 1920, American college rowing, revolutionized by the coaching of a remarkable ex-baseball coach, Hiram Conibear, dominated eight-oared events, winning every Olympic eights title from 1920 to 1956. On the Continent, Swiss, German, and Italian crews all triumphed for periods between the two world wars, although British crews competed only in Olympic rowing and continued to do well in sculling and coxless events on these occasions.

By 1936 Germany had become a force to be reckoned with, but after World War II neither of the German federations competed until 1953. By then, Russian crews, with a strange stop-go rhythm, were beginning to dominate the international scene. It did not last long: by the end of the 1950s West German crews, using even more revolutionary methods introduced by the most successful coach of recent times, Karl Adam, not only began to carry off the major European titles, but also ended the American monopoly of the Olympic eights.

5 West German methods soon influenced world rowing, and crews from as far afield as Australia and New Zealand, who began to shine at the Olympic Games during the 1960s, could be said to owe their successes to having absorbed the lessons taught by Adam.

After 1966, East Germany began to compete separately and soon became established as a major rowing force in the world. Within four years they were setting the international pace.

The most difficult event to win in international championships is the eights, and now only composite crews, made up of the best men drawn from a wide area, have much chance of a medal. In the small boat events, however, it is possible for talented individuals from quite small clubs to win top honours. This is particularly true in coxless pairs and in such individual events as the single and double sculls.

PAGE 216

Syd Hynes in pursuit of the Northern Rugby League Championship for his club, Leeds.

Rugby League Football

Ray Green

Rugby league players have to be tough. These three fowards are preparing to take a ball in the face from a penalty kick.

Rugby League is a major sport in four countries of the world—England, France, Australia, and New Zealand—far fewer than follow the game it sprung from, rugby union. And only in Australia does it consistently draw larger crowds than its parent. In England, France, and New Zealand rugby union has so far contained the break-away code's influence. But in all four countries rugby league draws fervid, undivided allegiance from its supporters, who view it as a tougher, more spectacular, and more intellectually satisfying sport than rugby union. To them its combination of planned pattern and improvisation strikes the happy medium between the free play of union and the formalized moves of American football.

Like rugby union, league could be called a 'war game', for its basic aim is to break the 'enemy' line or to halt his advance. Forwards correspond to infantry, the backs to the cavalry of a 19th-century military exercise. But unlike union it is basically a professional sport, and like all professional sports its ultimate concern is for the spectator. All of the code's rule changes have been made with him in mind. It is no accident that top rugby league players are sometimes referred to as 'gladiators'.

Development of Rugby League

Rugby league was born on August 29, 1895, in a hotel in the north of England. The representatives of 21 northern rugby union clubs who gathered at the George Hotel, Huddersfield, were totally unaware that they were founding what would become a major professional sport. They thought merely that they were creating an organization within which the best traditions of northern rugby union could flourish, unhampered by petty financial restrictions.

The issue behind the meeting was 'broken time', the name given to expenses paid by clubs to working men who forfeited a Saturday shift to play rugby. It was rarely more than a few shillings, but it was enough for the Rugby Union's annual meeting in London in 1893 to crush an amendment allowing 'compensation' by 282 votes to 136. The northern clubs, however, insisted on paying 'broken time', and when relations with the parent Rugby Union became strained beyond repair, they formed the Northern Union at the George Hotel. The first Northern Union fixtures followed on September 7 that year.

At first the new organization made no attempt to tamper with the laws and spirit of the traditional game. Teams of 15 took the field, but men who were missing a shift at work received expenses up to 6s a day. In 1897 an attempt was made to improve the game as a spectacle—the value of a goal of any kind was reduced to two points. Other changes followed, until in 1906 rugby league emerged in more-or-less its modern form by reducing the number of players in a side from 15 to 13.

The breakaway clubs soon found themselves excommunicated by the English Rugby Union. Clubs loyal to the union were forbidden to play against Northern Union clubs. But the ban had little effect—two competitions, the Lancashire and Yorkshire Senior, were launched, and this additional competitive element began to attract the crowds and lay the foundation for rugby league as a spectator sport. (Runcorn, a

J. A. Saville

Syndication International

1 Huddersfield's 'Team of all the Talents' which won everything available in 1914-15.
2 Wigan's New Zealand captain Ces Mountford (centre) passes.
3 Leeds fullback Lewis Jones (kicking) found league fame following a successful union career. 4 The solitude of the rugby league supporter.

the game, and the 6s a day restriction had gone. The 1898-99 season was the first to accept full professionalism.

The money the new game offered began to attract players from areas well outside the northern counties of Lancashire, Yorkshire, and Cumberland. The fruitful rugby ground of South Wales began to feed the northern clubs with players recruited by Northern Union emissaries. Rugby

Cheshire club, won the first Lancashire competition, and Bradford-based Manningham the Yorkshire competition. Both clubs are now defunct.) New clubs rushed to secede from the Rugby Union and join the ranks of the northern rebels. In 1896, 59 clubs applied for membership, and it became necessary to form auxiliary or 'second' competitions in Lancashire and Yorkshire. In 1897 came another innovation that was to prove an outstanding success. A Northern Union Challenge Cup competition was launched, and when the first final was played on April 24 at Headingley, Leeds, between Batley and St Helens, 13,492 fans paid £620 to see Batley win 10-3. The Northern Union had really arrived, and from this point on grew and prospered, slowly but perceptibly moving away from its position as a rebellious offshoot of rugby union into a major game in its own right.

The number of clubs in membership slowly increased—80 in 1897, 98 the following year. Attendances soared, and the 1898 Challenge Cup final between Batley and Bradford attracted 27,941 spectators to Headingley. Professionalism was now an accepted part of union clubs resented the visits of these 'poachers', who came in for occasional rough treatment, but their persistence and the lure of cash usually succeeded. It was the beginning of a tradition, for throughout the 20th century South Wales has provided some great league players, and many fine ones. Attempts to spread the new code to Wales, though, have persistently failed. In 1907-08 Ebbw Vale and Merthyr Tydfil were admitted to the Northern Union, and at various times since Welsh clubs have tried to make rugby league a viable proposition. None succeeded. Crowds were good at first, but eventually dwindled. The long distances involved in travelling to and from the north proved tiring and expensive, and the Welsh clubs suffered beating after beating. A similar fate has befallen attempts to branch out elsewhere in Britain. The mid-1930s saw short-lived professional teams appear in London, and Glasgow and Newcastle have also fielded teams.

The new code's growth has been halted in England, but overseas it was a different matter. Seeds planted by the Northern Union among members of the touring New Zealand rugby union team of 1905 bore fruit when they returned to New Zealand. In the face of intense opposition, a team—ironically labelled the 'All Golds' because they accepted payments—were formed and toured England under the auspices of the Northern Union in 1907. At the same time in Australia a 'broken time' and professionalism dispute broke out, and a successful tour by the New Zealand team en route to England for the first rugby league 'tests' led directly to the formation of New South Wales and Queensland rugby football leagues. (The Northern Union changed its name to Rugby Football League in 1922.) At first, competition was limited to Sydney clubs, but the new sport spread rapidly. The first New South Wales-Queensland match was held in the first season, 1908, and the same year an Australian team toured Britain.

Rugby league soon developed into the major winter sport in both Australian states. Tours of Australia by English teams became major events, heralded by enormous publicity, intense rivalries on and off the field, huge crowds, and tough and spectacular games. By the start of the 1970s the two countries were still finely balanced by skill and prestige. Great Britain—the title supplanted 'England' in 1950—won the 1972 World Cup series in France, but Australia squared matters by winning the 1973 test series in England, two to one.

Rugby league in New Zealand failed to develop on the same scale as in Australia, largely because of the entrenched interest in rugby union and the great All Black sides. It remained an amateur

game with less drawing power than major union matches. By 1974 New Zealand had never won the World Cup or a series against Great Britain in England. But the lively and enthusiastic Kiwis have often shaken Britain, Australia, and France in test matches in their home islands, and in 1965 New Zealand won the special award—the Courtney Trophy—for the best record in international matches over a five-year period.

France entered the rugby league lists in 1933-34, after a group of French rugby union officials had put out 'feelers' to rugby league officials in London. In December 1933 Australia played England in Paris in the first rugby league match to be held in France—and attracted a crowd of almost 20,000. Enough top French players defected to the new code to form a party to tour England the next year. They lost five of their six matches, but won applause for playing sustained open football even when beaten—a quality that France has retained in both league and union codes. A representative match played in Paris at the end of the tour attracted 20,000 spectators to see an England team win 32-21. This game persuaded enthusiasts to set up a French rugby league management committee, and in August 1934 it came into being with 12 founder clubs.

Since its formation, the French Rugby League—La Federation Francaise de Jeu a Treize—has known many vicissitudes. There have been times when clubs have been in dire financial straits, and representative teams have performed badly at international level. French teams are dangerous to underestimate, however, for they have often confounded forecasters with unexpected test wins. Their record against Australia is good—by 1971, of four tours of Australia since 1951, they had won two, drawn one, and lost one. Their 1951 side was acclaimed by many experts as the best rugby league combination ever seen.

Efforts to spread the game in other parts of the world have failed. In the late 1950s and early 1960s attempts were made to introduce the code to South Africa and Italy, and Australian and New Zealand teams played exhibition games in the United States in 1954. The infant leagues in South Africa and Italy opened on a wave of enthusiasm, but fierce opposition from rugby union authorities soon choked the life from the teams.

The international development of rugby league produced cross-fertilization of players and ideas. Although a ban has occasionally been imposed on international transfers, some of England's greatest club players have come from Australia. And even the ill-fated South African venture brought several fine union players to try their luck in Britain.

Australian News & Information Bureau

Above, **A notable feature of rugby league is the play-the-ball rule. When tackled, the ball-carrier invariably plays the ball back to any team-mate standing behind him.** *Left,* **The field of play.**

[Field diagram with labels: Dead Ball Line, In-Goal Area, Goal Line, 6-12yd, 8ft 6in, 10ft, 10 yd, 10 yd, 25yd Line, 10 yd, 110 yd max, Halfway Line, 10 yd, 25yd Line, Goal Line, In-Goal Area, Dead Ball Line, 6-12yd, Touch Line, 75 yd max]

Eric Jewell

Basic Rules

In rugby league, as in rugby union, two teams, controlled by a referee, attempt to score points by running the ball over their opponents line or kicking it over their goal-posts. The side without the ball defends its territory by tackling the ball-carrier. In contrast to American football, obstruction of attackers or defenders by any player other than the tackler of the man with the ball is not allowed. The ball is moved towards the line either in passing rushes (in which the ball can be passed only backwards) or by kicking. A *try*—the grounding of the ball over the opponents' line—is worth 3 points and gives the scoring side the right to attempt a *conversion*—a kick between the goal-posts from a point in line with where the try was scored—for a further 2 points. A *penalty try* can be awarded between the posts by the referee if an infringement by the defending side prevents a certain (in the referee's opinion) try. Penalty tries, too, can be converted. A *penalty goal*—a kick at goal awarded for an infringement—earns 2 points. A *dropped goal*—kicked on the bounce from open play—2 points in club matches, 1

point in internationals. (All national rugby league administrators are expected to adopt the system of 1 point for a dropped goal in 1974).

A team consists of 13 players, 2 fewer than in rugby union. Two substitutes are allowed, and, as in soccer, they may be employed for tactical reasons. (In England during the 1970-71 season, the rule was amended to allow a team to withdraw a substitute and re-enter the player he had replaced.)

If a ball-carrier goes into *touch*—over the sideline—play resumes with a *scrum*. If he is effectively tackled on the field of play he invariably *plays the ball* to the *acting half-back*—any team-mate standing behind him—by rolling the ball with his foot back between his legs, though he is, in fact, not obliged to play the ball backwards.

Each team is allowed to retain the ball only for the duration of six tackles. After that a scrum forms and the tackle count begins again on the team that wins the ball.

If a player *knocks-on*—fumbles the ball forward onto the ground —a scrum is formed. But if the opposing side gain possession from the knock-on play continues under the *advantage* rule.

A player can gain ground in broken play by kicking for the sideline. But the ball must bounce on the field of play before it goes out, otherwise a scrum is ordered at the point the kick was taken.

However, if from a penalty kick a team elects to gain ground rather than kick for goal, the ball can be kicked out on the full. They can then take a *tap-kick* from the point where the ball went out. (After a player nominally taps the ball with his foot he is free to run or pass it.)

Above, **As he is tackled, the player looks for, and finds, support. Constant backing-up keeps the attack flowing.**

Right, **Split-second decisions become second nature to the scrum-half. He must know when to run the ball or pass it.**

Ray Green

Rugby League Play and Tactics

The pattern of rugby league play is markedly different from that of rugby union. League places greater emphasis on attacking moves by ball-carriers, less on tactical kicking. If a ball is kicked out on the full from broken play it gains no ground—an effective deterrent to indiscriminate kicking.

A fundamental reason for league's emphasis on attack is its play-the-ball rule. A tackled rugby union player must release the ball; a league player retains it and plays it to a player behind him. The defending player marking the man playing the ball can strike for it when it touches the ground; but he rarely wins it. Ground won is ground retained, and an attacking team can launch a series of attacks. Until the mid-1960s a team could retain the ball for an unlimited number of tackles. Then a rule was introduced to prevent a team dominating the match by retaining possession for long periods. It specified that a scrum form after four tackles had been made on the team in possession. But this four-tackle rule did not satisfy all critics. Some preferred

the old rule allowing unlimited possession; others wanted a longer period to build up attacking movements. Consequently, in 1972 the limit of possession was increased to six tackles. Most league men agree that this has produced closer, faster, and more open matches.

Significantly, the French call rugby league *jeu a treize*—game for 13. The elimination of rugby union's two loose forwards early in the code's history was, together with the play-the-ball rule, the most significant of all league's improvisations. At one stroke the scope for attack widened immensely. The loose forwards in union play mainly a defensive role, breaking from the scrum to attack the opposition's backs if they win the ball. Naturally the inside backs try to beat the defence by swinging the ball out along the backline. It can be spectacular, but opportunities for turning the ball back inside (towards the scrum) are limited. Rugby league backs, harassed by only one instead of three loose forwards, have more freedom to experiment with reverse passes that switch the point of attack.

The attacking role of the backs

in rugby league is also enhanced by the substitution of the scrum for the line-out of rugby union. The scrum, by removing most of the forwards briefly from the play, gives the side that wins the ball a chance to attempt back-line thrusts before the forwards can reinforce the defence. Most of league's open play comes from scrums, and teams have a wide variety of moves that they use for offensive or defensive situations.

The difference between the two codes is most marked in forward play. Many rugby union players have switched to league this century; their failure rate has been much higher among forwards than backs. Union forwards are essentially scrummaging machines whose main aim is to swoop upon the ball in loose play. Rugby league forwards, however, need to be able to participate in complex forward attacks against organized defences, as well as tackling well and wearing down the defence with hard running. Modern league forwards are often as fast and handle as well as most backs.

Rugby union backs have found league much easier to master than forwards. The essential skills required are much the same for both codes. Basic requirements

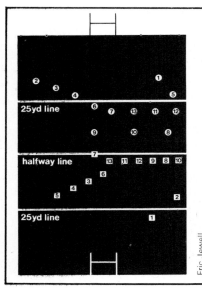

Eric Jewell

An example of field placing. The defending side (pink) should position themselves to field a kick to any part, and the full-back here appears to have left an alarming gap in front of his goalposts. The positions, Australian names in brackets, are: 1 Fullback, 2 Right wing-threequarter, 3 Right centre-threequarter, 4 Left centre-three-quarter, 5 Left wing-threequarter, 6 Stand-off half (five-eighth), 7 Scrum-half, 8 & 10 Front-row forward, 9 Hooker, 11 & 12 Second-row forward, 13 Loose forward (lock).

Right, **Especially in England, teams tend to favour the high 'smother' tackle to prevent the ball-carrier from passing, so committing him to play the ball back. In Australia, the low tackle is preferred.**

Fotosports International

then brings his left leg through. For the *swerve*, often used on slippery surfaces where side-stepping is impossible, the attacker runs on the inside of one foot and the outside of the other, leaning forward and swinging his hips away from the would-be tackler. The most common combination used by backs is the *scissors* movement, usually executed by the outside centre and winger. The winger runs towards the sideline, if possible drawing both the opposing centre and winger towards him. At the same time the winger starts a run in the opposite direction behind him. As their runs intersect the centre transfers the ball to the winger with a short backhand 'flick' pass. It calls for perfect timing, but can split a defence by suddenly changing the point of attack.

Most league back-lines in the late 1960s had at least one player adept at the dropped goal. Teams soon discovered that under the new four-tackle rule their best chance of scoring on the fourth tackle usually was by drop-kicking for goal. But when teams began to win matches with dropped goals rather than tries, pressure mounted to reduce the value of a dropped goal. In 1970 the International Board reduced it to one point in internationals, and all national authorities were expected to follow suit in 1974.

The International Scene
At the end of 1970 the fifth rugby league World Cup competition was held in England. Australia won it—a result that accurately reflected the strength of the game on a national level, even though a fine Great Britain combination started favourites.

Gates in England, although still healthy enough overall in 1970, had slumped in the 1960s. Attractive games in major rugby league centres such as Wigan and St Helens drew between 15,000 and 20,000 spectators, but unimportant matches sometimes attracted fewer than 1,000. French and New Zealand clubs also weathered some hard times. In Australia, though, rugby league boomed. Rising crowds forced Sydney clubs to increase the capacity of their grounds and the New South Wales Rugby League to take exploratory steps towards building their own sporting arena to replace the Sydney Cricket Ground—venue for most internationals and 'match-of-the-day' club games. The Sydney Cricket Ground can hold big crowds, but suffers from the disadvantages of being controlled by an independent authority.

The Sydney club competition dominates the Australian rugby league scene. Talent scouts from the 12 Sydney clubs are quick to snap up promising products from country, Queensland, or rugby union clubs. Sydney clubs provide most of the players for Australian test teams. In fact many of them are built around five or six players from an outstanding Sydney club —in 1970, South Sydney. Despite big gates, the Sydney clubs rely on legalized gambling—in the form of 'poker' machines—for the bulk of their revenue. It enables them

A perfectly executed scissors by Great Britain has the New Zealand Kiwis at sixes and sevens. Such ploys are often the only way of piercing a tight defence and call for perfect timing and handling.

are the ability to accelerate quickly, swerve, change pace, and side-step. The *side-step* allows an attacker threatened by a tackler to change direction without losing speed. A player side-stepping to the right forces his left foot down hard, moving his weight to the right. At the same time he throws his right leg to the right,

Ray Green

Radio Times Hulton Picture Library

Australian News & Information Bureau

Australia and France meet at Sydney in 1960. In two states of Australia, Queensland and New South Wales, league is the major winter game, and Australia, World Cup winners in 1957, 1968, and 1970, rivals Britain as the top nation.

to pay big signing-on fees for top players, whose total income can top $A200 (about £100) a week.

Rugby league players are not full-time professionals, and the money they receive from the sport only supplements their normal income. English and Australian clubs follow the same system of paying their players on results, employing a sliding scale of payments for wins, draws, and defeats. A leading English club such as Leeds, Wigan, or St Helens will pay a player a match sum varying from £40 to £50 for a good league win, and over £150 for a victory in the final stages of the Challenge Cup or Championship. Less wealthy clubs such as Batley, Huyton, or Doncaster may have to settle for sums ranging between £10 and £16 for a win, directors scraping together perhaps £30 to £40 a man if the team makes a good cup run. In the case of a defeat a top club might pay between £8 and £16 a man; a lesser club player would have to be satisfied with as little as £6 or £8. For these purposes, a home draw is usually counted as a defeat, an away draw as a victory. Most clubs survive only with the help of supporters' club 'pools', or the income from social clubs' amusement machines. Time and again distress signals are hoisted by club treasurers, and one club, Hunslet, was reformed as New Hunslet for the 1973-74 season.

English rugby league has been called a parochial game, since it is played only in Lancashire, Yorkshire, and Cumberland. The live televising of Saturday afternoon games in the 1960s changed this by introducing the game to a national audience, but it also split the rugby league world into two camps. Those who supported the move claimed that television has widened rugby league's popularity in England, but its opponents contend that it lowers attendances—not only at the game being televised, but also, if the television match is an attractive one, at other fixtures. In the 1969-70 season the BBC reached an agreement with rugby league authorities that guaranteed each of the 30 clubs in the Northern Rugby League about £4,000 a season for three seasons in return for television rights. This money, a lifesaver for many of the poorer clubs, stifled some opposition.

Despite falling attendances—a problem it shares with soccer— English rugby league remains the second most popular spectator sport in the north of England, and the Wembley cup final, highpoint of the season, attracts near six figure crowds.

Until 1948 the English Rugby Football League was the ultimate authority in rugby league. Its successor, the International Board, is composed of delegates from each rugby league-playing country —England, France, Australia, and New Zealand. Its meetings, which usually coincide with international tours and competitions, are concerned mainly with arranging international series and with the introduction of new rules.

In the 1950s and early 1960s, efforts were made to establish rugby league in South Africa, and in 1963 a South African side (green) undertook a tour of Australasia, winning 4 and losing 9 of their 13 games.

Australian News & Information Bureau

The job of the rugby league forward is not an easy one: he must win the ball and wear down the opposing defence.

Ray Green

Rugby League Positions

The collective task of a rugby league team's six forwards is to overpower and out-think the opposing pack and win a major share of the ball from them in scrums and loose play. The task of the seven backs is simple—to combine to score points preferably through tries. But each position has its specific responsibilities.

Front-Row Forwards These two take the brunt of the opposing pack's attack with hard head-on tackling, and in attack wear down the opposition with hard running. The front-row prop forward, who packs down on the side the ball enters the scrum, has the greater responsibility to combine with the hooker to win the ball.

Hooker The most brilliant back-line is useless without the ball, and the hooker is the man who must win it for them in the scrums. This function is so important that some teams will carry a player of indifferent ability in general play as long as he dominates the scrums.

Second-Row Forwards The two second-rowers should include at least one fast, hard runner who specializes in splitting the defence. Both must have strong defence and be adept at backing up in forward assaults. 'Running' second-rowers often play 'wide' in open play forming an extra man among the backs.

Loose Forward (*lock* in Australia) The ideal loose forward is a hybrid—half forward half back. Good defence and speed are essential, for if the opposition win the ball from a scrum he must be able to break from the scrum and 'cover' any player who breaches his back-line's defence. He is often called upon to make the extra man in back-line attacks and to replace a team-mate who has been sent-off or injured.

Scrum-Half This vital link between backs and forwards is usually the smallest man on the field. Essential requirements for his position are agility, footwork, acceleration, and judgement. The half-back must be able to make split-second decisions on whether to run the ball or pass it to the backs outside him. A good half-back runs judiciously against a strong defence, often waiting until the closing stages of a match before bursting from the scrum-base with the ball.

Stand-Off Half (*Five-eighth* in Australia and New Zealand) The stand-off half is the pivot of the back-line attack, linking the half-back with the point-scoring centres and wingers. He 'calls' and inaugurates most attacks. A good stand-off half's footwork and passing creates extra space for his centres to move in.

Centre-Threequarters The two centres should have good acceleration, speed, and all the tricks—change of pace, sidestep, swerve and dummy—necessary to beat a defender. And once in the clear they have to decide quickly whether to continue their run or off-load the ball to another centre or winger. Their defence must be good, for if an attacker breaches their defence he is in the open and threatening to score. Often a team will play a hard-running centre who can draw the defence inside a faster more elusive 'finisher'. England calls its centres 'right' and 'left'; Australia 'inside' (closer to the stand-off half) and 'outside'.

Wing-Threequarters The two wingers, who play on the right and left extremities of the field, should be the fastest men on the team. Their main function is to use their speed to finish off try-scoring movements.

Fullback This last line of defence stands alone behind the back-line. He needs to be a skilful handler of the ball for he covers most attacking kicks made by the opposition. He must be able to kick well under pressure, although modern full-backs tend to run the ball more from defensive situations. Coolness and a good positional sense are essential. He adds thrust to back-line attacks by joining in among the threequarters. The fullback must be capable of saving tries with last-ditch tackles.

A defensive slip, such as a missed tackle, can be fatal: the advantage it gives can soon be converted into points.

Ray Green

English rugby scenes: *Top* **Middlesex winger Hodgson tries to evade Durham's Walker in a County Championship semi-final.** *Above* **Oxford's Carrol gets his pass away in the 1970 Varsity match;** while *Below* **Redruth do battle with St. Luke's College.**

Central Press

Ed Lacey

Wilmik

Rugby Union Football

Rugby union football is not the only international sport that is strictly amateur. Field hockey and lawn bowling are other examples. But no other amateur sport has anything like the magnitude or is such 'big business' as this form of football. Not only do none of the thousands of players throughout the world receive any financial gain, but even the officials, apart from the few full-time employees such as the secretary of a Rugby Union, are unpaid workers performing their onerous and complicated rugby jobs outside their own business hours. In what other sport can one find a £300,000 operation such as a British Lions tour of New Zealand being master-minded by an official at his home phone in a London suburb?

For unpaid committees to be dealing with such huge money-spinners as international rugby tours might be regarded as unprofessional in the worst sense of the word. But the accent on amateur is the very life blood of rugby union. As Robin Prescott, a secretary of the Rugby Football Union, once put it: 'I'm the only pro in the business.' No true rugby man would want it any other way.

From what did it stem, this hyper-amateurism that even forbids a rugby player to accept any sort of gift—unless he is getting married? Basically it is contained in the very background of the game.

William Webb Ellis, a pupil at Rugby School, is supposed to have started it all in 1823 on the football field by picking up the ball and running towards his opponents' goal with it. It is a certainty that numerous other boys responded to this urge in the days when football was predominantly concerned with kicking the ball, but for some reason young Ellis has been singled out as the originator of 'the handling code'. From being a game at which any

Africamera

1 To the newcomer it may not always seem obvious that the purpose in rugby is to gain possession and score goals.
2 George Barnard's painting of Rugby School in 1852 *'The School from the Close'* **has a group playing rugby football.**
3 The 1871 England team that played Scotland at Edinburgh in the first rugby international, won by the Scots.

Rugby School

number could play it was whittled down to 20-a-side and finally to the present 15.

From Rugby School the game spread to other public schools and, inevitably, on to Oxford and Cambridge. From the outset it was primarily a sport for those of this type of background. Association football was taking formal shape at the same time, and when it 'went commercial' a number of soccer players saw the game as a means of augmenting the meagre pay of a mill worker, say, or miner. But many 'rugger types', especially in the South, did not need the money, and those in the North who did broke off to form the professional version of the game, rugby league. This left the hard core of those who, as players and administrators, wanted to keep rugby purely amateur: not even a hint of professionalism was going to taint their game.

When the game went from Britain to the colonies, it was the same public school and varsity people who carried the message— 'A game for ruffians played by gentlemen'. In New Zealand, Australia, and South Africa it became the game of the common people, yet for some odd reason they still wanted to keep it un-sullied by any hint of professionalism. Perhaps even more odd is this: Why was it that New Zealanders and South Africans of the old rough, tough colonial days took to their hearts a game identified more than any other with the 'old school tie'? That is one of the imponderables of what the grand old men of Twickenham are wont to call 'This Greatest of All Games'.

Development of Rugby Union

Whether the Romans playing a game known as *harpastum*, the drapers of Chester celebrating Shrove Tuesday, or Cornish villagers in the early 17th century were the first to play something vaguely resembling rugby football are matters of uncertain historical value—besides being in dispute. What is certain is that for more than 40 years after William Webb Ellis had run with the ball at Rugby School, the need for some form of organization among the clubs and players was not thought necessary—not even when the Football Association was formed in 1863.

It was in that year that Blackheath, who have the unique distinction of having been represented

Radio Times Hulton Picture Library

at the first meetings of the Football Association and, in 1871, of the Rugby Football Union, left the Football Association because that body prohibited the unsavoury tactic of hacking opponent's shins. Rugby football was beginning to steer a firmly separate course.

The inaugural meeting of the Rugby Football Union was at the Pall Mall Restaurant, near Trafalgar Square, on January 26, 1871, when 21 clubs and schools were represented. And in little more than 10 years within the date of foundation, most of what are still regarded as the game's principal fixtures had been arranged: in 1871 England v Scotland; in 1872 Oxford v Cambridge; in 1875 England v Ireland and the Hospitals' Cup; in 1877 Scotland v Ireland. By 1882 Wales was playing each of the other Home Countries.

These were the years of urban sprawl and new-found mobility, and rugby football, originally the privileged, if manly, exercise of the former public schoolboy and pursued by an elite few in South-East England and Edinburgh, spread rapidly. Soccer, too, was making swift advances, though not everywhere. In the North of England, for example, rugby football could, and did, rival it in universal appeal; so, too, in Wales and in England's West Country. In Scotland and London, however, the game remained the recreation of the former public schoolboy.

The game's appeal in the North and its rapid development did not please everyone. Early on there were murmurings, even outright requests, about payment for broken time—recompense for lost earnings. In 1879, it became permissible to pay expenses to internationals for travelling and accommodation, and later small amounts could be paid by clubs to their players for matches away from home. But at all times the Rugby Union reiterated its opposition to any form of payment or allowances for loss of earnings while playing or travelling to and from matches.

The matter came to a head in 1893, though a couple of years previously, because of growing professionalism in the North, restrictions had been placed on the transfer of players and the formation of leagues—as was again done in 1971. It was also agreed that only clubs composed wholly of amateurs might be members of the Rugby Union. At the Union's annual meeting in September 1893, Yorkshire proposed that players be allowed compensation for bona fide loss of time. But an amendment that 'this meeting, believing that the above principle is contrary to the game and its spirit, declines to sanction same' was carried by 282 votes to 136. Of the votes cast for, 120 were by proxy, which suggests the canvassing by the South was

1 All Blacks fullback George Nepia swoops in for a loose ball as Welsh forwards bear down in the 1924 international. Nepia played in all 30 of the tourists' matches, becoming the first of the game's immortals. 2 Another 1924 match, between the United States (white) and Devonport Services. Later in the year, the Americans won the last Olympic title ever contested. 3 The end of the drought for France as they gain their first victory in 50 years by beating Wales 16-6 at Cardiff in 1958. 4 New Zealand Maoris on the attack against the Springboks. Rugby history was made in 1970 when Maoris were included on an All Black tour of South Africa for the first time.

rather more persuasive (and successful) than that of their opponents. That year, 22 Yorkshire and Lancashire clubs left the Rugby Football Union to establish the Northern Union, the fore-runner of the present Rugby Football League.

Further laws prohibiting the donation—or acceptance—of money testimonials, medals, and prizes without the Union's permission, and the playing of matches where there was agreement to have less than 15 players a side, caused more withdrawals by Northern clubs, and by 1896 the Rugby Football Union had lost 98 of its 400 or so clubs.

After the formation of the Rugby Football Union, the game was enthusiastically adopted in many countries overseas. Within 10 years, rugby football was being played in Australia, Canada, France, South Africa, and North America. In 1888 New Zealand, where rugby union rapidly became the national game, sent a team comprising mostly Maoris to England. England went to New Zealand and Australia between March and November that year, but the tour did not have the approval of the Rugby Union. In all, 53 matches were played, some under local rules, but if 53 sounds a lot, the New Zealanders played 74 on their tour, winning 49, drawing 5, and losing 20.

In 1905 New Zealand's All Blacks were the first fully representative side to tour Great Britain and were beaten only by Wales. They scored 55 points against Devon, who were the county champions that season, the smallest winning margin in the first six matches being 28 points. The Second All Blacks, touring in 1924, won all their 30 matches and scored more than 700 points. Vast superiority in basic technique, support, fitness, and superb teamwork swept British teams to one side.

In Australia, rugby union developed a big hold in New South Wales and, to a lesser extent, in Queensland, but Australian Rules football and rugby league were strong rivals, eclipsing rugby union totally in other areas. By 1904, however, three British touring sides had played in Australia, and by 1908 the first Australian side had visited the British Isles.

There was a long struggle in South Africa before rugby became a greater attraction than soccer or a local sport which embodied points from both codes. British sides went to South Africa in 1891, 1896, and 1903, finding the opposition stronger each time. The South African Springboks toured the British Isles in 1906 and 1912, on each visit being beaten because of forward inadequacy. That was a lesson they never forgot and accounts greatly for the manner in which they have developed their game.

The International Scene

When rugby began at an international level, it did so without benefit of any over-all controlling body. England and Scotland played the first ever rugby international in 1871 purely as the result of an invitation issued by a group of Scottish enthusiasts to the newly formed (English) Rugby Football Union. The first tour by a British side to Australia and New Zealand in 1888 was a private enterprise, with the blessing of the Rugby Football Union but not under its direct control. Such pioneer internationals and overseas tours were not under the auspices of an international body for the simple reason that none existed. It was not until 1890 that the International Rugby Board was set up; and even then, despite what its name implied, it was not brought into being to control rugby around the world.

The word 'International' in the title was limited to cover matches between the Home Countries (England, Ireland, Scotland, and Wales), and in the Southern Hemisphere they are not even called internationals but 'tests'. The Board was formed as the outcome of a dispute between England and Scotland over their match of 1884. It was felt that there should be a central court of appeal, as it were, to make definite rulings.

It was not until many years later, though, that it achieved its present stature of a governing body for world rugby. After years of chaffing, the dominions were granted one seat each (to the Home Unions' two) in 1948, and then 10 years later they gained equal representation. The Board's purpose was 'to frame and interpret the laws of the game, settle disputes arising out of international matches and control all matters regarding international tours'. But even now there is still confusion in the minds of outsiders as to how rugby actually runs its international affairs.

As regards the countries outside Britain, it is simple. The New Zealand, South African, or Australian rugby unions organize everything as far as outgoing and incoming tours are concerned. But in Britain, each of the four Home Countries is so jealous of its autonomy that there is no central organization that could logically be called the British Rugby Union to run outgoing tours by the British Lions and incoming tours by the All Blacks, Springboks, and others. There is a Committee of the Four Home Unions that does liaison work, but it is on a muddling-through basis —the amateur attitude of the game carried to its ultimate.

The team Britain sends abroad —officially the British Isles Rugby Union Team, but commonly known as the Lions—is the oldest of rugby's international touring sides, and also its most unsuccessful. In the 19th century they were indomitable, undertaking two tours of South Africa, in 1891 and 1896, on which they carried all before them. There followed a long period of deterioration, during which the national teams of South Africa and New Zealand established themselves as world leaders of Rugby Union. Not only did these two teams consistently beat the Lions at home, but their dominance was paralleled on their touring visits. Of the four Home Unions, only Wales put up any sort of challenge to these two great sides.

But all this was to change in the 1970s. Following defeats inflicted on New Zealand, the Lions went to South Africa in 1974 confident that they were one of the strongest national teams ever assembled. Not only did they win the test series by three games with one drawn, but they finished the tour unbeaten in 22 games.

Due to its isolated position in world sport, South Africa was not the force it had once been, but the tour demonstrated the resurgence of British rugby.

France v Wales at Colombes, and highly rated scrum-half Gareth Edwards scores despite being collared by the defence.

There are eight major rugby countries in the world—England, Scotland, Ireland, Wales, France, New Zealand, Australia, and South Africa. Why is it then that the main strength has always been with New Zealand, South Africa, and Wales? The short answer is that, with each, rugby is the leading sport, the great preoccupation—a religion. The hold of soccer on the public of England and Scotland naturally relegates rugby to a secondary sport in each of those countries. In Ireland the followers of Gaelic games do all in their power to hold rugby back. In Australia, rugby league is so strong that rugby union has to fight for its very existence. France, where anything as British as rugby should never have stood a chance, was easy meat for the other countries for half a century, but since the 1950s has fought its way up to the top rungs of world rugby.

There was no logical reason why New Zealand and South Africa should have embraced rugby rather than soccer, but having done so, it became a matter of national pride to do well. 'Colonials' could not help but have an inferiority complex as regards the Old World. Even if subconsciously, New Zealanders and South Africans saw in rugby the opportunity to be equal or even superior to the more sophisticated, more rounded-out young gentlemen of what is still called the 'Old Country'. Down there in the isolated Southern Hemisphere they might be able to produce only the occasional author, scientist, or whatever of world class, but rugby, by crikey!, was a whole field of endeavour where they could show every other country where to get off.

To help them in this, the colonials seemed to have the advantage of physique. They could rely on their 'out door' forwards being harder and stronger than any that Britain could call on. But by the same token the more worldly Britain could always produce backs who were much cleverer players. And that has been the continuing story of the dominions versus Britain. Always it has boiled down in essentials to forward power versus sophisticated back play. And the structure of rugby is such that the team that dominates up front will always win, for no matter how brilliant a team's backs may be, it is to no avail if they are denied possession of the ball.

Allied to the highly developed brute strength of the All Blacks and the Springboks is dedication. It is *important* for them to win. If they do not, the folks back home virtually go into mourning. For England, Scotland, or Ireland to be beaten by these hard-rocks from down under is not a national calamity. It is of little or no concern to the man in the street. In Wales, however, it is a matter of

Colour Sport

Popperfoto

Popperfoto

Press Association

Africamera

Syndication International

1 The Fijians warm up with a war dance during their 1970 tour of England. Their ebullient brand of rugby wins friends wherever they go.
2 Hard running, quick passing, and 'kamikaze' tackling are a feature of rugby in Japan.
3 Rugby union visits Italy, where a London XV play a national side at Milan. **4** Scotland's halfbacks in action against the 1969-70 South Africans, who experienced a disastrous tour.

5 But later in 1970 the Springboks surprised the rugby world by defeating the All Blacks and so ending the New Zealanders' decade of rugby dominance. Their last series defeat had been in South Africa in 1960. **6** The teams were colourful enough, but the rugby was dull when Ireland beat the touring Wallabies in 1968.
7 England's problems were not only in the line-outs at Colombes in 1970: France won 35-13.

6 national prestige.

No one has yet been able to come up with an explanation as to why Wales, alone of the Home Countries, is obsessed with rugby. Why is it that Glasgow, Manchester, Liverpool and London are soccer-mad and Cardiff is rugby-mad? Only when someone is able to explain why Australians, who by nature should be quite uninterested in anything as slow-moving as cricket, are instead among its greatest adherents, will it be possible to answer the question of the Welsh preoccupation with rugby.

The spread of rugby to countries other than the Big Eight also has its question marks. It is logical that Canada, with all its British immigrants, should have a rugby following. It is only the climate that holds the game back there, preventing Canada from becoming one of the world's top rugby countries. The long freeze-up of the Canadian winter necessitates a split season in autumn and spring, and it is difficult for a game to thrive on that basis.

Fiji, long a mandate of New Zealand, naturally followed that country in taking to rugby. Only native exuberance and love of the spectacular prevents the Fijians from having greater success against countries more prepared to get down to the solid basics of **7** scrummaging and line-out work.

But though it is understandable for such countries, British in outlook, to embrace the game, why Japan, Argentina, and Romania —three of the important 'emerging' rugby countries?

A Japanese university man who had studied at Cambridge introduced rugby to the Japanese universities, and the game has grown to such an extent there that Japan has more rugby clubs than England. Whether or not the Japanese will ever attain international success, though, is debatable for their size alone may always be a handicap. Yet the 1968 side that toured New Zealand both surprised and delighted New Zealanders with their style of play, and their 23-19 victory over New Zealand Juniors could be a portent of things to come. Intelligent use of the short line-out, well timed jumping, and correct packing more than made up for lack of height and weight, and the backs ran and passed brilliantly.

The Argentinians came into rugby through its introduction there by British engineers building their railways. Today their skill at the game has risen to the level that they have been able to upset the full-strength touring teams of Wales, Ireland, and Scotland. They can be said to be knocking at the door of full recognition in test series with the Big Eight.

Even more entitled to such recognition is Romania. Rugby went to Romania by virtue of well-to-do Romanians sending their sons to Paris to study. They

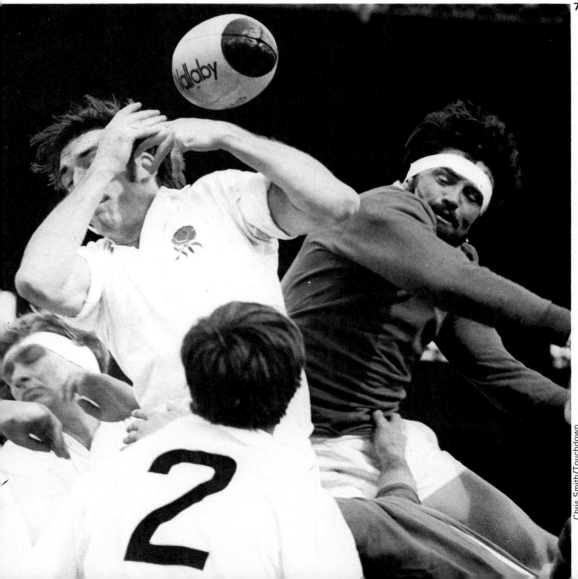

Chris Smith/Touchdown

played the game at university level there and started up teams when they got home. Since the early 1960s, Romania has surprised the rugby world by twice beating France at a time when the Tricolours were dominating the International Championship, and rugby followers wonder how long Romania can be denied full internationals with the Home Countries and others of the Big Eight.

It all boils down to the attitude of the International Rugby Board, which, although international in name, remains solidly British in outlook. It was purely for political reasons, extraneous to rugby, that two of the members—Ireland (the Republic only) and South Africa—became non-British. But France has never been a member of 'the British family'. Now, with two of the original members outside the family, there is an argument for the inclusion of France—an unsuccessful argument, however.

This rather unfair situation whereby France is in full participation in international rugby yet has no say whatsoever in how it is run makes it difficult for a country such as Romania to get a look in. France is only too willing to recognize Romania's stature

and play against her under the auspices of FIRA, the International Amateur Rugby Federation, which has 13 member countries on the Continent. But the International Rugby Board is hesitant.

The question is: can the Board continue to cold-shoulder countries such as Romania? Rugby followers as a whole would like to see such new blood injected into the International Championship. The All Blacks, Springboks, and Wallabies would find it interesting to add Romania to their fixture list on tours of Europe. But when rugby entered the 1970s Romania still remained outside the closed shop.

The International Board argue that they are not satisfied that rugby in Romania is conducted in the true spirit of the game. In this day and age, when paid coaches are an accepted thing and some of the Home Countries have squads that go into training months before taking the field for an international, such arguments carries less and less weight.

Fast, attacking backs, such as England's John Novak, are typical of British rugby; in New Zealand and South Africa forward play prevails.

Rugby Play and Tactics

Despite the attraction of backs throwing the ball around, forward play is the most important aspect of rugby. As the game has developed, far more time has been devoted to scrums and line-outs than back movements, and for a team to win it must get things right up front.

The scrum consists of the 'front five' and the three loose forwards. The vital five in 'tight' play consist of the front row of the *hooker* supported by a *prop* on each side of him, with the two *locks* of the second row binding them together. The loose forwards—a *flanker* on each side and the *No. 8* at the back—contribute their weight to the scrum but once possession has been gained they break away as speedily as possible. If their opponents get the heel, it is up to the three loose forwards to spoil the activities of their backs; if their own team heel they link in attack with their own backs.

In the early 1920s England had a great back row (as the loose forwards were called) in Wakefield, Voyce, and Blakiston. More than anything it was they who were responsible for England's Golden Era of that period. More recently New Zealand's Nathan-Tremain-Lochore combination **2** and South Africa's trio of Greyling-Ellis-Bedford have been the outstanding exponents of this aspect of forward play.

Scottish forwards were the early masters at wheeling the scrum (twisting it around on its axis), their object being to start a dribbling rush, spurred on by the famous Scottish cry of 'Feet! Feet! Feet!' But with dribbling very much a lost art, one of the main reasons for wheeling the scrum in modern rugby is to spoil possession gained by the opposing pack. Consequently when they do manage to complete their heel, they present their backs with what is called 'bad ball', the term originated by All Black captain Wilson Whineray to describe the ball not coming back to the backs efficiently.

The line-out should by rights be the simple matter of one or other of the two lines of forwards gaining possession and transferring the ball to their *scrum-half*. But only rarely these days is this done cleanly. The line-out remains rugby's most unsatisfactory manoeuvre, despite numerous law changes aimed at clearing up the indecisive huddle of players that invariably follows the throw-in. Now, the side with the throw-in has been allowed to withdraw some of their men from the line-out, opponents having to do likewise. But even in the 'short line-out', such is the barging and other interference, seldom is the ideal achieved of one player cleanly catching the ball in two hands and sending his backs away.

Behind the scrum one of the

great innovators was Danie Craven, outstanding Springbok scrum-half between the wars. At the end of the 1920s he originated the dive pass, his idea being to pass farther and so give his fly-half more space, and also to free himself from the attentions of bulky breakaway forwards. Today, however, the dive pass is out of favour, except under special circumstances. Modern scrum-halves prefer to 'spin' the ball—getting distance with a spinning flick imparted by the hand projecting the ball. This method gets around the great disadvantage of the dive pass—the scrum-half, on completing his dive, momentarily putting himself out of play.

The *fly-half* (variously called a stand-off, an out-half, or a first five-eighth) is invariably the key man of the backs, a team's tactician. In his hands lies the choice of trying to make a break through the defence, of sending the ball speedily along the line, or of kicking tactically. With his boot, he can either move play upfield for a line-out, put the ball 'up-and-under' for his forwards to follow up and exploit a confused defence, or kick diagonally towards the corner flag for his centre or the wing to try to beat

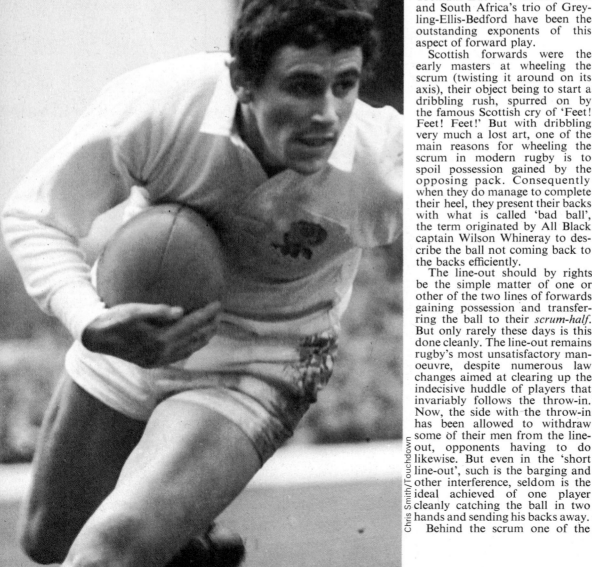

Chris Smith/Touchdown

1 The ball moves faster than the man, and there is little substitute for crisp passing with backs and forwards linking to make the overlap.
2 Though the subject of many law changes, the line-out is still one of rugby's problems. In theory one side should win the ball and transfer it to the scrum-half: in fact the line-out often ends in what is best described as 'a mess'.
3 Shadows in the afternoon. The camera catches the poetry that rugby can be. The dive-passing scrum-half went out of vogue in the mid-1960s.

Press Association

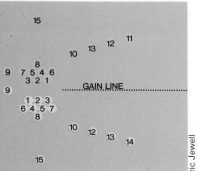

The basic formation at a scrum. Positions, with alternative names given in brackets, are: 1 Loose-head prop, 2 Hooker, 3 Tighthead prop, 4 & 5 Lock, 6 & 7 Flanker (wing-forward, break-away, or side-row), 8 No. 8, 9 Scrum-half (halfback), 10 Fly-half (stand-off or first five-eighth), 11 Left wing-three-quarter, 12 Left centre (in New Zealand the inside centre is the second five-eighth), 13 Right centre (centre), 14 Right wing-threequarter, 15 Fullback.

Eric Jewell

Peter Henderson, to name but two. One of the great sights of rugby is to see a wing in the clear at full throttle, with defenders converging and giving chase. But running is not the be-all and end-all of the position. A good wing is adroit at the cross-kick—the kick from the wing into the centre of the field for colleagues to follow up and exploit holes in the defence created by their converging onto the wing. The French are pastmasters at this manoeuvre.

The *fullback*, being the last line of defence, has more required of him than any other member of the team. He must be able to kick

3

Syndication International

Chris Benfield

their opposing numbers in the chase.

The main qualities required of the two *centre-threequarters* are the ability to run hard and fast, to be elusive either with swerve or side-step or both, and to be solid tacklers.

Through the years the Welsh have been outstanding at producing great centres, from the days of Gwyn Nicholls and Rhys Gabe at the beginning of the century on to such as Bleddyn Williams and Jack Matthews in more recent times. Almost invariably the British are much better in this aspect than their rivals of the Southern Hemisphere.

On the wing are the real speed merchants, and it is not uncommon for the position of *wing-threequarter* to be occupied by a champion sprinter—Ken Jones of Wales and New Zealand's

long and accurately with either foot; he must have a good sense of positional play, so that he can anticipate where to be at the right moment; and he must be a shattering tackler. And if he is a really great fullback, he has the flair to come into the back line on attack at just the right time to make the extra man for a try that would not have been on except for his intervention.

Although there are notable exceptions, fullbacks tend to be responsible for kicks at goal, and in this field one fullback, All Black Don Clarke, stands supreme. He scored 201 points in tests, and his nearest rival, Ireland's Tom Kiernan, is the only other player to have topped the 100, let alone 200 mark. The interesting aspect of Clarke's ability to put them over consistently from all angles and, when

the need arose, from inside his own half was that he always kicked with the ball upright. This went right against the textbook advice to place the ball lengthwise for long shots and upright when close to the posts. One would feel that budding place-kickers would ignore the textbooks and try to model themselves on the acknowledged master. Instead, however, in the late 1960s and early 1970s there was an increasing tendency to ignore both the textbooks and Don Clarke.

The vogue was 'round the corner'—the indirect, soccer style of running up to the ball. This may have its merits for the right-footed kicker attempting to goal from the left-hand side of the field, the automatic hook imparted to the ball helping it curve in between the uprights. But for a right-footed kicker to use this technique on the right-hand side of the field is technically unsound, since the curve becomes an outward one, away from the posts. In the early 1970s, however, Welsh wizards Barry John and Phil Bennett, and the great French full-back Pierre Villepreux brought consistency to this technique.

Second-Phase Play
At the beginning of the 1960s New Zealand revolutionized rugby thinking by their development of *second-phase play*. What lay behind this was the simple fact that they, along with all other rugby people, realized that it had become increasingly difficult to score from set pieces, ie scrums and line-outs, because of highly developed defence systems and

close marking. So they trained their forwards to be quick to reach the point of breakdown, and there to form a ruck, which would speedily get possession for their backs, who could then exploit their opponents' out-of-position defence.

So adept did they become at exploiting the breakdown that they went a step further. They purposely created breakdowns. Getting possession from scrum

1 The prince of goalkickers, Don Clarke. Standing the ball in an upright position, he kicked goals from any angle, at times from within his own half. **2 The All Blacks use of breakdowns to set up a second-phase was a feature of their play in the 1960s. 3 Making the tackle, Tony Bucknall smothers the ball, preventing Gareth Edwards from feeding it back to his forwards.**

or line-out, one of their inside backs would 'take the tackle' committing not only his opposite number but also other opposing backs to coping with him. Possession from a quick ruck would then present gaps to be explored.

This creating of new situations away from the set pieces, and thus dictating their own terms of attack, was something the All Blacks brought to such an art that from the mid-1960s there was no country capable of coping with their slickly executed second-phase play. It carried them to 17 successive test victories from 1965 to the end of the 1960s. The Home Countries decided there was nothing for it but to try to emulate them at this new technique, and long hours were put in practising the art of rucking and the other aspects of second-phase.

But in 1970 the South Africans, those other great rugby thinkers, decided not to bow down to New Zealand's supremacy at this new approach to the game. When the all-conquering All Blacks went to South Africa that year, the Springboks did not try to beat them at their own game. They decided they would just nullify it. This they did with such devastating tackling of first the New Zealand inside backs and then their midfield men that they were given virtually no chance to set up their second-phase situations. The Springboks were adroit enough to realize that second-phase works properly only when a team is going forward, ie when its backs have progressed beyond the advantage line and are invading enemy territory. If they are stopped before they get there, their forwards are in effect 'rucking backwards', having to retreat to join the ruck. No longer, therefore, are *they* dictating the terms of attack; the initiative has been taken away from them. So effectively did the Springboks of 1970 impair the All Blacks' second-phase rhythm that New Zealand lost the series 1-3.

As rugby advanced into the 1970s, rugbymen wondered whether this proof that second-phase play could be countered would mean that the revolution it had brought in the game had run its short course.

Laws of the Game

Rugby union is played by two teams of 15 a side, their object being to progress up the field by passing to one another (except forward) or kicking until such time as they are able to score. There are six ways of scoring. The grounding of the ball over the opponent's goal-line is a *try* (four points), which can be *converted* to six if the kick at goal that follows is successful (it must pass over the cross bar and between the line of the posts). The kick is taken from any point on a line perpendicular to the point of touchdown. The opposition must stand behind the goal-line until the kicker steps forward, when they may charge the kick. A *penalty try* is awarded if the opposition illegally prevent what the referee considers a certain try; the conversion is taken from in front of the posts. The *penalty goal, dropped goal,* and *goal from a fair catch* are each worth three points.

A team consists of eight forwards and seven backs. Substitution of injured players is permitted in internationals and in matches against touring teams. The field must not exceed 110 yards in length from goal-line to goal-line and 75 yards in width. The ball is oval in shape.

The Laws (which rugby people like to write with a capital 'L') are not the easiest for the newcomer to follow, but to understand the game it is most important to appreciate the *offside* law. In open play, a player is offside when he is in front of a member of his own team who has the ball, or last played it. When offside he can take no further part until being put onside by any team-mate running in front of him from behind the place the ball was kicked. Nor must a player in an offside position stay within 10 yards of an opponent waiting to catch the ball. He must retire a statutory 10 yards—immediately. He becomes on-side in open play if the opponent kicks, passes, or deliberately touches the ball but does not catch it.

As it is illegal to throw or knock the ball forward, the only methods of gaining ground in rugby are to run or kick. Opponents may be tackled or stopped only if they have the ball. They must not be tackled or stopped dangerously.

A *knock-on* is defined as occurring when the ball hits a player's hand or arm and goes forward towards the opposition dead-ball line — the line running the width of the field behind the goal-posts. But there are exceptions. If a player knocks-on and an opponent makes a fair catch from the mistake, the knock-on is ignored. And if a player charges down an opposition kick, if there is no loss of control, though there may have been a technical knock-on, or if a player fumbles a ball direct from a kick and the ball does not hit the ground, no knock-on is given.

At a *set scrum* the heads of the two front-rows must interlock so that adjacent heads belong to opposing teams. The hooker, the middle man, must put his arms either under or over his props' arms and they must bind around the body—not across the shoulders. The scrum-half must stand one yard from the scrum, midway between the front-rows, and put the ball down the middle of the tunnel, quickly, so that it touches the ground just past the first prop forward. Until the ball touches the ground no front-row forward may raise a foot.

The offside law at a set scrum operates in two ways. For scrum-halves, the offside line runs through the ball, and so long as the ball is in the scrum each scrum-half must stay on his own side of it. For everyone else the set scrum offside line runs through the tail-end of their side of the scrum.

At a *line-out* the two lines should be straight and there should be a clear place down the middle. The front man in the line-out must be at least five yards in from touch, and the end man of the side throwing in determines the length of the line-out. The offside line for players not in the line-out is 10 yards behind the line-out. Until the line-out ends, all players not in that line-out must remain behind this 10 yards line, except the scrum-half. The line-out ends when the ball touches the ground and a ruck is formed; if a player carrying the ball leaves the line-out; when the ball is passed or knocked back; or if the ball is thrown beyond the end of the line-out.

In the area between the 25 yard lines, which are that distance from the respective goal lines, it is illegal to kick directly into touch, ie on the full. The infringement brings a line-out at the point where the kick was made. Behind the 25 yard lines, a player may kick the ball directly to touch.

Hard at work in a set scrum. A penalty is awarded if the front row strike before the ball touches the ground.

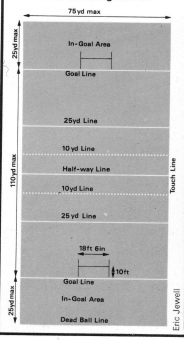

Eric Jewell

Sportography

233

A fisheye lens-view of a scrum gives an impression of how the ball might feel: and this is not even a full scrum. The minimum number for a scrum is three per side, but in practice there are eight, who pack in a 3-4-1 formation.

Good Ball Possession, by correctly timed feeding of the ball from scrum, line-out ruck, maul and elsewhere in broken play, from which something constructive can be achieved.

Hand-off Method by which a player with the ball pushes away a prospective tackler. The hand must be open, not clenched.

Line-out The means of restarting play after the ball has gone into touch.

Loose Head For a particular team, the side of the scrum at which their scrum-half puts the ball into the scrum. They are said to be hooking *with the head*.

Maul The situation when players of both sides gather around and mask the ball. It is similar to a *ruck* except that the ball is carried.

Offside When the ball is in play except at a scrum, line-out, ruck, or maul, a player is offside if the ball has been kicked, touched, or is being carried by one of his own team behind him. Other off-side laws apply to the exceptions.

Penalty Kick Awarded to the non-offending team after an infringement of certain Laws. It may be a place kick, drop kick, punt, or tap kick. If holding the ball, the kicker must kick it out of his hands, but if the ball is on the ground, for the *tap kick,* he may keep his hand on the ball and he kicks merely a visible distance from the mark before picking it up. The opposing side must retire 10 yards from the mark, and must not move until the kick is taken.

Ruck Sometimes called a *loose scrum.* A situation involving at least one player from either side, on their feet, pushing each other, with the ball on the ground between them. The ball must not be handled.

Scrum Method of restarting play in which a minimum of six men, three from each side, pack and push against each other. In practice a scrum involves eight players from either side, generally packing in a 3-4-1 formation though 3-2-3 was once standard.

Tackle Occurs when the man with the ball is held by one or more opponents so that there is a moment when either he cannot play the ball or the ball touches the ground. The tackled player must release the ball immediately.

Tight Head For a particular team, the side of the scrum at which the opposition scrum-half puts the ball into the scrum. They are said to be hooking *against the head.*

Touch-down The act of a defending player grounding the ball in his own in-goal, the area between his goal-line and the dead-ball line. It is a defensive action and not a synonym for a try, though the term is frequently used.

Gerry Cranham

Glossary of Terms

Advantage Law Gives the referee the opportunity to exercise his discretion. If one side offends, the other gets the advantage in that play continues for a couple of seconds to determine whether or not they benefit.

Advantage Line See *Gain Line.*

Blind Side The side of the scrum opposite that on which the backs line out in usual formation.

Box The open space behind the scrum or line-out between the scrum-half and the fullback. The *kick into the box* is usually employed, by the opposing scrum-half, to commit the fullback into coming forward for the ball and so be caught by the loose forwards. The term box is also used, somewhat injudiciously perhaps, to describe the open area behind the three-quarters.

Drop Kick A method of kicking in which the ball is dropped from the hands and kicked on the half-volley. A *dropped goal* is a means of scoring, counting three points. Until 1947-48 it was worth four points.

Fair Catch Catching the ball direct from an opponent's kick, knock-on, or throw forward when standing still with both feet on the ground. Because the player must shout 'Mark!' when he takes the ball, it is often called a *mark*! The player gets a *free kick,* which he must take, unless injured. The kick must be taken behind the mark on a line through the mark, or it is void. The opposition may stand on the mark and may charge as soon as the ball is placed on the ground (in case of a place kick) or as soon as the kicker runs to make his kick (for a punt or drop kick).

Forward Pass Exactly what it implies. The passing of the ball in a forward direction, which is illegal. Defined as a *throw-forward* in the Laws.

Gain Line The line behind which gain is made towards the opposition goal-line from the original source of possession (eg scrum).

Ed Lacey

Ball tucked under one arm, French loose forward Dauga uses the other to hand-off gifted Welsh fullback John Williams. The hand-off is an effective deterrent to the prospective tackler.

Show Jumping

For a sport that started only in the latter half of the 19th century, show jumping has grown rapidly in popularity, both among those taking part and as a spectator sport. In Britain, millions of viewers are glued to their television sets every evening during the Royal International and the Horse of the Year shows; in the United States, the New York International at Madison Square Garden is one of the highlights of the season; and in Germany, show jumping ranks second only to soccer. Perhaps the most surprising aspect of this dynamic growth is that, internationally, show jumping has become the province of the civilian as well as the military rider only since World War II.

There are various reasons for show jumping's popularity: the combination of man and horse make a more appealing picture than just man alone; the sport is easy to understand, although this has not always been so; and most

Ed Lacy

Two great names in British show jumping—controversial Harvey Smith *(Left),* **and Anneli Drummond-Hay.**

Gerry Cranham

of all, perhaps, it is a sport that
tends to build up to a climax, the
prize still being in the balance
until the last horse has jumped.
The more one learns about the
sport, the greater its interest
becomes, closer examination
showing not merely who is doing
well but how and why. As the
rapier of Broome combats the
cudgel of Mancinelli, then absorption is complete.

Development

Jumping is a comparatively
recent development in the 3,000-
year history of men riding horses.
Cavalry schools virtually ignored
it until the early 1800s, and
hunting men took it up only
because the increased division of
fields by fences and hedges made
it necessary if they were to keep
up with the hounds. It is generally
accepted that it was these same
huntsmen who held the first
jumping competitions. Usually,
the hunters were raced over the
flat, but as jumping became more
accepted, so the hunters were
tested over a few fences before the
actual race began. Perhaps, in a
way, the origin of show jumping
can be attributed to these contests.

In the 1860s, competitions for
jumping horses were organized
as far afield as Dublin, Paris, and
Russia, each apparently independent of the other, and in the
following decade the sport became
popular in Britain. In 1876,
'leaping classes' were included in
the schedule for the five-day show
at the Agricultural Hall, Islington,
London, but these were of little
import—scarcely more than a
diversion for the owners of
horses entered in the show classes.
The entrants were judged, by
Masters of Foxhounds, solely on
style! In 1883, the United States
also got into the act with the
foundation of the National Horse
Show at Madison Square Garden.

The sport's growth in various
countries was often in keeping
with differing social spheres. In
Germany, for example, it became
so popular with the public that
many towns organized shows,
whereas in France the jumping
shows tended to be affairs for the
social *elite*. The 1900 Olympic
Games in Paris included three
jumping competitions—'High
Jump', 'Long Jump', and 'Prize
Jumping'.

Apart from the Olympics, the
first international show recorded
was at Turin in 1901, with
German, and possibly Swiss, army
officers competing against the
Italians. In 1906, Count Clarence
von Rosen of Sweden proposed
the regular inclusion of equestrian
events in the Olympics, his
immediate intention being the
1908 Games scheduled for London, where the inaugural International Horse Show was held at
Olympia in 1907. At first the
British representatives on the IOC
agreed to stage equestrian events,
but at a late stage the idea was

dropped. Equestrian events did come in, however, when the Olympics were held at Stockholm four years later.

The three events were fundamentally the same as they are now: dressage, a three-day event —known as 'Military'—and show jumping. Although the rather nebulous 'style' was not a factor, the rules for the show jumping were complicated in the extreme, placing considerable reliance on the judges to decide whether knockdowns had been made with fore- or hind-legs. The Swedish team, appropriately, won the first show jumping Olympic gold, and the individual went to France's Captain Cariou on Mignon.

The 1920 Olympics, from which the British and the Swiss were absent, were notable for the successes of the Italians, who provided first and second in the individual. Both were pupils of Federico Caprilli, whose theories of riding have had more effect internationally than those of any other single man. Then the following year saw the formation of the Federation Equestre Internationale (FEI) with eight founder members: Sweden and France— the two prime movers—Belgium, Denmark, Italy, Japan, Norway, and the United States.

In Britain, show jumping after World War I was in a fairly moribund state, though it did produce some of the greatest characters of the sport. Judges were allowed so much latitude in reaching their decisions and competitors had such unlimited time to complete the course that spectator interest was minimal. In 1923, however, the British Show Jumping Association was formed, under the presidency of Lord Lonsdale, for 26 years the leading light of the International Horse Show at Olympia. It set out to impose some uniformity on a decidedly muddled situation, and by the 1930s the improved standards of course and judge had combined to produce riders and horses of international standard. In 1930 Jack Talbot-Ponsonby won the first of three King George V Gold Cups, and in 1937 Don Beard on Swank set a British high jump record of 7 ft. 6¼ in., which was still standing in the early 1970s.

Germany gave a taste of the might she was to show again after World War II by taking team and individual gold medals in all three equestrian sports at the Berlin Games in 1936. Three years later came the hostilities in which a young British officer and leading show jumper, Mike Ansell, was blinded and taken prisoner. And it was during his two years of captivity that Ansell gave considerable thought to improving his sport. Repatriated in 1944, he was invited to become chairman of the BSJA, and immediately set about making changes, both in the running of the sport and in its

1 Italy's Raimondo d'Inzeo was a dominant force in the 1950s and 1960s, winning two world championships, in 1956 and 1960, and taking the Olympic gold medal at Rome in the latter year.
2 Show jumping in Japan received an enormous stimulus when Baron Takeichi Nishi won the gold at Los Angeles on Uranus.
3 Hans Gunter Winkler contests the Prince of Wales Cup, the British Nations Cup, on Torphy. The German's earlier teaming with the mare Halla had brought him a world championship and three Olympic golds. He won further golds in 1964 and 1972.
4 The 1966 European champions Pierre d'Oriola and Pomone compete for the 1969 title. Olympic gold medallist in 1952, he turned in a brilliant performance at Tokyo 12 years later to win the title again, as well as a silver in the team event.

Ed Lacey

Ed Lacey

Official Report of Olympics

presentation to the public.

Grading was introduced, according to money won, to give young horses a chance; a stop was put to the unlimited time taken to jump a round; and in September 1945 a show was held at the White City, London, followed two years later by the Royal International, which stayed there for 20 years. That show saw the introduction of Harry Llewellyn's Foxhunter, unquestionably the most popular British show jumper of all time. And in 1947 Pat Smythe made her international debut, in Ostend and Le Zoute.

The Olympic Games were restarted in London in 1948, when both team and individual gold medals went to Mexico. Britain, with a third in the team event, gained her first show jumping medals, and then four years later won the gold through Harry Llewellyn on Foxhunter, Wilf White on Nizefela, and Duggie Stewart on Aherlow.

The first world championship, a year later in Paris, went to the most successful rider Spain has produced, Francisco Goyoaga. Until 1956, this championship was held each year—now it is every four years—and the 1954 victor was Hans Gunter Winkler, who had made his international debut only two years earlier. With the great mare Halla he retained the title in 1955, and won individual and team gold medals in the 1956 Olympics in Stockholm. That was the first of three successive team gold medals for Germany, with Winkler in the team each time. He also won the inaugural European Championship in 1957.

Raimondo d'Inzeo won the first of two successive world championships in 1956, followed by Pierre Jonqueres d'Oriola in Buenos Aires—the first time it was held outside Europe—in 1966 and David Broome in 1970. Broome was also Britain's first European champion, in 1961, winning again in 1967 and 1969.

For team competition on an international level, the President's Cup—a team championship based on Nations Cups—was started in 1965 and has rapidly become one of the established tests of skill.

Competitions

Basically, show jumping can be divided into three types of competition: those that are against the clock from the start; those that are primarily a test of jumping, but with the clock called in if necessary to decide a jump-off; and those that are purely to test jumping, with time not a factor.

Speed competitions are designed to test a horse's handiness, obedience, and training, as well as his jumping ability, and consequently the fences jumped are often—but not always—lower and easier than average. Results are determined by one of two methods, the first being that the horse with the least number of faults wins. Should two or more have the same number of faults, the result is decided by the fastest time. In the other method, each fault is converted to a specified number of seconds, theoretically from 3 to 17 seconds a fault, but usually about 5 to 7 seconds a fault, and the winner is decided on corrected time (time taken plus faults).

Most major competitions consist of one round in which all competitors jump. Those 'clear'— that is, without faults—go into a jump-off, usually over about two-thirds of the original fences, the height of which may be increased. If there is only the one jump-off, any still clear will be placed according to their speed: if two jump-offs, the 'clears' go into the second, which is decided, if necessary, on time.

The most popular competitions not including time are the *puissance* events. These are run over a smaller number of fences which, usually, are eventually reduced to two—an upright, generally a wall, and a spread fence, such as a triple bar or an *oxer*. As long as two or more horses are clear, these fences will be raised until there is a decision, or until the judges—or the competitors, with the judges' agreement—decide to call it a day.

Faults

One of the reasons why show jumping is so popular is the ease of judging the competitions. At one time, faults were dependent upon whether a fence was knocked down by fore- or hind-legs, or whether a horse landed within a demarcation area around a fence. Even touches were penalized, and

the fences were often surmounted by slats—thin laths of wood— that could be blown off as easily as knocked, so costing a vital half-fault.

Now, a fence lowered, no matter how, costs four faults. The first refusal in a round earns three faults, the second six, and the third elimination. And that, except for penalties for exceeding the time allowed for the course, is virtually all there is to it.

The great bugbear is the water jump, for this alone is still dependent on the human eye, with all its fallibility. Most dissensions have resulted from water-jump judging, but in 1970 the FEI brought in a possible end to future disputes. They decreed that all official international shows, championships, and Olympic Games must use, to mark the edge of the water, a strip of rubber covered with a white or brightly coloured plasticene material that would show beyond any doubt whether or not a horse has landed on the 'tape'.

Courses

The aim of a show jumping course is to test both horse and rider in one or more specific direction: for speed and handiness, for sheer show jumping ability, or for a combination of both. The good course-builders will produce a result without reverting either to tricks or, except for puissance events, to sheer height.

Their secret is in the siting of fences, either one with another, or in relation to the arena. Therefore a double that would be straightforward in the centre of the ring can be made much more difficult if it has to be jumped after a sharp

The type of course a rider would experience in a CHIO grand prix event. The course is 450 metres (492 yards) long and the rider has 76 seconds to get round. The fences, with their height (and spread in brackets) are as follows: 1 Parallel bar, 4′ 6″ (4′ 4″). 2 Triple bar, 4′ 8″ (5′ 6″). 3 Gate, 4′ 9″. 4 Combination a table with post-rails, 3′ rise and 4′ 9″ drop; b & c parallel bars, 4′ 9″ (4′ 9″). 5 Post-rail, 4′ 10″. 6 Gates, 4′ 7″. 7 Wall, 4′ 11″, 8 Double oxer, 4′ 10″ (5′). 9 Wall, 5′. 10 Combination a water 6′ with rails, 4′ 11″; b triple bar, 4′ 9″ (5′); c parallel bar, 4′ 10″ (4′ 10″). In the case of a jump-off, obstacles 1, 2, 3, 4, 5 & 10 would have to be jumped. The distance would be 270 metres (295 yards) with the time allowed 46 seconds.

turn. Fences within 39 ft. 4 in. of each other are accounted as parts of the same fence, and the distances within a combination can be varied from easy to difficult. For example, if the distance between two upright fences is 26 ft., it would be reckoned right for one stride between jumps, and if 35 ft. for two strides. But if it were, say, 30 ft., the rider would have a considerable problem in adjusting the horse's stride for either one very long stride or two short ones. This is why short-striding horses can have an advantage in show

jumping.

As the rider never knows the actual course until he walks it before the competition, an important part of the successful show jumping rider's armoury is his ability to 'read' a course during this walk. And it is perhaps not too surprising that many top course-builders were also successful riders. Two prime examples are Jack Talbot-Ponsonby, triple King George V Gold Cup winner, who for a long time built the courses for the Royal International and Horse of the Year shows, and Hans Brinckmann, a

4

have settled on a formula of three competitions: the first a speed, the second of Nations Cup type (two rounds over the same course), and the third, also of two rounds, incorporating fences of speed, Nations Cup, and puissance type. Points from the three competitions are then accumulated to decide the winner.

The men's world championship is run on more controversial lines, which have variously been described as the true test of a horseman, and a gimmick. Three qualifying rounds produce the top four riders and horses, who then go into a final in which all four ride their own horse and then each of the other three horses. In this way, although a rider needs a good horse to get through to the final, once there the more difficult his horse the better. Thus Raimodo d'Inzeo, although a worthy winner, largely owed his 1960 success to the difficulties his three rivals had with Gowran Girl. And in 1970 David Broome clinched his championship with his immaculate handling of Graziano Mancinelli's intractable Fidux.

1 Britain's Hickstead arena, venue of many international events. A well-designed course should produce the top horse-and-rider combinations, and also provide entertaining sport for the spectators.
2 The arena at Wembley during the 1970 Royal International Horse Show, **3** The bank at Hickstead is an integral part of the British Jumping Derby.
4 During the 1960s, the young French rider Janou Lefeovre enjoyed remarkable success, climaxed by her world title victory in 1970 at the expense of holder Marion Mould (**5**). The British girl had won the first women's world event.

leading German rider before World War II, who builds at Aachen. Brinckmann's talents in this field were recognized when he was chosen to be responsible for the courses at the Munich Olympic Games. Others, however, such as John Gross, senior course-builder for the BSJA for 10 years until his death in a car accident in 1970, learn the job 'on the ground' from people such as Talbot-Ponsonby and Brinckmann.

International Competitions

The most important competitions are the team events known as Prix des Nations, or Nations Cups. In Europe, each country may stage only one Nations Cup, which must be at its CHIO—Official International Horse Show. Such countries as the United States and Canada, however, can have two. Because a minimum of three countries must take part, Australia and New Zealand have, by the early 1970s, been prevented from staging their own Nations

Cups, distance and strict quarantine regulations being handicaps.

Each team consists of four riders and horses, each jumping the same course twice, with the best three in each round counting towards the final total. If a team can field only three riders, then all three have to count. At one time, riders could use more than one horse, and in 1926 America's Fred Bontecou rode two of the three in a team that failed by only half a fault to beat Britain in the Prince of Wales Cup—Britain's Nations Cup.

From Paris in 1924 until and including the 1968 Mexico City Games, the Grand Prix des Nations at the Olympics were restricted to teams of only three, all of them counting. This inevitably made for the elimination of many teams—in 1932 none finished complete—and for possibly false results. In 1970, therefore, the FEI General Assembly approved new rules to allow the Olympic team event to be run on the same lines as all other Nations Cups.

The men's and women's European championships and the women's world championship

Training of Horse and Rider

Millions of words have been written through the ages about the training of horses, and the men and women who ride them. The ancient Greek Xenophon, and even before him Simon of Athens, propounded truths that are by no means out of date today. For them the training of a horse, to produce actions done happily and beautifully, was basically a matter of kindness. Unhappily this has not always been so since, and indeed even today there are those who, through greed—trying to

5

Ed Lacey

Gerry Cranham

Gerry Cranham

find short-cuts to a quick profit—and perhaps even more through ignorance, inflict cruel or unkind 'training' methods upon horses.

Among those who are neither ignorant nor unkind there is plenty of room for diversion in theories of training, with perhaps the one universal precept—there is no substitute for patience. How long it will take to train a horse, whatever is wanted of him, will vary tremendously according to the horse's mental and physical make-up. It may be said that the better a horse is bred the more gentleness and patience will be needed, but as a result the rewards will be greater.

No mention of training can be made without reference to Frederico Caprilli, who was born in Leghorn, Italy, in 1868. By theory and practice at the Italian cavalry schools at Tor di Quinto and Pinerolo, he evolved the system known generally as 'The Forward Seat', which, although adapted to national schools of thought, had a revolutionary effect upon riding in general, and riding over jumps in particular. Basically it is a matter of partnership with the horse, seen most clearly in the riding of Raimondo d'Inzeo and David Broome, as opposed to the domination of horse by rider, which is a German characteristic and is more suited to their powerful, heavy horses than to a thoroughbred.

A well trained show-jumping horse will be one possessing three important qualities—balance at all times; obedience to the rider's wishes, for time saved in turns between fences often means the difference between winning and losing a competition; and impulsion. Impulsion is often confused with speed, but the two are not related. Impulsion has been likened to a clockwork spring, the releasing of which enables a horse to come into a big fence at

Britain was well represented in the 1970 men's world championships with Harvey Smith (1) and David Broome (2) both making the final four. Broome went on to take the title, on Beethoven, and Smith finished in third place.

an awkward angle and clear it, or to jump faultlessly through a *combination*, the fences of which may be at difficult distances from each other.

The show-jumping rider has to learn not merely the rudiments of riding over fences, but certain points that will enable him to save time. For slow clear rounds, except over the biggest of courses, rarely achieve the winner's rostrum.

In speed competitions, especially those in which the rider can choose in which order he will jump the fences, cutting to a minimum the time spent between jumps is obviously vital. No one is better at working out the quickest way round a course than Harvey Smith, and although he may sometimes be too adventurous, at others his dash will land him home well in front of the field.

In a jump-off, it is cutting corners in the timed round that counts. Usually the course plan, pinned up in the collecting ring or where the riders can easily see it, will merely make a note of the fences to be left in for the jump-off, and it is up to the rider to see how they can best be approached. This will depend as much as anything upon the horse, whether it is a nippy one who can be taken the shortest way to a fence, or a long-striding animal who needs plenty of room to manoeuvre.

It is in this combination of a rider's ability to 'think-out' a course and his horse's ability to perform what is asked that show jumping's principal fascination is to be found.

Glossary of Terms

Barrage Alternative term for a jump-off.

CHI (O) Concours Hippique International (Officiel): (Official) International Horse Show.

Combination A fence with two (a *double*), three (a *treble*), or more separate parts not more than 39 ft. 4 in. from each other.

Cup The support in which a pole or supported part of a fence rests.

Derby A competition that includes permanent 'natural' fences, such as a *bank*. The first derby was in Hamburg.

FEI Federation Equestre Internationale, the world ruling body of equestrian sport, founded in 1921, with headquarters in Brussels.

Groundline Line at the bottom of a fence that a horse uses to calculate his jump. The absence of a groundline makes the jump

more difficult.

Hand Term for measuring a horse, equal to 4 inches.

Nations Cup (or **Prix des Nations**). International team competition.

Oxer Brush fence with a pole on the take-off side. A *double oxer* has a pole on each side.

Parallel Poles—sometimes planks or walls. Often the take-off pole is lower than the landing pole; if exactly the same height, it is usually described as 'true parallel'.

Rapping Method of making a horse jump higher. As he jumps a practice fence, a pole is raised to rap him.

Triple (or **Triple Bar**) A fence with three poles on separate supports, progressively higher from front to back.

Upright A straight-up fence, usually of poles or planks.

SHOW JUMPING Olympic Champions

Year	Individual	Horse	Team
1912—Stockholm	J. Cariou (France)	Mignon	Sweden
1920—Antwerp	T. Lequio (Italy)	Trebecco	Sweden
1924—Paris	A. Gemuseus (Switzerland)	Lucette	Sweden
1928—Amsterdam	F. Ventura (Czechoslovakia)	Eliot	Spain
1932—Los Angeles	T. Nishi (Japan)	Uranus	Not awarded
1936—Berlin	K. Hasse (Germany)	Tora	Germany
1948—London	H. Mariles Cortes (Mexico)	Arete	Mexico
1952—Helsinki	P. J. d'Oriola (France)	Ali Baba	Great Britain
1956—Stockholm	H. G. Winkler (Germany)	Halla	Germany
1960—Rome	R. d'Inzeo (Italy)	Posillipo	Germany
1964—Tokyo	P. J. d'Oriola (France)	Lutteur B	Germany
1968—Mexico City	W. Steinkraus (USA)	Snowbound	Canada
1972—Munich	G. Mancinelli (Italy)	Ambassador	West Germany

There was no award in the 1932 team event because no nation had all three riders complete the course

SHOW JUMPING World Championships

Year	Venue	Winner	Horse
Men			
1953	Paris	F. Goyoaga (Spain)	Quorum
1954	Madrid	H. G. Winkler (Germany)	Halla
1955	Aachen	H. G. Winkler (Germany)	Halla
1956	Aachen	R. d'Inzeo (Italy)	Merano
1960	Venice	R. d'Inzeo (Italy)	Gowran Girl
1966	Buenos Aires	P. J. d'Oriola (France)	Pomone
1970	La Baule	D. Broome (Britain)	Beethoven
Women			
1965	Hickstead	M. Mould (Britain)	Stroller
1970	Copenhagen	J. Lefebvre (France)	Rocket

Ski-Bobbing

'How to succeed on skis without really trying' is an apt summary of ski-bobbing, a winter sports pastime that became an organized sport in the early 1950s. It is an unquestionable attraction for non-skiers who lack either the time or the patience to learn the major snow sport but still want the thrill of speeding down a slope. Within 10 minutes of first sitting astride a ski-bob and coasting down the nursery snow slopes, the rider starts looking for somewhere steeper. Once proficient, he can take the steepest descents in much the same way as the skier, even to the extent of jumps around 20 ft.

Made of wood, metal, or plastic, a ski-bob looks like a bicycle with short skis where the wheels should be. The rider wears miniature foot-skis that only slightly overlap the length of his boots, and his skis are fitted with metal claws at the heel to assist braking. The four points of ground contact make injury rare,

and speeds of around 60 mph are frequently attained. Experts have been timed in excess of 100 mph. Because of ski-bobbing's ever increasing popularity, many winter resorts have made special provision for the sport, designating specific areas and arranging hire facilities. Most ski-bobs fold, making them easy to carry in cable cars and chair lifts.

The first known 'ski-bike' was patented by a Connecticut American named Stevens in 1892, and it evolved as transport in Alpine villages, used particularly by Swiss, Austrian, and German delivery boys. The competition bob was introduced by Englebert Brenter and in 1962 the International Ski-Bob Federation was formed at Innsbruck. The Austrians, Swiss, and West Germans were prime movers, but within the next five years the number of member nations had swollen to 20. The official world championships have been held biennially since 1967, and combined titles are awarded for the best overall performances in downhill and slalom events.

George Konig

Ski-bobbing experts have been known to attain speeds of 100 mph.

SKI-BOBBING World Champions			
Year	Venue	Men	Women
1967	Bad Hofgastein	S. Schauberger (Austria)	G. Schiffkorn (Austria)
1969	Montana	P. Bonvin (Switzerland)	G. Schiffkorn (Austria)
1971	Reno	J. Estner (W. Germany)	G. Gerberth (Austria)
1973	Garmisch	A. Fischbauer (Austria)	G. Gerbert (Austria)

1

Popperfoto

2

George Konig

Ski Jumping

It is doubtful whether any other sport is so spectacular or so awe-inspiring as ski jumping, that aspect of Nordic skiing in which courage and grace are so closely combined. Even the most experienced jumper feels apprehensive during the last nerve-wracking moments in the lofty tower before he takes off. It is strangely quiet: the wind can muffle all sound, even the expectant murmuring of thousands of spectators waiting below. Then comes the moment of truth as each jumper in turn steps into the twin iced grooves, curls into a tight ball, and gathers speed down the long ramp—reaching up to 75 mph—until exploding into the air.

But even then the man who jumps farthest does not necessarily win, for in the air a man can soar to greatness or fade to obscurity. Five judges award each jumper marks for style; the highest and lowest marks awarded are discarded and the remaining three count. The important factors are posture and technique: points assessed are whether the jumper reduces speed on his way down the ramp, whether his spring is properly timed—neither unduly late nor too early. In the air, the judges look for the jumper's straight knees, an extreme forward

3

4

Colour Sport

1 Birger Ruud won the 1936 Olympic ski jumping title in the Games at Garmisch. 2 32 years later it was the turn of Vladimir Beloussov of the USSR to take the gold. 3 A jumper skids to a halt on the outrun at St Moritz. 4 The judges mark for grace as well as distance.

Colour Sport

lean from the ankles—the *vorlage* position—and just a very slight curve of the hips and back. The skis should be held parallel, and, during the final part of the flight, should be inclined upwards at an acute angle to the trajectory, so that the air presses up underneath them.

Certain obvious faults are penalized, such as an unsteady or oblique position of the body and arms, a curved or hollow back, bent knees, or unsteady skis. The jumper should maintain his forward lean all the way to the landing slope. Officials, stationed an arm's length apart, record the middle point between the feet of the jumper when he lands.

During the last seconds before landing, the jumper moves one foot forward into the *telemark* position, with knees bent to absorb the shock. Unsteadiness or stiffness here can still lose points. As connection is made with the snow, the arms are spread as stabilizers—but they must not contact the ground. Finally, the jumper skis along the flat 'outrun' and skids to a halt. So that wind resistance is minimized, the ski jumper does not use the ski sticks so essential to Alpine skiers, and this in itself tends to give this Nordic event a dare-devil appearance.

Organized ski jumping meetings first took place at Iverslokka, near Oslo in Norway, in 1866. The nearby Huseby hill was used for major Norwegian events from 1879 to 1891, and in 1892 they were moved to Holmenkollen. Ski jumps have been erected in many other places, including, of course, Winter Olympic Games venues. Each hill is different in height, construction, and wind patterns, and thus there can be no 'world ski jumping records' that are universally valid. The hill at Oberstdorf in the Bavarian Alps, for example, possesses particularly favourable conditions for long jumps because its vertical height is 528 feet.

But the most famous ski jumping site is still Oslo's Holmenkollen hill. The Holmenkollen Week every March is the highlight of the Scandinavian winter sports season, and it has been said that what Cowes means to yachtsmen, Holmenkollen means to Nordic skiers. For over 80 years, the Holmenkollen competitions have been the most popular ski meetings in the world. The jumping final each year attracts crowds of well over 100,000, usually headed by the Norwegian royal family.

The first international ski jumping championship was held at Chamonix in 1924, with the Olympic and world titles at stake. They were won by Jacob Tullin-Thams of Norway. Until 1964 there was only ever one jumping competition in these championships. But for the 1964 Olympics at Innsbruck there were two separate events, one from a height

of 90 metres and the other from 70 metres.

The most successful ski jumper was Birger Ruud, who won two Olympic and five world championships. He was one of a whole army of Norwegians who almost monopolized the world and Olympic titles, and only 4 times in 16 championships did the world title leave Norway before World War II. After the war, and especially in the 1960s, the top honours were no longer a Norwegian or even a Scandinavian prerogative, but Norway still produced the greatest number of star performers.

Today, the best jumpers are exceeding 150 metres, a distance which was first beaten by Lars Grini of Norway in 1967 at Oberstdorf. In 1969, Manfred Wolf of East Germany cleared 165 metres at Planica in Czechoslovakia. But almost a century earlier, in 1879, the longest ski jump had been a mere 23 metres

by Troj Hammestweit of Norway, at Huseby. In 1915, Amble Amundsen of Norway passed 50 metres for the first time with a leap of 54 metres at Holmenkollen. And it was an Austrian, Sepp Bradl, who flew more than 100 metres: he cleared 101 metres at Planica in 1936.

The Nordic Combination
The Nordic combination is an event devised to test the overall ability of skiers in jumping and cross-country (15 km). The winners are determined on a points basis after the two competitions. Norway's Thorleif Haug won the first world and Olympic contest at Chamonix in 1924, and after that, as happened with the ski jump, the Norwegian predominance was only gradually eroded.

Daring ski jumpers eschew the use of ski sticks in this spectacular Scandinavian sport which began in 1866.

SKI JUMPING Olympic and World Champions

Year	Venue	Special Jump	70-metre Jump	Nordic Combination
1924*	Chamonix	Jacob Tullin-Thams (Norway)	—	Thorleif Haug (Norway)
1925	Johannisbad	W. Dick (Czechoslovakia)	—	O. Nemecky (Czechoslovakia)
1926	Lahti	Jacob Tullin-Thams (Norway)	—	Johan Grottumsbraaten (Norway)
1927	Cortina	T. Edman (Sweden)	—	R. Purkert (Czechoslovakia)
1928	St Moritz	Alf Andersen (Norway)	—	Johan Grottumsbraaten (Norway)
1929	Zapokane	Sigmund Ruud (Norway)	—	Hans Vingarengen (Norway)
1930	Oslo	Gunnar Andersen (Norway)	—	Hans Vingarengen (Norway)
1931	Oberhof	Birger Ruud (Norway)	—	Johan Grottumsbraaten (Norway)
1932*	Lake Placid	Birger Ruud (Norway)	—	Johan Grottumsbraaten (Norway)
1933	Innsbruck	Marcel Reymond (Switzerland)	—	Sven Eriksson (Sweden)
1934	Solleftea	Kristian Johansen (Norway)	—	Oddbjorn Hagen (Norway)
1935	Hohe Tatra	Birger Ruud (Norway)	—	Oddbjorn Hagen (Norway)
1936*	Garmisch	Birger Ruud (Norway)	—	Oddbjorn Hagen (Norway)
1937	Chamonix	Birger Ruud (Norway)	—	Sigurn Roen (Norway)
1938	Lahti	Asbjorn Ruud (Norway)	—	Olaf Hoffsbakken (Norway)
1939	Zakopane	Josef Bradl (Austria)	—	Gustl Berauer (Germany)
1948*	St Moritz	Petter Hugsted (Norway)	—	Heikki Hasu (Finland)
1950	Lake Placid	Hans Bjornstad (Norway)	—	Heikki Hasu (Finland)
1952*	Oslo	Arnfinn Bergmann (Norway)	—	Simon Slattvik (Norway)
1954	Falyn	Matti Pietikainen (Finland)	—	Sverre Stenersen (Norway)
1956*	Cortina	Antti Hyvarinen (Finland)	—	Sverre Stenersen (Norway)
1958	Lahti	J. Kerkinen (Finland)	—	Paavo Korhonen (Finland)
1960*	Squaw Valley	Helmut Recknagel (East Germany)	—	Georg Thoma (West Germany)
1962	Zakopane	Helmut Recknagel (East Germany)	Toralf Engan (Norway)	Arne Larsen (Norway)
1964*	Innsbruck	Toralf Engan (Norway)	Veikko Kankkonen (Finland)	Tormod Knutsen (Norway)
1966	Oslo	Bjorn Wirkola (Norway)	Bjorn Wirkola (Norway)	Georg Thoma (West Germany)
1968	St Nizier	Vladimir Beloussov (USSR)	Jiri Raska (Czechoslovakia)	Franz Keller (West Germany)
1970	Vysoke Tatry	Garij Napalkov (USSR)	Garij Napalkov (USSR)	Ladislav Rygl (Czechoslovakia)
1972*	Sapporo	Wojciech Fortuna (Poland)	Yukio Kasaya (Japan)	Ulrich Wehling (East Germany)
1974	Falun	Hans-Georg Aschenbach (East Germany)	Hans-Georg Aschenbach (East Germany)	Ulrich Wehling (East Germany)

*Olympic Games and World Championship events decided concurrently

Colour Sport

Rudi Sailer, member of a
famous alpine ski-racing
family, in thrilling action in
the slalom.

Skiing

Skiing and flying have been roughly parallel phenomena in the 20th century. Both activities have expanded within a similar period, and both have done so at a startling rate. It is perhaps because of this that many people still regard flying and skiing with equal awe. Skiing, as a sport and as a recreation, is one of the most rapidly growing activities in the world of leisure and sport.

Skiing is not, as some might think, confined to countries in higher latitudes, but is possible at high altitudes in some unlikely areas—the Lebanon, Greece, India, and Turkey. Eight South American nations are actively concerned in skiing, and millions of people ski in Japan. In Africa the sport is practised in Morocco, Kenya, and on the Drakensburg Mountains only 150 miles from Durban. However, most skiing takes place in the more 'traditional' areas—the European Alps, Scandinavia, and in the mountainous areas of North America.

Even when the weather lets the skier down, it is possible for snow to be induced. When snow becomes sparse, whole areas can be sprayed with ammonium nitrate so that any subsequent falls harden and form a crisper surface for skiing. Snow can be 'sprayed' by mixing water with compressed air: snow-making machines can produce snow to order, varying its texture from powder to larger granules. In lowland areas where there is no snow, plastic ski slopes can be erected. On such surfaces, which have no snow but have a type of slippery brush texture, the elementary skills of skiing can be learnt before a skier embarks on more ambitious outings.

Skiing—as an essential part of man's way of life—started some 3,000 years BC. The most ancient ski known was found in a peat bog in Hoting in Sweden and is claimed to date from 2500 BC. A rock carving of two men on skis hunting elks was discovered at Rodey in Norway and attributed to a Stone Age artist operating in about 2000 BC. The techniques of skiing are, therefore, very old.

The first skis were made from the bones of large animals, and strapped to the feet with leather thongs. The use of wooden skis appears to have spread into Europe from Asia. A single wooden staff, sometimes as much as 8 feet long, was used for balancing and braking. The use of shorter pairs of ski poles is a relatively new innovation. Skiing as it is known today dates from the invention of ski bindings in the 1880s by Sondre Nordheim, of Mordegal in Norway. Norwegians from Nordheim's area—Telemark—became pioneers of skiing all over the world through emigration in the 19th century.

As early as 1841 they skied in Wisconsin. In California in 1856 John 'Snowshoe' Thompson, who was born in Telemark, used to carry mail by ski across the Sierra Nevada. Gradually the use of skis spread all over the world, to Australia, New Zealand, South Africa, Japan, and South America. In 1896 Norwegian gold prospectors were going to Alaska—by ski.

The first organized ski club was the Trysil club in Norway, formed in 1861. The Kiandra club in

The slalom is a challenging test for the Alpine skier— he does not get a trial run over the course beforehand.

Australia dates from 1870, and America's first—the Mansen club in Berlin, New Hampshire—from 1872.

Downhill skiing, that part of the sport later known as Alpine skiing—was evolved by an Austrian, Mathias Zdarsky, in 1896. He published the first methodical analysis on how to turn on skis, and developed the first skis and bindings specifically designed to assist turning. An Englishman, E. C. Richardson, was the man who initiated the first skiing proficiency tests. In 1903 he helped found the Ski Club of Great Britain, which, though it may sound unlikely, was the world's first national skiing

administrative body. (It was superseded by the National Ski Federation of Great Britain in 1964.) The National Ski Association of America (now called the United States Ski Federation) was formed in 1908, and the International Ski Federation, the sport's world governing body, came into being in 1924.

That year, 1924, saw the first Winter Olympic Games, held at Chamonix in France. Held regularly at four-yearly intervals thereafter, except during World War II, these celebrations have brought skiing into the world's sporting limelight to such an extent that the names of the great skiers, especially in the spectacular

Colour Sport

Equipment

The important aspect of the skis is their length: the most suitable length is roughly equal to the height from the ground to the skier's palm when the hand is held directly overhead. Beginners may, however, find shorter skis more suitable, and many schools provide sets of graduated lengths to assist progress. During the 1960s the metal ski replaced the wooden one in the high-quality ranges, but shortly afterwards some people were working on a plastic ski. The strength and durability of the more flexible plastics being developed could provide a better form of ski. But even the plastic skis would require steel edges for protection.

The binding, which clamps the boot to the ski, normally includes a safety quick-release mechanism. Because the ski is not, of course, all that flexible, the soles of the boots should be rigid, and the uppers of stiff, thick, waterproof leather. This ensures that the feet and ankles receive sufficient support.

Ski poles are used for balance and to assist in turning, braking, and climbing. The shafts are made of metal, bamboo, or fibreglass. The small, disc-shaped 'baskets', some three inches from the pointed ends, prevent their sinking into the snow.

Technique

The essence of successful skiing—at recreational or competitive level—is in a correct distribution of weight on one ski or the other, the proper movements of the body to move the skis in any particular direction, and knowledge of the use of the edges of the skis in side-stepping uphill or side-slipping downhill.

The basic Alpine skiing technique is based largely on the *stem turn*, in which the heel of one ski (or both) is pushed outwards to change the direction of movement.

The more advanced *christiana* is a medium-to-fast swing turn. Mastery of this technique gives a skier a high degree of control, and after this the more sophisticated techniques can be learnt. Skiing skill improves rapidly with the use of the ski edges.

Nordic or cross-country skiing involves different techniques, more suited to less undulating terrain. It is becoming increasingly popular in countries better known for Alpine skiing. The basic equipment is different: cross-country skis are longer and narrower, and the bindings allow more heel movement. The Nordic technique, which is more like walking—though more energy-sapping—is based on a long, rhythmic stride, a pronounced arm swing, and use of the longer poles to give added propulsion.

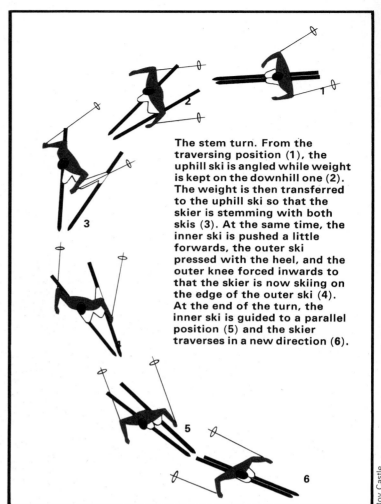

The stem turn. From the traversing position (1), the uphill ski is angled while weight is kept on the downhill one (2). The weight is then transferred to the uphill ski so that the skier is stemming with both skis (3). At the same time, the inner ski is pushed a little forwards, the outer ski pressed with the heel, and the outer knee forced inwards to that the skier is now skiing on the edge of the outer ski (4). At the end of the turn, the inner ski is guided to a parallel position (5) and the skier traverses in a new direction (6).

Roy Castle

Alpine events, such as Toni Sailer and Jean-Claude Killy, have become household words even in the 'lowland' countries where skiing is not a major sport. Also, increasing interest in the sport has coincided with the setting up of fully equipped ski-centres.

1 Nordic skiing, or cross-country skiing, is based on a long rhythmic stride and a pronounced arm swing.
2 The earlier the start the better: children under tuition at Val d'Isere in the French Alps. **3** Leaving the starting gate for a downhill event.

Popperfoto

George Konig

Colour Sport

Ski Racing

The Olympic slalom course at Chamrousse, 1968, scene of Jean-Claude Killy's clean sweep.

As the man said, he was racing 'toujours à mort'. And that was why millions of televiewers sat spellbound as he hurtled down the Alpine slopes at breakneck speeds, sending snow flying as he careered through slalom gates. His name was Jean-Claude Killy; his sport—Alpine ski racing.

A relatively new sport which acquired Olympic recognition only in 1936, Alpine ski racing is now practised in more than 40 countries. As the name suggests, the sport was developed in the high terrain of the European Alps which produces far more exhilarating slopes than the more gently undulating snowfields of Scandinavia (where the established competitions in Nordic ski racing—the cross-country kind—originated).

Alpine ski racing was devised by British skiers, notably Sir Arnold Lunn, who instigated the world's first downhill race in 1911 at Montana in Switzerland. The prize was a challenge cup presented by Lord Roberts of Kandahar. Unlike present downhill races, early competitions involved racing down wide courses, with the first past the flag winning. Fortunately for the competitors, this was soon abolished in favour of the obviously safer method of timing each contestant, starting at one-minute intervals. The modern-style slalom race was first held in 1922 at Mürren, Switzerland, which in 1931 saw the first world championships in Alpine ski racing.

The world titles are now contested every two years, and the Winter Olympics every four. In non-championship seasons, the most important event is the Arlberg-Kandahar ski competition. Each season, the top skiers also compete for the World Alpine Ski Cup awards. Inaugurated in 1967, these are based on each racer's highest score in any 3 of some 15 selected top international events at different venues throughout the season. The first ten skiers in each event score 25, 20, 15, 11, 8, 6, 4, 3, 2, 1, according to their placings. This new series has become increasingly popular with both skiers and spectators, and proves the value of continuous competition.

As many of the leading skiers practically live on the slopes, they have a distinct advantage over those not resident in mountain resorts. However, the non-resident skiers do have their own exclusive competition, a special category of races classed 'citadin'. The most important annual international meeting of this kind is the Martini Kandahar Citadin, which has attracted entries from as many as 18 nations. This joint promotion stemmed from co-operation between the Kandahar Ski Club, experienced since 1924 in organizing international races, and the Martini International Club, which was formed in 1960 to sponsor and support the best kind of sporting and cultural events.

Alpine ski racing comprises downhill and slalom events, and the major championship meetings normally recognize four titles—downhill, slalom, giant slalom, and combined. The latter is academic, being calculated on a points basis to decide the best all-round performance.

Downhill courses are set with length, steepness, and degree of difficulty appropriate to the standard of competitors. The average senior championship course has a vertical descent of between 2,500 and 3,000 feet and a length varying from 1½ to 3 miles according to the nature of the terrain available.

A winner's average speed is usually between 40 and 50 mph, although Jean-Claude Killy averaged 53.93 mph at the 1968 Olympics. Skiers have exceeded 100 mph, however, on extra steep, specially prepared courses, usually to test or publicize a particular piece of equipment.

The aim of downhill racing is to cover the course from top to bottom in the quickest possible time, with freedom to select whatever route is considered most suitable. Competitors are allowed to practise on a downhill course and acquaint themselves with its characteristics before a race is due to take place.

Slalom courses are considerably shorter than downhill, and comprise a series of pairs of poles with flags, known as gates. These are carefully positioned at different angles to test the judgment, fluency of movement, power of control, and skill in turning and pace-checking rather than the sheer speed of the skier.

There are officials at each gate,

247

and a racer who misses one is disqualified unless he climbs back to pass through it. Men's world championship courses have 50 to 75 gates, and a vertical drop between 650 and 975 feet. Women's courses are shorter and less difficult.

A slalom event normally consists of two runs, either over the same course or over two different tracks, the winner being the competitor with the fastest aggregate time for both runs.

In contrast to downhill races, slalom competitors are not permitted to try the course beforehand. They have to memorize the gate positions while ascending to the starting point. The distance between the two flags of each gate should be not less than 10 feet, and the distance between gates must be at least 2 feet 6 inches. The flags are 6 feet above the snow, and each pair is distinguished by red, yellow, or blue colours.

Giant slalom courses blend characteristics of the downhill and slalom in one event. The trail is longer than the slalom and the gates are set wider and farther apart.

Should a racer lose a ski in any Alpine event he is not disqualified if able to finish the course on the remaining ski. But a competitor is not permitted to descend any part of the course ski-less. Nor is 'stick-riding', holding both hands on the same stick, or 'tobogganing', deliberately slithering down on part of the body, allowed.

There is extremely keen rivalry among ski manufacturers and, aided by highly scientific research and the finest precision instruments, they have produced ever-improving equipment for the present-day racer. This, in turn, has improved the equipment for the ordinary skiing enthusiast.

But while the latter normally uses one all-purpose pair of skis, the top-class racer requires a diff-

World downhill and combined champion in 1962, Karl Schranz of Austria has been in the forefront of world skiing since 1957.

George König

Olympic Champions

Men Venue	Downhill	Slalom	Giant Slalom	Combined	Women Venue	Downhill	Slalom	Giant Slalom	Combined
1936 Garmisch				Franz Pfnur (Germany)	1936 Garmisch				Christel Cranz (Germany)
1948 St Moritz	Henri Oreiller (France)	Edi Reinalter (Switzerland)		Henri Oreiller (France)	1948 St. Moritz	Hedy Schlunegger (Switzerland)	Gretchen Frazer (USA)		Trude Beiser (Austria)
1952 Oslo	Zeno Colo (Italy)	Othmar Schneider (Austria)	Stein Eriksen (Norway)		1952 Oslo	Trude Beiser (Austria)	Andrea Lawrence (USA)	Andrea Lawrence (USA)	
1956 Cortina	Toni Sailer (Austria)	Toni Sailer (Austria)	Toni Sailer (Austria)		1956 Cortina	Madeleine Berthod (Switzerland)	Renee Colliard (Switzerland)	Ossi Reichert (Germany)	
1960 Squaw Valley	Jean Vuarnet (France)	Ernst Hinterseer (Austria)	Roger Staub (Switzerland)		1960 Squaw Valley	Heidi Biebl (Germany)	Anne Heggtveit (Canada)	Yvonne Ruegg (Switzerland)	
1964 Innsbruck	Egon Zimmermann (Austria)	Josef Stiegler (Austria)	Francois Bonlieu (France)		1964 Innsbruck	Christl Haas (Austria)	Christine Goitschel (France)	Marielle Goitschel (France)	
1968 Chamrousse	Jean-Claude Killy (France)	Jean-Claude Killy (France)	Jean-Claude Killy (France)		1968 Chamrousse	Olga Pall (Austria)	Marielle Goitschel (France)	Nancy Greene (Canada)	
1972 Sapporo	Bernhard Russi (Switzerland)	Francisco Fernandez-Ochoa (Spain)	Gustavo Thoeni (Italy)		1972 Sapporo	Marie-Therese Nadig (Switzerland)	Barbara Cochran (USA)	Marie-Therese Nadig (Switzerland)	

World Alpine Ski Cup

Men				Women			
	1967 Jean-Claude Killy (France)	1971 Gustavo Thoeni (Italy)			1967 Nancy Greene (Canada)	1971 Annamarie Proel (Austria)	
	1968 Jean-Claude Killy (France)	1972 Gustavo Thoeni (Italy)			1968 Nancy Greene (Canada)	1972 Annamarie Proel (Austria)	
	1969 Karl Schranz (Austria)	1973 Gustavo Thoeni (Italy)			1969 Gertrud Gabl (Austria)	1973 Annamarie Moser-Proel (Austria)	
	1970 Karl Schranz (Austria)	1974 Piero Gros (Italy)			1970 Michelle Jacot (France)	1974 Annamarie Moser-Proel (Austria)	

George Konig

Colour Sport

Colour Sport

George Konig

erent, highly specialized type of blade for each of the downhill, slalom, and giant slalom events. Similarly, the choice of ski wax for the racer has developed into a very fine art. The racer has to choose the correct wax to suit prevailing snow conditions and temperature, and the correct choice, plus the amount of wax applied to the underneath of the skis, can make a vital difference to his time.

The newcomer to Alpine ski racing is quite likely to be bewildered when he goes to buy his equipment. Confronting him may be a glistening forest of skis in every colour of the rainbow and every permutation of wood, metal, and plastic. He will have a staggering choice of safety toe-release and heel-release gadgets, boots with laces or clips, sticks to aid balance, and a range of accessories from ski wax in aerosol cans to goggles with adjustable ventilation. One item he should not have too much difficulty choosing is the protective helmet. It is a compulsory part of every racer's kit.

Like equipment, techniques have also changed over the years. Although the early racing techniques were developed and advanced in Switzerland, Austria, and France, modern styles are based on an international blend of the best. Gone are the days when the tourist promoters from leading racing nations could attract more holiday skiers in the belief that their national ski schools must be the best.

The French tendency to dominate Alpine ski racing in the mid-1960s was a triumph for the modern technique advocated by Honoré Bonnet, the French team manager. The style he adopted was not entirely that handed down by successful fellow countrymen like Emile Allais, Henri Oreiller, and Jean Vuarnet. For eight years,

Bonnet meticulously studied technique in Austria, and much of what he learnt there was incorporated in a revised system which most countries have adapted in varying degrees. Characteristics are a pronounced forward lean from the waist coupled with a hip-swinging 'wedeln' style.

The French have not always dominated, though, and championships have usually been shared among the Alpine nations. In fact, it was not until 1952, 21 years after the first world championships, that a title was won by someone not representing an Alpine nation. That year, Stein Eriksen won the giant slalom for Norway, and two years later he won the slalom, giant slalom, and combined. His victories helped give the Alpine racing events a much wider following than the Nordic racing which had previously been dominant.

In 1956, Toni Sailer of Austria won all three Olympic Alpine events by impressive margins, and was hailed as the most brilliant and daring exponent of Alpine racing yet seen. His feat was not equalled until 1968, when, at Chamrousse, Jean-Claude Killy climaxed a career which for three years had spearheaded France's bid for world supremacy. Before and during the 'Killy' period, Marielle Goitschel led an outstanding group of French women racers.

The longest career of distinction is that of the Austrian Karl Schranz, whose remarkable series of world, Olympic, Arlberg-Kandahar, and World Cup successes spanned 13 seasons from 1957. The German girl, Christel Cranz, won the greatest number of world titles, 12 in all—4 slalom, 3 downhill, and 5 combined—between 1934 and 1939. Sailer won most

1 Jean-Claude Killy, world Alpine ski champion in 1966 and 1968, won all three Olympic events in the latter year.
2 British stars Divina Galica, *left,* and Gina Hathorn. As 'lowlanders' they did very well in the 1966 and 1968 world championships.
3 A view of the Bernese Oberland, showing the steepness of a slalom course.
4 Marielle Goitschel of France won six world titles in the 1960s.

men's world titles, 7, and these in just two seasons, 1956 and 1958.

As with so many sports, British pioneers were initially prominent. Esmé Mackinnon was the first women's world champion in both downhill and slalom, and Evie Pinching later won the downhill and combined titles. But since then no Briton has won a major title, although in the 1968 Olympics Gina Hathorn was fourth in the slalom, only three-hundredths of a second from the bronze medal, and she was placed seventh in the world combined rating. British skiers, however, are hampered by geographical handicaps which restrict the amount of snow time available for training.

The sport is governed by the International Ski Federation, best known by its French initials, FIS, and has 47 member nations. Among these are Australia and New Zealand, where racing facilities have improved rapidly, attracting a number of European and American coaches. Thus, by 'following the snow', these coaches are able to instruct nearly all the year round, and this trend among leading skiers looks likely to create, as in tennis, an almost continuous international circuit for the stars of the future.

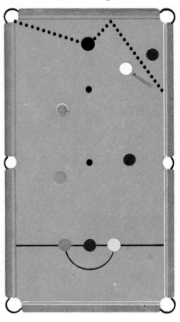

Ray Green

Below, **The crucial shot in Joe Davis' maximum break of 147 was the 14th red. Having taken the first 13 reds and 12 blacks, Davis attempted to get a position to pot the 14th red in the top pocket. His intention (diagram 1) was to pot the black and stun the cue-ball off the side cushion to leave a short pot. But he struck the cue-ball too low and finished the wrong side of**

the red. The break seemed to be at an end, but Davis summoned up all his nerve to bring off a remarkable pot, sending the red some 10 feet at the narrowest of angles into the baulk pocket (diagram 2). At the same time, he left himself an angle to pot the black again and travel down for the last red. He then proceeded to pot the black and clear the colours for his record break.

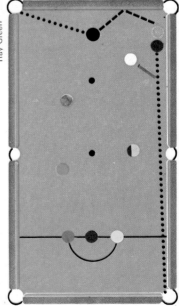

Snooker

The most popular cue-and-ball game in Britain, snooker has five times as many adherents as billiards. But snooker was a very minor sport until the late 1920s, and would probably still be virtually unknown but for the efforts of one man—billiards champion Joe Davis.

Before Davis came on the scene, few people had even heard of the game, and its origin is still vague. The earliest snooker reference mentions British army officers playing a form of the game in late 19th century India, and in 1900 the Billiards Association published a set of snooker rules. An English amateur championship began in 1916, but the game did not enter the professional billiards ranks until the 1920s—and then in a very humble capacity. When a billiards session finished early, the players would sometimes indulge in a couple of frames of crude knockabout snooker as light relief to the serious business of billiards.

Only Joe Davis saw the potential mass appeal of the game. Singlehanded, he developed the complex positional strategies and techniques of the modern snooker game, and threw his weighty talent for business and publicity behind the sport. Pushed by

Snooker is more than potting balls: it is the execution of chess-like calculations.

Davis, the ruling authority of the billiards table, the Billiards Association and Control Council (BACC), held the first world snooker championship in 1927. Davis won it, defeating T. A. Dennis 20 frames to 11. He retained the world title for a further 20 years before relinquishing it in 1947 to concentrate on exhibition play.

Davis was given some close matches during his long unbroken reign, especially by the Australian Horace Lindrum, who went down 32-29 in 1937, and by his younger

brother, Fred Davis, who lost 37-36 in 1940. Fred was, in fact, the only player to defeat his brother on level terms in a week's match in the 1950s. After Joe's retirement, Fred fought out five consecutive world snooker finals with Scotland's Walter Donaldson. He won three, although Donaldson's superb long potting and vice-like safety play thwarted him in 1947 and 1950.

In 1952 a dispute over terms between the professionals and the BACC split the billiard-table world. The professionals formed a breakaway ruling body called the Professional Billiard Players Association, which ran championships won by Fred Davis and former amateur champion John Pulman. By 1964, however, the breach was healed, and the championship again came under the control of the Billiards Association. Pulman retained the title until 1969.

With public interest now running at a record level, the professional game attracted the greatest influx of newcomers since the war.

One of them, John Spencer, English amateur champion in 1966, became a popular champion in 1969. The appeal of his game came from its all-out attacking style, marked by prodigious potting and screwing ability. Ray Reardon—another new recruit to the professional ranks—took the title the following year, but Spencer regained it in Australia in November 1970 with a brilliant display that included three centuries in four frames.

Although snooker has become an extremely popular sport in Australia, South Africa, New Zealand, India, Pakistan, Canada, Ceylon, Malta, and elsewhere, Britain has continued to dominate it on both amateur and professional levels. However, Australia's Eddie Charlton gave Pulman a close match, 39-34, for the professional title in 1968, and recorded a unique feat in 1967 by clearing the table with breaks of 135 and 137 in consecutive frames without allowing his opponents a single shot. Another Australian, Warren Simpson, beat leading players

1 Joe Davis advances to a break of 146, one off maximum, in 1950. Five years later he achieved the ultimate.
2 John Spencer, 1969 world professional champion, in play against runner-up Gary Owen.
3 Snooker is by no means a male preserve. **4** Former world champion Fred Davis tries the now illegal jumping shot.

Pulman, Gary Owen, and Charlton to reach the November 1970 final before going down to an inspired Spencer.

The standard of snooker has improved immensely since the 1930s. Century breaks, very rare in the 1930s, have become relatively commonplace among both professionals and the top amateurs. Joe Davis made 687 century breaks before his retirement from public engagements in 1965, with a world record of 147 in 1955 as the pinnacle of his achievements. This, the first time a player had potted 15 reds, 15 blacks, and all the colours, was the game's first maximum break. It was a record equalled by British professional Rex Williams in South Africa in 1965, but it is one that can never be beaten.

In November 1970 the professionals again split from the BACC and formed the World Professional Billiards and Snooker Association. They have complete autonomy over the professional game, but the amateurs remain under the control of the Billiards Association, which changed its name from BACC to the Billiards and Snooker Association Control Council in January 1971.

The Billiards Association had instituted a world amateur snooker championship in Calcutta in 1963. Birmingham fireman Gary Owen won it, retained the title in Karachi in 1966, then

Ray Green

Equipment and Rules

Snooker is played on the 12 ft. by 6 ft. 1½ in. English billiards table and with the standard billiards equipment (see article on BILLIARDS). Most games are between two players, although any number can take part, either as individuals or as part of a team. A set of 22 balls—1 white cue-ball, 15 reds, and 6 colours (yellow, green, brown, blue, pink, and black)—is used.

At the start of the game the *black* is placed on the *billiard* spot (12¾ in. from the mid-point of the top cushion), the *pink* on the *pyramid spot* (midway between the centre spot and the top cushion), the *blue* on the *centre spot,* and the *yellow, brown* and *green* on the *baulk spots,* from right to left. The 15 *reds* are arranged in a 'pyramid' by means of a triangular wooden frame, with the red ball at its apex as near as possible to the pink without touching it after the frame has been removed. Behind that red is a row of 2 reds and further rows of 3, 4, and 5. The cue-ball may be placed anywhere in the 'D' for the first stroke of the game, but after that it must be played from wherever it comes to rest.

Points are scored by *potting*—knocking an object-ball into a pocket with the cue-ball—or by *penalties.* Each player must first attempt to strike a red and, preferably, pot it. This scores 1 point, and gives the player the option of attempting to pot one of the 6 coloured balls—black (value 7), pink (6), blue (5), brown (4), green (3), or yellow (2). The player must nominate the ball he is aiming for, although in fact this rule is enforced only when the choice of colour is not obvious. After potting a colour, the player then has to pot another red before he can nominate another colour. And at each separate turn at the table he must start with a red. Potted red balls remain out of play, but when a colour is sunk it is returned to the table (on its spot) until all the reds have been sunk. (If a colour's own spot is occupied, it is respotted on the highest spot available, or, failing that, as near as possible to its own spot in direct line between the spot and the top cushion.) When all the reds have been potted, yellow, green, brown, blue, pink, and black are potted in rotation.

Failure to strike a red carries a penalty of 4 points—or 5, 6, or 7 respectively if the blue, pink, or black is struck first instead. An *in-off*—inadvertent sinking of the cue-ball—is a foul carrying a penalty of 4 points (or more if the ball struck is of higher value) in favour of the non-striker. (After the cue-ball has been sunk, the opposing player restarts from the 'D'). Failure to strike a nominated colour carries a penalty of 4 points or the value of the ball nominated if it is higher. The potting of a ball not 'on', whether or not it is struck first, is a foul, with a penalty of 4 points or the value of the ball potted if it is higher. If more than one foul is committed at the same time, only one (the highest) is counted. For example, if the cue-ball goes in-off a red (the ball 'on') and the pink also finishes up in a pocket, the penalty is 6 points.

Penalties may be due to the offender's lack of skill or to bad luck, but many are also the result of skilfully laid *snookers.* A snooker is a situation of the balls that prevents a player striking directly the ball he is due to strike at. For example, a player is snookered on the reds if a colour intervenes between the cue-ball and the reds in such a way that the cue-ball can strike the reds only by means of a swerve shot or off a cushion (jump shots are no longer legal). A snooker may earn points, but this becomes its primary purpose only in the later stages of a game (or *frame*), when the margin between the two scores is greater than the total value of the remaining balls. Otherwise, the main purpose of the snooker is to force one's opponent into leaving a good opening.

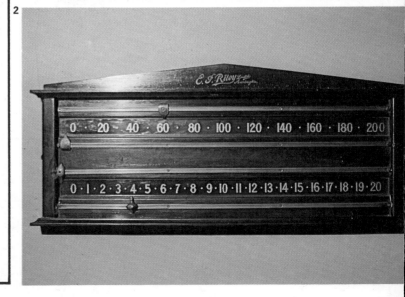

Above, English world snooker champion John Spencer and an old friend—his cheap and crooked cue. Together they won the world title in 1968 and 1970. Spencer's superb attacking style helped to make the sport even more popular in the late 1960s.
1 The referee or the marker sets up the balls for a snooker frame. He uses a wooden pyramid to place the 15 reds close to the pink, without actually touching it.
2 The snooker scoreboard—adjusted by the marker in formal games—records the point-by-point progress of the two players or teams.
3 Unable to hit the white cue-ball where he wants to, this player has been forced to use the spider rest.

3

Ray Green

Techniques

Stance, grip, and the basic techniques of *screw*, *stun*, and *side* are exactly the same in snooker as in billiards, although a snooker *break*—a sequence of scoring shots—is compiled through potting alone. Billiards breaks are compiled through a combination of potting, in-offs, and cannons. To compile a snooker break calls for a combination of potting ability, positional play involving manoeuvring the cue ball in such a way that following pots are as easy as possible, and a clear enough brain to plot these chess-like sequences.

One snooker shot rarely needed in billiards is the *swerve*, which may be used to get out of a snooker, but only if there is some distance between the cue ball, the intervening ball, and the ball 'on'. A player imparts swerve by raising his bridge (the hand he rests the cue on), lifting the butt of the cue, and striking the cue-ball a short, sharp stroke on the side to which he requires to swerve it.

Technique with the *spider* rest is a valuable snooker requisite, as this instrument, which is rarely needed in billiards, is often employed in snooker, where the cue-ball is likely to finish up in an inaccessible position. It is used when another ball is behind and so close to the cue-ball that the player cannot strike the cue-ball where he wants to, even with an elevated bridge. He must be careful to avoid touching any balls with the spider either when placing it near the cue ball or when removing it from the table.

Glossary of Terms

Angled A player is angled if he finds the cue ball in the jaws of a pocket after an opponent's foul and he cannot play the ball 'on'. He has the choice of a **free ball** or he may play from hand (and still claim a free ball if he is snookered).

Ball 'on' The ball to be played by the cue-ball.

Break A sequence of scoring shots.

Break off The first shot of a frame in which the striker contacts the unbroken triangle of reds.

Clear-the-table A sequence of shots that pots all the balls left on the table.

Colours The six object balls other than the reds—yellow, green, brown, blue, pink, black.

Cue-Ball The white ball.

Double A ball that enters a pocket after striking one or more cushions.

Frame A game.

Free ball If a player is snookered after a foul shot by his opponent he may nominate any coloured ball as a red or as the ball 'on'. If the nominated ball is potted as a red he scores 1, and then can nominate a colour in the normal way. If all the reds have left the table, the free ball is valued at the same number of points as the lowest-valued ball on the table and the colours are then taken in sequence. It is a foul not to hit the nominated ball, even if the ball originally 'on' is struck instead. A player is held to be snookered under the free-ball rule if he cannot hit both extremities of the object ball directly, unless, in the case of the reds, it is partially obscured by another red. It is a foul to leave a snooker behind the ball that has been nominated as a free ball.

Marker The official in charge of the scoreboard.

Maximum break A sequence of shots in which a player pots all 15 reds, 15 blacks and all the colours to score 147.

On the black When there are fewer than 7 points between the players and only the black is left on the table, the game is said to be **on the black**. In this case, when the black is potted or there is a foul (one player misses the black or goes in-off) the game is over. If there are exactly 7 points between the players and a pot or a foul brings the scores level, the black is respotted and the cue ball played from hand. The players toss for first strike (it is usual to ask one's opponent to restart).

Plant A position in which the first object-ball is played against the second object-ball in such a way as to make the second ball enter the pocket.

Play from hand Play from the D.

Pyramid The 15 reds as arranged at the start of a game in triangular formation.

Referee The official who controls the game, giving rulings, resetting the balls, calling the scores, etc.

Safety shot A shot made with the intention not of scoring, but of leaving the opponent unable to score.

Set A position in which two object balls are touching in such a way that the second ball is certain to be potted no matter how the first object-ball is struck.

Shot to nothing A shot in which a player attempts to pot in such a way as to leave himself in a position to continue his break if successful, and to leave the cue-ball in a bad position for his opponent if unsuccessful.

Snooker A position in which the cue-ball cannot hit an object-ball directly because of an intervening ball.

turned professional. Other English players succeeded him as champion. David Taylor, who later turned professional, won in Sydney in 1968, and Jonathan Barron took the 1970 Edinburgh championship.

The English Amateur Championship remains the leading British event, but in spite of the many pockets of intense local interest the Billiards Association has found it surprisingly difficult to promote other competitions on a national level. The British Junior (under 19) and boys (under 16) championships have become permanent events, but a national team championship and national pairs championship were both discontinued, partly through lack of finance. On the other hand, the initiative of the Welsh Association led to the first of a home international series at Port Talbot in June 1969.

Rex Williams prepares to break off. In 1965, he compiled the maximum break of 147, so equalling Joe Davis's 1955 record.

Fotosports International

WORLD PROFESSIONAL SNOOKER CHAMPIONSHIP

Year	Winner	Runner-up	Final Score (Frames)
1927	J. Davis	T. Dennis	20-11
1928	J. Davis	F. Lawrence	16-13
1929	J. Davis	T. Dennis	19-14
1930	J. Davis	T. Dennis	25-12
1931	J. Davis	T. Dennis	25-21
1932	J. Davis	C. McConachy	30-19
1933	J. Davis	W. Smith	25-18
1934	J. Davis	T. Newman	25-23
1935	J. Davis	W. Smith	25-20
1936	J. Davis	H. Lindrum	34-27
1937	J. Davis	H. Lindrum	32-29
1938	J. Davis	S. Smith	37-24
1939	J. Davis	S. Smith	43-30
1940	J. Davis	F. Davis	37-36
1941-45	*no contest*		
1946	J. Davis	H. Lindrum	78-67
1947	W. Donaldson	F. Davis	82-63
1948	F. Davis	W. Donaldson	84-61
1949	F. Davis	W. Donaldson	80-65
1950	W. Donaldson	F. Davis	51-46
1951	F. Davis	W. Donaldson	58-39
1952*	H. Lindrum	C. McConachy	94-49
1964†	J. Pulman	F. Davis	19-16
1964†	J. Pulman	R. Williams	40-33
1965†	J. Pulman	F. Davis	37-36
1965†	J. Pulman	R. Williams	25-22‡
1966†	J. Pulman	F. Davis	5-2‡
1968†	J. Pulman	E. Charlton	39-34
1969	J. Spencer	G. Owen	37-24
1970	R. Reardon	J. Pulman	37-33
1970	J. Spencer	W. Simpson	37-29
1972	A. Higgins	J. Spencer	37-32
1973	R. Reardon	E. Charlton	38-32
1974	R. Reardon	G. Miles	22-12

*Only two entrants owing to a dispute between the professionals and the BACC, which led to the abandonment of the championship until 1964, when it was reformed on a challenge basis
†Challenge system
‡Matches, not frames

WORLD AMATEUR SNOOKER CHAMPIONSHIP

Year	Venue	Winner (country)	Runner-up (country)
1963	Calcutta	G. Owen (England)	F. Harris (Australia)
1966	Karachi	G. Owen (England)	J. Spencer (England)
1968	Sydney	D. Taylor (England)	M. Williams (Australia)
1970	Edinburgh	J. Barron (England)	S. Hood (England)
1972	Cardiff	R. Edmonds (England)	M. Franscisco (South Africa)

Soccer

Eight hundred million people are estimated to have watched the 1970 World Cup final on television. There could be no more impressive or alarming evidence that soccer is the world's most popular spectator sport, not to mention its most popular team game. Though North America has remained largely immune to it, its scope and sweep are astonishing. In Britain, where it began, crowds of 130,000 and more can attend Scotland-England matches in Glasgow, and Wembley could usually fill its 100,000 capacity stadium five times over for the FA Cup final; in Rio, 120,000 crowds are common at the Maracana Stadium, which absorbed nearly 200,000 for the decisive World Cup match of 1950 between Brazil and Uruguay; the Aztec Stadium in Mexico City has crowds of 105,000 and more, and the Lenin Stadium in Moscow has seen attendances of 100,000; 90,000 crowds have frequently been known in the Roman Olympic Stadium, and San Siro, in Milan, and the Stadio Comunale, in Turin, have taken over 80,000.

The passions aroused by the game are infinite and even lethal. On May 24, 1964, when Peru played Argentina in Lima and a goal was disallowed, the riot that followed led to over 300 deaths and 500 injuries. In Brazil, the crowd has been known to set fire to stadiums. And Glasgow has known violence and tragedy at Rangers-Celtic matches since early in the century; in January 1971, 66 people died at Ibrox Park on a dangerous exit stairway.

In Buenos Aires, the use of tear gas by the police to quell disturbances on the terraces has long been almost commonplace, while in Italy, one hears all too frequently of referees being besieged in their dressing-room after a home team has lost. In one case, at Naples—always notorious for crowd violence—a referee actually prolonged the game and contrived to award Naples a questionable penalty so that they could win.

The future of the game, however, is guaranteed for decades to come by its astonishing popularity among the young of Europe and Latin America, its increasing vogue among boys in North America and Japan, and its emergence in Africa. Television and newspapers in Europe and South America are saturated with reports and news of professional football. Players such as Pele, in Brazil, and George Best, in Britain, can earn immense sums, both inside and outside the game, and in Italy the market is so healthy that one player cost £440,000, while a moderately good one will change clubs for £250,000.

The reasons for this frenetic popularity are obscure. Probably they have something to do with the fact that soccer is at once a very simple and very dramatic game, with that fine consummation—the ball hitting the back of the net—its equivalent of bullfighting's 'moment of truth'. But though it is an easy game to follow and comprehend, it is at the same time a complex and subtle one that lends itself to infinite disagreement and analysis. Professionalism came naturally to it, because people were prepared to pay to watch it, and working-class boys, originally from Scotland and the North of England, saw in it a means to a good and pleasant livelihood. Today, it is the way out of the slums and trash heaps of Lima, the awful *favelhas* of Rio, and the shanty towns of Africa.

In Britain, where it began, the pendulum swung away from the university and public school men who initiated it, with the sport turning into a working-class game administered by the middle class. Abroad things were different, and such distinguished writers as De Montherlant, Camus, and Giraudoux played and wrote about the game. In Britain the pendulum has swung again, and the sport is now followed, played, and celebrated by writers, actors, and intellectuals. It remains, however, very much the favourite of the 'man in the street'.

Arsenal and Liverpool fans present a cheerful picture before the 1971 Cup Final, later won by the Gunners.

History of Soccer

The origins of soccer, otherwise association football, are at once readily accessible and profoundly obscure. Accessible, because we know very well how it began in the late 19th century, when the various public schools, all playing their own different codes, eventually formulated a unified set of rules, splitting with the handling devotees in 1863. But speculation on the origin of the game can be protracted indefinitely. Since kicking a ball, even if it be the wickerwork ball that was favoured in ancient China, is a simple human activity, claims can be made for the origin of the sport in Ancient Rome, Japan, Greece, or China.

It may well be that the first international matches were played between the Chinese and the Japanese. The Munich Ethnological Museum contains a text written by Li Ju, who lived about 50 BC, which mentions games between Chinese and Japanese, playing their respective codes. There are records indicating that in 1004 BC the Japanese played a football game of a sort on a tiny field, delineated by trees at each corner. The Chinese had a game in which a leather ball (filled, allegedly, with female hair) was kicked, and it is certain that in the ancient Japanese capital of Kyoto a football game was played in AD 611. Among the Ancient Greeks, the ball game of *episciro* was very popular. Rome adapted it, as it took so many Greek things, calling it *harpastum*. Caesar is said to have played it, once winning 50 talents in a contest with Cecilius; Virgil and Horace knew and disapproved of it; Ovid advised women against playing it. It was, in fact, a robust sport, in which the object was to win the ball from all one's opponents. The Roman legions may well have brought it to Britain, and legend has it that a British team beat a legionary one in a famous victory of AD 276. Certainly a rough kind of football had taken root by the Middle Ages—much to the displeasure of a succession of kings, who wanted the peasantry to apply itself to the martial arts. There is abundant documentation of this. There is a record by Fitz-Stephen to the effect that London schoolboys would play football after dinner on Shrove Tuesday. In 1314, Edward II issued his famous proclamation banning the game, with its 'hustling over large balls', in the city, with prison as the punishment for disobedience. Richard II had cause to issue a further proclamation in 1389, so clearly the game's popularity was such as to make it resilient. His complaint was that it interfered with archery practice. This Act was confirmed by Henry IV in 1401 and Henry VIII in the following century. James I of Scotland condemned it, but in 1497 James IV's High Treasurer is known to have purchased two

Calendar of Events

1846	First soccer rules formulated at Cambridge University
1857	Sheffield, the oldest football club still in existence, founded
1862	Notts County, the oldest Football League club, came into being
1863	Football Association founded at Freemasons Tavern, Great Queen Street, on October 26
1867	Queen's Park, the oldest Scottish club, founded
1871	FA Cup introduced
1872	First official England-Scotland match at Glasgow, with Scotland represented by 11 Queen's Park players
1873	Scottish FA formed: Scottish Cup inaugurated
1876	Welsh FA formed; Wales play first international, against Scotland
1878	Referee's whistle introduced to replace handkerchief
1879	Cliftonville, oldest Irish club, founded; England first play Wales
1882	Ireland first play England and Wales; England won 13-0 (still Home International record) in Belfast
1884	With Scotland playing Ireland, the Home International Championship was born
1885	Professionalism legalized in England
1885	Arbroath beat Bon Accord 36-0 in the Scottish Cup, the record score for a first-class game in Britain
1886	International Caps awarded for the first time
1887	Preston North End beat Hyde 26-0 in FA Cup, the record for a first-class game in England
1888	Football League formed with 12 clubs
1889	Preston win the FA Cup without conceding a goal and the Football League title without losing a game
1889	Dutch FA, the oldest outside Britain, formed
1890	Irish League formed
1891	Scottish League formed
1892	Goal-nets used for the first time in the cup final, between WBA and Aston Villa
1892	Second Division of the Football League started with 14 clubs
1893	FA Amateur Cup inaugurated
1894	Corinthians supply whole England side against Wales at Wrexham, and win 5-1
1895	Argentina and Chile first South American countries to form governing bodies
1897	Aston Villa become the second club to do the 'double' of League and Cup
1898	Players Union formed (now the Professional Footballers Association)
1901	Tottenham Hotspur, then of the Southern League, take the FA Cup to London for the first time
1902	25 people die after the collapse of terracing during the Scotland-England match at Ibrox Park
1902	Austria beat Hungary 5-1 at Vienna in the first full international played between non-British sides
1904	Federation Internationale de Football Association (FIFA) founded in Paris
1905	The first £1,000 transfer: Alf Common moves from Sunderland to Middlesbrough
1905	Argentina draw 1-1 with Uruguay in first South American international
1906	England join FIFA
1907	Wales win the home international tournament for the first time
1908	England play their first match against foreign opposition, beating Austria 6-1 in Vienna
1908	Football introduced to the Olympics, in London; the United Kingdom beat Denmark in final
1910	Scotland, Wales, and Ireland join FIFA
1912	United Kingdom again beat Denmark in Olympic final, at Stockholm
1915	Football League and FA Cup suspended for the duration of World War I, but Scottish League continues
1923	Bolton Wanderers beat West Ham United in the first Wembley cup final, watched by crowd of over 150,000
1925	Offside law altered from three to two defenders between attacker and goal
1926	Huddersfield Town become the first club to win a hat-trick of League Championships
1927	Cardiff City beat Arsenal to take the FA Cup out of England for the first time
1928	British associations leave FIFA owing to dispute over definition of amateurism
1928	Everton's 'Dixie' Dean scores record 60 goals, in 39 League matches
1928	Uruguay retain their Olympic title by beating Argentina in Amsterdam
1928	The first £10,000 transfer: David Jack moves from Bolton Wanderers to Arsenal for £10,890
1929	England lose their first match on foreign soil, going down 4-3 to Spain in Madrid
1930	13 nations enter for the first World Cup; the hosts, Uruguay, beat Argentina in the final
1931	West Bromwich Albion win the FA Cup and promotion from Division II
1932	Motherwell win the Scottish League after 27 years of domination by Rangers and Celtic
1934	Hosts again win the World Cup, Italy beating Czechoslovakia in Rome
1934	England (with 7 Arsenal players) beat Italy (with 9 World Cup medal winners) 3-2 at Highbury
1935	Arsenal emulate Huddersfield by winning third successive League Championship
1936	Steve Bloomer's aggregate of 352 League goals passed by Dean, who eventually finished with 379
1937	British record crowd of 149,547 see the Scotland-England match at Hampden Park
1938	Jimmy McGrory of Celtic retires after scoring 550 goals in first-class football
1938	Italy retain World Cup, beating Hungary in Paris
1939	Numbered shirts made compulsory in Football League matches
1939	Official British competitions suspended for the duration of World War II
1946	British associations rejoin FIFA
1946	33 killed and over 400 injured at Bolton during FA Cup match with Stoke City
1948	Stanley Matthews voted first Footballer of the Year by the Football Writers Association
1949	Aircraft carrying Torino, the Italian League champions, crashed near Turin, killing 8 full internationals
1949	Rangers become first to win the Scottish League, Cup, and League Cup in the same season
1949	England lose their unbeaten home record to foreign sides, losing 2-0 to Eire at Goodison Park
1950	Uruguay win the World Cup by beating Brazil at Rio in front of world record crowd of 199,854; England, in their first competition, lose to the United States and Spain
1950	Scotland lose their unbeaten home record to foreign sides, losing 1-0 to Austria at Hampden Park
1952	Billy Wright passes Bob Crompton's England record of 42 caps
1953	Stan Mortensen scores the first FA Cup final hat-trick at Wembley, and Blackpool beat Bolton 4-3
1953	Olympic champions Hungary crush England 6-3 at Wembley; the following May they win 7-1 in Budapest

Arsenal Football Club

1954	West Germany upset Hungary to win the World Cup final at Berne
1956	Real Madrid win the first European Cup final, beating Reims 4-3 in Paris
1958	Manchester United lose eight stars in the Munich air crash
1958	Sunderland the last club to hold continuous membership of the First Division, are relegated
1958	Brazil beat Sweden in Stockholm to win World Cup; England, Scotland, Wales, and Ireland had all qualified
1959	Billy Wright retires after winning 105 England caps
1959	Alfredo di Stefano is voted European Footballer of the Year for the second time
1960	Real Madrid win the European Cup for the fifth consecutive time, beating Eintracht Frankfurt 7-3 in Glasgow
1960	Russia beat Yugoslavia in Paris to win the first European Nations Cup
1961	Tottenham Hotspur become the first club to do the League and Cup double in the 20th century
1961	Fiorentina of Italy beat Glasgow Rangers to become the first holders of the European Cup Winners Cup
1961	The PFA win their fight for the abolition of the maximum wage
1962	Brazil retain the World Cup, beating Czechoslvakia in Chile
1963	The FA celebrate their centenary, and England beat the Rest of the World at Wembley
1964	Jimmy Dickinson of Portsmouth becomes the first player to make 700 League appearances
1964	Over 300 people crushed to death during a match between Peru and Argentina at Lima
1964	Spain beat the champions, Russia, to win the European Nations Cup
1965	Arthur Rowley retires, having scored a record 434 goals in the Football League
1966	England win the World Cup, beating West Germany after extra time at Wembley
1966	First £100,000 transfer between two British clubs—Alan Ball from Blackpool to Everton
1967	Celtic become the first British team to win the European Cup, beating Inter-Milan in Lisbon
1968	Manchester United keep the European Cup in Britain by beating Benfica at Wembley
1968	Pietro Anastasi transferred from Varese to Juventus for a world record £440,000
1968	Italy beat Yugoslavia in the European Championship final; England win third place
1969	Leeds United win the League Championship with a record 67 points
1969	Pele scores his 1,000th goal in first class football
1970	Martin Peters transferred from West Ham to Spurs for £200,000, including Jimmy Greaves
1970	Bobby Charlton wins his 106th cap in England's World Cup quarter-final defeat by West Germany in Mexico
1970	Brazil win their third World Cup, beating Italy in Mexico City
1971	66 people killed when crush barriers collapse at Ibrox during a league game between Rangers and Celtic
1971	Arsenal emulate Tottenham's feat of League and Cup double
1972	West Germany beat USSR in the European Championship final
1973	Bobby Moore wins a record 107th cap for England
1974	Bob Latchford transferred from Birmingham City to Everton for British record £350,000
1974	FA Amateur Cup contested for the last time

For centuries, football was no more than a disorganized street brawl, until rules were formulated in 1846.

footballs. so that the King might play football at Stirling that April. In 1572, it was the turn of Queen Elizabeth to condemn the game.

A contemporary scribe, Sir Thomas Elyot, complained that it was 'a pastime to be utterly objected by all noble men, the game giving no pleasure, but beastlie furie and violence'. Those who deplore these qualities in the game today may note that it was in them from the beginning. Stubbs, the antiquarian, was still less enamoured of it, dismissing it as 'a friendlie kind of fighting', rather than recreation, while another Elizabethan coined the memorable phrase, 'a bloody and murthering practice' in describing the football played by apprentices in the Crooked Lane, Cheapside, and Covent Garden areas.

Shrove Tuesday football grew in popularity in the North and Midlands, where large groups roamed and raged through the town or village, playing against one another, the goal being at one and the other end. In 1829, an account of such a match in Derbyshire spoke of 'broken shins, broken heads, torn coats and lost hats'. The Industrial Revolution gave a great impetus to the game, but the pitch, ball, and rules continued to vary from place to place.

1 Perhaps it was this sort of behaviour by football players that led to the game's being officially discouraged in the Middle Ages and Tudor times in England and Scotland. But it survived.
2 'Calcio' the Florentine branch of football, was played between two teams sponsored by their royal masters. Betting was heavy.
3 'Indiens jouent au ballon avec le pied': the simplicity of the game of football has given it universal appeal through the ages.
4 International football arrived officially in 1872 when Scotland played England in Glasgow, the game being a 0-0 draw.

It was the public schools who domesticated this rough sport, as they did so much else. Eton, Harrow, Winchester, Charterhouse, Rugby, and Cheltenham all had their own special codes, which blended when their boys went to Oxford and Cambridge. Eton gave the game its conception of offside—which they typically called 'sneaking'—and also initiated the practice of changing ends at half-time, rather than at every goal; at Harrow, the goals stood 150 yards apart, the clear precursor of the rugby try-line; Cheltenham originated the throw-in from touch, the word 'offside', and the crossbar—though for many years soccer goals made do with tapes.

In 1862, matters came almost to a head when a Mr. J. C. Thring, from Uppingham School, drew up a code of 10 rules called 'The Simplest Game', which was believed to have had its origins at Cambridge University. Hands could still be used, but only to stop the ball; goals were scored when forced between the posts and under the bar or tape, but not when thrown; when the ball was kicked out of play, the 'offender' had to return it into play, in an undeviatingly straight line. But one rule at least had more to do with rugby—a player in front of the ball was 'out of play'.

The following year soccer and rugby split, soccer gaining its name when a famous centre-half, Charles Wreford-Brown, was asked in his Oxford rooms whether he was that day playing rugger. No, he replied facetiously, he was playing 'soccer', an evident play on the word 'association'.

The rugby men wanted to retain hacking (the unpleasant habit of kicking an opponent's shins) the soccer people did not. So, in a meeting at the Freemasons' Tavern in Great Queen Street, London, the Football Association was born.

Under the early rules the field could be 200 yards long, but there was no minimum width. Goalposts already stood 8 yards apart, though there was no provision for tape or bar. There was to be no hacking and no running with the ball. The early clubs, such as the Wanderers, had a strong public schools basis and bias. Many of their players, and those of such successful teams as the Royal Engineers, were from Eton. But it was an Old Harrovian, C. W. Alcock, who in 1870 became a dynamic secretary of the FA, using his memories of the Harrovian Cock House tournament to initiate the FA Cup in October 1871.

By now there was a maximum length of 200 yards, a maximum width of 100, and the goals had tapes. Emphasis was on dribbling, possession, and individualism. But the Scots, led by the fine Queen's Park amateur team from Glasgow, initiated the passing game and changed the whole pattern of football.

It was from Scotland, too, that most of the first disguised professionals, traditionally finding their money in their boots, came south to Blackburn and Preston in the 1880s, when the balance tipped away from the public school teams. In 1885, after intense debate, the FA wisely legalized professionalism. In 1888 the Football League was founded by William McGregor, a Scot transplanted to Birmingham, and the professional clubs had an economic context in which to operate.

From that time the game never looked back. Europe soon followed Britain—Austria played Hungary in 1902—and in 1904 Belgium, France, the Netherlands, Spain, Sweden, and Switzerland founded FIFA. By World War I many European countries had national league competitions, and soccer was firmly established in South America. Since then the story has been one of constant growth, both as a spectator and as a participant sport.

The International Scene

International soccer is inevitably overshadowed by the quadriennial World Cup. Initiated in 1930, it grew slowly in stature, but by the 1950s was big enough to withstand the challenge of international club competitions and the reluctance of clubs to release players for internationals.

The World Cup has been won, in its first nine series, by only five countries, all of which are European or South American. Though North Korea beat Italy and almost upset Portugal in 1966, and though Africa supplies an increasing flow of good players to Europe, it is these two older footballing continents which continue to dominate the game.

There are two principal factors in the superiority of Europe and South America. First, soccer is the major game in almost every country, superseding such spectator sports as cycling in Belgium and Italy and bullfighting in Spain. Second, the game is highly professional, at least at the level that would produce internationals, and highly organized. (The position is complicated by the fact that the Communist bloc countries practise, but do not officially recognize, professionalism, and for years have kept up the pretence that their best players are primarily soldiers, students, or factory workers, though it would clearly be impossible to maintain such high standard if they were.)

It is the lack of organization that, more than any other factor, has restrained African football, good enough to produce talents such as Benfica's Coluna and Eusebio (from Mozambique), and St Etienne's Keita (from Mali). The innovation of the 1970 World Cup, whereby for the first time both Asia and Africa were allowed one automatic qualifier, may have provided the requisite encouragement. Israel and Morocco acquitted themselves well, even if Israel failed to scale the heights achieved in 1966 by the mysterious North Koreans (who had this time withdrawn on political grounds). It should also be noticed that it was an Arab country that represented Africa—further evidence that African football did not yet express the full potential of its individual abilities. It was, however, an advance for Afro-Asia on the 1966 tournament, when there had been a mass withdrawal following FIFA's decision to produce only one finalist from the two continents.

Soccer in Europe and South America has, of course, the added advantage of deeper roots. Having started in Britain, the game already had thousands of converts in Europe by World War I, while teams such as Southampton, Everton, Spurs, and the Corinthians had been on tour to South America. The war, indeed, caught Italy's Torino on tour in Argen-

Australian News and Information Bureau

Rod McLeod

Syndication International

1 11 boys from 10 different countries form this team in Perth, Australia. They have one thing in common—soccer.
2 Uwe Seeler (left) and Bobby Charlton (9) were their countries' most-capped players: by 1971 Charlton had won 106, Seeler 72.
3 The 1970 World Cup final—the ninth in a series of quadrennial showpieces of what is the best—and worst—in the world of football.

tina, and kept them in Latin America for several months.

It was the Italian mass immigration that lit the spark in Argentina at about that time, for as late as 1911 the national team consisted largely of British migrants, one of whom actually withdrew from an important match in order to play rugby. The non-involvement of Latin America in the war certainly expedited the game's progress there. Argentina and Uruguay set the pace, and Brazil, lagging at first, quickly caught up in the 1930s when black players at last became recognised, then fashionable, and eventually dominant.

FIFA—the Federation Internationale de Football Association, founded in 1904—controls its ever increasing membership (some 140) from its headquarters in Zurich. It not only controls the World Cup and the Olympic tournaments, but regulates the international movement of players; professionals cannot join a foreign club unless a transfer is duly completed with the appropriate release and fee. This avoids 'poaching', though in the late 1940s and early 1950s Argentinian players and several Britons went to earn high wages in Colombia.

From Berne, UEFA—the Union of European Football Associations, founded in 1954—controls the European Championship, competed for by its members over the two years after the World Cup, and is also in command of the European Cup (for national champions), the Cup Winners Cup (for national cup winners), and, from 1971, the European Union Cup, formerly called the Fairs Cup. In South America the countries unite under the banner of the South American Confederation, formed in 1916 and based in Peru.

Though many expensive attempts have been made to introduce professional soccer to North America, that continent has proved largely resistant to the game. In 1967 two professional leagues emerged playing in the summer. One was made up of teams of rather obscure or elderly professionals, and had no FIFA sanction; the other used established European and South American clubs to play its matches. In 1968 they merged in the insecure North American Soccer League, but the only true

London Express News & Feature Service

hope of the game's success there lies in the schools and colleges, where in the late 1960s there was a remarkable explosion in popularity. Americans, however, seem to require a game that is at once more and less continuous: that is, which is punctuated by intervals but does not have the bewildering ebb and flow of soccer. They also seem to prefer a greater measure of organization and sheer brute force.

Soccer in the Antipodes is not a particularly hardy plant, though the incessant immigration worked changes in Australia, whose national team qualified for the 1974 World Cup finals and have recorded many notable wins. Many of the best players are now native-born Australians. But though New Zealand has played the game since the 19th century, rugby union remains unchallenged and they do not even have the semi-professionalism of Australia.

Africa, whose national cup competition (started in 1958) takes place every two years, would seem to be the continent of the future, while the increasing popularity of the game in Japan, and the possible involvement of China, suggest that Asian standards will also continue to improve.

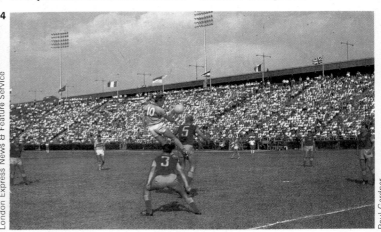

London Express News & Feature Service

Paul Gardner

1 Israel (white) beat Australia in the Asian group to qualify for the 1970 World Cup finals in Mexico City. 2 An enormous crowd, typical of those that pack South American stadiums, is entertained by a sparkling Brazil at Chile's expense. 3 The dramatic emergence of African nations in the 1960s and early 1970s could well be a portent of similar success in soccer. 4 West Ham and Dukla Prague drew the crowds when they played in New York in 1963, but later attempts at domestic competition in the United States failed. *Opposite Page.* **Bobby Moore of West Ham and England, one of the finest defensive footballers of his era. During the 1960s his name was inextricably linked with the fluctuating fortunes of the English soccer team. He played in the 1962, 1966 and 1970 World Cups and in two, 1966 and 1970, he was captain. After his triumphant leadership in the 1966 World Cup, he was voted Player of the Tournament. Cool, calm and a great leader, Moore lacks some speed and mobility, but more than compensates for these shortcomings by his unerring reading of the game and his superb tackling.**

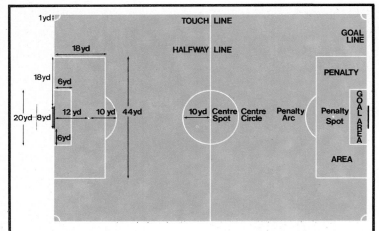

The field of play is drawn to scale for a pitch of 110 yd by 75 yd—the exact size of the pitches on which Arsenal, Bury, Coventry City, Crystal Palace, Halifax Town, Lincoln City, Liverpool, Oldham Athletic, and Swansea City play. The biggest playing area in the Football League is that of Doncaster Rovers—119 yd by 79½ yd. Pitches vary within internationally recognized limits.

Soccer, like other football codes, is a bodily contact sport. But whereas in rugby, for example, the contact is in tackling and scrummaging, in soccer contact occurs when playing the ball or by means of the approved shoulder charge. The referee has the unenviable task of making the fine distinction between what is fair play and what is foul, and also whether the foul was intentional. Nor is he helped, especially in professional football, by players who know, and are prepared to use, the devious tricks of their trade.

1 One cause for contention is the sliding tackle. In this instance, the tackler has missed the ball. The man in possession either hurdles the outstretched foot or is tripped by it. In the latter case a foul should be given and a direct free-kick awarded. **2** There are times when players give as good as they receive, and it is often difficult to distinguish between offenders. The laws state that a player must not

How the Game is Played

A bodily contact sport—something important to remember—soccer is played by two teams of 11 players, one of whom is a goalkeeper. Though it requires immense skill at the highest level, and can have great tactical subtlety, it is essentially a simple game. Its object—perhaps a little obscured by the defensive tendencies of the 1960s—is to score more goals than the opposition: that is, to propel the ball with the foot, head, or any other part of the body other than the hand or arm, through the space formed by the goalposts and the crossbar.

The equipment, too, is simple: a shirt, shorts, stockings, and boots. The only complications arise with the bars and studs on the boots, but the laws lay down strict regulations for their size, number, and suitable materials. The ball must be spherical, of leather or other approved materials, and be 27-28 inches in circumference, 14-16 ounces in weight, and have a pressure equal to atmospheric pressure at sea level (approximately 15 pounds per square inch).

Rules

Soccer is played on a rectangular pitch 100-130 yards long and 50-100 yards wide (for internationals the dimensions must be 110-120 yards and 70-80 yards). The pitch is marked out with lines, more than 5 inches wide and usually in white. The longer lines are called *touchlines*, the shorter ones *goal-lines*. A *halfway line* is marked out across the field of play, with its *centre spot* having a *centre circle* of 10 yards radius drawn around it. Flagposts must be placed at each corner (where there is a quarter-circle of 1 yard radius drawn inside the field of play) and may be placed opposite the halfway line not more than 1 yard outside the touchline.

The *goal area* at each end is formed by two lines drawn at right-angles to the goal-line 6 yards from each goal-post, joined by a line drawn 6 yards away from, and parallel to, the goal-line. The *penalty area* is similarly proportioned, but with dimensions of 18 yards. A mark 12 yards from the centre of the goal-line forms the *penalty spot*, and an arc of a circle 10 yards from the spot is drawn outside the penalty area.

The goals are placed at the centre of the goal-line and consist of two upright posts 8 yards apart, joined by a horizontal crossbar 8 feet from the ground. The width and depth of the posts and crossbar must be 5 inches or less, and the same for both. Nets may be attached to the posts and crossbar to receive the ball.

A game of soccer lasts for 90 minutes (two periods of 45 minutes) unless otherwise agreed on by the two teams concerned. Allowance must be made by the referee for time lost through injury and other causes, and time must be extended to permit the taking of a penalty at the end of either half of the match.

At the start of a match, the team winning the toss has the option of either choice of ends or *kick-off*. The game begins with a player kicking the ball off the centre spot into his opponents half. Both sides must be in their half, and the team not kicking off must be at least 10 yards from the ball, until the ball is kicked. The ball is in play once it has travelled the distance of its own circumference, but the kicker must not play the ball again until it has been touched by another player. The same process applies after a goal has been scored (with the team who have conceded the goal kicking off) and at the start of the second half, when the teams have changed ends and the side who did not start the match kick-off. Any infringement of the rule results in the kick being retaken,

Diagram labels: 1yd, TOUCH LINE, HALFWAY LINE, GOAL LINE, 18yd, 18yd, 6yd, PENALTY, 20yd, 8yd, 12 yd, 10 yd, 44yd, 10yd, Centre Spot, Centre Circle, Penalty Arc, Penalty Spot, GOAL AREA, 6yd, AREA

Roy Flooks

Fotosports International

Colour Sport

Roland Leach

Fotosports International

Ray Green

6

Syndication International

Ray Green

7 hold an opponent with his hand or any part of his arm.
3 Using the arms to keep an opponent at bay and so shield the ball is a common ploy, but as the ball is being played there is no obstruction. A player causes obstruction by interposing himself between an opponent and the ball with no intention of playing the ball. **4** The man in possession has slipped the ball past an opponent, who is, however, still committed to the tackle. Unscrupulous players will go through with the tackle deliberately, so endangering their opponent. **5** A shoulder charge is fair when the ball is within playing distance of the players concerned. If they are not trying to play it, however, an indirect free-kick is awarded. **6** A player with cause to protest: Terry Cooper is pushed aside, so being obstructed from chasing after the ball he nudged on.
7 Chorus-line kicking often looks spectacular but it can constitute dangerous play. So too can a player's going down too low to head the ball.

except if the player kicking off touches it again before another player, in which case an indirect free-kick is awarded against his side. A goal cannot be scored direct from a kick-off.

The ball is out of play when all of it has crossed the touchline or goal-line, or when the game has been stopped by the referee. It is in play at all other times, including when it rebounds off a goal-post, crossbar, or flagpost into the field of play, when it rebounds off the referee or linesmen when they are in the field of play, and in the event of a supposed infringement of the laws until a decision is given.

Apart from a goal, there are three ways in which the ball is returned to play after leaving the pitch. If the whole of the ball goes over the touchline, a *throw-in* is awarded to the team opposing that of the player who last touched it. The player throwing-in must face the field of play and have part of both feet on or outside the touchline at the moment of delivery and use both hands in bringing the ball from behind his head. As at the kick-off, he may not play the ball again until it is touched by another player, and a goal cannot be scored direct from a throw-in. If the ball is not thrown in correctly, a throw is awarded to the other side, and if the player throwing in plays it twice in succession an indirect free-kick is awarded against him where the infringement occurred.

If the whole of the ball passes over the goal-line (except between the posts) and was last touched by a player of the attacking side, the defending side gains a *goal-kick*. It can be taken by any player from any point inside the half of the goal area on the side where the ball crossed the line (though usually from the 6-yard line, and most often by the goalkeeper), and must travel outside the penalty area; if it does not the kick is taken again. A goal cannot be scored direct from a goal-kick and the players of the opposing team must remain outside the penalty area while the kick is being taken.

When the ball passes over the goal-line but was last touched by a player of the defending side, a *corner-kick* is awarded to the

The International Board
The laws of the game are the province of the International Football Association Board, consisting of 20 representatives—four each from the FA, the Scottish FA, the FA of Wales, and the Irish FA, and four from FIFA. It meets in June in rotation—England, Scotland, Ireland, Wales—except when the FIFA Congress and the World Cup coincide, in which case FIFA will convene the assembly, if possible at the World Cup venue. Business can only proceed with at least four associations represented, one of whom must be FIFA. The four British associations each have one vote and FIFA has four, and a majority of three-quarters is required to execute any change in the laws. If passed they are binding on all FIFA members.

1 One unwholesome aspect of British soccer in the late 1960s was the increasing use of the 'tackle from behind'. But how often can a player take the ball from behind without first fouling his opponent? **2** When tripped by an opponent, players tend to fall in a diving motion. Some just 'dive' in an attempt to gain a free-kick or penalty. **3** Using another player to gain leverage is a foul, no matter whether the player is a team-mate or an oponent. But there are times when the opponent backs into the player heading (making a back) and is not interested in going up for the ball. **4** The penalty: the price paid for certain offences in the penalty area. **5** One of soccer's peculiar sights is the defensive wall for free kicks. Opposing players must be at least 10 yards from the ball when the kick is taken. **6** No player, except the goalkeeper, may handle the ball.

attacking side. The whole of the ball must be inside the quarter-circle at the corner on the side on which the ball went out of play, but the taker cannot remove the flagpost to take it. Players of the defending side must be at least 10 yards from the ball, and the player taking the kick may not play the ball again until another player has touched it. If he does, an indirect free-kick is awarded to the defending side. A goal can be scored direct from a corner.

The referee may restart play with a *dropped ball* where play has been temporarily suspended with the ball in play and no other decision given. In this case any players involved may not play the ball until it has touched the ground.

In addition to these methods of restarting the game—kick-off, throw-in, goal-kick, corner, and dropped ball—there are the two types of free-kick that join corners and throw-ins as the 'set pieces' at which predetermined tactics can be practised: the *direct free-kick* (or a *penalty* if the offence is committed by the defending side inside their penalty area), from which a goal can be scored by the taker, and the *indirect free-kick*, from which a goal cannot be scored direct.

When a player takes either a direct or an indirect free-kick inside his own penalty area, the opposing side must be outside the area and at least 10 yards from the ball, and the ball must travel outside the area from the kick. For a kick outside the penalty area, the opposing side must all be at least 10 yards from the ball until the kick is taken; for an indirect free-kick in the opposing penalty area, the opposition may stand on their own goal-line, between the posts, even if they are closer than 10 yards to the ball. For a free-kick the ball must be stationary and the taker may not play the ball again until it has been touched by another player. If he does, an indirect free-kick is awarded to the other side.

For a *penalty*, taken from the penalty spot, all players except the taker and the opposing goalkeeper must be outside the penalty area and at least 10 yards from the ball. The goalkeeper must stand on his goal-line, without moving his feet, until the ball is kicked, and the taker cannot play the ball again until it has been touched by another player. The game must be extended either at half-time or full-time to allow a penalty to be taken. For any infringement by the defending side, the kick will be retaken if the goal was not scored; for any infringement by a member of the attacking side, other than the taker, the kick will be retaken if a goal was scored; and for any infringement by the taker after the ball is in play, the defending side are awarded an indirect free-kick.

The laws of soccer are wide-

The laws of soccer are relatively simple. But one criticism of the game is that the laws are open to too wide a range of interpretation. Managers, players, referees, spectators, journalists, and commentators tend to throw accusations at each other when a controversy develops or when foul play prevails. But the very basis on which the whole game is founded—namely, the laws—is too vague to stand up to the demands of modern soccer.

In what other game is it possible to gain an advantage by means of a deliberate breaking of the law? So-called 'tactical fouls', such as holding, obstruction, or hand ball, are being increasingly used to prevent a certain goal or to stop a dangerous situation developing. The referee is empowered only to award a direct free-kick at the point where the offence was committed (a penalty, if it took place in the penalty area) or, in the case of obstruction—however threatening the attack—an indirect free-kick. He may also caution the offending player. On the other hand he may not. And this is a frequent criticism of refereeing: it is far too arbitrary and inconsistent in such matters.

Perhaps the most controversial of soccer's laws is the offside rule. Apart from the inability of certain players and officials—and a large proportion of spectators—to appreciate the 'when the ball is played' aspect of the rule, there is the perennially controversial question of whether a player in an offside position is 'interfering' with play. As this has never been even loosely defined in the laws, its interpretation varies drastically. A player in an offside position is liable to be whistled up, even if he makes no attempt to play the ball, if he is adjudged to be interfering with play. The increasing trend since the mid-1960s has been, at least in British football, for the referee to give offside as soon as he sees the linesman's flag go up—before, for example, the ball has a chance to hit a defender, with the 'offside' player being thus 'played on'. This apparent fear on the part of officials to use their judgement is due more than anything else to the ill-defined nature of the law.

Other aspects of the laws that might profitably be examined and improved include the system of awarding free-kicks (it is not the type of offence but the seriousness of the offence that should determine whether a free-kick is direct or indirect), the possibility of penalty kicks for certain offences committed outside the penalty area (for the 'tactical' or 'professional' foul that stops a near-certain goal), and the introduction of a system of standard signals for referees. The aim always should be to ensure that a team does not gain any advantage from unfair tactics—i.e. to make the punishment fit the crime—to keep pace with modern tactical developments and make sure that the game does not suffer as a spectacle, and to improve understanding between the officials, players and spectators so that not only is justice on the field done, but is seen to be done.

6

Colour Sport

ranging on the subject of fouls and misconduct. A player who kicks or attempts to kick, trips, jumps up at, charges in a violent manner, strikes or attempts to strike, holds, or pushes an opponent, or handles the ball, is penalized by the award of a *direct free-kick* to the opposing side. If a player intentionally commits any of these offences inside his own penalty area, he concedes a penalty, which can be awarded irrespective of the position of the ball at the time. An *indirect free-kick* is awarded against a player for dangerous play, charging (fairly) an opponent when the ball is not within playing distance, obstructing an opponent, and charging the goalkeeper (except when he is holding the ball in his goal area, obstructing an opponent, or is outside his goal area); and against the goalkeeper if he takes more than four steps while holding, bouncing, or throwing up the ball without releasing it so that it is played by another player (he may, however, roll it on the ground), or if, in the referee's opinion, he is guilty of deliberate time-wasting.

A player may be officially *cautioned*, or 'booked', if he enters the field of play to join or rejoin his side without the permission of the referee while the game is under way—and unless an offence worthy of a free-kick has been committed the referee restarts with a dropped ball—or if he persistently infringes the laws, shows dissent from the referee's decision, or is guilty of ungentlemanly conduct. The last three automatically warrant the award of an indirect free-kick to the opposing side. A player may be sent off if, in the opinion of the referee, he is guilty of violent conduct (including spitting at opponents or officials) or serious foul play, if he uses foul or abusive language, or if he persists in misconduct after being cautioned. If play is stopped by a player's being sent off, without a separate offence being committed, the game is resumed with an indirect free-kick to the opposing side.

There remains the *offside* law, probably the most contentious of soccer's rules and almost certainly the cause of most frustration. The law states that a player is offside if he is nearer the opponent's goal-line than the ball is at the moment the ball is played, with the following exceptions: first, if there are two or more opponents nearer the goal-line than he is; second, if the ball was last played by an opponent or touched by him; third, if he received the ball from a corner, a throw-in, or when the referee used a dropped ball; and last, if he is in his own half. A player in an offside position will not be penalized unless the referee considers him to be interfering with the play or an opponent, or seeking to gain an advantage by being in that position.

265

Techniques

Soccer is a team game, the basic object being to both initiate and execute attacks with passing movements until a player is in a position to shoot or head at goal. The days of dribbling—in the 1870s, when each player held on to the ball with the intention of beating as many opponents as possible—were soon overtaken by the passing game. Every generation includes its individualists, but it is in the nature of football that each player is ultimately dependent on the other members of his side.

The basic skills, however, are inherently individual. The first and most obvious is kicking the ball—passing and shooting. Three main parts of the foot are usually employed: the instep (where the boot laces up), more often than not for power and shooting; the inside of the foot, with which a player can obtain accuracy and spin; and the outside of the foot, particularly useful for a pass that can curve round an opponent to a colleague, without risking interception in the air. Good players can use either side of the foot to bend a powerful kick—the 'banana' shot perfected by the Brazilians. In exceptional circumstances players use the heel (for a back-pass), or, if unable to reach the ball for full control, the toe or even the sole.

There are several guidelines to kicking a ball. In most cases it is important, for the sake of balance, to have the non-kicking foot alongside the ball and keep the weight of the body above it. But the primary rule is the one that applies to all ball games: to keep the eye on the ball while it is being played.

The basic pass of soccer is placed in front of a colleague so that he does not have to alter his pace or direction drastically when running on to it. But the occasions when there is sufficient space or time, except when moving out of defence, are few, and a player is expected to control passes that arrive at all speeds, heights, and angles. Trapping a ball is the basic method of bringing it under control before deciding how to utilize it. The first way is with the sole, or sole and inside, of the foot, for killing a ball that arrives on the bounce. The side of the foot can be used to control a low pass, and the shin for an awkwardly bouncing ball. There are also several other parts of the body commonly used: the head, the chest (taking a high ball and dropping it down to the feet), the stomach (hunched over for a rising ball), and the thigh.

Running with the ball—dribbling—is usually associated with the feet, though on occasions a player finds it necessary to take the ball on the chest, thigh, and so on. Dribbling has come back into the limelight in the era of packed defences: first, through players

attacking frontally and trying to beat several opponents, and second, through the return to favour of wingers who can beat a man, get round the back of a square defence, and cross the ball, or centre. But whether in vogue or not, dribbling has always been an integral part of soccer.

So too has heading, which is unique to the game among major sports. It is done with the forehead, at the area where the top of the head modulates into it. The thickness of the bone there pre-includes the chance of injury or brain damage, and the ball can be

1 Derby County's Alan Hinton, renowned for his fierce shots at goal, lets fly, using the instep. **2** Chelsea's Charlie Cooke uses the side of the foot for a short, precisely placed pass. His team-mate Alan Hudson (**3**) gets well over the ball for a long pass up the field, **4**. Allan Clarke shows captain Billy Bremner his trapping ability. The ball is caught on the foot, which drops with the ball to prevent it bounding off. **5** With the defence closing in, Ray Kennedy chests the ball down. **6** Goalkeepers have numerous ways of preventing goals. One of them is to punch high balls away rather than risk catching them. **7** Sudden change of pace, body swerve, ball control: George Best has them all, and few can answer his dribbling ability.

propelled with great accuracy and force—provided the timing is correct and the muscles of the neck are properly utilized. Eyes must be kept fixed on the ball, and timing is something that comes, to the majority of players anyway, only with constant practice.

Goalkeeping, like wicket-keeping in cricket, is in a category of its own. Though the goalkeeper will probably be a useful sort of player in any position, and may well have started his career in another spot, he is less of a footballer than a gymnast with superb reflexes, a keen eye, safe hands—and courage. He has three main ways of saving the ball: catching it cleanly, tipping it round the posts or over the crossbar (when it is unsafe to try to catch it, or when he is under pressure, or when he cannot reach it to hold) and punching it (when he is under pressure or unable to hold the ball). There is also the more recently developed goalkeeping technique of coming out to save with the feet and legs foremost. Though the goalkeeper has the advantage of arms' length and a certain amount of protection from the laws, he is expected to put himself in situations that expose him to great risk, such as diving at an opponent's feet. Most forwards, however, have a certain respect for the unique nature of the goalkeeper's tasks.

A goalkeeper must learn timing and positioning (for corners, free-kicks, etc) and be particularly adept at 'narrowing the angle'—coming out of his goal to reduce the effective area at which an oncoming opponent can aim. His most obvious mistake, in both this and most of his situations, is hesitation.

Despite the skills in contact with the ball, it is, by the law of averages, highly unlikely that any player will be in possession for more than a few minutes during a match, and in the case of strikers it is probably less than a minute. Thus the vast majority of a player's time on the field is taken up with movements and actions that do not necessitate possession: 'running off the ball' (running 'into space' and taking up positions for a pass), covering defending colleagues when they are committed to an opponent or a tackle, and marking opponents at set pieces (and perhaps throughout the game in the case of a defender). Because the spectator follows the ball, he is normally unaware of what each player does for 95% of a match. He merely expects him to be in the right place, at the right time, and do the right thing when he receives the ball.

Heading the ball is unique to soccer among major sports. It is not something that usually comes naturally, but requires great practice. Neck muscles play an important role and the forehead is the part used.

Ray Green

Tactical Systems

The development of soccer tactics has in essence been the story of a gradual reduction in the number of forwards in favour of the number of midfield players and defenders. In 1870 there would have been as many as eight forwards; a century later there might well be as few as one.

The early forwards were expected to dribble past man after man until they scored—or, more likely, lost the ball. It was the Scots who first evolved the passing game, and with their progress and superiority it quickly became the norm. The basic configuration of 2-3-5 (which is still often used for line-ups on paper, and which gives the positions their traditional names of right-half, inside-left, and so on) then held sway for about 40 years.

It was the change in the offside law in 1925, required by the extravagant use of the offside trap, that sparked off the next major change. The new rule stipulated that only two players, and not three, had to be between the player and the goal-line when the ball was played, and it resulted in a steep increase in the number of goals being scored. In the first season with the change (1925-26) the number in the Football League rose by almost a third, and it was inevitable that it would provoke tactical reorganization. Herbert Chapman, Charlie Buchan, and Arsenal were the pioneers. The centre-half, previously the midfield 'general', was moved back between the full-backs to become a third- or centre-back, and the area he vacated was filled by the two inside-forwards, who retreated behind the wingers and centre-forward to produce the configuration descriptively called the 'W' formation.

Though some European and South American countries persisted with the attacking centre-half—Austria were still using him in the early 1950s—the third-back game was the basic structure in soccer for a quarter of a century. It was, of course, like all systems, merely a model, and each team had its own variation moulded round the players it possessed.

Despite some successful developments—Karl Rappan's 'bolt' defence in Switzerland (the forerunner of *catenaccio*) and Hungary's use of the deep-lying centre-forward, copied by Manchester City through Don Revie—it was not until the 1958 World Cup and Brazil's spectacular performances with their 4-2-4 system that the game took its next big tactical turn. This employed two centre-backs (the old centre-half and a wing-half) between the two full-backs, two midfield players (a wing-half and an inside-forward), and four attacking forwards (two wingers, the old centre-forward, and an inside-forward). It was almost universally imitated, but by 1962 the Brazilians had refined it to 4-3-3, with Zagalo dropping back to midfield. Some continental and South American countries took the process a stage farther in the mid-1960s with *catenaccio* (in effect 1-4-3-2 or 1-4-2-3) which was epitomized by Inter-Milan under Helenio Herrera. The marked drop in the size of scores at European club matches illustrated the grip that the system, with its sweeper behind the defence, and its use of defensive absorption and quick breakaways, took on the continental game. Inter-Milan's progress to the 1966-67 European Cup final is typical: 1-0, 0-0, 2-1, 2-0, 1-0, 2-0, 1-1, 1-1, and 1-0.

3

England team manager Alf Ramsey, after persevering with wingers for some time, eventually discarded them, and his side won the 1966 World Cup with what was in effect a 4-3-3 system—though Peters, like Zagalo, was expected to perform a dual role. For 1970 he was kept for the most part in midfield, and England were reduced to virtually 4-4-2. The strikers (usually Hurst and Lee) found it hard going, and the midfield—where matches are in the main won and lost—suffered from overcrowding.

There are, of course, qualifications in talking of tactical systems. They are only simplified models, useful frameworks, and are open to numerous permutations and refinements. This is governed not not only by the players available —it is easier and more profitable to adapt a system to suit the talents and shortcomings of a team, than expect players to tailor their styles to fit a plan— but also by the type of match being played; thus a team may well adopt vastly different tactics in the two legs of a European club competition. It also depends on how the system is employed: in theory West Germany lined up in a *catenaccio* formation during the 1970 World Cup, but their displays bore little resemblance to the practices of the Italian clubs who follow the same pattern. Soccer tactics, like the game itself, are the source of infinite variety.

4

Mary Evans
U.P.I.
Colour Sport

A. Wilkes & Son

TACTICAL SYSTEMS

Simplified examples of the main tactical formations. In each case the numbers refer to the way the team would appear on paper, that is, in the old classic fashion

```
                          1
                      goalkeeper
          2                               3
      right-back                      left-back
   4                    5                        6
 right-half        centre-half              left-half
              8                10
          inside-right     inside-left
       7              9                11
 outside-right   centreforward      outside-left
```

1. 4-2-4—Brazil's World Cup winning side in 1958:

```
                          1
                       Gylmar
     2              5              6              3
  N. Santos      Bellini        Orlando      D. Santos
              4                        8
            Zito                     Didi
     7           9            10              11
  Garrincha    Vava         Pele           Zagalo
```

2. 4-3-3—Everton's League Championship side in 1969-70:

```
                          1
                        West
     2              5              10             3
   Wright        Labone         Hurst          Brown
          4              8              6
        Kendall        Ball         Harvey
          7              9              11
        Husband       Royle        Morrissey
```

3. 4-4-2—England's side in the 1970 World Cup quarter-final at Leon

```
                          1
                       Bonetti
     2              5              6              3
   Newton        Labone         Moore          Cooper
     4              8              9              11
  Mullery         Ball        Charlton        Peters
              7                        10
            Lee                       Hurst
```

4. Catennacio—Inter-Milan's European Cup winning side in 1965:

```
                          1
                        Sarti
                          6
                       Picchi
     2              4              5              3
  Burgnich        Bedin        Guarneri       Facchetti
          9              10             11
        Peiro         Suarez          Corso
          7                              8
        Jair                          Mazzola
```

1 Before more intricate tactics evolved, the dribbling game was in vogue. Forwards dribbled past man after man until they either scored or lost the ball. **2** The Brazilian side that won the World Cup in 1958 introduced the 4-2-4 formation. **3** But in systems employing packed defences, it was left to one or two front-runners, or strikers, to win the ball. **4** Arsenal's Herbie Roberts became soccer's first stopper centre-half, or third back, in the tactical evolvement following the change in the offside rule. **5** Numbers have grown insignificant: Everton gave their second centre-half, John Hurst, the No. 10 shirt.

Ray Green

Goal Average

Goal average is used to decide who gets the verdict when two sides in a league are level on points, and is derived from dividing the number of goals a team scores by the number of goals that team concedes. In the Football League it has decided the First Division winners on four occasions—1924, 1950, 1953, and 1965—with Huddersfield Town squeezing out Cardiff City in 1923-24 by only .024.

When the Football League was formed in 1888, the principle of goal average was written into its first set of rules. That it has never been discarded is thought by some to be a condemnation of the law-making body, for the ratio of goals for to goals against, arguably bears little relation to the game itself. At the top of the table it favours defence: for example, a goal average of 40-20 is superior to one of 79-40. (Whereas, at the other end of the table, 40-79 is better than 20-40.) Used to determine the leading clubs in small groups, goal average can seem unjust. It has been used in the World Cup on a number of occasions, and, fortunately, there have been no instances of apparent injustice through its use in the finals. But with only three matches, should a ratio of 5-1 be better than 14-3 ? Strangely enough by adding the same score, 3-2, to each of these, which then become 8-3 and 17-5, the second average becomes superior !

Apart from counting teams level on points as inevitably equal (as in the Home International Championship), there are four main alternatives to goal average, each of which is employed by at least one national league: a play-off (only really applicable in the case of a dispute at the top or bottom of the table); goal difference (the number of goals scored minus the number of goals conceded), as used in the 1970 World Cup and first used in major competition in the 1964 Olympics; giving the benefit to the side with the highest number of wins; and using the results of the matches during that season between the two or more teams concerned.

Peter Robinson

Referees

An average and out-of-touch amateur who makes gross errors in the interpretation of the laws, or a brave figure doing his best in an increasingly difficult situation? The referee and his art are the subject of endless controversy, and it needs only one bad decision in an important match to set the old debate rolling.

The referee is in some ways an anomaly in football. In an era of intense professionalism and specialization, at least at the top levels, he remains the unglamorous part-timer who once or twice a week dons his black gear and takes complete control of a match, perhaps a vital one, for its whole duration.

His job is thankless; good decisions (using the advantage where applicable) and quietly firm control (well-chosen words to a player off the ball) go largely unnoticed—that is what makes them good. A bad or controversial decision gives a referee a stigma that takes a long time to lose. The abuse and comments — some funny, some unnecessary, some cruel—are probably an occupational hazard he soon learns to tolerate or ignore.

Each referee is, of course, a human being with human faults. There is no evidence to support the view that full-time professional referees know or apply the rules any better. Those in Latin America, who sometimes earn over £100 a week, are by no means doyens of their craft.

In the early days of football the game was controlled by two umpires, one from each club. But the increased and keener competition made it imperative that the men in charge be neutral, and a referee was added to the number of match officials with the task of settling any disputes between the umpires.

The referee gained complete control in 1891, when the umpires were converted to linesmen. He moved from his place on the touchline to the field of play, and was given the power to make decisions without consulting his colleagues. In Britain referees were sufficiently established by 1893 to form their own association.

For 1970-71 the Football League had 76 referees on its list, plus 36 auxiliary referees-cum-linesmen. They receive expenses and a match fee, which in 1974 was £12.50 (£6.40 for each linesman) for all Football League games. The fees for FA Cup ties are the same, except for duty in the final, for which the fees are £15.75 and £8.00, while the payment for internationals is a little higher—£18.00 and £9.00.

The problems of the referee were accentuated in the 1960s. The trends of the modern game—speed, the crowded defences, the tactical foul—and the increased rewards for success, have all helped to heighten the difficulty of

Syndication International

Colour Sport

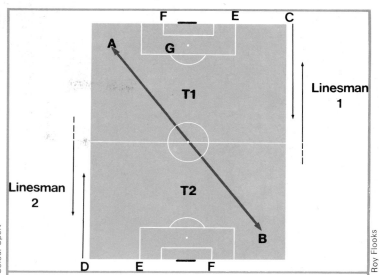

Roy Flooks

his task. Television, too, with its sterile and unemotional 'instant replays' and slow-motion analysis, has often proved a necessarily quick decision on the field to be wrong and the 'man in the middle' has come under criticism. The pressures of the game have discouraged many potential referees from joining the ranks, and the number of referees with character who exercise a grip on the game and earn the respect of the players is dwindling throughout the advanced footballing nations.

1 Referee Tschenscher hunts for the yellow warning card used in the 1970 World Cup.
2 The referee is not always subjected to intimidation.
3 Ken Aston's gesture can have only one meaning—off! Ferrini (head bowed) received vociferous support from his Italian team-mates in this 1962 World Cup match against Chile, but Aston stood firm.
4 Referees do not always get the players' support over even the more basic rules.

Referees normally follow the diagonal system of controlling a match, on the line A-B. When the referee is at point A, linesman 1 should be on his touchline in line with him, thus providing two judges of play. Linesman 2 watches the team playing into his half (T2), and as that team advances he keeps in line with the second-last defender of team T2 (usually the player nearest the goalkeeper). Thus he will rarely cross the halfway line. There are also standard positions for set pieces. For corners and penalties, for example, the appropriate linesman positions himself at the point where the penalty area joins the goal-line (E), while the referee stands at F or halfway along A-F (or B-F) for a corner, and approximately position G for a penalty. If the referee prefers to work the alternative diagonal (C-D), the linesmen adjust accordingly. Though many suggestions have been put forward—a referee for each half, a referee for each half diagonally, linesmen-control with a referee as adjudicator—the diagonal system remains the best method while a single referee is the ultimate authority on the field of play.

The laws state that the referee shall:
a) enforce the laws and decide any disputed point and his decision on facts connected with play is final. His jurisdiction starts from the kick-off, and continues when play is temporarily suspended or when the ball is out of play. He should refrain from penalizing in cases where by doing so he would be giving advantage to the offending team.
b) keep the score, act as timekeeper, and add all time lost through accident or other cause
c) have discretionary power to stop the game for any infringement of the laws and to suspend or terminate the game when by reason of the weather, spectators, or other cause he thinks such action appropriate
d) have discretionary power to caution a player guilty of misconduct or ungentlemanly behaviour and, if he persists, to suspend him from further participation in the game
e) allow nobody but the players and linesmen on the field of play without his permission
f) stop the game if he considers a player to be seriously injured, have the player removed from the pitch as quickly as possible, and resume the game. If a player is slightly injured the game will continue until the ball goes out of play, and if a player can reach the touchline for attention he must not be treated on the field of play
g) have discretionary power to suspend from further participation in the game, without previous caution, any player guilty of violent conduct
h) signal for the resumption of play after all stoppages
i) decide that the ball meets the specifications laid down in the laws
The duty of the two linesmen (subject to the referee's decision) is to indicate when the ball is out of play and which side is entitled to the resulting goal-kick, throw-in, or corner. They shall also assist the referee to control the game in accordance with the laws, but in the event of undue interference or improper conduct the referee shall dispense with his services and arrange for a replacement. The linesmen's flags should be provided by the home club.

On September 22, 1930, at Hampden Park, referee Mr J. Thomson of Burnbank was 'sent off' by Jimmy Seed, the Sheffield Wednesday and England inside-forward. Seed was captaining Sheffield, who were playing in white shirts and black shorts, in an inter-city game against Glasgow, and he found himself passing to Mr Thomson, who wore a white shirt but no jacket. He asked the referee to stop the game and don a jacket, and Mr Thomson obliged.

U.P.I.

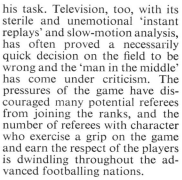

Ray Green

Glossary of Terms

Blind side The side of a player or defence away from the play or ball.

Catenaccio Literally, 'big chain'. Very defensive tactics first evolved in Switzerland in the early 1950s and later employed with great success, particularly by Italian clubs. Consists of a sweeper behind the four defenders, with three midfield players and two strikers.

Centre or **cross** A pass, most often in the air, played from the area of the pitch near the touchline into the penalty or goal area.

Chip A short-range lob with back-spin; often used from free-kicks taken in an attacking position.

Containing When a defending player prevents an opponent from attacking at speed by slowly retreating.

Covering When a player fills a position vacated by a colleague who has committed himself to a tackle, or when he forms a second line of defence behind him.

Cross See Centre.

Crossfield pass/ball A pass made from one side of the pitch to the other with the intention of changing the source of the attack.

Dead ball When the ball is kicked from a stationary position (corner, free-kick, etc).

Far post The goalpost, or side of the goal, farther away from the player in possession.

Four-four-two (4-4-2) Defensive formation with four defenders, four midfield players, and only two permanent strikers. Used by England in the 1970 World Cup.

Four-three-three (4-3-3) Formation first illustrated by Brazil in the 1962 World Cup and employed by England in 1966. Uses one more midfield man (and thus one fewer striker) than 4-2-4.

Four-two-four (4-2-4) Formation devised in Brazil and first on general display by them during the 1958 World Cup. It comprises four defenders, two midfield players, and four strikers.

Funnelling When a defence retreats, converging on their own goal.

'Hospital' pass/ball A pass played too near an opponent for which the intended receiver will have to struggle and risk injury.

Inside The goal or non-touchline side of a player.

Killing the ball Rendering the ball stationary.

Linkman See Midfield player.

Marking Keeping within playing distance of an opponent, particularly at set pieces, to discourage his colleagues from passing to him and to hamper or tackle him quickly if he does receive a pass.

Midfield player or **linkman** A player operating for the most part in the central areas of the pitch, whose job it is to connect defence and attack.

Near post The goal post, or side of the goal, nearer the player in possession.

Outside The wing or touchline side of a player.

Overlapping When a player, often a full-back, goes outside his winger or fills the area where his winger would normally operate.

Over the top/ball Going into a tackle over the ball and kicking the opponents legs; a serious foul.

Reverse pass/ball When a player runs one way and passes the other.

Running off the ball The movement into 'space' of players not in possession in order to be available for a pass from a colleague who has the ball.

Selling a dummy Feinting to dribble or pass one way and then going another in order to beat an opponent.

Set piece A predetermined situation (corners, free-kicks, throw-ins, etc) from which practised moves can be executed.

Shoulder charge A legal charge, shoulder to shoulder, in competition for the ball.

Sliding tackle Sliding into a tackle on one leg, to attempt to take the ball with that leg.

Square pass/ball A pass made laterally. A square defence is one all of whose members are in a line at right-angles to the touch-line.

Stopper One or other of the two centre-backs in a defensive line, originally used to denote the centre-half of the third-back game.

Striker The centre-forward, inside-forward, and sometimes the winger or wingers, who stay upfield with the intention of scoring. An all-out attacking player.

Sweeper or *libero* The player operating behind the defensive line of four in a catenaccio system. He 'sweeps up' loose balls.

Tactical foul A foul (or hand-ball) committed to gain an advantage; a free kick or even a penalty may be conceded in order to prevent a certain goal or to nullify a highly dangerous situation.

Third-back game Initiated as a response to the change of the offside law in 1925. The centre-half was converted from a midfield attacker to a centre- or third-back.

Through pass/ball A pass to a colleague running through that splits the opposing defence.

W formation Another facet of, and name for, the third-back game, deriving its name from the 'W' formed by the disposition of the five forwards, with the two inside-forwards playing behind a spearhead (centre-forward) and the two wingers.

Wall pass or 'one-two' When a player receives a quick return from a colleague, using him like a wall, in order to beat an opponent.

Work-rate A term that emerged in the 1960s to assess and describe a player's capacity for running, chasing, etc.

In an age when many teams adopted negative, defensive tactics, the genius of such individuals as Celtic winger Jimmy Johnstone provided fans with moments of magic always hoped for but so rarely seen or, for that matter, allowed.

Coaching

'Coaching', observed Walter Winterbottom, in his days as the FA Director of Coaching, 'is simply a means of showing how to practise'. Few men did more to disseminate the practice of coaching in Britain than the former Manchester United centre-forward, appointed to his job in 1946, and retaining it until 1963.

He and his scheme had many hurdles to surmount, for coaching had long been distrusted in Britain. It was considered something needed only by foreigners, the lesser breeds without the law, who had been brilliantly shown how to play the game by such as Jimmy Hogan (Austria, Hungary, Germany), John Dick (Czechoslovakia), and William Garbutt (Italy). Between the wars, a few perceptive critics such as Ivan Sharpe—'they coach, we don't,' he lamented—preached the gospel in

Malcolm Allison, among soccer's finest coaches.

Britain. But though Hogan was appointed as chief coach by the Football Association just before World War II, progress was slow and opposition large.

Winterbottom broke through with his pioneering zeal and his establishment of equally zealous cadres—Ron Greenwood, Alan Brown, and the rest. Gradually these men gained key managerial positions in British football, and when they had the natural drive and talent of such later arrivals as Malcolm Allison, their worth was indisputable.

Less acceptable was the 'new orthodoxy' of jargon and set attitudes, protecting the uncertain and the insecure. The double-talk about 'environmental awareness', 'work rate', 'positive running', and so on alienated many players and managers.

Coaching, it may be said, is of vital importance provided the coach is talented and he encourages his players to develop and express their own natural strengths, rather than conform to his rigid pattern. For the 1970s a productive balance appears to have been reached between the doctrinaire and the reactionary.

Training

Training is a vital part of a team's preparation: the tactical discipline imposed by coaches is wasted if the basic fitness is missing. In the old days, training consisted largely of laps round the pitch, but the programme is now compiled and following with military thoroughness. The concentration on aspects with the ball is fairly recent, particularly in Britain, but the actual amount of fitness and ball training is still the subject of some controversy.

In the weeks before the start of a new season the training staff bring their men to a physical peak, to be maintained for nine months. Most clubs now train for about two hours a day on four days a week, but the amount of work packed into those brief periods is immense: sprint after sprint, with only a few seconds of rest between body-building, ball-control, five-a-side games, head tennis, and a wide range of physical exercises. Several players transferred to leading clubs have admitted to actual physical sickness after their first training sessions. The object is to concentrate so much effort into the workouts that actual matches do not prove so taxing.

The consequent increase in overall standards of fitness is both an effect, and a cause, of the speed of modern football. The greater pace and the wider concentration on tactics probably mean that the stars of the past would be caught out if they could be restored to their prime and put into a modern side. But they are still at liberty to argue that, given the facilities of the moderns and a few months in which to adjust, their skills would be equally obvious.

Ray Green

Above, **Wilf McGuinness proved an effective coach during Manchester United's reign in the 1960s, but found managerial success elusive.** *Below,* **Team training is essential at all levels.**

Keystone

273

The Transfer System

Transfer fees have been a source of controversy in football since the very early days of professionalism. Successive generations of critics have claimed that no player can be worth the escalating sums expended, from the £1,000 Middlesbrough paid to Sunderland for Alf Common in 1904 to the £200,000 sale of West Ham's Martin Peters to Spurs 66 years later.

While demand exceeds supply, fees are likely to remain high—although there were signs after the Peters move that British clubs were being more cautious, because of the shortage of class performers and the difficulties of obtaining the necessary cash. In the lower divisions of the Football League 'credit' transfers are common, with fees paid in instalments by clubs too poor to afford lump sums. The buying club can offset fees paid against tax on profits, although the sellers become liable for duty on the amounts received. In some countries, notably Italy, some players are even sold on a shared basis, with two teams holding half a registration, and a player having alternate seasons with each one.

Although the transfer system is far from perfect—with the main criticism being that it enables wealthier managements to buy success rather than breed it—at least the money stays in the game. Several Fourth Division clubs in the Football League, some higher

Colour Sport

1 Spurs paid an estimated £200,000 for West Ham's Martin Peters in 1970, less than half the £440,000 that Juventus paid Varese for Pietro Anastasi (2) in 1968.
3 George Eastham (left) was the centre of a legal storm in the 1960s: his stand ended the retain-and-transfer system that bound players so inexorably to their clubs.
4 At the end of the 1970-71 season, Newcastle paid Luton a reputed £180,000 for Malcolm MacDonald, a player without any experience of First Division football.

Peter Robinson

up the scale of which Burnley in the 1960s is a good example, have remained in business solely through their ability to recruit players at small cost and then sell them at inflated fees.

The system had been modified in Britain since the celebrated Eastham case in 1963, when the Newcastle United forward claimed that his club were acting unlawfully in retaining him and refusing him a move. After a lengthy hearing, the High Court upheld his submission, with the result that contracts are now for set periods, not indefinite terms, with either party free to renew them.

Although the players have welcomed the increased freedom, they are still tied by 'options' and they do not have an automatic right to leave at the end of a contract. However, it is a vast improvement on the old method, which was heavily biased towards the clubs—players such as the great Wilf Mannion were virtually starved out, and had to submit and re-sign at the old terms after going on strike for months. In the later system, players can still 'work their ticket' although officially contracted to stay. The art, as far as the players are concerned, is in obtaining a move without deman-

ding one in writing, which would invalidate the claim to a 5% share of the fee involved. This method, instituted in an effort to get rid of the 'backhander' payments rumoured to have been rife, has caused considerable problems.

The transfer record by 1970 was the £440,000 Juventus paid Varese for Pietro Anastasi in 1968. World stars such as Pele and Eusebio would no doubt have fetched more had they been allowed to move, and keeping them involved their clubs in enormous expense. In the late 1950s and early 1960s, Italian

clubs made several forays into Britain, recruiting such players as John Charles and Jimmy Greaves (who had both joined their English teams as schoolboys) in return for huge sums. A subsequent ban on importations only inflated the Italian market still further, and in 1970 every senior club in the country was in debt, some for hundreds of thousands of pounds.

But, irrespective of nationality, the transfer market remains the same in one important aspect. Spending money, if the money is there, is comparatively easy: what counts is how you spent it.

1 Johnny Haynes, the Fulham and England forward, was the first English £100-a-week footballer. The 'greats' before the abolition of the maximum wage were, by comparison, rewarded with a pittance.
2 George Best, proud owner of shops and a £30,000 house (3), was not untypical of the successful player of the 1960s in any country. Pele was reputedly a dollar millionaire, and the fringe benefits of football—such as advertising and television— make the footballer an envied, character in the social scene.

Remuneration

The top professional footballer now has a merited place in a money-orientated British society, and has at last caught up with his continental counterparts, who have long been financially envied.

The abolition of the maximum wage in 1961, after threats of strike action by a militant Professional Footballers Association, means that pay-packets of £100 a week are now commonplace in the First Division of the Football League, with liberal additional revenue for the stars by way of advertising, journalism, television, and business opportunities. Success is rewarded by various bonus systems geared to attendances, positions in tables, cup victories, and so on, and the elite have various fringe benefits—free travel, sometimes free cars, free meals, and the chance to see much of the world at no personal cost.

In Italy and Spain, where bonuses tend to be bigger, salaries are rapidly reaching absurd levels and there is no doubt that Brazil's Pele became a dollar millionaire. Even in Communist countries players are well rewarded, with nominal jobs and distinguished titles.

The British footballer has come a long way from the early days of illegal payments in shillings before the general acceptance of professionalism in 1885. Even in those days money played a large part in the game, and the varying sums paid led to difficulties over 'poaching' before the League standardized wages at £4 a week (in season) in 1901. This went up to £5 in 1910 and £9 in 1920, but was cut to £8 in 1922, with only £6 in the summer months. Soccer giants such as Dixie Dean and Alex James spent their careers on this sum: the next rise was not until 1947, when the maximum was lifted to £12 for players with five years of unbroken service. Further increases culminated in a £20 maximum in 1958, but although such sums were niggardly reward for such men as Stanley Matthews and Tom Finney, the post-1961 revolution brought several clubs to the verge of bankruptcy, with income from sidelines such as weekly draws and social clubs playing an ever-increasing part in finances.

Although the publicity given to the earnings of leading players obscures the scant returns in the lower grades—with their growing reliance on part-time players— the fact remains that wages are far too high to be compatible with revenue in a great many cases. In 1970-71 some Second Division clubs paid out more in wages than they took at the gate. As a result, some form of standardization may be needed unless the number of clubs is to be drastically reduced—a blow to the League's fundamental principle of equality for all.

The players, of course, claim that they earn all they get. Certainly they are subjected to more rigid authority than in the old days, sometimes fined for breaches of discipline, often away from home—for seven weeks in the case of England's 1970 World Cup party—and with their food, alcohol, tobacco, and even leisure habits strictly controlled. Certain well-publicized lapses show that healthy young men can rebel against a regime imposed by older officials, but in general the modern player seems to take his off-field responsibilities seriously. Rightly so: the money now to be made from the game is directly related to dedication.

Scouting

As football has widened its scope, so the search for talent has become more intense. The network of scouts run by the top clubs—a format pioneered by Major Buckley at Wolves in the 1930s—in now such that the average age of players under review is dropping lower and lower. Brilliant teenagers have emerged throughout the game's history, but never has the industry been so closely concentrated on youth. Clubs in Britain are now able to sign pre-teenage boys on associate forms, and the battle to snap up the best of each succeeding generation is becoming increasingly fierce.

Because of the nature of their trade, scouts prefer to remain anonymous. The leading members of the fraternity are known to all club managements, but only rarely do their names become common knowledge among supporters. How many West Ham followers, for instance, would know that Wally St Pier brought on Moore, Hurst and Peters. Although many of them are former professionals (Bill McCracken at Millwall, Alf Sherwood at Liverpool), a great number have never played the game at any high level, but have the innate judgement of talent that makes their long hours worthwhile. They go to matches anywhere and everywhere—in minor leagues, parks, back streets, and beaches—in the hope of finding a jewel.

Scouts in a club's employ work for retainers and expenses, plus

1 Wally St Pier, who brought on Moore, Peters, and Hurst, with some West Ham hopefuls. 2 In games such as these, on public recreation pitches, future stars may be found.

a bonus if a youngster they discover turns out to be really good. Such payments are usually geared to the amount of games played in the first team over a set period.

The unearthing of a genius such as Jimmy Greaves, found by Chelsea's Jimmy Thomson at the age of 11, can save a club thousands of pounds in transfer fees. But the cost of running a scouting organization—with its endless travelling, reports, and phone calls, checks by managers and directors, and the expense of maintaining junior teams in virtually spectator-less leagues—can be as big a drain on finances as an actual transfer fee. And there is another aspect to consider: the 'hawking' of a talented teenager from club to club, with the consequent haggling over terms. Many parents have made various profits, from cases of whisky to lump sums in cash, before allowing their offspring to sign.

A scout's job, never easy, has become all the harder as society in general has become more and more dominated by material gain. But while football, a microcosm of that society, retains its intensely competitive nature, no club can afford to be without the men who first give them news of a possible star.

Violence and Foul-Play

The increase in violence is one of the crosses that football has to bear. Although the mindless hooliganism of crowds in the late 1950s and the 1960s seemed to have been stemmed to a considerable degree in the early 1970s, the on-field atmosphere of many matches was still distressingly ill-tempered.

Football had always been a hard game—'Let us have hacking' said Lord Kinnaird, a Scottish international, a century ago—but the recent proliferation of incidents could be blamed to a great extent on the increased rewards for success. The spread of defensive tactics also contributed, building up frustrations that could easily explode into one of the unseemly brawls that littered the soccer scene.

'Strong-arm' methods were not new, of course. Veterans still spoke with reverence of such rugged tacklers as 'Nudger' Needham and Wilf Copping, and the advent of such graceful full-backs as Jimmy Armfield and Ray Wilson did not entirely dispel the memory of those awesome mountains of muscle, all thighs and toothbrush haircuts, who figured in so many defences during less cultured days.

But the emergence of cash as the dominating factor brought with it an overall cynicism and disregard for the spirit of the laws, coupled with a growing ability to bend those laws as far as possible through the so-called 'tactical' or 'professional' foul—the deliberate handling of a pass out of heading distance, the jersey-tugging, the obstruction, the verbal goading of opponents.

England players, felled like skittles in the notorious match against Argentina in the 1966 World Cup, complained about the flying boots, but were even more bitter about the unseen methods: the apparently friendly ruffling of the hair disguising a sharp tug, the equally 'sportsmanlike' helping hand that covered a quick twist of the flesh.

Not all British players reacted so stoically. A couple of years later the Celtic team responded with brutality in the World Club Championship play-off with another Argentinian side, Racing Buenos Aires, and their directors fined them all £250, even after making allowances for the appalling provocation in their two previous matches. At half-time winger Jimmy Johnstone had to wash the spittle out of his hair and goalkeeper Ronnie Simpson was felled by a bottle before the game had ever begun.

So Britain was feeling the backlash of ill-feeling that had built up over the years, a resentment against the strong tackling of players brought up on physical challenge. In contrast, the Latin countries preferred to use the ball rather than the body, did not

relish the muscular approach, and treated goalkeepers—fair game for such forwards as Dean and Drake—as if made of rare jade.

When referees of clashes between the two methods could not agree on a standardized interpretation of the rules, the situation was plainly open to the sort of explosion that earned the 1934 England-Italy match the tag of 'The Battle of Highbury'. This unsavoury affair led to one sportswriter signing his report 'From our war correspondent', and also provided one of the great photographs of soccer history: that of Drake on his knees with an Italian arm round his throat.

The World Cup, with its many contrasts of national temperament, has a gory history bearing out the Orwellian theory of sport being an unfailing source of ill will. The worst incidents were in 1954, when the Brazil-Hungary 'Battle of Berne' was carried over into the dressing room, with boots and furniture used by both sides, and in 1962, when a journalistic hate campaign resulted in a dreadful clash between Italy and the host country, Chile. And the way in which opponents can be inflamed and authority influenced was ably demonstrated in 1966 by the West Germans, whose skill as footballers was only a little better than their acting ability. Man after man collapsed in histrionic agony . . . and four of the five players sent off during the tournament incurred that punishment when playing against the Germans.

Fortunately for the game's reputation, or what remained of it, the 1970 World Cup was in general well handled by a panel of referees specially briefed on interpretation and at last certain of authority's support. Despite the high stakes, the players behaved themselves in a sportsmanlike way.

But all countries still had their own domestic problems, and none greater than Britain. The growth of television coverage brought bad behaviour into millions of homes, and there would be little doubt that this was an influencing factor on the sharp rise of disciplinary cases in minor soccer. Youngsters who emulated the stars in dress, hair style, and mannerisms were also copying their violent habits, for no good reason.

Opposite, **Niggling fouls such as shirt-pulling can lead to retaliation from even the most mild-mannered player. And then it is the man who hits back who is booked or sent off. Failure to see the first foul is a fault not exclusive to soccer referees. 1 Violence flares in a Greek football match in 1970. The action on the field is often transmitted to the terraces. 2 English soccer is often the scene of the mass melee—when players try to settle their disputes the traditional way.**

Keystone

Syndication International

1 There's a time and a place for everything, and many players have learned, during suspension, that a football field is no place for fights.
2 Amateur football clubs eke out a precarious existence, with very little gate money.

Having beaten Britain in the 1964 Olympic qualifying tournament, Greece then withdrew voluntarily because of their own lack of definition of amateurism. Yet only the next year UEFA began a new competition for amateurs, Austria beating Scotland 2-1 in the final in Palma. In the semi-final, when Scotland beat Spain 3-1, the Spanish right-back was Gonzales, who had played for Real Madrid against Manchester United in the European Cup semi-final two months previously. In the second European Amateur Championship in 1969, England were beaten by Spain, who fielded almost an entire team of players from the leading league clubs, four of them from Real Madrid.

Football is retained in the Olympic Games—despite all the difficulties of definition—because it usually attracts more spectators than the athletics programme; the most ironic example of financial expediency. In Britain, amateurism lingered on until its abolition in 1974. It was abused on all sides, not because the players wanted it (though their under-the-counter payments were conveniently tax-free), but because its opponents alleged, its existence supported a body of officials who would lose their position and power if amateurism were ended. Finally, the Football Association, with an objective view of the abuses, decided to call everyone 'players', and so ended the charade which had been so stoutly defended for several decades. It is unlikely that Football, as a whole, will suffer.

Amateurism, by definition, should be voluntary, yet throughout the history of the game there have been attempts to impose amateurism on those who were quite clearly not amateur or did not wish to be. In between is the hard core of hypocrisy which says 'we want to be amateur, but we want to pay our players'. By terminating the Amateur Cup, the FA, almost at one blow, eliminated the abuse of 'amateurism', for the Cup was the *raison d'etre* of most of the 'shamateurism'. The one disadvantage of this, however, is that the Amateur Cup provided considerable impetus in the early part of the season to the small, genuinely amateur clubs who battled through the qualifying stages with the dream of reaching the Wembly final. It is difficult to see how another competition, open to semi-professional clubs as well, can provide the same appeal.

But the decision to ban amateur football at a 'senior level' was inevitable. For almost 70 years there had been a running fight between the officials of amateur and professional football. There were ridiculous anomalies—one of the most blatant being the fact that, until 1935, amateur international teams were chosen by a selection team which had not seen the players in action.

The players continued to complain, with considerable justification, about varying methods employed by referees and the inconsistent punishments imposed by higher authority. But the League and the FA do not kick and punch each other. Referees do not steal yards for free-kicks, or drag players across to consult a linesman. Journalists and commentators do not incite crowds by gestures and play-acting.

Though the blame for violence rests, in the last count, with the players, it falls in the first instance on the press and the public, who create and sustain the pressures, and on the managers, coaches, and directors who are responsible for applying them. With success of such paramount importance—few people remember the runners-up—the indications early in the 1970s were that the problem was no nearer a solution.

Amateur Football

It is symptomatic of the general state of amateur soccer that the day before the 1971 Amateur Cup final at Wembley, one of the finalists, Skelmersdale, were the subject of an investigation into . . . their amateurism. Indeed it is doubtful whether any amateur side of consequence could bear a close scrutiny of the basis on which its affairs are conducted, how its players are remunerated for 'expenses': certainly not Bulgaria, Britain's opponents in the qualifying competition for the 1972 Olympics. Like all Eastern European countries, they admit to no professionalism, and so fielded seven of the same team in almost successive weeks against Britain at Wembley and against Greece in a full international.

The amateur world is a confusion of blurred distinctions.

Speedway

Speedway—motor-cycle racing on short, loose-surfaced tracks—has had a chequered history since its birth in a small Australian town in 1923. Its growth has been phenomenal—in 1971 speedway's world championship attracted entries from 19 countries and tracks were appearing in Africa and North and South America—but at times the sport has been in danger of extinction in its major centre, Great Britain. The crises, however, seem to be over. Speedway has emerged as one of Britain's top spectator sports, drawing an estimated 150,000 spectators to its tracks each week. This firm base, combined with expanding international horizons, seems to assure speedway a rosy future in the 1970s.

There are references to forms of motor-cycle short-track racing as far back as 1907—in Pietermaritzburg, Natal—but historians generally agree that speedway's real beginning was in West Maitland, New South Wales, in 1923. The man behind it was a New Zealander, Johnnie Hoskins. (Hoskins retained his interest in the sport he created. In 1971 he was promoting speedway at Canterbury in the British League's

second division.) The restless and energetic Hoskins, responsible for a West Maitland 'Electric Light Carnival', decided to inject some interest into the event by introducing short-track motor-cycle racing on a dirt track. There were virtually no rules, although riders were told they could not put their foot down to help them round corners. Mounts were stripped-down road machines.

The success of the meeting left no doubt that this new form of racing was more than just a gimmick. More meetings were arranged at West Maitland and

speedway was born. Tracks appeared at New South Wales centres such as Newcastle and, more important, Sydney. Organization became more sophisticated. The Australian riders of the time —including such now-legendary figures as Vic Huxley, Billy Lamont, and Frank Arthur— were joined by a sprinkling of Americans, notably the giant Sprouts Elder.

News of a new daredevil sport in Australia filtered through to Britain, but just how speedway arrived there remains a controversial question. The Speedway

Above, **The sport of the 1970s? Since its invention in Australia in 1923, speedway has spread all over the world and continues to expand.** *Below,* **This 1928 meeting at High Beech in Epping Forest brought speedway to England.**

Control Board says that a licence was granted by the Auto-Cycle Union (ACU) for a meeting at Camberley Heath in Surrey in May 1927. But this meeting, on a sandy surface, would appear to resemble modern grass-track racing more than speedway. Northern followers claim the first meeting was at Droylsden, near Manchester, on June 25, 1927. This meeting, held on a $\frac{1}{2}$-mile trotting track, was organized by the South Manchester Motor Club. It is said that riders raced in a clockwise direction and that the meeting bore little resemblance to a modern speedway meeting. Most historians believe that Britain's first meeting was at High Beech in Epping Forest on February 19, 1928. The ACU definitely issued a permit for this meeting to the Ilford Motorcycle Club. And there is no doubt that two Australians were present at High Beech that day to demonstrate the art of broadsiding, by then the accepted form of cornering in

Syndication International

Australia. (One of the British riders at this historic meeting was Phil Bishop, who was killed in Belgium in 1970 while acting as team manager to West Ham speedway team.)

After High Beech, speedway mushroomed all over the country, and by 1929-30 the sport was developing into an organized business. The great names of Australian speedway such as Huxley and Arthur had moved to Britain, with the larger-than-life American Sprouts Elder possibly the biggest drawcard of them all. By 1929 league competitions had started, and Britain had begun to produce riders of the calibre of Roger Frogley and Colin Watson to match the Australians. Equipment and techniques were changing and improving all the time, and enthusiasts who recall these infant days of speedway in the late 1920s and early 1930s still claim that they were the most exciting of the sport. Wimbledon, White City, Stamford Bridge, West Ham, Crystal Palace, and, a little later, Wembley developed into famous tracks in the South. In the North, speedway centred upon Manchester's Belle Vue circuit.

In 1930 the first England-Australia test matches put the sport on an international basis, and in 1936 the World Championship began. This was another brainchild of Johnnie Hoskins who had moved to Britain after hearing of the success speedway was enjoying there. There were efforts, too, to spread the speedway word farther afield. Places as far apart as South America and Egypt saw speedway, while North America produced successors to Sprouts Elder in the form of the brothers Jack and Cordy Milne and Wilbur Lamoreaux. Australian Lionel Van Praag had won the first World Championship in 1936, but a year later the Americans scored a remarkable 1-2-3 success, with Jack Milne winning from Lamoreaux and Cordy Milne. Australia recaptured the title through Bluey Wilkinson in 1938.

Efforts were even made to introduce speedway to Hitler's Germany. Scandinavians had already adopted it, and they produced a top-class rider in Morian Hansen of Denmark. Sweden for a time banned the sport on the grounds that it was too dangerous—an ironic move in view of Sweden's domination of the sport in later years.

The outbreak of war brought to an end fully organized speedway—a costly activity—although there were regular meetings at Belle Vue and occasional meetings in the London area throughout the war. In common with other sports, speedway went through a boom period with the return of peace, and as early as 1946 the sport was running smoothly again. Speedway flourished in Britain, Australia, and New Zealand.

The World Championship

The most important event on the speedway calendar, the World Championship was first held in 1936 at Wembley. In its early years the competition attracted only riders based in Britain. Not that it mattered much—before and immediately after World War II any speedway rider of talent was competing in Britain. But when European speedway began to bloom, the structure of the championship had to be revised. In 1936-37-38 tournaments had consisted of a series of British qualifying rounds in which the riders picked up bonus points. The 16 top scorers qualified for the final and the bonus points were added to the score each rider made in the final. Hence, in the inaugural year of 1936, Australian Bluey Wilkinson scored a 15-point maximum in the Wembley final but failed to win the championship because he had scored fewer bonus points than Lionel Van Praag.

When the championship was reintroduced in 1949 the bonus points system was dropped. Instead a series of qualifying rounds and semi-finals decided the 16 men for the final, and the points scored on final night determined the winner. Today the qualifying rounds are split up into three zones—Great Britain, Scandinavia, and the Continent. Each area runs a series of qualifying rounds, semi-finals, and finals to determine the final 16. In the final, each rider meets every other opponent only once.

Not only the organization, but also the site of the championship has changed. Wembley was long synonymous with the World Championship, but with the overseas boom in speedway outside Britain it came as no surprise when the FIM—Federation Internationale Motorcycliste, the international ruling body of all two-wheeled sport—delegated the final to another country. Sweden staged the first world final outside Britain in 1961 at Malmo, and has played host at Gothenburg's Ullevi Stadium in 1964, 1966, and 1968. They were scheduled to host it again in 1971. Strong Polish claims were answered in 1970, when a capacity crowd of 65,000 watched the final in Wroclaw. At the start of the 1970s, the USSR were pressing for the right to stage the final.

Ove Fundin of Sweden, with five victories, has the best record of any rider in the championship up to 1971. New Zealand's Barry Briggs—four wins—has appeared in 17 finals since making his debut in 1954. Another New Zealander, Ivan Mauger, became the first man to win the title three years in a row when he won at Wroclaw in 1970—a performance all the more creditable in view of the fact that his two previous wins were at Gothenburg and Wembley. Riders from one country have finished 1, 2, 3, in the final on three occasions. America did it in 1937, England in 1949, and Sweden in 1961. Most winners have come from New Zealand, Sweden, and, in early years, Australia. England has produced only two winners—Tommy Price and Peter Craven (twice), but Welshman Freddie Williams won the crown in 1950 and 1953.

In the United States, though, it was a different story. Within a few years of the end of the war the influence of American riders was almost non-existent.

From 1946 to 1948 speedway's World Championship was replaced by a British Riders Championship. In domestic competition there were three divisions, and with crowd restrictions in force at the time, many meetings were held before capacity crowds. In 1949 the World Championship was reinstated, and Tommy Price became the first Englishman to win the crown. There were also signs that Sweden was beginning to take the sport seriously—something that became apparent in the mid-1950s with the emergence of Olle Nygren and Ove Fundin, the rider who went on to win the world final a record five times. The New Zealanders, too, became a force after Ronnie Moore and Barry Briggs arrived on the British scene. And England, in addition to 1949 world champion Price, boasted such riders as Jack Parker (who had ridden superbly since 1928), Bill Kitchen, and Split Waterman. Later there followed Peter Craven who won the world title twice before being killed in 1963.

Yet even during the boom years of 1950 and 1951 there were signs of danger ahead. Crowds were falling off after the immediate post-war upsurge, and interest in Australia, for more than 20 years a pipeline of fresh talent, was on the decline—even though an Australian, Jack Young, won the world crown in 1951 and 1952. By the middle of the decade the danger signals were there for all to see. Following the death of Sir Arthur Elvin, a long-time ally of speedway, Wembley closed down in 1956. And when West Ham also closed, many assumed that speedway itself was dying. From a bustling, healthy three-division set-up in the early 1950s, speedway slumped to a mere one division and nine tracks in 1959. In London, once the home of top-flight teams Wembley, West Ham, Harringay, and New Cross, only Wimbledon survived. Without the perseverance of the nine tracks that held on through the bitter years of the speedway recession, it is doubtful if speedway would be alive today in Britain.

Many reasons can be advanced for the speedway slump. Perhaps speedway had expanded too quickly after World War II and left itself open to a sudden falling away of interest. It was, too, the period of 'tele-mania', with many people for the first time finding entertainment brought to them in their own homes. Speedway survived—just—and in 1960 traces of a silver lining appeared in the speedway cloud of depression. A bunch of enthusiasts, some of them former riders, linked up to form the Provincial League. Old tracks were revived and new tracks

Gerry Cranham

Popperfoto

Sportography

1 Sweden produced a 5-times world champion in Ove Fundin. **2** Wembley v West Ham. British club competition is the heart of speedway. **3** Australian Jack Young waits his chance behind New Zealand's Ronnie Moore in a 1951 world title race. A crowd of 93,000 saw Young triumph in the final. **4** Tony Clarke slams his left foot down hard in a British Southern Riders Championship.

introduced. In a matter of months the number of speedway tracks in Britain more than doubled. And although Australian interest in speedway continued to decline, the scene in Europe was improving. Swedish speedway was thriving, and Poland, Czechoslovakia, and the USSR were coming into the picture. In 1960, too, inter-

national competition received a great fillip by the introduction of the World Team Cup.

The Provincial League continued to prosper in Britain until another crisis hit the domestic front in 1964. The Provincial League newcomers rebelled against the ruling Speedway Control Board (SCB) and operated without official licences. Their protest turned out to be a blessing in disguise. At the end of 1964 the Royal Automobile Club held an inquiry into speedway with Lord Shawcross as its chairman. It upheld many of the protests of the Provincial League promoters and completely revamped speedway's organization. The inquiry decided that the Provincial League and the seven-strong National League should merge to form a British League,

which first appeared in 1965 with 18 teams. The new set-up gave the promoters a larger say in how speedway was to be run, and a new body, the British Speedway Promoters' Association (BSPA), was given the task of handling the day-to-day affairs of speedway. A restyled Speedway Control Board took over the remainder of administration with power to accept or reject the decisions and recommendations of the promoters. It proved a much better arrangement than the old. West Ham, back in speedway in 1964, won the first British League Championship a year later.

The new-found harmony in the British ranks gave speedway a chance to expand. Early efforts to form a second division failed at first, but by 1968 the British League was strong enough to

embrace 10 new tracks and form another division. A year later the total increased to 35, and in 1970 and 1971 the number remained at a constant 36. The fact that Wembley returned in 1970 confirmed the healthy rebirth of speedway in Britain. The British League's policy of cautious advancement has given the sport a firm foundation, while the BSPA has proved a constant source of new ideas for expansion. More areas were being probed for possible centres, and plans advanced for a third division—in its own right or by regionalizing the second division—in 1971. Speedway has been called a family sport, and it seems to have captured the imaginations of enough households in the late 1960s to make the catastrophic days of the 1950s a mere bad memory.

281

Associated Press

International Speedway

Although Australia was the birth-place of speedway, Britain became, after the huge successes of speedway meetings there in the 1930s and 1940s, the home of the sport. Since the revival of speedway there in the late 1960s, strenuous efforts have been made to spread the speedway gospel to far-flung parts of the world.

The worth of international competition had been proved as long ago as 1930, when the first test series was held between England and Australia. Internationals between the two countries lapsed in the mid-1950s, when Australian speedway went into a decline deeper even than in Britain. In 1966, however, the tests were resumed. Australia caught the backlash of the formation of the British League, and interest in speedway improved markedly in all major Australian cities. The young Australian rider is now prepared once again to give the

**1 When speedway came to New York's Madison Square Garden in 1971, a huge crowd cheered the fall of Barry Briggs, the New Zealand 'villain' of the night. The meeting's success encouraged hopes of an American speedway revival.
2 Subtle cornering technique from another New Zealand world champion—Ronnie Moore. 3 Ivan Mauger, a Kiwi in Lion's clothing, leads top Russian ace Igor Plechanov.**

sport a fling, knowing that if he displays talent he is virtually assured of a place in British League racing. New Zealand, too, fulfils the same role of an English nursery, and Barry Briggs, Ronnie Moore, and Ivan Mauger have really put New Zealand on the speedway map. These three giants have been the backbone of a New Zealand international squad, and as they hold British racing licences they have also been permitted to represent Great Britain.

Gerry Cranham

Ray Green

Speedway has spread remarkably in Europe since the end of the war, and most continental countries have staged the sport. From humble pre-war beginnings, Scandinavian speedway advanced to the stage where its riders were able to challenge British and Commonwealth domination of the sport. By 1971 Sweden, with Ove Fundin as its standard-bearer, had won the World Team Cup six times since its inauguration in 1960, compared with one solitary success by Great Britain.

Norway, with riders such as Sverre Harrfeldt and Reidar Eide, and Denmark, with Ole Olsen, have helped considerably in widening speedway's international horizons, while Finland too have shown considerable interest in the sport. But speedway's biggest success story has probably been Poland—Eastern Europe's leading speedway nation and four-times winner of the World Team Cup. Official figures show that in 1969 speedway overtook soccer as Poland's number one spectator

Above, **It's not only when they're on the track that the riders risk injury. Russian riders and other team members shield their faces from shale flying off the track during an event at Manchester's Belle Vue stadium,** *Below,* **Out on the track, the Russians find a safer place—leading the way from Barry Briggs in the Great Britain-USSR match. In the white helmet is two-times runner-up in the world championship—Igor Plechanov.**

sport. Speedway has also caught on in the USSR. Since Moscow staged the first meeting in 1958, Russian riders have enjoyed reasonable international success. Igor Plechanov, their 1971 chief trainer, twice finished runner-up in a World Championship final. By the start of the 1970s most experts rated the USSR fourth—behind Britain and the Commonwealth, Sweden, and Poland—in world ratings. They were, however, strongly challenged by Czechoslovakia—a country that has

Ray Green

Equipment and Techniques

Speedway is a rough-and-tumble sport, so the speedway rider outfits himself accordingly. As well as encasing himself in leather and a crash-helmet, he usually wears both goggles and face visor to protect himself from falls and churned-up dust. His left boot has a lot of work to do on corners, so he clips a steel sole onto it.

The machine he rides is in a class of its own. In fact, anyone taking one of these powerful motor-cycles on the road would face prosecution —they have no brakes, and only one gear, although this can be adjusted to various conditions and tracks.

The special speedway machine was evolved in Britain. At first, British riders followed the Australian pattern of stripping down their road machines for speedway meetings, but it soon became plain that specialized machinery was necessary for such specialized racing. By the end of 1928, 17 well-known manufacturers were displaying speedway machinery at the London Motorcycle Show. At first the Harley 'Peashooter' proved the most popular bike, but already several leading Australian riders had adopted modified Douglas machines. Douglas were the first concern to set about making a pure speedway motor-cycle, and despite the efforts of well-known names such as AJS, BSA, Cotton, New Imperial, Scott, and Triumph, their creation was selected by most of the star speedway riders. This horizontal twin-cylinder machine is still held in great affection by those who rode it or saw it raced, although it lasted only a short time as top machine. It was supplanted by the Rudge, but this bike, too, was destined for a short career. By 1932 the top men in speedway were opting for the JAP, and they continued to do so for more than 30 years. Until 1966 all of speedway's world champions gained their titles on JAP motor-cycles powered by engines basically the same as the JAP powerplant of the early 1930s. Only the frames of the machines had changed drastically. In the late 1950s Poland introduced the FIZ, but it failed to catch on, and it was not until Czechoslovakia came up with the JAWA-ESO that the JAP found itself facing a serious rival. At first the JAWA won a reputation as a tough bike able to smooth out bumpy East European circuits, but New Zealand ace Barry Briggs proved its suitability for British circuits by winning the 1966 World Championship on one. By 1971 the JAWA was probably a more popular machine in Britain than the JAP.

Today's speedway motor-cycles are powered by a 500 cc engine, except for those taking part in domestic British meetings, which allow a maximum of 510 cc. Before the race they are bump started, then held on the clutch until the race starts. (In the earlier days of the sport some narrow tracks such as Stamford Bridge allowed rolling starts). The rear tyre—larger than the front because of the drive needed for quick acceleration and broadsiding—has a nominal dimension of 19 by 3.50 inches. Frames and handlebars have changed over the years, largely because of the drastic changes in cornering technique that modern riders have pioneered. Early machines had low-slung handlebars and long frames suitable for the spectacular trailing-leg technique. This involved the rider broadsiding round the bends with his left, or nearside, leg trailing behind and his knee almost touching the track. As a spectacle this style has no equal, but it has been ousted by the more efficient foot-forward technique. It means that the rider now sits in a much more upright position on a machine with upswept handlebars and short frames.

Although it is difficult to improve on today's sophisticated machinery, many riders do make minor modifications to their machines to suit their own style. Limited markets have so far deterred manufacturers from producing new speedway machines, but there is some hope that America or Japan might come up with something new if speedway catches on in a big way there.

Popperfoto

Gerry Cranham

produced some good international riders despite a dearth of local speedway meetings. At the end of the 1960s Czech riders began moving to Britain to appear for British League clubs in much the same way as Swedish, Norwegian, Danish, and, 10 years previously, Polish riders. Another communist country, East Germany, is a rapidly improving speedway force that has produced riders good enough to ride in a world championship final. All the other East European nations take an active interest in speedway.

Scandinavia apart, Western Europe has not taken to speedway on anything like the same scale. At one time or another, however, most of its countries have staged the sport. West Germany has been the venue for some big meetings—and they have always drawn the crowds. Austria and France stage a handful of meetings each year, and interest is growing in Italy. Plans are also afoot to take the sport to the holiday island of Majorca in the early 1970s.

Speedway's export drive for the 1970s seems to have got off to a good start outside of Europe A track at Costa Mesa in California has successfully reintroduced speedway to the Americans. A number of British League

1 Speedway's international appeal is illustrated by the appearance of a Dane and a Briton in an East German race. 2 Crash helmets, goggles, face visors and leather suits are necessary to save the rider from possible injury.

riders have raced there, and more tracks are being opened, mainly in California.

Farther south, Brazil is likely to take over from Venezuela and Argentina in staging speedway—in 1969 Brazil asked Britain's SCB for advice on how to run it. Speedway even has a foothold in the east, where Japan, very much a law unto itself in the speedway world, is the only country that allows betting on speedway events. Jimmy Ogisu became the first Japanese rider to appear in Britain when he took part in a few meetings in 1970. There are also reports that Chinese observers have watched speedway meetings in the USSR. South Africa showed some interest in speedway in the 1950s, but for some time little was heard of speedway in the African continent. This has been changed by the successful introduction of speedway to Rhodesia, where the sport got under way at Salisbury, Bulawayo, and Gwelo late in 1970.

Squash Rackets

Give any small boy a ball and a piece of wood and he will soon discover what fun and exercise there is to be had batting the ball against the nearest available wall. The game he has invented has the same essential elements and appeal as squash rackets, the 19th-century British invention that, after sweeping Australia in the 1950s, emerged as Britain's fastest growing sport.

A player-against-player (singles) sport, squash rackets is played on an enclosed, rectangular, four-walled court. Walls are of wood or composition material. Players enter through a door set flush into the court's back wall. The basic aim of each player—they hit the ball alternately—is to make a stroke that sends the ball above a 19-inch-high tin strip on the front wall so that his opponent cannot reach it until it has bounced twice, or is forced into the error of hitting the ball onto the floor, tin, or outside the boundary lines painted on the side and back walls. The ball need not go directly from racket to front wall, but can hit any number of other walls first so long as it does not touch the ground before reaching the front wall.

Played at championship level, squash makes tremendous demands on stamina and skill. But at the other end of the scale it is childishly simple to play and enjoy, provided that the two novices are of similar basic skill. The size of the court and the number of rebounds enables an active player to reach most strokes made by an opponent of comparable standard. And as the size of the court and the height of the boundary lines afford a tremendous margin of safety against hitting out, an average club session of 40 minutes provides ample exercise for all but keen competitive players. Exhilarating and

Above, **Squash is not a noted spectator sport, but a glass wall allows the small number of onlookers to be augmented** *Below,* **Hashim Khan (right) won the Open championship seven times: his brother, Azam Khan (left), four times.**

Sunday Times Magazine

Popperfoto

Central Press

Glossary of Terms

Board The equivalent of the net in tennis: a line, the top edge of which is 19 inches above the floor, extending the full width of the front wall.

Boast A shot in which the ball is hit onto the nearer side wall before rebounding onto the front wall, ideally falling where the other side wall joins the floor.

Game ball The state of the game when 'hand in' needs only one point to win it.

Hand in The player who serves.

Hand out The player who receives the service.

Hand The period from the time a player becomes 'hand in' until he becomes 'hand out'.

Marker An official appointed to control a match and call the score.

If no referee sits beside him, he also assumes the referee's duties.

Nick The junction of walls and floors; also a shot that sends the ball into the nick for it to bounce unpredictably.

Not up An expression used to denote that a ball has not been returned in accordance with the rules. Frequently heard when a scrambling player hits the ball desperately just after it has bounced on the floor a second time.

Penalty point If a player seems deliberately or unnecessarily to obstruct an opponent in play, the referee can award a penalty point against the offender.

Referee An additional official appointed for important championships to assist the marker and adjudicate on difficult decisions,

particularly penalty points.

Reverse angle A shot hit onto the side wall opposite the one the striker is facing, the ball then rebounding onto the front wall. Used sparingly, this stroke is surprising and effective.

Rally The continuous exchange of shots between players during the playing of a point.

Set A marker must remind 'hand out' at 8-all that he must decide how to 'set' the game before receiving the next service. The 'hand out' may decide 'set 2' (best 2 out of 3 points) or 'no set' (next point scored by player 'in hand') decides the game.

Tin See *Board*.

Volley As in all ball games, a shot made before the ball hits the ground.

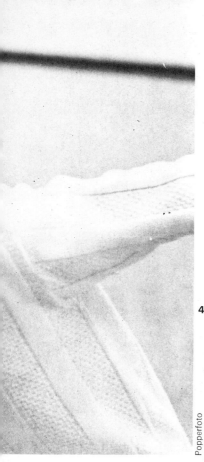

1 Australia's Heather McKay was almost unbeatable in the 1960s and 1970s, winning the British amateur title from 1962 to 1974.
2 Cornishman Jonah Barrington became a squash addict and was rewarded with six wins in the British Open. It is Barrington, more than anyone else, who typfies the new professional approach to the game in Britain.
3 His great rival Geoff Hunt won the first two ISRF titles.

Popperfoto

Eric Jewell

4 The squash court. Squash derives little income from 'gates', as few spectators are able to watch any game. It remains, essentially, a participant sport for enthusiasts of all ages.

Diagram labels: FRONT WALL LINE, SIDE WALL LINE, BACK WALL LINE, CUT LINE, SERVICE BOX, FLUSH FITTING DOOR, 19in, HALF COURT LINE, FOREHAND COURT, TELL TALE, BACKHAND COURT, SHORT LINE, SERVICE BOX, 15ft, 6ft, 21ft, 5ft 3in, 7ft, 5ft 3in, 14ft, 32ft

exhausting, it is a game that appeals equally to both sexes.

History

The ancient Lydians reputedly invented the ball. Whether they did or not, they were certainly fond of games, and it is easy to imagine of a Lydian child batting the new invention against a wall with a piece of wood. That, surely, was primitive rackets—a game that did not become clearly identifiable until the 19th century, although the work 'racket' appears in Chaucer's *Troylus and Cryseyde* (about 1380). Inferences about the existence of rackets can be drawn from Joseph Strutt's 1801 work *The Sports and Pastimes of the People of England*, but the best starting point for the game of rackets is probably 1820, when a court was built at Harrow School. A fast game played with a hard ball, it demanded practice, and pupils found the Harrow boarding houses particularly suitable for the purpose. Nearly all had an area where a blank wall ran at right-angles to another. A

chalk line at the correct height across the blank wall, a soft ball, an asphalt sheet on the ground, and the training game 'baby rackets' was born. So was squash. By 1886 the smaller-court, soft-ball game had gained individual recognition, and it grew at a steady if moderate pace in Britain until the mid-1960s. By then social conditions made squash an ideal recreational activity, and by 1970 there were an estimated 500,000 players in the country.

Before the 1960s, squash was essentially an upper- and middle-class sport, mainly because of its historic associations with the public schools and the armed forces. But the construction of new multi-courts, such as those at the National Sports Centre at Crystal Palace, opened up the game to other groups of people: overweight business executives, typists, bored factory workers, and schoolchildren in need of more stimulating physical training than their schools offered. Nevertheless, the venues for the major championships—the Lansdowne, RAC, Naval and Military, Manchester Northern, and similar clubs—retained their air of exclusiveness.

Britain, however, was not the first officially to organize the game. That first took place on the

North American continent with the formation of the United States Squash Rackets Association in 1907 and the Canadian Squash Rackets Association in 1911, although the game played there differed slightly then—and still does—from the one met elsewhere in the world. (In North America the court and racket have different dimensions, doubles are played, and there is no need to be the server to win points.) The first organized body to adopt the English game was the South African Squash Rackets Association, in 1910. Early control in England was exercised by the Tennis and Rackets Association, the inaugural meeting of the Squash Rackets Association (SRA) not taking place until 1928, when about 30 clubs affiliated. By 1955 the total in England had risen to 350, with a further 250 overseas clubs supporting them. At the start of the 1970-71 season there were 605 affiliated bodies listed in the SRA handbook.

Competitive play preceded the formation of the SRA. The first professional championship took place in 1920, C. R. Read beating A. W. B. Johnson in a two-match series played at the Queen's and Royal Automobile Clubs. The Amateur Championship followed in 1922 at Lord's. The Women's

Championship also appeared that year, Miss J. Cave defeating Miss N. Cave in the final. One or other of these sisters appeared in every final of this event until 1933. The Oxford-Cambridge universities match following in 1925, and Yorkshire won the first inter-county championship in 1929.

The first international matches were held at Philadelphia in 1923, Great Britain winning against Canada but losing to the United States. But the game did not take on a truly international aspect until 1930, when the first English Open Championship was held. This remained the unofficial world championship until 1967 when, following the birth of the International Squash Rackets Federation (ISRF) in January, the first ISRF Championships were held, in Australia. Geoff Hunt showed how far squash had advanced in that country by winning the individual event, and Australia took the team championship. The founder countries of the ISRF were Australia, Great Britain, India, New Zealand, Pakistan, South Africa, and the United Arab Republic.

Most of the hundred plus meetings on Great Britain's tournament schedule for the 1970-71 season were open to non-British subjects—but not to the touring professional 'circus' headed by Jonah Barrington, who were playing exhibition matches and competing in the few tournaments open to them. The situation was approaching that of the pre-Open days of lawn tennis, when 'shamateurism' brought discredit on the game. With this in mind the SRA wanted to eliminate all distinctions and call all competitors simply 'players', but this move to make squash 'open' has been resisted.

Steeplechasing

A sport of thrills and spills in which the least significant contest may prove spectacular, steeplechasing reached a peak of popularity in Great Britain and Ireland in the 1960s. That decade a number of factors combined to make horse racing over jumps one of the most popular spectator sports in Britain. Several great personalities —equine and human—won new followers, press coverage increased and, above all, television brought the sport to millions. By 1970 it was rivalling flat racing in public appeal.

The attraction of this exciting sport to the British is tied up with their love of the amateur. While flat racing is essentially an industry, concerned with bloodstock breeding and high finance, steeplechasing remains much more of a pure entertainment. The prospects of personal gain in this highly dangerous sport are so remote that the usual motivation for entering it is a love of horses and the spur of competition. Luck, good or bad, so governs the steeplechasing world that every contestant soon learns to lose graciously and to be happy for another's success. The spirit of camaraderie that exists on the jumping circuits is almost unknown in flat racing, where the greater sums of money at stake are apt to make every rival a deadly enemy and defeat something to be dreaded. Steeplechasing trainers and jockeys do professional jobs while retaining the amateur spirit, many of them carrying on through sheer enthusiasm, with no hope of making more than a bare living.

From the spectator's point of view, steeplechasing has arguably more to offer than flat racing. How can the frenzied scurry of a flat race, lasting perhaps less than a minute, compare with the prolonged excitement of a race over fences or hurdles, with its ever-present promise of drama and heroics? And as far as betting is concerned, jumps are no barrier to success. Form works out as well over the sticks as on the flat, the additional factor of jumping ability—when known—being in favour of the punter. Steeplechasing's popularity as a betting medium is best exemplified by the Grand National. Despite 30 formidable fences and a casualty list that usually includes about two-thirds of the starters, few races in Britain attract such a volume of betting. Millions of pounds change hands each year on the result.

The Grand National is also—at £15,000 plus to the winner—the richest steeplechase in Britain. But in 1971 the two other top events of the season, the Champion Hurdle and the Cheltenham Gold Cup, were still worth less than £8,000 to the winner. With no international bloodstock market behind it, because most 'chasers are geldings and useless for breeding, jumping is, compared with the flat, very short of money. Sponsorship, however, holds out hopes of increased jumping prosperity. The introduction of the Hennessy and Whitbread gold cups in the late

Mary Evans

Steeplechasing has come a long way since the days when a church steeple showed the way to the winning post and an artist's impression of 'The First Steeplechase' was a moonlight gallop by the military. In modern steeplechasing, obstacles are skilfully prepared to test both horse and rider, and riders have more protection than night-cap and nightshirt.

Gerry Cranham

1950s started the movement, and by the end of the 1960s over 10 per cent of all prize money in British steeplechasing came from sponsors. Their contribution is likely to increase still further in the 1970s, as more firms discover the value of this cheap form of nation-wide advertising.

History

Why steeplechasing? The term originates from the 18th century, from such contests as the earliest recorded cross-country race, held in Ireland in 1752. A Mr O'Callaghan and Mr Edmund Blake matched their horses to race 4½ miles between Buttevant Church and St Leger Church. There was no more prominent landmark than a church steeple, so this made an admirable finishing post —a goal that was always in sight.

Steeplechasing developed naturally out of hunting. What better way for these gentlemen who rode to hounds to settle their arguments over whose horse was the better jumper or who the better horseman than simply to dispense with the hounds and race over a set distance? Races always took place over normal hunting country with natural obstacles. Refinements were nil; riders just agreed to race between points A and B without mention of which route should be taken. An amusing, though probably typical, example of the sort of incident that took place comes from a race in Leicestershire in 1792. The distance was 8 miles and a resident in the area who had doubtless backed the favourite told that horse's rider, Lord Forester: 'You'll save 100 yards if you come through my garden and jump the gate into the road.'

Leicestershire, always a great hunting area, provided another historic steeplechase in 1792. This was a match for 1,000 guineas between horses owned by Mr Willoughby and Mr Hardy, and for the first time in a 'chase the riders were professional horsemen instead of gentlemen. Contemporary accounts indicate that the race created great excitement locally. The next important date was 1811, when the first race over made fences was held at Bedford. More than 40,000 spectators saw Fugitive beat Cecilia over a 3-mile course in which four 4 ft. 6 in. fences were each jumped twice.

Despite the apparent success of this venture, there are no more records of steeplechases over manufactured fences for many years. The next great landmark came in 1830 when Tom Coleman —called the 'Father of Steeplechasing'—instituted the St Albans races. Before then, almost all races had been matches made

Mr. F. Colling on Romany Queen leads the Spanish Duke of Alberquerque on Nereo, which went on to win, over the last flight in an international race for amateur riders.

between gentlemen. Coleman organized a series of events at St Albans between 1830 and 1839 that really put steeplechasing on the map. Backed by such influential men as Squire George Osbaldeston and the Reverend Lord Frederic Beauclerk, the St Albans steeplechases thrived. Soon there were other important meetings at Newport Pagnell, Aylesbury, Leamington, and, for the first time, in 1836, Liverpool.

The winner of the first steeplechase at Liverpool was a horse called The Duke, who returned a year later to win the same race, which some authorities regard as the first Grand National. It

1

2

Barnaby's

certainly did not bear that name, being described as a 'Sweepstakes of 10 sovs each, with 100 sovs added by the Town of Liverpool'. The course was described as 'over a country not exceeding five miles'. Although it attracted only four runners, one—the favourite, Dan O'Connell—had come from Ireland, so the event was obviously regarded as of some importance. The establishment of Liverpool as a centre of steeplechasing placed the sport on a sound footing, but there were many who viewed the growth of this branch of racing with misgivings. For the purist, steeplechasing was the bastard offspring of hunting and flat racing, and for at least another 50 years it was often referred to as the 'illegitimate sport'. In fact, its detractors were generally those with vested interests in flat racing, who were jealous of the success attained by the new sport.

By 1840 there were accounts of steeplechases in provincial France and Spain and in 1844 a race over four 4-ft. hurdles took place at Hoboken, New Jersey. This initial American event was run in three heats and won by a Canadian-bred 4-year-old called Hops, who appears to have been the only proficient jumper in the field of four.

By the mid-1850s steeplechasing had lost public favour in Britain. The hierarchy of the Jockey Club steadfastly refused to take upon itself the government of racing over obstacles, so there was no body to which disputes could be referred and local stewards possessed no real powers. In consequence, the sport became, in the words of one contemporary writer, 'the recognized refuge of all outcasts, human and equine, from the legitimate Turf'. A vast number of badly organized meetings had sprung up all over the country, chicanery was rife, and good racing the exception rather than the rule. No wonder that public confidence was lost. But amazingly the sport was allowed to continue in this haphazard manner until 1866. Then a number of Jockey Club members, concerned about the future image of all racing, successfully established the Grand National Hunt Committee. This body formulated rules for steeplechasing which were rapidly adopted throughout

the land, and employed the Jockey Club secretaries, Messrs. Weatherby, to issue a Steeplechasing Calendar on the lines of the Racing Calendar. The National Hunt Committee was to rule British steeplechasing until the end of 1968, when it merged with the Jockey Club.

The institution of law and discipline paved the way for genuine progress in the conduct of the sport in Britain. Other countries had not been so slow. France had already put her house in order with the formation of the Societe des Steeplechases in 1863. The American Jockey Club was not established until 1866, but three years later steeplechasing was being properly conducted under its auspices at Jerome Park, and

hurdle races had come within its jurisdiction from the outset.

Whereas European riders and race crowds had always shown a preference for contests over fences, ditches, banks, and stone walls, the Americans at first contented themselves with less formidable hurdles.

The first American race over European-style hunting country came in 1865, when four hurdle racers lined up for a handicap event over stiffer obstacles at

Paterson, New Jersey. It was a fiasco. The winner, Nannie Craddock, fell and was remounted, the runner-up also fell and was ridden home by another jockey who happened to be standing by the fence, while the third ran a most peculiar race, which was blamed variously on the dishonesty or drunkenness of his rider.

Jump racing in America remained a novelty entertainment for another 30 years and most of the entertainment was for the participants. But at the turn of the century there was a sudden great upsurge in public interest. The reason was primarily the formation of the National Steeplechase Association in 1895, which focused more attention on the sport. Other factors included the imaginative

introduction of races such as the Maryland Hunt Cup (1894) and the American Grand National (1899).

In Britain the National Hunt season still revolved around the Aintree Grand National, although Scotland (1867) and Ireland (1870) had long since instituted their equivalent contests. France staged its counterpart, the first Grand Steeplechase de Paris, at Auteuil in 1901.

But the National remained *the*

race for jumpers. The sport as a whole was not yet strong enough to sustain interest in the host of minor meetings, and even top-class races at other courses could not compete with the ultra-spectacular Liverpool event. One of the saddest losses was the Croydon fixture, which closed in the 1890s. Three very important races—the Great Metropolitan Chase, the Grand National Hurdle, and the Grand International Hurdle—were run there.

Steeplechasing was becoming an international sport in the first decade of the 20th century. It had entrenched itself firmly in Australia and New Zealand, and giant New Zealander, Moifaa, won the 1904 Grand National. American-bred Rubio took the 1908

National, and the following year the race went to French-bred Lutteur III. In 1910 the English gelding, Jerry M, crossed the channel to land the Grand Steeplechase de Paris.

After World War I steeplechasing entered a prosperous phase when many new and wealthy owners began to take an interest. Jock Whitney and Ambrose Clark were two of the most important Americans to enter the sport, while Miss

The water jump is a compulsory feature of the steeplechasing course, but it is by no means popular with trainers and jockeys, for the water is where a fair percentage of falls occur.

Sportography

1 Steeplechasing over timber at Middleburg, Virginia. In the United States, the sport has fallen away in popularity and there are now relatively few events in the calendar.
2 In France the situation is different, with large crowds packing Auteuil for big races like the Prix du President de la Republique. 3 Though not in the healthiest of states Australian steeplechasing was still able to produce such a potential champion as Crisp, leading at Cheltenham in 1970.

Keystone

Parkin

3

In the 1960s the great Irish 'chaser Arkle bestrode the British scene, his 27 wins in 35 outings including a hat-trick of Cheltenham Gold Cups.

Keystone

Dorothy Paget and Lord Bicester were the most prominent new English owners.

This influx of money and enthusiasm helped to gain publicity and interest. A number of really top-flight jumpers such as Easter Hero, Golden Miller, Thomond II and a crop of wonderful riders such as the Rees brothers, Billy Stott and Gerry Wilson pulled in the customers. And the institution of the Cheltenham Gold Cup (1924) and the Champion Hurdle (1927) established championships for the 'chasers and hurdlers respectively.

Surprisingly, while Americans poured fortunes into British steeplechasing and won Nationals with Kellsboro Jack (1933) and Battleship (1938), the sport in the United States was fast declining. In 1940 there was steeplechasing in only three states—New York, Maryland and Delaware. In 1938 only two runners lined up for the American Grand National at Belmont Park. The sport was also on the decline in Australia, and when World War II ended it was dead in New South Wales. Post-war steeplechasing was confined to Victoria and South Australia.

After World War II a wonderful 'chaser called Elkridge helped to repopularize the sport in America with a number of memorable victories. The support of rich owners such as Paul Mellon, Mrs Isabel Dodge Sloane, and Mrs Marion du Pont Scott ensured a revival—but only to a limited extent. Modern American racing is geared entirely to betting, and as race-goers tend to bet far less on steeplechases, tracks are unwilling to stage them. Consequently there

are few races (the 1969 champion jockey rode 32 winners, while the leading flat rider had 352) and prize money for big races has not improved. Australian steeplechasing, too, runs a poor second to flat racing, although it made considerable ground in Victoria at the end of the 1960s. In 1971 the Australian jumper, Crisp, displayed potential greatness with two fine English wins.

Among the 'chasers of post-war years, Prince Regent, Cottage Rake, Pas Seul and Mill House each thrilled the crowds in his time. But none rivalled the feats and popularity of the remarkable Golden Miller in the 1930s, until the emergence of Arkle. Incomparable Arkle won three Cheltenham Gold Cups, and numerous other races giving stones away to the best of the rest. When Arkle was entered for a handicap there were often two sets of weights—one for if he did not run—for his appearance in a race telescoped the weight range of the rest of the field. He was struck down by injury at the height of his powers. But the hold he had gained over the public—and his benefit to steeplechasing—is illustrated by the fact that he was front-page news in the national press throughout his recuperation and a major news story again at his death in 1970.

Hurdling's post-war stars include Hatton's Grace (1949-51), Sir Ken (1952-54), and Persian War (1968-70), who each recorded three consecutive victories in the Champion Hurdle.

The Races
There are two types of jumping races—hurdles and steeplechases. In Britain, hurdlers tackle $3\frac{1}{2}$-ft-high wooden frames tightly packed with gorse; 'chasers $4\frac{1}{2}$-ft-plus fences. A horse can often knock down a hurdle and keep going, but fences leave much less room for error. And British courses add further hazards for the 'chaser—for every mile there must be at least one ditch, 6 ft. wide and 2 ft. deep on the take-off side, guarded by a band and a rail. A water jump at least 12 ft. wide guarded by a fence of up to 3 feet is also compulsory. (Water jumps have become unpopular with trainers and jockeys, who argue that they are unnecessary hazards. Certainly, a fair proportion of falls occur when horses fail to clear the water and slip on landing. It would not be surprising to see them removed in the 1970s).

Hurdle races are faster than 'chases, and usually shorter. Most of them are run over the minimum jumping distance of 2 miles, in contrast to the 4 miles 856 yards of the Grand National 'chase. British rules state that there must be at least 8 flights of hurdles over 2 miles, and an additional flight every $\frac{1}{4}$-mile after that. A 2-mile 'chase contains at least 12 fences, with at least 6 more obstacles for

Gerry Cranham

Fox Photos

each additional mile.

Jumping races are held for 10 months of the year—from August to June—on more than 40 tracks scattered across Britain and Ireland. A steeplechase fan can usually find a meeting on one or more of them on any day of the week except Sunday during this period.

An added attraction each spring to British steeplechasing cards is the inclusion of *hunter 'chases*, confined to horses that have been regularly hunted. In the early days of the sport hunter 'chases attracted horses that were not in the same class as racehorses. But times change, and since World War II they have unearthed some top-class horses such as Freddie, Halloween, Teal, Oxo, Merryman II, and Highland Wedding.

The Horses
All hurdlers and 'chasers have one thing in common—strength. In Britain, weights range from a minimum of 10 stone to a maximum of 12 st 7 lb, and a horse

must be exceptionally strong to carry that sort of burden over 2 miles or more.

While a lot of horses are still bred specifically for jumping—notably in Ireland—many jumpers are recruited from the flat, and graduate to fences after a year or two of hurdling. In the 1960s a higher class of flat racer has been recruited to hurdling. Aurelius, winner of the 1961 St Leger, was put to hurdling after an unsuccessful spell at stud. He hurdled well, finishing second in the 1967 Champion Hurdle, only to be disqualified for failing to keep a straight line on the run in. National Hunt owners are now prepared to outlay heavily on likely hurdle or 'chase prospects from the flat. Major Rose, winner of a Chester Cup and the Cesarewitch, fetched 16,000 guineas in 1969 after he had won four hurdle races. He went on to record places in both the 1970 and the 1971 Champion Hurdle. Good flat horses, however, do not automatically make top-class hurdlers. But

1 Large fields may make for a great spectacle, but when horses tumble at fences the less congested the traffic the better the jockeys like it. Too often one horse takes others down with it.
2 The other type of jumping, over hurdles, lacks both the suspense and danger of the 'chase. Usually the hurdler is able to knock down the hurdle and keep going, but the steeplechaser, taking a higher fence, is rarely so lucky. **3** Up and almost over.

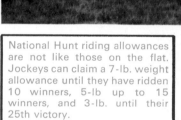

nor does moderate flat form condemn a horse's prospects as a hurdler. Some very moderate flat horses have blossomed into excellent jumpers. A perfect example is the gallant gelding Persian War, whose two wins on the flat in modest company gave no real clue of his hurdling potential. He proceeded to win three Champion Hurdles in a row from 1968, and finish second in the fourth, leading home horses that were easily his superior on the flat.

The best hurdlers win their races by a combination of stamina and speed allied to fast, clean jumping. By flicking over the hurdles with minimum effort they gain priceless lengths. Yet it is a strange fact that most truly brilliant hurdlers have failed to make the grade when put over fences. Often they try to hurdle the big fences instead of standing off and arching their backs to

jump truly like a 'chaser.

Although ex-flat racers and hurdlers make up a big percentage of the runners in steeplechases, the majority of top-flight 'chasers still tend to be horses specially bred for the purpose. Not running them on the flat gives them valuable time to grow to their full strength. They might be given an educational couple of runs over hurdles before being put to fences when five or six years old. Before they run on the course all novice 'chasers should have a thorough schooling over fences on their home gallops. Some horses are natural jumpers but many need to be quietly schooled before they gain confidence. Jumping ability and courage are vital if a horse is to make his mark as a 'chaser. Without jumping ability a horse may as well stay in his box, and the faint-hearted soon realize that there are easier ways of life.

4 A frequent sight in most steeplechases; sometimes the fallen rise and walk away, at other times they are not so fortunate. However, safety measures such as back-pads (**5**) and 'crash-helmet' caps give the jockey needed protection.

The Jockeys

Jockeys come to steeplechasing from all walks of life. Some, such as former champion, Josh Gifford, are forced by increasing weight to switch from successful careers as flat-race apprentices. Others start as stable lads hoping for the odd chance mount. A typical example is John Cook, a brilliant rider over fences, who won the 1971 Grand National on Specify. John started in racing as a 15-year-old apprentice, but he did not have his first ride, and later his first win, until he was 25.

Many good jockeys start off their racing life as unpaid amateurs who ride solely for fun and enjoyment. Champion Stan Mellor, Terry Biddlecombe, and Bob Davies all had their first successes as amateurs. But as soon as they began to ride regularly they were politely, but firmly, asked by the stewards of the Jockey Club to turn professional. The stewards feel strongly that amateurs should not take too many rides from the professionals, and at the start of the 1970-71 season a new rule was brought in that makes it necessary for owners to pay the full professional fee into a fund when employing amateur jockeys who had had more than 75 rides against professionals.

That fee then stood at £13.50.

National Hunt riding allowances are not like those on the flat. Jockeys can claim a 7-lb. weight allowance until they have ridden 10 winners, 5-lb up to 15 winners, and 3-lb. until their 25th victory.

Deductions for insurance, valets, and other items make quite a hole in it, and the money is very little for the enormous risks these riders take. The jockeys at the top of the tree make a substantial living from the game—far less, however, than their equivalents on the flat—but the rest struggle along on very minor rewards. If a rider is injured his income automatically drops to the weekly £15.05 from the Racing Industry Benefit scheme. And, unfortunately, injury is an inevitable part of any jump jockey's life. Some who have been at the game for a long time, have broken just about every bone in their bodies. Royal jockey David Mould, a supreme stylist, openly jokes that he would fall apart if all the pins in his body were taken out.

Steeplechase jockeys, for all their bravery and skill, are an unassuming bunch of sportsmen. They take the good with the bad, shrugging off the pain and frustration of today's injuries in the stoical belief that tomorrow will bring better fortune. Great advances have been made in the provision of financial benefits and practical rehabilitation for badly injured jump jockeys, but the lists of dead and crippled riders suggest that they are still grossly underpaid for the risks they take.

Ed Lacey

Swimming

The second most important Olympic sport, swimming is practised almost universally. Competitions are organized at all levels, and though younger swimmers tend to be the most successful competitors in the major championships, swimming is a sport and recreation that can be indulged in by all sorts of people.

The inherent buoyancy of the human body makes swimming an ideal pursuit for the disabled and the old, who can exercise without endangering their health from falls and knocks. Swimming's usefulness when adapted to life-saving and personal survival in areas which abound with lakes and rivers and along the coast cannot be questioned.

But it is as a sport that swimming makes the biggest impression. Perennial record breaking keeps it in the public eye. It is a strictly amateur sport, so far as participants are concerned, and is free from any rumours of corruption or drugs.

Although swimming competitions did not form part of the Greek Olympic Games, the classical world was not blind to the advantages of proficiency in the art, and swimming was highly regarded in the training of warriors and practised very widely in Ancient Greece and Rome. Bas-reliefs in the British Museum in London depict soldiers swimming, and some can be seen to be using an inflated animal skin as a type of primitive Aqua-Lung. But although bathing was popular among the Romans, in the Middle Ages the pastime fell into disrepute, swept away by the general belief that bathing helped to spread epidemics, and it was not until the 19th century that the sport again became popular.

In Japan, meanwhile, swimming continued to be widespread. In 36 B.C. competitions took place, and in A.D. 1603 an Imperial edict made swimming a compulsory part of the school curriculum. But although swimming continued to be an important part of Japanese school life, the isolation of the country inhibited the spread of ideas, and competitive swimming in its modern context really began, inevitably, in mid-19th-century Britain.

Above and Right. **Swimming, a useful art in itself, has become one of the most widely practised sports in the World.**

Men such as George Poulton, George Pewters, Samuel Hounslow, and Harold Kenworthy (who beat American Indians of the Ojibway tribe in races at the Holborn Baths in London in 1844) were all renowned at that time. Nobody thought about amateurism and professionalism then, when money was to be made out of competing. Side bets and money prizes, and payments for exhibitions of trick and ornamental swimming—the forerunners of the modern synchronized swimming—were common.

Organization

An embryonic swimming organization—the National Swimming Association—was formed in London in 1837, but the oldest acknowledged national body was formed in 1869. On January 7 that year, at the German Gymnasium in London, the Associated Metropolitan Swimming Clubs was formed, known later as the Amateur Swimming Association,

the governing body of swimming in England. The first acts of the AMSC were to define an 'amateur' and establish rules of competition. As a result, the first amateur swimming champion in history is recognized as Tom Morris, who won the mile championship, then swum in the River Thames, in 1869.

Other national associations followed. The American Athletic Union (AAU) was founded in 1878, the German Federation in 1896, and the French in 1899. The New Zealand ASA (1890) preceded by one year the foundation of the ASA of New South Wales. These two bodies organized Australasian championships until the Australian Swimming Union came into being in 1909, although combined Australasian teams competed in the Olympics until 1912.

It was not until 1908 that a world governing body, the Federation Internationale de Natation Amateur (FINA), came into being. The initiative came from an Englishman, George W. Hearn, then president of the ASA, who, at the time of the London Olympic Games, called a meeting of nations to discuss the problems

Records

FINA first approved world records in 1908, and in the ensuing 60 years tremendous changes came about. Altogether no fewer than 105 different events have been recognized for world records, though in Mexico City in 1968 a tidy all-metric list was drawn up. This comprised the following distances for both sexes:

Freestyle : 100, 200, 400, 800, 1,500 metres ; 4 x 100 metres relay, and for men only the 4 x 200 metres relay
Breaststoke : 100 and 200 metres
Butterfly : 100 and 200 metres
Backstroke : 100 and 200 metres
Medley : 200 and 400 metres individual ; 4 x 100 metres relay

This list, except for the men's 800 metres and the women's 1,500 metres, made up the programme for the Olympic Games and all other major competitions.

Until May 1, 1957, after which FINA decided that world records could be set only in international-size 50-metres pools, it had been possible to establish records for distances under 800 metres in short-course pools (minimum 25 yards). The reason for this change was the difficulty of comparing long-course and short-course performances. Swimmers in short pools make extra turns, and as each extra turn represents a time advantage of about 0.7 sec it is easier to make better times in a short pool than a long one. Most countries, however, keep records for both long-course and short-course performances.

Swimming Competitions

Pride of place in the world's swimming calendar is taken by the Olympic Games. On the women's side, more titles are decided in the pool than in the athletics arena. In fact, in the 1968 Games in Mexico City, men and women competed in the same number of individual events—12—in the four competitive styles (freestyle, breaststroke, butterfly, and backstroke) and medley. But there were three men's relays (two freestyle and one medley), to only two women's (one freestyle and one medley).

Naturally, the aim of every competitor is to represent his country in the Olympic Games, and this opportunity has been available to men since 1896 and women since 1912. The events at those first modern Olympics, in Athens, were three freestyle races, and one confined to sailors on ships anchored in the port of Piraeus.

Three years after the Athens Games, in 1899, the Erste Wiener Amateur Swim Club of Vienna organized contests entitled 'European Championships', but they were unofficial and were discontinued after 1903. It was not until 1926, after many years of pressure from Hungary, that official European championships were held. International championships—in name at least—were held in Europe in the years around 1900, and the English championships were often won by the top swimmers from Europe, America, and Australia. In 1911, an Inter-Empire contest, with teams from Australasia, Canada, South Africa, and the United Kingdom, was held at the old Crystal Palace in London in conjunction with the Festival of Empire, which celebrated the coronation of King George V. And in 1912, women's swimming events were included in the Stockholm Olympic Games.

The first in the series of British Empire Games was held in Hamilton, Ontario, in 1930, thanks to the initiative of Canada. With the changing nature of the Empire, the title of the Games was changed to the British and Commonwealth Games (1954 to 1966) and to the British Commonwealth Games in 1970. Swimming always occupied an important place in these events.

The Olympic and British Commonwealth Games, and the European championships, take place every four years. The Olympics

of the sport. Eight nations attended that first meeting, at the Manchester Hotel on July 14, 1908—Belgium, Denmark, Finland, France, Germany, Great Britain and Ireland, Hungary, and Sweden. Hearn became FINA's first secretary-cum-treasurer.

The Federation immediately set about drawing up rules for competition and an official world record list. Present at the first meeting and much involved in the early work was a young German, Max Ritter, who swam for Germany in the 1908 and 1912 Olympics, and later became an American citizen. He was in turn secretary, president, and a life president of FINA, and was still involved in the sport at the beginning of the 1970s. From this small beginning, FINA's membership grew until it included almost 100 nations, the only power not belonging being Communist China, who withdrew in the late 1950s.

1 Daring Victorian maids in an early swimming gala.
2 Eight men go down for the 110 yards freestyle final at the 1966 Commonwealth Games. Most important Games feature swimming as a major section of their programmes.
3 Three timekeepers on every lane minimize timing errors.

The Spearhead Principle

Swimming is essentially a time sport. It lacks the tactics and jockeying for position of athletics, and in promoting competitors from heats to final, time alone is the deciding factor. (This has been the case in the Olympic Games since 1952).

In an eight-lane bath, the normal facility for major competitions, the swimmer with the fastest heat time goes in lane 4, the next fastest in lane 5, and so on, in lanes 3, 6, 2, 7, 1, and 8. This is called the 'spearhead' principle and has two purposes : it gives the better swimmers (theoretically speaking) the chance to see and race against each other, while it also helps the judges place the finishers in the correct order.

For the 1972 Olympics it was decided to use the spearhead principle not only for the finals but also for the heats, based on the swimmers' best pre-Games performances.

are held in the years divisible by four—1896, 1900, etc.—and the European and Commonwealth events in the even years between—1958, 1962, etc. Other important multi-sport events in which swimming plays a major part are the Pan American Games (instituted on a four-yearly basis in 1951), Asian Games, Mediterranean Games, and World Student Games.

There is no lack of domestic events, and each national association organizes its own championships annually. Following the example of the United States, the modern fashion is to have two meetings every year: a spring meeting (often short course) in April, and a summer meeting (long course) in late July or August. The inversion of the seasons in the Southern Hemisphere necessitates the Australian championships' being held in February. These various domestic events may be open to the world, like the English summer championships have always been, or confined to residents and nationals of a particular country.

Another type of top-class competition is the international meeting. The traditional type is a match between two teams, but meetings between many countries are held. The most notable team events are the European Cup competitions inaugurated in 1969 and organized in two or more divisions. Invitation internationals in which the best swimmers from many countries test their strength against each other are another form of international competition. But the increasing cost of travelling and the growth of sponsorship for training and competitions are such that swimming may be hard pressed to maintain its jealously guarded amateur image.

Development of Techniques

The first swimming style was breaststroke, and the other three modern styles were developed from it, though this may be hard to imagine when one appreciates the differences in the stroke techniques. Even the importance of the simultaneous arms and frog-like leg-kick actions of the breaststroke in the early days is quite different from the modern approach to the same style. Charles Newman, a noted teacher of his

1 The start, as used in freestyle, breaststroke, and butterfly events. Backstroke swimmers start in the water. **2** The first stroke was the breaststroke, in which the arms and legs remain underwater and move simultaneously. **3** The front crawl has undergone many changes and is now the fastest technique known. **4** Swimming on the back: once a trick, now an Olympic event. **5** The butterfly was born in 1935, and became official in 1952.

1

2

3

4

5

time, wrote in *The Swimmer's Album* of 1898: 'The arms should be used principally as a lifting power in order to inhale breath', and 'too much importance cannot be attached to the straightening of the legs in the outward movement, to give width and thus more propelling power as the legs are brought together'. The situation is now very different. The arm stroke is an important propulsive action, and the head is lifted only just clear of the water for breathing. The leg-kick in the sprinting stroke (the 100 and 200 metres Olympic events are basically sprints) has been narrowed so that almost all the propulsion comes from the backward surge of the feet, which are turned out to present the instep surface of the foot to the water.

From the classic breaststroke came the sidestroke, which was the breaststroke performed on one side. Emil Rausch of Germany, winner of the 880 yards and 1 mile events at the St Louis Games of 1904, was the last person to win an Olympic title using this stroke. From the side-stroke came the over-arm stroke, in which the upper arm, the main propelling agent, was carried forward over the water. Then there was the trudgen, in which both arms were moved over the water in an alternate action as the legs executed a froglike movement. This stroke, the forerunner of the front crawl, was demonstrated by John Trudgen in London in 1873 and named after him. But as the bas-reliefs in the British Museum indicate, this stroke was in reality very ancient.

There is also evidence that the front crawl, developed and popularized by Richard Cavill (one of a family of swimming brothers) in Australia in 1900, was no new discovery and that the natives of the Pacific islands had used it for as long as the oldest islanders could remember. However, Richard Cavill is credited with being the pioneer of the front crawl stroke. Cavill's important discovery was that the breaststroke-like leg action of the trudgen was a retarding factor. He recalled a rapid, vertical leg movement used by Alec Wickham of Colombo, and by adapting this to the alternating over-arm stroke, Cavill gave birth to the 'Australian crawl'.

The Americans were quick to react to the news of Cavill's revolutionary stroke. But as they had only vague newspaper reports to go on, they unwittingly developed a faster leg drive, with four vertical kicks to each arm stroke, compared with the two used by Cavill. Further experiments with different leg actions, with major and minor kicks, produced astonishing improvements even in moderate swimmers. This inspired American coaches to try a six-beat action, with two major and four minor kicks, but this proved so tiring, except over

297

Gertrude Ederle broke the world 100 metres record in 1923 and three years later became the first woman to swim the English Channel.

shorter distances, that the idea was abandoned for a while.

Into the picture in 1917 came two members of the New York Women's Swimming Association —Charlotte Boyle and Claire Galligan. So convincing were their demonstrations of the superiority of the action, especially over longer distances, that coaches had to reconsider their views. Some swimmers even experimented with eight-beat and ten-beat kicks, notably Gertrude Ederle who set a world 100 metres record in 1923 and swam the English Channel in record time in 1926 using the eight-beat style. But neither kick lasted very long, and swimmers almost universally adopted some sort of leg kick with a maximum of six beats.

Meanwhile, swimmers were learning more about swimming on their backs. Until the turn of the century, swimming on the back had been little more than a trick, combining a sculling action of the hands and a flutter kick. But in 1902 swimmers began to use an inverted breaststroke on their backs (known later as the Old English backstroke). As soon as the front crawl was developed, it was realized that the same principles of front crawl could be applied to the supine stroke, and so the back crawl was born.

The next major stroke development came in 1935, when Henry Myers of the United States recovered his arms over the water while swimming breaststroke. The flying appearance of his stroke gave it the name by which it is now known—the butterfly. There was consternation at the time, but the supporters of the classic underwater style had to face the fact that the rules did not prohibit this unorthodox arm recovery. One new idea fathered another, and in the same year Jack Sieg of the University of Iowa found that he could swim the butterfly by beating his legs in unison like a dolphin's tail—the

vertical dolphin kick. This kick was at once ruled illegal, as it contravened the basic premise of the breaststroke kick—the backward thrust of the flat feet. But when separate rules for butterfly and breaststroke were drawn up in 1952, this vertical kick was specifically permitted. Before this happened, however, America's Jack Kasley found a way round the rules, by spreading his knees slightly and turning his toes inwards so that the leg-kick retained a semblance of the orthodox breaststroke kick. Using this style, he set a world 200 metres breaststroke record in 1936.

The years of World War II delayed swimming development in general and especially postponed a final decision on the interloping butterfly stroke. As a result, it was not until after the 1952 Olympic Games in Helsinki that butterfly was separated from breaststroke and became a fourth official swimming style.

Americans were also responsible for developing a further swimming event—the medley. This consisted of swimming equal distances using each of the recognized styles, whether the race was for individuals or teams. Before butterfly was made official, the individual medley consisted of breaststroke, backstroke, and freestyle, and in teams backstroke, breaststroke, and freestyle.

Team events have always been popular races, for competitors and spectators alike. Freestyle relay events were included for men in the 1900 Olympic Games, and for women in 1912. The classic men's international distance of 4 by 200 metres was first swum at the 1908 Olympics in London, but it was not until 1932 that relays were recognized for world record purposes, when the winning Olympic times of Japan (men's 4 by 200) and the United States (women's 4 by 100) became the first ratified marks. Records for the three-stroke medley relay were first recognized in 1946, but medley relay events did not feature in the Olympic programme until 1960, although the British Empire Games had included them since 1934.

1 Captain Matthew Webb swam the English Channel on his second attempt, in 1875, and thereby popularized swimming immensely.
2 Australia's Frank Beaurepaire swam in four Olympic Games, did not win a title, but set eight freestyle world records.
3 They're off! The start of the 1908 Olympic 200 breaststroke.

Competitive Development

The history of modern competitive swimming has been dominated by the tremendous strength of the United States. The Americans have excelled in international swimming consistently, although other nations have had their moments of glory. The Olympic results and world record lists can be taken as reliable guides to national prowess and individual achievement.

The first decade of the 20th century was a triumphant period for British swimming. John Jarvis and Henry Taylor were both double Olympic champions, Jarvis in 1900 and Taylor in 1908. Jarvis, supreme from 1897 to 1906, used the right over-arm sidestroke and developed his own leg-kick which was named after him and his professional rival Joey Nuttall. At the 1900 Olympics in Paris, Jarvis won the 1,000 and 4,000 metres races in the River Seine.

Britain was not represented at the 1904 Olympics in St Louis, where the United States championships also served as Olympic events. Not surprisingly, Charles Daniels became the first American holder of an Olympic title: he won

the 220 and 440 yards in 1904, and in 1908 won the 100 metres. An early exponent of the American crawl, Daniels had a great influence on the development of the stroke in Britain through his visits in 1906 and 1907 when he won the ASA 100 yards title. Very few countries competed at St Louis, and Germany won the most titles, while Hungary's Zoltan Halmay won the 50 and 100 yards, beating Daniels in both.

At the first London Olympics, in 1908, Britain won four of the six races, with Henry Taylor taking the 400 and 1,500 metres in world record times and anchoring the winning relay team. But by 1912 the United States had taken over from Britain, despite being at that time outstanding only in the sprints. It was the winner of the 100 metres, Duke Kahanamoku, who was in the forefront of America's rise to world domination in the 1920s.

A tall and powerful Hawaiian, Duke Paoa Kahinu Makoe Hulikohoa Kahanamoku was one of the first to use a purely vertical six-beat flutter kick with his American crawl. A factor which may have helped Kahanamoku

was the size of his feet, which were abnormally long and broad. At the 1920 Olympics, after a gap of World War I, he retained his sprint title—at the age of 29 years—and his team-mate Norman Ross took the 400 and 1,500 metres. America also won the 4 by 200 metres relay for the first time. The breaststroke titles, hitherto the preserve of Germany, went this time to Sweden.

Kahanamoku was still at the top in 1924 in Paris, but he was relegated to second place in the 100 metres by a young team-mate of 18, Johnny Weissmuller, who completed a sprint treble—which was not emulated until 1964—by winning the 400 metres and being in the winning 4 by 200 metres relay team. He also introduced new and significant developments into the crawl stroke. The star of future 'Tarzan' films, Weissmuller added a push phase to his arm pull, turned his head to breath independently of his arms, and substituted a deep leg action for the old shallow flutter kick. His

upper body thus had a much higher position in the water. By the time of the 1928 Games, in Amsterdam, Weissmuller (who retained his 100 metres title) was acknowledged to have the best speed stroke in existence, and many thousands of feet of slow-motion film were taken of him from all angles.

Quick to make use of these were the Japanese, who also obtained films of the other world stars. Inspired by the victory of Yoshi-yuki Tsurata in the 200 metres breaststroke at Amsterdam in 1928, they went to Los Angeles in 1932 determined to do even better. Adapting the techniques of the former champions to their generally shorter limbs, the Japanese trounced America's stars in Los Angeles, winning every men's title except the 400 metres, which went to Clarence 'Buster' Crabbe.

America's stock was almost as low at the Berlin Games of 1936. The Japanese won three titles, the 200 metres breaststroke, the 1,500 metres, and the 4 by 200 metres

6

7

4 Johnny Weissmuller, winner of a record five Olympic gold medals, three of them in individual events, setter of 24 world records, and future 'Tarzan' of the film world.
5 Backstroker Adolph Keifer brought in a new style and was reputedly unbeaten for eight years in the 1930s.
6 Ethelda Bleibtrey was once prosecuted for swimming without stockings at New York's Manhattan Beach. Her other claim to fame is her winning every event (100, 300, and 4 x 100 metres relay) at the 1920 Olympic Games.
7 Incomparable Helen Madison held every world freestyle record in 1930-31 and won three 1932 Olympic golds.

relay. And Hungary's Ferenc Csik sprang a surprise in the 100 metres. America's men had to settle for two titles—the 400 metres and the backstroke. But the backstroke win was a sweeping 8-foot victory for a Chicago schoolboy, Adolph Kiefer, using a completely new stroke. It had three distinguishing features, which started a new line of thinking. He kept his arms straight, and recovered them low and sideways. His hands entered the water just above his shoulders (instead of straight up beside his head), and he used a shallow pull, instead of the deep, under-the-body technique formerly used.

Women's swimming had become part of the Olympic programme in 1912, anticipating athletics by some 16 years. The first champion was Australasia's Fanny Durack, who set a world record in her 100 metres heat (1 min 19.8 sec) and won the final in 1 min 22.2 sec. Britain won the women's 4 by 100 metres freestyle relay. By 1924 the women's programme had expanded to include a 400 metres freestyle, and backstroke and breaststroke races. American girls dominated the freestyle events in the Olympic Games of the 1920s, but the Europeans as a group were just as successful on the other strokes. America, traditionally weak in the breaststroke events, won only one medal in the 200 metres breaststroke until 1964. British girls excelled in the backstroke.

One of the truly great woman swimmers appeared at the 1932 Olympics in Los Angeles. This was Helene Madison, the fastest

swimmer in the world at every distance in the early 1930s, who won the 100 and 400 metres, and collected a third gold in the relay. Behind Miss Madison in second place in the 100 metres was Willy den Ouden of the Netherlands, who set a world 100 metres record of 1 min 4.6 sec in 1936 that was not beaten until almost 20 years later, by Australia's Dawn Fraser. Yet it was not Miss Ouden, but her team-mate Rie Mastenbroek, who took the honours at Berlin. Rie won gold medals in the 100, 400, and 4 by 100 metres freestyle, and a silver in the backstroke.

World War II and its aftermath affected the careers of two great swimmers who are significant names in the history of the sport, but who never won Olympic titles. Denmark's Ragnhild Hveger, runner-up in the 1936 Olympic 400 metres, broke 42 individual world records for 15 distances between 1936 and 1942 with her high-riding, arms-flying front crawl. For good measure she also set three world marks on backstroke, and was deservedly nicknamed the 'Golden Torpedo'. Hironashin Furuhashi, who emerged at the end of the war, was a Japanese antithesis of the flying Dane. Everything about his swimming appeared to be technically wrong. He swam low in the water, rolling violently onto his side in order to breathe. He lollopped almost as strongly the other way to take his other stroke. And his leg-kick, viewed from underwater, was quite remarkable: one leg swept round and down, while the other moved only to act as a counterbalance. But despite this

unorthodox appearance, he did not violate the fundamentals of good technique, as his six ratified world records proved. In 1948, when both Japan and Germany were excluded from the Olympic Games, Furuhashi stole the headlines from the Olympic champions. On the day America's Jimmy McLane won the 1,500 metres in 19 min 18.5 sec, Furuhashi returned 18 min 37.0 sec in Tokyo, but his mark was never recognized as a world record, as Japan was not a member of FINA at the time.

The United States had things much their own way in the 1948 Games, winning all six men's events and two of the five women's. But in 1952 the Hungarian women's team emerged as the top squad, winning four of the five titles (the other went to South Africa's Joan Harrison in the backstroke). America's men, however, won five out of six titles to confirm their hegemony of the world scene.

The Modern Age
The 1952 Olympics were the last of an old era; the 1956 Games in Melbourne were the beginning of a new one. The Melbourne Games marked the beginning of a period of record breaking that knew no parallel in any other sport. They also saw the first signs of a domination of the world of swimming by two powerful teams: Australia and the United States. The four Olympiads from 1956 to 1968 were a period when other nations had only a minor part to play.

Above, **Olympic, Commonwealth, and European backstroke champion Judy Grinham. Three great freestylers: 1 Australia's John Marshall revolutionized the world records in the middle-distance events in the 1950s. 2 Lorraine Crapp did the same in the women's events, and 3 John Konrads made even Marshall's marks look antique towards the decade's end.**

Glossary of Terms

Age-group swimming Development system in which children compete against others of the same age from ages 9 to 17.
Australian crawl Early crawl stroke; first to involve alternate vertical leg-kicks.
Dolphin kick Leg action—vertical symmetrical movements—used in butterfly stroke.
Fast pool Swimming bath with qualities tending to minimize wave-making.
Flutter kick Alternative vertical kick used in front crawl and backstroke.
Freestyle Common term for front crawl stroke.
Individual medley Races consisting of equal legs of butterfly, backstroke, breaststroke, and another different stroke (front crawl).

Interval training Method of training, not exclusive to swimming, which involves performing a certain number of repeat swims with a set rest interval.
Kicking board Training aid to support the upper body when swimming, using the legs alone.
Life saving Swimming techniques for saving people from drowning.
Long course Baths 50 metres or 55 yards long.
Long-distance swimming Open-water swimming in lakes, rivers, and the sea; races range from 1 mile to 40 miles.
Medley relay 4-man relay of equal legs of backstroke, breaststroke, butterfly, and another different stroke (front crawl).
Old English backstroke Early technique of swimming on the back using a kind of inverted breaststroke.

Personal survival Techniques of keeping alive in open water using clothes, etc, as flotation aids.
Plunging Event to determine who can get farthest simply by diving—not using arms or legs and lasting a maximum of 60 seconds.
Recovery The non-propulsive phase of a stroke, when the limb is moved forward to begin the propulsive action.
Repetition training Form of training in which swimmer tries to reproduce pre-set times, eg 16 times 100 metres all under 64 seconds.
Salt water Some swimming baths are filled with salt water. This is more buoyant than fresh water but is also denser and there is thus little advantage to be gained from it.
Screw-kick Colloqualism for an irregularity of the breaststroke kick.
Short course Any bath length

under 50 metres: usually refers to 25-yard or 25-metre courses.
Slow pool Bath in which waves build up and inhibit speed.
Spearheading Method of arranging competitors with the fastest in the centre lanes and the slowest on the outside.
Synchronized swimming A competitive form of 'water ballet', for women only. In format, competitions are similar to ice skating.
Throwaway, or grab, turn A freestyle turn in which the swimmer pushes himself round by hand, or by holding a rail or scum trough to do it.
Trudgen Early ancestor of the crawl stroke: breaststroke legs action with alternate arm recovery over the water.
Tumble turn Somersault turn in freestyle or backstroke; faster than the rather easier grab.

Australia's Murray Rose (*left*) and America's George Breen (*above*) were rivals in the 1950s. In the 1956 Olympic 1,500 metres heats, Breen broke Rose's world record, but came third in the final while Rose won.

Above, Lynn Burke looks happy with news of yet another world backstroke record. She set five—all in 1960.
Below, Anita Lonsbrough led British swimming in the 1960s.

The pioneers of this age of record breaking were Australians. Preparing for their own Games in Melbourne, they introduced interval training, in which their swimmers—under the guidance of such famous coaches as Harry Gallagher, Sam Herford, and Forbes Carlile—did numerous repetitions of their racing distances at just under full speed. In consequence they produced stars of the calibre of Lorraine Crapp and Dawn Fraser, Murray Rose, Jon Henricks, John Devitt, and David Theile. These six swimmers won a total of six individual gold and three silver medals, and helped Australia to world record wins in both relays. It was a tremendous shock to the Americans, who won only two events—the two new butterfly races.

Australia's men held their lead —just—at the 1960 Games. They shared the eight golds with the Americans, and won three silvers and two bronzes to America's two silvers and three bronzes. But of

Central Press

1

2

Ed Lacey

3

Another double winner at Mexico City was East Germany's Roland Matthes, who showed the most devastatingly relaxed and effective backstroke yet seen, winning both backstroke titles. The East Germans, as a team, emerged as the top nation at the 1970 European championships in Barcelona, taking the lead from the USSR.

In western Europe, ambitious swimmers began looking more to the United States for improvement. The successes of West Germany's Hans Fassnacht and Sweden's Gunnar Larsson can be traced directly to coaching in America. Australia, meanwhile, pursued a home-grown policy, and early in 1971 this was seen to be bearing fruit. Swimming in an invitation international at London's Crystal Palace, Karen Moras set a world 400 metres record (4 min 22.8 sec), and Shane Gould, a 14-year-old sensation, equalled Dawn Fraser's 100 metres mark (58.9 sec) and beat Debbie Meyer's 200 metres record with 2 min 6.5 sec.

U.P.I.

4

A.P.

the Australian girls, only Dawn Fraser could reproduce her Melbourne performances.

By 1964, and the Tokyo Olympics, America had done some re-thinking. This was the result not only of specialized training, but of specialized competitions—a nationwide age-group swimming programme begun after the Melbourne debacle. This programme of regular races within age divisions discovered tremendous talent in depth.

The most obvious product of age-group swimming was Don Schollander, whose seemingly effortless freestyle won him four golds—two individual and two relays—in the 1964 Games, the first such aggregate at one Olympics by a swimmer. Altogether, America won 13 of the 18 championships, including all 5 relays. Australia were first in three men's events—Bob Windle in the 1,500 metres, Kevin Berry in the butterfly, and Ian O'Brien in the breaststroke—and Dawn Fraser made history by completing a hat-trick of 100 metres titles, the first swimmer ever to win the same title three times.

Tokyo was the last Olympics at which Germany—though politically separated, entered as a combined team. They had fair success in the men's events, but the only

European to win was the young Muscovite Galina Prosumenschikova in the 200 metres breast-stroke. This was Russia's first ever success in the Olympic pool.

The tempo of training, already heavy in most countries, increased even more between Tokyo and the Mexico City Games of 1968. Daily stints of 10,000 metres or more were commonplace. This distance would be broken down into a series of repeat swims, such as 20 times 100 metres, 10 times 400 metres, or 3 times 1,500 metres, with other series of kicking (legs only) and pulling (arms only), and short wind sprints—and all this controlled by the stopwatch. It was boring in some cases, but it was the only way of gaining any kind of reward in the Olympics.

This kind of work had its effect. It produced swimmers such as Debbie Meyer from Arden Hills, California, who in Mexico City won three individual titles in the enlarged programme, the first time a swimmer had made such a haul in the same Games. Australians still had a measure of success in Mexico City, however. Mike Wenden won the 100 and 200 metres freestyle and Lyn McClements won the 100 metres butterfly. But Americans still won 21 of the 29 swimming titles.

7

Gerry Cranham

A.P.

8

9

Tony Duffy

1 Don Schollander won a record four golds at the 1964 Olympics. **2** Australia's Kathy Wainwright won the 1966 Commonwealth Games 440 yards in world record time. **3** Donna de Varona was the first great female individual medley swimmer. **4** South Africa's Karen Muir was sport's youngest world record holder at 12 years 328 days in 1965 when she set a world 110 yards backstroke record. **5** Dutch girl Ada Kok was a popular winner of the Olympic 200 metres butterfly in 1968, and was European champion in 1962 and 1966. **6** British international Tony Davison demonstrates the backstroke. **7** Australia's Shane Gould removed Debbie Meyer (**8**) from the world 200 metres record list. **9** Gunnar Larsson set world freestyle and medley marks.

SWIMMING Most Olympic Medals

Most medals: **Men**   11 (9 gold, 1 silver, 1 bronze) Mark Spitz (USA)
               Women   8 (4 gold, 4 silver) Dawn Fraser (Australia)

Most gold medals in career:
              Men   9 Mark Spitz (USA) 4 x 100 metres freestyle, 4 x 200 metres freestyle 1968; 100 metres freestyle, 200 metres freestyle, 4 x 100 metres freestyle, 4 x 200 metres freestyle, 100 metres butterfly, 200 metres butterfly, 4 x 100 metres medley 1972.

Most gold medals in career:
              Women   4 Dawn Fraser (Australia) 100 metres freestyle 1956, 1964, 1968; 4 x 100 metres freestyle 1956.

Seven gold medals in one Games:
1972—Mark Spitz (USA)   100 metres freestyle, 200 metres freestyle, 4 x 100 metres freestyle, 4 x 200 metres freestyle; 100 metres butterfly, 200 metres butterfly; 4 x 100 metres medley

Four gold medals in one Games:
1964—Don Schollander (USA)   100, 400, 4 x 100, 4 x 200 metres freestyle

Three gold medals in one Games:
Since 1904, twelve swimmers have won three medals in one Games. They are: Charles Daniels (USA) 1904, Henry Taylor (GB) 1908, Ethelda Bliebtrey and Norman Ross (USA) 1920, Johnny Weismuller (USA) 1924, Helene Madison (USA) 1932, Rie Mastenbroek (Netherlands) 1936, Murray Rose (Australia) 1956, Chris von Saltza (USA) 1960, Sharon Stouder (USA) 1964, Debbie Meyer and Charles Hickcox (USA) 1968, Melissa Belote and Sandra Neilson 1972

Table Tennis

In 1971, a game still somewhat jokingly referred to as 'ping pong' made newspaper headlines throughout the world. Table tennis had achieved perhaps the international breakthrough of the later 20th century. The People's Republic of China invited English and American table tennis teams to make a private visit, making a gap in the 'bamboo curtain' that diplomats had been attempting for years.

Almost 100 years before, two Cambridge University under-graduates had indulged in an activity credited with introducing the idea that became table tennis. In 1879, they hit champagne corks across a table with the remnants of a cigar box. Later, small rubber balls were hit over books placed across the centre of the table. In 1899, James Gibb, an engineer and a founder of the Amateur Athletic Association tried placing a clamp midway along each side of the table and putting a piece of string across, in the manner of the modern net. As there were no rules, the Gibb family improvised their own. If a player missed the ball, he conceded the point, the first to score 21 winning.

When Gibb introduced his game, it became known as *gossima*, but after Gibb's return from America with some toy celluloid balls, he used these instead of the rubber variety. Friends laughingly referred to the pastime as *ping pong*, because of the sound of the ball hitting the bat, and the name stuck. When a sports goods firm became interested in the game, it began to thrive throughout the English-speaking world.

In 1902, a Ping Pong Associ-ation was formed in England to supervise tournaments, but limita-tions in play resulted in boredom, and within two years interest had slumped. It took two years for a revival, and the rubber-surfaced bat of Percy Bromfield was the instrument. Hitherto, all types of wooden bats had been used, but when Bromfield played such fantastic shots and spins using the rubber surface, a whole new game appeared and ping pong flourished. Problems followed, however, when it was discovered that ping pong was a registered trade name, so the English associ-ation changed its name to the Table Tennis Association, and in 1927 to the English Table Tennis Association.

By this time, table tennis was also popular on the Continent, and European championships

Originally known as 'ping pong' and still thought of by some by that name, table tennis has developed into a dynamic sport requiring the most subtle skills, a high standard of fitness, and the fastest possible reactions.

Ed Lacey

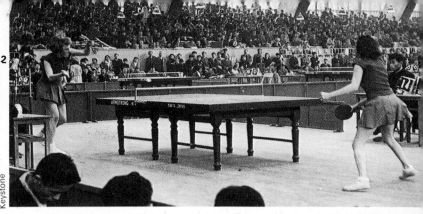

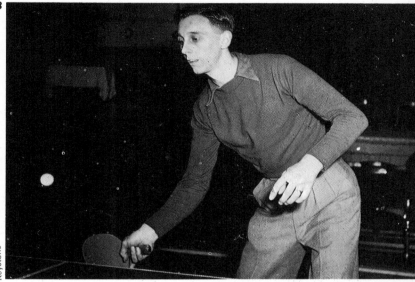

were planned in London for that year. But with India joining Austria, Czechoslovakia, England, Germany, Hungary, and Wales as participants, the title was changed to world championships. A trophy was donated for the men's team competition by Lady Swaythling, whose son, the Hon Ivor Montagu, was responsible for organizing the tournament and was elected first president of the International Table Tennis Federation (ITTF), a post he held until 1967. Apart from World War II, the world championships were held annually up to 1957, after which they have been held every two years. The question of amateurs and professionals was soon settled. In 1935, the category of 'player' was introduced, dispensing with the need for other terms.

Though Asian players held sway in the 1950s and 1960s, the pre-World War II years were the province of the Europeans, especially the Hungarians. Victor Barna won the men's world title five times between 1930 and 1935, and Maria Mednyanszky took each of the first five women's titles. Her record stood until Romania's Angelica Rozeanu brought off her sixth successive triumph at Utrecht in 1955. Hungary won the Swaythling Cup eight times in its first nine years, but by 1934, when

the Corbillon Cup was introduced for women, other nations were challenging.

The late 1930s saw the advent of the extreme defensive tactics that eventually led to changes in the rules. In 1936 at Prague, Romania, playing in their first Swaythling Cup, shocked Hungary with their stonewalling tactics and reached the final. This turned out to be a marathon affair, which Austria won 5-4 thanks largely to the young Richard Bergmann, who won his three matches. The most extraordinary match of the whole championships, however, had been between Ehrlich of Poland

and Romania's Paneth in the semi-finals. Romania had already qualified for the final, yet the first point of this match took 2 hr 5 min to complete! The Pole eventually won it with a net cord, and, after officials had cautioned the two contestants, needed less than 20 minutes to finish the job. To prevent the sport from becoming a farce, the ITTF decided to limit a five-game match to 1 hr 45 min —and disqualify both players if they exceeded this. It was not until the 1938 championships that they introduced the 20-minute rule. Under this, if a game was still in progress after 20 minutes it was awarded to the player in the lead at the time. If both players were level, they were given 5 minutes and the first to win the next point was awarded the game. Also at these championships, the finger-spin was outlawed and the height of the net was reduced from $6\frac{3}{4}$ to 6 inches.

The time-limit rule went through various stages—it was reduced to 15 minutes, with reduced limits for succeeding games—until the present expedite rule was introduced in 1963. Adopted internally by the Americans much earlier, this restricts the number of strokes in a rally when a game lasts more than 15 minutes.

The 1950 tournament saw Richard Bergmann, now playing as a naturalized Englishman, win his fourth world title. But the days of European domination were ending, and in the 1950s the Asians stamped their authority on world table tennis—but not without initial misunderstandings and controversy. The 1952 world title was won by Japan's H. Satoh, by common consent not a world-class player. But he was using a newly developed sponge surface on his bat, and the extraordinary spins he produced foxed much better players. There followed a period of confusion, in which some authorites banned the 'sponge bat' and others accepted it. And it was not until 1959 that laws were introduced to standardize a maximum thickness, and the sandwich bat was introduced.

Nevertheless, there was no stopping the Asian invasion. Japan's Ichiro Ogimura and T. Tanaka shared the men's world title from 1954 to 1957, and China produced one of the game's foremost players in Chuang Tse-tung, who won three successive world titles in the 1960s.

Always as fit as any boxer going into the ring or an athlete entering the Olympic arena, Chuang Tse-tung was the product of the national Chinese system that regards table tennis as the country's No. 1 sport. In outlying districts all over China there are outdoor tables available for anyone wishing to play. University degrees are made available in the sport, and the best players, like Chuang, become Chinese Masters of Sport.

1 Gizi Farkas featured in all the women's world championship singles finals from 1946 to 1953, but only in the first three was she victorious—in the other four honours went to Angelica Rozeanu (**2** playing British left-hander Ann Haydon in the 1956 Corbillon Cup). Mrs Rozeanu won the match and with Ella Zella went on to defeat Japan for Romania's fifth cup win of the decade. **3** Johnny Leach's world titles came at the end of the European era in table tennis. Soon the Asian penholders such as **4** Toshiaki Tanaka were to reign supreme. **5** In the late 1960s and early 1970s, though, the play of such Europeans as Norway's Christer Johansson (left) and Sweden's Stellan Bengtsson gave promise of a possible swing from east to west.

1 A front view and **2** a back view of the penhold grip used by China's three-times world champion Chuang Tse-tung. As only one side of the bat is covered, the player relies almost exclusively on attacking strokes made from all parts of the table. **3** Chuang follows through after a forehand drive, and **4** used the 'backhand' once considered impossible for the penholder. The stroke is executed by turning the bat to the left and holding it above wrist level. **5** Japan's Shigo Ito won the 1970 world championship using the penhold grip, but it was the Asians' superior speed, fitness, and dedication rather than their grip that gave them their supremacy in world table tennis during the latter part of the 1950s and in the 1960s.

Rules and Equipment

Table tennis is played indoors with rubber-covered bats and a white (or yellow) celluloid spherical ball on a rectangular table. The table is 9 ft. long by 5 ft. wide, standing 2 ft. 6 in. from a floor of hard, non-slippery wood or thermoplastic. A net 6 inches high is stretched across the middle, dividing the table into two equal courts. The minimum playing area for championship matches is 46 ft. by 23 ft., and the light should be of a specified uniform strength over the table, and not less than half that strength over any part of the playing area.

Doubles is played on the same regulation-size table, but with the playing surface divided into halves by a centre line.

The bat may be of any size, shape, or weight, but the blade must be made of wood, of even thickness, flat and rigid. If the blade is covered on either side, this covering must be: plain, ordinary-pimpled rubber with pimples outward of a total maximum thickness of 2 mm; or sandwich, with pimples outward or inward, of a total maximum thickness of 4 mm; or a combination of any of these surfaces. Sandwich consists of a layer of cellular rubber (sponge) surfaced by plain, ordinary-pimpled rubber. Since its introduction, play has become much faster, with even greater emphasis on spin.

The ball should have a diameter not less than 1.46 inches and not more than 1.50 inches (37.2-38.2 mm). It should weigh not less than 37 grains and not more than 39 grains (2.40-2.53 grammes).

One point is scored when a player fails to return a ball, or strikes the ball into the net or off the table. The winner of a game is the one who first scores 21 points or, at the score 20-20, is first to establish a 2-point lead. The best of five games normally constitutes a championships match for men, best of three for ladies. Service changes every five points, but at 20-20 service alternates point by point until the end of the game. If a game should be unfinished 15 minutes after it began, the *expedite system* is applied for the rest of that game and for the remaining games of the match. Under this system the server is allowed his service and 12 subsequent strokes in which to win a point, otherwise he forfeits one; players serve alternately.

Service must be made from the palm of the free hand. The ball must rest on the palm without being cupped or pinched by the fingers, and should then be tossed into the air as near vertically as possible, straight up without spin. As the ball descends it must be struck by the bat so that it first touches the server's side of the table, then, passing directly over or around the net, the receiver's side. At the moment of striking, the bat's position must be behind the end of the table, or any imaginary continuation of the table. In doubles, the ball must first touch the server's right-half court or the centre line on his side of the net and then, passing directly over or around the net, touch the receiver's right-half court or centre line. The ball must then be hit by each of the four players in turn.

For a good return, the ball must be struck after one bounce (volleying is illegal) so that it passes directly over or around the net to touch the opponent's court.

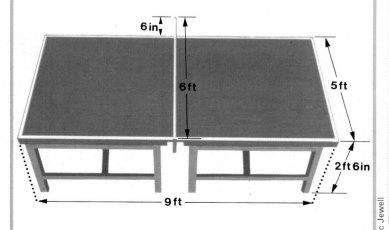

Techniques

There are two basic styles of play, Western and Asian. For the former the bat handle is normally held in a 'shake hands' grip, and strokes are played from either side of the bat from the appropriate sideways-on body position. For Asian style, only one side of the bat is covered and used, the handle being held in a *penhold* grip. This is virtually 'one stroke' table tennis, exponents relying almost exclusively on attacking forehand strokes they make from all parts of the table.

A right-handed western-style player aims whenever possible to have his left shoulder and left leg nearer the table when playing a forehand stroke, and the right shoulder and leg leading when playing backhand. Body weight, which starts on the back foot, is transferred to the front foot during the playing of the stroke.

The basic stroke is the simple 'push', played forehand or backhand. The bat, tilted slightly backward, is moved steadily forward and slightly downward to return the ball over the net to an intended target area. A full follow-through is important for maximum accuracy and control. From the 'push' stem the main attacking and defensive strokes, for which two main spins are employed—backspin for defence, and topspin for attack. Also used, especially in conjunction with these basic spins, is sidespin.

Backspin makes the ball rotate backwards while it is moving forwards, and is produced by chopping the bat downwards, behind and underneath the ball at the moment of striking. On touching the table, a ball carrying backspin tends to check its forward movement and, unless counteracted, causes the receiver to hit the ball into the net.

Topspin makes the ball rotate forwards while moving to the other side of the net, and is produced by brushing the bat upwards and forwards across the top of the ball as it is struck. The ball will tend to dip in flight over the net and, on striking the table surface, to shoot forward and upward, and, unless counteracted, cause the receiver to return it too high.

Sidespin makes the ball spin horizontally to either left or right, and is imparted by moving the bat across the ball from one side to another as it is struck.

With the aid of a sandwich bat, which accentuates both speed and spin, almost any ball can be returned simply by placing the bat in the path of an opponent's shot. The *half-volley*, made with very little follow through, is often a valuable weapon. The natural counters to attacking topspin are forehand or backhand *chop* strokes, sometimes made at long range. They slow down an opponent's attack and often set him problems of judgement. A feature of the Asian game is the use of topspin against topspin, or *counter-hitting*, and this is also now practised by top-class western-style exponents.

As it is virtually impossible to give equal attention to both forehand and backhand attacking strokes at match-play speed, the majority of players compromise with a safe, modified backhand. It is thus easier to bring a much stronger forehand into action as conveniently and as frequently as possible.

A useful variation of the topspin drive is the *loop*, produced on similar lines but with a heavily accentuated action that tends to make the ball kick up on bouncing. The way to counter the loop is to take the ball very early with a smothering shot, or very late with a defensive chop.

A ball arriving at a height above net level is normally killed with a flat hit. Another point winner, perhaps the most deadly though most difficult to produce, is the *dropshot*, normally played when one's opponent has been driven back some distance from the table edge. For this, an approach is made as if to drive, but just before contact the forward motion of the bat is arrested and the ball is lifted gently just over the net.

Asian penhold-style players employ a wide range of spin services with which they sometimes score service aces. But their main asset is their exceptionally nimble footwork that enables them to play hard and fast forehand drives from almost any range and angle. The Chinese differ from the Japanese in their use of a short backswing, which enables them to make sudden, devastating changes of direction in their shots. Some of their players have also perfected a powerful backhand drive. Once considered impossible for the penholder, it is achieved by turning the bat to the left and holding it above the wrist level. The Asians' dominance during the 1950s and 1960s, however, was due to their superior fitness, speed, and dedication—not to their grip nor to their style of play, which clearly offers less scope than that of the west.

6

7

8

9

6 The service is made from the uncupped palm of the hand. The ball is tossed into the air, without spin, and is hit as it descends so that it touches the server's side of the table and then the other side. **7** The forehand topspin drive and **8** the backhand topspin drive. Topspin is produced by brushing the bat upwards and forwards across the top of the ball as it is struck. **9** A unique feature of the doubles game is that the ball must be struck by each of the four players in turn, so a close understanding between partners is essential.

Gerry Cranham

Peter Madge

Colour Sport

Gerry Cranham

Tennis

In 1970 Rod Laver, currently the world's best tennis player, won $201,453 by playing tennis. In the first two months of 1971, when experts began wondering whether anyone would beat him that year, he amassed $115,000. With endorsements and consultant's fees, his gross income probably doubled—all because of his prowess at the game of tennis. Laver was among the richest sportsmen in the world, but he was only one member of a vast army of tennis players most of whom regularly participate in the game merely for pleasure.

History of Tennis

Ball games were popular in Egypt, the rest of northern Africa, and Asia Minor before the birth of Christ, and movements of armies and peoples resulted in a spreading of these games throughout Europe. The first ball game to be played with rackets appears to have been the Persian *tchigan*, but there is no clear connection between this game and tennis.

Tennis can be traced to France, and the origianal game was played with bare hands. During the 14th century, an indoor form of the game became very popular. This indoor game became known as *jeu de courte paume*, and the outdoor game as *jeu de longue tennis*. (The word 'tennis' derived from the command 'tenez', or 'hold this', uttered by the server before beginning a rally.) Though gloves were at first worn to protect the hands of dedicated players, in time wooden *battoirs*— simple clubs like rounders bats— and then more sophisticated implements came to be used. The first strung racket was introduced in the 15th century by Antonia Saino da Scalo, an Italian priest who wrote a book, *Trattato del Giucco della Palla* which was really a general treatise on ball games, but contained a major section on tennis. The diagonal stringing of this racket gave way in 1583 to the straight version of E. Nanteuil. At this time the game was essentially a preserve of the upper classes, and because it was played in the cloisters of many churches and similar places, many of the irregular features of such courts have been perpetuated in the eccentricities of royal tennis or real tennis.

Early Lawn Tennis. In the mid-19th century a whole spate of new games were formalized, and the ancient game of tennis did not escape being amended. It was in the 1860s that lawn tennis detached itself from its predecessor, when Messrs T. H. Gem and J. B. Perera played a game very akin

Almost a generation apart, Pancho Gonzales *Right,* **and John Newcombe** *Left* **have thrilled countless fans.**

Keystone

to modern lawn tennis at a house called 'Fairlight' in Ampton Road, Edgbaston, and later on a lawn alongside the Manor House Hotel, Leamington Spa, where, in 1872, the world's first Lawn Tennis Club was formed. They thus preceded Major Clopton Wingfield's 'sphairistike' by a matter of a few months. This gentleman, in December 1873, published his first book of rules for this new game and was granted a patent to cover his 'New and Improved Court for Playing the Ancient Game of Tennis' on July 24, 1874.

Unlike the game played by Gem and Perera, which took place on a rectangular court 30 yards long and 12 yards wide, Wingfield specified an hour-glass-shaped court 12 yards wide at the baselines and narrowing to 7 yards at the net, which was 14 yards away from each baseline. His scoring followed the badminton pattern of 15-up with special rules to operate whenever the score reached 13- or 14-all.

In 1877, when the All England Croquet Club invited entries for the first ever 'Wimbledon' Championships to be played that July, there were at least five major variations of tennis being played. The three men who had been detailed to propound the championships rules—Julian Marshall, Henry Jones, and C. G. Heathcote—did not like any of them. So they drew up a new set containing three major departures from other rules: the court would be rectangular, 26 yards long and 9 yards wide, the net being 3 ft.

3 in. high in the centre suspended from posts 3 ft. outside the court and 5 ft. high; royal tennis scoring would be adopted in its entirety; and one service fault would be allowed without penalty. These rules remained substantially unchanged for a century, so well did they conceive the game. The net posts were later reduced in height from 5 ft. to 3 ft. 6 in. and the height of the net in the centre to 3 ft., and the size of the service court was changed slightly.

The entry for those 1877 championships was only 22 gentlemen. The winner was Spencer W. Gore, an Old Harrovian who was adept at rackets. He beat W. C. Marshall 6-1, 6-2, 6-4 in the final, which was played in front of 200 spectators who each paid one shilling for the privilege of watching. Gore was a volleyer of such aptitude that the rules had to be changed in order to assist baseliners to overcome these new attacks. Although he was beaten the next year by the lobbing tactics of Frank Hadow, the rules were changed in 1880 to prohibit players hitting the ball before it had crossed the net.

The entries rose, to 34 in 1878, 45 in 1879, and 60 in 1880, when the profits reached £300. The 1880s saw the arrival of the Renshaw twins, Willie and Ernest, who dominated the game; Willie won the Wimbledon singles seven times and Ernest once between 1881 and 1889. Willie, with his ability to force the ball while it was still rising, added a new dimension of speed to tennis, and

although the twins' ascendancy seemed to discourage opposition, by 1884 the 'Renshaw boom' had crowds flocking in, and the South Western Railway began stopping trains outside the ground to unload spectators.

Meanwhile, the game was becoming popular abroad. In 1881 the United States championships were launched, and the South African and French championships in 1891. Croquet, the game which had first brought men and women together in serious competition and whose superbly true lawns had first tempted members of the All England club to try them for tennis, gave way in popularity to the new, more vigorous game. Women could not be excluded for long, and in 1884 Maud Watson became the first women's champion at Wimbledon. Like her great successor of recent years, Margaret Court, she developed her considerable powers through practising the sport with men—in her case male undergraduates attending her vicar father for 'cramming'. Three years later Lottie Dod— 15 years and 10 months old— became the youngest ever champion (an age limit of 16 was later imposed) and demonstrated that women need not be weak either technically or physically.

Tennis as an international game received an immense boost in 1900 when Dwight Davis donated his famous cup and started a men's team championship. He saw in tennis and its players a valuable way of spreading friendship

1 A group of early Wimbledon stars. Standing, l-r: E. Browne, John Hartley (winner of the singles in 1879 and 80), C. W. Grinstead, Maud Watson (who beat her sister Lilian, seated, in the 1879 final), Herbert Lawford (champion in 1887), William Renshaw and Ernest (seated) who dominated the game of the 1880s.

among nations. In 1900 the United States beat the British Isles 3-0 with one match unfinished and one not played at Longwood, near Boston. The British, however, recovered from this set-back and won in the years from 1903 to 1906. The heroes of this run were the 'princes charming' Reginald and Laurence Doherty. Neither of these brothers was particularly strong, nor especially aggressive, but their strokes were technically perfect. The manner of their winning, and occasionally losing, was the start of a tradition of sportsmanship in the game which persisted even through the pressures of professional and open tennis. The British tenure of the cup was halted in 1907 by a successful challenge from Australasia in the persons of Norman Brookes and Tony Wilding. In 1914, when World War I stopped any international competition involving the Empire, Australasia, despite brief tenures by Britain and the United States, still held the trophy, and defended successfully in 1919, though they lost to the United States in Auckland in 1920.

The Inter-War Period. The 1920s saw the emergence of two of the greatest personalities in tennis, and indeed in any sport, one male, and the other female. The female was Suzanne Lenglen of France, and the man, American Bill Tilden. Suzanne favoured a loose fitting, one-piece dress of calf length and with a wide skirt to allow plenty of movement, which in itself was enough to draw the crowds. Added to her Gallic adventurousness was a dynamism, grace, and flamboyance, and wherever she played, the crowds arrived in droves. At Wimbledon in 1919 a record crowd of 8,000 headed by the King and Queen saw Suzanne save two match points before wresting the singles title from the great pre-war champion Mrs. Dorothea Lambert Chambers. From that day until the end of her amateur career she was beaten only once in an important singles event—by Molla Mallory in the 1921 American championships. Never before had anyone—man or woman—exercised such control over the game. Success against her was measured in terms of points. Tournament organizers immediately saw her potential as a money-spinner, and the Manchester Northern club was one of the first to approach her father-

manager-coach about her participation. 'She will play,' he answered. 'My fee for bringing her will be £100.' Thus the incipient 'shamateurism' which had made a shadowy appearance before the war took a major step towards the lucrative 'trade' which eventually resulted in the open tennis of the 1960s.

The tall, gangling and theatrical Bill Tilden won his first tournament at the age of eight. But he was so interested in learning about the game and teaching others that he did not win his first major singles title until he was 27—the Wimbledon singles in 1920. From then until 1927, when it took the manifold talents of the famous French 'musketeers', Borotra, Cochet, Lacoste, and Brugnon, to knock him off his pedestal, he dominated the world game. He mixed sheer power, technical excellence, and

2 The outside courts during the All England championships at the end of the 19th century. 3 New Zealand's Tony Wilding shared Australasia's Davis Cup success before World War I with Norman Brookes. 4 The greatest player ever? Bill Tilden certainly made a hit in his famous teddy bear sweater. His influence on the game was inestimable.

Press Association

4

Mansell

Radio Times Hulton Picture Library

2 tactical wizardry to such an intense degree that many critics rate him as the greatest player ever to grace the game. He came back to win at Wimbledon at the age of 37, in 1930, and continued to excel as a professional in later years.

The newspapers and radio nourished a public craving for heroes and heroines and accelerated the cult of personality. The game grew concurrently, and in 1929 the total number of Davis Cup challengers had reached 29. The growth of men's international tennis had not gone unnoticed among the women, especially an American, Mrs. Hazel Wightman. A notable player in her own right, and impressed with the standard of play of American, British, and

3 French women, she broached the idea of the competition for women's teams from those three countries. Received coldly at first, the idea gradually took hold, and three years after the original advance the Wightman Cup match came into being as an annual match between teams of women from Britain and the United States. The first encounter took place at Forest Hills in 1923, and the United States won 7-0.

The increase in the number of tournaments, and the growth of tennis as an international game, demanded an administrative efficiency and enterprise which never completely materialized. In March 1913, 12 national associations had joined forces in Paris to form the International Lawn Tennis Federation. But this body did not cater

for professionals. The first portent of impending trouble arose in 1926 when Suzanne Lenglen, following a series of misunderstandings at Wimbledon which had—in effect—affronted the Queen, quit the amateur game to play a series of professional matches against Mary K. Browne, a former American champion. These proved highly profitable, although the matches were banned from the courts of affiliated clubs and so had to be played on improvised courts in stadiums.

This tour opened a number of wounds that were never completely healed even with the advent of the open game in 1968. It became clear, however, that many players could not hope to compete without some sort of backhand remuneration. 'I left the amateur ranks to maintain my wife and child', claimed Vincent Richards, the 1924 Olympic champion. The more conservative elements in the amateur game ignored professionalism until they were forced to accept the principle of paid players or find that control of the game had passed out of their hands altogether.

In 1928, the US LTA launched the American Professional Championships, Richards winning the title. Tilden, constantly at odds with officialdom, added his glittering name to the groping professional game. More important, he took with him all his flair and energy for promotion, frequently travelling all night from place to place, playing in the evening, and then moving on again.

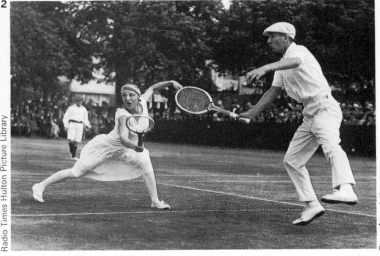

1 With her voracious appetite for tennis, Bunny Ryan won an estimated 659 tournament events between 1912 and 1934.
2 A strangely ungainly Suzanne Lenglen partners another outstanding French player, Rene Lacoste, one of the famous 'Four Musketeers' who won the Davis Cup for France in 1927 and retained it until 1933. The others were Jean Borotra (**3**), Jacques 'Toto' Brugnon (**4**), and Henri Cochet (**5**).

6 Bobby Riggs won all three events at Wimbledon in 1939, and joined the professional ranks after his United States victory in 1941. But only a fortnight before his All England triumphs he had lost the Queen's Club final to Gottfried von Cramm 6-1, 6-0. (Von Cramm's entry was not accepted at Wimbledon). **7** Don Budge completed a grand slam in 1938 and immediately became a professional to tour with Ellsworth Vines.

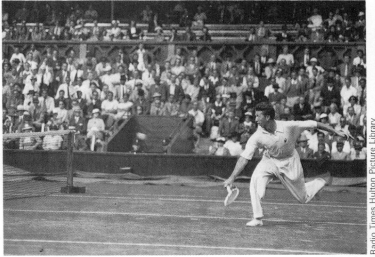

Meanwhile, the rising star of the amateur game was a 6 ft. 3 in. tall, stringy Californian named Ellsworth Vines. In 1932 he won the Wimbledon singles, and many experts think that in his last three matches he reached a standard of play of such high quality that it had never been seen before or repeated afterwards. Losing form slightly in 1933, Vines decided to join Tilden in 1934 and on a tour won a series of matches by 47 to 26—which speaks volumes for Tilden's greatness: he was then 41.

The gay, socialite tennis world of the 1920s had as four of its major personalities the French foursome—Jean Borotra, Rene Lacoste, Jacques Brugnon, and Henri Cochet. As a team they were responsible for France's winning the Davis Cup for the first time, in 1927. They held it until 1932—and 40 years later France was still looking for another victory. Borotra, with his black Basque beret and extravagant leaps, was ranked in the world's top ten from 1924 to 1935, though never at No. 1. He lost a monumental Wimbledon final in 1927 to the delicate touch player Cochet, who was 2-5 down in the fifth set and saved six match points. French tennis was never the same after they dropped out of the top class in the mid-1930s.

The French supremacy was followed by a brief resurgence of the British game thanks largely to Bunny Austin and Fred Perry. Perry gave everything to the game as an amateur, winning Wimbledon in 1934, 1935, and 1936, and the American title in 1933, 1934, and 1936. He and Austin were instrumental in winning the Davis Cup for Britain in 1933 and retaining it in 1934, 1935, and 1936. Perry joined the pros in 1937, and toured with Vines in 1938, Vines winning the series 47-26.

Perry's abdication of the amateur crown left the field open for Donald Budge, a red-headed Californian who rates as one of the greatest players of all time. In 1937 he became the first man to complete the 'grand slam'—the singles titles of Australia, France, All England (Wimbledon), and the United States in one year. But he, too, turned professional, beating Vines 21-18 in their 1938 tour. And when Bobby Riggs, who won all three events at the 1939 Wimbledon, turned pro in 1941, the professional game was beginning to hurt the amateur game, though World War II obscured the issue.

The Post-World War II Era. Sports quickly revived after the ravages of the world war: none more so than tennis. British writers were quick to point out, as their players were beaten, that the Americans were much better fed and equipped. But a lot of this was just sour grapes. The decade after the war was dominated by American men and

women. Jack Kramer, Bob Falkenburg—whose stalling tactics earned him an undeserved notoriety—Ted Schroeder, Budge Patty, and Dick Savitt successively carried off the Wimbledon title and were no less prominent elsewhere. Savitt was only the second American to win the Australian singles, in 1951.

On the women's side the big names in the American ranks were those of Louise Brough and Maureen Connolly. Miss Brough won Wimbledon three times in a row (1948-50), and in 1950 missed the 'grand slam' by failing in the United States championships: she won all the others. The grand slam was completed by Maureen Connolly in 1953, the first time a woman had achieved this statistical feat. Over a period of three years, 1952, 1953, and 1954, Miss Connolly was beaten on only four occasions, and never in the final of a major championship. Her tennis career was cut short by a riding accident in which she broke a leg. She, in turn, was followed by a whole series of great Americans. The first of these was Althea Gibson, whose serve and volley technique carried her to United States and Wimbledon wins in 1957 and 1958, as well as the world No. 1 ranking in those years. She was the first black American to reach the world top class.

Meanwhile, the men's balance of power had swung drastically towards Australia. Frank Sedgman, winner of the French, All England, and American singles in 1952, was the first to hit the top after the war. He turned professional, but was succeeded by a group of players who kept the Davis Cup in Australia from 1950 to 1967. These were basically the Harry Hopman 'chain gang', so

called because of the strict training they underwent with this legendary figure in world tennis. The group included, in the days of amateur tennis of course, Ken Rosewall, Lew Hoad, and Rod Laver, all of whom came up through those ranks. And once these three had turned professional by the beginning of the 1960s, the Australian flag was kept flying by Fred Stolle and Roy Emerson. Stolle, labelled as one of Wimbledon's unluckiest losers, reached three consecutive singles finals only to go down each time, twice to Emerson, but reached world No. 1 status after winning the United States title in 1966.

The women's game in the 1960s was graced with the suntanned figure of the Brazilian bombshell Maria Bueno. Though dogged by ill health, she won Wimbledon twice (1959 and 1960) and was twice runner-up (1965 and 1966), won four American singles titles (1959, 1963, 1964, and 1966) and was the world No. 1 on three occasions. Her style of play is perhaps best described as 'feline', and it well epitomizes this player of Latin blood and an ice-cold tactical brain.

After Miss Bueno's withdrawal from the scene, two women players almost monopolized the top honours—Margaret Court of Australia and Billie Jean King from the United States. Mrs. King started her own women's professional tour, and was instrumental in helping women to demand—and receive—prize money more

in keeping with their prowess. Mrs. Court, a rather more establishment figure, amassed an extraordinary number of major and minor titles, and completed the second women's grand slam by winning all four major singles titles in 1970.

With the coming of open tennis in 1968, most of Australia's men stars joined the contracted ranks, including the last winner of 'amateur' Wimbledon, John Newcombe. As a result, his country was relieved of the Davis Cup in 1968 by the United States, many of whose players remained independent. But Australians still collected most of the major men's prizes. Rod Laver, who turned professional after doing a men's grand slam in 1962, won the first

Popperfoto

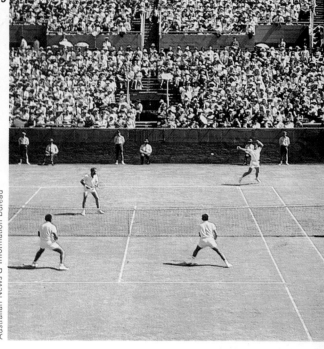

Australian News & Information Bureau

8 Two singles stars—Darlene Hard (left) and Althea Gibson combined to win the doubles at Wimbledon in 1957.
9 Kooyong stadium, Melbourne, has often been the scene of a Davis Cup challenge round.

open Wimbledon in 1968 and then repeated his grand slam feat—in far more trying circumstances—in 1969. Rosewall, too, proved that age had not blunted his ability by winning the first ever open championship, the 1968 British Hard Courts at Bournemouth, and the first open national championship, the French.

Post-1945 Professionalism. The first full post-war season, 1947, was, perhaps, the critical year. Jack Kramer, a disciple of Budge, who stood head and shoulders above all other amateurs as a player, toured with Riggs and amassed a considerable fortune, though he realized it was still small compared with the money made by the promoter. A man of great integrity and a shrewd negotiator, Kramer decided to promote himself, and seized his chance in 1952 by signing the Wimbledon winner, Frank Sedgman of Australia. Sedgman, a great sportsman with a sunny disposition, was a favourite with the crowds, and hordes of fans flocked to see his matches with Kramer. Each man netted $128,000 as a player, and Kramer probably took as much again as a promoter. Encouraged by this *coup*, he quickly signed up a band of top players—Tony Trabert, Ken Rosewall, Lew Hoad, Ashley Cooper, Malcolm Anderson, Alex Olmedo, and many who were already professionals, notably Pancho Gonzales. More important from the public relations angle, he transformed the professionals from being an unorganized army of mercenaries into a respected body of players who, although their monetary demands were high, gave splendid value in return.

Clearly the two separate games of tennis—amateur and professional—could not remain apart much longer, especially as 'under the table' payments of as much as $1,000 a week as expenses for amateurs had become commonplace and public knowledge. Furthermore, the 'shamateur' tag was bringing the game into disrepute. The first important efforts at ILTF level were made in 1959, and in 1960 an official proposal for open tennis was debated, and almost inevitably defeated. Only five votes divided the two factions: one man misunderstood the proposal and cast his two votes in the wrong lobby; another vote was lost because, at a critical moment, a delegate was temporarily attending a call of nature; more votes were lost as a French delegate had left the building to settle details of a reception being staged by the French LTF that evening. Subsequent efforts fell short of success, and it was clear that multilateral action was not

Jack Kramer with his pro 'troupe' in 1968. Conflicts between the contracted groups and the ILTF were softened, but not settled, by the 1968 decision on 'open' tennis.

going to have any effect.

It fell to Herman David, the Wimbledon chairman, to take the decisive step. He published a long interview in the British magazine *Lawn Tennis* condemning the 'Living Lie of Amateurism', and announced that Wimbledon would 'go it alone' on open tennis in 1968. This stunning news flashed round the world in seconds, and Britain was promised with expulsion from the ILTF. But at a special ILTF general meeting on March 30, 1968, most of the British proposal was accepted. The ILTF did not agree to abolish all distinctions and designate all tennis players as simple 'players'. Instead there were to be no fewer than four new categories.

The first category was the *Contract Professional*. This was a player under contract to an independent promoter, such as Lamar Hunt. Such players were outside the jurisdiction of their national associations and so could not be called upon to play in the international team competitions such as the Davis, Federation, or Wightman cups. *Independent Professionals*, on the other hand, recognized the control of their national bodies, but because they were not contracted in a group, each individual had to extract his own appearance money from promoters of tournaments. And not all tournaments were open to independent professionals. *Authorized Players*, however, are not too different from professionals. This category was invented to include players whose countries (especially those behind the Iron Curtain) did not recognize professionalism. In practice, their position was similar to the independent professionals. And there was still a category of *Amateurs*. They could accept no prizes, and their expenses were now strictly controlled.

This new classification imposes

restrictions on players under contract to the two big professional promoters Lamar Hunt and George MacCall (who later sold out to Hunt's group, World Championship Tennis Incorporated).

Hunt, a sports-loving Texan oil billionaire, negotiated, through his executive director Mike Davies, the erstwhile British No. 1 player, to organize his own series of tournaments. And by the end of 1970 32 of the world's best male players were signed up to play in them. Also in 1970 came a new idea from Jack Kramer. He and the ILTF evolved an internationally linked scheme in which 20 tournaments not only put up substantial prizes of their own but also contributed to a central fund to be allocated to the men earning most points in those tournaments. Later, Pepsi-Cola added their own sponsorship, and so the Pepsi-Cola/ILTF Grand Prix was born.

But all was not peaceful between the professional groups and the ILTF. In September 1970, Hunt announced that his own world championship series of 1971 would offer $1 million. Only hours later the ILTF announced that they would repeat their 1970 Grand Prix series but with the prize money increased. It was, in effect, a tennis war. Such escalation threatened to kill off the game as a big time sport. But after a period of snarling at one another, the ILTF and Hunt's WCT reached an uneasy compromise peace in which contract players would participate in ILTF events as well as their own, while the ILTF players could also take part in some WCT events. All this was basically sensible, because only if the professionals were prepared to compete on the open market, so to speak, could they retain their images as the world's best players.

Central Press

Topix

Colour Sport

1 All games begin with the service. The player must be grounded behind the baseline on impact, and the ball has to pitch in the service court over the net. The two basic strokes in the game are the forehand (**2**) and backhand (**3**) which can be used as groundstrokes (after a bounce) or volleys. To deal with a high ball a player 'smashes' (**4**), and a good smash will win a point.

How the Game is Played

Tennis is a one- or two-a-side game played on a regularly marked-out court divided by a net. The object of the game is to beat the opposition by making them hit the ball out of court or into the net or by hitting the ball accurately into their court so that they do not even reach it.

To start with, imagine a game of singles. Two men walk onto the court, they toss up, and the winner of the toss can elect to serve or choose ends. Thereafter, they change ends after each odd game—after the first, third, fifth, and so on. After a preliminary knock-up, which allows both players to loosen up and to test the condition of the court, play begins. The player due to serve serves. If he delivers the ball into the service court diagonally opposite him (and commits no foot fault in serving), the service is good and must be returned. Play then continues with each player hitting the ball alternately—on the volley or after one bounce—until the point is won or lost. If the server wins, the score becomes 15-love. If the receiver wins, love-15. Four points—15, 30, 40, and game—decide a game. If the scores are 40-all, *deuce* is called, and the first player to be two points ahead wins the game. The first player to win six games and be two games ahead wins the set (subject in some cases to tie-breaking conditions), and the winner of a majority of sets (two in the case of a three-set match, three in a five-setter) wins the match. Service changes as usual at the end of each set, but players stay at the same end for the first game of the next set if the completed set consisted of an even number of games, or change ends for one game after a set with an odd number of games.

Each sequence of shots (a rally) to decide a point commences with a service. The first service is made from the right-hand side of the server's baseline, and he changes sides on every point. The ball is served by projecting it into the air and then hitting it before it hits the ground over the net into the service court diagonally opposite. If the server fails to do this properly, he has another chance, but if the second chance fails, then a point is scored by the receiver. Services that touch the net and then fall into the correct court are termed 'lets' and are replayed without penalty.

Points are not only lost because the ball is missed, hit out, or hit into the net. A player loses a point if he allows the ball to bounce twice. It is a foul to hit the ball before it has crossed the net, to throw the racket at the ball and hit it, to strike the net with person or racket, or to touch the ball with anything but the racket.

In a doubles match between two pairs, say A1 and A2, and B1 and B2, each pair decides on its order of serving. Service must go A-B-A-B and so on, with 1 and 2 of each pair alternating during a set. But the precise order may be changed after each set. The receivers receive from the same courts throughout a game, while the server changes his court as in singles after each point.

Play in tennis is, according to the rules, continuous. But the players normally stop for a few seconds while changing ends to towel themselves and perhaps take a drink. Tennis crowds, not normally slow to show their feelings, can be relied on to make any player violating the conventions of the game feel so uncomfortable that he refrains thereafter.

Syndication International

Mansell Collection

1 Bunny Austin's eperimental racket did not bring him the success he hoped for. It did, however, anticipate the metal rackets used by Arthur Ashe (**3**) in the 1960s. The tennis racket developed from the implement used in real tennis (**2**), as illustrated in Diderot's 'Encyclopedia'. There is no restriction on the size or shape of a racket, but few weigh more than 1 lb, and shapes and sizes change little.
4 Sun, shade, and doubles: a perfect Wimbledon evening combination. The three forms of tennis—singles, doubles, and mixed doubles—have not been altered for decades. The fast men's game is well complemented by the more tactical play of the women, with mixed a healthy hybrid.

Popperfoto

Equipment. The rackets and balls used in tennis have, like almost everything else, been affected by changes in technology and production processes, while the mass market in tennis goods has meant that more research goes into design and manufacture than perhaps used to be the case.

Tennis balls were originally made of uncovered rubber, but by the time of the first Wimbledon championships in 1877, they were being covered with white cloth which was shaped and stitched over the rubber core. No cross-stitching was permitted, and unbleached carpet thread was compulsory. In order to ensure that pressure inside the balls was uniform, they were inflated by gas liberated from a pellet put inside the core during manufacture. Towards the end of the 1920s, stitching gave way to a special cement. Wool as a cover was largely superseded after World War II by mixtures of wool and man-made fibres, though pure wool remains the most responsive surface. The diameter of the ball is between 2.575 and 2.675 inches. When dropped from 100 inches onto a concrete base, it must bounce to between 53 and 58 inches.

In top-class tournament tennis, six balls are normally in use at any particular time, and these are changed regularly. The umpire calls for new balls after the first seven games (plus the knock-up) and thereafter after every nine games. The balls are kept at a temperature of 20°C before being used. The player serving with new balls is reckoned to have a slight advantage, as they will be springier.

There has also been a constant change in the types of rackets used. Because of the close connection between lawn tennis and real tennis and rackets, the original tennis rackets followed the patterns set for those other games. One primary difference was that the head and handle were not in a straight line: in some cases the section of the racket was convex, and in some others concave. Fred Taylor, who developed time and motion study, won the first American doubles championship using a racket which curved in *both* directions. Flat rackets have, however, been the general rule.

The best racket strings have always been made from lamb's gut, but rising costs have led to the development of substitutes, including one type which boasts oil-filled plastic capillaries.

Laminated wooden frames became common in the 1930s, and before that time one-piece frames were normal. The only great departure in design came in the 1960s, when metal-framed rackets became popular. But because steel does not have the elasticity of wood, it causes 'tennis elbow' more readily. Metal rackets had been developed in 1928, but they were also strung with steel, and this rusted!

The Court. Tennis (officially lawn tennis whatever the playing surface may be) is played on a rectangular court—78 feet long by 27 feet wide for singles, and 78 ft. by 36 ft. for doubles. The court is divided into halves by a net, which is suspended from posts. The net is 3 feet high in the centre of the court, and 3 ft. 6 in. high at the posts, which are positioned on the sidelines. Each half of the court is divided by a service line, 21 feet from the net, while another line runs from the centre of the net to divide the service area into two service courts.

Although tennis can be played on almost any flat, true surface, international matches are confined mainly to grass, clay (ground-up brick dust), cement, wood, linoleum, artificial grass carpets, and tarmacadam. Of these, closely cut grass and wood offer the least surface resistance to the ball and are, therefore, the 'fastest' surfaces. They greatly assist players who rely on power, and it is customary of men such as Rod Laver and Arthur Ashe and women such as Margaret Court and Billie Jean King to follow every service to the net in anticipation of weak returns which they can volley out of reach. Red clay courts abound on the European mainland and Asia. They are relatively soft, so the ball digs in before bouncing up slowly and high. On this surface, defence and subtle tactics reap dividends, enabling players with the imagination and touch of Manuel Santana or the baseline skills and persistence of Ann Jones to come into their own.

Of the other surfaces, cement plays rather like grass, and linoleum plays somewhere between clay and grass until it becomes shiny and worn, when it is very fast. Artificial carpet surfaces vary according to the thickness and tightness of the underlay, irrespective of the surface of the carpet itself, which of course adds a further variant.

The proliferation of rich tournaments has meant that players can no longer afford to become experts on one surface and duffers on another, so it is now rare to consider players as good only on grass or clay. Laver, Rosewall, Newcombe, and Gonzales have been equally deadly on them all.

5 Tennis scoreboards show the state of the game in terms of sets, games, and points, who is serving (red dots), and, in the 1970s, the situation in a tie-break. This is essential information for anyone trying to follow this rather involved sport.

6 The umpire on his high seat is in control of a match, and in important fixtures is assisted by a number of line judges and a net-cord judge— not to mention the players.

Scoring. A tennis encounter between individuals (singles), two teams of two men or women (doubles), or teams each containing a man and a woman (mixed doubles) is termed a 'match'. The match itself is divided into sets and games. Normally, play is the best of three sets (the first player to win two sets being the winner), though in some major men's events it is the best of five sets. A set continues until one player wins 6 or more games with a certain advantage over his opponent. The game is the shortest division of a match, and consists of one player beginning each rally with a service until the game has been won. A game is won by the first player to win four points, but a special rule operates if the score reaches three points each. In this situation, play continues until one side is two clear points ahead.

Straightforward 1, 2, 3, 4, scoring is not used. Instead, the traditional '15' (one), '30' (two), and '40' (three) have been retained from royal tennis. When 'deuce' (a corruption of '*quarante a deux*' or 40-all) is reached, the game progresses until one player is two points clear: these points are measured as 'advantage server' or 'advantage receiver', and then either 'deuce' or 'game' depending on who wins the next point.

In traditional tennis scoring, a set is won by the player or pair who wins six games, or are two games ahead after the score has reached 5 games all. With the modern serve-and-volley game, a stalemate situation can go on and on, and sets of 10-8, 11-9, and 16-14, are common. One doubles set in America went to 49-47. Such games, though in certain circumstances exciting, can become extremely boring and disrupt the scheduled programme of events in a tournament.

For this reason, a handful of reformers, led by the American millionaire James van Alen, fought for and achieved recognition that life was simply too short for these long matches to continue. After a series of experiments, a number of tie-breaking systems were devised. In general, they operated once the score had reached 6 or 8 games each.

A popular tie-breaking system was the one adopted by the British LTA as an experiment during 1971, named the '12 point' system. This arrangement was used in outdoor matches after 8-all, and indoors after 6-all or 8-all, but never in the final set. It was thought wrong for a match which had gone to five sets to be decided on a tie-breaker. When the score reached 8-all, the system changed: the server at 8-all served for one point, then his opponent for two, then the original player for two, until one player had scored seven points or was two points ahead. If the score reached 6-all, the game was extended until one player had a lead of two points. Another version of the '12 point' system was mooted. In this method; each player served twice in turn, but if 6-all was reached the system changed to one serve each. A further method was based on the best of nine points—sometimes referred to as the 'sudden death' system. If the score reached 4-all the game and set went to the winner of the next point.

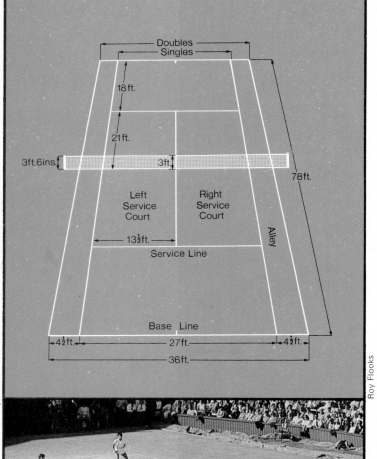

Radio Times Hulton Picture Library

Fox Photos

Left, **Mrs. Ethel Larcombe in the 1914 Wimbledon challenge round. Freedom of movement was not considered important.** *Above,* **Gorgeous Gussie Moran scandalized and entranced the crowds with her lace panties.** *Right,* **A 1970 style worn by Britain's Virginia Wade.**

Ed Lacey

Tennis Fashions

Tennis abounds in healthy, attractive young women who, as a group, are extremely fashion conscious. Long past are the days when a well-dressed woman player went on court wearing a tightly waisted shirt or blouse with a high neck and, perhaps, a tie, a voluminous skirt that reached the ground, a pill-box hat, leather shoes, and fiercely restraining underwear. Indeed, in one of the earlier American championships, two sisters went on court to play a doubles semi-final dressed in long satin skirts so that they could go straight from a game to a garden party.

Keen women players of the Victorian and Edwardian eras thought only of tennis when selecting, in Mrs Dorothea Lambert Chambers's words, 'a plain, gored skirt—not pleated—about four or five inches from the ground. It should just clear your ankles. A plain shirt without frills or furbelows, a collar, tie, and waistband go to make an outfit as comfortable as you could possibly desire . . . I prefer white shoes and stockings'.

Not until 1919, and the arrival of Suzanne Lenglen, did women shed, so to speak, their clothing fetters. Mlle Lenglen favoured a shorter, one-piece dress, with knee-high stockings, and was reputed to wear only the flimsiest of underclothes. Stockings were not discarded as almost compulsory tournament wear until the late 1920s, and the first woman to appear shamelessly without them was 'Bobby' Tapscott, a South African. Shorts were introduced to women's tournaments by Miss G. A. Tomblin, at the Chiswick Hard Court

meeting in 1933; they were exactly like the *culottes* of later days. Helen Jacobs's shorts were better cut, though considerably longer, than the relatively brief, functional shorts worn by Alice Marble when winning the Wimbledon singles in 1939.

During the Lenglen era, a young designer, Teddy Tinling, slowly began to build the reputation which was to make him a virtual dictator of women's tennis fashion for a quarter of a century after World War II. He understood the requirements of top class players, and possessed a rare sense for fabrics and designs. A picturesque giant of 6 ft. 3 in., he became famous in 1951 when an outfit he had designed was used by Augusta 'Gorgeous Gussie' Moran at Wimbledon. Part of the ensemble was a pair of lace-trimmed panties, which were a sensation in a Britain still suffering from rationing.

His name made, Tinling became more adventurous. He found Maria Bueno the perfect model for some truly regal designs, one of which was purple-lined with purple pants to match. Shocked, the Wimbledon committee imposed a ban on colour that was to last for a dozen years after. In the 1960s the standard playing wear of women was either a dress with frilly panties, or separates—shirt with shorts or skirt. The use of artificial fibres has eliminated much of the laundry problem for women, though none of them have adopted the common men's practice of stepping under a shower and washing body and clothes simultaneously.

Men's wear, on the other hand, has remained almost exactly as it was 60 years ago, except that shorts have superseded long trousers.

Tennis in the 1970s

Tennis has remained essentially an upper and middle class game. The inauguration of open tennis in 1968 enabled many young people to become career players, and so time spent playing tennis is part of their work. Before 1968, 'shamateurism' enabled many stars to enjoy luxury living on vastly inflated expenses. Before that a number of regular tournament players either possessed private means or worked in jobs that allowed them plenty of time off.

The basic structure of tournaments has changed little since the 1890s. It is usual to offer five events, men's and women's singles and doubles, and mixed doubles, together with occasional veterans', junior, and handicap events. Most tournaments operate on a knock-out basis, though some professional events are leagues.

Normally, play in a tournament begins at 10 a.m. on a Monday morning and continues until late

The modern tennis player is one of the most highly paid animals in the sporting world. Even quite lowly players can accumulate enough money to allow them to play tennis all the year round and all over the world. The richest tournaments at the start of the 1970s were the linked grand prix competitions. Thus the actual cash winnings at individual tournaments are far from the only awards. Spearheaded by the whisky firm John Dewar—whose indoor winter tour in Britain, the Dewar Cup, quickly became known as the 'whisky circuit'—these linked tournaments caught promoters' imaginations in a big way. In such events the players finishing high up according to a predetermined points formula gain bonuses at the end of the events. The system became international in 1970 when the ILTF, aided by Pepsi-Cola, sponsored a worldwide Grand Prix spread over 20 countries. Cliff Richey from the United States won the most

'And in the blue corner, Tony Roche!' Coloured shirts and shapely ballgirls were features of the later professional game.

points and thus took the $25,000 bonus. Arthur Ashe, second, picked up $17,000, and third-placed Ken Rosewall $15,000. Altogether, $150,000 was given out to the top 20 players.

Endorsements and advertisements are another rich field for the top players. Arthur Ashe signed a contract for $50,000 a year for using a steel racket manu-

factured by the Head Ski company. Rod Laver contracted to use three different rackets, depending in which continent he played. Laver's contracts are said to be worth $110,000 a year. Others receive from $25,000 a year downwards, and quite moderate players may be paid as little as $600 a year for using a particular make of racket.

The decade 1960-1970 was dominated by two Australians, Margaret Court (*above*) and Rod Laver (*right*). Both did a grand slam—Court in 1970, Laver in 1962 and 1969.

on Saturday. Most women's events are played in the morning, and the men's in the afternoon, but this is only a hangover from the days when women did not work and the men could afford to have only the afternoons off. In practice, those who enter tournaments are expected to be on call all day, whenever it suits the referee. The world's chief referee is Captain Mike Gibson, a former army officer who referees at Wimbledon and all other important British events, as well as a number of overseas events including the United States and South African open championships.

Laver also began a clothing business, and became a consultant to a petrol company who sponsor tennis. But he is managed by the American lawyer Mark McCormack, who is also the agent of millionaire golfers such as Arnold Palmer, Gary Player, and Jack Nicklaus. Many players, especially Australians, have invested some of their money in tennis 'farms'. Lew Hoad opened a monster residential centre near Malaga in Spain, and John Newcombe one in Texas. Newcombe made a series of TV casettes for home tuition, and Hoad a gramophone record. Yet had he been born 30 years later, Britain's Fred Perry might have been richer than anyone else. In his Wimbledon winning days, he was offered a shilling royalty on every pair of Daks trousers sold during his lifetime, a figure running into many millions. The rules then forbade endorsements, and so he had to refuse the offer.

This enormous prize money is not lightly gained. The season begins early in January, covers the globe, and ends in December. It is common for players to contest finals in the United States one day, and be on court in Europe the following afternoon. Because the prizes are so great, many players compete too much

John Newcombe (*above*) **won the last amateur Wimbledon and was open champion in 1970 and 1971. 1 Ken Rosewall proved tennis players were not over the top when they were 30. He was Australian champion in 1953 (age 18) and 1972 (37). 2 Young Evonne Goolagong won the French title in 1971 and looked set to take over Mrs Court's mantle as the world No. 1 after beating her in the Wimbledon final.**

and suffer physical and psychological strain. Most of the top players are afflicted by various muscular ailments. Bob Hewitt, his nerves perhaps frayed by too much competition, once argued with an umpire and a spectator who remonstrated. Though 75, the spectator was a karate expert, and when Hewitt left the court he was felled by a blow which put him in a Los Angeles hospital with concussion.

Hewitt and other colourful players are great crowd pullers, and in a sport where entertainment is a vital ingredient, many players cash in on this quality. Willie Alvarez, an itinerant Colombian of the pre-open days, admitted that he played up this side of his nature so that he would be invited to more tournaments. The glamourous Karol Fageros loved tennis and travel, and in order to further her career made herself front-page news with her gold lame panties, a pair of which once fetched £25 in an auction at the Manchester Northern tournament.

Professional and amateur tennis players continue to co-exist in an uneasy harmony despite the coming of open tennis. But the enormous financial rewards affect only the top players. To the spectator, the game is still the most important thing, and it is on the spectator that the health of the game depends. This is the reason for Laver's success: though he is highly paid, he offers superb entertainment value. Quiet and modest, he is extremely thorough, but has an attacking flair which is traditionally associated with the old school of amateur cricketers. His counterpart in the women's game is his fellow-Australian Margaret Court, who in 1970 emulated Laver's grand slams of 1963 and 1969. A superb athlete,

Glossary of Terms

Ace A service which the receiver cannot touch. Some consider a service which the receiver touches with his racket, but without any chance of returning it, as an ace, but this should really be classed as a service winner.

Advantage After a game has gone to deuce, the player who is a point ahead is said to have 'advantage'. If he wins the next point he wins the game: if he loses, the score reverts to deuce.

Alley or **tramlines** Those parts of the court lying between the lines marking the lateral extremities of the singles and doubles courts.

Backhand shot Stroke played with the reverse side of the racket, i.e. with the back of the hand facing the ball.

Backstop The netting or canvas at the back of the court. Under championship conditions this must be at least 21 feet from the baseline.

Ballboy or **ballgirl** Boy or girl with the duty of collecting stray balls around the court and feeding them to the players.

Baseline The line marking the end of each half of the court.

Centre line The line dividing the service court into two halves.

Chop A stroke that imparts backspin and causes the ball to stay low after bouncing.

Cross-court drive A shot that directs the ball diagonally across the court.

Deuce If each player wins three points, the score in a game is deuce. After that, if they have both won an equal number of points, the score is again deuce.

Dink A medium to slow return hit low over the net and usually at an acute angle, but also at the feet of an opponent if he is inside the service court area. Used especially to neutralize the effectiveness of volleying attacks.

Double Fault See *Fault*.

Doubles Match of two players against two.

Drop shot A shot dropped just over the net, normally hit with back spin to prevent the ball bouncing too high.

Fault A service that sends the ball into the net or outside the service court. Two faults on one service lose the point—a *double fault*.

Foot fault Certain radical foot movements are prohibited when serving (such as walking or running) and neither foot may be placed over the baseline. Any contraventions of these rules are known as *foot faults* and count as serving faults.

Forehand Any shot made with the front of the arm facing the ball.

Ground stroke Generic term for all shots played after the oncoming ball has bounced.

Half-volley Stroke made at the moment the ball bounces.

Let A term common to many ball games to describe the replaying of a point without penalty in the event of an unusual occurrence. In tennis, a let is played if the service hits the net and bounces into the service court or touches the receiver and anything he carries. A let is also played if, for instance, the receiver of a service is not ready to start; if one player involuntarily hinders his opponent; or if a player is hindered in playing by an external agency.

Major championship Four international championships are rated 'major' by the ILTF—the Australian, French, All England (Wimbledon), and United States. The tennis 'grand slam' constitutes winning all four in the same year.

Match point When a player requires one point to win the match, he is said to hold *match point*; if, say, he leads 40-15, he has two match points. Likewise, the terms 'set point', 'game point', and 'a point for a break' (of service) are also used.

Mixed doubles Doubles played between partnerships of man and woman.

Net cord When a player hits the ball and it hits the top of the net (the cord) and goes over the net (often dropping dead in an unplayable position), the player making the shot is often, justly, described as having had a 'lucky net cord'.

New balls During play, the covering of balls becomes scuffed; so that the balls used are consistent in behaviour, balls are replaced at regular intervals in important matches.

Open tournament Any tournament that accepts entries from all categories of players, including those under contract to outside agents and not subject to control by national associations.

Passing shot Any shot which goes by (passes) an opponent at the net.

Ranking A list of players drawn up in order of ability. National lists are normally official, but international rankings are not.

Referee The arbitrating and organizing official in charge of all players and facets of the game at a tourna-

ment: he can overrule the umpire.

Seeding Method of distributing players within a draw so that the best players do not meet in early rounds. The number of seeds is governed by the rules and in a draw of 32 places must not exceed 8. Numbering the positions 1 to 32, the seeds are placed according to their estimated ability (1-8) to meet in the third round thus: 1 v 8, 6 v 3, 4 v 5, 7 v 2.

Service The stroke which starts each point. It must, to be valid, pitch in the opposition's service court. The receiver must allow the ball to bounce.

Set point See *Match Point*.

Singles A one versus one match.

Smash A powerful overhead stroke played in response to a high ball, usually without letting the ball bounce. Often played near the net.

Tie-breaker A means of resolving sets that have reached a certain stage (6-all or 8-all, for example). See section on *Scoring*.

Top spin A stroke which imparts forward rotation to the ball. The ball dips in flight; the shot is used extensively to pass opponents attacking at the net.

Slice A shot hit with a mixture of back- and side-spin.

Umpire A man or woman in charge of a match, normally seated in a high chair by the net post. At important events linesmen and net-cord judges assist the umpire.

Volley Any stroke made before the ball bounces. In modern tennis the server often rushes to the net to volley the return beyond the receiver's reach, hence the term 'serve-and-volley'.

---

she learnt her game on public courts and was discovered and sponsored by Frank Sedgman, another great Australian champion.

If Mrs Court is the epitome of sheer athleticism, Britain's Ann Jones is a living testimony to the heights that can be reached through intelligence and application, and she eventually won the Wimbledon title in 1969.

Yet all these players yield to Ken Rosewall, Australia's 'Little Master', in popularity. Small and intense, he remained at the top of world class for almost two decades, winning the French championship in 1953 and 1968, and

The great American, Billie Jean King, won five Wimbledon titles, three in a row.

the Australian in 1953, 1971 and 1972, the biggest winning spans in the history of major tennis championships.

Rosewall, with Pancho Gonzales, proved that tennis players are not over the hill at 30, and that they can win major titles at 35 or older. It proves that the game can be enjoyed by men and women of all ages, and it is this, together with the fact that men and women can compete together, that gives the game its world-wide popularity.

Australian News & Information Bureau

LONGEST MATCHES AND SETS IN TOP-CLASS TENNIS

Men's singles match: 126 games. Roger Taylor (GB) beat Wieslaw Gasoriek (Poland) 27-29, 31-29, 6-4 in the King's Cup, Warsaw, 1966.

Men's singles set: 70 games. Bill Brown (USA) beat John Brown (Australia) 36-34, 6-1 in the Heart of America tournament, Kansas, 1968.

Women's singles match: 62 games. Kathy Blake (USA) beat Elena Subirats (Mexico) 12-10, 6-8, 14-12 in New York, 1966.

Women's singles set: 36 games. Billie Jean Moffitt (USA) beat Christine Truman (GB) 6-4, 19-17 in Wightman Cup, Cleveland, 1963.

Men's doubles match: 147 games; set: 96 games. Dick Leach and Dick Dell (USA) beat Len Schloss and Tom Mazur (USA) 3-6, 49-47, 22-20 at Newport, Rhode Island, in 1967.

Women's doubles match: 81 games; set 64 games. Nancy Richey and Carole Graebner (USA) beat Justina Bricker and Carol Hanks (USA) 31-33, 6-1, 6-4 in the Eastern Grass Courts championships at Orange in 1964.

Mixed doubles match: 71 games; set: 52 games. Bill Talbert and Margaret du Pont (USA) beat Bob Falkenburg and Augusta Moran (USA) 27-25, 5-7, 6-1 at Forest Hills in 1948.

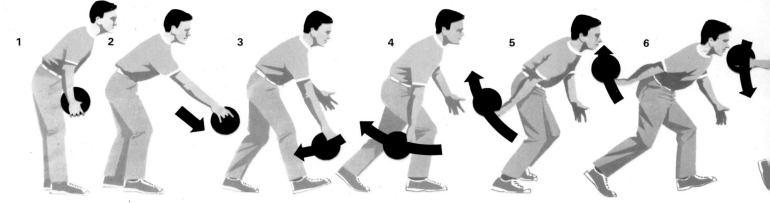

Tenpin Bowling

The lure of tenpin bowling is its apparent simplicity: even a novice can score a strike. The therapeutic value of heaving the ball down the lane to smash into the pins has made the game an almost universal anodyne for the stresses of the modern world. Technology has been enlisted to make this game both simple and complex. Automatic machines set up the pins after each person has bowled, clean the balls and return them to the bowler, detect feet that creep over the foul line, and project scores onto a screen so that spectators can follow a game easily.

Tenpin bowling claims 60 million adherents in 45 countries. Richard Nixon, president of the United States, is said to be a regular on the lanes in the basement of the White House. In Tokyo, the world's largest tenpin emporium has 258 lanes situated in a nine-storey building. World championships are organized by the *Federation Internationale de Quilleurs* every four years.

Bowling of one kind or another is as old as history, and objects for a game similar to bowling were discovered in an Egyptian child's tomb dating from 5200 BC. The ancient Polynesians played a bowling-type game—*Ula Maika*—using small elliptical balls and round, flat discs of stone. The roots of tenpin bowling, however, go back directly to the region of Germany in the third or fourth century AD. The peasants carried clubs called *kegels*, and they would set these clubs up in the cloisters of churches and bowl large round stones at them. The *kegel* was said to represent the heathen, and a hit was praised, while a miss meant that more religious devotion on the part of the bowler was required. In time the priests themselves began to play, and in the Middle Ages *kegelspiel* was very popular in Germany. The game spread, and in 1365 Edward III of England was forced to forbid the game lest it interfere with more martial activities. But the game was too popular, and in various forms it survived. The pins varied in number from 3 to 15, the balls in size and weight, and the distance from foul line to the pins varied as well. A form of tenpin bowling on a triangular base was played outdoors in Essex in the early 19th century.

Dutch migrants took bowling to the United States, and by the 1820s ninepins was a flourishing pastime in New York City. But later this game was banned because the alleys were the scene of much illicit gambling. To circumvent the law an extra pin was added and the pins rearranged into a triangle. This new form of bowling quickly became the dominant variety in America.

In 1895, the American Bowling Congress was formed and standardized the sport; by 1971 it had four million members. Tenpin was largely a male preserve until 1916, when the Women's International Bowling Congress was started. Large numbers of women took up the game, but the revolution which made a minority pastime into a major sport was yet to come.

This revolution began in the 1950s. Automatic pinspotters eliminated pin boys (boys employed to reset the pins), speeded up play, and ushered in the era of modern, air-conditioned lanes which, in some places, stay open all night. Manufacturers saw the possibilities in the sport, and in 1959 the pinspotter was exported to Britain. Coupled with the automation came changes in environment. The alleys were brightened up, with bars and spectator accommodation available.

The essence of tenpin bowling is competition, and this is organized at all levels. In the United States, the game is professional at almost every level, but elsewhere it is amateur. Competitions are normally for individuals, two-man teams, and five-man teams, and all-events (a combination of those three). For the not-so-expert, handicaps ensure that competitions remain interesting. A tenpin bowler, it is said, never retires: he just steps down in class.

How the Game is Played

Tenpin bowling, the basic object of which is to knock down all 10 pins, is played on an alley or *lane* of maple and pine boards. The pins, numbered from 1 to 10, and 15 inches high, are automatically set on spots within a 36-inch triangle at the far end of the alley. The distance over which the ball is bowled, from the *foul line* to the *head pin* (No. 1) is 60 feet, and the alley is approximately 42 inches wide. On either side of the alley are shallow grooves, called *gutters*, and on the alley itself there are two sets of guides spots—7 feet and 13-16 feet beyond the foul line—to help the bowler aim. Behind the foul line is an approach area of roughly 15 feet.

The ball, made of hard rubber, is 27 inches in circumference, and has three finger holes in it. Most bowlers use the three-finger grip—thumb, middle finger, and ring finger—but some prefer the two-finger grip using the thumb and middle fingers. The thumb and fingers should slip into the holes to the second knuckle.

A bowling game consists of 10 frames, each bowler rolling his ball twice in each frame unless he scores a *strike*. Then he forgoes his second bowl. Games can be played as singles, doubles, or between teams of up to five players. The result can be determined either by the total pins scored or by the number of games won or lost.

A game is won by the player with the highest score at the end of the 10 frames. A strike, the knocking down of all 10 pins with the first ball of a frame, is worth 10 pins, plus a bonus—the pins gained from his next two bowls. If the bowler knocks all the pins

down with his two bowls in a frame, he scores a *spare*, which is also worth 10 pins but has a bonus only the value of his next bowl. If neither a strike nor a spare is scored, only those pins knocked down count. If no pins at all are knocked down in a frame, the bowler scores an *error*. A *perfect game* brings a score of 300, and comes from 12 consecutive strikes —one strike for each frame, plus 20 bonus points per frame (a strike on the last—10th—frame wins a player two more turns in which to score his bonus points— hence the total of 12 strikes).

Though the method of bowling

Above, **The four-step delivery. The bowler starts with feet together and body bent forward from the hips (1). Holding the ball out in front of him, he steps off on the right foot (2) and begins the down- swing (3). As the ball goes into the backswing (4 & 5) he steps onto his left foot (6). With the forward downward swing (7), he brings his right foot forward, then slides the left foot forward (8 & 9), releasing the ball with thumb to the front (10) and following through smoothly (11).**

differs from person to person, the majority of bowlers use the *four- step delivery*. The bowler starts about 12 feet from the foul line, and, if right-handed, he steps forward on the right foot, pushing the ball forward and down as he does so. On the next step he swings the ball back behind him, and his left arm comes forward to main- tain balance. The ball reaches the end of its backswing (about shoulder height) on the third step, and as the final step, with the left foot, brings the bowler up to the foul line the ball is released and the arm follows through smoothly.

If the bowler touches or crosses the foul line when delivering his bowl, an automatic device or a foul judge signals, and the ball is illegal. If the foul is committed on the first ball, all pins must be reset and the bowler is entitled to a second ball. Should he knock all the pins down with that ball, how- ever, he scores only a spare, not a strike. If he fouls on the second ball, he scores only the number of pins knocked down by the first.

The bowler aiming for a strike aims for the *strike pocket*, the space between the No. 1 and No. 3 pins (or No. 1 and No. 2 pins if he is left-handed). The ball itself hits only three or four pins, which in turn knock down the remaining pins. The bowler can choose between two methods of aiming— *pin-bowling* or *spot-bowling*. In the former he keeps his eyes on the pins throughout his approach and delivery; in the latter he chooses a spot on the alley that the ball must pass over to hit the pins correctly, and he aims at that spot instead, lining up his right shoulder with the spot and the strike pocket. Spot-bowling has a number of advocates who reason that it is easier to hit a spot say 14 or 15

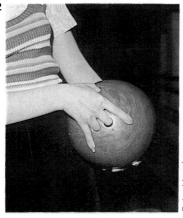

1 A congenial atmosphere and automation have helped bowling enjoy a great popu- larity boom. **2** Most bowlers use the three-finger grip, with the thumb, middle finger and ring finger slipping comfortably into the holes to the second knuckle. **3** Strike or split?

feet away than one 60 feet away.

Bowlers throw one of three types of ball—the straight ball, the hook ball, and the curve ball. Because it is the easiest to throw accurately, the *straight ball* is the best for the beginner. The *hook ball* rolls down the side of the alley and then turns in sharply towards the pins. The *curve ball* is rather like an exaggerated hook, following a wider arc than the hook, but its angle gives it a greater range of impact among the pins. For both the hook and the curve balls, the bowler twists his wrist as the ball leaves his hand.

Not every bowler scores a strike every time, however, and con- sequently he is going to be left with a number of pins remaining, which are known as *splits* if they are not grouped together. The removal of the splits shows the difference between the average bowler and the skilful one, for the latter will carefully calculate the positions instead of bowling and hoping.

Volleyball

From a game that began with exercise-seeking businessmen knocking a basketball bladder over a 6-ft. high net, volleyball has become one of the world's foremost recreational team sports. It is played by more than 50 million people in over 100 countries, in about a third of which it is recognized as a top level competitive sport, and in some countries, such as Czechoslovakia, Russia, Romania, Bulgaria, Japan, Mexico, and Brazil, it draws similar crowds to football matches. In Japan, its popularity is such that a league held in one factory takes almost a year to play off and there are leagues for 'street teams'. At the 1970 world championships in Bulgaria, ticket touts did business on a scale normally associated with England's FA Cup final.

Volleyball was invented in America in 1859 by William Morgan, director of physical recreation at the Holyoake, Massachusetts, YMCA. He wanted to provide some form of exercise for large groups of businessmen, and as he thought basketball too strenuous for them he devised volleyball. His original game was extremely simple, and any number could play.

As American interests and the YMCA movement spread abroad, so volleyball found adherents in other countries. Its simplicity accounts for its fantastic increase in popularity, for it is ideally suited to the beach or the park. Relatively little space is needed and the equipment is both simple and inexpensive. Yet at the top level, it is a demanding and fiercely competitive sport.

International organization of the sport stems from the 1936 Berlin Olympic Games, where representatives of 22 countries met to discuss the world-wide administration of volleyball. As a result, volleyball was placed under the jurisdiction of the International Handball Federation until a year later the International Volleyball Federation was formed and its headquarters set up in Paris. The first world championships were held in Prague in 1949 with men and women from 11 countries taking part. Indicative of the sport's rising popularity is the fact that 24 countries contested the the men's title and 16 the women's title in 1970.

Volleyball was introduced to the Olympic Games for the first time at Tokyo in 1964, its acceptance as an Olympic sport being very much due to the pressure of the host country. Russia emerged gold medallists in the men's event, with Czechoslovakia and Japan taking the minor placings, and Japan, followed by Russia and Poland, emerged successful in the women's event. Four years later, the Russians made a clean sweep. In Mexico City, the competition was played on a 'round robin' basis, which took far too long to complete, and so it was decided that at Munich in 1972 there would be two preliminary groups of six teams in the men's competition and two of four in the women's.

As the Olympic and world championship results show, the East European countries and Japan have dominated the sport, and it would appear that they will continue to do so for some time. The huge crowds the sport draws in those countries and extensive television coverage give them financial backing and they also get considerable government help. In their society, it is possible for players to train often and for long periods, and they tend to have a much more professional attitude than their counterparts in the West.

Colorsport

How the Game is Played

From its original form, in which any number could play, volleyball was modified into a game for 12 players, 6 on either side. Each team, however, can have as many as 12 players including substitutes. It is played on a court measuring 18 metres (59 ft.) by 9 metres (29 ft. 6 in.), with the net at a height of 2.43 metres (7 ft. 11⅝ in.) for men and 2.21 metres (7 ft. 4⅛ in.) for women. The court must be free of obstructions to a height of 7 metres (23 ft.), and should be marked at least 2 metres (6 ft. 6 in.) from any obstruction all the way round.

Play is started by one player hitting the ball with his hand or arm over the net. He stands in the service area behind the base line, and the other players line up in a specified formation as front-line players and back-line players, but as soon as the ball is served players may move in any part of their court. Once the ball passes over the net, the receiving team are allowed to touch the ball three times with their hands or arms before it must go back over the net. No player, however, may hit the ball twice in succession. The object of the game is to ground the ball within the opposition's half of the court or to force them into making errors so that they are unable to return the ball.

The ball may be played back on either the first, second, or third touch, but it is the basis of modern tactics to use all three touches to build up a strong attack. The normal pattern is to use the first touch to get the ball up close to the net, then play it high above and close to the net so that for the third touch a player can run in and jump up to smash the ball down into the opposition court.

The opposing team try to intercept the smash by using one, two, or three players jumping up together and reaching over the net to block the path of the smash or force the ball back into the attackers' court. If the blockers do not cut out the smash, the rest of the team try to control it and build up their own attack.

If the serving team win the rally, they score a point, but if the receiving team win it they gain the right to serve. A team winning the right to serve rotate one place round so that during a game the players have to play in all positions. The first team to 15 points by a margin of 2 points wins the set. Ordinary club matches are the best of three sets, and championship and international games are the best of five sets.

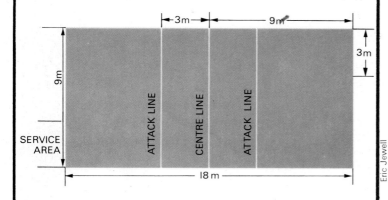

court diagram labelled: 3m, 9m, 3m, 9m, SERVICE AREA, ATTACK LINE, CENTRE LINE, ATTACK LINE, 18m

Eric Jewell

Equipment

One of the great advantages of volleyball is the minimal amount of equipment required. The ball is made of leather with stitched panels or is of a laminated composition, and has a circumference of 65-67 cm (26-26.8 in.). Its weight must be between 250 and 280 grammes (9-10 oz). The net should be 1 metre (3 ft. 3 in.) deep and 9.5 metres (30 ft.) long, with its mesh 10 cm (4 in.) square.

Players wear vests or jerseys, shorts, and light rubber or leather shoes without heels. They must have numbers on both their chest and their back. A player must not wear any object or article that might cause injury during play.

1 An incident from a volley-ball international between Japan and Czechoslovakia shows how players go up at the net to intercept smashes. 2 Volleyball's popularity in Eastern Europe is reflected by the large Moscovite crowd that saw Russia beat Bulgaria in the first women's world championships. 3 Later, the balance of power in women's volleyball shifted to Japan, who were Olympic champions in 1964, when the game was given Olympic status. 4 Schneider of East Germany overcomes a triple Bulgarian block during the 1970 men's world championship final.

VOLLEYBALL

Olympic Champions	Men	Women
1964—Tokyo	USSR	Japan
1968—Mexico	USSR	USSR
1972—Munich	Japan	USSR
World Champions		
1949—Prague	USSR	
1952—Moscow	USSR	USSR
1956—Paris	Czechoslovakia	USSR
1960—Rio de Janeiro	USSR	USSR
1962—Moscow	USSR	Japan
1966—Prague	Czechslovakia	
1970—Sofia	East Germany	USSR

4

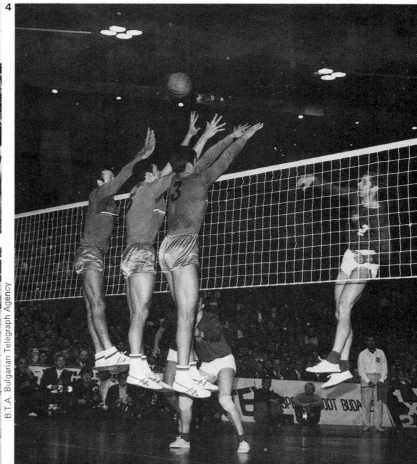

B.T.A. Bulgarian Telegraph Agency

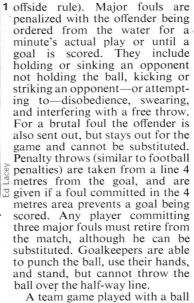

Water Polo

To its devoted adherents, water polo is the world's toughest and most demanding team game. At international level two teams of superbly fit athletes, fast swimmers, expert ball handlers, and excellent tacticians, vie in a most physical and exciting sport.

In order to make the game more attractive for spectators and to reduce the amount of violence to which players are apt to resort, the rules of water polo have been changed regularly. The changes made at the 1968 Olympic Games seemed to be designed to make the game more fluid, and appeared to have succeeded. A team consists of 11 players, 7 of whom may be in the water at any time: substitutions may be made after a goal has been scored and at the intervals (of which there are three, between the four periods of play). The object of the game is to score goals, and this may be done by propelling the ball into the goal by any means except punching or using two hands on the ball.

In order to regulate the game, the referee can penalize a player in three ways. Ordinary, technical fouls are penalized with a free throw to the opposition: they include standing while handling the ball, taking the ball underwater, putting the ball out of play, splashing, touching the ball with both hands, impeding, and being within 2 metres of the opponents goal without the ball (there is no

1 Hungarian goalkeeper Molnar lunges across to save during a 1968 Olympic water polo game. **2** What the public—and at times the referee—does not see. **3** The ball drifts off while several players indulge in other activities.

offside rule). Major fouls are penalized with the offender being ordered from the water for a minute's actual play or until a goal is scored. They include holding or sinking an opponent not holding the ball, kicking or striking an opponent—or attempting to—disobedience, swearing, and interfering with a free throw. For a brutal foul the offender is also sent out, but stays out for the game and cannot be substituted. Penalty throws (similar to football penalties) are taken from a line 4 metres from the goal, and are given if a foul committed in the 4 metres area prevents a goal being scored. Any player committing three major fouls must retire from the match, although he can be substituted. Goalkeepers are able to punch the ball, use their hands, and stand, but cannot throw the ball over the half-way line.

A team game played with a ball

in water—the direct ancestor of water polo—was first played in Britain in the 1870s, though it was not until 1885 that the English ASA recognized the game and formulated rules. In 1877, however, a set of rules had existed in Scotland. In 1888 the first English club championship was held, and in 1896 an inter-county championship was instituted. Britain, who led the world in the game at the turn of the century, not surprisingly won the water polo competition at the 1900 Olympic meeting in Paris, and though no European teams competed at the St Louis Games of 1904, the European ascendancy was confirmed at the 1908 Olympics in London. Only occasionally, in fact, has there been any challenge from non-European teams in the Olympic Games, and the main interest has revolved around the relative merits of the Europeans.

By 1890 water polo was being played in America, and in the 1890s it spread to the European mainland, reaching Hungary in 1897. From 1900 to 1920, Britain won four out of five Olympic titles (aided by the outstanding Welshman, Paul Radmilovic, in 1908, 1912, and 1920) but thereafter met with little success. The balance of power shifted, and seemed to settle in Hungary. Before World War II, Hungarian sides won the Olympics of 1932 and 1936, and were European champions five times out of five. Supreme in the Magyar side was Oliver Halasy who had only one foot but was in both the winning Olympic teams and in three European championship sides.

After World War II the Hungarians were rivalled by Italy, the USSR and Yugoslavia. With superbly conditioned sides, adept at the intricacies of ball handling, and extremely fast swimmers, these four nations monopolized the medals at the Olympics from 1952 to 1968. Indisputably the best player of this period was Hungary's Dezso Gyarmati, three times an Olympic champion, who survived a brief defection to the West to return to Hungary to play more international polo.

WATER POLO Olympic Games

Year	Gold	Silver	Bronze
1900	Great Britain[1]	Belgium[2]	France[3]
1904	USA[4]	USA[5]	USA[6]
1908	Great Britain	Belgium	Sweden
1912	Great Britain	Sweden	Belgium
1920	Great Britain	Belgium	Sweden
1924	France	Belgium	USA
1928	Germany	Hungary	France
1932	Hungary	Germany	USA
1936	Hungary	Germany	Belgium
1948	Italy	Hungary	Netherlands
1952	Hungary	Yugoslavia	Italy
1956	Hungary	Yugoslavia	USSR
1960	Italy	USSR	Hungary
1964	Hungary	Yugoslavia	USSR
1968	Yugoslavia	USSR	Hungary
1972	USSR	Hungary	USA

[1]Osborne SC, Manchester   [2]Club Natation, Brussels
[3]Tie for third place between two French teams, Libelulle, Paris and Enfants de Neptune, Tourcoing
[4]New York AC   [5]Chicago AC   [6]Missouri AC

Water Skiing

The pier at a British seaside resort has displayed the sign: 'Water skiing £1.50 for one hour. Old Age Pensioners half price'. It underlines the fact that there is no age limit to this pastime if one is able to swim in an emergency. Clubs and facilities are multiplying fast throughout the world on the sea coasts and at inland lakes wherever water conditions are suitable.

Unknown before World War I, water skiing made tremendous progress during the 1950s and 1960s. As with snow skiing, it developed in two distinct ways—as a holiday recreation providing invigorating exercise for all the family, and as a highly competitive sport with exciting spectator appeal.

Recreatively or competitively, water skiing is the art of travelling on water with the aid of two skis—and often only one—in the wake of, and while holding a rope from, a towing motor launch. The skier holds on to a bar handle attached to the tow-rope, which is usually made of polypropolene and limited to 75 feet.

A development from aqua-planing, water skiing is traceable to 1922, when Ralph Samuelson used water skis on Lake Pepin, Minnesota. Two years later, an American, Fred Waller, was awarded a patent for water skis which he had designed. An independent beginning in Europe is attributed to Count Maximilian Pulaski, who accidentally discovered the possibilities in 1929 while experimenting with two narrow aquaplanes at Juan les Pins, France.

In 1928, Dick Pope Sr, one of the sport's most energetic pioneers, gave the first public demonstration of jumping on water skis, at Miami Beach, Florida, which has always been the sport's leading stronghold.

The American Water Ski Association was founded in 1939 by Dan Hains, and from that year United States national championships have been held annually except for wartime suspension. The World Water Ski Union (WWSU) was founded in 1946 and the first European championships were contested at Evian, France, in 1947. The same year, the first official jump record of 49 feet was set by Chuck Sligh at Cypress Gardens, Florida. The WWSU, which gained official IOC recognition in 1969 (though water skiing is not an Olympic participating sport), has a membership exceeding 50 nations. The first world championships took place in 1949 at Juan les Pins. The dominant nations since have been the United States, France, Switzerland, Austria, Italy, Australia, and Great Britain.

In 1955, Esther Williams starred in a colour feature film, *Easy to Love*, which promoted public interest in water skiing just as Sonja Henie films had influenced the popularity of ice skating. Spectacular water ski shows have become an offshoot of the sport and a more recent development has been speed racing.

The earliest recorded water skiing in Britain took place off the coast at Scarborough in 1936. Despite the generally unhelpful climate and water conditions, progress in Great Britain was astonishing, with a national federation growing to become Europe's largest and second in the world only to the United States. The British Water Ski Federation was formed in 1951, with its first club at Ruislip Lido. By 1971 there were over 100 affiliated clubs representing more than 35,000 active skiers.

American men have largely dominated the world championships. Alfredo Mendoza took two overall titles in the 1950s, a performance equalled by Mike Suyderhoud in 1967 and 1969. In neither of his wins, however, did Suyderhoud manage an individual title. In contrast, Elizabeth Allan, also from the United States, won all three individual events in 1969, when chalking up her second overall title. She first won in 1965, but two years later lost her title to Britain's Jeannette Stewart-Wood. The first winner of the women's world championships, Willa Worthington (USA) in 1949, set a record for overall wins in 1955 when she won her third title as Willa McGuire.

Man's desire to take to the air finds expression in water skiing— often at speeds of around 50 mph.

How to Water Ski

For the beginner, preliminary dry practice on land with an instructor is advisable. Attempting to ski on water without prior knowledge of how to control the feet or balance is likely to provide similarly embarrassing sequels to those which befall the novice on skates.

There are standard initial principles. First, the skis should be placed parallel on the ground and the skier pushes his feet forward into the binders as far as possible before pulling the rear part of each binder up around the heels. The skis are easier to put on if the feet are wet.

Next, the tow-rope handle is grasped tightly. The instructor keeps the rope taut while lowering the skier into a sitting position on the rear of the skis. Arms should be fully extended, parallel to the skis, with knees between and almost touching the elbows and with chest nearly resting on the knees.

The position from sitting to crouching is achieved as the arms remain fully extended while moving high above the knees. The back is nearly straight with a slightly forward body lean. Repeated rehearsal of this starting movement while still on land will accelerate progress in this most important technique of starting.

Another dry technique to practice is careful control of the skis by turning the foot with an ankle movement while keeping the toes pointing forward. Sudden turning of the toes would tip the skier into the water.

After mastering these basic dry-land lessons, the skier is ready to step out of the skis and carry them out into the water to a depth of several feet. There the skis are put on again in the manner already learned, making sure that the binders are correctly adjusted. Skis too loose can pull off and skis too tight can induce cramp.

When making a real start in the water—and this is the most difficult moment for many learners—care must be taken to have the ski tips above the water and evenly spaced apart, with the tow-line held firmly and equidistant from each ski. The slack is taken out of the rope and, when the signal is given, a gradually increasing start is best at first, to allow the beginner time to check balance and position. Quicker starts are mastered with further practice.

As the boat gathers speed, the new skier repeats the starting action learned on land, rising slowly from sitting to standing, with weight balanced directly over the feet in a half crouched stance and knees bent to act as shock absorbers. The elbows should be kept straight as the skier resists an early natural temptation to pull the towing handle towards the chest or above. Experienced skiers take off from a sitting position on a jetty if using two skis, or a standing position if using one, taking care not to let the ski ends dip under the water.

Crossing the wake of the boat provides one of the thrills of the sport. This is achieved by transferring the weight to the right when crossing to the right, bending the right knee and pulling to the right while slightly raising the left foot. Only a slight lean is necessary. Once the start and turn have been learnt, water skiing is largely a question of acquiring the right degree of weight distribution and balance for all manoeuvres.

To stop, the skier lets go of the rope and spreads the arms out to the sides for balance. Speed quickly decreases and the properly balanced skier will sink slowly into the water. The skis are bouyant and so help to keep the skier afloat until the boat driver can return for the pick-up. Skiers should always come ashore at an angle, allowing space and time in which to slow down.

1

2

Associated Press

Popperfoto

Central Press

Colorsport

3 Skier's Signals to Boat

Faster Disengaged palm raised upwards or, if both hands are in use, a nod of the head.
Slower Palm lowered downwards, or thumb-down sign, or shake of head.
Speed OK An 'O' made with thumb and forefinger.

Turn Vertical palm turned down in direction required.
Stop Hand held up with fingers out-stretched, policeman style
Return To Base Arm swung downwards, with index finger pointing towards water.
Cut Motor Finger drawn across throat.

Equipment

Most general purpose pleasure skis are made of solid or laminated wood, approximately 5 ft. 9 in. long and 6½ in. wide, weighing about 15 lb. They are fitted with a wooden stabilizing fin on the underside of the blade near the heel. Each ski holds the foot by tight-fitting rubber bindings which stretch to release the foot safely in the event of a fall.

For figures or trick skiing, special skis, shorter and wider, are used. Normally they are about 4 ft. 6 in. long and 8 in. wide. They have no fins, thus enabling skiers to turn completely round. Some are squared at the rear ends, others rounded for faster turning.

For the slalom, skiers use a single ski, fitted with a large metal fin to assist sharp turns. The ski is usually tapered near the heel. There are bindings for both feet.

For jumping, skis are of conventional size or slightly longer and heavier.

Water skiing clothing consists simply of normal swimwear or, especially in cold weather, a rubber wet suit.

---

1 Liz Allan, competing in the tricks final at the 1969 world championships, won all four titles that year and in 1971 won her fourth consecutive US overall title. 2 Not only backwards but barefoot too! 3 It looks disastrous, but 1967 world tricks and jumping champion Alan Kempton is just going through a somersault routine. 4 The spectacular slalom calls for skill in timing, turning, and crossing the wake of the towing boat.

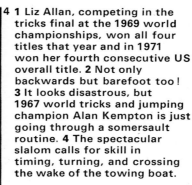

Types of Water Skiing

Water Skiing championships are divided into three specialized sections—figures (freestyle tricks), slalom, and jumping—and the championship is awarded to the best overall performer.

Slalom competitors are pulled through a course containing six diagonally placed buoys. Progressively increasing speeds up to 34 mph are achieved as the skier negotiates a zigzag path between the buoys. It is a test of skill in timing, turning, and crossing the wake of the towing boat.

Jumping is achieved at speeds around 50 mph over a 20-ft.-long, waxed wooden ramp, 6 feet high for men, 5 feet for women and juniors. At a speed of 36 mph, the skier cuts across the boat's wake so that he is well out to the side as he hits the ramp often at speeds in excess of 50 mph. A world record of 162 feet was achieved twice in 1969 by Mike Suyderhoud, first at Callaway Gardens, Pine Mountain, Georgia, on July 15, and again at Berkeley Aquatic Park, California, on September 7 the same year. In 1971 the women's record was officially 106 feet, set by Elizabeth Allen at Callaway Gardens on July 17, 1966. Britain's Jeannette Stewart-Wood beat that distance by 3½ in. at Ruislip, London, on June 11, 1967, but this did not gain recognition as a world record because of a WWSU rule requiring a minimum improvement of 8 in. Nevertheless, Miss Stewart-Wood could justly claim to have made a longer clearance on water skis than any other woman.

Figures, alternatively called tricks, are a form of freestyle competition, providing a choice of repertoire to suit the performer's individual ability. Different kinds and numbers of turns, either on one ski or both, may be made on the water, in mid-air, or on the jumping ramp. Special tow bars are available if and as required for holding the line with a foot. A competitor has two runs, each lasting 20 seconds, in which to score points from manoeuvres varying from simple turns to difficult somersaults. This event, more than any other, favours the skier from the warmer climate because training for it involves a greater incidence of falling in the water.

Ski racing is a quite separate, specialized form of competition from the conventional championships in figures, slalom, and jumping. Speeds of 70 mph are often reached. A skier may resume after falling, provided he does not touch the boat. A speed record of 122.11 mph was achieved by Chuck Stearns (USA) at the Marine Stadium, Long Beach, California, on January 11, 1969. Sally Younger, at the age of 15, set a women's record of 92.68 mph at the same venue on the same day.

Long-distance skiing is a further variation of the sport. A record non-stop distance of 818.2 miles was covered by Martin Shackleford (USA) on McKellar Lake, Memphis, Tennessee, in September, 1960. The feat was accomplished in 35 hr 15 min.

Photo credit: Gerry Cranham

Weightlifting

Men have always sought to prove themselves stronger than one another. From the earliest days they have vied with each other by lifting heavy weights of any description—rocks, people, or animals. In the modern world, the strongest men in sport are found in weightlifting, an activity that has had a permanent place in the Olympic Games since 1920.

Controlled by the Federation Internationale Halterophile (International Weightlifting Federation), which was founded in 1920, this amateur, men-only sport has proved enormously popular, especially in Russia where by the end of the 1960s there were over 300,000 registered lifters. And in 1971 it was a Russian, Vasily Alexeyev, who was the world's strongest man. During the 1970 world championships, he became the first person officially to raise 500 lb above his head. But the strongest man in the world *pound for pound* at the time

was Poland's Waldemar Baszanowski, who won Olympic gold medals in 1964 and 1968 in the lightweight class.

Modern weightlifting is contested in nine bodyweight categories and on the basis of three lifts—all two-handed. They are: the *clean and press* ('press'). the *snatch*, and the *clean and jerk* ('jerk'). There is also the *power set*, which is not held at the Olympics or world championships but which is contested between countries and in national championships. The power set consists of three lifts which depend less on technique and more on sheer strength: the *bench press* (with a pause of the bar on the chest), *the squat* (bending the legs to just below the 'thighs parallel with the ground' position), and the *dead lift* (lifting the bar by straightening the thighs and back until the body is straight with the bar touching the thighs.)

The first international meeting that can reasonably be classed as a world championship was held in London in 1893. The winner was

Opposite and Above. **All the strain, effort and concentration that go into weightlifting are reflected by Britain's Louis Martin.**
Right. **Such has been the progress in weightlifting in the last 20 years, that middleweight Victor Kurentsov's total in 1968 topped the Olympic heavyweight total.**

an Englishman, Lawrence Levy, after a series of events that involved mainly repetition or alternate pressing of 56 lb and 84 lb weights with each hand. An unlimited weight category event was held at the 1896 Olympics in Greece, and another Briton, Launceston Elliott, won a gold medal with a right-hand lift of 156½ lb, and Viggo Jensen of Denmark won the two-handed event.

With the founding of an international federation in 1920, the sport of weightlifting gradually became more strictly organised. One-hand lifts gradually disappeared from international com-

Photo credit: Popperfoto

1

2

3 petition, and the three-lift Olympic set became established at the 1928 Games, when there were five weight categories.

No one country has had a monopoly of world honours in the sport. For many years France, Germany and Italy shared most of the Olympic honours. Then the Egyptians became prominent, to be succeeded by the Americans. But since the mid-1950s it is the Russians who have been supreme.

4

5

6

In Olympic Games and world championships, there are three lifts: 1 the clean and press ('press'), 2 the snatch, and 3 the clean and jerk ('jerk'). In the press, the lifter has to raise the barbell above his head without any jerking, bending of legs, or moving of feet, but in the jerk, in which the heaviest weights are lifted, he splits his legs to effect the lift. In addition to these three lifts are those of the powerlifting set, which are not recognized by the IWF: 4 the bench press, 5 the squat (or deep knees bend), and 6 the dead lift. 7 Super-heavyweight Vasily Alexeyev, world record-holder at press, snatch, and jerk, won the 1970 world championships at Columbus, Ohio, with an astounding total of 1,350 lb.

7

Weightlifting Competitions

Olympic-style weightlifting requires not only strength, speed, skill, but subtle strategy. A quick-thinking brain will often win a contest between two physically equal opponents.

A competitor must first decide which of the nine weight categories he is best suited to. These classes are:

flyweight	up to 52 kg (8 st 0¼ lb)
bantamweight	52 to 56 kg (8 st 11¼ lb)
featherweight	56 to 60 kg (9 st 6¼ lb)
lightweight	60 to 67½ kg (10 st 8¾ lb)
middleweight	67½ to 75 kg (11 st 11¼ lb)
light-heavyweight	75 to 82½ kg (12 st 13¾ lb)
mid-heavyweight	82½ to 90 kg (14 st 2¼ lb)
heavyweight	90 to 110 kg (17 st 4½ lb)
super-heavyweight	over 110 kg

Most competitors train over the maximum limit and then slim down for competitions. Each lifter has to weigh within the upper and lower limits of the category on the day, but most are very close to the upper limit because a competitor can lift heavier weights the heavier he is.

The competition is decided on the aggregate of a lifter's best attempt on the three separate lifts—the press, snatch, and jerk. If two competitors have the same total, the lighter man is the winner. Each competitor is allowed three attempts at each lift. The key to the tactics of the sport is that a competitor having tried for a poundage cannot take a lighter weight for any subsequent attempts, though he may try the same weight again. Thus, if he selects 300 lb for his first press and misses it, he cannot ask for 290 lb on his second or third try. If he fails with all three attempts on any of the lifts he is automatically eliminated from the competition.

The weights are lifted on a wooden platform, measuring 4 metres on each side, and the competition is adjudicated by a referee and two side judges. They signal their verdict by means of white lights (a fair lift) and red lights (a failed lift). A majority is needed for the attempt to be successful. A jury of appeal, consisting of five people, supervises the contest.

The weights on the bar are progressively increased, and the difference must be 5 kg after the first lift, and 2½ kg after the second. Most lifters aim to have one attempt they are certain to get, one which is a 'probable', and another which is a gamble for victory. Thus, a lifter, who is invariably advised by at least one coach, must not only watch his own figures but those of his opponent as he makes split-second decisions to try to put the pressure on an opponent by suddenly increasing his poundage for the next attempt.

Wrestling

Throughout history, wrestlers have been admired for their strength, speed, stamina, and skill. Almost every civilization has had its champion wrestlers as its heroes. In Ancient Greece, Milo of Croton was as famous a figure as George Hackenschmidt was in Britain at the beginning of the 20th century. Ability in this basic sport, where man faces man in unarmed combat, has brought wrestlers fame and fortune. Different countries have their own styles and champions: sumo in Japan, yagli in Turkey, sambo in Russia, glima in Iceland, and Cumberland and Cornish in Britain.

But wrestling is a truly international sport, and the two major styles—freestyle and Graeco-Roman—are part of the Olympic Games. World championships are staged annually under the organization of the Federation Internationale de Lutte Amateur (International Wrestling Federation). The Olympics and world championships are, of course, amateur events. But professional wrestling also attracts huge crowds, particularly in America and Britain, and it is very popular on television. This aspect of wrestling should be

The same name but hardly the same sport: 1 freestyle, one of the two major styles of amateur wrestling that are in the Olympic programme, and 2 professional wrestling, an entertainment rather than a true sporting contest.

Central Japan Photo Service

London Weekend Television Ltd

classified as entertainment rather than pure sport, however. International control of professional wrestling is non-existent, and the participants, though often very skilled and athletic, aim to please a crowd more than win bouts. New gimmicks are introduced to keep up the interest of the fans—'tag' matches, women's bouts, contests between midgets, and even fights in mud and against animals are staged.

History

Although the international wrestling federation was not formed until 1921, the sport had been organized in some way or another for thousands of years. Techniques used at the Olympic Games are almost exactly the same as those used in the ancient civilizations of China and Egypt, and especially Greece. But the origins of wrestling almost certainly antedate these eras, for it is likely that primitive man practised throws and strangles to defend himself from his enemies. Wrestling was respectable enough to feature in Egyptian wall paintings at Beni-Hassan. It was in Greece, however, that the sport really developed. Wrestling was introduced to the Olympic Games in 704 BC—the Games of the 18th Olympiad — though some 200 years earlier a set of rules had been in existence. In the Greek Olympics, the winner was the man who twice forced his opponent to touch the ground with any part of his body except his feet.

The greatest wrestler of the Greek age was probably Milo of Croton, who won five Olympic titles altogether. He is also famous for the training he undertook by carrying a calf around a field on his back. Milo thus anticipated the basic principles of weight training, for as the calf got bigger, so Milo got stronger, his body adapting itself to greater resistance.

Although *pankration*, a vicious form of fighting which included kicking, punching, gouging, strangling, and throwing, was brought into the Games in 648 BC, classical wrestling remained very popular. The eventual downfall of the sport was the introduction of professionalism, with competitors being bribed to lose. But the Romans, who conquered the Greek empire, adapted the Greek style of wrestling and called it Graeco-Roman, which is used with minor modifications in modern events. The important feature of Graeco-Roman wrestling is that the use of the legs in either attack or defence is forbidden.

Wrestling, though attracting interest during the Middle Ages, became outstandingly popular only in the 18th century. Even so, there were many references to the sport, including a legendary bout between King Henry VIII of England and King Henry I of

333

Styles of wrestling individual
to countries around the world:
1 Sumo, the traditional
spectacle of Japanese
wrestling. **2** Yagli, a Turkish
form in which the contestants
smear themselves with grease
to make holds difficult.
3 Sambo, the FILA's third
official style after free-style
and Graeco-Roman, is a
Russian form of jacket
wrestling similar to judo.
4 Cumberland wrestling, an
ancient style that continues
under traditional rules in
England's Lake District.

Glossary of Terms

Catch-as-catch-can Another
name for freestyle wrestling, but an
expression falling out of use.

Cornish A form of wrestling in
jackets practised in the West of
England.

**Cumberland-and-Westmore-
land** Form of wrestling in which
competitors start with their arms
clasped behind each other's backs
and maintain their grip throughout
a bout.

Fall Another name for a pin, when
a competitor has both his shoulders
pressed to the floor.

Freestyle The most popular type
of wrestling, and one of the three
styles recognized by the FILA.

Full Nelson A hold allowed in senior
amateur wrestling in which a
wrestler places both arms beneath
his opponent's armpits and clasps
his hands behind his opponent's
neck.

Glima A form of harness wrestling
popular in Iceland.

Graeco-Roman A mixture of the
ancient styles of Greece and Rome.
Now an official FILA style, it is
similar to freestyle except that the
use of the legs and holding below
the waist are forbidden.

Half Nelson A common hold
secured when one arm is placed
under the opponent's corresponding arm and around his neck.

Lancashire style An ancestor of
freestyle wrestling which was popular in Lancashire.

Pin Holding an opponent's shoulders on the mat: it automatically
ends a contest in both freestyle and
Graeco-Roman.

Sambo Russian form of jacket
wrestling similar to judo. Accepted
by the FILA as their third official
style.

Slam A technique illegal in amateur
wrestling in which a wrestler lifts
his opponent above his head and
then slams him to the mat.

Sumo Traditional Japanese form
of wrestling fought out with tremendous ceremony by huge men
weighing in excess of 25 stone.

Take-down Technique whereby a
competitor brings his opponent
from a standing position onto the
mat, thus securing an advantage.

Wing Way of grasping an opponent
in tight and then rolling him over.

Yagli Form of Turkish wrestling
where competitors smear their
bodies with grease, thus making
holds awkward.

1

2

3

Turkish Tourism Information Office

4

Novosti

France at the Field of the Cloth
of Gold. Despite the interest in
the sport in other parts of the
world, organized wrestling grew
up in Western Europe. And in the
United States, a land peopled by
Europeans, regional championships were held and wrestling was
the leading combat sport until
boxing took over in popularity, a
development due mainly to the
exploits of John L. Sullivan. For
a number of years, in fact,
Sullivan toured America challenging all comers in company with
Bill Mudoon, who was a leading
wrestler. Mudoon claimed the
world's championship in Graeco-
Roman in 1883, but catch-as-
catch-can (freestyle) was the more
dramatic style, and at the
beginning of the 20th century
professional matches in this
version aroused great interest.

The outstanding figure in world
wrestling was not Mudoon, but

George Hackenschmidt, a
Russian-born wrestler based in
Britain, who took the world title
from Tom Jenkins, a one-eyed
Cleveland mill-worker, in 1904.
Hackenschmidt, backed by his
smart manager C. B. Cochran,
was hero-worshipped in Britain
where he settled. He lost the world
title in 1908 to another American,
Frank Gotch, who did an
enormous amount to publicize
the sport in what, in retrospect,
can be described as wrestling's
golden era.

But professional wrestling,
conscious of the counter-attraction of boxing, had to introduce
showmanship to keep the crowds.
And after World War I this
aspect of the sport slowly moved
away from competition to entertainment. Fortunately, however,
amateur wrestling filled the void,
though in the past amateur
wrestling had been of a consider-

ably lower standard simply
because the best amateurs turned
professional. The establishment
of the international wrestling
federation in 1921 ensured that
'straight' wrestling would continue, and, indeed, wrestling had
featured in the first modern
Olympic Games in 1896.

The international federation
brought in new weight categories,
and world Graeco-Roman championships were held in Scandinavia
in 1921. Then, in 1925, the first
European championships were
staged, and five years later wrestling (freestyle) was one of the
sports at the first British Empire
Games. Before World War II, the
United States and Scandinavia
—Sweden produced two wrestlers,
Carl Westergran and Ivar Johann-
son, who won three Olympic
gold medals each—dominated the
sport.

Wrestling expanded tremendously after the war, and in 1948 Graeco-Roman was included in the London Olympics. The star performers there were the Turks, who captured six gold medals. Turkey maintained this superiority at the world freestyle championships in 1951, taking six titles. But at the following year's Olympics their entry forms arrived late and four of their stars could not compete. As a result, the USSR won most medals. Britain's sole moment of glory at Helsinki came through Ken Richmond, who won a bronze medal in the heavyweight freestyle, his country's first, and after 1968 still the only, wrestling medal in the Olympics since World War II. The rest of the first 25 years after the war saw a continued battle for supremacy between Turkey and

5 A Graeco-Roman bout. This style is similar to freestyle except that the use of legs and holding below the waist are forbidden. **6** Ireland's Joseph Feeney is caught in a double hold by Gaetano de Vescovi in an Olympic bout. **7** The great Russian heavyweight Alexandr Medved (left) in a 1965 freestyle world championship bout against Jutzeler of Switzerland. **8** Britain's Brian Sparks gets a strangle hold on his Greek opponent. The hold is illegal in amateur wrestling.

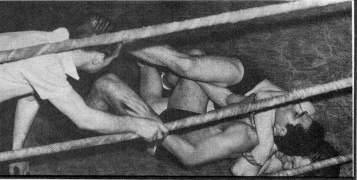

Russia. At Melbourne the USSR swept off with six gold medals, two silver, and five bronze—and their selection had deliberately ignored all former world and Olympic

Organization of Competitions

The object of both freestyle and Graeco-Roman wrestling is to pin both one's opponent's shoulders on the mat for a count of one second from the referee. This gives a clear-cut victory in both styles and thus ends the bout. However, nearly always in international competitions decisions are given by the referee according to the relative merits of the participants.

All competitors are divided into 10 weight categories in senior events and 11 in junior matches. The senior classes are:

Light-flyweight	under 48 kg (7 st 7 lb 13 oz)
Flyweight	under 52 kg (8 st 2 lb 10 oz)
Bantamweight	under 57 kg (8 st 13 lb 10 oz)
Featherweight	under 62 kg (9 st 10 lb 10 oz)
Lightweight	under 68 kg (10 st 9 lb 15 oz)
Welterweight	under 74 kg (11 st 9 lb 2 oz)
Middleweight	under 82 kg (12 st 12 lb 12 oz)
Light-heavyweight	under 90 kg (14 st 2 lb 7 oz)
Heavyweight	under 100 kg (15 st 10 lb 7 oz)
Heavyweight-plus	over 100 kg

A competitor has to weigh within the upper and lower limits of his class on the day of competition, and in tournaments which last several days they have to weigh in each day.

Wrestlers wear a one-piece leotard costume, which is either red or blue depending on which colour they draw in the event. Wrestlers are forbidden to wear either oil or a sticky substance, and any rings or buckles which may cause an injury. They also wear leather wrestling boots or ordinary gym shoes.

The fight takes place on a thick mat. A 6-metre square is compulsory for international matches, but for Olympic Games and world championships the mat must be 8 metres by 8 metres. A free space of 2 metres is left round the edge, and the centre of the mat is marked with a circle.

Three officials control a bout—mat chairman, referee, and judge—and international events are under the control of the technical committee of the FILA. The mat chairman is the chief official in charge of a bout, and his decision in the event of a dispute is final. The referee controls the contest from the mat, while the other two sit on the edge of it. The referee wears a red band on one arm and a blue band on the other and signals the points scored by the wrestlers by raising their particular colour with the number of points indicated by his outstretched fingers. If the judge agrees he will raise his baton with the appropriate number and colour. If the referee and judge do not agree, the mat chairman decides.

Bouts consist of three 3-minute rounds with a minute's rest between each. The duration is timed by a timekeeper.

Wrestling competitions are conducted on an elimination basis, which is complicated but avoids the injustices of shock defeats. All fighters have at least two bouts and often more. They begin with a clean sheet and continue until they have had 6 or more penalty points scored against them. These penalty points range from winning by a fall—no penalty points—to losing by a fall—4 penalty points. Between these extremes, the narrowness of the verdict is reflected in the distribution of points. The competition continues until there are three fighters left to contest the final in a 'round-robin' form.

The referee awards points for aggressive and successful moves as the wrestlers attempt to end the bout by pinning each other. The degree of danger is indicated by the number of points allocated in bouts which do not end in a fall.

champions.

But at the 1960 Olympics Turkey were back on top, taking seven gold and two silver medals, although the outstanding individual was the West German heavyweight Werner Dietrich, who was first in the freestyle and second in the Graeco-Roman. An even finer heavyweight appeared at the 1961 world championships —Russia's Alexandr Medved— who was to dominate for the rest of the decade.

In the lighter classes, however, Japan, with their tradition of judo, provided Russia with most opposition. Most of the top Japanese wrestlers were originally judo fighters with a background of devastating throws ideal for wrestling. And at the 1964 Olympics they grabbed five gold medals. Their pride was Osamu Watanabe, who won the featherweight crown with his 186th consecutive victory. Meanwhile, in the Commonwealth, India and

Pakistan were the masters, as they showed at the 1966 Commonwealth Games where together they took seven of the eight championships.

At the Mexico City Olympics in 1968, Russia and Turkey were again the most outstanding countries. However, the most outstanding competitor was the Hungarian 'Pici' (Tiny) Kozma, a huge man who died in a car crash two years later. It was at the Mexico Olympics that the Olympic Congress decided to add two new weight categories—light-flyweight and heavyweight-plus—to bring the number of classes to 10. By this time it was clear that the regular winners — Russia and Turkey — would be challenged in future by a new name in world wrestling, East Germany. East Germans won two Graeco-Roman titles in Mexico City, and in 1970 they won three gold medals in the European championships—held in East Germany.

Yachting

The 'Sport of Kings' is a title long associated with horse racing, but it could also be easily bestowed on yachting. From its very origins yachting has had royal connections: the first recorded instances of using a boat for pleasure concerned King Charles II of England. And still today yachting has the stamp of kings about it. King Constantine of Greece won an Olympic gold medal in Tokyo, and Norway's King Olaf and Crown Prince Harald are familiar names in top yacht racing. Yet for all yachting's royal associations, there is no more cosmopolitan sport, and it is increasing in popularity all over the world with a growth rate few sports can rival.

This, however, was not always so, and between the world wars yachting was without question the sport of the rich. Yachts were large affairs on which the owner lived for perhaps a month a year in luxury. If they were racing yachts, they were reserved exclusively for that purpose, with a team of paid hands and a professional skipper, whose word was law and who treated the owner to his face with a certain deference—and behind his back referred to him with a certain derision. There were but a few amateur yachtsmen throughout the world who sailed in small yachts, with a consider-able amount of discomfort, and it is to their credit that their enthusiasm encouraged many others.

That yachting has become a major sport is due to those who sailed and kept alive the smaller classes. Dinghy sailing, for example, was virtually unheard of until the late 1930s, yet it was mainly through dinghies that the post-World War II surge into yachting came about. Just how popular yachting has become is illustrated by the fact that, by the early 1970s, there were over two million participants in England alone.

Yachting—the pastime of the leisured classes that became the sport of millions.

History

King Charles derived such pleasure from sailing in one of the small vessels of his navy that he commanded the building of several similar craft so that racing could take place. History does not, however, record whether or not this merry monarch took the helm of his own yacht or if he won any of his races.

Little is known about the sport from that period until more than a century later, when the water became an attraction for the 18th-century gentry looking for ways to pass their long leisure hours. There was also an added advantage in yachting. At the time the navy was a private affair, and yachts were one way of supple-

John Watney

Left, **The One Hundred Guinea Cup won by the schooner 'America'** (*below*) **now known as the America's Cup.** *Right* **with spinnakers billowing, yachts leave Sydney Harbour at the start of the Australian ocean racing classic to Hobart. In 1969, it was won by 'Morning Cloud', skippered by Ted Heath (1), who, two years later and now the British Prime Minister, led the British to victory in the Admiral's Cup, the virtual world championship of ocean racing. 2 High speed racing in a 505 brings out both skills and courage.**

Radio Times Hulton Picture Library

Mary Evans

menting the numbers in an emergency—and of getting cheap crews and maintenance. The oldest yacht club still in existence is the Royal Cork Yacht Club in Ireland, which was founded in 1720, largely as a dining club for the local gentry who went afloat for pleasure.

But it was during the 19th century that the real growth in yachting began. With the Industrial Revolution came a slightly greater spread of wealth, and with it the desire for ostentation. Naturally, with the peerage and the rest of the aristocracy already showing an interest, the *nouveaux riches* of industry took to the water. By boosting the numbers, they gave yachting the impetus it needed to develop into a major sport.

Development in other countries at this time, however, was slow. In the Netherlands the stirrings were just beginning, as they were in the United States. But in 1851

came what has turned out to be the most important single event in the history of sport. The schooner yacht *America* arrived in Cowes. It had been designed and built by a syndicate under Commodore Stevens of the New York YC with the sole purpose of beating the English yachts of the day, their intention being to cover their costs by the wagers they confidently expected to win. Their confidence in the yacht was not unfounded, for *America* trounced the cutter *Laverock* in her first race in British water. But the victory was so devastating that other would-be opponents were put off, and it was not until an invitation came from the Royal Yacht Squadron to take part in a race around the Isle of Wight for a bulbous jug called the One Hundred Guinea Cup that *America* raced again. The black schooner was opposed by 15 home contestants all determined to uphold the reputation of British

builders and designers, especially as the race was being watched in some of its stages by Queen Victoria. The result is best summed up in the now famous reply to Queen Victoria when, in the final stages, she enquired of a signalman as to the state of the race: '*America* first, your Majesty. There is no second.'

Commodore Stevens and his syndicate were naturally delighted, and some years later presented their prize to the New York Yacht Club as a 'perpetual challenge cup for friendly competition between foreign countries'. The America's Cup was open for attack, but as the years passed the task of removing it became increasingly difficult. The New York YC have become so possessive of this trophy that few would be surprised if there was some truth in the apocryphal story that the helmsman of the boat that loses it will replace it in the trophy room with his head.

Early yacht racing was done on a crude handicap basis, with yachts allowed time for each particular race against the scratch yacht. As racing became more popular, though, it became more and more obvious that this was quite unsatisfactory. It would be much more exciting if boats could race each other on level terms. Consequently rules were drawn up so that yachts built within certain measurement restrictions would have no handicap allowance. These moves proved popular, and by the beginning of the century yacht racing had taken a firm hold, even if it was still only the sport of the rich. The 'metre' classes were beginning to attract competition, with the gaff-rigged 15 metres perhaps the most popular of the era. As today, the term '15 metres' bore no direct relationship to any of the yacht's principal measurements, but was the result of a complex formula taking into account overall length, waterline

338

length, draught, beam, and sail **1**
area.

In the United States at this time, the sport was undergoing even more important developments, with small-boat sailing achieving popularity. The more democratic peoples of America were not tied by tradition and believed that it should be anyone's prerogative to sail for pleasure. As early as 1906 William Gardner designed an 18-foot-long keelboat called the Bug, which was to be the forerunner of the Star class. Because its owner, Pop Corry, thought the Bug too small, he had a larger successor constructed four years later (from the same designer), and during that winter 22 Stars were built. It was the first small one-design class to catch on internationally.

After World War I, yachting and yacht racing began to grow, with development running apace. A new metre-boat formula was evolved as the Bermudan rig came into being, and the largest of these was the J class, which usually raced together with the 23-metres. King George V's own *Brittania* was one of these, perhaps the most successful ever built. The in-between classes did not attract big fleets, but the 12-metres (then regarded as a small class), 8-metres, and 6-metres did get a large following. And as these metre boats spread through Europe, Scandinavia began to emerge as a yacht racing force. America and, to a lesser extent, Canada were already established. In Australia, however, the trend was to smaller-boat sailing. The development of the surf boats and of skiffs had provided open boats with large areas of sail and centreboards to cater for a wider and more democratic participation.

It was also during this period

between the wars that ocean racing came into its own as an integral part of yacht racing. This side of the sport began in 1906 in the United States, with the Newport (Rhode Island) to Bermuda race that has since established itself as an ocean racing classic. The first ocean race held in British waters was in 1925 and attracted a good deal of attention from the press at the time, many considering it foolhardy to race from Cowes, round the Fastnet Rock off the coast of County Cork in Ireland, and back to Plymouth in a yacht. The progress from the humble beginnings of 7 starters in the first race to 236 in the 1971 event is a pointer to the growth in the sport.

After World War II came the emancipation of yachting. A social revolution was abetted by a technological one, and the age of do-it-yourself hit yachting with a vengeance. Marine plywood and resin glues made boat building possible for amateur carpenters who before had tackled little more than kitchen shelves. Suddenly dinghy sailing was available to everyone. At first the designs were for boats for young people or for pottering about in, and though greater varieties were available in America and Australia the majority of them were unsophisticated. Gradually the metre boats dropped out of the scene. The vast J boats were beyond the pocket of even millionaires, and today it generally needs a syndicate of millionaires to raise the money needed for a 12-metre yacht to challenge for or defend the America's Cup.

Multihulled boats such as catamarans and trimarans, which had long been considered freaks, also achieved acceptance, appearing at first as fast day-sailing and racing craft. But as they became more popular, they also made strides in the cruising and cruiser-racing fields.

Glossary of Terms

Bearing away Altering course away from the wind until the yacht begins to gybe. Also known as *falling off the wind.*

Beating Sailing as close into the wind as possible. Also known as *close-hauled.*

Bermudan rig A rig for a yacht carrying a high, tapering sail.

Gybing Altering course from one tack to another with the wind aft.

Handicap The time allowance given to yachts. The smaller a yacht's rating, the greater its handicap.

Hard chine boat A boat the bottom of which is made up of straight sections instead of one curved section.

Leeward That side of the yacht away from the wind.

Luffing Altering course towards the wind until head to wind.

Mark Any object which a yacht must pass on a specified side.

Obstruction to see room Any object, including craft under way, that makes a yacht alter course to avoid it.

Pay off To turn away from the wind.

Port The left-hand side of the yacht.

Port tack Sailing with the wind coming from the left-hand side.

Proper course The fastest course a yacht might sail to the next mark. It is not necessarily a straight line but makes allowances for the wind and tidal streams.

Reaching Any other point of sailing other than close-hauled (beating) or running.

Reefing Reducing sail area.

Running Sailing with the wind dead aft.

Sheets Ropes that control the sails.

Starboard The right-hand side of the yacht.

Starboard tack Sailing with the wind coming from the right-hand side.

Tacking Altering course from one tack (port or starboard) through the eye of the wind.

Trimming the sails Adjusting the balance of the sails.

Windward That side of the yacht on which the wind blows.

Eric Jewell

How to Sail

To most people it is obvious that a yacht is propelled by the action of the wind on its sails What is not always realized is that the action of the wind blowing across the *leeward* side of the sail plays an equal part with the wind pushing into the *windward* side of the sail. Sails are cut with an aerodynamic curve, so that when filled out by the wind, they are shaped in a similar way to the wing of an aeroplane. The wind blowing across this curved surface becomes a pull away from the sail·towards the bow of the boat, while at the same time the wind pushes against the other side of the sail. These two actions combine to force the boat forward and make it possible to sail in almost any direction. The shape of the underwater parts of the hull, such as the keel or the centreboard, counteract the sideways movement of the boat.

There are three different points of sailing a boat : *running*, with the wind from astern ; *reaching*, with the wind abeam ; and *beating*, when the wind is as close to the bow as possible for forward motion.

The easiest point of sailing is reaching. The boat is pointed in the desired direction and the sails trimmed accordingly. In strong breezes, dinghies can hydroplane on the reach, achieving speeds well in excess of their designed waterline length, and this ability to hydroplane, used in conjunction with the wave patterns, makes reaching the most exciting part of dinghy racing. As the wind comes further astern, the reach is said to broaden (broad reach), and with the apparent wind aft of the beam yachts and dinghies will hoist spinnakers. There are now three sails to be kept in balance, and the spinnaker is the most unstable of them all.

Running, with the wind dead aft, needs continual concentration. The wind must not be allowed to come from the 'wrong side' of the boat or the boat will gybe involuntarily. *Gybing* is the most difficult manoeuvre to make because the change in wind forces are altered radically without any reduction in their effect on the boat's rig. Consequently bad gybes in heavy weather can easily cause dismasting in big yachts or capsizing in dinghies.

The most difficult point to master is beating, which is also the point of sailing that provides the greatest differential between good and bad yachtsmanship. It is when beating to windward that races are generally won or lost.

Though the basic skills are soon mastered, the finesse takes considerable experience to acquire. Most yachts have a mainsail and foresail (jib). Pulling in the sheet of the mainsail will tend to make the bows of the boat turn into the wind, whereas pulling on the foresail sheet makes the boat's head turn away from the wind (*pay off*). Therefore a balance must be achieved between these two sails, for to windward both are *sheeted* well in. This is a factor of design and tuning. It is imperative that the sails are set so that their full efficiency is obtained and so that they do not disturb one another.

Once the sails are properly trimmed, the helmsman then aims to sail as close to the wind as possible. If he goes too close, the front part of the sail begins to lift as the sail itself starts to stall and, efficiency reduced, the boat slows down. If the boat is too far off the wind, then the flow of air across the sail is reduced and the side-pressure forces of the sail are increased, causing the boat to heel more, another loss in efficiency. Performance can always be further improved by fine trimming of the sails, and the boat's performance can be judged in relation to one nearby or, in the case of many large yachts, from the speedometer.

It is not, however, possible to sail directly into the wind. The closest

a yacht can get is about 45 degrees to the wind, and so a zig-zag course must be steered to get to a point dead to windward. This manoeuvre is called *tacking*. As the wind is never completely constant in direction, the choice of which tack, port or starboard, to be on is important. A 5-degree shift in the wind makes a 10 degree advantage or disadvantage depending which tack the boat is on. With bigger boats, the action of tacking may take a lot of time, causing a loss of speed for a considerable period, so this factor must be taken into account before tacking on a wind shift.

Dinghy-sailing techniques for getting to windward in a short steep sea are now being adopted by the ocean racing fraternity. In order to maintain maximum speed through oncoming waves, the yacht *luffs* slightly up the face of the wave, *bears away* through the crest to obtain more speed when it is most likely to be stopped, and returns to the correct course down the back of the wave and into the trough. However, smoother seas make the going easier for both big yachts and dinghies, and it is always wise to look for smoother water when racing, even if it means making a small detour to get to it.

Tidal current is the other major factor that affects the speed of a yacht, and this can be considerable. In light airs a yacht may be able to make only 3 knots through the water, and so if there is a foul tide of 4 knots, the yacht is actually going backwards 'over the land'. Other effects of the tide are to increase or to decrease the height and steepness of waves. For example, consider the 4-knot tide again but this time in a true wind of 25 knots (force 6 on the Beaufort wind scale). If the tide is running in the same direction as the wind, it is reduced to 21 knots (force 5) but if it opposes the wind direction, its effect is increased to 29 knots (force 7). As wind increases, it may provide too much power for the yacht or dinghy; the side forces may cause too great an angle of heel for efficient sailing or, in the case of a dinghy, result in capsizing.

This is easily remedied. Reduction in sail by changing down to a smaller headsail or *reefing* the mainsail is the recognized method in keelboats, whereas dinghies would use flatter sails than normal and then *feather the rig* (allow the boom to sway out to leeward as much as necessary) to partially stall the sails. On a reach, both yachts and dinghies would be constantly trimming sheets in order to get the best out of the boat. The acknowledged maximum for the amount of sail reduced is to shorten for best performance in the lulls and spill a little wind in the gusts.

1 The three different points of sailing a boat. In all three instances, the wind is blowing in the direction of the arrow. *Left:* beating, or sailing into the wind, in which the boat tacks at a 45-degree angle to the direction of the wind. *Centre:* reaching, or sailing with the wind abeam. *Right:* running, with the wind coming from astern.
2 Hauling down the foresail before hoisting the spinnaker.
3 Sailing on tidal waters requires consideration of the tide as well as the wind.

London Express News and Feature Service

Classes

Though racing yachts are divided into a number of individual classes, they fall into three main categories: *ocean racers*, *keel boats*, and *dinghies*.

Ocean racers. Because it would be virtually impossible to sell exactly the same type of boat to those wishing to indulge in this aspect of yachting, ocean racing is a handicap affair. Yachts needed for ocean racing can cost anything' upwards of £25,000, and so the owner is more than entitled to have his boat designed to cater for his own personal preferences. In addition, the opportunity to build a yacht to an owner's tastes allows designers to exploit their skills.

For many years there were several rating rules in existence, but in 1970 the International Offshore Rule (IOR) was formulated. A highly complex rule, the product of many years' work by some of the world's leading yachtsmen, designers, and administrators, its object was to level the handicap of yachts throughout the world and at the same time to encourage production-line yachts. In both objects it has been successful, as was reflected by the 17 countries that entered that same year for the 1971 Admiral's Cup—the virtual world championship of this branch of yachting. Within the ocean racing framework, the boats are again subdivided into classes, encompassing small differences in their rating length. This helps cut down the effect of weather changes that are unfair to boats at the far ends of the scale.

The design of ocean racers has altered radically since the 1920s, when many of the boats were of the very heavy displacement type, needing a considerable sail area to drive them. Some were schooners, but most were cutters. In the United States, the Cruising Club of America rule favoured the development of beamy, shallow-centreboard yawls, but alterations to this rule tended to eliminate two-masted boats, to the regret of many. In Britain, alterations to the Royal Ocean Racing Club rule encouraged the trend towards lighter-displacement sloops with less sail area, and towards the end of this rule's existence mainsails were getting very small while headsails were becoming gigantic in proportion.

The new IOR has continued to exploit light displacement, with very flat-floored boats and an accent on large headsails, smallish mainsails, and penalty spinnaker booms (spinnakers which, because they are over the normal length, alter the boat's rating, causing its handicap to be lowered). There

Left, '**Wizard of Paget**' a Class 1 ocean racer. Classes are determined by the rating length of the yachts.

has even been some experimenting with extremely light displacement boats that will plane down-wind like a dinghy. One of these, *Improbable*, won the Miami to Montego Bay race in a heavy-going downwind, but the designers still had to reach a reasonable compromise, which is what a successful ocean racer must be.

Keel boats. Day-racing keel boats come in numerous classes. Many may be local classes, where the fleet comprises no more than a couple of dozen boats, or they may be an international class with more than 5,000 of their type spread throughout the world.

The most famous of the keel boat classes is the 12-metre yacht used for the America's Cup, the Blue Riband of yacht racing. By modern standards these are vast yachts, 70 feet overall with 2,000 square feet of sail, and their purpose is now limited to the America's Cup. Rule changes have now permitted construction in aluminium, making the building of new boats cheaper but at the same time outclassing the existing 12-metres.

There are three main international classes, each of them quite different in concept. The *Star* is a hard-chined, narrow boat that is tremendously over-canvassed, whereas the *Soling* is a boat that needs three fit crew to sail it. The third, the *Tempest*, is a two-man boat reminiscent of a dinghy and is sailed with the crewman riding a trapeze. There is a fourth international class, the *Dragon*, but its prohibitive costs and its somewhat old-fashioned design have numbered its days as such.

Keel-boat racing did not develop apace with dinghy racing in the yachting boom just after the war, and it took the development of glassfibre boatbuilding to give keel boats a much needed shot in the arm. Then it appeared that the designers had been holding cards up their sleeves, for a rash of new boats suddenly appeared. At first they tended to replace local classes that were growing old and beyond repair, but later

1 The 12-metre yachts are the most famous of the keel boat classes. 2 Since the boom in keel boats, many new classes, such as the Redwing, have come into being. 3 Solings, one of the three main international keel boat classes.

Sunday Times

they catered for dinghy sailors who had decided to move into keel boats. This further boost meant there had to be some narrowing of designs for major international racing, and after trials the Tempest and Soling were chosen.

By the early 1970s, the keel boat revival was in full swing, and even the metre boats were being raced again: the sixes became popular in America, Canada, and Australia with some signs of emergence in Britain: eights were racing as a class on the Clyde in Scotland; and the 5.5, despite its demise from the Olympic Games, still looked healthy.

Dinghies. Dinghies of a type were sailed for years before the bug really hit Britain, and in the mid-1920s there were only two dinghy classes of note—the International 12s and 14s. But interest in small-boat racing was stimulated in 1927, when the Prince of Wales donated a trophy to the International 14 ft Class that became one of the most sought-after prizes in the dinghy world. Then, with the post-war boom in home building, the dinghy came into its own and for a time the centre of dinghy racing shifted to Britain. The main reason was Jack Holt, a designer whose plans of numerous dinghies became available through the magazine *Yachting World*. His earliest published plans were for a racing dinghy for young people that has become the International Cadet. The spread of the design was worldwide, and scores of children were introduced to yacht racing through this 10 ft 6 in pram-bowed dinghy. Some of them have gone on to win Olympic medals.

Now the yachting scene is full of dinghies. Each week, it seems, a new class emerges. But the established classes continue to enjoy their own particular popularity, having national, continental, and world championships that give the weekend sailor the chance to pit his skills against the best from other countries and to enjoy the camaraderie that goes with yachting. Other influences have also been felt. The Enterprise class was the first in Britain

4 An Enterprise dinghy. This class was the first in Britain to be sponsored. 5 Dinghy sailing's popularity reflects the growth of yachting as a sport.

John Watney

John Watney

Rules

Yacht racing rules are few but mandatory, and infringement results in immediate disqualification. All disputes are settled by protest before the Race Committee, for yacht racing is the one sport without referee or umpire.

The rules are framed to avoid collision between boats and to encourage fair sailing, with encouragement to the attacking boat but allowing the boat ahead to defend her position. Some rules apply at all times, others on specific occasions. A yacht is racing under rules from the five-minute signal before the start until she has finished.

Those rules that always apply :

a yacht that makes no attempt to avoid a collision resulting in serious damage, even if she has right of way, may be disqualified ;

a yacht with right of way shall not alter course to prevent another yacht from keeping clear ;

a yacht with right of way must hail before making an alteration of course that may not be foreseen by another yacht ;

a port-tack yacht shall keep clear of a starboard-tack yacht.

The start

There are two warning signals for the start, one 10 minutes before, when the class flag is hoisted, and the other 5 minutes before, when the international code flag P (for Blue Peter) is hoisted with the class flag. Shots are fired to bring the competitors' attention to these flag signals. At the start both flags are dropped and there is another shot. If any boat is over the line, a second shot is fired and the class flag held at half-mast until the boat or all boats have recrossed the line and started correctly. A yacht that has crossed the line before the starting gun and has to go back has no right of way whatsoever when going back. If there has to be a complete restart it is signalled by the hoisting of the First Substitute of the international code and the firing of three shots. A yacht is considered to have started when any part of her crosses the line in the direction of the first mark after the start.

When yachts are on the same tack

a windward yacht shall keep clear of a leeward yacht ;

a yacht clear astern shall keep clear of one clear ahead ;

a yacht that establishes an overlap to leeward from clear astern shall allow the windward yacht to keep clear and must not sail above her *proper course;*

a yacht clear ahead or to leeward may *luff* to try to prevent a windward yacht overtaking until the helmsman in the windward boat is forward of the mainmast of the leeward yacht which must then return to its proper course ;

an overlap exists only when the boats are within two lengths of each other ;

a yacht must not sail below her proper course when she is within three lengths of a leeward yacht or a yacht clear astern that is steering a path to leeward.

When changing tacks

a yacht *tacking* or *gybing* shall keep clear of all others ;

a yacht shall not tack to get right of way unless it does so in sufficient time to allow others to keep clear.

When rounding marks

the yacht inside has right of way over all those outside her ;

an inside overlap must be established before the leading boat is within two lengths of the mark.

At one time a yacht that touched a mark had to retire immediately, but now most sailing instructions allow the correction of this mistake by a complete re-rounding of the mark. In such circumstances the yacht has no right of way whatsoever.

When approaching shoal water or an obstruction

a yacht may hail a right-of-way yacht for room to manoeuvre.

Yachts must not receive outside assistance while racing, including advice from the shore, another boat, or by radio, and must be propelled only by the natural action of the wind on the sail and the water on the hull. This stops unnecessary rocking and the pumping of sheets to induce wind flow across the sails. Nor must a yacht eject or release any substance which will reduce friction.

A yacht finishes when any part of her crosses the line from the direction of the last mark.

The end of a day's racing. Yachts moored at Cowes, home of British yachting.

to be sponsored, and within a few years had grown to 10,000 boats. In Denmark the Optimist class was proposed by a newspaper for cadet sailing and it emerged as the largest class in the world, with the Mirror dinghy, also newspaper-influenced, its biggest rival. It is generally reckoned that a top dinghy-racing helmsman has the world at his feet in yacht racing, and this is borne out by the number of former dinghy sailors found at the front of the fleet in international competition.

In dinghy-racing circles it has been said that the greatest test of skill is rewarded by a gold medal in the Finn single-handed class. These one-design dinghies are supplied to the competitors at the Olympic Games, each with a bag of identical equipment that the helmsman can use as he wishes. This eliminates almost any difference in boats and puts the accent fully on sailing and tuning skills. From this demanding competition has emerged perhaps the greatest sailor of all time, Denmark's Paul Elvstrom, who won the Olympic single-handed gold medal four times in succession, the last three times in Finns.

Organization

Yachting throughout the world is organized by the International Yacht Racing Union (IYRU) on which each country is represented through its National Authority. The union meets in London each November to discuss the year's business, and to legislate, if necessary, on the racing rules and the management of the international classes. But the IYRU does more than just concern itself with racing. Its general-purpose committee is more widespread in its functions, having at heart the problems of all yachtsmen, both cruising and racing.

The racing rules as constituted by the IYRU are now universally used. They were completely revised in 1964, and since then have been subject to only slight alterations. Any proposal for alteration must be considered by the member countries for a year before it is ratified.

The national authorities that feed the IYRU themselves deal with the majority of the legislation and protection of yachting rights. They have been known to extract large sums in compensation from industry for clubs whose amenities have been threatened by development, and they have also stopped development where it was proved to be environmentally unsuitable.

The final link in the administrative chain is through the member clubs, whose reports and proposals to their national authorities are the prime movers of legislation.

Ed Lacey